The Logic of International Relations

The Logic of International Relations

Fifth Edition

Walter S. Jones

Professor of Political Science, Senior Vice President for Academic Affairs and Provost, Wayne State University

Previously authored with Steven J. Rosen

Little, Brown and Company
Boston Toronto

To Sally and Doug,
whose generation may have the final opportunity
to answer the question,
"Will man survive?"

And to Barbara—and *Jupiter,* Rachmaninoff, and *Bon Appetit*

Library of Congress Cataloging in Publication Data

Jones, Walter S., 1938–
The logic of international relations.

Includes index.
1. International relations. I. Title.
JX1395.J66 1985 327 84-26152
ISBN 0-316-47288-3—SUPPLIES AS ART

Library of Congress Catalog Card No. 84-26152

ISBN 0-316-47288-3

9 8 7 6 5 4 3 2 1

MV

Published simultaneously in Canada by Little, Brown & Company (Canada) Limited

Printed in the United States of America

Preface

Readers familiar with earlier editions of *The Logic of International Relations* will find that the new edition, though having no additional chapters, is substantially revised throughout. Part I, "The Logic of National Perceptions," is revised in all but its historical sections. The world outlooks of the principal actors are displayed with the most recent official statements about relations among nations, particularly with respect to the deterioration of Soviet-American relations during the current decade; the evolving world view of China; the further awakening of European, Japanese, and Canadian economic and strategic autonomy, and the rapid industrialization and accumulation of debt in the Third World. In Part II, "The Logic of Power," current data have been added to the chapter "Regional Military Balances," and the chapter "The Balance of Terror" has been thoroughly revised. "Principal Causes of War," previously entitled "Twelve Causes of War," has been revised, reorganized, and expanded to accommodate new theoretical approaches to an understanding of armed international conflict. Part III, "The Logic of International Trade and Exchange," concentrates on the reversal of trends stressed in the fourth edition, especially with respect to the loss of unanimity among the OPEC states and the continuing imbalance of trade among the industrialized nations, now less preoccupied with Middle Eastern oil supplies. Other major emphases are the return of the American dollar to global prominence, post-recession economic growth, and the financial crisis of the Third World together with its implications for international finance and the banking systems of the capitalist countries. The concluding part, "The Logic of World Order," contains numerous revisions of data, many new illustrations of organizational and transnational activity, and some theoretical readjustments.

The content of the fifth edition is enhanced enormously by the extraordinarily precise and helpful comments of Henry P. Jones, Stephen F. Austin State University, Nacogdoches, Texas; William K. Domke, University of California, Davis; and Herbert K. Tillema, University of Missouri, Columbia. I trust that they will recognize their many contributions, and that they will forgive my judgment in those areas in which I have chosen to go my own way.

The patience and guidance of several people at Little, Brown have been major factors in the timely completion of this edition which, like the earlier ones, was prepared in the midst of a major geographic move. Previous editions were undertaken principally in Boston, Canberra, Boston, and Annapolis; this one began in Annapolis and was concluded in Detroit. Schedules could not have been met without the gracious coaxing of Don Palm, John Covell, and Cynthia Chapin. And behind them, as always, has been the steady and fine creative work of the many production people whom the author is never privileged to know.

I particularly desire to acknowledge the role of the readers and the professors who have used this and previous editions of *The Logic of International Relations*. It is clear that the message of this book—that an effective understanding of contemporary international relations requires a method that is interdisciplinary and multinational—has reached many thousands of young people throughout the English-speaking world. These students have been alerted to the need to view world politics through more than a single set of national lenses. This is the author's everlasting reward.

My appreciation goes also to my many work colleagues, first among them Richard F. Neville, whose pressing business was delayed by my impatient desire to complete work on the manuscript. I also want to express my profound sense of obligation to Steven J. Rosen, with whom this book was written originally, but for whom a major change in professional duties prevented further co-authorship. Similarly, this is the first edition of *The Logic of International Relations* that was not influenced by James J. Murray III, formerly the president of Winthrop Publishers. Much of the success of this book is attributable to Steven and Jim, and it has been a lonelier task without them.

But only my wife, Barbara, has endured the wasted weekends, sacrificed beautiful spring days on Chesapeake Bay, quietly accepted long delays at the Library of Congress en route to the Kennedy Center, and feigned sleep through the pounding of the typewriter and glare of the desk lamp long into the evening. She has ridden the emotional crests and troughs with me, from the small triumph of a minor argument proved to profane anger over misplaced datum or agony over the phrase reluctant to find its way to paper. Hers is a contribution of patience, encouragement, even temperament, and an inexpressible understanding of my passion for this work. For these and many more of her characteristics, I am so grateful.

For any shortcomings and imperfections that may have survived all of this assistance the author alone is responsible.

W.S.J.
Detroit, 1985

Contents

IV: THE LOGIC OF WORLD ORDER

Introduction

There are several questions of style and organization in this book that may at first seem odd and will be misleading without an explanation. The book begins, in the first five chapters, with an analysis of the world outlook of five key "actors" in the contemporary international system: the Soviet Union, the United States, the major Western allies, China and a composite of the Third World. We begin with an examination of how each point of view is influenced by concepts, values, national interests and ideologies, rather than a statement of universal laws and regularities describing *all* actors, as is done in most texts. This emphasis on *perceptual analysis* is based on the belief that differences in national goals and perceptions are the origin of the two overarching conflicts of our time: the dispute between East and West and the conflict between North and South.

For the fullest appreciation of the differences among perceptions of the international system, this book uses an experimental method of presentation. Instead of taking a detached, objective, "scientific" perspective and looking at each actor's view critically, we try to step into each nation's shoes to look at the world from its own point of view. This is an exercise in role-playing, or more exactly, in role-writing, imagining first the outlook of a Soviet citizen, then seeing the world from an American point of view, then from that of an ally of the U.S.A., then as a Chinese communist and finally from a synthesized Third World perspective. This differs greatly from the usual approach of newspapers, histories and most of our sources of information, which stand above their subjects as "neutral and objective" observers. We believe that the task of understanding points of view that differ profoundly from our own is so difficult that it is necessary temporarily to suspend judgment the better to appreciate the perspective of the other. To judge is to be separate from. We use the Stanislawski theory of Method Acting: we try temporarily to *be* the figure we wish to understand.

We must interject several reservations and caveats about our experiment at this point. First, we will not present each perspective in the original words of national leaders, but rather interpret and organize their expressions and perspectives for an American audience. We believe that primary sources written for foreign audiences do not communicate successfully when taken into another context. Thus, we are intermediaries between the various actors and the reader, and we explain the five perceptual frames in their own terms. Original materials are available elsewhere.

Second, we concentrate on idealized pictures of each actor, emphasizing values and professed beliefs. There is a danger here of mistaking mere rhetoric for the actual motives; we know that speechwriters often use idealistic disguises for less lofty goals, such as the pursuit of power. The differences between nations are undoubtedly exaggerated when we concentrate on ideals, but they would be understated if, like most introductory texts, we concentrated instead on universal modes of behavior that ignore critical differences between actors. In a sense, we are choosing to err on the side of principles, drawing caricatures that highlight the unique and defining features rather than a completely proportioned portrait.

Third, we must concede that it is partly artificial to speak of *the* perceptual system of the United States or of its major allies, or of China or the Soviet Union or, especially, the Third World. Within each of these actors there are elites with differences of opinion regarding the national interest, the optimal course of strategy, and other issues. We try to develop in each case a characterization that subsumes these differences, at least as far as the dominant elites are concerned. However, our analysis will give less importance to dissenting opinions within each actor that have not in the post-war period influenced policy directly and substantially. For example, in the American case our analysis will concern mainly the anticommunist perspective that has in fact guided policy since 1948, and only in passing will we review various revisionist challenges to the dominant outlook. In other words, we are interested primarily in the various orthodoxies, not in minority views or factions which have been consistently out of power.

Fourth, we must explain one feature of our presentation that some may find controversial. We give considerable attention to internal political features and to problems of the various actors that shape their external outlooks. Conventional analysis draws a fairly sharp distinction between domestic politics and foreign policy, but many international relations specialists are finding this rigid boundary a hindrance to understanding the roots of international behavior. To a considerable degree, the foreign actions of a nation are continuations of essentially domestic processes and demands, and certainly international perceptions cannot be separated entirely from the broader value base that gives rise to them. Therefore, we feel justified in our emphasis on domestic matters at certain key points.

Fifth, our analysis takes the basic actor in international relations to be the nation-state. Some specialists believe that the nation is becoming less important as the key unit of analysis and is being supplanted by the multinational corporation, the nongovernmental organization, and other transnational and supranational entities. We are sympathetic to this view, and later in the volume we treat some of these actors at length. But we believe that the key actors in the Cold War system are still nations and official bureaucracies, accounting for perhaps 80 percent of real power in international relations, while the other actors account for the balance. For the first section of the book, the basic unit of analysis will therefore be individual states.

Sixth, since the publication of the first edition of *The Logic of International Relations* in 1974, the role and character of the Cold War have changed considerably. For about half the life of this book, détente between the Soviet Union and the United States and the relaxation of Sino-American tensions have reduced the probability of serious confrontation, except between China and the Soviet Union. In more recent years, however, détente has failed as a regulator of Soviet-American relations, and the new decade is marked by mutual suspicion, accelerated arms production, and angry rhetoric. The new wave of American conservatism has coincided with the revival of Soviet adventurism (as in Afghanistan) and tightening of the Soviet grip on Eastern Europe (as in Poland), so that the celebrated period of détente seems only to have been a brief interlude in the Cold War. This book accepts the viewpoint that Soviet-American relations continue to be ruled more by hostility than by emerging common interests.

Finally, we must say a word about the political implications of perceptual analysis. It has been said that this method tends to be forgiving of sins, and to view the behavior of each actor in the sympathetic light of its own values and experiences. Ultimately, each actor is free of responsibility, each the victim of respective misperceptions. We concede that an agnostic analysis of positions, giving the internal logic of each case and avoiding absolute external judgments, may introduce greater moral ambiguities than fixing a single position from which to assess all the alternative views. We believe that these dilemmas of relativism and ambiguity are inherent in international relations, and that it is necessary to leave the comfort of one's own belief system. Relations between nations are in their very nature a meeting place of divergent perceptions.

I

The Logic of National Perceptions

1

The Soviet Perspective

The Soviet point of view has two core themes: a theme of Russian *nation* with a long history of goals and conflicts before communism, and a communist theme based on a universal *ideology,* which is a system of beliefs and values purporting to apply equally to all countries. The revolutionaries of 1917 were probably motivated more by communist ideology than by Russian nationalism: one of their first acts was to sign away large portions of Russia (containing one-third of its population and three-quarters of its iron ore) in a very unfavorable peace treaty with Germany at Brest-Litovsk to preserve a kernel, however reduced in size, for the world's first communist state. Russian national interests were subordinated to the communist ideological goal of establishing a revolutionary base.

In recent years, the mixture of goals may have shifted to a greater emphasis on national interests and a reduction of communism's universal goals. More attention is given to the problems of Russian society and the demands of the Russian people, and less to world revolution. To understand the Soviet view, it is necessary to see the basic tenets of communist ideology as intertwined with the historical interests of the Russian nation.

What Is Communist Ideology?

Communist ideology introduces a unique analysis of the basic behavioral laws that underlie the spectrum of human relations and explain in an orderly way the otherwise unintelligible complexities of society. Karl Marx and Friedrich Engels provided the basic analysis of capitalism and the state, and Vladimir Lenin, using Marx's "objective truth," contributed the main analysis of the international system.[1]

Fundamentals of Communism

Economic Determinism

Marxist-Leninist philosophy holds that the foundation of society is the economic system and the social relationships it produces. Stalin said, "The basis is the economic system. . . . The superstructure consists of the political, legal, religious, artistic, philosophical views of society, and the political, legal, and other institutions corresponding to them." Communism is thus a branch of the materialist school of philosophy.

What distinguishes Marxism-Leninism as a materialist philosophy is its conception of class relations as the root of social interaction. In *The Communist Manifesto* Marx declared:

> The history of all human society, past and present, has been the history of class struggles.
>
> Freeman and slave, patrician and plebeian, baron and serf, guild-burgess and journeyman—in a word, oppressor and oppressed—stood in sharp opposition each to the other.

This theory holds that in every organized society, one class controls the ownership of the means of production, and it uses political authority and all-powerful institutions to maintain this control. The ownership class extracts surpluses produced by the laboring masses. Society is a pyramid in which the broad working class at the bottom produces wealth for the privileged elite at the top.

Feudalism and Capitalism

This principle is seen in the feudal pattern of agriculture where ownership of land was concentrated in the hands of a small nobility, the "lords," for whose benefit it was worked by impoverished peasants.

1. Alfred G. Meyer, *Communism* (New York: Random House, 1967), pp. 11–22, 51–58.

The laborers lived in shanties on a minimum subsistence, sustaining themselves from disaster to disaster. The lord lived in a baronial mansion at leisure, enjoying his daily diet of sport and cultivation of the arts. The landlords were not, of course, chosen by God; they achieved their position initially by conquests, foreclosure on usurious loans, and royal grants, and they passed on their control through inheritance. Government was intertwined with feudal landownership: the lords gave a portion of their wealth and power to support the state, and the state used its physical force to guarantee the rights of property—that is, the position of the lords. The whole system was sanctified by the church, the "opiate of the masses."

Industry, the second and more modern form of production, displaced feudalism. A new class of owners was created, the capitalists, whose interests were tied not to land, but to factories. In the capitalist mode, the bourgeoisie monopolizes control of machinery, assembly lines and other modern means of production plus a financial infrastructure. Now, the labor power of the workers itself has become a commodity, to be sold in the market to the highest bidder. By maintaining a surplus labor force—the pool of the unemployed—the price of labor (wages) is depressed. The industrial workers become proletarians where before they were serfs. The emergence of the capitalist mode of production shifts the center of power from landlords to industry. After a period of struggle, the bourgeoisie seizes the reins of state from the landed gentry. Now the power of the state is used to provide infrastructure and supports for capitalist manufacture, trade and finance. This is not to suggest that feudalism disappears altogether; even today, in certain underdeveloped outposts of the imperial world, landlords collect rents of 60 percent and more of the workers' wages. But the controlling interests of the "free market" industrial state are the capitalists.

Origins of the State

Economic exploitation creates political relations in society. "The state," Engels wrote, "has not existed from all eternity. There have been societies that did without it, that had no conception of the state and state power. At a certain stage of economic development which was necessarily bound up with the cleavage of society into classes, the state became a necessity owing to this cleavage."[2] Lenin added, "History shows that the state as a special apparatus for coercing people

2. Friedrich Engels, "Origin of the Family, Private Property, and the State" in *Selected Works of Marx and Engels* (Moscow: Foreign Languages Publishing House, 1951), vol. 2, p. 239.

arose only wherever and whenever there appeared a division of society into classes, that is, a division into groups of people some of whom are permanently in a position to appropriate the labor of others."[3] The state, he concluded, "is an organ of class rule."[4]

Social Controls

This is not to suggest that the physical might of the state is the only (or even main) means whereby the elite protects its position. No social system, however oppressive, habitually uses force where there are less expensive and more efficient means of control available.

Coercion is the most visible form of control, but it is the least reliable. It requires vigilance and an elaborate network of enforcing agents who themselves are loyal to the system, and it raises a constant danger of rebellion. A social system that is forced to fall back on extensive coercion is on the point of collapse.

More efficient than coercion are *market* controls, meaning a structure of material rewards keyed to positive behavior; the carrot rather than the stick. Capitalism, for example, is superior as a form of exploitation to slavery, because now the workers have the illusion of free choice. Their victimization is masked by what appear to be impersonal "market forces," rather than naked threats by identifiable enemies.

But the most effective form of behavioral control is neither coercion nor the market, since both of these depend on external regulation of the individual. *Normative* controls work through education and social training to produce a set of norms and to identify expectations which act as internal regulators of behavior. Individual consciousness is patterned to fit the desired social model. "False consciousness" exists when deceptive morals, ideologies and religions are used to mask injustice behind a façade of legitimacy and legality. Individuals are betrayed by their own education, and they come to revere the very institutions that exploit them.

In general, normative social controls, supported by a structure of market rewards for cooperative behavior, are capitalism's first line of defense. Only in the last resort is brute force on the part of the state necessary. Control by the state ensures the smooth operation of all three forms of control. Public law and administration are thus extensions of the relations of production.

3. Lenin, "The State" (1919) in *Selected Works* (London: Lawrence & Wishart, 1939), vol. 2, p. 644.
4. Lenin, "State and Revolution" in *Selected Works* (New York: International Publishers, 1943), vol. 7, p. 9.

The Meaning of Revolution

Marxism prescribes a revolutionary solution to the problem of class rule.[5] The aroused proletariat rips the instruments of control from the bourgeoisie and uses the state apparatus to seize the means of production, thus changing the entire basis of social relations. "Expropriation of the expropriators" gives land to the peasants, factories to the workers. A certain amount of violence may be necessary, since the ruling class will not give over its position voluntarily, but this is nothing next to the much greater violence of the everyday capitalist system. As Khrushchev said, "The use or nonuse of violence in the transition of socialism depends on the resistance of the exploiters, on whether the exploiting class itself resorts to violence, rather than on the proletariat." Communism does not romanticize violence, but it regards pacifism as bourgeois sentimentality. No matter how many crumbs the ruling class may let drop from its overloaded tables, the capitalist system will always rest on foundations of injustice and suffering, and it must be overthrown.

Marxism regards revolution not just as desirable, but also as inevitable. History is progressive, and each epoch represents an inevitable advance from the preceding period. Capitalism itself outdates all previous forms of social order; no poet could compose an ode to capitalism as flowery as Marx's celebration of its accomplishments. But capitalism rests on class exploitation, so while it is necessary and progressive, it is also unjust. Eventually, it produces the seeds of its own destruction. Mature capitalism is increasingly monopolistic and insatiable in its profit hunger. Eventually, a point is reached at which the economy is saturated with enterprises, and the relentless search for investment opportunities drives the weaker capitalists back into the proletariat. The competition of the workers becomes more severe, driving wages down; and the misery of the proletariat grows.

Capitalism, which began as a progressive force leading humanity to the possibility of fulfilling all human needs through industry, becomes an obstacles to the next step. The army of the unemployed grows, production cannot be consumed, rates of profit fall, general desperation prevails. Capitalism has created the machinery to satisfy human needs, but it cannot use this machinery rationally. It is driven by its inner dynamic to amplify its contradictions until only revolution can rationalize society again.

Soviet faith in the inevitable march of history from its capitalist phase to socialism is unchanged from the early days of Leninism. In

5. Robert C. Tucker, *The Marxian Revolutionary Idea* (New York: Norton, 1969).

1982, in a speech commemorating the sixtieth anniversary of the founding of the Soviet Union (dated not from the 1917 revolution but from the close of the unionizing civil ware in 1922), Yuri Andropov noted that:

> The imperialists have not given up the schemes of economic war against the socialist countries, of interfering in their internal affairs in the hope of eroding their social system, and are trying to win military superiority over the USSR, over all the countries of the socialist community. Of course, these plans are sure to fail. It is not given to anyone to turn back the course of historical development. Attempts to 'strangle' socialism failed even when the Soviet state was still getting on its feet and was the only socialist country in the world. So surely nothing will come out of it now.[6]

Despite the presumed inevitable results of historical development, Marx's prediction that capitalism would collapse of its own weight has not yet been fulfilled. While he apparently expected the collapse of advanced capitalist states by 1900, these centers have become progressively more secure. Meanwhile, revolution has occurred in the Soviet Union, China, Cuba and North Vietnam, none of which conformed to the Marxist premise that mature capitalism must precede communism. How has this paradox occurred? In the Soviet view, the answer lies in the subtle ways in which capitalism manipulates the international system.

Lenin's View of the International System

Lenin extended Marx's analysis of society to a conception of international relations. Capitalism saved itself, according to Lenin, by reaching the stage of imperialism in which international dynamics temporarily ameliorate the conflicts at home. Borrowing from the English economist Hobson, Lenin showed that capitalism depends not only on oppression within the borders of the home state, but also on the external oppression of whole peoples in other parts of the international system. Lenin called this the "internationalization of the class system."

Searching for the Highest Rate of Return One imperial drive given particular emphasis in Lenin's analysis is the search for the highest rate of return on capital. In the advanced stage of development, the

6. Yuri Andropov, "Sixty Years of the USSR," December 12, 1982. English translation from *Moscow News* (No. 52, 1982), and reprinted in Martin Ebon, *The Andropov File: The Life and Ideas of Yuri Andropov, General Secretary of the Communist Party of the USSR* (New York: McGraw-Hill, 1983), pp. 249–264, at pp. 259–260.

centers of capital become saturated with investment, and the rate of return on new investment is relatively low. Less developed portions of the world still have not had production raised to its full level of exploitive efficiency, so new capital realizes a higher rate of return. Capitalists therefore compete with each other for investment opportunities and concomitant "spheres of influence" around the world. Imperialism is, in this model, mainly a search for high-return investment opportunities for surplus capital.

Searching for Markets Another factor cited by theorists of imperialism to explain the international nature of capitalism is the search for markets for surplus production. The capitalist system of production rests on a fundamental inefficiency in distribution. The workers must be paid less than the full value of their product if the capitalist is to retain a large share of production for profits. But this means that the workers are unable to buy all that they produce. Other markets must be found for the surplus products. So in addition to providing investment opportunities, colonies and spheres of influence can provide captive markets. This can be seen in many historical cases of colonial empires.

Controlling Raw Materials A third reason for the internationalization of capitalism is the need to control the richest sources of raw materials wherever they exist. Monopoly capital minimizes the costs of production by suppressing wages and by developing the cheapest sources of supply. Thus, the bounties of nature located in the undeveloped world are important prizes for international capital.

In this way, the international class system reduces the poor nations of the world to the status of suppliers of raw materials and cheap labor, as well as captive centers of foreign investment and import dependency. The colonies must not be permitted to develop on their own, free of foreign control, but rather are kept as dependent subsystems in the empire of capital. As in the home system of exploitation, the capitalists reinforce their international position with a preponderance of physical might. Controlling the government of their own states, they use its power to secure their own positions. Naturally, this international system of exploitation is disguised by legal and moral principles that give a veneer of legitimacy to the capitalists' plundering. Much of international law, for example, was written by the imperial states to protect their position; an example is the Treaty of Berlin (1885) in which the European powers delineated the future legal borders within Africa.

Source: Tass from Sovfoto

Mayday celebration in Red Square, Moscow, May 1984.

The Growth of Imperialism During the earlier period of this international system of exploitation, capitalists were very crude in competing with each other for the most profitable prizes. In the days of colonialism, the capitalist states actually fought wars over who was to benefit from which subjugations. In the resulting colonies, bourgeois functionaries developed a political system and an infrastructure (rails, ports and so on) conducive to profitable investment.

In later years, this system has (with exceptions) become more subtle and durable. Direct control offended the national spirit of the subject peoples, so international capital has relinquished formal colonialism. Titular control has been passed on to the *national bourgeoisie,* a native class of capitalists comprising a subsystem of the international system. The native bourgeoisie are co-opted by giving them a small share in the profits of national exploitation (for example, the royalties from a mining investment). There is a pleasant illusion of self-determination. In case of trouble, the imperialists can use their overwhelming position in the international economic system to deny markets to any subject state that refuses to comply (the boycott of Cuban sugar by the United States, for instance), and the national bourgeoisie can be relied upon to put the recalcitrant former colony back on course. Very occasionally, it is necessary to use direct force to stop a revolution by those who see through this delusional system. In these and other ways, neocolonialism preserves and even extends the imperial system while giving the Third World a false sense of independence.

The development of the imperial system gives capitalism a temporary reprieve, postponing its inevitable collapse. A portion of the gains of imperialism has been passed along to the organized workers in the centers of capital, raising their living standard and thus preventing an alliance with the unemployed. This, combined with the promotion of racism and ethnic divisions, has enabled the ruling class to forestall revolution. In the poor countries, however, the class basis of the international system is only too visible. Hence, the paradox that revolution seems to be ripest where capitalism is least mature. Stalin explained this phenomenon in *The Foundations of Leninism:*

> Formerly, it was the accepted thing to speak of the existence or absence of objective conditions for the proletarian revolution in individual countries, or, to be more precise, in one or another developed country. Now this point of view is no longer adequate. Now we must speak of the existence of objective conditions for the revolution in the entire system of world imperialist economy as an integral unit. . . .
>
> Where will the revolution begin? . . .
>
> Where industry is more developed, where the proletariat constitutes the majority, where there is more culture, where there is more democracy—that was the reply given formerly.
>
> No, objects the Leninist theory of revolution (imperialism); *not necessarily where industry is more developed,* and so forth. The front of capital will be pierced where the chain of imperialism is weakest. . . .[7]

Revolution may come first in the most progressive states of the underdeveloped world, and the centers of capital may be the last, rather than the first, to fall. But eventually communism will be universal.

The State Withers Away

What form will communism take after the revolution against capitalism succeeds? Marx and Engels were not very specific on this critical question. Because of this ambiguity, it has been possible for Trotskyists and other so-called "independent socialists" in Western countries to build an anti-Soviet propaganda campaign that accuses the Soviet state of "betraying the revolution" and even of being "non-Marxist."

7. Joseph Stalin, *The Foundations of Leninism* (New York: International Publishers, 1931).

One point in this anti-Soviet line is based on Engels's prediction in his *Anti-Duhring* that after the victory of the socialist revolution, the state would "wither away" and be replaced by a society without coercion. Obviously the Soviet state has not disappeared. But "Engels' formula had in view the victory of socialism in all countries or in most countries." The reality of today is that socialism is surrounded by a hostile "capitalist encirclement," so the country "of the victorious revolution must not weaken but must in every way strengthen its state, the state organs, the organs of the intelligence service, the army, if that country does not want to be smashed by the capitalist encirclement."[8] Stalin knew that the old Russia was repeatedly beaten by foreign enemies—the French and English in the Crimean War (1856), the Japanese in 1905, the Germans in 1917—precisely because of its political and industrial backwardness. The new Russia would have to use the most modern and practical means to ensure the survival of the first communist advances in a still-capitalist world, and to protect the Russian nation.

"Democracy"

Western critics accuse the Soviet Union of suppressing democratic principles by not adopting the Euro-American concept of "electoral democracy" based on the ideas of Locke and Rousseau. But in the Soviet view, bourgeois elections are part of the state apparatus of capitalism. Even if balloting is conducted without deceit, and a decision made by a voting majority, the outcome could not correspond to the objective interests of the masses anyway. False consciousness, perpetuated by class control of the mass media and the educational system, blinds the voters. Pious electoral candidates, most of whom are leading capitalists, further obscure the issue, often using a false demonology of "the Communist Threat" to stir up fears. Marxist-Leninists reject this as a meaningless version of "democracy."

Real people's or workers' democracy in the Marxist-Leninist conception emphasizes the objective nature of the social system, rather than the formal decision process. Work is available to all in the Soviet Union, and slums and poverty, which are the hallmark of the Western so-called democracies, do not exist. The substantive question is whether a social system, especially in the ownership of the means of production, can serve the interests of the masses. The meaning of social justice is not a spurious procedural question, but one of real outcomes; substance rather than process.

8. Joseph Stalin, "Reply to Comrades," *Pravda,* August 2, 1950.

Diplomacy

Leninism also has its own view of making foreign policy, one that prevails in the Soviet view yet today. Unlike the pre-Soviet Russians who formulated foreign policy in secret forums and without consultation with the masses, Lenin's "new international policy" required a "new socialist diplomacy" that was:

> . . . destined to break down the wall which the exploiters had always carefully raised between foreign policy and the mass of working people, and thus to turn the masses from a mere object of foreign policy into a force actively influencing international affairs in their own interests. The birth itself of socialist foreign policy made it immediately possible to move crucial international problems out of the secrecy of closed tsarist offices into the street, which the bourgeoisie so completely scorned, and bring them within reach of the workers and all working people. This was a thoroughly class, thoroughly Party-type kind of change. For the first time, it enabled the masses effectively to influence politics. . . .

In contrast, however, non-socialist diplomacy continues to be conducted beyond the reach of working people.

> What is Washington busy with now? One hysterical propaganda campaign after another. First the public is told of a "Soviet military threat." Then it is sold a bill of goods on the subject of the USA "lagging behind" the USSR strategically. People are also either being intimidated with tales of "international terrorism" or told cock-and-bull stories regarding the events in Poland, Central America and South and Southeast Asia. All this has its own logic, of course: the imperialists are able to indulge in creating new weapons of mass destruction only as a result of deceiving the masses.[9]

Russian National Interests

We have seen in a selective discussion of key issues in Soviet ideology that communist thought is an analytical scheme of universal applicability adapted to the specific situation of the first communist regime. This adaptation imposed on Marxism-Leninism compelling issues of Russian *national* interest, since defense of Russia became the essence of defending communism. Stalin intertwined national and ideological

9. Yuri Andropov, "Leninism: A Source of Inexhaustible Revolutionary Energy and Creativity of the Masses," April 22, 1982, in English translation by the Soviet press service, Novosti, and printed in the Soviet press on May 15, 1982. Reprinted in Martin Ebon, *The Andropov File*, pp. 224–238, at p. 235. A different translation of the same address appears in Y.V. Andropov, *Speeches and Writings* (New York: Pergamon Press, 1983), pp. 216–234, particularly pp. 228–229. There the final sentence appears as follows: "There is a logic, albeit perverted, in this propaganda: indeed, to advertise weapons of mass destruction and to prod the world to war the imperialists have to deceive the masses."

imperatives in 1927 when he defined a "revolutionary" as "he who without arguments, unconditionally, openly and honestly . . . is ready to defend and strengthen the USSR, since the USSR is the first proletarian, revolutionary state in the world." Moreover, "to advance the revolutionary movement is impossible without defending the USSR."[10] Thus, an historic accident married communism to the international position and national interests of a particular country.

Marx and Engels had been skeptical of nationalism and predicted its early demise as the interests of both the workers and the capitalists were internationalized. Polish and French workers would be united against capitalists of the two countries; and class, rather than nationality, would survive as the critical line of division. In this view nationalism is nothing more than a false consciousness dividing the proletariat.

But the First World War convinced Lenin that communist ideology would have to adjust to the continued potency of the national idea. The workers of every country dropped all pretense of proletarian internationalism when war broke out, and marched blindly behind the various national flags. The Second International in 1907 had called upon all European socialist parties and trade unions to resist an international conflict, which would serve none but competing capitalist interests. But grand expectations of worker solidarity were shattered in the summer of 1914, when not a single major socialist party in Europe opposed war, and the German Social Democratic Party, the leading Marxist group, voted unanimously for government war credits. The lesson for Lenin was that communism must join with nationalism rather than oppose it.[11] The power of this merger became visible thirty years later when communist parties emerged from the Second World War leading patriotic resistance movements in China, Indochina, Yugoslavia, Greece and elsewhere.

The Russian revolutionaries of 1917 found themselves at the head not just of a nationalist movement but of a national state. They were an opposition party whose entire organization and philosophy had been geared to destructive action, suddenly in a position of responsibility rather than insurgency. Not just grand principles but physical Soviet realities had to be dealt with.

The first national issue was the challenge of unifying the vast Soviet land mass and the diverse peoples of the Soviet state into a cohesive nation under effective administration from Moscow. This would entail

10. Joseph Stalin, "The International Situation and the Defense of the USSR" (August 1, 1927), *Sochineniya* (Moscow: Gospolitizdat, 1949), vol. 10, p. 61.

11. Adam B. Ulam, *Expansion and Coexistence: The History of Soviet Foreign Policy 1917–67* (New York: Praeger, 1968), pp. 13, 18–19, and 24–25.

giant logistical difficulties under the best of conditions. In Russia, it was compounded by vexing nationalities problems, from oriental minorities in the maritime provinces to Ukrainian separatism on the European border, with the Turkic peoples of Central Asia in between. "Russification" of the nationalities of the Caucasus and the Baltic littoral had resisted the best efforts of the tsars. The first vital necessity imposed upon the communist government was the amalgamation and federation of many separate pieces into a Union of Soviet Socialist Republics.[12]

Another condition imposed upon the Soviet government was the necessity to insulate the state from excessive economic, cultural and military penetration by the expansionist powers of Western Europe. From 1917 to 1940, the communists used an economic policy of autarky, a political policy of limited intercourse, and a strategic policy designed to equilibrate a European balance of power. Some Western observers dismissed these defensive maneuvers as Stalinist paranoia overlaid onto a traditional Russian xenophobia,[13] but the same actions can also be seen as a realistic response to a distinct external threat.

Another part of the historic Russian policy that preceded communism but has been continued is the pursuit of influence in critical border areas: Poland, the Balkans, the Bosporus and Dardanelles Straits, Manchuria, Finland and elsewhere. The value of these policies is economic, strategic and even cultural (pan-Slavism), in addition to the impetus given by communist ideology. Indeed, it is argued by some that the whole modern Soviet policy is nothing more than a continuation of the imperialism of the tsars, even in Korea, Iran and Mongolia.[14] The Balkan wars, the Crimean War, the Russo-Japanese War—all anticipated the broad pattern of Soviet policy in later years, except that Soviet leadership has succeeded, where the tsars failed, in achieving influence in Eastern Europe. Churchill said that Soviet policy is "a riddle wrapped in a mystery inside an enigma. . . . But . . . the key is Russian national interest."[15]

The relative position of various national interests and ideological goals in Soviet foreign policy changes over time. But it surely cannot be said that the USSR is little more than a conspiracy disguised as a

12. For a thorough, current study of the contemporary consequences, see Basile Kerblay, *Modern Soviet Society* (New York: Pantheon Books, 1983), particularly chapters II and VIII–IX.
13. Basil Dmytryshyn, *USSR: A Concise History* (New York: Scribners, 1965), pp. 143–53, 200–207, 247–59.
14. Tsarist and communist imperialism are compared in Michael Karpovitch, "Russian Imperialism or Communist Aggression," *The New Leader,* June 4, 1951, p. 18.
15. Winston Churchill, *The Gathering Storm* (Boston: Houghton Mifflin, 1948), p. 449.

state. Indeed, it is probable that Russian national demands have overshadowed questions of communist principle, particularly in more recent years.

The Soviet View of the International System

The interplay of national and ideological themes in Russian policy can be seen in the Soviet interpretation of major events in international relations since 1917.

America's participation in the 1918–19 War of Intervention which attempted to overthrow the Bolshevik regime is now virtually forgotten in the USA—though it is well-remembered in the USSR. Here, the bodies of 111 American soldiers killed in Russia lie on the Army Piers at Hoboken, New Jersey. About one thousand Americans died in the war, early martyrs in the struggle against communism.

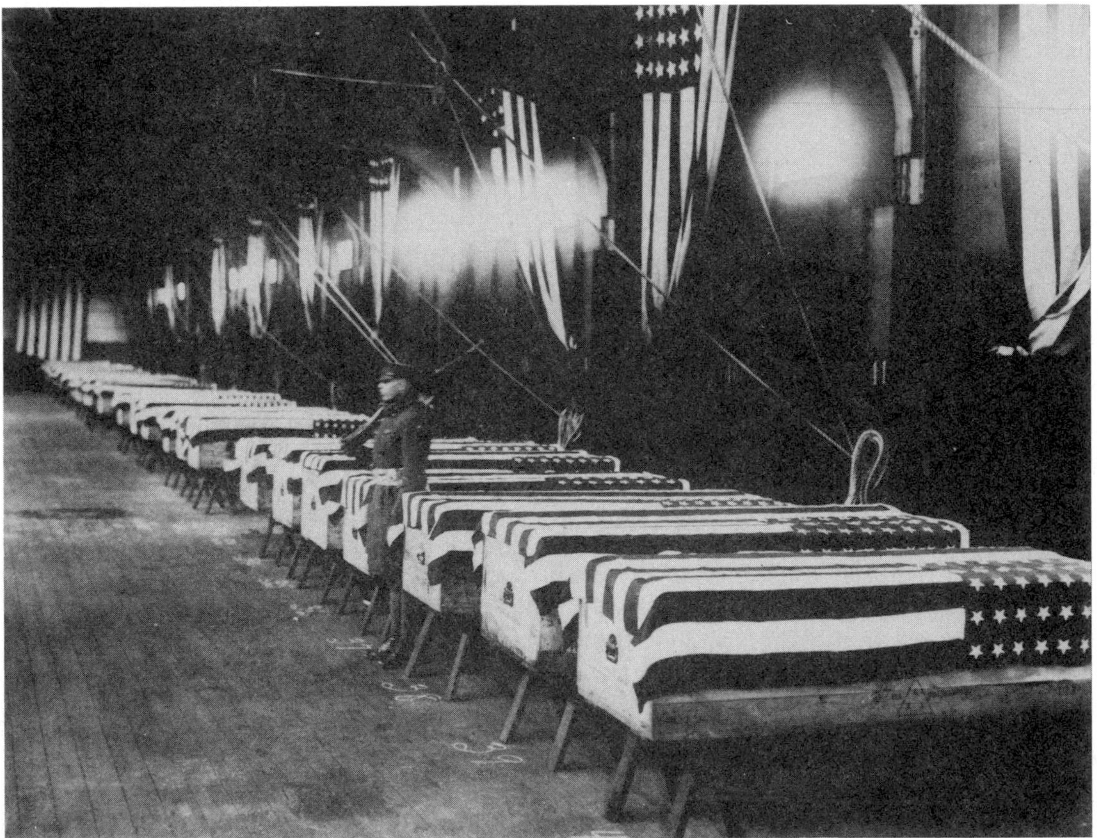

Source: Wide World Photos

The First World War and the Russian Revolution

Until 1917 capitalist countries controlled the entire international system. All regions not part of the advanced capitalist world were dominated, directly or indirectly, by it, and exploited as subject markets and sources of raw materials. The capital-exporting countries divided the world among themselves, and periodic readjustments, sometimes involving wars, occurred. Russians call the First World War the Imperialist War because they see it as having been a struggle between rival imperialists for the most desirable spoils.

The capitalist countries understood from the outset that the Bolshevik Revolution of 1917 posed a threat to their international system. Britain, France, the United States and other imperialist powers sent an international army to join domestic counterrevolutionaries (the "White" armies) in a struggle that lasted from 1917 to 1921. (The United States played a relatively minor role, sending 14,000 troops and suffering 1,000 casualties. The intervention is relatively unknown to Americans today, though it is well remembered by Russians.) For a while, the tides of battle gave the imperial powers hope of preventing Russia's defection from the capitalist world, but the Red armies finally prevailed and revolution was secured. From the outset, therefore, the hostility of the capitalist world to socialism was manifest. But could it have been otherwise, when the very existence of the Soviet Union would encourage other revolutionary movements?

The capitalists did succeed in preventing other revolutions for many years by a combination of clever anti-Soviet propaganda and the repression of revolutionary movements. The Soviet Union was an island in a hostile sea, and as such needed to spend huge portions of its resources on its defenses. Nonetheless, great progress was made from 1917 to 1940 in developing a revolutionary society, and in rebuilding the Soviet economy from the ravages of the First World War.

The Second World War and Subsequent Hostilities

The second great European war erupted when a particularly virulent form of imperialism took hold in Germany, a late starter in the imperialist division of the world. Its leadership was determined to extend its hegemony at the expense of the other capitalist states, making war inevitable. The lunatic Hitler also proposed to lead a holy war against communism—that is, against the Soviet Union. The German-Italian-Japanese Anti-Comintern Pact led some of the Western powers to flirt briefly with the idea of neutrality, to turn Hitler east and let the Nazis and communists bleed each other dry. Harry S Truman, then a US senator, said on the occasion of the Nazi invasion of Russia, "If we see that Germany is winning we ought to help Russia and if Russia is winning we ought to help Germany and in that way let them kill as many as possible" *(New York Times,* June 24, 1941). But Hitler's expansionist aims forced the other capitalist states into a wartime alliance with the Soviet Union. The United States and Britain, still deeply anticommunist and dedicated to the overthrow of the Soviet government, temporarily suspended this goal to deal with the more immediate danger of fascist Germany.

The Western powers did succeed, however, in shifting most of the burden of the European war to the Soviet Union. The great victory over fascism was paid for by Russian blood and by the heroic efforts of the Soviet people while the capitalist allies delayed opening the "second front" on the West until 1944. Of the 22 million Allied lives lost in the war, an estimated 20 million were lost by the Soviet Union. The United States, by comparison, though it made an important fi-

The Soviet Union's suffering during the Second World War was intense; an estimated twenty million Soviet citizens lost their lives. A feature of the fighting on Hitler's "Eastern Front" was the huge number of civilian casualties.

Source: Sovfoto

nancial and military contribution, lost only 300,000 (1.5 percent of the Soviet loss). The Nazi invaders destroyed and plundered more than 1,100 Russian villages and towns, razing many, while the Western Allies suffered only minor damage. Many historians hold that the Soviet Union came very close to defeating the Germans single-handedly. Churchill said that Russia's fighting men "did the main work of tearing the guts out of the German army."

These great human and material sacrifices did bring some gains for Soviet revolutionary and national interests after the war. The Red armies were decisive in liberating a number of countries from fascist occupation in 1945/46, particularly in Eastern Europe. Following the war, socialist governments were established with Soviet aid in Poland, Hungary, Bulgaria, Czechoslovakia, Rumania, Albania and the Soviet-occupied sector of (East) Germany. Other communist movements, with lesser amounts of Soviet aid, established socialist regimes in Yugoslavia and China. Within three years of the war's end, the Soviet Union had moved from isolation in a world of capitalist powers to partnership and leadership in a communist bloc comprising half the world's population! Thus, the anticommunist fanaticism of the fascists had a reverse effect in the long term.

As in 1917, the Western capitalist powers wasted no time developing a propaganda offensive against socialist gains. The establishment of communist governments in Eastern Europe was characterized as Soviet imperialism, while the restoration of capitalist forms in the West European countries was, of course, portrayed as the will of the people. The imperialists demanded that the financiers and landlords be returned to their "proper" position in the East European states, including even East Germany. The Soviet Union, it would seem, was expected to reproduce exactly the conditions that led to the two world wars and then sit back politely and wait for the next invasion. Instead, the Soviet Union committed itself to the establishment of a new order in Eastern Europe in cooperation with its new allies. The peoples of the communist world were not deceived by Western propaganda, though the Western governments did succeed in reinforcing the false anticommunist perceptions of their own peoples in some cases.

By 1950, the new imperialist NATO alliance system was developed against the Soviet Union and its allies. More than fifty hostile military bases were constructed by the Americans around the Soviet periphery, reinforced by the American lead in the development of atomic weapons. This capitalist encirclement forced the socialist states to spend an inordinately large portion of their productive efforts on defensive capabilities to prevent imperialist adventures. It is ironic that the imperialists have managed to convince some people that the Soviet Union has aggressive designs, when it is the Americans who keep their bases far from home on the borders of the Soviet heartland, and not the other way around! Leonid Brezhnev, General Secretary of the Central Committee of the Communist Party of the Soviet Union, protested on March 30, 1971:

> The peoples will not be deceived by the attempts to ascribe to the Soviet Union intentions which are alien to it. We declare with a full sense of responsibility: we have no territorial claims on anyone whatsoever, we threaten no one, and have no intention of attacking anyone, we stand for the free and independent development of all nations. But let no one, for his part, try to talk to us in terms of ultimatums and strength.[16]

In the less developed portions of the world still under their control, the imperialists have intensified their exploitation of Afro-Asian and Latin American peoples and resources. These poorer countries have, in most cases, been given technical independence, but they remain under the control of neo-imperialism through reactionary puppet governments, military interventions and the manipulation of international markets. Within the capitalist countries, privileged segments of the working class have been given a small share in the wealth extracted from the Third World to buy their complicity in the imperial system.

The Soviet view finds the capitalist countries aggressive and the revolutionary countries defensive. The revolutionary movement is strong, but its final victory is postponed by the might of the imperialists. The Soviet Union has assumed the burden of defending the revolutionary advances that have been gained against imperialist reaction, while giving extensive aid to advance new anti-imperialist movements where they develop. The world system thus consists of an imperialist bloc led by the United States, a socialist bloc led by the USSR, and the Third World nations at various stages of development toward socialism but in many cases still dominated by the imperialists.

American Economic Imperalism

From the Soviet perspective the United States is uniquely important in modern imperalism. American foreign investors play critical roles in the economies of more than seventy-five foreign nations. The gross value of goods and services produced in foreign countries by American-owned facilities is over $60 billion per year. If we consider United States enterprises abroad as an aggregate, they would comprise the fourth largest "country" in the world, with a gross annual product

16. M. Gribanov, *Security for Europe* (Moscow: Novosti Press Agency, 1972), p. 19. Originally stated at 24th Congress of the Communist Party of the Soviet Union.

larger than that of any country except the United States itself, Japan or the Soviet Union.[17] Some large American firms dwarf the national economies in which they operate. Among American-owned multinational corporations, those companies that produce their goods in more than one country outside of the United States, several had total sales in 1982 of $20 billion or more. Exxon, for example, rose to more than $97 billion and both General Motors and Mobil Oil to $60 billion. Together, the fifteen largest of these corporations had sales in 1982 of $570 billion. This amount is almost a quarter of the American gross domestic product for 1982; and, more strikingly, it is 21 percent of the gross domestic products of all developing countries combined for the same year! Furthermore, one-half of all American exports goes to the developing world in terms of trade, which keeps the developing economies in constant debt to the United States. This debt is covered by loans from American banks and increases by 20 percent per year. By 1982, the debt of the entire developing world was 104 percent of its total exports. In many of those countries, total debt is more than 60 percent of gross national product. In some, the annual cost of that debt in interest exceeds 10 percent of gross national product.[18]

For some small countries, the operations and decisions of one or two large private investors are more important to national welfare than are the decisions of the highest domestic political officials, resulting in external control. The lust for overseas investments exists mainly because American investments in less developed countries return, according to Marxist computations, higher rates of profit than is normal within the home countries of the capitalists. This is, of course, a boon to the Americans, but a disastrous drain of wealth from the poor countries. United States investments in Latin America, for example, totaled less than $4 billion from 1950 to 1965. The returns on these investments that went back to the United States during this period were over $11 billion, almost three times as much.[19] For many individual countries, the outflow of profits to the United States is two to four times as great as the inflow of investment from the United States every year. This is one crude indicator of the exploitative character of the system of American economic dominance.

The highly favorable economic position of the American capitalists

17. Leo Model, "The Politics of Private Foreign Investment," *Foreign Affairs,* July 1967, pp. 640–41.
18. For data on American corporations, see *Fortune,* August 22, 1983, pp. 170–171. For data on the developing countries, see "International Bank for Reconstruction and Development," *World Development Report, 1983,* especially Part I and Annex Table 16.
19. N. Simonia, *The Third World and the Struggle for Economic Independence* (Moscow: Novosti Press Agency, 1972).

is secured and advanced by military force, just as the earlier imperialists used conquests and invasions to gain and protect a foothold for economic penetration. The United States protects its traders and investors by maintaining American armed forces in no fewer than sixty-four countries, truly a record in the history of empires. Naturally the hundreds of bases that are involved are rationalized in terms of "protecting" these countries from "Soviet imperialism" and "internal subversion," the American euphemisms for revolution. The American world system reaches farther and deeper than any previous imperial system in history, approximating a truly worldwide system of military, political and economic control.[20]

The United States has achieved this dominant position by pushing aside older imperial systems, and also by extending the range of the imperial system beyond its former reach, partly as a result of two world wars. The United States entered each of these wars only after

America's foreign trade: the Soviet view.

Source: Izvestia/World Press Review

20. V. Panov, *The Economic Weapons of Neo-Colonialism* (Moscow: Novosti Press Agency, 1972).

the other major capitalist powers were already weakened, and it emerged with the most nearly intact economy. Meanwhile, it exacted colonial and other enriching concessions from its allies and defeated enemies. Indeed it even went so far as partly to colonize the European countries themselves. Of course, the Europeans are not quite as helpless as some Third World states, and they are attempting to counterbalance the weight of American economic power by developing institutions to defend their own interests.

In addition to assuming the colonial enterprises of the older capitalist states, the United States has also deepened its penetration of the world market areas that were formerly not fully exploited. This is reflected in the spread of foreign branches of United States banks all over the world. Table 1–1 shows how bank branches have grown, and how this growth is due partly to a great increase in the number of countries in which United States financial institutions operate. Sometimes, the subject governments do not resist the invasion but rather welcome it. This is partly because of the control exerted on these governments, but also because of the poverty of such countries from long years of exploitation. As a result of the extraction of capital from them over many years, they are not able to develop enterprises of their own, and consequently depend on outside aid. This makes them vulnerable to American firms looking for profitable investment, and of course it makes the future of these countries even more dependent on foreign influence.

Owing to these patterns of investment and ownership of foreign production, the American role in the world imperial system is huge and growing. American capitalist imperialism dominates the economic and political order in many countries, often with substantially negative effects in the dominated countries.

We turn now to a second Soviet proposition, that this imperialist behavior is rooted in the nature of American capitalism. This theory that imperialism is caused by capitalism distinguishes the socialist view

TABLE 1–1
US bank branches outside the United States.

	1918	*1939*	*1950*	*1955*	*1960*	*1967*	*1975*
Number of branches	61	89	95	111	124	298	732
Number of countries	16	22	24	26	33	55	n.a.

Source: Through 1967, Harry Magdoff, *The Age of Imperialism* (New York: Monthly Review Press, 1969), p. 56. Copyright © by Harry Magdoff, and reprinted with permission of Monthly Review Press. For 1975, Andrew F. Brimmer and Frederick R. Dahl, "The Growth of US Banking Abroad," *Journal of Finance,* May 1975, pp. 341–63.

from other critiques of American foreign policy. American liberals, for example, also tend to see United States foreign policy in a critical light, but trace its failings to excessive anticommunist zeal or to misperceptions of the objective situation in other countries, rather than to the basic nature of capitalism. If capitalism inherently tends to be imperialistic, the problem of imperialism will be more difficult to solve within a capitalistic framework than if the cause of imperialism is the more superficial issue of mistaken policies. Thus, the relationship between capitalism and imperialism is a critical difference between socialist views of American imperialism and other theories.[21]

In the Leninist view, there are three needs that make capitalism externalize itself to imperialism: (1) the need for raw materials; (2) the thirst for captive export markets; and especially (3) the search for secure, high-yield foreign investment opportunities. All three of these dynamics operate in the American case.

Raw Materials

The huge American industrial apparatus consumes immense quantities of imported raw materials without which it would suffer a severe decline. While the United States was a net exporter of raw materials until 1920, since that year it has been increasingly dependent on imports, including reliance on foreign sources of vital petroleum fuels. Sixty-two industrial raw materials are listed by the Department of Defense as "strategic and critical materials" crucial for the warmaking ability of the United States, of which more than half of the annual consumption must be imported. For most of these materials, more than 80 percent of the supply is imported. It is obviously in the interest of American capitalism to secure these foreign sources of supply and to control the cheapest sources of raw materials. Both goals are served by American politico-military domination of the supplier countries.

Profits and Foreign Markets

Serious as it is, the raw-material issue is a relatively small point compared to the other two themes of the Leninist analysis: the issues of controlling foreign markets and investment opportunities. The very profits of American firms are tied closely to the control of other countries. To assess this proposition, consider the relative magnitude of foreign sales by American producers compared to sales within the

21. This critical distinction is developed in Robert Tucker, *American Foreign Policy and the Radical Left* (Baltimore: Johns Hopkins University Press, 1971).

United States. Taking the total of exports and sales abroad by American-owned enterprises located outside the United States, the foreign market is equal to approximately 25 percent of the total output of US-owned farms, factories and mines, and a somewhat higher percent of profits.[22] (Furthermore, while in 1961 American manufacturers exported $15 billion in goods and foreign affiliates of American industries sold $25 billion in goods, in 1970 the values increased to $35 billion in exports from the US and $90 billion for sales by foreign affiliates. Thus in that decade exports increased by 133 percent, while the sales of foreign affiliates skyrocketed by almost 400 percent.[23])

A brief look at annual performance reveals the extent to which individual American manufacturers rely on foreign markets. In 1982, for example, America's fifty largest exporting corporations produced a total of almost $629 billion in goods, of which they exported approximately $59 billion, or about 10 per cent. However, a look at some specific corporations dramatizes the potential for exploitation of external markets. Table 1–2 presents such a look. Table 1–3 reorders the principal exporting corporations on the basis of rank as measured by the percentage of total sales that are export sales. Note that in each table, the companies listed are not the largest American cor-

TABLE 1–2
Ten leading American exporting manufacturers by dependence on foreign markets, 1982, ranked by export sale in dollars.

Rank as Exporter	*Name*	*Rank in Total Sales*	*Total Sales*	*Export Sales*	*Percent of Total Sales Exported*
1	General Motors	2	$60.0 bil.	$4.7 bil.	7.8
2	General Electric	11	26.5	3.9	14.9
3	Boeing	34	9.0	3.9	43.0
4	Ford	5	37.1	3.7	10.0
5	Caterpillar	45	6.5	2.6	40.5
6	duPont	8	33.3	2.6	7.7
7	United Technologies	20	13.6	2.3	16.7
8	McDonnell Douglas	43	7.3	2.1	28.3
9	IBM	6	34.4	1.9	5.5
10	Eastman Kodak	26	10.8	1.9	17.1

Source: "The 50 Leading Exporters," *Fortune,* August 8, 1982, p. 89.

22. Harry Magdoff, *The Age of Imperialism* (New York: Monthly Review Press, 1969), pp. 173–202, esp. pp. 177–78.
23. "The Multinational Corporation and the World Economy," Committee on Finance, United States Senate, 1973, p. 12.

TABLE 1–3
Ten leading American exporting companies by dependence on foreign markets, 1982, as measured by percent of total sales exported.

Rank by Exports as Percent of Total Sales	*Company*	*Number of Exports as Percent of Total Sales*
1	Boeing	42.9
2	Caterpillar	40.5
3	Northrup	33.3
4	McDonnell Douglas	28.3
5	Hewlett-Packard	25.5
6	Harris (Florida)	24.7
7	Archer Daniels Midland	23.6
8	Ingersoll-Rand	22.3
9	Weyerhaeuser	22.1
10	Signal Companies	21.8

Source: Fortune, August 8, 1983, p. 89.

porations in terms of total annual sales. Hence many of the most familiar names in American industry are omitted, including all of the huge oil companies that dominate the largest list of the largest fifteen (nine). The two lists are limited to corporations that produce their entire output in the United States, but rely heavily on foreign sales. These companies are distinguished from the many American-based corporations that produce in several countries, the "transnational corporations" that are studied and listed in Chapter 16. Taken together, reliance on foreign sales by American producers and the gross world sales of the American-based transnationals is so extreme that it is now virtually self-evident that without foreign markets, countless American corporations could not survive.

Foreign Investment Opportunities

But even these figures understate the linkages between American imperialism and the class interest of capitalists, in the socialist view. An important additional point is the concentration of foreign interests compared to the domestic American economy. Only about fifty firms control more than half of all United States foreign investments; fewer than two hundred control more than 80 percent. Thus the foreign operations of American capital are far more monopolistic than the domestic operations: The largest and most powerful corporations tend to have a disproportionate interest in the foreign market.

From the socialist perspective this is significant because concentrated economic interests are better organized and more influential politically than dispersed economic interests. Thus a large industry that is concentrated, such as the General Electric Company, has more influence than a large industry that is dispersed, such as the retail drugstores, even though the total sales of all retail drugstores may be larger than General Electric. The huge concentration of power in the foreign investment and export sectors gives added weight to these interests.

The Military-Industrial Complex

Another link between imperialism and the interests of capitalism is the military-industrial complex, even though it serves a domestic rather than a foreign market. Military spending comprises another 10 percent of the profits of capitalism, and again more for large firms than small ones. In addition, a large percentage of the United States labor force is involved in defense production. If we add defense to exports and foreign investments and count only the largest firms, we may estimate that the world structure accounts for 35–40 percent of the profits of the top capitalist interests. The proposition is demonstrated: There is a clear linkage between capitalism as a socioeconomic system and the tendency to imperialism seen in American foreign policy.

How does this connection between the economic sectors of capitalism and the political policies of the United States government operate? There are both direct and indirect linkages. By studying the personal backgrounds, career origins and bureaucratic job cycles of the 234 top American foreign policy decision-makers from 1944 through 1960, the years in which the American empire absorbed the older imperial structures and became the dominant force in the world system, it can be shown that a relatively small number of individuals circulated among the top policy bureaus during these years. Moreover, about 60 percent of these came from big-business, investment and major law firm backgrounds.[24] There is an equally impressive circulation of personnel between the armed services and the top defense-supply firms. For example, more than 2,000 retired officers above the rank of colonel or naval captain are now in executive positions with the largest defense corporations. One linkage between imperialism and capitalism is the shared interests of the top capitalists and key government officials in the United States.

Another link is the influence that foreign-oriented capitalists are believed to exercise within the Congress and the American public. The Pentagon alone commanded in 1968 a force of 6,140 public relations officers assigned to sell the armed services point of view around the world. Of these, 339 were "legislative liaison" lobbyists assigned to

24. Gabriel Kolko, *The Roots of American Foreign Policy* (Boston: Beacon Press, 1969), pp. 16–26.

The White House and the business community serve the Pentagon: the Soviet view of America's military-industrial complex.

Source: Krokodil/World Press Review

the United States Congress. In addition, the private defense firms, the exporters and the foreign investment interests all had lobbying and public relations operations of their own, including sophisticated Washington law firms to exercise influence with members of Congress.

To suggestions that the Soviet Union, too, might have a military-industrial complex, there are stern denials. When the leading Soviet expert on the United States was asked about the "Soviet military-industrial complex. . .which also plays a decisive role in the arms race," he replied:

> You should not try to create symmetry where the situation is very different. Besides, to have a good arms race, you really need just one military-industrial complex.

The Soviet Union does, of course, have a defense industry and modern armed forces.

> But our defense industry does not operate for profit and thus lacks the expansionist drive that characterizes the arms industry of the West. Besides, our economy does not need the booster of military spending that has been turned on more than once in the West to tackle the problem of insufficient demand in the economy.[25]

This statement is consistent with the historic Soviet view that Western arms policy is linked directly to economic imperialism and the inherent weaknesses of capitalism.

Capitalism and National Interest

Another connection between the economic interests of capitalism and the political behavior of American officials operates through the perception of most officials that what is good for capitalism is good for America. In allocating defense spending, for example, members of Congress compete to get the juiciest prizes and largest military projects for their own districts. Mendel Rivers was the Chairman of the House Armed Services Committee, which is supposed to keep military expenditures under control. Mr. Rivers' Charleston, S.C., district had an air force base, an army depot, a naval shipyard, a marine air station, the Parris Island boot camp, two naval hospitals, a naval station, a naval supply center, a naval weapons station, a submarine training center, a Polaris missile facility, an Avco plant, a Lockheed plant, a GE plant and a Sikorsky installation. The annual military payroll in this district alone is over $2 billion. It has been said that if any more defense plants were put in Charleston, it would sink. Naturally, Representative Rivers was only too happy to go along with the military-industrial complex, justifying his position in terms of defending the "Free World" (the international capitalist system) from "Soviet imperialism" (revolutionary movements against Western imperialism).

American Militarism and Anti-Soviet Hysteria

Because of Washington's loss of world military superiority, the changing role of the Third World, the deterioration of American control over the Western allies and political changes in the United States affecting the conduct of foreign relations, the United States has, since the demise of détente, become increasingly militaristic. This is evi-

25. Statement by Georgi Arbatov in Georgi Arbatov and Willem Oltmans, *The Soviet Viewpoint* (New York: Dodd, Mead, 1983), pp. 110–111.

denced not only in military budgets and propaganda, but in Washington's international behavior as well.

This militarism is built upon the myth of a Soviet threat or of a global Soviet military build-up, a myth created in Washington with the assistance of the defense industries, the Pentagon, the government bureaucracy, the academic community, and the news media. "They thrive and prosper on the phantom of the 'Soviet threat.' They always take good care to nurture it when it gets too worn out through heavy use."[26] It is the work of Americans "who simply longed to be provoked and were desperately searching for a pretext"[27] for resumption of the Cold War. Then, having created the fable, these elements have doubled spending on weapons of mass destruction and threatened all socialist and Third World peoples with annihilation. For both economic and imperial purposes, the United States is determined to regain military superiority over the Soviet Union, the motherland of socialism, which is increasingly surrounded by the threat of Western aggression, now with the assistance of two huge and powerful Asian allies: Japan and China.

Washington's allies are almost as much the victims of this policy as is the Soviet Union. Much of the anti-Soviet hysteria emanating from Washington is designed to perpetuate fears of the Soviet Union among the allies in order to gain control of Western European, Japanese and Chinese foreign policies. By tactics of fear, the United States is attempting to generate the energy that its policy lacks virtually everywhere except in North America. Ample evidence was supplied in 1983 during the European debate about deployment of new American Pershing II and Cruise missiles. When the issue of the necessity of the weapons was raised, one senior State Department official declared that the principal issue at hand was not strategic parity with Soviet SS-20 missiles, but "alliance management."[28]

The improvement of Sino-American relations was a deliberate provocation of the Soviet Union by both the United States and China. It resulted in closing the ring around the Soviet Union and requiring that Moscow revise its targeting strategy in the Pacific. It was a major contributor to the deterioration of détente. While Americans were busily concocting stories about Soviet expansionism, the new military and diplomatic policies of the United States, that included China and

26. Georgi Arbatov and Willem Oltmans, *The Soviet Viewpoint, op. cit.* (1983), p. 107.
27. Georgi Arbatov, "A Soviet Commentary" in Arthur Macy Cox, *Russian Roulette: The Superpower Game* (New York: Times Books, 1982), pp. 182–183.
28. Richard Burt, *Time*, Dec. 5, 1983, p. 29. The complete statement: "The purpose of this whole exercise is maximum political advantage. It's not arms control we're engaged in, it's alliance management."

Western Europe as well as a strategy of limited nuclear war, provoked the Kremlin into new defensive strategies in such places as Afghanistan. All Soviet ventures were defensive in nature and "extraneous" to the context of détente; hence it was American policy which led to its demise.[29]

The militant tone of the Reagan administration at the time of the deployment of new missiles in Europe impelled Yuri Andropov to release a statement on Soviet-American relations in which he wrote:

> In their striving to justify in some way their dangerous, inhuman policies, the same people pile heaps of slander on the Soviet Union, on socialism as a social system, with the tone being set by the President of the United States himself. One must say bluntly—it is an unattractive sight when, with a view to smearing the Soviet people, leaders of such a country as the United States resort to what almost amounts to obscenities alternating with hypocritical preaching about morals and humanism.[30]

Two weeks later, another attack was made on the Reagan administration. This one acknowledged that while all American presidents are elected on the basis of their connections with the economic elite and oligarchy, Ronald Reagan in particular "was pushed upward by a group of 'the powers that be,' who discovered in him a cynical demagogue and obedient apostle of big business." It declared that "a policy of madness is gaining the upper hand" in Washington, one exceeding a mere "flurry of great-power messianism" to "an obsession with attaining world domination. . . ."[31]

This is the theory of American imperialism as viewed by Soviet observers and socialists around the world. The United States is the dominant power in the global system of imperialism that exercises control almost everywhere outside the communist world. Domination takes military, political and economic forms, and is motivated by interests that are rooted in American capitalism. Thus, Lenin's perception that capitalism tends to produce imperialism because of foreign investment dynamics, the need for export outlets and the search for cheap sources of raw materials describes, in the Soviet view, the reality of American behavior today. The theory of American capitalist im-

29. For specific comments, see Georgi Arbatov, "A Soviet Commentary," in Chapter VII of Arthur Macy Cox, *Russian Roulette: The Superpower Game* (New York: Times Books, 1982), pp. 173–199; and Georgi Arbatov and Willem Oltmans, *The Soviet Viewpoint,* especially pp. 62, 86, 104, 107, 167, 178.
30. Yuri Andropov, "Text of Soviet Statement on Relations with U.S.," *The New York Times*, September 29, 1983, p. A14. The text was released by Tass the preceding day.
31. Alexander Yakovlev, "The Harsh Soviet Line on Reagan," *The Washington Post,* October 16, 1983, p. B5. The author is Director of the Soviet Institute of World Economics and International Relations.

perialism is not just a rhetorical device employed by Soviet propaganda, but a real analysis of America's role in the world that is shared by Soviet communists and other observers who consider themselves anti-imperialist.

While the theory of imperialism and the role of the United States in the international system dominates the Soviet view, two other questions must be raised: the position of Europe and relations with China.

The Soviet View of Europe

Europe is the most immediate geopolitical issue in Soviet foreign policy. The Soviet Union has been subjected to three major invasions from the West in the past 150 years—twice from Germany. Any Soviet government would have as a paramount interest the question of European security and defense. Today these traditional issues are compounded because three of the world's six nuclear powers (USSR, Britain and France) are European, and the line of division between the capitalist and socialist worlds runs right through the heart of Europe. On the Western side of the line of demarcation, the NATO alliance members maintain armed forces in excess of five million troops organized in twenty-four divisions, armed with 7,200 nuclear warheads and an abundance of conventional air, sea and land materiel. On the communist side of the line, the Warsaw Pact nations maintain a defensive shield. All of the world's largest economies (except Japan) are engaged in this massive confrontation of forces in Central Europe. Quite naturally, the issue of security in Europe looms large in the Soviet view.

From the beginning in 1949, the Soviet Foreign Ministry objected to the formation of the NATO alliance. The Soviet government favored an all-European security conference to conclude a nonaggression, collective security treaty instead of constructing two opposed systems of alliances. Signatories to the treaty would pledge themselves to refrain from attacking one another and renounce the threat and use of force. Hostile coalitions would be prohibited, and in the case of an armed attack on one or several of the signatories, the others would regard this as an attack on themselves and would render the necessary military aid. This system would be maintained by forming political and military consultative committees.

The Western states consistently rejected this proposal, doubting Soviet intentions and, in the Soviet view, preferring to maintain the network of hostile and aggressive alliances in the hope of restoring capitalism in Eastern Europe, or at least preventing the further spread of revolutionary movements. Thus the socialist states were forced to form the Warsaw Pact counteralliance in their own defense. The defensive nature of the Warsaw Pact organization is shown by the provision that, in case of the discontinuance of the North Atlantic (Western) alliance, the pact would be invalidated automatically. Thus, according to the Soviet view, the responsibility for the system of Cold War alliances lies with the West.

To accomplish the key goal of preventing an attack from the West in the absence of a European security system, three elements of Soviet policy are paramount:

1. Governments sympathetic to the USSR and socialist in orientation must be maintained in the belt of Eastern European countries which lies between the Soviet heartland and the powerful countries of Western Europe, especially Germany. In the West, these East European states are considered a "buffer zone" of "satellite states."
2. Germany, the most powerful and historically the most aggressive country of Europe, responsible for the terrible suffering and depredations of the war, must be neutralized as a threat. Germany cannot be permitted to reunify under a capitalist government that is still tied to the imperialist camp. Preserving the division of Germany into East and West is a necessary and expedient means of reducing the German threat. A government sympathetic to the USSR is maintained in the East.
3. The military powers of the West European countries must be counterbalanced by the military power of the USSR and the East European countries. This is the mission of the Warsaw Pact.

Soviet policy since the Second World War has achieved all three of its aims in Europe. As an outcome of the war, Poland, Czechoslovakia, Hungary, Rumania, Albania, Yugoslavia and Bulgaria are now communist countires, most of them reliable allies against the possibilities of a Western invasion. The strategic location of Czechoslovakia, through which there is direct access to Soviet territory from West Germany, helps to explain why the Soviet Union invaded that country in 1968 rather than risk its move out of the Soviet camp and into a friendly relationship with West Germany. Such an alteration in position would have jeopardized the entire Soviet-Eastern European defense system.

The problem of an immensely powerful Germany, once so threatening, has been reduced by partition and by the Soviet-American agreement at Helsinki in 1975, which recognizes as permanent the post-Second World War boundaries. The division of Germany into two

FIGURE 1–1

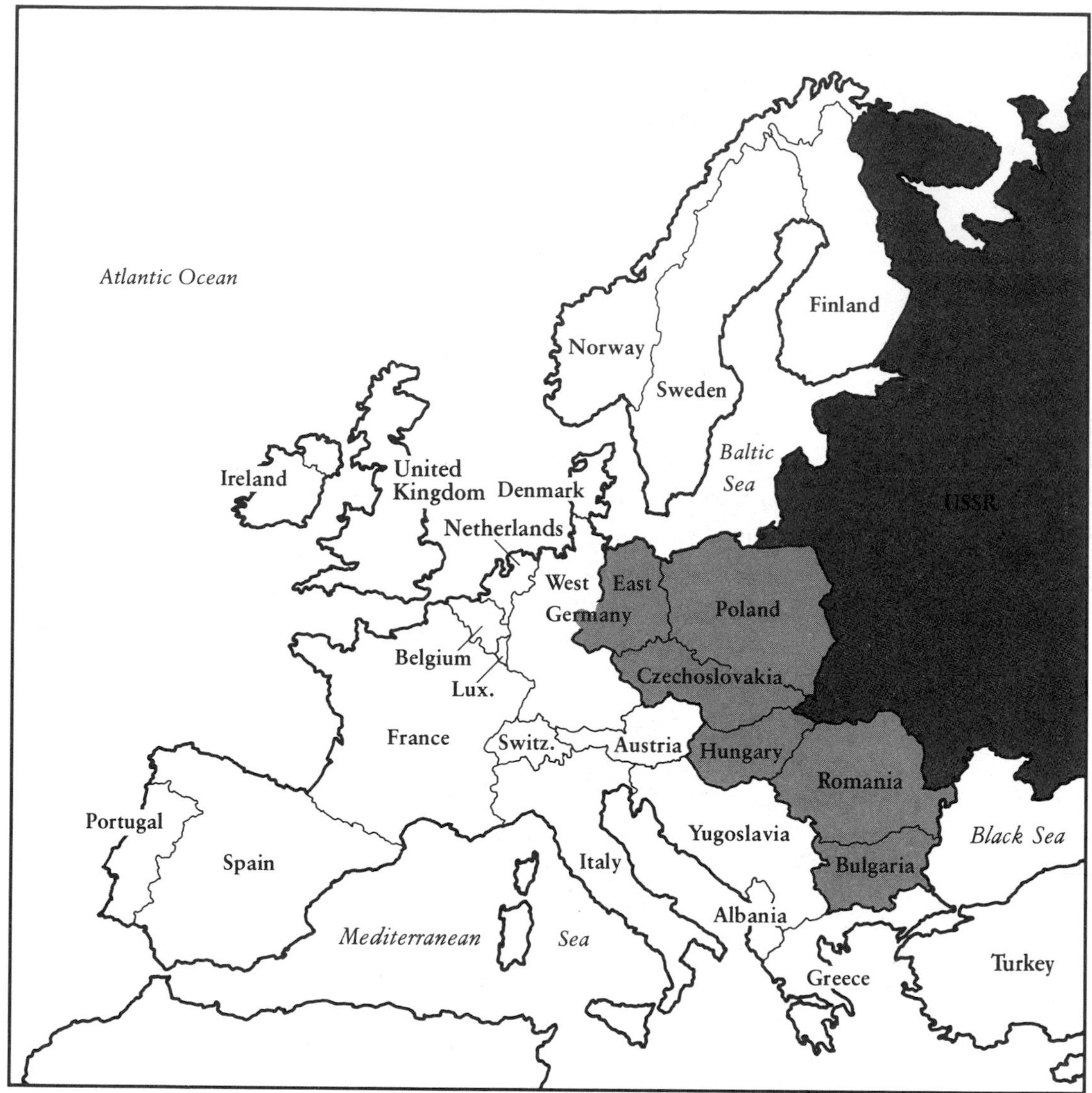

Eastern Europe seen as a buffer for Soviet defense.

zones, originally a by-product of a 1945 military convenience, had become a reality prior to Helsinki. The USSR obviously cannot allow the zone under its influence to rejoin the western half while West Germany maintains a capitalist social system and an alliance with imperialism. In addition, the Soviet Union strenuously opposes nuclear development in West Germany. An aggressive West Germany armed with atomic bombs could have nightmarish consequences not only for the Soviet union, but also for Poland, Czechoslovakia and other East European countries.

Finally, to secure control in East Europe and to counterbalance NATO, Soviet and other communist forces are maintained at levels superior to Western ground forces. Communist division in Central Europe have outnumbered those of the NATO countries since the Second World War. While the West considers this a menace to the capitalist international order, in Moscow it is seen as a simple necessity for preserving the Socialist commonwealth.

In recent years several issues outstanding in the postwar division of Europe have been settled. Most significant among them has been the conclusion of a treaty between the Soviet Union and West Germany in 1970, paving the way for the solution of all outstanding questions between these two crucial countries. The realistic *Ostpolitik* of West Germany has created the possibility of an acceptance of the de facto situation in Europe as the basis for new relations in this region. In particular, Germany accepted the Oder-Neisse line as Poland's western border with East Germany, and recognized the permanence of the two Germanies. The two signatories also pledged themselves to refrain from the use or threat of force and to guide their relations by the principles of the United Nations Charter.

The treaty was followed a year later (1971) by the signing of a four-power agreement on West Berlin by France, the United States, Great Britain and the Soviet Union. The agreement detailed a basis for relations between that city and West and East Germany, prohibited the use of force, and resolved many technical issues that had been barriers to the relaxation of tensions and the opening of borders for the freer passage of visitors. Although this agreement did not satisfy all sides, it did lay a realistic basis for the improvement of relations, bypassing the insistence on absolute principles that always leads to an impasse. Thus, some of the key issues in Central Europe have been resolved by political moderation.

The Soviet Union has paralleled this "peace offensive" with a renewed call for a general European Security Conference. In 1966, at a conference in Bucharest, Romania, the Soviet Union and six other socialist countries proposed the holding of an all-European conference on security and cooperation. It aimed at expanding nondiscriminatory East-West trade and at reducing military tension in Europe by gradual dissolution of military blocs, dismantling of foreign bases, withdrawal of foreign troops and renunciation of the use of force.

At a subsequent meeting in Budapest in 1970, this proposal was expanded to emphasize economic, scientific and environmental issues with a view to promoting political cooperation among the European states. And, most significantly, the Budapest Memorandum proposed the establishment of a permanent all-European political body to deal with questions of security and cooperation. The European Security Conference held in Madrid in 1980 was sabotaged by American insistence upon attacking the human rights record of the Soviet Union. The Conference met periodically through 1981 and 1982, although the opposing sides were deadlocked over security issues. Both Western condemnation of Soviet behavior in Afghanistan and Poland, and NATO's determination to deploy new theater nuclear weapons that jeopardize the security of the Soviet missile force from a first nuclear strike have contributed to the impasse. The Conference concluded at the end of 1983 with a call for a first phase European Disarmament Conference, which convened in Stockholm early in 1984.

Before the severe break-down of relations in the 1980s, however, there was an eight-year period that promised a thaw in Soviet-American relations, despite differences over Soviet policy in Africa and generally over the subject of human rights. From the Soviet perspective, the thaw rested on several bases. From a strategic point of view, increased fear of Chinese strength on the Asian borders was an incentive to more peaceful relations in Europe (although, paradoxically, improved relations between Peking and Washington resulted in renewed suspicions in the Kremlin of American motives). Secondly, the phenomenon of Eurocommunism further loosened the economic dependence of Eastern Europe upon the Soviet Union. It opened both intergovernmental (official) and transnational (popular and unofficial) avenues to improved relations between Eastern Europe and the countries of the European Common Market, thus greatly strengthening the potential for international trade balances among the Eastern European countries. Thirdly, and a matter of utmost importance to Soviet planners in all areas pertaining to economic modernization, agricultural production and military preparedness, Moscow increasingly recognized its need for access to the superior technological capabilities of the United States, Japan and Western Europe. While American critics of technological trade with the Soviet Union argued that it merely strengthened the military potential of their country's principal adversary, the Soviets, in acknowledging that the gap between the two countries can be closed through such trade, recognized that its continuation depended upon moderation in their foreign policy.[32]

Despite these reassuring trends, however, Soviet policy was scarcely free of age-old distrust of Western military and diplomatic strategies.

32. Mark E. Miller, "The Role of Western Technology in Soviet Strategy," *ORBIS*, Fall 1978, pp. 539–68.

Three issues in particular continue to strain relations between the Kremlin and the West, even at a time when Soviet preoccupation with the growth of Chinese influence in Asia continues to mount.

Détente and its Demise

A popular attitude prevailed from the end of the Vietnam War through the 1970s that fundamental changes in East-West attitudes had called a halt to the Cold War. This attitude was expressed as *détente,* and was seen by both East and West as a promising new foundation for foreign policy. But in the Soviet view, the specific conditions and political assumptions of détente, as applied in American diplomacy and in American political expectations, was unreasonable, one-sided and generally unfair. Détente, after all, was only one characteristic of complex international dynamics subject to change at all times and places. Therefore, in the Soviet view, the playing out of competing interests is a natural part of international politics, and should be allowed to continue without the fearful assumption that every Soviet-American competition will result in a severe deterioration of relations between the two great capitals. Thus, while Americans were quick to assume that every new Soviet move was a threat to détente, Soviet planners argued instead that détente was "the art of tradeoffs between competitors, not an arrangement whereby new friends solemnly swear to end the contest." Far from being an agreement to preserve a status quo or a particular world power distribution, détente was a theory of international politics that enabled the Soviet Union to pursue its interests without direct military involvement in areas of specific American dominance, to the end that the Soviet Union might fulfill its goals of full superpower status. The Kremlin regarded détente not as a set of global rules preventing the acquisition of its goals, but of ensuring the peaceful evolution of a world order in which every important international issue would require Soviet participation.[33]

However it was interpreted in the West, détente did not survive the 1970s. Increasing Western hostility to the Soviet Union and its internal and external policies made it clear that the West understood détente to apply restraint to Soviet pursuit of great power interests. Examples abound: American destruction of the Socialist regime of Chile; constant American attacks on the human rights policies of the Soviet Union; NATO charges of aggressive Warsaw Pact intentions in Europe; reconstruction of Sino-American relations as a form of tacit aggression against the Soviet Union by both Washington and Peking;

33. Dimitri K. Simes, "Détente, Russian-Style," *Foreign Policy,* no. 32 (Fall 1978), pp. 47–62.

continued American intrusion in the affairs of the Eastern bloc by condemnation of Soviet actions in Poland, together with American economic retaliation; American plans to deploy an MX missile system, a major variant of the nuclear arms race threatening its stability; failure of the United States to ratify the SALT II treaty; change of American nuclear targeting strategy from one of counterforce (aimed at military installations only) to countervalue (aimed at population and industrial centers); deployment of highly accurate Cruise and Pershing II missiles in Western Europe; inflammatory rhetoric of the Reagan administration accusing the Soviet Union of planning military superiority designed to enslave the world; and so on. The militarism and anti-Soviet hysteria of the United States, together with the expanded threat of nuclear war following the deployment of new American weapons, struck the Soviet Union as signs of hostility, not of an enlighted Western attitude called détente, which provided assurances of great power, peace, and freedom of action in areas not directly under the control of one another. Détente had been merely a ruse under which the West perpetuated the Cold War.[34] In such an environment, it was necessary for the Kremlin to discontinue the Intermediate-range Nuclear Forces (INF) talks regarding Europe and the Strategic Arms Reduction Talks (START) on intercontinental nuclear weapons. While the Soviets longed for the return of détente and normalization of relations with the United States, their moves were based on the "gaping discrepancy between U.S. policy and today's realities. Officials in Washington have forgotten, or simply do not want to remember, that successful talks on arms limitation and the very prevention of nuclear war call for normal relations, relations of peaceful coexistence and détente between countries with different social systems. . . . One cannot count on the preservation of peace, or on the success of the negotiations, while at the same time unleashing a wholesale political war against the socialist countries, spurring on the arms race, and fanning hatred and mistrust of the Soviet Union."[35]

Mutual Force Reductions in Europe

Since 1973 the Soviet Union, together with its Warsaw Treaty Organization allies, and the Western powers have been discussing the subject of mutual and balanced force reductions (MBFR) in Europe.

34. John Lewis Gaddis, "The Rise, Fall and Future of Détente, *Foreign Affairs,* Winter 1983/84, pp. 354–377. Gaddis presents the revisionist interpretation that détente from the American viewpoint was not a new strategy, "but a means of updating and reinvigorating containment."
35. Georgi Arbatov in Georgi Arbatov and Willem Oltmans, *The Soviet Viewpoint,* p. 86.

Each party recognizes the explosive potential of continued arms buildups in Europe, with respect to both nuclear and conventional forces. As the title of these talks suggests, a formula is being sought that would ensure the reduction of total forces but in a manner that requires each party to contribute to the reduction by mutual responsibility. The objectives, then, in simple terms are: (l) establishment of a stable military balance in Europe with (2) reduction in total deployment of troops and weapons, and (3) responsibility shared among the participants to contribute to the reductions.

The principal issue of contention is that while Moscow interprets the reality of capitalist encirclement as limiting its obligation to *mutual* reduction (MFR), the West continues to try to weaken the Soviet defenses by calling for mutual and *balanced* reductions (MBFR) on the basis of an abstract and politically unacceptable principle.

Beyond these basic objectives, however, few successful principles have been elaborated. The Soviet Union objects to American skepticism as to the accuracy of Soviet figures on the strength of the Warsaw Treaty forces; and the two sides cannot agree on mathematical formulas for achieving mutually acceptable reductions. Specifically, should reductions be determined by percentage withdrawals or by the withdrawal of specific numbers of troops and weapons? To the Soviets the former is desirable, on the the grounds that the current balance is at least effective—even if too much military potential is tied up in it at a time when more attention needs to be given to the China front. The second approach, labeled the common-ceiling approach, is viewed by Moscow as a Western ploy to substitute absolute numerical equivalence for a system of effective balance and, through that equivalence, to gain an advantage in the European power distribution. There is further fear that such "asymmetrical" reductions will enable the United States, which is viewed as a stabilizing force within NATO, to withdraw a disproportionately large share of its commitment (an act that Congress has repeatedly threatened as an economic measure), thus enabling the dreaded German forces to be increased. With these and other fears in mind, the Soviet negotiators have repeatedly charged the West with approaching MBFR with an aggressive, obstructionist and militarist attitude.[36]

Modest progress was achieved in 1982, when both the Warsaw Treaty Organization (WTO) and the North Atlantic Treaty Organization (NATO) presented draft treaties. Though far from achieving a settlement, these two attempts did estabish some common ground,

36. See particularly John Borawski, "Mutual Force Reductions in Europe from a Soviet Perspective," *ORBIS,* Winter 1979, pp. 845–73. Borawski's text draws heavily on Russian-language sources.

including eventual total number of troops on each side (900,000), autonomous authority to determine the national proportions within the total number, establishment of verification stations on each side, and agreement on non-interference in satellite verification measures. Prospects for further progress were dimmed by an exchange of charges between Moscow and Washington regarding the propaganda objectives of one another as the United States attempted to solidify Western European public opinion in preparation for the deployment of new theatre weapons. By the end of 1983, as that deployment began, the Soviet Union reacted to the insincerity of American arms negotiations by postponing further MBFR talks, much like what occurred with both theater weapons negotiations (INF) and intercontinental force reductions (START).[37]

Strategic Arms Limitation

Since the conclusion of the first phase of the Soviet-American Strategic Arms Limitation Talks (SALT I) in 1972, the parties have been striving for a formula that would go beyond limitations on antiballistic missile systems and ceilings on the deployment and replacement of nuclear-weapon-bearing vehicles.

In the intervening years, the development and deployment of additional weapons systems has clouded the future of the SALT negotiations, and has repeatedly been used in the United States to call into question its own military preparedness. In response to accusations that the Soviet Union is attempting to deploy new missiles under the guise of having redesigned old ones, the Soviets charge that American development of cruise missiles undermines the spirit of the SALT deliberations. Americans charge the Soviet Union with equipping intercontinental ballistic missiles (ICBMs) with more independently targeted warheads than the parties agreed in principle to be permissible; whereas Soviet critics of American policy deplore the American development of the Triton submarine and the capacity to launch nuclear attacks from the ocean floor.

A few areas of agreement on principles do exist. The parties agree, for example, that SALT should result in a stable nuclear balance in which neither side is disadvantaged by dismantling requirements or by ceilings on production. Both, too, have agreed that the essential goal of the talks is the establishment of mutual deterrence through the preservation of adequate second-strike capability. This, it is hoped, will dissuade the other side from attacking because, even after having

37. For a summary of the 1982 occurrences, see *SIPRI Yearbook, 1983*, pp. 595–605.

sustained an attack, there will be enough nuclear capability to retaliate. The United States has conceded that the issue of parity (the attempt to make nuclear arsenals as nearly identical in size and capability as possible) is unimportant, because it is in the nature of nuclear weaponry that there is reached a point of "sufficiency" beyond which it becomes tactically unimportant whether or not the other side has a few more weapons! The Soviet view is complicated, of course, by the fact that while the Pentagon needs to think of nuclear strategy almost exclusively with respect to the Kremlin, the latter must also take into account the growing threat of Chinese military and even nuclear power.

Under these circumstances, Soviet planners regard themselves as more eager to conclude SALT II than their American counterparts. They consider the United States to have violated the spirit of the talks by new weapons developments that are disproportionate to the expansion of Soviet capabilities, and to have damaged the prospects for successful agreement by reviving Cold War rhetoric about the Soviet military threat. This excerpt from *Pravda*, the official press of the Kremlin, sets the tone of the Soviet attitude on the American commitment to SALT II:

> Reactionary circles in the US have been trying, among other things, to impede the current Soviet-American strategic arms limitation talks. The noisy propaganda campaign that has been launched recently in the US Congress and the United States' mass news media is clearly aimed at casting aspersions on the Soviet Union as far as the fulfillment of the agreements currently in effect is concerned, sowing doubts among the American public and members of Congress as to the viability of documents worked out in this field, and hampering the process of the strengthening of trust between our countries' peoples. As is known, most of the initiators of this campaign have long since proved themselves to be outspoken opponents of the improvement of Soviet-American relations. Among them one could list such figures as Democratic Senator H. Jackson, former Republican Senator J. Buckley, former Defense Secretary Laird, retired Admiral Zumwalt and others.
>
> The fabrications of these figures are as numerous as they are groundless. They include fantasies about the alleged construction in the USSR of ICBM silo launchers in contravention of the interim agreement, about some kind of opposition to technical means of verification, and other fabrications having nothing in common with the actual state of affairs.
>
> What is the real purpose of these allegations? There can be only one answer: They are aimed at impeding the ongoing and—it should be noted—highly complex Soviet-American talks on strategic arms limitations and at throwing a monkey wrench into the policy of detente.[38]

In 1981, Washington and Moscow agreed to pursue separate but related negotiations on intermediate-range nuclear forces in Europe,

38. From *The Current Digest of the Soviet Press,* February 4, 1976, pp. 1–4.

the so-called theatre forces, and on the problem of eventually reducing intercontinental nuclear forces. These two sets of talks, called respectively INF and START (for Strategic Arms Reduction Talks), proceeded in parallel fashion through 1983. In December 1983, deployment of new American Pershing II and Cruise missiles began with the result that the Soviet Union declined to agree to dates for continuation of either set of talks. The negotiations and the principles behind them are discussed in detail in Chapter 9, "Military Regional Balances," and Chapter 10, "The Balance of Terror."

The Soviet View of China

The persistent conflict between the Soviet Union and China has grown in importance to the Soviet world outlook in recent years, contributing to the desire for reduced tensions in Europe. This antagonism is a very old issue, predating communism in the two countries. The historical fact of an expansionist Russia relentlessly pressing eastward has naturally brought conflict between two giants who share a 7,000-mile border. The issues dividing the USSR and China today include both ideological questions and historical national interests that would conflict regardless of ideology.

National Border Disputes

Western Region The border may be separated into three general regions of conflict. In the western region the 1,850-mile border between Soviet Central Asia and China's Sinkiang Province divides homogeneous ethnic minorities (Uighurs, Tadzhiks, Kazaks) whose movements do not always observe the legal boundaries. China conducts it atomic testing and some atomic production in Sinkiang, raising other special issues. The most serious problem from the Soviet point of view is that China controls the Ili Valley gateway to Turkestan, making the protection of Soviet Central Asia militarily difficult. This "Great Gateway of the Nations"—the Dzungarian Gates—was the route through which the hordes of Genghis Khan invaded Europe, and it has long been a problem of Russian (and later Soviet) defense.

Eastern Region In the eastern region the 2,300-mile border separating the Soviet maritime regions and Pacific ports from Chinese Manchuria is a special problem. These Soviet Far Eastern assets are vital commercial and military links, but they are logistically remote from the Soviet heartland and are difficult to defend. On the Chinese side of the border in the main Manchurian industrial region, which confers logistical advantages. China's claims for revisions of the existing line of demarcation, based on historical issues, would bring Chinese power right up to the city limits of Khabarovsk and in other ways substantially weaken the Soviet position. Therefore, the Soviet Union insists on the principle of sanctity of treaties, and denies the ambitious Chinese claims.

Central Region In the remaining region, the 2,650-mile Chinese border with Outer Mongolia, the issue is not border delineation or the strategic balance, but the question of control over Outer Mongolia itself. This quasi-independent nation is now under Soviet influence. China asserts a historical right to suzerainty—a claim that the Soviets regard as pure troublemaking.

This 7,000-mile border cannot be directly defended mile-by-mile, so defense depends on a system of mutual threats and general military preparations. Hundreds of thousands of troops are deployed on each side. Several skirmishes resulting in deaths occurred during the late 1960s and the early 1970s, and pessimistic predictions speak forebodingly of the potential for much larger encounters.

The potential for military conflict reaches beyond the common boundary of the two giant powers. For almost twenty years they have competed for Mongolia, now in the Soviet orbit, and for as long they have nervously watched one another's interests, maneuvers and investments in India, Pakistan and Bangladesh. During the Vietnam War, Peking and Moscow competed for dominant influence over Hanoi, with Ho Chi Minh playing a coy game of accepting the assistance of both without succumbing to the control of either. There were unconfirmed reports, however, that Soviet goods bound for the North Vietnamese war effort were being held up on railroad sidings in China, in order that the dominant military aid might be thought to be from China.

More recently, continental Asian events have taken a number of peculiar turns. First, Japan has reached formal peace with both China and the Soviet Union. Second, Peking and Washington have exchanged diplomatic recognitions, putting an end to a bitter mutual antipathy and the sponsoring of wars through their surrogates; and the rapprochement of China with the West has improved China's conventional military potential as well as its political-military relations with NATO on the Soviet western front. Third, and of most immediate apparent value, China has invaded Vietnam as an act of punitive aggression for Hanoi's conquest of Kampuchea (formerly Cambodia).

In an effort to offset this apparent Chinese advantage in the competition among the nonnuclear areas of Asia, the Soviet Union has moved naval vessels into Cam Rahn Bay, a huge naval facility built by and for the use of the US Navy during the Vietnam War. Furthermore, the military relationship among China, NATO and Japan has called for an increase in Soviet vigilance throughout the North Pacific; Soviet air, naval, submarine, intelligence and communications activities have been expanded there, particularly in the Soviet-held islands north of Japan. These are not aggressive moves, in the Soviet view, but the necessary defensive consequence of a new and ever more threatening form of encirclement by imperial and ideologically revisionist forces.

Ideological Disputes

In addition to this conflict of national interests, there are key ideological issues in dispute between the two communist giants. Since the death of Stalin in 1953, Chinese propaganda has portrayed the Soviet Union as a center of "new imperialism" just as abhorrent as that of the Western capitalists. China has called for "alternative paths to socialism" in the communist bloc, in which the central determination of bloc policy by the Soviet Union would be ended in favor of a concept of self-determination by each country. China even laid claim to the mantle of ideological leadership, portraying Mao Tse-tung as a contemporary and coequal of Lenin, while the present Soviet leadership is seen as a gang of bureaucratic hacks. Chinese propaganda has made virulent attacks of all kinds on the intentions and integrity of the Soviet Communist party. The Soviets regard the Chinese charge that the broadening of Soviet interests to Afghanistan and other areas in the Third World represents the establishment of "social imperialism" as a particularly repugnant ideological diversion. Pure Marxism-Leninism reserves the charge of imperialism for capitalists and other fascists.

The Soviets reject these claims as irresponsible, ill-founded and motivated by wild ambition. Both "alternative paths" and Chinese leadership are invalidated by the simple reality that only Soviet might, backed up by the huge Soviet economy, can in fact defend the revolutionary states from capitalist encirclement and promote revolutionary gains in the Third World. Only Soviet nuclear power deters the American colossus—the Chinese capability could never do it alone. And only Soviet technology and production can supply the most advanced weapons and aircraft to aid the struggling peoples of Indochina and the Middle East. Thus, the Soviet Union is the shield and the arsenal of the revolutionary world.

In addition, the "alternative-paths-to-socialism" slogan causes disunity in the socialist camp and creates a false idea of relativism. The Soviets have never denied that revolutionary principles must adjust to the special conditions in each country, but they firmly reject the extreme go-it-alone lengths to which this idea is carried by China. The ideal form is collective determination of bloc policy by international party congresses, as practiced since 1945 and even earlier. The Soviet Union does not propose to rule by arbitrary and unilaterial fiat, but neither does it propose to allow purely national interests within the bloc to rise above the collective interests of the bloc as a whole. The Brezhnev Doctrine, pronounced in 1968 in justification of the Warsaw Pact countries' invasion and occupation of a liberalizing Czechoslovakia, reaffirms the primacy of the collective socialist good over the particular interests of any single country within the camp. United, the socialist world will prosper; but divided it will fall to hostile capitalist encirclement. This maxim is complicated by Peking's improving ties with the communist parties and governments of Eastern Europe, thus accelerating the erosion of socialist solidarity.

The Soviet Union itself, it is argued, must be the first among equals. The USSR was the first revolutionary state and spawned the others. The Soviet Communist Party is the direct heir of Lenin and is ideologically and materially best prepared for the leadership position. Thus, the Soviets reject the ideological as well as the territorial claims of the Chinese adventurists, and increasingly hold them responsible for the deterioration of the Socialist Commonwealth, both by undermining Soviet superiority and by making threatening accommodations with the West.

The deterioration of détente with the West has occurred simultaneously with major changes in China and in Chinese foreign policy. The passing of Mao Tse-tung in 1976 brought enormous changes to Chinese relations with the West, with obvious implications for Soviet foreign policy. But the emergence of a new Chinese political outlook has not had direct benefits for the Kremlin and has not yet eased the necessity for vigilance on the Eastern front. Thus the new Chinese diplomacy presents a triple cost to the Soviet Union: (l) the Chinese connection with the West and with its economic, technological and military capabilities increases the Chinese threat in Soviet policy; (2) the opening of China to new ideas and new modes of diplomacy and commerce threatens to erode Moscow's position as the unchallenged pinnacle of the Socialist Commonwealth, as China works out new relations with Eastern Europe; and (3) the new Chinese leadership has taken fewer steps to improve relations with the Kremlin than with Washington and the other NATO capitals. Hence, while the West has largely been freed of the burden of countering Chinese foreign policy in Asia and elsewhere, the burden for the Soviet Union has multiplied.

Summary of the Soviet View

The Soviet point of view is a combination of Russian national interests and communist ideological principles. The contemporary international system is seen as largely unjust and threatening to the Soviet Union, whose main role is to defend itself and its allies and to combat international injustice.

The dominant theme in the Soviet view of the international system is the *theory of imperialism*. Capitalism, which is still the social system in most of the advanced and powerful countries, is supported by class exploitation, and imperialism is simply the international expression of this exploitation. Capitalist systems need empires that provide (l) raw materials, (2) markets for domestic exports, and (3) high returns on investments. The imperialist states therefore dominate most of the poorer countries.

The communist countries have defected from this international class system. As the first and strongest socialist state, the USSR is the natural leader. The military might of the imperialists is such that direct challenge to the imperial system is not possible. But it is the obligation of the USSR to defend the communist states that already exist from capitalist-inspired counterrevolution or invasion and, insofar as is possible, to help other countries on the path to revolution.

As the leading imperialist power, the United States has a special role in the international system. It controls more than half of the imperialist system of exploitation, and it is immensely powerful militarily. It maintains a vast network of alliances designed at the minimum to keep control of all countries not already communist, and possibly even "to roll back communism" (that is, recapture the liberated countries for the imperial system). The United States is also important in that it is most skillful in hiding its true position behind moral and ideological disguises that continue to befuddle many non-Marxists.

The capitalist world encircles socialism, and only the Soviet shield protects and advances the world revolutionary movement. Yet a dissident faction within the socialist camp, led by China, divides and disunifies revolutionary states and creates an internal opposition to the Soviet leadership. Only the solidity of the Warsaw bloc in Eastern Europe prevents renewed aggression from the capitalist world. The unity of the socialist commonwealth must stand above the claims of factions within individual countries. Chinese adventurism must be opposed at every point, and the solidarity of the revolutionary world must be maintained. Only in this way can the final victory of socialism be achieved over the long run.

2

The American Perspective

Ironically, for most of the lást two decades it has been easier for many Americans to entertain a friendly picture of the Soviet or the Chinese view than to appreciate the role of an official of their own country. Particularly in the wake of the twin calamities of Vietnam and Watergate, together with the fall and rise of Cold War rhetoric, there was a willingness to look closely at the communist side, a willingness that made the shortcomings of their own country seem all the more glaring.

During the 1980s a revised view of the American role in world affairs developed. Growing awareness of the Soviet military strength after a decade of curtailed military sentiment at home called into question the adequacy of national preparedness in a manner unknown since the 1930s; and the presidential election of 1980 as well as the congressional elections of 1980 and 1982 seemed to be, among other things, a repudiation of post-Vietnam War foreign policy and a call for a new national outlook. President Reagan called for a renewed vigilence against Soviet expansionism with its threat to democratic principles the world over and against the efforts of the Third World to command world events in a way that could diminish the standard of living in the United States. A wave of conservatism and patriotism swept the country, as much among young people as among their elders.

With the major exception of student reaction against compulsory registration for Selective Service (though the actual draft did not exist), most youthful political activity leaned sharply toward conservative policy proposals, both domestic and international.

In these changes of view, perceptual analysis need not imply that a particular outlook is "correct" and another "incorrect"—only that when attitudes about world perspective change, there is a strong internal logic consistent with the evidence when it is ordered in a certain, even if changed, way.

Roots of the American World View

Whereas Marxist thought begins with a theory of class conflict and revolution, the American world view turns on questions of political freedom and tyranny. Freedom—understood as self-determination, majority rule and the right of dissent—is the highest goal in the hierarchy of core values. "Give me liberty or give me death," demanded Patrick Henry. When Americans evaluate other social systems, the first questions they ask usually concern the degree of freedom of speech and religion, the right to vote and tolerance of dissent. Political and religious liberty are put above economic well-being and questions of economic justice.

The relative unconcern of Americans for class injustices, compared to other peoples, has been credited to the lack of a feudal experience. Absentee landlordism and other abuses of feudalism left in many other countries a bitter heritage of class conflict, which was much less pronounced here.[1] The promise of open land beyond the frontier before 1900 made America a "land of opportunity" where wealth was the direct reward for hard work and poverty the punishment for laziness or stupidity.[2] The early settlers who came to the New World sought not class revolution, but religious tolerance (for example, Puritans, Mennonites) and economic opportunity. Capitalism itself demanded a free market, entrepreneurial liberty and political self-determination, at least for the commercial classes.

These origins were consistent with the evolution of a philosophy of the "social contract." In this theory, the state is constituted, by freely consenting individuals, to protect the security and advance the com-

1. The importance of a nonfeudal past is explored by Louis Hartz in *The Liberal Tradition in America* (New York: Harcourt Brace and World, 1955).
2. The significance of the frontier is explored in Frederick Jackson Turner, *The Frontier in American History* (New York: Henry A. Holt, 1920). See also David Potter, *People of Plenty* (Chicago: University of Chicago Press, 1954).

mon interests of society. Government "derives its just powers from the consent of the governed," in Jefferson's words. Revolution is justified not in terms of class upheaval, but as a legitimate response to political tyranny.

The principal danger to liberty is the inherent tendency of government to expand without limitation and to extinguish the rights of citizens. Power corrupts and absolute power corrupts absolutely. Tyranny is averted and governmental power is limited in the United States by constitutional restraints, majority rule, guaranteed minority rights, checks and balances among 80,000 separately elected governmental units, and the separation of executive, legislative and judicial powers. Power is at every point balanced against power: civilian control of the military, judicial oversight of the constitutionality of legislative and executive actions, state versus federal authority, direct election of high officials and other checks. The obsession of the entire design is eternal vigilance against despotism.

The American Image of International Relations

The problem of defending freedom against tyrannical tendencies exists not just within individual societies, but in international relations as well. The parallel to individual freedom in international society is the principle of national independence and self-determination, and the parallel to infringement of individual rights is the violation of territorial sovereignty and foreign interference in the internal affairs of a free nation. Civil freedom is threatened when uncontrolled authority expands to tyranny. International freedom is threatened when one nation or coalition undertakes to extend its power to the domination of others. In both cases, injustice begins when one power center upsets the natural balance of forces and seeks an unwarranted expansion.

Historically, internal and external tyranny are linked in the American view. Democratic governments and free peoples are thought to be naturally peace loving, while tyrannies and dictatorships have an innate tendency to expand beyond their own borders to make demands on their neighbors. An unchecked tyranny in one country is soon a danger to the entire world.

The Image of the Aggressor

The image of the International Aggressor is a critical component of the American belief system. An image is a simplified representation of reality that serves as a mental ordering device. The Aggressor is a bully

"On the Threshold!"

Source: © Gale, *The Los Angeles Times*

who employs military threats and actions to subdue weaker states and to seize from them any assets he wishes. He is immune to normal considerations of justice, and regards international law and morality as mere sentimentality. His appetite for expansion is insatiable, especially when motivated by a messianic ideology, and success in one conquest does not appease him but whets his appetite for more. He is cunning in the use of propaganda to conceal his intentions, and he regards agreements and treaties as mere expedients rather than obligations.

The only restraint that the Aggressor truly respects is physical opposition. If the world is to be ruled by reason and not by force, and if weak members of the international community are not to be left at the mercy of the strong, it is the special responsibility of the larger democratic states to oppose international lawlessness. The United States in particular is obligated by its vast resources and its historic ideals to play a role of leadership in guaranteeing minimum standards of international behavior.

The dominant theme of American diplomatic history during the twentieth century has been the search for an appropriate role. On the one side are the ideals of the American people and the perceived problems of the international system; on the other side are the limits of American commitment to external affairs. Repeatedly, the United States has been called upon to respond to aggression in other parts of the world, but the American people have continued to find the role of "world policeman" unnatural.

Aggression in the Twentieth Century

Before the First World War the United States was relatively uninvolved on the world stage. Though potentially powerful, it was insulated from foreign conflicts by vast oceans on both shores, and the dominant position of the United States in the western hemisphere assured safety within this zone. Moreover, the global system from 1815 until 1914 was relatively stable and rarely called for active American military participation. The major European states that dominated the world system pursued essentially conservative policies of maintaining the status quo (though redistributive goals were pursued in relation to colonial issues), and the security of American interests was hardly affected by the tides of world politics.

American foreign policy during this period had three cornerstones:

1. *Isolationism:* nonentanglement in the complex web of European military alliances and intrigues. These were perceived as having little consequence for Americans.
2. *The Monroe Doctrine:* an insistence on European nonintervention in the western hemisphere, in effect declaring Latin America as the United States' sphere of influence.
3. *Commercial expansion:* full participation in free international trade and access to world markets while avoiding foreign conflicts.

In general, these principles asserted for the United States a major role as a world economic actor but a minor role in world political and military affairs.

This relatively harmonious world was thoroughly upset in 1914 with the outbreak of the First World War. For the first time since 1815, a major power seemed bent upon fundamental redistribution and alteration of the European balance, with vast consequences for the rest of the world. Within months, most of the big powers and their allies and colonies were drawn into the complex struggle, and a variety of regional antagonisms separate from the main issues were added to the conflict. The United States, protected by geographic position from the main issues and confused by the morass of charges and counter-charges, claims and counterclaims, stayed out of the war for three years.

But as the war progressed, America's early neutrality and isolationist attitude gave way to growing hostility toward Germany and an increasing sympathy to the Allies, especially Britain. Ties of language and custom with England, as well as strong commercial links, made true neutrality impossible. Moreover, the struggle was increasingly viewed as a deeply moral issue of democracy and decency (England) versus dictatorship and barbarism (Germany). This image of the German Aggressor was promoted by British propaganda, and was taken up by President Wilson to build public support for entry into the war on the Allied side. When German submarines began sinking American commercial vessels with civilian passengers aboard, American opinion was enraged, and the image of the Aggressor was driven deep into the public consciousness. President Wilson's memorable war message on April 2, 1917, spoke directly to the key themes in the image. The war was caused by an attempt at territorial expansion by tyrants.

> We have no quarrel with the German people. . . . It was not upon their impulse that their government acted. . . . It was a war determined as wars used to be determined upon in the old, unhappy days when peoples were nowhere consulted by their rulers and wars were provoked and waged in the interest of dynasties or of little groups of ambitious men who were accustomed to use their fellow men as pawns or tools.

The United States had tried to stand apart, Wilson declared, but had discovered to its sorrow that it could not escape the responsibility to oppose massive aggression.

> A steadfast concern for peace can never be maintained except by a partnership of democratic nations. We are glad . . . to fight thus for the ultimate peace of the world and for the liberation of its peoples, the German peoples included; for the rights of nations great and small and the privilege of men everywhere to choose their own way of life and of obedience. . . . America is privileged to spend her blood and her might for the principles that gave her birth and happiness and the peace which she has treasured. . . . The world must be made safe for democracy.

The United States would fight not for narrow national interests, but for the restoration of an international system based on principles of justice and nonaggression.

> We have no selfish ends to serve. We desire no conquest, no dominion. We seek no indemnities for ourselves, no material compensation for the sacrifices we shall freely make. We are but one of the champions of mankind.[3]

This break with historic isolationism signified for the United States the beginning of an active role in the defense of Western democracy.

The 1919 Settlement

The leadership's approach to the Peace Conference after the German defeat in 1918 provides further clues to the operation of the Aggressor image in the American world view. Since Wilsonian thought traced the origins of German external aggression to roots of internal tyranny, the first task was to redesign the German political order. The Weimar Constitution, which was drafted largely by Americans and which borrowed heavily from Anglo-American constitutional experience, projected for Germany a model democratic system eliminating all traces of autocratic rule. Combined with a compulsory program of disarmament and industrial limitation, it seemed to guarantee that Germany would never again attempt aggressive expansion.

On the international level, the Wilsonian design was to seek new systematic guarantees against potential future threats to stability. The idea of *collective security* was founded in the institutional form of the League of Nations (precursor to the United Nations). In effect, this modeled future international relations on the principle of an alliance of major powers permanently committed to oppose aggression. Unfortunately, the League had little success in fulfilling these goals when new threats to international peace developed. Domestic political opposition and a resurgence of isolationism prevented the United States from actively supporting the League in the way that Wilson had designed. Moreover, the major powers were not, in most cases, able to agree on joint policy toward expansionary movements, and it became clear that opposition to aggression on grounds of principle was less important to most leaders than the pursuit of more narrowly conceived national interests. The dream of collective security evaporated and international relations reverted to the more familiar pattern of power politics from which, in fact, it had never varied.

3. Woodrow Wilson, *War Message*, 65th Congress, first session, Senate document no. 5 (Washington 1971), pp. 3–8.

The Second World War

Within fifteen years of victory in the Great War, three new Aggressors moved to subdue new victims. First, in a mounting series of crises, militant Japan seized control of the crucial Manchurian industrial region of China in 1931. In 1933, Adolph Hitler used the ill-conceived emergency-powers clause of the Weimar Constitution to overthrow the German Republic and establish the fanatical and aggressive Third Reich dictatorship. In 1935, Benito Mussolini led Fascist Italy into a war of conquest in Ethiopia. In 1936, Hitler remilitarized the Rhineland in preparation for war. In 1937, Japan extended its movement in China with an eye to total conquest.

President Franklin Roosevelt tried to warn the American people in 1937 that "the epidemic of world lawlessness is spreading," but Americans remained firmly isolationist. Reluctance to get involved was based on retrospective doubts about the First World War, including scandalous revelations about the activities of munitions profiteers and British propagandists in promoting the earlier war policy. A January 1937 poll showed that 64 percent of Americans questioned thought that it had been a mistake to enter the previous war. Many Americans resolved not to be trumpeted into foreign troubles a second time. The Neutrality Act of 1937 formalized this attitude in law.

Critical events in the deepening European crisis began in 1938. The German *Anschluss* absorbed Austria into Germany in March, signaling the opening of military advances in Europe. The democractic powers stood by, helplessly making indignant statements. When Hitler subsequently demanded that Czechoslovakia surrender the Sudetenland on the grounds that its population was German-speaking, the war alarm sounded across the continent. Czechoslovakia counted on its defensive alliances with France and Russia, while Hitler confidently expected that the Allies would balk at war.

In September the United States requested, and Hitler and Mussolini agreed to, a big-power crisis conference at Munich. Included were the two Fascist leaders and the premiers of Britain and France (but not of the Soviet Union), who met to discuss the Czech crisis and how war might be averted. At Munich the democratic leaders took Hitler at his word that he would make no further demands if given the Sudetenland, and the Allies abandoned Czechoslovakia to its fate. Prime Minister Chamberlain returned to London with the wishful declaration that he had achieved "peace in our time," on the grounds of Hitler's promise that this was "the last territorial claim which I have to make in Europe." These are now remembered as some of the most tragic statements in diplomatic history.

The Munich sellout is universally cited as a classic case of appeasing an aggressor. The futility of this policy was immediately apparent when Hitler absorbed the remains of Czechoslovakia and went on to the invasion of Poland, which finally triggered British and French resistance. Many historians believe, in the light of the documents that have since become available, that the Allies could have stopped Hitler at the Sudetenland before he captured the Czech munitions industry. This might have deterred further expansionary moves. An additional cost of appeasement was the stimulus it gave to Soviet fears that the Allies were trying to "turn Hitler East" at Soviet expense, a perception that led to the infamous Hitler-Stalin nonagression pact, which temporarily took Russia out of the antifascist alliance. Americans took from this bitter experience a deep skepticism about "appeasers" who would compromise with aggressors (a practice subsequently known as "Munich-mindedness").

As German armies rolled over Denmark, Norway, Belgium, Holland, Luxembourg and finally France, and as the nightmare of Nazi rule was extended across the continent, American isolationist feeling began to give way to alarm. President Roosevelt reported to the American people that even the security of the United States itself was not absolutely guaranteed.

> Armed defense of democratic existence is now being gallantly waged in four continents. If that defense fails, all the population and all the resources of Europe, Asia, Africa and Australasia will be dominated by the conquerors. Let us remember that the total of those populations and their resources in those four continents greatly exceeds the sum total of the population and the resources of the whole of the Western Hemisphere many times over.

Roosevelt asserted that beyond considerations of domestic security, "We know that enduring peace cannot be bought at the cost of other people's freedom." What was truly at issue was the ability of a tyrannical movement to commit aggression against other people at will.

> Every realist knows that the democratic way of life is at this moment being directly assailed in every part of the world—assailed either by arms, or by secret spreading of poisonous propaganda by those who seek to destroy unity and promote discord in nations that are still at peace.
>
> During sixteen long months this assault has blotted out the whole pattern of democratic life in an appalling number of independent nations, great and small. The assailants are still on the march, threatening other nations, great and small.[4]

4. *Congressional Record,* 87 (January 6, 1941), p. 46.

The American people did not fully throw off the philosophy of isolationism and enter the struggle against fascist aggression until the Japanese surprise attack on the American naval and air base at Pearl Harbor on December 7, 1941. The purpose of the attack was to immobilize American defenses against Japanese seizures of American, British and Dutch possessions in the Far East, but many Americans perceived the event as a step toward a move on Hawaii or even California. An enraged public gave overwhelming support to a declaration of war against Germany as well as Japan. But once in the war, broad principles of an allied defense against aggression took precedence over purely national concerns. For example, a frequent poll question during the war was, "If Hitler offered peace now to all countries on the basis of not going further but of leaving matters as they now are, would you favor or oppose such a peace?" Support for peace on these terms was generally below 20 percent. In many concrete ways, American war conduct manifested a broad commitment to principles of non-aggression and universal self-determination, rather than a pure concern with American self-interest.

The 1945 Settlement

Following the war, the United States and its allies once again set about to secure the future international system. The German and Japanese political systems were redesigned by Occupation authorities along modern democratic principles, and the United Nations was founded to re-establish the machinery of collective security that had failed in the League of Nations. Americans took the lead in proposing a reformation of the world system; more than half of the respondents in several polls favored the idea of a world government with the power to control the armed forces of all nations, including the United States. The United States joined the United Nations immediately (whereas it had stayed out of the League) and was from the beginning one of its most active and supportive members.

The greatest shift in American policy, then, was a strategic reorientation from isolationism to a permanent commitment to world responsibilities. In contrast to the almost complete disarmament after 1918, demobilization after 1945 left a standing army of more than a million and a global network of active American military bases. Americans had concluded from the experience of "coming to Europe's rescue" in two world wars that a position of responsibility in world politics was an inescapable obligation of the most powerful democracy, and that the interests of world stability and American security would be best served by involvement rather than by isolation.

This shift in perception characterized mass opinion as well as the views of policymakers. In various polls on isolationism since 1949, between two-thirds and four-fifths of respondents have favored the option of an active international role for the United States, working closely with other nations rather than taking an independent position. However, when the question is posed in the form, "Has this country gone too far in concerning itself with problems in other parts of the world?" opinion is more evenly divided.[5] It appears that the United States should, in the majority view, play an active role in defense of certain interests and principles, but should not attempt to be "policeman of the world." National exhaustion over the Vietnam War served to deepen this sentiment.

Several points should be made about the terms under which the United States entered the world arena between 1914 and 1945. The tragic course of world history during these four decades convinced Americans that Europe had failed in its stewardship of world order. Twice the New World had been forced to rescue the Old from its own contradictions. The United States entered the world arena flushed with tremendous success at home in building the world's most dynamic economic and political entity and bursting with ideas for international reform. It had emerged from the two wars as the only major actor that had not been subjected to invasion, humiliating occupation or the terror of aerial bombardment. The decisive role of its power in the two victories reinforced a sense of invincibility, built on the innate optimism of a people who had little experience with tragedy. America based its new image of "leader of the free world" on this foundation of pride and self-confidence.

It has been argued that the unique innocence Americans brought to international politics has been a liability as well as an advantage. An optimistic people has a tendency to reduce burdensome complexities to simplistic explanations and easy formulas, and Americans have often compressed their understanding of difficult issues into purified political and moral principles.[6] Not every conflict can be understood as a struggle between good and evil. In particular, the tendency to interpret the motivations of all adversaries through the lens of the Aggressor theory may distort reality and lead to false solutions. This is especially dangerous when America's response is founded on the anti-appeasement principle of countering perceived aggression by a strong willingness to use force. The twin problems of accurately defining threats to the peace and formulating an appropriate response

5. See John E. Mueller, *War, Presidents, and Public Opinion* (New York: Wiley, 1973), p. 110.
6. Henry Kissinger, *American Foreign Policy* (New York: Norton, 1969), for example.

by the United States reached a more acute stage as the shape of the postwar world emerged from the fog of the battle against the Axis imperialists.

Origins of the Cold War

The settlement of 1945 that ended the violence of the Second World War created at the same time the basis of the Cold War. The United States and the Soviet Union ceased to be allies in the common struggle against fascism and initiated a prolonged competition for the political mastery of Europe, Asia and the world. There are profound differences of opinion among informed Americans about the origins of the Cold War, and alternative interpretations greatly affect the understanding of many other issues.[7]

The alliance with the Soviet Union against Hitler was undertaken by the United States out of necessity. Before 1941, a deep-seated suspicion of Stalin and Soviet communism had severely restricted commercial and political relations with the USSR. These fears were amplified during the decade before the war by reports of massive purges in Moscow, the virtual extermination of several million farmers of the kulak class and other denials of human rights. Soviet foreign behavior was typified in the American mind by subversive activities of the Comintern that seemed to threaten the democratic states, by the hated Hitler-Stalin nonaggression pact and by a brutal attack upon tiny Finland.

But the wartime alliance of necessity, once undertaken, generated a warmth between the two peoples. There was a new respect in the United States for the deep commitment of the Russians to their struggle against fascism. Some American officials projected a new era of cooperation between dissimilar but friendly societies after the war, including cooperation in guaranteeing collective security through the Security Council of the United Nations. Other possible contingencies

7. Studies of the origins of the Cold War abound. Among the most thorough full-length studies that represent a spectrum of viewpoints ranging from strongly pro-American to equally strongly critical of the United States are these: Herbert Feis, *From Trust to Terror* (New York: Norton, 1970); Denna F. Fleming, *The Cold War and Its Origins* (Garden City, N.Y.: Doubleday, 1961), two vols.; John Lewis Gaddis, *The United States and the Origins of the Cold War* (New York: Columbia University Press, 1972); David Horowitz, *Free World Colossus* (New York: Hill and Wang, 1965); Vojtech Mastny, *Russia's Road to the Cold War* (New York: Columbia University Press, 1979); Hugh Seton-Watson, *Neither Peace nor War* (New York: Praeger, 1960); Martin J. Sherwin, *A World Destroyed* (New York: Random House, 1973); Ronald Steele, *Pax Americana* (New York: Viking, 1967); and Daniel Yergin, *Shattered Peace* (Boston: Houghton Mifflin, 1977).

in relations with the USSR were not thoroughly examined by Washington before the end of the war, and little realistic and systematic planning was done for the design of the postwar world beyond the United Nations. In Moscow, however, some fateful and extensive decisions were being taken on postwar policy and actions. This difference was later to produce deep American shock at Soviet designs.

Some joint discussion of the postwar liberation took place at the Teheran, Yalta and Potsdam conferences. The three Big Powers—the USA, USSR and Britain—agreed on several essentials. The Nazi war machine would be destroyed by Soviet armies moving from the east and American and British forces moving from the west. Temporarily, each of the Allies would be responsible for establishing civil order in the territories liberated by its forces, pending the assumed restoration of self-determination and free elections. Eventually, the occupation forces would withdraw and the various nations would resume their independent lives.

It was understood that as a matter of simple realism, the Soviets could not be expected to tolerate potentially hostile alliances along their borders again, and that the new East European governments would have to respect this principle in their foreign affairs. An informal understanding provided this formula to guide political development during the transitional period:

Rumania	90 percent Soviet
Bulgaria	80 percent Soviet
Hungary	50/50 Soviet/West
Yugoslavia	50/50 Soviet/West
Greece	90 percent British

It was also understood that the Western European countries, including France and Italy, would not be under Soviet influence, but that Soviet security needs would have a large say in Poland and Czechoslovakia. Germany, the most serious problem, would be divided into four zones—under American, Soviet, British and French control—disarmed, and eventually reunified after pacification and political reconstruction. Other understandings applied to Korea, Japan and other countries, and to the United Nations.

What was not intended in these agreements, and was definitely not anticipated in the West, was that the Soviets would leave the Red armies permanently in control of the Eastern European states, creating a satellite chain linked by virtual puppet governments. Americans were outraged by the naked use of Soviet power to create colonies. In Poland, for example, the Soviets shocked world opinion by abetting in the extermination of antifascist but noncommunist freedom fighters, and after they were destroyed, putting in their place an all-communist government reporting directly to Moscow. In Czechoslovakia, a democratic coalition of communists and noncommunist leftist parties was destroyed by a Moscow-ordered communist coup. In Germany, the Soviet zone of occupation was converted into a permanent puppet state, and the agreed goal of reunification was scuttled. The idea of free elections was forgotten. "Across Europe," Winston Churchill declared to the American people at Fulton, Missouri on March 5, 1946,

> from Stettin in the Baltic to Trieste in the Adriatic, an Iron Curtain has descended across the continent. Behind that line lie all the capitals of the ancient states of central and eastern Europe. Warsaw, Berlin, Prague, Vienna, Budapest, Belgrade, Bucharest, and Sofia, all these famous cities and populations around them. . . . The Communist parties, which were very small in all these eastern states of Europe, have been raised to prominence and power far beyond their numbers and are seeking everywhere to obtain totalitarian control. Police governments are prevailing in nearly every case.[8]

Even more alarming was what was perceived as the effort by the Soviet Union to push this Iron Curtain forward and bring additional lands under communist control. Subversive activities were encouraged in France and Italy; claims were advanced against Iran; the communist-controlled Viet Minh moved against French control in Indochina; threats were made against Turkey; and an insurgent movement was mounted in Malaya. In China, the communists reopened their struggle against the Kuomintang government.

Throughout the world, insurgent parties fomented disorder and revolution in the name of communism. Many in the West concluded that the USSR sought not just security on its frontiers but expansion everywhere, and possibly even mastery of the earth.[9] Dissenters argued that not every revolutionary event could be traced to a conspiratorial command center in Moscow.

The Truman Doctrine

The case that finally produced a crisis atmosphere in Washington was that of Greece. There, the retreating Germans had destroyed railways, ports, bridges, communications facilities and the network of orderly civil administration. More than a thousand villages were burned. By 1947 a majority of children tested were tubercular. In this atmosphere,

8. *New York Times,* March 6, 1946, p. 4.

9. See, for example, Elliot Goodman, *The Soviet Design for a World State* (New York: Columbia University Press, 1960).

rival communist and monarchist factions of the former antifascist resistance were locked in civil war. It was believed in Washington, though there were dissenters, that Stalin had given the go-ahead signal to the insurgents and that Soviet arms were flowing freely to the communist side in violation of the understanding that Greece was to be under Western influence.

This crisis had special significance for the assessment of Soviet intentions. If indeed this were a Soviet move against Greece, Russian expansionary goals evidently included political issues quite remote from critical zones of national defense. Stalin seemed to have in mind ambitious plans for the destruction of capitalism, in disregard of his agreements. On the other hand, some continued to see the Soviet Union pursuing essentially defensive goals, or at worst regional expansion along the familiar lines of tsarist imperialism, rather than a truly global power grab in the name of communism. A great debate about Soviet motives, and a search for the wisest response, began in the United States.

The dominant school of thought, given its classic expression in the "containment" philosophy of diplomat and scholar George Kennan, was that Soviet policy served ideological imperatives demanding global struggle and opposition to capitalism. He explained:

> Of the original ideology, nothing has been officially junked. . . . The first . . . concept is the innate antagonism between capitalism and socialism. . . . It means that there can never be on Moscow's side any sincere assumption of a community of aims between the Soviet Union and powers which are regarded as capitalist.[10]

The responsibility to oppose this policy of limitless conflict fell to the United States which, Kennan said, must base its actions on the principle of containing Soviet power within its existing boundaries until internal changes within the Soviet leadership produced an abandonment of aggressive intentions.

> The Soviet pressure against the free institutions of the Western World is something that can be contained by the adroit and vigilant application of counterforce at a series of constantly shifting geographical and political points, corresponding to the shifts and maneuvres of Soviet policy.

This point of view was shared by President Truman, who incorporated it in his enunciation of the Truman Doctrine on March 12, 1947. His speech made the analogy between communist aggression and the Nazi aggression that preceeded it: The "fundamental issue" in the war with

10. George Kennan (writing under the pseudonym "Mr. X"), "The Sources of Soviet Conduct," *Foreign Affairs*, July 1947.

Germany and Japan had been "the creation of conditions in which . . . nations . . . will be able to work out a way of life free from coercion." Now, once again, we had to be "willing to help free people to maintain their free institutions and their national integrity against aggressive movements that seek to impose upon them totalitarian regimes." Note the themes of aggressive dictatorship versus peaceful democracy in the following passage from Truman's address.

> The peoples of a number of countries of the world have recently had totalitarian regimes forced upon them against their will. . . . At the present moment in world history nearly every nation must choose between alternative ways of life. The choice is too often not a free one.
>
> One way of life is based upon the will of the majority, and is distinguished by free institutions, representative government, free elections, guarantees of individual liberty, freedom of speech and religion and freedom from political oppression.
>
> The second way of life is based upon the will of a minority forcibly imposed upon the majority. It relies upon terror and oppression, a controlled press and radio, fixed elections and the suppression of personal freedom.
>
> I believe that it must be the policy of the United States to support peoples who are resisting attempted subjugation by armed minorities or by outside pressures.
>
> I believe that we must assist free peoples to work out their own destinies in their own way.[11]

Note also that the United States will "support peoples who are resisting attempted subjugation by armed minorities." This suggests intervention against aggression even when the rebels are nationals of the same country, blurring the distinction between international aggression and civil war.

Critiques of the Truman Doctrine

The Truman-Kennan perspective was criticized from several camps. The "realist" school, headed by Hans Morgenthau, accused it of "sentimentalism" and "moralism." The containment strategy was justified

> not primarily in terms of the traditional American interest in the maintenance of the European balance of power, but in terms of a universal moral principle. This principle is derived from the assumption that the issue between the United States and the Soviet Union . . . must be defined in terms of "alternative ways of life" . . . [and] proclaims the defense of free, democratic nations everywhere in the world against "direct or indirect aggression". . . . Thus the Truman Doctrine transformed a concrete interest of the U.S. in a geographically defined part of the world

11. *Congressional Record,* 93 (March 12, 1947), pp. 1999–2000.

> into a moral principle of worldwide validity, to be applied regardless of the limits of American interest and of American power. . . . As a guide to political action, it is the victim, as all moral principles must be, of two congenital political weaknesses: the inability to distinguish between what is desirable and what is possible, and the inability to distinguish between what is desirable and what is essential.[12]

Journalist Walter Lippmann, another realist, called the Truman Doctrine "a strategic monstrosity" that could not succeed in changing the situation in Eastern Europe. "No state in Eastern Europe can be independent of the Kremlin as long as the Red Army is within it and around it," he wrote. And the Red Army would remain as long as Russia was threatened with hostile encirclement across the military line of division in Western Europe. "The presence of these non-European armies in the continent of Europe perpetuates the division," he continued. The wise course of American response would be to offer the Soviets a mutual withdrawal, United States forces to leave the Western sector and Soviet forces to return to the USSR. "If the Red Army is in Russia, and not on the Elbe . . . the power of the Russian imperialists to realize their ambitions will have been reduced decisively." The containment policy was seen as having exactly the opposite effect and therefore as an incorrect response to Soviet expansion.[13]

The "liberation" school of dissenters, headed by John Foster Dulles, who later became Secretary of State to Republican President Dwight David Eisenhower, took a position opposite to the realists. Dulles objected that containment was a passive policy that always left open the question "Which of us will be the next victim?" It projected for the United States a static political role, allowing the Kremlin to determine the place and terms of conflict. "Ours are treadmill policies which, at best, might perhaps keep us in the same place until we drop exhausted." It was a law of history that "the dynamic prevails over the static," and the correct response to Soviet imperialism was not mere defense but an active offense. We could not just contain communism at its present boundaries but had to carry the struggle across the Iron Curtain to pursue the liberation of captive nations that have already fallen to Soviet imperialism.[14]

12. Hans J. Morgenthau, *In Defense of the National Interest* (New York: Knopf, 1950), pp. 120–21.
13. Walter Lippmann, *The Cold War* (New York: Harper and Row, 1947), p. 61. See also Ronald Steel, *Walter Lippmann and the American Century* (Boston: Atlantic-Little, Brown, 1980), Chapter 34.
14. John Foster Dulles, "A Policy of Liberation," *Life,* May 19, 1952, pp. 147–48. See also Townsend Hoopes, *The Devil and John Foster Dulles* (Boston: Atlantic-Little, Brown, 1973), Chapter 13.

The third and final major school of dissent may be called, in the parlance of later Vietnam debate, the "dove school." Climaxing in the unsuccessful 1948 presidential drive of former Secretary of Agriculture Henry A. Wallace, the doves argued that the containment policy itself endangered peace and provoked the very Soviet posture that it deplored. Wallace asserted that "a great part of our conflcit with Russia is the normal conflict between two strong and sovereign nations and can be solved in normal ways. . . . When Britain competes for resources, we settle our differences as friends. When Russia competes for them, we sound a fire alarm and thank God for the atom bomb. Why?" Wallace argued for cooperation in the UN rather than a worldwide anticommunist military crusade. He predicted that containment would force the United States to support dictators everywhere in the name of defense: "Every fascist dictator will know that he has money in our bank. . . . Freedom, in whose name Americans have died, will become a catchword for reaction."[15]

A similar view was argued by Robert A. Taft, the leading conservative of the time, who objected to the North Atlantic Alliance as "a treaty by which one nation undertakes to arm half the world against the other half," and predicted that "this treaty . . . means inevitably an arms race." Taft, like the doves, feared that "if Russia sees itself ringed gradually by so-called defensive arms, from Norway and Denmark to Turkey and Greece . . . it may decide that the arming of Europe, regardless of its present purpose, looks like an attack upon Russia."[16]

The "containment" and "liberation" schools portray the Soviet Union largely in terms of the Aggressor, while "realist" and "dove" schools of thought take a more limited view of the threat posed by communism. To simplify and organize the key distinctions, the various views are condensed into a "hard" and a "soft" line in Table 2–1.

The magnitude of the Soviet threat has been a question of fierce controversy among American scholars and Kremlinologists. Inferences about Soviet motives have ranged from a portrayal of designs for world domination[17] to the view of a defensive Soviet Union acting more in fear of the West than in pursuit of an autonomous hegemonial will.[18] In a survey of twenty-two major American writings on Soviet foreign conduct, nine authors were found to take ultrahard positions (sub-

15. Speech by Henry A. Wallace at Madison Square Garden, New York City, on March 31, 1947, printed in *Congressional Record,* 80th Congress, 1st Session, Appendix, pp. A1572–1573.
16. Speech by Robert A. Taft, *Congressional Record,* 81st Congress, 1st Session, pp. 9208–10.
17. Goodman, *The Soviet Design for a World State, op. cit.* (1960).
18. Denna F. Fleming, *The Cold War and Its Origins, op. cit.* (1961).

TABLE 2–1
Two views of the Soviet Union.

	Hard Line	*Soft Line*
Russia's primary goal	Worldwide communist expansion	National and regional defense
Communism	A centrally directed aggressive conspiracy	Only partly controlled by Moscow; not a monolithic bloc
New revolutionary crises	Most coordinated from the Kremlin	Most responses of local movements to particular conditions, aided but not controlled by Moscow
America's responsibility	Worldwide containment of communist-led movements	Maintain European balance of power, but not play role of reactionary policeman of the world
Effects of US alliances	Stalemate communist aggressive moves	Stimulate defensive arms race and troop deployments on Soviet side

scribing to the Aggressor image), seven hard, and six mixed hard-soft. None gave a soft or ultrasoft portrayal.[19]

In this survey, an *ultrahard* view saw as Moscow's purpose a boundless expansion in pursuit of total worldwide revolutionary victory, accepting no restraints but those dictated by the ebb and flow of opportunity. The *hard* image saw the Soviet Union seeking a global improvement in its political, economic and military position. Ideology to these authors played a secondary role in Soviet intentions, and the Kremlin's motivation for expansion outside areas of immediate national concern was considered moderate. The *mixed hard-soft* writers saw the Soviets as expansionist, but only as a continuation of the historic Russian reaction to repeated foreign invasion, and motivated by defensive concern for security rather than by dreams of a Soviet world state.

The majority of Americans followed President Truman's lead in

19. William Welch, *American Images of Soviet Foreign Policy* (New Haven, Conn.: Yale University Press, 1970), especially pages 30–58. Welch selects Robert Strausz-Hupe, William R. Kintner, James E. Dougherty, and Alvin J. Cottrell, *Protracted Conflict* (New York: Harper and Row, 1963) to represent his ultrahard image; Marshall Shulman, *Beyond the Cold War* (New Haven, Conn.: Yale University Press, 1963), to represent his hard image; and Frederick Schuman, *The Cold War: Retrospect and Prospect* (Baton Rouge, La.: Louisiana State University Press, 1967), 2nd ed., to typify the mixed hard-soft image.

taking the hard line. The Gallup poll asked, "As you hear and read about Russia these days, do you believe Russia is trying to build herself up to be *the* ruling power of the world, or do you think Russia is just building up protection against being attacked in another way?" In June 1946, just after Churchill's Iron Curtain speech, 58 percent favored the "ruling power" interpretation to 29 percent for the "protection" interpretation. By November 1950, after the adoption of the Truman Doctrine and the onset of the Korean War, 81 percent favored the "ruling power" theory to only 9 percent for the "protection" theory. In January of 1948, 83 percent of Americans favored stopping all trade with Russia. The ratification of the NATO pact "to stop Soviet expansionism" was endorsed by 67 percent. On November 8, 1954, *Time* magazine defined the communist idea of coexistence as "a period of deceptive docility while gathering strength for a new assault." Clearly, the great debate had been won by the containment theorists.

Deepening Hostility

Hostility between the United States and the Soviet Union deepened after the promulgation of the Truman Doctrine and the establishment of the North Atlantic Treaty. A constant stream of negative headlines concerning events in the communist world reinforced and strengthened the convictions of the containment model. The Soviets suppressed liberalization movements in East Germany in 1953, in Hungary in 1956 and in Czechoslovakia in 1968, to mention only the large-scale coercive actions. Oppression against captive peoples was also perceived in China's forcible annexation of Tibet and Soviet policy toward non-Russian minorities within the USSR. These negative impressions were confirmed by millions of refugees who voted with their feet by fleeing communism to seek new homes in the free world. Three million left East Germany for the West (prompting the construction of the Berlin Wall to stop the outflow); 180,000 left Hungary in 1956; 500,000 came to the United States from Cuba. Even relatives of the ruling elite, including Josef Stalin's own daughter and Fidel Castro's sister, defected to the democratic world. Some of these migrants were motivated by economic considerations (foreign workers also came to Germany from Italy and Greece, without apparent political motivation, and more Puerto Ricans have come to the United States than Cubans), but many others described themselves as political refugees and reported their former countries to be hostile to basic human rights. It appeared to the majority of Americans that these outer signs were the tip of an iceberg of repression, and that the communists retained power only through the massive use of police coercion.

In addition to political repression, Americans saw the Soviet Union impose a system of economic imperialism on the captive nations after 1945. While the United States poured billions of dollars in Marshall Plan aid into the devastated economies of former allies and enemies, restoring Europe and Japan to economic health, the Soviet Union milked approximately $20 billion out of its zone of occupation, through four devices:

1. Billions of dollars in "war reparations" were assessed against East Germany, Hungary and Rumania.
2. A "special price system" was imposed for trade within the communist bloc, characterized by high prices for Soviet goods and low prices for exports by satellite nations,. One result was losses to Poland of about $500 million in discounted coal exports to the USSR between 1946 and 1956.
3. "Joint stock companies" were established as a highly exploitive form of Soviet foreign investment in East European economies. Former German firms were expropriated by Russia under the Administration for Soviet Property Abroad, and their value was counted as Moscow's investment against which fair returns to Russia were calculated. Joint stock companies of this and other types transferred additional billions of dollars in value to the USSR.
4. Interdependence of production was forced on the satellite economies, restricting their trade with the West and giving priority to Soviet deliveries. Raw-material dependency is illustrated by the case of Poland, which in 1957 imported from the USSR 100 percent of its oil, 70 percent of its iron ore, 78 percent of its nickel, and 67 percent of its cotton. From 1945 through 1956, exploitation of Eastern Europe was ruthless, though economic relations were more nearly equal after 1956.[20]

The Continuity of Policy: Korea and Vietnam

For twenty-five years American policy remained firm and unvarying in its opposition to what was perceived as communist aggression. Isolationist impulses were suppressed, and the most extensive commitments ever undertaken by a single power were honored. The essential continuity of the policy can be seen in a comparison of state-

20. Zbigniew Brzezinski, *The Soviet Bloc* (Cambridge, Mass.: Harvard University Press, 1967), pp. 124–28, 282–87, and 376. See also Paul Marer, "The Political Economy of Soviet Relations with Comecon," in Steven Rosen and James Kurth, eds., *Testing the Theory of Economic Imperialism* (Lexington, Mass.: D. C. Heath, 1974).

ments in the Korean and Vietnam wars, separated by a span of fifteen years.

President Truman explained the problem in Korea to the American people in bleak terms in a radio address in April of 1951:

> The Communists in the Kremlin are engaged in a monstrous conspiracy to stamp out freedom all over the world. . . . The whole Communist imperialism is back of the attack on peace in the Far East.

Truman said that American strategy was based on the lessons of dealing with communist aggression.

> In the simplest terms, what we are trying to do in Korea is this: we are trying to prevent a third world war. . . . If [the Free World] had followed the right policies in the 1930's—if the free countries had acted together to crush the aggression of the dictators, and if they had acted in the beginning, when the aggression was small—there probably would have been no World War II. If history taught us anything, it is that aggression anywhere in the world is a threat to peace everywhere in the world.[21]

US Marines of the international security force in Beirut, Lebanon, 1983.

Source: Patrick Chauvel/Sygma

21. *The New York Times,* April 17, 1951.

Strikingly parallel themes were later used to explain the necessity for American military intervention in Vietnam. The notable State Department White Paper of 1965, significantly entitled "Aggression from the North: The Record of North Vietnam's Campaign to Conquer South Vietnam," portrays that struggle as a typical attempt at communist aggression.

> South Vietnam is fighting for its life against a brutal campaign of terror and armed attack inspired, directed, supplied, and controlled by the Communist regime in Hanoi. . . . Aggression has been loosed against an independent people who want to make their way in peace and freedom.[22]

President Nixon said in 1969:

> If Hanoi were to succeed in taking over South Vietnam by force—even after the power of the United States had been engaged—it would greatly strengthen those leaders who scorn negotiation, who advocate aggression, who minimize the risks of confrontation. It would bring peace now, but it would enormously increase the danger of a bigger war later.[23]

In both wars, American policy was based on four key propositions:

1. Conflict is due to communist aggression against the free world.
2. The communist appetite for expansion cannot be appeased and will grow without limit unless checked.
3. The United States, as leader of the free world, is obligated to act as a counterweight to communist aggression.
4. By fighting a small war now, we avoid a bigger war later.

This was the stern formulation of American ideals from 1947 to approximately 1970.

America's Post-Vietnam World View

The withdrawal of American troops from Vietnam in 1973 signaled the end of an age of United States foreign policy. To be sure, the event itself was uncharacteristic of Washington's policy since the enunciation of the Truman Doctrine. But the abandonment by the Nixon administration of the costly anticommunist crusade in Asia gave larger meaning to the event: The United States was engaged in a major reassessment of its foreign commitments, of its place in the international system,

22. US Department of State, *Aggression from the North: The Record of North Vietnam's Campaign to Conquer South Vietnam* (Washington, D.C.: US Government Printing Office, 1965).
23. "Address to the Nation on Vietnam," May 14, 1969. See *The Public Papers of the Presidents of the United States: Richard M. Nixon, 1969,* pp. 369–375 at pp. 370–371.

and of the means that it would invoke henceforth to influence significant international events. It seems irrational that the immense investment of lives, resources and political fortunes in Vietnam in the name of freedom should suddenly have been overturned in favor of a unilateral withdrawal that would inevitably lead to reunification of North and South Vietnam under a communist flag. Quite clearly, such a decision could have been made only in the context of other changes in the American world view.[24]

In fact, many converging perceptions and policy shifts rendered the American departure logical. First, the communist bloc had come to be seen as having several (though not necessarily equal) competing centers of power rather than a unified command center in Moscow. In particular, the growing Sino-Soviet dispute had alerted the West after 1960 to China's independence from the Soviet yoke, and the competition between Moscow and Peking over the policy of North Vietnam during the war served to strengthen the American expectation of a deeper rift between the two communist giants after its conclusion. Thus the prevailing image of communism shifted from the fearful monolithic one to a more differentiated theory of polycentrism, which implied the possibility for Americans of exploiting a more fluid international political scene by dealing with different factions of the splintered communist world. This same view led President Nixon to begin the process of normalization of relations with China, a policy consummated by formal diplomatic recognition in 1979 by President Carter.

Second, some amelioration now seemed to moderate the relentless hostility of Soviet actions. After fifty years of revolution and rapid economic growth, and twenty years after the death of Stalin, the Soviet Union had grown soft and somewhat more satisfied with its own position in the world. The dominant elites in Moscow clearly favored coexistence with the West and minimizing the risks of war. Like the American government, Moscow was under continuing pressure from various industrial, regional and consumer interests to hold down defense spending. The hawk group in the Politburo was on the decline, and new possibilities for cooperation with the West were open.

Third, the Cold War itself had come to be presented in less strident ideological terms. Whereas attention to communist events in the early years had been highly selective, concentrating on negative news, later impressions included positive achievement in the USSR, China and the

24. For a major treatment of the Nixon diplomatic strategy involved in these changes, see Tad Szulc, *The Illusion of Peace: Foreign Policy in the Nixon Years* (New York: Viking, 1978), particularly Book Four ("The Year of Détente") and Book Five ("The Year of 'Peace' ").

East European states. Some observers saw a gradual process of convergence between the two economic systems, with the Soviets instituting managerial reforms ("Liebermanism") and loosening other tendencies toward free enterprise, while the capitalist states accepted increased government planning and participation in their economies. Also, increased awareness of continuing injustices in the West itself, such as the suppression of black people in the United States, weakened the moral righteousness of anticommunism.

Many people had come to see the problem of dealing with the USSR as a practical balance-of-power issue instead of a battle between the forces of light and the forces of darkness. A less moralistic foreign policy permitted a more pragmatic exploration of options. As perceptions of the USSR shifted from the image of Aggressor to one of more complex, less dangerous patterns of motivation, cooperative proposals were less vulnerable to charges of appeasement by domestic opponents.

In this atmosphere the United States was able to open a new phase in its dealings with the communist world during the 1970s, particularly after withdrawal from Vietnam. The reversal of twenty-five years of hostile relations with China is only one pertinent example. In addition, several major agreements on arms control and political settlements were reached with the Soviet Union, notably the strategic arms limitation agreements (SALT I and SALT II, the latter of which was not ratified by the United States Senate), the interim agreement on arms limitation and human rights at Vladivostok, and the long-awaited settlement of the German borders, a problem remaining from the collapse of Nazi Germany in 1945. Western European trade with Eastern Europe had already increased tenfold during the 1960s, but in the 1970s the volume continued to climb, particularly with the emergence of Eurocommunism. Trade between the United States and the Soviet Union increased as well, and American firms and corporations based in the territories of American allies entered into agreements with Moscow to establish production plants in the Soviet Union. Trade agreements blossomed for shipment to the USSR of American computers and other state-of-the-art technological materials, many of which were known to have immediate use in military development and application.

Sino-American trade grew from nothing to a thriving exchange (the first Chinese ship to visit an American port since 1949 arrived in early 1979). The Coca-Cola Company was even invited by the Chinese to establish a bottling facility on Chinese territory. Due to the improved atmosphere that made possible all of these and other changes, American officials began trumpeting, in the mid-1970s, that the Cold War was over. This, of course, could not be taken literally, since over $400 billion in defense expenditure continued annually by the Soviet Union and the United States alone as they glared, even if more tolerantly, at one another across military lines the world over. But it seemed clear, nevertheless, that by the time of the American withdrawal from Vietnam, a new era of de-escalation was in progress, however gradual and interrupted. The revised international climate, and particularly the consequences for Soviet-American relations, ushered in the era of détente.

Like most significant changes in political relations, détente did not occupy a fixed period of time, having had no precise beginning and no identifiable termination. It characterized a stretch of time marked more by evolving attitudes than by dates and events. Though not dated with the American withdrawal from Vietnam, it was surely permitted by the spirit in which that withdrawal occurred; and while not brought to a close by any single incident, it was extinguished by a gradual loss of American confidence in the fidelity of new Soviet attitudes toward world politics. One American observer interprets détente as a loss of consensus about the basic anticommunist goals of American foreign policy.[25] Another summarizes the history of détente as a self-imposed public mood in the United States resulting from exhaustion over Vietnam, loss of confidence in the morality and judgment of American leadership, discontent over global responsibilities and skepticism over activities undertaken in the name of national defense. Under these circumstances a charitable view of the Soviet Union was preferred to the tough-minded decisions and policies that the United States needed to take to maintain its vigilance against the Soviet challenge.[26] Détente, therefore, came and went with attitude, not with events and landmark years. Unlike peace and war, which have precise anniversaries to celebrate, conflicts such as the Cold War and times of tranquil confidence such as détente do not.

While in 1975, then, it might have seemed that détente was a solid and reliable foundation for American foreign policy and arms development, the next year revealed its transparency. The Soviet-Cuban intervention in Angola on behalf of communist independence forces raised fresh questions about Soviet expansionist aims. Still aching from the Vietnam experience, the nation debated its response. A bitter battle raged between President Ford and Secretary of State Kissinger, on the one hand, and Congress on the other, over whether or not the United States should intervene indirectly by assisting noncommunist forces in

25. George Quester, "Consensus Lost," *Foreign Policy,* no. 40 (Fall 1980), pp. 18–32.
26. Dimitri K. Simes, "The Anti-Soviet Brigade," *Foreign Policy,* no. 37 (Winter 1979–80), pp. 28–42, especially pp. 28–29.

the struggle for independence from Portuguese colonialism. The rancor of the battle, which Congress won by denying supporting funds for an indirect counterintervention, threw a dark shadow over détente and severely embarrassed the president in the presidential primaries and election of 1976. Ford declared the word "détente" to have been removed from the American political lexicon; Secretary Kissinger countered with the prediction that long-term improvement in Soviet-American relations would soon revive the word and the concept. Indeed, despite upheavals of faith, "détente" was not long out of use.

Despite the lingering sentiment of détente, however, a succession of events gradually eroded American faith. During the last two and one-half years of the 1970s, American officials saw troubling evidence that the Soviet Union intended to exploit détente to its political and economic advantage, while still pursuing familiar, ideologically inspired ends and enforcing familiar forms of domestic oppression. The principal evidence was threefold. First, Moscow had vastly increased its military capabilities by every measure: annual cost, deployment of new weapons systems, increase in size of armed forces and so on. Moreover, contrary to a common Western perception, most of the build-up of the most modern arms was not along the Chinese front, but in Central Europe. Second, in spite of its agreement at Vladivostok to curb its assault on political dissenters, the Soviet government continued to impose brutal punishment on those who were publicly critical of its policies. And third, the pattern of Soviet arms sales indicated to American observers that Moscow was intent upon disrupting the global balance of forces and the regional balances in the Middle East, Africa and Europe, on extending its naval forces to areas of Western interest, and on sponsoring armed communist revolution in Central America and the Caribbean. These observations reawakened concern about the long-range intentions of Soviet foreign policy and about the trustworthiness of Soviet commitment to détente.

Specifically, the strategic build-up was seen by Western skeptics as evidence that the Soviet Union was intent upon maintaining a level of tension in Europe aimed at preventing economic ties between the eastern and the western sectors from eroding Moscow's economic, military and ideological stranglehold on its Warsaw Pact allies. The maintenance of continental tension was a way for the Soviet Union to prevent any deterioration in the Socialist commonwealth. The arms transfer policy of the Soviets, in turn, was seen as a means of preparedness for exploiting tactical situations—not for random advantage, but as a means of developing and expanding the number of socialist centers in the world. Together, they will eventually integrate into a larger Socialist commonwealth. A study of official Soviet statements regarding the ideological foundations of foreign policy by an American observer has been summarized in this manner:

> The growing "organic" relationships within the socialist commonwealth are represented as a "law-governed" process; this process is "organically" linked with "proletarian internationalism"; "proletarian internationalism" is "organically" combined with "peaceful coexistence"; and "peaceful coexistence," defined as a product of the changed balance of forces, is "organically" tied to the ideological struggle between social systems. Thus, the processes that are effecting the triumph of socialism over capitalism are functionally interconnected; a change in one structural relationship produces change in the others.[27]

Détente, then, had become a camouflage for a subtle, ideologically inspired renewal of determination to alter the international system in such a way as to promote the triumph of socialism over capitalism, to bring an end to the American era, to to reinforce Moscow as the center of a worldwide Socialist commonwealth. Another observer concluded from similar evidence that while the strategic policy of the Kremlin was to instill fear of its power everywhere, its diplomatic practice was an act of seduction designed to persuade others that Moscow had accepted its role in the contemporary world order and had abandoned aspirations for a Soviet world state.[28]

The turn of the decade demolished détente, and optimistic claims of the Cold War's demise were replaced everywhere in the West by declarations that it had been revived. The first indicative event occurred in the waning days of 1979, when the Soviet Union replaced the government of Afghanistan with Kremlin-oriented leadership and expelled the foreign press. Thereafter, Soviet troops put down dissent, patriotism and unrest with brutal force. And as events in the Persian Gulf rose from tepid to boiling, Soviet troops moved ever closer to the Iranian border, arousing fears of expanding Soviet activity, intervention in a revolutionary Iran and direct Great Power confrontation over the Gulf area. This event, coupled with redoubled Soviet arms development and an increasingly bellicose tone regarding the American role in Western Europe, seemed testimony to the four-year-old view that détente had expired, and to the persistent view of some that the Cold War had never ended.

Interbloc events of 1980–81 added further to this grave interpretation. During the summer of 1980, Polish labor became restive over wages, conditions of work and food prices. As the country went onto

27. R. Judson Mitchell, "A New Brezhnev Doctrine: The Restructuring of International Relations," *World Politics,* April 1978, pp. 366–90.
28. Kenneth L. Adelman, "Fear, Seduction and Growing Soviet Strength," *Orbis,* Winter 1978, pp. 743–65.

strict meat rationing, the unrest grew into the first organized labor strike in Poland since the establishment of the Soviet bloc after the Second World War. The shipyard strike at Gdansk resulted not only in major concessions (at least on paper) regarding the right of Polish laborers to organize in unions outside of government control; it also resulted in the Kremlin's removal of the Polish leadership. Moreover, Warsaw Pact troop maneuvers and scantily veiled Soviet threats to strikers, particularly as unrest moved to other industries and other parts of Poland, brought back memories of forceful Soviet interventions in East Germany (1953), Hungary (1956), and Czechoslovakia (1968). The West waited to see if Polish dissent would be crushed in the name of a unified Socialist commonwealth. The United States applied economic sanctions against Poland, verbally encouraged the Solidarity movement and repeatedly condemned both the Polish and Soviet governments. Though the dissent was not forcefully crushed, countless political activists were incarcerated and the threat of force was ever present. Lech Walesa, leader of the movement, was unable to leave the country to receive his Nobel Peace Prize in 1983 for fear that he would not be permitted to return. At Walesa's urging, the United States began easing sanctions more than a year after the discontinuation of martial law, since more harm was being done to Polish citizens than to the intransigent government.

With hawks now seemingly in control of Soviet policy, fear was rampant in the West that a struggle for power within the Kremlin might touch off an irresponsible, politically inspired military adventure somewhere other than in Afghanistan or Poland. Secretary of State Edmund Muskie reported after a meeting of the NATO Foreign Ministers that the allies were united as they had not been for decades, even after the OPEC petroleum embargo of 1973–74. Policies of rearmament dominated the American presidential and congressional campaigns of 1980. If the outcome of the elections was unclear on other issues, it was certain that on the matter of American military status the election spoke with historic voice: détente was dead, the Cold War had returned, and once again the United States must multiply its arms development effort in face of the Soviet challenge.[29] A congressional study made public before President Reagan's inauguration estimated that the effort to catch the Soviets in both conventional and strategic military potential might take as much as eight years and $80 billion.

29. In an apparent epitaph to détente Aleksandr Solzhenitsyn, Russian Nobel Prize winner now in exile, wrote that "even after Afghanistan the Soviet leaders will be only too happy to restore détente to the status quo ante—an opportunity for them to purchase all that they require in between acts of aggression." See "Misconceptions About Russia Are a Threat to America," *Foreign Affairs,* Spring 1980, pp. 597–834, at p. 807.

Japanese officials examining débris from Korean jetliner downed by the Soviets in 1983.

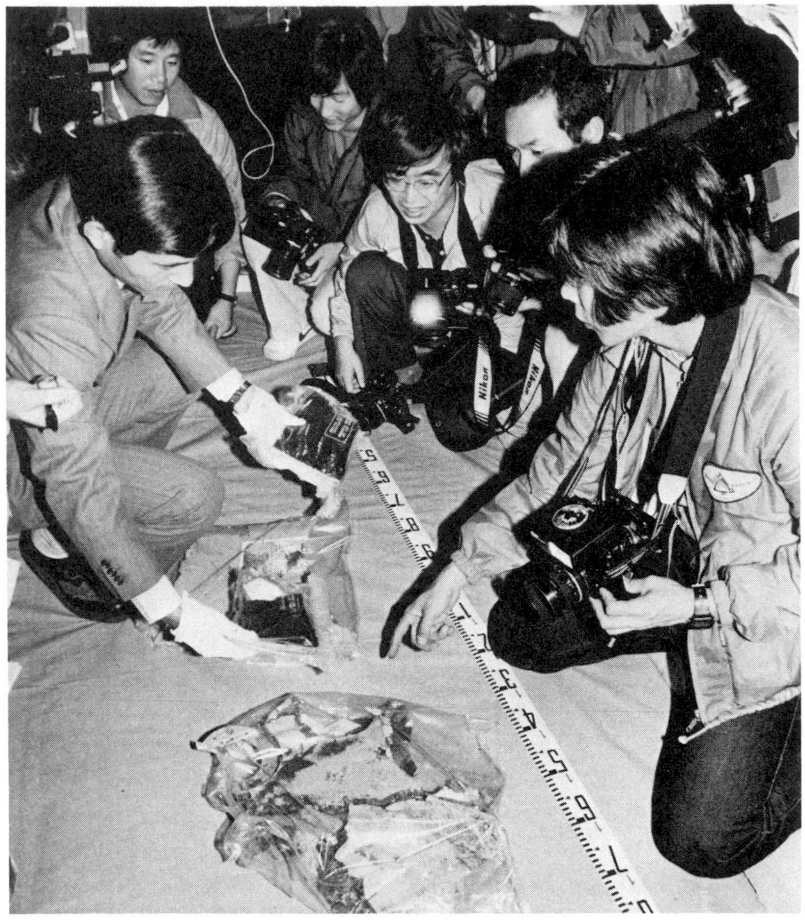

Source: Wide World Photos

Despite the magnitude of the estimate, the American taxpayers were quietly resigned to the need. And SALT II, withdrawn from the Senate's ratification process by President Carter ostensibly as a protest of Soviet behavior but probably because of fear that the Soviet-wary Senate would reject it, was declared by the Reagan administration to be defeatist and void in its negotiated form.[30]

Brezhnev's death on November 10, 1982, was followed by a peaceful succession which brought to power Yuri Andropov, former director of the dreaded KGB, the Soviet secret police. Andropov had already

30. For a representative spectrum of American positions on the SALT II agreement concerning both international strategic and domestic political questions, see the five-article section entitled "SALT and Beyond," in *Foreign Policy,* Summer 1979, pp. 49–123.

been the target of much Western criticism, for it was he who had initiated the policy whereby KGB psychiatrists declared political dissenters emotionally unfit, and then had them committed to mental hospitals as a form of imprisonment. He had also been the Soviet ambassador to Hungary during the forceful suppression of revolt there in 1956.[31] He was no friend of the West, and the Reagan administration greeted his rise to power with unabashed verbal attacks on Soviet intentions around the world. Within a year, much of which Andropov spent in illness and away from public life, all arms negotiations had been suspended, both the Soviet Union and the United States had deployed new-generation missiles in Europe, and Soviet-American relations were at their lowest point since the height of the Cold War in the 1950s. American condemnation of continued Soviet policies in Poland (despite the formal lifting of martial law) and Afghanistan, together with proof that the Kremlin was providing arms to the leftist government of Nicaragua and the rebels in El Salvador, fueled the revived image of the Soviets as the Aggressor. The shooting down of a civilian Korean airliner in 1983 was seen as a statement of the inhumane Soviet character; and a brief American invasion of Grenada to depose a leftist government and rid the population of communist influence was an announcement of Washington's intention that it would no longer take a passive position on Soviet interferences in the inter-American community.

Soviet behavior from 1976 through the mid-1980s persuaded many Americans that the USSR was no longer the revolutionary center of Marxism-Leninism, but an expansionist empire in the classic tradition. Suffering from political, ideological, economic and agricultural failure, and eager to establish political, regional and strategic security, the Soviet Union was poised to expand everywhere and anywhere Western vigilence was perceived as unsteady.[32]

Paradoxically, then, while the early post-Vietnam American world view was built upon the notion that peaceful relations with Moscow and Peking would create a balanced pentapolar world (with Japan and Western Europe also playing independent roles) to the advantage of American foreign policy, a decade later Soviet-American relations were at their lowest point in a quarter-century. In the same short time, Sino-American relations went from warlike to friendly, and then leveled off at mutually wary friendliness. No longer is the American

31. Martin Ebon, *The Andropov File* (New York: McGraw-Hill, 1983), Chapter VI, "The Hungarian Connection," chronicles Andropov's "duplicity" during this episode, but holds open the possibility that Andropov attempted to prevent military intervention.
32. Edward N. Luttwak, *The Grand Strategy of the Soviet Union* (New York: St. Martin's Press, 1983), especially Chapters V and VI.

perspective governed by optimistic assumptions about Soviet motives and the feasibility of arms limitation, whether unilateral or bilateral. Instead, the guiding assumption is borrowed from the Cold War: Every Soviet action anywhere is a threat of war, and the United States can rely only upon strong alliances and a vigorous program of rearmamentation in order either to meet the threat or to reestablish a precarious East-West peace through a balance of strategic and conventional forces appropriate for use anywhere on short notice.[33]

The United States and the Third World

Although much of the American world perspective centers upon its relations with the two communist giants and upon its allies, the Third World, too, plays an increasingly important role. Much of the northern hemisphere (including China) is industrially and economically underdeveloped, as is most of the southern hemisphere (excluding Australia and New Zealand). While prior to 1945 most of the Third World peoples lived in the imperial possessions of the European powers, their emancipation through the processes of the United Nations, particularly after 1960, has made them independently-governed. They comprise the vast majority of the world's population; they are the most rapidly growing populations; and they have rising expectations regarding global status and sharing the world's economic distribution which result in their having a major voice in world politics.

In the early post-war years, the United States selflessly supported both the independence and economic aspirations of the Third World. From 1950 to the present, American taxpayers have given scores of billions of dollars to the improvement of nutrition, transportation, health, population control, agricultural development, industrial development, education, etc. in areas of the world with which they are unfamiliar. This generosity was motivated in part by humane concern, and in part as ideological competition with the Soviet Union, a competition in which both Washington and Moscow attempted to secure the loyalty of these peoples as they became politically independent.

Although the United States continues, both on its own and through international organizations, to provide considerable assistance to the Third World, the American attitude about such foreign aid has shifted.

33. On the general subject see "The Soviet Threat: Myths and Realities," *Proceedings of the Academy of Political Science,* vol. 31, no. 1 (1978), edited by Grayson Kirk and Nils H. Wessell. The volume contains comments on economic, strategic and geographic policies of the Soviet Union from the vantage points of several important American commentators.

Americans have grown weary of the waste and corruption to which their aid has been subjected. They have tired of giving funds to people who have rejected American principles in favor of authoritarian governments, often socialist or communist, and most frequently anti-American. That governments receiving American funds in turn should condemn the United States' relationship with Israel or its determination to prevent the spread of communism in Latin America is an incomprehensible contradiction. Since 1960, the frequency with which the United States has voted with the majority in the United Nations has declined steadily, demonstrating that the political voice of the Third World has steered the organization away from the course of pro-Western democracy upon which it had embarked before these lands became independent.

Whereas Third World peoples often regard American economic policy and the activities of its transnational corporations as imperialistic, Americans hold the view that without American public aid and private capital, these peoples would still be impoverished, unemployed and generally backward. Indeed, the two places in the Third World to which the most American aid and investment have gone—Taiwan and South Korea—enjoy the highest standards of living anywhere in the non-oil-producing Third World. The New International Economic Order, declared by the United Nations as a result of the political coalition of the Third World governments, is accepted by the United States in principle, but is feared nonetheless as an instrument capable of disrupting free trade in favor of preferential treatment of the poor nations. A new economic order in which the recipient states are habitually unable to pay their monetary debts, affecting negatively both the trade and payments balances of the United States, is a difficult economic order for accounting-conscious America to understand. The economic demands of the Third World are regarded by Americans as unending, unreasonable, non-reciprocal, unruly and a costly burden for the United States, both politically and economically.

If the politics of the Third World in general causes discomfort for Americans, the economics of the oil-producing members is particularly irritating. Since the coming of age of the Organization of Petroleum Exporting Countries (OPEC) in 1973, American consumers of oil and petroleum products have been at the economic mercy of a handful of states, some radical in their demand that the industrialized West pay the social and economic costs of modernization, and some more moderate. Together, however, they raised the cost of imported oil by a multiple of almost ten, which caused domestic prices to skyrocket, the cost of industrial production to rise, severe inflation, and a tremendously disruptive redistribution of foreign currency reserves. And to add insult to injury, on most critical issues of world politics, particularly those pertaining to the Middle East, most of these governments are the outspoken opponents of American policy.

During the 1980s, the United States retaliated against this uneven relationship. It has announced its withdrawal from the United Nations Educational, Social and Cultural Organization (UNESCO) in protest of that agency's anti-Westernism. It has increased its support to anti-government forces in Nicaragua, and to the pro-American government of El Salvador, despite that government's poor record on matters pertaining to human rights. It forcefully rid Grenada of communism and pro-Soviet influences. ("In Grenada," declared President Reagan during a celebration honoring the completion of the third year of his presidency, "we set a people free.") Congress has passed legislation preventing the release of financial aid to communist-dominated countries, and the Reagan administration has used its voting strength in the World Bank to prevent an increase in the Bank's maximum authorization for loans to the Third World. And in a rare breach of inter-American solidarity, President Reagan broke from neutrality and openly assisted Britain against Argentina in the Falkland Islands war.

Rebuttal to the Theory of American Economic Imperialism

Throughout the years since World War II, one obstacle to improved relations between the United States and the major communist governments has been the contention of the latter that the United States pursues a design of world economic imperialism and hegemony. Although this claim is heard infrequently from post-Maoist China and more frequently from the post-détente Soviet Union, this is a basic ideological difference between East and West that guides perceptions and obstructs peaceful relations. According to neo-Leninist critics, the mature phase of capitalism is characterized by a saturation of the domestic market with surplus capital and by overproduction. The maintenance of the profit structure depends on penetration of foreign markets for high-yield investment opportunities, export outlets and secure sources of the cheapest raw materials. For the United States, the necessary expansion has been justified behind a disguise of anti-communism and defense of the Free World. This is said to explain the basic dynamic of US Cold War policy and domination of much of the Third World. The neo-Leninist analysis, presented at length in the preceding chapter, is rejected by orthodox theorists on the following factual grounds:

1. *Foreign investment profits are not higher* Over the past twenty years, American manufacturing investments at home have returned a profit slightly higher than have investments abroad. It is false, therefore, to argue that American capital is being driven from the domestic market to foreign markets for higher profit.
2. *American capitalism does not depend on foreign markets* It is true that American foreign investments total in value more than the national economies of all but the US itself, Japan and the Soviet Union. But these foreign assets are only a fraction of the book value of American corporations. In most industries, exports account for less than 10 percent of total sales, though a few industries depend heavily upon sales abroad: computers, aerospace and farm machinery in particular.
3. *American capitalism does not depend on exploitation of the Third World* Less developed countries are only a small portion of the market for US foreign investment and exports, and they are gradually declining in importance except with respect to arms. American capital increasingly finds it more profitable to invest in developed countries than in underdeveloped areas, in large part because of the differences in political stability and, therefore, the safety of investments. It is not plausible to argue that American capitalism needs to dominate small countries or to retard their growth.
4. *Vietnam cannot be explained as economic imperialism* The natural resources and market value of Vietnam or all of Southeast Asia could not begin to repay the costs of the war: $150 billion, ten years of war, 50,000 American lives. The rice, tungsten, teak and small offshore oil deposits of Indochina are relatively minor in value. American policy in Vietnam cannot be explained by the imperatives of capitalism. The stock market averages, which Leninists would have predicted to rise with the war, instead fell sharply, indicating that Vietnam was not good for business.
5. *There is not a clearly defined capitalist ruling class in America* The neo-Leninist theory assumes that major multinational corporations are owned and managed by a small, definable class with vast influence in the American political process. In truth, the means of production are widely owned, including millions of successful small businesses. Even the large industries have widely dispersed ownership through shareholding. Sixty-seven percent of Americans—about 140 million people—own stocks directly or indirectly (through pension funds, insurance companies and other collective "institutional investors"). Thirty-five million Americans own shares directly in the stock markets. While there are some very large stockholders as well, to some degree America has achieved "peo-

ple's capitalism." There is not a sharp line between rich and poor.

Morevoer, the rich/poor division is just one way of slicing the pie in pluralistic democracy. Catholics are sometimes opposed to Protestants, men to women, black to white, Irish to Italian, farmer to worker, young to old, urban to rural, North to South, hawk to dove, among other divisions. Each conflict crosscuts the others, and instead of immutably opposed permanent classes, pluralism offers shifting coalitions and factions. Government is not the permanent agent of one class, but an arbiter standing above the various divisions, favoring first one, then another.

6. *Economic interests do not determine American foreign policy* Even if the neo-Leninist can demonstrate that America profits from a foreign market, it does not follow that policy toward that country is guided by material gain. In general, security interests and ideological principles tend to override limited economic gains in the determination of foreign policy, according to the orthodox view. If, like many neo-Leninists, we discount Soviet imperialism as an official mythology created by American propaganda, we must rely on exotic explanations such as economic determinism to explain American policy. But if we accept the reality of the Soviet threat, the primacy of security interests in determining US policy is apparent. The theory of American economic imperialism is, in the dominant American view, a tired set of worn shibboleths to be mouthed without conviction by Soviet speechmakers on state occasions.[34]

Conclusion

The twentieth century has seen a radical alteration in the world position of the United States. It entered the epoch clinging to isolation, but was forced twice in twenty-five years to intervene in critical European conflicts that threatened world stability. After 1945, with American influence and prestige still intact among the noncommunist Allies, an obligation was accepted to play a permanent international role. Thus America twice went to war against spreading communism, once in Korea and once in Vietnam. The close of the latter conflict occurred in a global environment that seemed a portent to improving relations between the communist and noncommunist worlds.

34. This analysis borrows heavily from Robert W. Tucker, *The Radical Left and American Foreign Policy* (Baltimore: Johns Hopkins University Press, 1971), especially pp. 124–38.

With the failure of détente, however, that premise once again needs evaluation. At a time when America's principal allies are becoming increasingly independent and more of a challenge to America's economic supremacy in the nonsocialist world, relations with the Soviet Union are at their lowest point in three decades. The 1980s began with the Soviet Union occupying Afghanistan and suppressing Poland; and as the decade approached its mid-point, Soviet strength in Europe, Asia, Africa, Central America and the Caribbean appeared ominous. Meanwhile, relations with China had leveled off with improved economic, political and military communication. Once the outcast of Asia contained throughout Asia by American military might, China is now seen as a rapidly developing friendly power where economic growth is the first priority. Class struggle and Marxism have been subordinated to the practical problems of development, arbitrary administrative rule has been replaced by an attempt to build a government of laws, and non-Chinese ideas and commerce are welcomed.[35]

The economic recession that plagued the Western world during the first two and one-half years of the 1980s made the United States' relationship with the Third World all the more difficult. While high interest rates, business failures, record inflation and other symptoms may have been due in part to domestic policies, Americans tended to focus their frustrations on the New International Economic Order, the pricing and production policies of OPEC, and the ceaseless demand of the Third World for economic assistance and preferential treatment in global trade. The contradiction between financial demands and the rejection of American foreign policy, even within the inter-American community, tested the patience of many Americans, including President Reagan. The Third World's apparent disregard for human life (as evidenced in genocide in the Nigerian civil war, the massacre of civilians in Lebanon, the killing of American churchwomen in El Salvador, the marauding of right-wing "death squads" in El Salvador and the presumably official killing of an opposition leader in the Philippines after his return home from exile in the United States with guarantees of safety), added to the American frustration: We are paying the price of Third World development, but for what?

The fundamental dilemma of American foreign policy under these circumstances was thoroughly debated in the elections of 1980, 1982 and 1984. Conservative elements called for military expansion to meet the Soviet threat, a tough line on conditions for assisting the Third World, and protection of American produce in world trade. More liberal elements called for rhetorical restraint and hard negotiations

35. Ross Terrill, "China Enters the 1980s," *Foreign Affairs,* Spring 1980, pp. 920–35.

in dealing with the Kremlin, a more tolerant attitude with the Third World conditioned upon improved performance related to human rights, and the restoration of reciprocal trading relations with the European partners, Japan and China. Conservatives accepted the resumption of the Cold War and proposed accordingly; liberals charged the Reagan administration with encouraging the resumption of the Cold War and urged policies that would revive détente. Declining power nor world policemen—neither is a role the United States can play.

3

The Perspectives of America's Major Allies

The concept of a multiparty balance in world politics, together with the reality of the burgeoning importance of the nonmilitary components of power, calls for a review of the international perspectives of those modern industrial nations which contribute independently to the world balance. To achieve this balance they must remain free from foreign economic and military domination. These two conditions—modernity and autonomy—typify some of America's principal allies, particularly Japan, the European Community countries and Canada. Each of these countries has achieved a high level of industrial activity, a major competitive position in world economic affairs and a sophisticated security system. Yet in both military and economic relations, each is intertwined with the interests and capabilities of the United States. There is a delicate balance between independent decision making and domination from Washington and Wall Street. For each, accordingly, a world view is colored as much by the ambivalence of relations with closest friend as by the fear of potential enemies.

Japan

A paradox of forces shapes the Japanese world view. On the one hand, Japan is intensely nationalistic and has a proud history of cultural continuity and empire. Yet on the other hand, Japan removed itself entirely from world affairs from 1640 to 1854, when it was "opened" by threat of force by the American fleet of Commodore Matthew C. Perry. After the First World War Japan was humiliated by the refusal of the Western powers to include in the Covenant of the League of Nations a declaration of racial equality. In 1945, under relentless fire-bombing and two atomic attacks, Japan was forced into unconditional surrender; and after six years of occupation by American troops, a peace treaty was arranged at the price of a series of military and economic agreements that compromised Japan's self-determination.

Yet despite these restraints, in the years since the Second World War Japan has undergone a remarkable economic recovery that survived even the severe world economic fluctuations of the 1970s. At present rates of growth, this small nation, which fits a population half that of the United States into a territorial mass only the size of Montana, may well exceed the gross national product of the United States by 1990. But in order to understand the unique elements of the Japanese world view, it is necessary first to examine the evolution of modern Japan.

The Opening of Japan

Like China, Japan fell into the covetous orbit of American "Manifest Destiny" in the nineteenth century. As the China trade multiplied after 1844, American merchants eyed Japan as an additional source of Oriental goods, and as a supply station and refuge that would minimize the hazards of the long Pacific journey. Already Americans had absorbed the idea of this new land and it had inspired their missionary zeal: popular tales about the Japanese treatment of shipwrecked sailors had prompted some Americans to brand the Japanese "enemies of mankind." After two unsuccessful diplomatic efforts, in the wake of expansionism in the Mexican War and the acquisition of the Pacific coast, American nationalism and the idea of "opening" Japan converged. The departure of Perry's squadron was appropriately festive to the anticipated results; for it was to mark the first time Americans would deal directly with Japanese since the Napoleonic Wars, during which a few Americans had carried on the trickle of Dutch trade that Japan permitted. (Ironically, one of the sites of that trade was Nagasaki, the second of the two "atomic cities" destroyed a century later by America.)

In 1854 the Japanese entered reluctantly into a treaty with the United States, seeing it as an opportunity to learn industrial science. If the commercial treaty opened the door to Japan, the immediate evolution of Japanese-American relations propped it wide. For by 1858, while

Japan had gained few concessions, Americans had acquired most-favored-nation status (granting automatic improvement of trading conditions if Japan were to offer more liberal terms to any other party), the right of extraterritoriality (Americans charged with crimes in Japan were to be tried in American courts by American laws), and the rights to teach Western religions and to establish religious institutions. As was the case in early Sino-American relations, then, the principal mark of these early dealings with the West was imbalance: Japan was assigned the obligations, while America gained the lucrative and enviable benefits.

Japanese Expansionism

As exploitative as the American presence might have been, it was not pervasive. As Japan became more aware of the industrial revolution elsewhere and commenced its own modernization, it was free to conduct its own foreign policy (except as its external interests were limited by its trade treaties with Washington and other capitals). Hence, despite a watchful eye from America, Japan was able to begin, in the last decade of the century, a quest for its *own* empire. Control of Korea, long an object of competition among China, Japan and Russia, prompted the Sino-Japanese War of 1894–95, a war that Japan won because of its superior arms and modernization. Though Chinese interests were uprooted from Korea and Taiwan (Formosa), Japanese acquisitions on the Asian mainland were seized by Russia with the assistance of France and Germany. It was clear that if Japan were to achieve status as the dominant modern Asian state, the influence of the Western states within the region would have to be restricted.

Peace was but a lull, as the Russo-Japanese War (1904–05) ensued, largely over competing claims to Manchuria and Korea. Again, however, a Western state's policy was to dominate the outcome. Having acquired the Philippines in 1898, the United States hoped that Asia and the Pacific would be stabilized by a Russo-Japanese stalemate. In view of Russia's apparent edge, President Theodore Roosevelt's policy was to encourage Japan to limit the Russian successes by dangling postwar rewards. But when Japan won decisive land and sea battles and appeared ready to seize Eastern Siberia, Roosevelt saw urgent need for a peace that would ensure the stalemate, as war apparently could not. While giving his assent in the Taft-Katsura Agreement of 1905 to Japanese control of Korea, Roosevelt urged moderation of Tokyo's other expectations of indemnification. Though he did not force these compromises upon Japan, popular and editorial opinion in that country focused dissatisfaction with the peace treaty on America: United States policy seemed to have betrayed the Japanese victory. The flames of hostility were fanned by frequent reports of anti-Japanese racial violence in California, and by American policies that excluded Asian immigrants. With Russia vanquished and China quieted by Western colonialism, redress of grievances with the United States became the focal point of Japanese politics.[1]

The tenuous understanding which was achieved through a visit of the American fleet (painted white) to Japanese ports and through executive agreements concerning immigration and mutual respect for Pacific territories, was broken by the First World War. When at the war's outset Germany vacated its China holdings, Japan moved swiftly to occupy them. Shortly thereafter Tokyo issued to China the Twenty-One Demands (1915), which sought to enlarge Japan's influence throughout China. Since wartime diplomacy did little to resolve these issues, their persistence accentuated the mutual distrust. At the Paris Peace Conference Japan, its economy vibrant, its navy among the world's most modern and its national spirit running high, attached the China issue to a demand that the Covenant of the League of Nations include a declaration of racial equality. Without it Japan would not bow to President Wilson's demand for a timetable for the return of Germany's former holdings to China. For their part, some European states rich in colonial holdings throughout the nonwhite world rejected Japan's demand. Western resistance prevailed, leaving the China question unresolved but, worse, leaving the Japanese more convinced than before of the untrustworthiness of Western intentions.

The breakdown of trust was recorded also in a division of Japanese opinion concerning the country's role in the postwar world. The civilian government and conservative elements readily subscribed to the Washington Treaties of 1922, which sought a permanent balance of interests in China and a restriction on naval armaments. But to expansionists and the military, naval arms limitation and the new diplomatic regime for China constituted surrender to a Western design to regulate Japan's influence in Asia. The military slowly became virtually self-governing, and by 1931 the government denied that troops were moving into Manchuria even while the army was using a minor (and deliberately provoked) skirmish at Mukden as the pretext for a massive invasion of Manchuria and eventually of China, Asia and the Pacific. To the expansionists this was a policy born of having been denied, through habitual Western interferences, the prizes of conquest

1. Raymond A. Esthus, *Theodore Roosevelt and Japan* (Seattle: University of Washington Press, 1966); Howard K. Beale, *Theodore Roosevelt and the Rise of America to World Power* (Baltimore: Johns Hopkins University Press, 1956), particularly Chapter 5; and Charles E. Neu, *An Uncertain Friendship* (Cambridge, Mass.: Harvard University Press, 1967).

in 1885, 1905 and 1918. Consistent with this thinking were the decisions to withdraw from the League of Nations, to create the Greater East Asian Co-Prosperity Sphere and to join the Axis Alliance (1940) with Germany and Italy. These moves were additionally encouraged by the imperfections of American neutrality and its tendency to favor China, and Washington's economic sanctions against Japan. Prevention, then, or at least delay, of American intervention in the Asian war necessitated the Japanese attack on the American fleet at Pearl Harbor on December 7, 1941.[2]

The horrors of the Second World War in the Pacific reached their climax with several events that apparently were indicative of Western attitudes to the Orient. On the tactical front, as an alternative to invasion, the US chose to fire-bomb Japanese population centers, a policy facilitated by the discovery of napalm (jellied gasoline); even worse, it used the only two atomic bombs in existence to devastate the industrial cities of Hiroshima and Nagasaki. Two political decision also stand out in Japanese memories. First, at the Potsdam (Berlin) Conference, held a scant three weeks prior to war's end, it was decided to force Japan into unconditional surrender and to reject an offer of surrender that had as its sole condition the preservation of the tradition of the Emperor's sovereignty. Second, the Soviet Union declared war on Japan on the day of the second atomic attack, giving Moscow five days of belligerency and almost no combat, but a claim to reparations despite five years of formal Soviet-Japanese nonbelligerency.

To the Japanese the fire-bombings were an unnecessary and heinous attack upon innocent civilian populations. These and the atomic bombings were wholly unnecessary in view of the offer to surrender on a single cultural condition. Since there was no strategic value to the use of atomic bombs, Japan already having reached virtual submission, these attacks are taken as evidence of the American intention to pulverize Japanese society, or to demonstrate American strength to the Soviet Union at great and indiscriminate cost. The opportunism of the Soviet Union was seen with equal suspicion.

One haunting question pervades all these arguments: Would the Second World War have been concluded in this manner had Caucasian rather than Oriental lives been at stake; Western civilization rather than Asian?

During the occupation that followed, the Japanese were faced not only with national reconstruction, but also with the need for a revitalization of self-esteem under a victor whose intentions they did not trust even in good times.

2. Herbert Feis, *The Road to Pearl Harbor* (Princeton, N.J.: Princeton University Press, 1950).

Ruins of Nagasaki after atomic bombing in August 1945.

Source: John Bennewitz, Black Star.

The American Occupation

The prevailing international climate when Japan embarked upon its program of restoration was one of utter turmoil. All Europe was in tatters; China was in the middle of a civil war; and the Soviet-American wartime rapport had broken down. Japan had to accept the United States as the sole occupying power, despite the intention of the Allies to have a multilateral policy. It also had to acknowledge General Douglas MacArthur as the Supreme Commander of the Allied Powers in the Pacific, even though he personified the Allied conquest of Japan.

The Japanese were still less pleased with the American estimate that nearly a quarter-century would be needed to achieve the objectives of occupation: democratization; industrial restoration at a level below war potential; land reform and agricultural self-sufficiency; and the purging of war criminals and imperialists. Remarkably, nearly all of these had been achieved, or set in irreversible motion, in little more than three years. Within that time MacArthur had authorized the drafting of a new constitution, and by the end of 1948 he and others were publicly calling for an expeditious termination of the occupation.

Although the Japanese attributed the speed to their own forbearance as much as to American policy, they recognized that a prolonged occupation, if not oppressive, might be preferable to speedy independence. The Cold War was under way; Korean reunification talks between Moscow and Washington had broken down; and the ideological future of Asia seemed written in the forthcoming victory of Chinese communism over the Kuomintang (the Chinese Nationalist Party). Independence would mean dealing with the Soviet Union; balancing the interests of two Chinas; accommodating American economic and military might when its right of intrusion was no longer acknowledged; and surviving on industries that would be long on productive capacity but short on raw materials and energy sources. Now was scarcely a propitious time for new Asian ventures.

Again, however, the decision escaped the Japanese, as occurrences within months of Mao's victory and the Korean War altered Japan's place in the American world scheme. No longer did the US look upon Japan as a pastoral and self-sufficient island kingdom, but rather as a powerful, industrialized and strategically located ally; an atomic fortress and haven for American investments; and a center of operations for American manipulation of Asian power. The cover of United Nations legitimacy in Korea could not conceal the fact that in its decision to contain communism in Asia, Washington had summarily transformed the purposes, the timing and the consequences of the Japan occupation.[3]

The Pacific Treaties and Japanese Prosperity

Amidst these new circumstances John Foster Dulles began to negotiate the Pacific Treaties of 1951. Dulles' zealous anticommunism, heightened by events in China and Korea, seemed to ensure a revised role

3. Frederick S. Dunn, *Peace-Making and Settlement with Japan* (Princeton, N.J.: Princeton University Press, 1963).

for Japan; his insistence on a "peace of reconciliation" rather than a "peace of retribution"[4] created a cordial negotiating environment. It was clear from the beginning, however, that within the framework of reconciliation, the United States would seek to acquire Cold War access to Japanese territory, and would insist on including Japan in a growing chain of anticommunist alliances. The peace of reconciliation would have to facilitate Washington's Cold War strategies.

Of the four Pacific Treaties that resulted from Dulles' diplomacy, two pertained directly to Japan. (The other two linked the Philippines, Australia and New Zeland to American alliances. Both the Soviet government and the Chinese government of Mao were excluded from the Pacific Treaties.) In the Peace Treaty, Japan was obliged to sacrifice virtually all territories acquired since 1895, and to enter into reparations negotiations with those Allied governments whose territories had been occupied by Japanese troops between 1931 and 1945. More important, however, were the clauses that prepared for Japan's inclusion in the American security system; as a consequence of these the Security Treaty went into effect simultaneously with the Peace Treaty.

In the early years of these agreements, great benefits accrued to Japan. Because of American willingness to bear the cost of Japan's security, the share of gross national product that would normally have gone to defense was invested instead in economic growth, leading to annual growth rates until 1981 of twice those of other industrial states. In fact, for the period 1960–81, Japan's average annual growth in GNP per capita was 3.3 times the combined average of the United States, Canada, Britain, France and West Germany. (The growth was reduced to about the same level of those states by the recession of 1981–83.) In terms of GNP (as contrasted with GNP per capita), Japan's productivity multiplied twelve times between 1950 and 1976, while the GNP of the United States multiplied only 2.3 times and that of Western Europe about three times.

Equally important, however, is the growth of Japan's manufacturing sector, since Japan's exports emphasize automotive and electronics manufactures. As Table 3–1 indicates, although the reduction of Japan's growth rate in the decade of the 1970s declined proportionally to the growth rates of its principal competitors, in absolute terms its growth rate in this sector compared with the growth rates of its Western trading partners actually increased by more than 50 percent.

4. As a young man, Dulles had been a member of the American Peace Commission at the Paris talks leading to the Treaty of Versailles. He came away from the conference with the conviction that the peace would not last because it was punitive, thus forming the basis for his later strategy of negotiating a Japanese peace treaty based on reconciliation rather than retribution. See Townsend Hoopes, *The Devil and John Foster Dulles* (Boston: Atlantic-Little, Brown, 1973), especially Chapters 2 and 7.

TABLE 3–1
Comparison of growth rates in the manufacturing sector, 1960–70 and 1970–81, for Japan and principal trading partners.

	1960–1970		*1970–1981*	
Japan	13.6		6.5	
United States	5.3	5.7 = av	2.9	1.7 = av
Britain	3.3		−0.5	
France	7.8		3.2	
Canada	6.8		3.2	
West Germany	5.4		2.1	
Ratio	13.6 / 5.7 = 2.4		6.5 / 1.7 = 3.8	

Source: The World Bank, *World Development Report 1983,* from Table 2, pp. 150–151.

Meanwhile, the favorable trade and payments balances which accompanied this seemingly miraculous recovery from the Second World War enabled the Japanese yen to share the spotlight with the German mark as the most valuable and desirable currency in the world. By all measures except military might, therefore, Japan's status as a major power has been taken for granted for one and a half decades.[5]

Despite these remarkable evidences of redevelopment, however, not all was well in the early and intermediate phases of Japan's return to principal power status. For even as the Japanese economy surged upward, external events imposed other burdens, many of which collided with the Japanese urge for more self-determined foreign policies.

Relations with China

China's need for industrial goods and Japan's need for raw materials and markets create a remarkable trading partnership. Yet as Japan's ability to promote this relationship matured, American's obsession with the isolation of China resulted in pressure against massive Japanese trading with China. The Japanese interpreted this not only as an interference with national decision making, but as an affront to national economic growth. They also viewed it as an American effort to use the isolation of China as an instrument for restricting Japanese competition with American manufacturers. Furthermore, it was seen as a cause of unnecessary delay in normalizing the international relations of Asia, a delay from which Japan might suffer and for which it might be held responsible.

5. For example, see Herman Kahn, *The Emerging Japanese Superstate: Challenge and Response* (Englewood Cliffs, N.J.: Prentice-Hall, 1971); Nobutaka Ike, *Japan: The New Superstate* (San Francisco: W. H. Freeman, 1973); and Frank Gibney, *Japan: The Fragile Super Power* (New York: W.W. Norton, revised edition, 1979).

Japan was not free to establish diplomatic relations and full activity with China until 1971 and 1972 when the United States began to reassess its Asian policy.[6] That trade, consisting principally of Japanese exports of steel, industrial machinery, industrial produce and imports of oil and coal, is shown in Table 3–2 for the years before and after normalization of relations. Today, Japan's trade with and investments in China lead those of all other nations, and the two have entered into a joint oil exploration agreement in the Pacific.

The changing Chinese global perspective has influenced the strategic relationship between the two Asian powers. During the period of closest Sino-American relations (1976–80), Japanese and Chinese anti-Soviet strategies were coordinated; but as the Chinese have embarked more recently on a policy of improved relations with both the United States and the Soviet Union, with dependence upon neither, the openness of the relationship has diminished. China's century-long fear of Japanese military power also contributes to skepticism regarding the value of too close collaboration on military matters. Nonetheless, the

TABLE 3–2
Japan's trade with China, 1970–1981, expressed in billions of US dollars.

		Imports	*Exports*	*Balance*	*Total Value*
1970		0.2	0.6	0.4	0.8
1971	(normaliza-	0.3	0.6	0.3	0.9
1972	tion of	0.5	0.6	0.1	1.1
1973	relations)	1.0	1.0	0.0	2.0
1974		1.3	2.0	0.7	3.3
1975		1.5	2.3	0.8	3.8
1976		1.4	1.7	0.3	3.1
1977		1.6	1.9	0.3	3.5
1978	(treaty	2.0	3.1	1.1	5.1
1979	concluded)	3.0	3.7	0.7	6.7
1980		4.3	5.1	0.8	9.4
1981		5.3	5.1	−0.2	10.4

Source: For 1971–1977, Chae-Jin Lee, "The Making of the Sino-Japanese Peace and Friendship Treaty," *Pacific Affairs,* Fall 1979; for 1978–1981, Japanese Ministry of Finance as reproduced in the *Europa Yearbook, 1983,* Volume II, p. 668.

6. Chae-Jin Lee, "The Making of the Sino-Japanese Peace and Friendship Treaty," *Pacific Affairs,* Fall 1979, pp. 420–445. The article includes a history, economic data and the text of the treaty.

Japanese need for fuel and the Chinese need for technology transfer for military-related manufacturing leaves open the possibility of closer cooperation in the future.[7]

Okinawa

Of the many territorial questions left over from the Second World War, none has been more excitedly symbolic to the Japanese than Okinawa. Even after conclusion of the Pacific Treaties, this large territory, regarded by the Japanese as virtually a fifth home island, remained in American control, continuing as a major center for conventional and nuclear military strategies. Washington persistently rejected the growing demand for the reversion of Okinawa to Japanese sovereignty, particularly as the Vietnam War underscored the importance of Okinawa in American strategy. The question was further complicated in the Senate by powerful interests that insisted upon restricting Japanese textile exports to the United States as a condition for reversion of Okinawa. Finally in 1972, amid global trade negotiations, the American reassessment of its policy in Vietnam and normalization of relations with China, Okinawa was returned to Japan by treaty, subject to American rights under the Mutual Security Treaty of 1950.

American Military Bases

Under the terms of the Security Treaty, the United States was allowed to maintain military bases throughout Japan. These bases were a source of particular resentment. They were viewed as remnants of the occupation, as symbolic of something less than sovereignty for Japan, and as a potential danger to Japan should the enemies of the United States take retaliatory action. Most annoying to the Japanese was the continued use of their ports and territorial waters for servicing the nuclear submarine fleet, a presence that the bomb-conscious population detested. Successful efforts to negotiate the removal of nuclear weapons from the home islands, and the requirement that the Japanese government be afforded the right of "prior consent" for the combat use of American bases on the home islands, only partially allayed national dissatisfactions. A succession of American-oriented govern-

7. William T. Tow, "Sino-Japanese Security Cooperation," *Pacific Affairs,* Spring 1983, pp. 51–83. See also Chalmers Johnson, "East Asia: Living Dangerously," *Foreign Affairs,* America and the World 1983 issue, pp. 721–745.

ments desperately sought compromise on these issues lest popular demand weaken the government and lead to a movement for national rearmament. With increasing fretfulness, a Japan restored to economic power and revitalized in national purpose reached for ways to effect its role in a world where the most troubling restraints were perceived as emanating from its closest partner.

The Vietnam War

The enlarged military presence of the United States in Asia after 1965 brought new strains to Japan's foreign policy and to its internal politics. Although the government tacitly supported the American commitment in Vietnam, the war became increasingly unpopular among Japanese. In particular, it accentuated fears of Japanese involvement should excesses of American strategy (such as B-52 launchings from Okinawa) result in retaliatory actions. The war also hardened the American position on the Okinawa issue, just as the balance-of-payments deterioration suffered by the United States during the war heightened American intolerance of Japan's export capability. Finally, to the extent that American involvement was motivated by the desire to isolate China and to contain its influence, the war threatened to prolong the restrictions on Sino-Japanese trade. Underlying all of these fears, however, was a prevailing apprehension that through its policy in Southeast Asia, the United States was attempting to adjust the Asian power distribution in directions that would measure the benefits to the United States partly by costs to Japan.

Japan in a Changing World

From a century and a quarter of relations with the West, the Japanese learned that international decisions concerning Asia tend to be made less by coordinated diplomacy than by the rush of events. Not inconsistently, then, just when the opportunity for consideration of Asian issues seemed possible in the diminished fighting in Southeast Asia, the Japanese found new disrupting problems. At a time when an independent role for Japan in Asian and world politics might have evolved, many of the basic assumptions on which Japan had built its political and economic policies were subverted.

The Nixon Doctrine In its search for methods of face-saving withdrawal from Vietnam, President Nixon's administration considered non-interventionary paths to Western-oriented political stability in the underindustrialized world. The Nixon Doctrine was first proclaimed during 1970.[8] Though its full meaning was never aired, in essence it meant that the United States would no longer intervene in civil or regional wars, but would provide arms and military information to help governments meet insurrections. The reaffirmation of the Japanese-American Security Treaty exempts Japan from the terms of the doctrine; yet its simple utterance nevertheless brings crisis to the issue of Japanese defense. What might the result be for the security of Asia and the Pacific? Is it now necessary for Japan to undertake a major remilitarization? Despite the formal status of the Security Treaty, do the Nixon Doctrine and the American withdrawal from Southest Asia portend reduced reliability in the Japanese-American security relation? Should Japan become a nuclear power?[9]

Regional events have compounded these problems. The rapid changes in Southeast Asia from 1973 to 1975—particularly full American withdrawal, and the exclusion of Western-oriented governments and factions from South Vietnam, Laos and Kampuchea—opened a potential sphere of influence to which the Japanese government and investors quickly responded. These opportunities seem offset, however, by the jeopardy to regional stability created by the precarious Soviet-American-Chinese triangle, and by the entry of India into the exclusive circle of nuclear powers (1974). At a time when the reliability of the American nuclear umbrella was in doubt, competitive ventures on an Asian continent between two regional nuclear powers (India and China) accentuated the urgency of whether Japan should "go nuclear." Long a heated issue in domestic politics between those who abhor nuclear strategy and those who consider it the only fruitful path to foreign policy independent of the United States, this topic was renewed by the Indian development.[10] It was not settled until 1976, when the Japanese government signed the Nuclear Non-Proliferation Treaty, a multilateral treaty prohibiting the spread of nuclear weapons by its signatories.

Military Expenditures In recent years, although economic matters have been at the heart of Japanese-American instability, the question of Japanese military expenditures has also been a source of contention. Throughout the 1970s, though Japan's military expenditures rose sometimes as much as 9 percent per year, the amount as a function

8. Richard M. Nixon, *US Foreign Policy for the 1970s,* Report to the Congress by the President of the United States, February 25, 1971.
9. For a detailed consideration of the Nixon Doctrine's implications for Japan, see Robert E. Osgood, *The Weary and the Wary: US and Japanese Security Policies in Transition* (Baltimore: Johns Hopkins Press, 1972).
10. Frank C. Langdon, "Japanese Reactions to India's Nuclear Explosion," *Pacific Affairs,* Summer 1975, pp. 173–80.

of gross national product remained consistently below one percent. As NATO began its planning for the deployment of new missiles in Europe, and as détente subsided and Cold War rhetoric again dominated East-West relations, Washington increased its pressure on Japan to absorb a larger share of its national defense cost. The Reagan administration, in particular, urged the Nakasone government to increase its annual military expenditure to 2 percent of GNP. By early 1983, during a visit to Washington, Prime Minister Nakasone began preparing his country for such a surge, and upon his return home he declared that Japan should become as "an unsinkable battleship" in the Pacific. At the same time he called for a review of Japan's basic political institutions, suggesting the possibility of revising the military prohibitions of the post-war constitution; and he announced as part of the Japanese-American anti-Soviet campaign that American nuclear aircraft carriers would be permitted to dock in Japanese ports.

Defense budgets became the central issue of Japan's 1983 general elections and, presumably as a result of Nakasone's strong stand, the Liberal Democratic Party lost its majority in the Diet for the first time since its emergence in 1955. Though Nakasone continued to rule by a coalition of his party and eight others, in 1984 the Diet cut substantially from his military budget proposals.[11]

The First Nixon Shock Events quickened in 1971 after President Nixon announced his intention to visit China the following winter. This decision, made without consulting Tokyo, took the Japanese by complete surprise. They could not comprehend even the remote possibility of Sino-American détente prior to complete resolution of the Southeast Asian war; and neither could they avoid suspicions about American motives in attempting to normalize relations with China while at the same time forbidding Japan to modernize its relations, particularly with regard to trade. To make matters worse, if the US ceased isolating China and enacted the Nixon Doctrine simultaneously, were the imperatives for Japanese security multiplied? Were the concurrent changes of the security and political relations of Asia cumulative, in the sense that the natural trading partnership between China and Japan might produce new forms of conflict? Once the national shock over the president's announcement had been digested, an anxiety of substantial change in Asia took root, one introduced

11. For two views of the Japanese rearmament dilemma and Tokyo's security options, see Joseph M. Ha and John Guinasso, "Japan's Rearmament Dilemma: The Paradox of Recovery," *Pacific Affairs,* Summer 1980, pp. 245–268; and Taketsugu Tsurutani, "Japan's Security, Defense Responsibilities, and Capabilities," *ORBIS,* Spring 1981, pp. 89–106.

unilaterally by the United States. The path to independent policy, so vivid only a few years earlier, now became cluttered by unforeseen, unknown and menacing complications.

The Second Nixon Shock Scarcely a month after the China visit announcement, the Nixon administration took steps to correct what it perceived to be the causes of economic recession. Among other things, to reduce foreign competition in the United States, the government imposed for ninety days an additional tariff of 10 percent on all imported goods, with certain exceptions for under-developed countries and specially protected commodities. The Japanese interpreted this as an attempt to force a revaluation of their currency—a long-held objective in Washington—and as an assault on Japanese-built automobiles. A measure of the shock wave is that in 1970 US-Japanese trade was valued at $10 billion and had grown in 1973 to $19 billion. In all of its trading history, only with Canada had the United States previously done in excess of $10 billion business in a single year. Furthermore, for Japan the larger share of the total amount was in exports, enabling it to maintain an enviable balance-of-trade surplus.[12] Yet another measure was the immediate effect of unemployment in the Japanese automotive industry.

By this act the United States had directly and boldly intervened in Japan's domestic and international economic policies as a reprisal for success, and had restricted Japan's ability to compete in the world's large industrial markets. Japan's postwar economic renaissance, supported by the United States as a way of controlling the Asian power distribution during the Korean War and the Cold War, had now become too competitive. Once again, by unilaterial American decision, the setting in which Japan would have to design its regional and world roles was fraught with the uncertainty of altered assumptions.

The Petroleum Crisis Japan's economic stability was now subject to new pressures. Caught in global recession and inflation, forced by Washington to revalue their currency in a direction injurious to their prosperity, and once again conscious of their vulnerability to foreign economic decisions, the Japanese also saw domestic capital flow out to lucrative investment opportunities elsewhere. As a result of all these

12. Hisao Kanamori, "Future US-Japanese Economic Relations," in Priscilla Clapp and Morton H. Halperin, editors, *United States-Japanese Relations in the 1970s* (Cambridge, Mass.: Harvard University Press, 1974), pp. 58–78. For a summary of Japan's export distribution, see Ernest H. Pregg, *Economic Blocs and US Foreign Policy* (Washington, D.C., National Planning Association, 1974), report number 135, pp. 124–26.

factors, they watched their remarkable growth rate slide toward zero, and their enviable payments surplus begin to dwindle.

Before effective changes could be made, in 1973 the Organization of Petroleum Exporting Countries (OPEC) threatened Japan with an oil embargo unless it either discontinued its relations and trading policy with Israel, or offered technological assistance to the OPEC members. Even after the embargo threat was withdrawn on the basis of an oil-for-technology agreement, the price of oil continued to rise to an intolerably high level, forcing Japan to petition the United States for a collective diplomatic offensive by the oil-consuming countries.

But the humiliation did not terminate with this new reliance on Washington. Nor did the danger end with removal of the embargo threat, for the Japanese have always been acutely aware of their dependence on external sources of raw materials and fuels. In the 1970s, with their economy the world's fastest growing, there could be no substitute for long-range certainty of stable fuel resources. After all, as early as 1972 it had been estimated that by 1985 Japan's annual consumption of energy would equal 40 percent of the total world use in 1970. In keeping with this prediction, the government had made plans for a twentyfold increase in electrical generation from nuclear fuels. It was also exploring for oil with South Korea and Taiwan, arranging for petroleum exploration in Siberia under contract with the Soviet Union and forging joint exploration arrangements with Canada and China.

In the meantime, there was a growing gap between Japan's position as a producer of energy and her rank as a consumer, as Table 3–3 indicates. By 1976, Japan had become the world's sixth largest consumer of fuel per capita and fourth largest in gross national consumption, while the country ranked only as the twenty-third largest producer, earning that position only by virtue of nuclear fuel development. Even today, nearly three-quarters of all energy burned in Japan is oil, approximately 80 percent of which is imported from the Middle East. Thus, fluctuations of supply occasioned by OPEC or by disruptive events in the Middle East (e.g., war between Israel and the Arab states, the curtailment of exports from Iran, etc.) are particularly threatening to Japan.

Japan's immediate response to the increased oil price was to expand industrial exports to the Middle East. Unable to compete with the United States and Europe in arms sales, however, Japan's ability to offset the rising price of oil was limited. Although it was able to increase the value of its exports to the region by more than five times in 1974, the first full year after the crisis commenced, the increased cost of petroleum importation, together with Japan's rising oil demand,

TABLE 3–3
Comparative energy consumption and production. Annual consumption measured in units of 1000 metric tons of coal equivalent, and per capita consumption measured in kilograms of coal equivalent per capita.

	World Rank as Consumer	*World Rank as Producer*	*Consumption per Capita*	*Annual Consumption*
US	1	1	10,204	2.335
USSR	2	2	5,738	1.536
China	3	4	578	.572
Japan	4	23	3,575	.421
West Germany	5	12	5,614	.346
UK	6	9	4,641	.259
Canada	7	6	10,070	.244
France	8	22	4,081	.220
Poland	9	7	4,507	.162
India	10	16	199	.136

Source: United Nations Statistical Yearbook, 1981.

resulted in a trade deficit with the Middle East of more than $11 billion, larger than that of any other state, and an increase of 320 percent over the preceding year.[13]

Still, the problem worsens. From 1973 to 1982, the price of OPEC petroleum increased by more than 1000 percent. The civil war in Iran (1978–79) resulted in a temporary discontinuation of oil exportation and in competitive bidding for Iranian oil, which pushed the price above OPEC levels. The war between Iran and Iraq that began in 1980 was catastrophic for Iranian oil fields, pipelines and refining facilities, thus increasing the burden on Japan to find alternative sources of oil and substitute fuels. By early 1981, Japan was purchasing coal mines in West Virginia, negotiating with Canada for a $5 billion purchase of coal for its steel industries over a fifteen-year period, investing in petroleum exploration in Canada's Beaufort Sea and considering a coal liquification plant with Canada.[14]

The combined effects of recent American economic and strategic policies and the petroleum crisis of the 1970s demonstrate the delicacy of Japan's transition from subordinate state to major power. Simply stated, despite the degree to which it commands world attention as an economic giant, Japan is a highly dependent state with respect to both fuel for industry and national security. Matters are further complicated by the constant economic strain in Japanese-American relations. Even while Japan opens joint ventures with both China and the

13. Atef Sultan, "Japan Sells Hard to Make Up Oil Deficit," *The Middle East Economic Digest,* December 5, 1975, pp. 5–9 and 29–30.
14. On the arrangements with Canada, see "Japan and Canada Develop an Energy Alliance," *World Business Weekly,* December 15, 1980, pp. 14–15.

Soviet Union, Americans look upon Japan as a threat to world markets and as an unfair competitor. One sympathetic American observer has noted that Americans are resistant to the notion that Japan has learned to compete better in the technological age than has the United States.

> It is easier to accept such explanations as Japan's industrial plants were devastated by a world war, and it could therefore build modern facilities; Japan copied Western technology; Japanese companies undersell American ones because they dump goods . . .; Japanese companies succeed because they are subsidized and protected by their government; Japanese workers receive low salaries; Japanese companies exporting to the United States violate antitrust and customs regulations.
>
> It is more comfortable to overlook Japan's continued modernization decades after rebuilding from World War II, its effective organization, its genius in adapting technology, its patience in marketing, its disciplined work force. It is more comfortable not to ask how its businessmen could remain so zealous in selling goods in America if they were basically selling below cost. It is disquieting to admit that the Japanese have beaten us [Americans] in economic competition because of their superior planning, organization, and effort.[15]

Fully aware of American resentment of their economic success, the Japanese find themselves asked repeatedly to diminish their international activity, to adjust currency values and to withhold goods from American markets. By the end of the 1970s there was an increasingly heated mood in Congress to take formal steps to reduce Japanese imports. The Japanese are aware that the words of former Texas governor John Connally have legions of sympathizers in the United States. In an early speech to test his popularity for a run at the Republican nomination for president in 1980, he warned that unless the Japanese open their markets more to American goods, they should "be prepared to sit on the Yokohama docks in [their] Toyotas and [their] little Datsuns and watch [their] own little portable TV sets because we have all of them we need."[16]

The Japanese are proudly aware of the statistical evidence from which this American attitude stems. Since 1970, the Japanese trade position with respect to the United States has improved steadily.

15. Ezra F. Vogel, *Japan as Number One: Lessons for America* (Cambridge, Mass.: Harvard University Press, 1979), pp. 225–26. See also James C. Abegglen and Thomas H. Hout, "Facing Up to the Trade Gap with Japan," *Foreign Affairs,* Fall 1978, pp. 146–168; Richard Tanner Pascale and Anthony G. Athos, *The Art of Japanese Management* (New York: Simon and Schuster, 1981); William Ouchi, *Theory Z: How American Business Can Meet the Japanese Challenge* (Reading, Mass.: Addison-Wesley, 1981); and Edson W. Spencer, "Japan: Stimulus or Scapegoat?" *Foreign Affairs,* Fall 1983, pp. 123–137.
16. Speech in Jacksonville, Fla. on April 27, 1979, as quoted in *The Christian Science Monitor,* May 2, 1979, p. 7.

TABLE 3–4
Japan's trade with the United States, 1971–1982, expressed in billions of US dollars.

	Japanese Exports to US	*Japanese Imports from US*	*Japanese Balance*
1971	7.3	4.1	3.2
1972	9.1	5.0	4.1
1973	9.7	8.3	1.4
1974	12.3	10.7	1.6
1975	11.3	9.6	1.7
1976	15.5	10.1	5.4
1977	18.6	10.5	8.1
1978	24.5	12.9	11.6
1979	26.2	17.6	8.6
1980	30.7	20.8	9.9
1981	37.6	21.8	15.8
1982	37.7	21.0	16.7

Source: International Monetary Fund, *Direction of Trade Annual,* 1971–1978; thereafter, U.S. Department of Commerce, *Business Statistics, 1982 (Supplement to the Survey of Current Business),* November 1983, pp. 75–79.

As Table 3–4 indicates, at the beginning of the 1970s the Japanese trade surplus with the United States, a measure of the relationship of exports to imports, was barely $3.2 billion; by the end of the decade it exceeded $10 billion and grew to nearly $17 billion in the next three years.[17] Furthermore, in 1982 the total American trade deficit was $31.7 billion (i.e., American imports exceeded exports by that amount). Japan alone counted for 53 percent of the total. Were it not for its trade with the United States, Japan would show a modest trade deficit of its own in any typical year, rather than a surplus.

Furthermore, American intolerance for Japanese success was accentuated during this period by two additional phenomena: American producers were losing their accustomed share of Japanese imports in virtually every commodity except wool and cotton, while at the same time Japanese manufacturers were capturing more of the world markets previously controlled by the United States. All of this evidence, by one standard a measure of Japanese success, was by American measurement a source of concern about the success of their principal Asian ally. As the decade closed, Japan feared the increasing American desire for commercial protection and retaliation against Tokyo.

Bilateral negotiations failed until 1981 to result in an agreement to restrict Japanese automobile exports to the United States; and in 1983

17. For an argument that Japanese-American economic conflict arises particularly from the misalignment of Japanese and American currencies and capital flows, see C. Fred Bergsten, "The U.S.–Japan Economic Conflict," *Foreign Affairs,* Summer 1982, pp. 1059–1075.

Tokyo announced that it would not impose export restrictions on its auto manufacturers beyond 1984. But in 1983 Japan also agreed for the first time to market liberalization so that Japan's import markets were opened to autos, pharmaceuticals, appliances, expanded agricultural sales, and investment capital.

Meanwhile, Japanese capital continued to sink more deeply into the economies of the world, just as Japanese goods became more and more evident. As Table 3–5 reveals, Japan's foreign investment in 1970 totaled about $3.3 billion, and by 1979 it had grown to about $31 billion, a tenfold increase. Furthermore, it was expected that by 1985 total foreign direct investment would climb to nearly $80 billion.

Matters are further complicated by Japan's awareness that the very success of in its economy creates regional problems. Japan's status as the dominant economic power of Asia cannot go unnoticed by its neighbors, who will eventually compete for its markets and who are already aware of the political costs of Japan's burgeoning private investment in Asia and the Pacific.[18] Furthermore, it may be in their interests to restrict the availability of fuel to Japan. This raises still a new security imperative in view of Japan's dependence on Middle Eastern oil; it could require more than a fivefold increase in naval strength to defend the 7,500-mile sea journey from source to home.[19]

The Japanese world view, then, is that of a nation that is developed economically, but that remains highly dependent upon the resources, markets and stable economic policies of others in order to prosper. Most especially, the view is shaped by having arrived at the threshold of world power status at a time when the power distribution is changing rapidly and the conditions of security on which Japanese economic

TABLE 3–5
Japanese foreign investment, expressed in billions of US dollars.

	1970	*1979*	*1985 (est.)*
North America	0.9	8.5	21.8
Latin America	0.5	5.0	11.8
Europe	0.6	4.0	5.9
Middle East	0.3	2.3	6.1
Africa	0.01	12.5	3.7
Asia and Pacific	1.0	9.7	29.7
Total	3.31	31.0	79.0

Source: Business Week, June 16, 1980, pp. 92–93.

18. Jon Halliday and Gavan McCormack, *Japanese Imperialism Today* (New York: Monthly Review Press, 1973).
19. Jay B. Sorenson, "Japan: The Dilemmas of Security," *Asian Affairs,* July/August 1975, pp. 363–70.

Newly imported Japanese automobiles sit on a dock in Baltimore. In 1980, Japanese cars accounted for 25 percent of total American car sales.

Source: Paul Conklin

growth has been predicated are in upheaval. As a result, the national role remains undefined, and national politics is a battleground for decisions about changes in economic and military policies.[20]

Summary and Conclusion

Japan's transition from occupied state to world power has had last-minute diversions. Although Japan's economic capacity as measured in gross national product is second only to the United States' in the non-Soviet world and third in the entire world, the independence of its policies remains in doubt. Highly dependent upon external supplies of natural resources—particularly fuel—and upon stable external markets, the economy is ever-vulnerable to foreign pressures. By the same token, domestic and regional sensitivity to Japan's rearmament places severe constraints upon the likelihood of diminishing reliance upon the American security system in Asia, despite the growing fear that the declining American presence in Asia reduces the probability that the United States would come to Japan's defense in case of nuclear or conventional war.

20. J. A. A. Stockwin, *Japan: Divided Politics in a Growth Economy* (New York: Norton, 1975), particularly Chapter 12, "Issues of Foreign Policy and Defense."

Western Europe

Until half a century ago, world politics was Eurocentric. Europe was the center of the Industrial Revolution, home of the world's great financial capitals, site of the principal military and political rivalries, and the metropole from which vast empires were directed. Much of the world's population outside of Europe, in Africa and Asia, was under European domination; and still more did Australia, North America, the Caribbean and the Near East owe allegiance to one or other of the European powers. Even the American role in the First World War, an intense but transitory plunge into global politics, did little to alter the fundamental structure of international politics. By refusing to join the League of Nations, the United States handed the management of international affairs back to the European governments. Neither could the defeat of Germany and the realignment of old empires change the fact that world politics revolved around Europe.

But the First World War set in motion certain inexorable trends. First, it gave Americans an external vision that they had not previously had (though in general their reaction was one of withdrawal). Still, the war demands on American industry produced a most modern and productive economy. Second, Russia's participation in the war ended with the Bolshevik Revolution in 1917, which gave birth to the Soviet Union and brought the Communist Party to power. With a government dedicated to the transformation of a feudal society, massive industrialization and the defense of state against capitalist encirclement, the Soviet Union meant change for Europe and the World. Third, in settling the issues involved in the First World War, it was broadly acknowledged that imperialism and colonialism were major causes of war. The doctrine of national self-determination emerged and foretold the eventual collapse of the European empires.

In a real sense, then, the First World War launched many of the forces that the Second concluded. While the Second World War left continental Europe in ruins, American industry had grown to unprecedented capability, as it had supplied all the allies including the Soviet Union since 1941. Similarly, while Western Europe depended upon the United States for reconstruction, the Soviet Union and the Eastern European states began recovery of their own. Together, these events rearranged the international power distribution so that virtually all effective power was clustered around either the United States or the Soviet Union. Europe was cordoned into the Soviet-allied Eastern sector and the American-allied Western sector. World politics was no longer Eurocentric but bipolar, a configuration in which, far from being the pivotal point of global relations, Western Europe was an object of conflict between the two giants.

From this unaccustomed position, Western Europe looked to the United States for both defense and economic regeneration, objectives in which the United States readily assisted. Apart from America's European roots and heritage, the Cold War confrontation with the Soviet Union dictated that the United States act to preserve democratic polities and free-market economies wherever possible, particularly in Western Europe. This policy, though always expressed in ideological terms, had the firm support of American merchants and manufacturers (whose production surplus cried out for external markets), and of American labor (which equally needed external buyers to maintain full employment). The investment community lent its support too, on the grounds that a reconstructed Europe would borrow American capital, and that a Western Europe staunchly defended from the menace of Soviet invasion would be a safe place for investment. Basic American Cold War foreign policies, enunciated from 1947 through 1949, arose out of the ideological threat and from the convergence of all these interests, and were aimed at the reconstruction of Europe. These included the European Recovery Plan (the Marshall Plan) of 1947, in which Washington committed almost $15 billion to Western Europe's revitalization; the Truman Doctrine (1947), which proclaimed Washington's intention to resist the territorial advance of communism, and on which the containment policy was based; and the institutionalization of European-American defense in the North Atlantic Treaty Organization (NATO) in 1949. Each of these moves presupposed a prolonged threat of Soviet aggression.

During the era of Europe's recovery and of agreement on the imminence of the Soviet threat, the cooperation forged by the Marshall Plan and NATO was constructive. But as Europe neared full restoration, and as the threat of war abated by the late 1950s, trans-Atlantic strains began to develop. Most of these occurred in the economic sphere, though there was a loss of harmony on security matters as well. Most important in both categories, however, was the uniting of Europe, a process of economic consolidation for more successful competition with the United States and a revitalized Japan. As the states of Western Europe grew more interdependent after 1958, they asserted greater independence of the United States. American efforts to maintain the tenor of the trans-Atlantic partnership after the restoration of Western Europe fueled the potential conflict among allies.

The Uniting of Europe

When the European Recovery Plan was launched in 1947, the United States encouraged common economic planning among the aid recipients. The strategy for designing grant requests was for the European governments to study their common needs, design a policy among them and submit a joint proposal to Washington. This was the beginning of cooperative economic planning, an idea that took firm root by 1958. At that time, the economies of the region were rapidly fulfilling their recovery expectations and the fear of invasion from Eastern Europe seemed remote. Now, however, while their individual economies were thriving (though not all equally), they realized their inability to compete with the United States. The American postwar starting point enabled the United States to outrace Europe in the production of goods that sold better even in European markets than did European goods. Another reason for the noncompetitive position of the Europeans was that their national economies were too small to encourage the most efficient production. Futhermore, Europe was slow to develop its own capital market, and American money for multiplication of production facilities was scarce in this period, though it later became so abundant that its value dropped drastically. For all these reasons and more, the states of Western Europe seized upon the idea of a supranational economy, where the economic needs of the group would supersede those of any single state, and where trade among members would be facilitated while the entry of foreign goods would become more difficult.[21]

The European Community (EC) is comprised of several constituent organizations, each designated a "community." Principal among these are the European Economic Community (EEC), the European Coal and Steel Community (ECSC) and the European Atomic Energy Commission (EURATOM). This text uses EC to refer to the larger community, and EEC to identify the economic subsystem alone.

Because of its traditional reluctance to enter continental affairs, and in part its unwillingness to join a French-inspired venture, the British government elected to take its own course. Hence as the European Economic Community (EEC, or European Common Market) was es-

21. For a review of the historical passage from cooperation to competition with an essentially European perspective, see Ernst H. van der Beugel, *From Marshall Aid to Atlantic Partnership* (Amsterdam: Elsevier, 1966), and Henry A. Kissinger, *The Troubled Partnership: A Re-Appraisal of the Atlantic Alliance* (New York: McGraw-Hill, 1965). For a study of European alternative strategies for effective global competition, see Alastair Buchan, *Europe's Future, Europe's Choices: Models of Western Europe in the 1970's* (New York: Columbia University Press, 1969). For an American interpretation sympathetic to the European, see Richard J. Barnet, *The Alliance* (New York: Simon and Schuster, 1983).

tablished by six European states, the British set up the competing European Free Trade Area (EFTA). Together the Common Market and the EFTA included virtually all of industrial Western Europe. The EEC, with its larger industrial potential and its greater demand for industrial goods (particularly as EFTA became weakened by the declining British economy), was measurably the more successful of the two and, accordingly, the one that tended to widen further the trans-Atlantic division. France blocked Britain's attempt to leave EFTA and join the EEC in 1963 because of President de Gaulle's fervent desire "to de-Americanize" Europe, a goal that he deemed unattainable if Britain were to enter while retaining its special relationship with the United States. It was not until 1973 that Britain joined the EEC, together with Denmark and Ireland, leaving EFTA divided but increasing the EEC from The Six to The Nine. Together, the enlarged Economic Community had a GNP of over $1 trillion that was equivalent to 83 percent of the United States' GNP. In the next three years, though the GNP of the EEC continued to grow, it dropped to 78 percent of the United States' GNP. In the years following, however, and with the addition of Greece to the Community in 1981, the economic performance of the European Community grew steadily in comparison with the United States. It grew to the extent that in 1983, with Greece contributing only $43 billion to the total economic performance of the Community, the total Community gross national product reached a level of 95 percent of the United States' GNP. Table 3–6 summarizes the 1983 performance.

TABLE 3–6
Comparison of economic performances of the United States and the European Economic Community, 1983.

	GNP (US$ bil.)	*Population (millions)*	*GNP Per Capita (US$)*
West Germany	830	61.7	13,450
France	658	54.0	12,190
Britain	510	56.0	9,110
Italy	391	56.2	6,960
Netherlands	167	14.2	11,790
Belgium	118	9.9	11,920
Denmark	67	5.1	13,120
Greece	43	9.7	4,420
Ireland	18	3.4	5,230
Luxembourg	2	0.4	5,806
Total EC	2,804	270.6	9,400 (av)
US	2,946	229.8	12,820

Source: The World Bank, *World Development Report 1983,* adapted from Table 1, pp. 148–149.

Beyond these raw facts lies a single compelling conclusion: Acting in concert, the member states of the European Community comprise one of the most productive, and therefore most powerful and influential, actors on the international stage. Despite their individual problems, their disparities, their separate national identities and the disagreements among them, it is as a composite whole rather than as individual states that they play a critical role in contemporary international relations. Together, they are working to restore Western Europe as a principal world center rather than an area of Soviet-American competition or a handmaiden of American foreign policy. It is the world perspective of this "United States of Europe" that we explore here.

One point merits emphasis. It cannot be said that on all issues there is a definable Western European world view; rather, there is a French world view, a German world view and so on. One French observer puts it this way:

> In order to do a better job of analyzing the relations between Western Europe and the United States, one has to consider successively the dialogues between Bonn and Washington, London and Washington, Paris and Washington, all of which differ from one another. More precisely, it is desirable to separate two problems: (a) the attitude of the American government toward the European Community, or more generally, the effort to create a European unity; and (b) the attitude of the American government toward the different European governments in respect to the various problems posed. *There is no global dialogue taking place between Europe as an entity and the United States.*[22]

But while, indeed, there may be no such dialogue at present, the issue at question here is somewhat different. Our concern is not with the unique national differences in relations with the United States, but with the common effort to establish an economic and security community from which to compete more effectively in global economic relations and to reduce security dependence upon Washington. Hence the focus of this analysis is on the compound force rather than on the individual member states.

European-American Trade

The prime economic rationale underlying the EC is the theory of customs union, which seeks to expand trade among the members by eliminating tariffs and other trade barriers among them, and to guard against foreign imports by setting a common trade policy toward nonmembers. Through this device, the EC pursues economic stimu-

22. Raymond Aron, "Europe and the United States: The Relations between Europeans and Americans," in David S. Landes, editor, *Western Europe: The Trials of Partnership* (Lexington, Mass.: Lexington Books, 1977), p. 27. Emphasis added.

lation by capturing a larger share of the European market, and by generating investment capital for expansion of production for external competition. The central objective is improved competitive position, though it was evident from the start that such competition would eventually run afoul of American economic nationalism. This was accepted by Europe as a natural extension of the cooperative recovery assisted earlier by the US.

While Europeans looked forward to trade equality with the United States and to the profitability of their customs union, Americans were quickly awakened to their potential losses. In a preventive step, Congress passed the Trade Expansion Act of 1962, which authorized the executive branch to negotiate sweeping tariff reductions. To Europe the objective was self-evident: Americans, concerned that the toddling European Community might erode their lucrative export surplus, were searching for ways to reduce its competitive position. Because of these negotiations, and despite dire American predictions of trade loss, the composite EEC trade balance for any typical year shows a slight deficit, with only Germany turning up a significant surplus. For the remainder of the Community, the trading relationship with the United States is stable, with only France showing a trend toward deepening deficit.

Europeans consider American efforts to manipulate the EC's trade balance, and particularly to undermine Germany's surplus, to be retaliations for Europe's success. This was especially pronounced in 1971, when the US increased import tariffs by 10 percent in an attempt at economic stabilization. Because they considered this an assault on European competition and on the value of German currency, the EC economic ministers jointly labeled the tariff increase a step short of an American declaration of trade warfare. They pledged that if the new and illegal tariff were not discontinued within ninety days, they would respond by increasing the barriers to American trade in Europe. A multilateral agreement on changes in currency valuations averted a showdown. The near-crisis demonstrated, nevertheless, the awareness by Europeans and Americans of the degree of damage that each can inflict upon the other in international trade. But from the European perspective, another issue fogs the route to full and equal competition: American ownership of European production through direct foreign investment.

American Direct Investment in Europe

The uniting of Europe commenced at a time when American investors were seeking external opportunities and when, in an effort to improve efficiency, industries were becoming multinational. Because the maturation of European customs unions threatened their exports, American manufacturers wished to get behind the tariff barriers presented by EFTA and the EC by buying and building plants in European nations as foreign subsidiaries. These would manufacture goods primarily for sale in Europe. Such goods, though bringing profit to American corporations, would be free of import duties in European markets. Subsequent increases in productivity would be financed not from fresh American capital, but from profit, the remainder of which would be repatriated and thereby removed from the European economy. The initial investment in this trend, recorded as capital leaving the United States, rose to such heights that the American balance of payments, already adversely affected by military commitment in Vietnam, slipped into severe deficit. President Johnson responded by introducing a voluntary restraints program in which American firms were requested to moderate their foreign capital expenditures. But despite these pleas, by 1967 American firms controlled nearly eight thousand foreign subsidiaries, of which nearly half were in the EFTA and EC countries.[23] Of these, two-thirds were in Britain, France, West Germany and Italy. The continuing outflow of capital for this purpose resulted in the imposition of mandatory controls in 1968.[24] Table 3–7 reveals the volume of direct American investment in the combined EC economy. Measured by the extent to which America's total world direct investment is located in the European Community, the facts are even more striking: in 1970 American investments in the EC totaled 27 percent of American worldwide investment, and by 1978 the amount had grown to 33 percent. In 1982, American direct investment abroad totaled $221.3 billion in book value, $163 billion of which was in

TABLE 3–7
American direct investment (Total Book Value) in the European Community, 1960–1981, expressed in billions of US dollars.

Year	*US$ (billions)*
1960	5.9
1965	11.4
1970	20.1
1973	31.3
1978	56.0
1981	80.5

Source: Statistical Abstract of the United States, 1975, 1977, 1979, 1981 and 1982/83. For the years 1960–70 the figures include Britain and the EC countries; for 1973 and after Ireland and Denmark are also included, and Greece is added for 1981.

23. Raymond Vernon, *Sovereignty at Bay: The Multinational Spread of US Enterprises* (New York: Basic Books, 1971), p. 141.
24. US Department of Commerce, *The Multinational Corporations: Studies in US Foreign Investment,* 1972.

industrialized countries. Of this investment, $100 billion was in Western Europe, where it returned earnings at a rate of 8.2 percent.[25]

The prevalence of American capital and the extensive American ownership of European production have led to severe disenchantment among those Europeans who previously expected effective competition with the United States both inside Europe and out. Some have called upon Europeans to restore their own economic destiny by adopting American managerial techniques.[26] Others, like President de Gaulle, have insisted that the only path to effective competition is the "de-Americanization of Europe." Though this theme is not universally espoused among the EC members, it is widely felt that continued American domination of European capital and production not only defers equal competition, but actually places Europe in a position of dependency and colonization. This makes a double blow of American retaliations for Europe's success. Furthermore, since American firms have effectively penetrated the customs union and thus prevent European firms from dominating their own markets, the latter's share of European markets is too small to stimulate the most efficient production. As a result, the regional idea is rapidly giving way to corporate demands for globalization of European industries. Thus, more and more European industries, which were previously considered the foundations of regional integration, are going multinational instead.[27]

In addition to persisting economic matters, which ensure that the Euro-American relationship will always be one as much of competition as of cooperation, there are a number of underlying issues in the relationship that lead to doubt and occasional disruption. One of these involved the natural tension between the United States as a trans-Atlantic power and the United States as a global power. Europeans have frequently objected to non-European American foreign policies that are inconsistent with Europe's aims in the world, or that are undertaken at risk to the trans-Atlantic community without consultation with the European partners.

Occasionally, this "fitful rush toward global unilateralism," as one European calls it, strikes directly at the partnership with considerable cost to the European interest.[28] The most outstanding example was the effort of President Ronald Reagan to prevent the construction of

25. For details on American investment in Europe and foreign investment in the United States, see U.S. Department of Commerce, *Survey of Current Business,* August 1983, p. 14.
26. J. J. Servan-Schreiber, *The American Challenge* (New York: Avon Books, 1968).
27. Raymond Vernon et al., *Big Business and the State: Changing Relations in Western Europe* (Cambridge, Mass.: Harvard University Press, 1974).
28. Josef Joffe, "Europe and America: The Politics of Resentment (cont'd)," *Foreign Affairs,* America and the World 1982 issue, pp. 567–590 at p. 567.

a gas pipeline from Siberia to Europe, through which the European governments would have bought millions of dollars worth of natural gas annually. When the Europeans themselves refused under American pressure to discontinue the contract with the Soviet Union, President Reagan attempted to thwart their desires by threatening with prosecution any American firm or European-based affiliate of any American firm which participated in any way in the sale, planning or installation of parts of the pipeline. The United States argued over a ten-month period in 1981 and 1982 that it opposed the pipeline because it did not want European economic and military strategies to become dependent upon a source of fuel that could be discontinued at any time. The Europeans, however, responded that the policy was inspired by an inappropriate attempt on the part of the Reagan administration to couple Europe's fuel needs with the American effort to impose economic sanctions on the Soviet Union for its use of martial law in Poland to crush the independent Solidarity labor movement. The matter was settled in favor of the European view after nearly a year of discontent, and in the context of larger trade issues involving European steel exports.

Contrary to public perception, European-American trade competition is not limited to industrial produce. Particularly during the 1980-83 recession, when world industrial trade dropped steadily and the American balance of trade fell dangerously, competition in agricultural trade eroded the spirit of partnership. As wheat prices fell and stocks accumulated, particularly in the United States, European grain exports doubled. The increase resulted in part from the Soviet preference for European grain (after the United States broke an agreement and embargoed grain to the Soviet Union in response to the Afghanistan and Poland events), and in part from a disagreement between the EEC and Washington on interpretation of certain export provisions of agreements resulting from the 1979 Tokyo Round of negotiations of the General Agreement on Tariffs and Trade.[29] This type of disagreement is likely to recur as the EEC seeks a diversified export base, and as the United States relies increasingly upon agricultural exports to balance its trade against superior competition in industrial goods from Europe and Japan.

Largest among the causes of European-American discord, however, is the widening gap in how Soviet foreign policy is interpreted, particularly in Europe. While the United States engages in an endless barrage of rhetoric about Soviet intentions of global conquest, the

29. Nicholas Butler, "The Ploughshares War Between Europe and America," *Foreign Affairs,* Fall 1983, pp. 105–122.

Europeans take the view that, although the Soviet Union is more powerful now than it was a decade ago, its influence has actually waned.[30] In a rare break from President Reagan's policies, British Prime Minister Margaret Thatcher said in 1984 that the West must do more to secure the confidence of the Kremlin on matters of arms competition and control, even while Washington blamed the discontinuation of three different arms negotiations on the Soviets.[31]

By 1984, the difference between the dominant European view of the Soviet Union and that of the Reagan administration was so great that many Europeans were questioning the capability of American foreign policy to adjust to world realities. The issue is sufficiently serious to merit the extensive quotation of one critical British writer. Noting that there are two views of the American understanding of Soviet policy, he rejects the first, namely, that after a decade of weakness and humiliation, America is now preparing to stall the spread of Soviet influence.

> The other view is shared to a greater or lesser extent by much of the rest of mankind. . . . It is that the Reagan Administration has vastly overreacted to the Soviet threat, thereby distorting the American (and hence the world) economy, quickening the arms race, warping its own judgment about events in the Third World, and further debasing the language of international intercourse with feverish rhetoric. A subsidiary charge, laid principally by Europeans, Canadians and many Latin Americans, is that in a desperate desire to rediscover "leadership," the United States under Reagan has reverted to its world unilateral habits, resenting and ignoring, when it deigns to notice, the independent views and interests of its friends and allies.
>
> It is in my experience almost impossible to convey even to the most experienced Americans just how deeply rooted and widely spread the critical view has become. It is, however, worth recalling . . . that a devastating but entirely reputable opinion poll taken in January [1983] . . . showed that no less than 70 percent of the British lacked any confidence in the judgment of the American Administration. This did not mean that they were neutralist or soft on communism or anything of the kind; on the contrary, their answers to another question proved that they were overwhelmingly in favor of NATO. It simply showed that they did not trust President Reagan and gave him no credit for successful leadership. Similar polls have been taken in other European countries, but the appearance of these sentiments in Britain, the most solid and phlegmatic member of the Alliance, may legitimately be regarded as a measure of the chasm that lies between current American perceptions of the world and the world's perception of America.[32]

30. For a detailed analysis, see Jonathan Steele, *Soviet Power: The Kremlin's Foreign Policy—Brezhnev to Andropov* (New York: Simon and Schuster, 1983). Steele is a British news correspondent.
31. *The New York Times,* Sunday, January 22, 1984, article on p. 1, quotations on p. 12.
32. David Watt, "As a European Saw It," *Foreign Affairs,* America and the World 1983 issue, pp. 521–532 at pp. 521–22.

Such a broad critique of American attitudes is symbolic of the deterioration of trust between Europe and the United States, an erosion which finds its way not only into economic affairs, but into commonly held security affairs as well. While NATO continues to play its original role of forming the first line of defense against the Soviet Union, it is the focal point of divergent notions about strategies, arms control, troop deployments, military appropriations and a host of other issues that lie at the interface of military strategy and the politics of alliance. Most distressing of all is the possibility that in preparing for limited nuclear war, and in declaring that limited nuclear war is both winnable and survivable, the Pentagon may be basing its nuclear strategy in Europe on an unspoken premise of using Western Europe as a line of defense for the United States.

The issue of the nuclear and conventional forces balances in Europe is left to subsequent chapters (Chapters X and IX, respectively); the following section deals only with the diplomatic aspects of intra-alliance strategies.

The European Community and Trans-Atlantic Defense

If the emphasis of the European Community is on regionalism, then the underlying postulate of the Western security system in Atlanticism. And if the United States relates to the European Community in the economic sphere as an overbearing competitor, then it presents itself to the European members of NATO as a dominant partner, unsure of its objectives, but resistant to change in its stature. As in the economic sphere, the Community members acknowledge their reliance on the United States, but deplore the political and economic consequences of imbalance. Is American control of trans-Atlantic defense policy an instrument for preventing marked alteration of political and economic relations? Is it a means by which Washington and its economic interests pursue economic Atlanticism as an alternative to effective competition from a united Europe? Is European integration feasible in the presence of a NATO as presently structured? Is NATO integrative of Atlanticism, but disintegrative of Europeanism?[33]

Despite the clear European dilemma on the security issue, however, there is among the NATO partners considerable fragmentation of perception. All suffer a degree of anxiety concerning the acknowledged superiority of the Warsaw Pact's conventional forces, though Germany and France seem more alarmed about the growing nuclear threat posed

33. Francis A. Beer, *Integration and Disintegration in NATO* (Columbus: Ohio State University Press, 1969).

by the strategic competition of the USSR and the USA. During the 1970s, Washington pressed the Europeans for a redistribution of the costs of the alliance, calling for a greater European contribution so that the US might diminish its burden. With the onset of the 1980s, Washington saw a need for allies on both sides of the Atlantic to increase their commitments, and talk in the Senate of a reduced American share vanished.

Nevertheless, Europeans continue to differ in their attitudes about the imminence of the danger from the East. The more liberal elements argue that the Soviet Union's demands for a stable European balance had been satiated by 1980, and that the NATO deployment of Pershing II and land-based cruise missiles beginning at the end of 1983 was a destabilizing event which called for further Soviet deployments. The more conservative, on the other hand, argued that the Soviet Union had been quietly building its strike forces in order to exploit any weakness in Western defenses. To these people, Soviet deployments following the arrival of the first new American missiles were evidence of aggressive Soviet intentions for both conventional and nuclear superiority across the East-West border of Europe. The Kremlin's refusal

Western Europeans protesting deployment of new American weapons, 1984.

Source: Wide World Photos, Inc.

to continue the Strategic Arms Reduction Talks (START), the Intermediate-range Nuclear Force Talks (INF) and the Mutual Balanced Force Reduction Talks (MBFR) at the end of 1983 was seen by the conservative camp as further evidence of Soviet intentions to secure superiority.

Of these two positions, the former is dominant in Europe and the latter in the United States. The difference between them goes beyond simple disagreement. That the views should have emerged into prominence during the debate over the new missile deployments indicates fundamentally different premises for the nuclear weapons of NATO. One European observer puts it this way:

> In the past, Europeans had tended to view nuclear weapons both as a means of last resort and as an alternative to expensive conventional defense. The United States, on the other hand, had increasingly come to regard nuclear weapons as an integral part of the military effort, designed to provide a spectrum of deterrence across the range of conceivable military contingencies. Both of these approaches were challenged by the missile controversy, and their contradictions revealed: in Europe, the unreasonably high dependence on nuclear weapons for defense; in the United States, the impermissible slide from deterring to contemplating fighting a nuclear war.[34]

But beyond questions of strategy are matters of dependence. Throughout NATO's history, the European partners have felt themselves subject to American strategy, command and equipment decisions. In response, the French in 1965 removed themselves from the NATO integrated command (though not from the organization itself), and ordered NATO headquarters and all military personnel and equipment not under the command of the French government removed from French soil. More typically, however, NATO members have attempted to resolve cooperatively the dilemma of Atlanticism and Europeanism. Within Europe, for example, both Britain and France have undertaken independent nuclear policies, each premised not on the thought of destroying a potential enemy but on that of developing the capability to inflict intolerable harm; a policy of minimal deterrence. These national developments have resulted in public debate about the creation of an Anglo-French deterrent, a prospective policy of combining British and French nuclear capabilities under a planning system that will reduce the dependence on American strategy. Furthermore, the Eurogroup within NATO continues to press collectively for a greater European voice in the strategic planning of NATO, an effort designed to take maximum advantage of the American commitment while at

34. Christopher Bertram, "Europe and America in 1983," *Foreign Affairs*, America and the World 1983 issue, pp. 616–631 at pp. 628–629.

Source: Steve Mendelson, *The Washington Post*

the same time minimizing European servitude to Washington's objectives for the alliance. None of these efforts, though, can deal effectively with a confrontation with the conventional military strength of the Warsaw Pact without American participation. Americans, then, ask the question, "How much longer must we bear the cost of Western Europe's defense even while suffering from increasingly effective European economic competition?" Simultaneously, Western Europeans are asking, "How can we reduce our reliance on the United States without emasculating the alliance to the point at which the balance of forces across all of Europe is irreparably damaged? And how can we promote Europeanism without eroding Atlanticism to the point of inviting American retaliation and coercion?" To Americans, the costs of NATO are unevenly divided because they carry the bulk of the economic burden. But Western Europeans believe that they themselves assume the social and political costs of the reliance of Washington. As long as the costs are perceived and measured differently, Atlanticism and Europeanism will persist, and the Western European perception of the international system will continue to focus most nervously on the dangers imposed by its closest non-European friend.

The Atlantic Alliance, for nearly four decades the cornerstone of American strategic policy and of European dependence upon Washington, is thoroughly familiar with discontent and disagreement. Often it has acted like a mighty arsenal in political disarray.[35] In times of threat, however, it has bound together. Secretary of State Edmund Muskie, on the occasion of the Soviet occupation of Afghanistan in 1979, declared that the trans-Atlantic allies were united in a manner not known in decades. More frequently, however, as the United States has engaged in unilateralism in Europe and elsewhere, as economic conflict has hardened the tone of trans-Atlantic diplomacy, and as divergent interpretations have divided the alliance over Soviet intentions, discord has reigned. While some observers regard such conditions as typical of specialized organizations and others attribute them to such factors as economic competition, still others are concerned that conflict is insuperable in the long run. For while NATO may be an organization of sovereign equals, it is not an organization of military equals, and in this respect Europe's dependence is permanant.[36] Indeed, it may be that except in the presence of a constant threat from a unifying enemy, NATO is incapable of sustained purpose.[37]

In the absence of significant arms reduction across Europe, however, the perception of a common enemy continues and, with it, the asymmetrical relationship within the Atlantic Alliance. Europeans recoil when they are informed that the American pressure for the installation of new missile generations is not for purposes of improving security, but for "alliance management."[38] They take as a more salient suggestion a proposal from a responsible American observer of foreign policy that NATO be restructured to enlarge the probability of Europe's military self-determination within Atlanticism.[39]

Eurocommunism: Europe Between East and West

Soviet domination of the world communist movement, commencing with the Bolshevik Revolution of 1917, has been based on a number of ideological goals. (For history and theoretical premises, refer to

35. For a sound general treatment of the politics of the alliance from a European perspective, see Alastair F. Buchan, "The United States and the Security of Europe," in David S. Landes, editor, *Western Europe: The Trials of Partnership* (Lexington, Mass.: Lexington Books, 1977), Chapter 9.
36. Raymond Aron, "Ideology in Search of a Policy," *Foreign Affairs,* America and the World 1981 issue, pp. 503–524. See also Eliot A. Cohen, "The Long-Term Crisis of the Alliance," *Foreign Affairs,* Winter 1982/83, pp. 325–343.
37. George Ball, "Europe Without a Unifying Adversary," in G. R. Urban, editor, *Détente* (New York: Universe Books, 1976), pp. 229–242.
38. Richard A. Burt, *Time,* December 5, 1983, p. 29.
39. Henry A. Kissinger (former Secretary of State), "A Plan to Reshape NATO," *Time,* March 5, 1984, pp. 20–24.

Chapter 1.) First, and in faithful compliance with the tenets of Karl Marx, the leadership has insisted upon an "international" model of communism, requiring that all communist parties adapt their domestic and foreign policies to those of the leader, and that the needs of the Socialist commonwealth rather than of individual nation-states be the focal point. Second, Moscow has insisted on "monolithic" communism, specifying that there is but one world communist movement, in which all of the far-flung parts (the various national communist parties) take their ideological and political direction from the Kremlin. Third, the Soviet version of communism requires that the Party serve as the "vanguard of the proletariat" in the challenge of the working class against bourgeois capitalists. Fourth, the international activities of communist states and parties must be based on the movement of the working class across national borders, thus prescribing a worldwide movement of "proletarian internationalism." Fifth, the communist state and party command the full allegiance of individuals, thus authorizing the ideological chieftans of communism to determine the meaning and content of liberty even if the advancement of the movement should require the outlawing of religion or freedom of expression. And sixth, the fixed objectives of communism dictate that parties should use political strategies that seek to rule, and that there be no recognition of pluralistic interests, no accommodation with divergent political elements, and no concession to nonproletarian minorities to exercise the power of government.

Modern history is filled with instances in which this creed has been violated. We have seen, for example, that the Chinese Communist Party departed entirely from the requirement of monolithic communism, a "crime" that the Soviet leadership denounced as a deviant aberration by a political movement parading under the title of communism in nonindustrial society! But even closer to Moscow, in European industrialized states such as Yugoslavia and Rumania challenges to the international model have been common, as communist parties have asserted their independence and have attempted to apply basic communist objectives to national problems, rather than to subordinate their national needs to international communism.

For the most part, however, the communist parties of Western Europe have been loyal to the Soviet line, not least because the Communist Party of the Soviet Union and other national communist parties were their only sources of support for the quarter-century during which the United States and its Western European partners strove relentlessly to contain Soviet influence and to crush national communist movements.

But Soviet-American détente, Sino-Soviet warlike posturing, and the decline of fear of a major European war have converged to give improved respectability to the Western European communist parties. And with this luxury, they have determined to exploit the environment of political change by challenging each of the basic tenets of Soviet leadership. This challenge, enunciated most vocally in 1976 at the Second Pan-European Conference of Communist and Workers' parties in Berlin, gave birth to Eurocommunism.

Far from being merely a regional variant of Marxist doctrine, Eurocommunism may eventually pose a major test of Moscow's leadership in the world communist movement, and of its hold over Eastern Europe. One observer has judged that the movement signifies a major shift in international communist influence—no longer from East to West but now from West to East.[40]

Eurocommunism is, first and foremost, built upon the "national" model: It calls for the application of Marxism to national problems rather than the sacrifice of local needs for those of the larger Socialist Commonwealth. The Italian Communist Party, which together with the French and Spanish parties initiated the movement, has gone so far as to declare that further development of communist influence in Italy will occur "within the framework of the international alliances to which our country belongs," referring presumably to NATO and the EC.[41] Not only does this depart from the dual notions of the international model and monolithic communism; it also declares an intent to work with one of the major armed threats to the Socialist Commonwealth, NATO.

Eurocommunism's erosion of international subservience and of monolithic leadership is apparent. But in addition, the Western European communist parties, together with some dissidents from the East, have abandoned the most important stage of Marxism, that of the dictatorship of the proletariat. "Abandonment of the dictatorship of the proletariat is not negotiable," in the worlds of one principal spokesman for the French Communist Party.[42] In its place has been substituted the notion of pluralistic democracy (the free competition of divergent interests in a political system). Similarly, the rigid communist notion that the Party can leave no room for minority challenges, and cannot concede to open competition for the authority to rule, has been replaced by the concept of electoral pluralism. As a final accompaniment, Eurocommunism is openly critical of Moscow's brutal suppression of religion and freedom of expression, and has called for a European

40. Charles Gati, "The Europeanization of Communism?" *Foreign Affairs,* April 1977, pp. 539–53.
41. Reported in *L'Unitá,* June 30, 1976, and quoted in Kevin Devlin, "The Challenge of Eurocommunism," *Problems of Communism,* January/February 1977, p. 16.
42. Reported in *Le Monde,* March 2, 1976, and quoted *ibid.,* p. 11.

communist movement that would endorse civil liberties. At issue, then, are all six building blocks of Soviet monolithic leadership.

But these descriptive passages reveal little of the potential consequences of Eurocommunism for global or even continental politics. Some expect that as the movement gains steam it will effectively diminish Soviet influence over Eastern Europe. Others retort that the maintenance of the Eastern European buffer zone is so crucial to the Kremlin that Eurocommunism in Eastern Europe will be held under control at all costs, particularly when Atlanticism is strong and when détente fails to guide Soviet-American relations.

One American observer offers the possibility that Soviet tolerance is based on a perceived advantage to the Kremlin. This conclusion is derived from five premises. First, Eurocommunism (at least in Western Europe) diminishes internal conflict, thus minimizing the invitation to American influence. Second, Eurocommunists have pledged not to disrupt the national economies of Western Europe, thus avoiding a major cause of conflict and potential American intervention. Third, tolerance of communism under its new doctrinal form in Western Europe will result in placing communists in critically important public positions, inside and outside of government, thus enabling Eurocommunism to neutralize counter-revolutionary forces. Fourth, as détente fails, and severe Soviet-American antipathy resumes, Eurocommunism might reduce Western Europe's commitment to the American cause, and possibly in the long run swing it to the Soviet. And finally, Eurocommunism assists the Soviet Union by lulling anticommunist factions in Western Europe and the United States, so that the Kremlin might pursue expansionist foreign policies without fear of retaliatory restrictions on trade and the import of Western technology.[43]

Eurocommunism is an ideologically profound, yet still an infant and inconsistent movement, subject to influence by a variety of conditions. As a result of the failure of détente, the reawakening of war-fears as a result of the Soviet invasion of Afghanistan, and the resumption of Soviet political intervention in Eastern Europe during the Polish crisis, severe limitations have been placed on Eurocommunism as an instrument of change in Western Europe and between East and West.

Canada

If there is one indicator to differentiate the relationship of the United States with Japan and Western Eruope from that with Canada, it is proximity. Like its Asian and European counterparts, Canada shares

43. Roy C. Macridis, "Eurocommunism," *The Yale Review,* March 1978, pp. 321–37.

an extensive economic and security relationship with the United States. But that relationship has the added features of a 3,000-mile undefended border and a long tradition of intimate economic cooperation. Though until the end of the Second World War Canadian economic and political relations were closely tied to the United Kingdom, the predominance of the American economy since the war, and the aggressive diffusion of American capital, have reversed this course. At present, the trading relation between Canada and the United States reaches an annual value exceeding that of any other bilateral economic relation in history; such has been the case for over a decade.

Canada's total economic capacity at present ranks ninth in the world by gross national product and thirteenth by GNP per capita.[44] Also, its capacity is increasing because of its vast mineral reserves. Supporting a population of only twenty-four million (10 percent that of the United States and only 20 percent that of Japan) in one of the world's largest territorial masses will enable Canada to preserve its natural resources longer than most nation-states, though at the present rates of extraction the petroleum and natural gas reserves (those presently known) will have been depleted within twenty-five years.

But despite these apparent foundations for national autonomy, the geographical closeness of the United States has fostered a pattern of investment, trade and managerial control leading to what some call partnership and others label a colonial relationship. Still others are tempted to refer to an integrated Canadian-American economy, though such an observation ignores the asymmetry of benefits. The conditions that surround the effort to establish full economic, cultural and political sovereignty out of this lopsided partnership govern the Canadian world perspective.

Domestic Influences Affecting the Canadian World View

Canadian domestic politics is divided along several firmly drawn lines. Most significant among them is the ethnic distinction between the dominant Anglo-Canadians and the French-Canadians, who are concentrated in Quebec Province. Although French-Canadians consider themselves a nation within a nation, only at the extreme is French-Canadian nationalism separatist. They are deeply persuaded that as a minority they have been exploited and oppressed by the English. Nevertheless, in their external outlook they are concerned for Canada's

44. In addition to the economies listed in Table 3–6 which exceed Canada in GNP, so does the Soviet Union. Those not appearing in the tables that have greater GNP per capita are the United Arab Emirates, Kuwait, Saudi Arabia, Norway, Sweden and Switzerland.

economic independence from the United States. As a self-proclaimed oppressed minority, they were unusually sympathetic to young Americans who emigrated to Canada rather than serve in the armed forces in Vietnam, and whose criticism of American foreign policy and of the American establishment accentuated the appetite for Canadian autonomy even more than for Quebec's secession.

For their part, the Anglo-Canadians have been slower to recognize the costs of economic ties to the United States, having for so long depended upon American capital for industrialization. Those who inhabit the industrial heartland, however, which for the most part is centered close to the American industrial complexes along the Great Lakes, have developed a new self-consciousness regarding managerial control, and are now eager to establish full Canadian economic sovereignty by reducing American ownership of the nation's industry. It is this geographic distinction that forms the second line of division among Canadians in determining the world outlook.

A third important line of difference in Canadian politics is that between continentalists and nationalists. Continentalists have resolved in their minds the partner/colony debate by declaring their preference for an economy integrated with that of the United States for the maximum profit of Canada. This view is now held most notably by mineral exporters who find that national pricing systems put them at a disadvantage with respect to profits that can be earned in the United States; and among those who reside at the industrial fringes, who believe that national investment policies favor the industrial heartland and retard the economic development of their own regions.

The nationalists, however—the growing number of Canadians who believe that American investment and ownership have already exceeded the desirable level—avidly support policies drawn to safeguard Canada from further encroachment, policies that will reduce American industrial ownership of Canada. It is principally the convergence of this sentiment among the Anglo-Canadians who comprise the new entrepreneurial class (and who yearn for national scientific and technological development) with the more traditional French-Canadian nationalism that has led to the now widely recognized era in Canadian-American relations.[45] The new Anglo-Canadian nationalists, who are amply and vigorously represented in government, particularly deplore the deleterious effects upon Canada of American legal control over

45. Robert Gilpin, "Integration and Disintegration on the North American Continent," *International Organization* 28, 1974, pp. 851–74. See also John Sloan Dickey, "Canada Independent," *Foreign Affairs,* July 1972, pp. 684–99; and Gerald F. Rutan, "Stresses and Fractures in Canadian-American Relations. The Emergence of a New Environment," *Orbis* 18, summer 1974, pp. 582–93.

foreign subsidiaries in Canada. The government recognizes this problem of extraterritorial control as a political instrusion more costly than mere foreign ownership.[46] It is with these thoughts in mind that the nationalists have sharpened their focus of the Canadian world view on the economic relationship with the United States. Nonetheless, "ambivalance concerning the choice of a proper balance between autonomy and integration has been a recurrent feature of Canadian foreign policy."[47] Ecological, security and cultural problems follow next, in that order.

As has been indicated, trade between the United States and Canada is of exceptional volume, and comprises the largest bilateral trading relationship in the world. In 1981, for example, as is indicated in Table 3–8, trade with the United States comprised $110 billion of Canada's total world trade of $165 billion, or fully 66 percent. In addition, however, because the value of Canada's exports to the United States exceeds the value of goods imported, Canada consistently runs a modest trade surplus in the bilateral relationship, as normally it does with the world. Preliminary figures for 1983, not shown on Table 3–8, indicate that Canada exported $53.4 billion to the United States in return for $42.8 imported, yielding a total trade value of $96.2 billion and a Canadian surplus of nearly $11 billion.[48]

But despite this apparently enviable position, the maintenance of a trade surplus with the southern neighbor has not been without high costs. In the long run perhaps the greatest cost will prove to be the premature depletion of natural resources. More immediately, however, Canadians are concerned with the American political and corporate controls to which their economy is susceptible. In the automobile industry, for example, stimulation of production occurred only as a result of an Auto Pact (1965), in which Canada sacrificed tariff revenues in return for anticipated employment benefits and lower consumer prices. But employment has been subject to economic fluctuations in the United States, and to the decisions of the multinational auto companies to relocate production. Furthermore, subsequent investment has come largely from profit, rather than from fresh capital flowing from the United States. At the intergovernmental level, in order to minimize Canada's trade surplus with respect to the United States, American policy on automobile trade ensures that in this single com-

46. "Foreign Ownership and the Structure of Canadian Industry: A Report of the Task Force on the Structure of Canadian Industry," January 1968, pp. 310–45.
47. Michael B. Dolan, Brian Tomlin and Harald von Reikhoff, "Integration and Autonomy in Canadian-United States Relations, 1963-1972," *Canadian Journal of Political Science,* June 1982, pp. 331–363 at p. 332.
48. The figures are at annualized rates after the close of the third quarter and appear in *The Economic Report of the President, 1984,* p. 335.

TABLE 3–8
Direction of Canadian Trade, 1969–1981, expressed in billions of US dollars.

	Import	*Export*	*Total Value*	*Balance*
1969				
Trade with US	9.5	9.8	19.3	0.3
Trade with World	14.3	13.5	27.8	(0.8)
% of total with US	66%	73%	69%	
1973				
Trade with US	16.5	17.1	33.6	0.6
Trade with World	24.0	26.4	50.4	2.4
% of total with US	69%	65%	67%	
1977				
Trade with US	27.8	29.1	56.9	1.3
Trade with World	40.8	43.1	83.9	2.3
% of total with US	68%	68%	68%	
1981				
Trade with US	54.4	55.4	109.8	1.0
Trade with World	79.1	86.2	165.3	7.1
% of total with US	69%	64%	66%	

Source: Adapted from *Direction of Trade Annual* for 1969 through 1977; *Europa Yearbook, 1983* for 1981.

modity, Canada will have a fluctuating deficit. Finally, Canadians fear that in their efforts to negotiate conditions that will enhance the industrial sector, they may be forced by Washington into a continental policy in natural resources that will both accelerate the depletion of reserves and further erode national autonomy.

Thus, behind the Canadian trade surplus lurk the dangers of extreme reliance on a single partner for both import and export markets, and the problems of external investment and foreign industrial ownership that give rise to these external controls. Furthermore, because Canada's trade base is small compared with those of the United States, Japan and Western Europe, it is unusually vulnerable to world trends toward protectionism (tariffs and other barriers to trade that governments use to protect their domestic economies against imported goods). For this reason, Canada attempted throughout the 1970s to expand trade relations with the Third World and to play a vigorous part in the frequent multilateral trade negotiations in order to encourage free international trade.[49]

49. See statement of the Honorable Don Jamieson, Secretary of State for External Affairs, on February 5, 1979, entitled "A Canadian View of the Multilateral Trade Negotiations" (Ottawa: Ministry of External Affairs, Paper Number 79/3).

Direct Private Investment

During the lengthy period of British influence in the Canadian economy, private investment was mostly of the portfolio type—that is, purchase of stocks and bonds on securities markets. As the era of American domination began, however, with investments rising from approximately $5 billion to $25 billion in twenty years, the pattern shifted from portfolio investment to purchase of Canadian firms and mineral deposits, and construction of foreign subsidiaries of American firms. In the immediate postwar years and in the early years (1955–65) of intense Canadian industrial development, government planning took for granted that this direct private investment was profitable. It brought needed managerial skills as well as capital into the country; it hastened industrialization and the ability to exploit natural resource reserves; it created profit and increased employment; and it generated public revenue as well as export surpluses. The rapid and sustained increases in the gross national product and in per capita income seemed testimony to the wisdom of an open policy on direct private investment from the United States.

As Canadian economic nationalism began to rise, however, this policy was reappraised. Between 1964 and 1967, for example, Canadians who thought that there was enough American capital in their economy rose from 46 percent to 67 percent of those questioned. Clearly the population was aware of how much the partnership with the United States was decaying into colonial subordination. Table 3–9 dramatizes the basis for this fear. By 1972, only 37 percent of Canadians polled felt that they shared with the United States an economic partnership, while 34 percent felt that they had become colonized. Only 34 percent felt that dependence on the United States was good for Canada; 53 percent thought it bad.[50] Table 3–9 summarizes direct American investment in Canada. It shows that while Canadian investments were becoming a smaller fraction of worldwide American investment, actual American ownership of Canadian industry actually doubled in value during the early 1980s.

After decades of satisfaction with the profitability of American investment, national preoccupation turned to the sordid side. The Gray Task Force in 1972 focused as much on the costs of dependence as upon the benefits. In a marked departure from traditional assumptions,

50. For an extensive statistical study of Canadian attitudes toward American domination, see John H. Sigler and Dennis Goresky, "Public Opinion on United States-Canadian Relations," *International Organization* 28, 1974, pp. 637–68. For a briefer survey pertaining specifically to attitudes on foreign investment, refer to John Fayerweather, *Foreign Investment in Canada: Prospects for National Policy* (White Plains, N.Y.: International Arts and Sciences Press, 1973), pp. 13–72.

TABLE 3–9
American direct investment in Canada, 1970–1981, expressed in billions of US dollars.

	1970	*1974*	*1978*	*1981*
US worldwide investment	$75.5	$110.1	$168.1	$227.3
US investment in Canada	$21.0	$28.4	$37.3	$47.0
Canada investments as percent of American worldwide investment	28%	26%	22%	21%

Source: Statistical Abstract of the United States, 1979 and 1982/83.

the Gray Report concluded that most of the profit accrued to Canada was actually drawn not from American investment capital, but from the American corporations' ability to exploit Canadian resources.[51] If this is the case, then the wise course for Canada is to distinguish between investment policy as a capital venture and foreign ownership, and thereafter to restrict foreign direct investment to a level below 50 percent ownership or control. As early as 1970, a plurality (though not a majority) of Canadians polled reported that they would approve a policy of restricting American ownership to 49 percent in any industry even if it meant a reduction in the national standard of living!

The Gray Report was followed only months later by an extensive government report on Canadian relations with the United States entitled *Options for the Future,* a statement on foreign affairs by Mitchell Sharp, Minister for External Affairs.[52] Major portions of this report deal with the question of whether asymmetrical interdependence with the United States automatically raises threats to Canada's economic sovereignty. For both trade and investment policies, the report suggests that Canada should measure permissible relations in how they will benefit Canada and Canadians. Since then, Parliament has entertained a variety of proposals for screening investments by foreign sources in accordance with the requirement that a project strengthen the Canadian economy without further deteriorating national control over economic activity. Recognizing that excessive nationalism might damage the economy by repelling useful investments, the government seeks

51. Gray Task Force Report, *Foreign Direct Investment in Canada* (Ottawa: Information Canada, 1972).
52. Published as a special issue of *International Perspectives* (Ottawa: Information Canada, Autumn 1972).

a policy that will run a delicate line between destructive nationalism and equally destructive continentalism.

Efforts at reducing the amount of foreign (and particularly American) ownership had resulted, by 1979, in a decline to 28.5 percent ownership by foreign investors of all Canadian industry. Of the total, 75 percent continues to be American-owned.[53]

Natural Resources

Canada's richness in natural resources permits a favorable trade balance with the United States. Though fuel products (including uranium) comprise the bulk of such resources, Canada is also plentiful in ore deposits. The United States is the largest customer, to the extent that by exporting half of its annual gas and oil production, Canada fulfills about 6 percent of the total American demand.

In an era of fuel shortages and gloomy predictions about exhaustion of resources, it would seem that it is the United States that is dependent upon Canada in this regard; and on the surface this is accurate. From the Canadian viewpoint, however, this is but part of the story. As Table 3–10 shows, the mining and refining facilities of Canada are heavily in foreign—and particularly American—control. As a result, the profit from these enterprises contributes little to the Canadian economy, but is repatriated to the United States. Moreover, the rate of production is determined less by Canadian public policy than by American demand and American corporate decisions. Of paramount importance is the tendency of Canadian fuel production to become enmeshed in American foreign policy. The OPEC threat of a total oil embargo as a lever on Israeli-American relations in 1973 heightened Washington's interest in a continental oil policy that would formally subordinate Canadian national policy to joint Canadian-American determination. The growing demand for fuel in the United States, the steady increase of OPEC petroleum prices and the increased reliance of the United States upon external sources of fuel (both petroleum and natural gas) in the remaining years of the 1970s made the attractiveness of Canada's riches even greater. Coupled with gradual depletion of Canada's reserves, such overtures continue to threaten Canadian autonomy, despite the fact that Canada's annual export volume of fuel to the United States is declining steadily, while its volume to Japan increases.

Canadian international affairs are centered upon another natural resource as well: its fishing industry. Long an exporter of fish and

53. *The Europa Yearbook, 1983.*

TABLE 3–10
Foreign and American ownership of selected Canadian industries, 1971.

Industry	*% Foreign Ownership*	*% American Ownership*
Motor vehicles and parts	95.7	95.6
Industrial electrical equipment	95.7	89.6
Iron mining	86.2	85.8
Rubber products	92.4	82.9
Petroleum refineries	99.9	72.0
Synthetic textiles	85.0	71.5
Oil and gas wells	82.6	65.0
Pharmaceuticals	82.2	68.6
Soap and cleaning compounds	92.5	62.1
Industrial chemicals	79.9	58.9
Aircraft and parts	91.6	48.3
Fruit and vegetable canners	67.4	62.3
Major appliances	58.5	58.5

Source: Adapted from 1967 Report of Corporations and Labour Unions Return Act as quoted in the Report of the Standing Committee on External Affairs and National Defence, on investigation into Canada-US relations ("The Wahn Report"), and as produced in Malcolm Levin and Christine Sylvester, *Foreign Ownership* (Don Mills, Ontario: General Publishing Co., 1972), p. 74.

other edible products of the sea, this portion of the Canadian economy was subjected to disruption as a consequence of extending the country's territorial waters to two hundred miles in 1977. The United States did likewise (despite its customary objection to the two-hundred-mile limit by other governments), and this change in policy gave rise to a fisheries dispute between Canada and the United States concerning (1) the establishment of their common border in the sea, and (2) the rights of their respective fishing fleets in the disputed waters until such time as the border issue might be settled. Differing attitudes over this issue led to a deep rift in relations until the matter was resolved in early 1979, a settlement which the Secretary of State for External Affairs labeled "an auspicious and promising development in Canada/USA relations."[54]

Added to its concern for preserving its natural resources is Canada's long-standing determination to avoid environmental spoilation. It is particularly concerned about the consequences of acid rain, precipitation that brings with it air-borne industrial pollutants that have a number of negative chemical influences upon the environment. These include stunting wheat and grain growth and killing all fish stocks in fresh water ponds and lakes. Since ecological pollution knows nothing

54. See statement by the Honorable Don Jamieson, "An Auspicious Development in Canada/USA Relations" (Ottawa: Ministry of Foreign Affairs, 1979), paper no. 79/4.

of national boundaries, Canadians continue to be concerned about the continental consequences of Washington's failure to attack the acid rain problem; and the Trudeau administration was openly critical of President Reagan in 1984 when he rejected all overtures, both domestic and international, to include in his budget message to Congress a fund for dealing with the problem.

Security

Although the principal Canadian-American links are currently economic, they were originally forged around the need for a continental defense policy during the Second World War. That partnership was epitomized by including Canada in the Hyde Park Declaration of 1941, which agreed upon a common production effort between the United States and Britain to meet wartime industrial and munitions needs. Later, Canada became an active member of the North Atlantic Treaty Organization, though it declined to participate in the Inter-American Treaty of Mutual Assistance, the military wing of the Organization of American States. The continental radar defense system, NORAD, is a joint Canadian-American undertaking of long standing, as are several bilateral defense planning boards.

Despite this cooperation in common security matters, Canada has steadfastly refused to endorse American defense strategy in its entirety. Ottawa was one of the first Western capitals to break with Washington over both Korea and Vietnam; it sold wheat to China and the Soviet Union during the era of containment; it opened diplomatic relations with China during the Vietnam War (though at a point at which this act probably facilitated American withdrawal from Southeast Asia and aided Sino-American normalization); and while reducing its commitment to NATO, Canada became one of the main contributors to the United Nations armed peacekeeping expeditions. It is evident that one of the central tenets of Canadian defense policy is to distinguish between Canadian-American relations on continental and on extracontinental matters, respectively.

This independent attitude results not simply from a different ideological view of the world, or from disavowal of a global role. It rises rather from the will to conduct foreign policies from which Canada will prosper without the constraints of the American world view. It assumes that transnational economic relations are more effective governors of the international system than are ideological confrontations and arms races. This attitude has enabled the Canadian government to reduce military expenditures over the last decade both in absolute number of dollars and as a percentage of GNP. Built into this policy is the realization that threats to Canadian security are extremely remote. Canada grows less responsive to what it considers excessive sensitivity in the United States to apparent threats to the security of North America and to the common economic interests of the USA and Canada.

During the 1980s Canadian-American relations have encountered unprecedented strain. The anti-Soviet rhetoric of the United States and the escalation of the strategic arms race during the Reagan years have made Canadians suspicious of the purported good will of the United States in global relations. A public opinion poll taken in mid-1983 by the Canadian Institute of International Affairs revealed that while 51 percent of those polled continued to regard the Soviet Union as the principal threat to world peace, fully 21 percent had come to regard the United States as a greater danger.

A somewhat more specific source of friction arose in 1983 over American testing of air-launched cruise missiles over Canadian territory. An initial agreement had been sought by the Carter administration, but it was not finalized until 1982. From mid-1983 to early 1984, when for the first time the missiles were transported across Canada fixed to the wings of an American bomber, public opinion rose in opposition to the tests. More than half of the Canadians polled on the tests opposed them.[55] Court efforts to prevent the flight failed and, despite a great public outcry, the first flight was made in March 1984. These are strategic arms rather than theatre arms, and Canadians are aware that in the event of a nuclear confrontation between the Soviet Union and the United States, the cruise missiles will be launched against Soviet targets from American aircraft in Canadian air space.

Canadian concern about the strategic arms race was symbolized by Prime Minister Trudeau's trip to all of the world's principal capitals during late 1983 and early 1984 seeking to stimulate new arms reduction talks and to secure commitments from heads of state on the principles for reducing tensions surrounding the arms race. Trudeau's visit to Washington was particularly disconcerting to him and to Canadians in general, for it was widely felt—and corroborated by the American press—that his efforts had been rebuffed tactlessly by the American President.

As one of the world's most productive states, Canada has all the ingredients of an independent and prosperous foreign policy, and of

55. For a review of the principal issues afflicting Canadian-American relations during the Reagan years—economic, ecological and military—see Adam Bromke and Kim Richard Nossal, "Tensions in Canada's Foreign Policy," *Foreign Affairs,* Winter 1983/84, pp. 335–353. The public opinion polls referred to here are cited in the Bromke-Nossal article.

continued national economic growth and autonomy. At present, however, neither of these goals is held in the tight control of Canadian decision-makers, inasmuch as the resources and production facilities on which each relies are controlled by foreign interests, mostly American. Since this degree of external control raises the specter of foreign interference, the Canadian world view is one that is especially wary of the motives, needs and machinations of its neighbor to the south, a neighbor that is friendly but rapacious; tolerant but ambitious beyond its means; libertarian in philosophy but determined that the foundations of its global supremacy will not be eroded. It is because Canada is so closely tied to those foundations, and because its quest for autonomy is perceived by the United States to contribute to their erosion, that the Canadian perspective of the international system is tinted by a growing sense of association with the dependent middle-ranking powers. Also, there is a commensurate sense of separation from the United States to the extent that Washington insists on those modes of interdependence that prevent Canada from achieving a full sense of autonomy in a world which it finds otherwise comfortably peaceful.

Conclusion

In a world of nuclear superpowers and economic upheaval caused by the new roles of the mineral-rich states, it is understandable that the American student of international affairs should fail to recognize the diversity of outlook to be found even among those states that are most interdependent. It is not the purpose of this chapter to argue that the Western alliance system is in imminent danger of collapse, or that the foundations of cooperation within it have deteriorated beyond repair. It is intended to demonstrate, rather, that the volume of political and economic transaction that occurs among the Western allies in North America, Western Europe and Asia creates internal problems, difficulties that are not related to attitudes concerning the Soviet Union or China or the Third World. Close mutual identity fertilizes inequalities, stimulates demands and breeds resistance. As the conditions of world order enable America's industrial allies to reduce their dependence on Washington, they find themselves facing an ally which, through military and economic preponderance, attempts to forestall changes that would advantage it allies but disadvantage itself. Because their own global perspectives differ vastly from those of the United States, these allies struggle to avoid subordination to American foreign policy.

4

The Chinese Perspective

National perceptions are not permanent. Just as events of the late 1970s brought about a reassessment of the American world position, so too did the Chinese attitude undergo major changes. From 1950 through 1976, the Chinese perspective was a product of Maoism, that is, of the leadership, domestic policies and foreign policies of Chairman Mao Tse-tung. With the death of Mao and the emergence of national leadership with a broader view of China's position in the world, new tolerances and aspirations developed, resulting in a marked revision of Chinese preceptions.

Nevertheless, for the most part the world perspective of the People's Republic is based on a fusion of two great forces: a *national* force developed out of China's long history, and an *ideological* force of Marxism-Leninism-Maoism. Both elements must contribute to an analysis of contemporary policy and outlook. The national force is a consequence of a continuous political experience spanning two thousand years. But the infusion of communist ideology has modified and reshaped China's self-perception and the image of the country in the outer world. Perhaps the historical force accounts for three-quarters of the national perspective and the ideology of communism for most of the remainder.

China's history falls broadly into three periods: (1) the long classical epoch of imperial greatness (the "Middle Kingdom"); (2) a century of degradation and Western domination from 1840 to 1945; and (3) the modern period of national revolution and rebirth. It is impossible to understand China today without at least a general comprehension of these three periods.

The Middle Kingdom Period: Classical China

Classical China was a vast empire comparable to the great Roman Empire in the West, but enduring over a longer historical period. Most of the people under the direct sovereignty of the Middle Kingdom were ethnic Chinese (that is, Han Chinese), but this included a multitude of regional, cultural, religious and linguistic differences. Chinese were as different from each other as the European peoples; and their integration into a single political unit was one of the great feats of early social engineering that is still not completely understood.

One factor behind this vast system of central government may have been that for its survival China requires a vast irrigation network to control the twin problems of flooding and drought that are characteristic of its rivers. The basic requirements of agricultural production depend on rigorous social controls to ensure orderly development of hydraulic works over the huge territory. Because of their mutual water needs, the diverse lands of China joined politically.

This is not to suggest that China was a fully integrated society. Local potentates known as "warlords" wielded great power in their regions throughout Chinese history, and during long periods the emperor ruled only at their discretion. When the imperial center was weak, the warlords carved out zones of control and reduced the emperor to a powerless figurehead dependent on the warlord armies. Only when the imperial court was strong, free of corruption and skillful in building necessary coalitions, could the power of the warlords be reduced and the central government truly able to rule. In a sense, the empire was a syndicate of local organizations; tension always existed between the central and regional powers.

The authority of the emperor was legitimized by the belief that he ruled by divine sanction as the Son of Heaven occupying the celestial throne. Emperors were dethroned throughout Chinese history, but this was explained by the convention that they had lost the mandate of heaven, as evidenced by the success of their enemies, and the divine sanction had therefore passed to the new rulers.

The officially encouraged culture of China was essentially conservative. It emphasized the Confucian virtues of obedience and "filial piety," a system of moral obligations guiding all social behavior. Individuals derived identity mainly as members of the nuclear family or community, and through other group identities. Within these units every individual had some importance; outside them the individual was nothing.

The educational system emphasized knowledge of the classic writings. It was more concerned with the development of values than with the acquisition of functional knowledge; and advancement in society, to the extent that it depended on education, stemmed more from command of the ancient texts than from expertise.

All segments of Chinese thought, even reformist and revolutionary, were portrayed as conservative and restorative of the principles in the venerated classics. Reforms were rationalized as reinterpretation of the great books, said to be more consistent with the original intentions of the texts than existing practices (comparable to the US Supreme Court's stimulation of social change by reinterpretation of the Constitution). This system of reverence for the classical texts served as a stabilizing element in Chinese history. It encouraged a profound respect for literacy; scholar/administrators were revered and powerful men, and the inventor of writing was deified. The nation was guided by the accumulated wisdom of a thousand years.

The Chinese believed themselves to be the center of world civilization, having relatively little contact with other peoples except weak states on the periphery of the empire. Many of these were periodically conquered by China during expansionist phases, only to regain independence when the warlord struggles reduced emperor's ability to exercise control in the outlying regions. (This expansion and contraction of China over time makes it difficult to define today exactly what the boundaries of the classical kingdom were. China's proper "historical borders," over which there is now so much contention, depend on the historical dates chosen as the base years.)

Under the *tribute system,* the rulers of the peripheral societies kept themselves in power by acknowledging the superiority of the Chinese emperor, sending gifts and offerings of homage. These gifts were not significant in economic terms, but they reinfored the Chinese national self-image as the Middle Kingdom at the center of known civilization. Non-Chinese were regarded as "barbarians." A new envoy would arrive with a caravan of gifts for the emperor, kneel before the Son of Heaven three times in the act of *kowtow* and present the tribute. This ritual set the tone for the entire relationship between China and other peoples, one not of equality but of dominance and submission. China saw little need for the outside world and therefore sent forth few explorers, traders or conquerors.

The Century of Humiliation: The Meeting with the West

This stable, conservative and self-confident Chinese society was in for a rude awakening when it came into contact with the dynamic societies of Europe and North America. The Chinese were very poorly prepared for this experience, and the shock of it reverberates even today.

The first Europeans came to China to spread Christianity and to find trading opportunities. Both the Christians and the merchants discovered that their arrival stirred relatively little interest. In other parts of the world, explorers had been revered as gods or at least as men of extraordinary power and inventiveness, but in China they were received as envoys from inferior civilizations. Early Chinese maps portray entities called "England," "France," "America," "Portugal" and so on, as small islands on the fringes of a world with a huge China at the center. The advanced products of Europe that so dazzled other peoples were received unexcitedly in China. The Son of Heaven wrote to the king of England in 1793:

> The virtue and prestige of the Celestial Dynasty having spread far and wide, the kings of myriad nations come by land and sea with all sorts of precious things. Consequently, there is nothing we lack, as your principal envoy and others have themselves observed. We have never set much store on strange or ingenious objects, nor do we need any more of your country's manufacturers.[1]

Christian missionaries were tolerated but were regarded as a nuisance.

China may not have been much interested in the Europeans, but the Westerners coveted China. By 1715, the British had established the first commercial base at Canton, and they were soon joined by French, Dutch and American traders who, under close Chinese control, were confined to tiny enclaves and hampered by travel and other restrictions. Europeans were required to deal exclusively with a government trade monopoly, and Chinese were forbidden to teach them languages. The traders grew increasingly unhappy with these restrictions, and energetic representations were made to the emperor, but to no avail.

Perhaps the most serious problem to the traders was the relative lack of interest in Western products. To buy from China they had to sell in exchange something that the Chinese wanted. The Europeans discovered that there was one major marketable product. Its nature,

1. Quoted in John K. Fairbank and Ssu-yu Teng, editors, *China's Response to the West: A Documentary Survey* (Cambridge, Mass.: Harvard University Press, 1954), p. 19.

and the fact that its open sale was encouraged, may surprise the modern reader: The product was opium.

Opium had been known in China for many years, but as in Europe and America, its sale and use were prohibited. Before the Europeans stimulated the trade, opium addiction was a minor problem, partly because Chinese cultural traditions discouraged personal hedonism and antisocial behavior. But after the European trade reached its peak, in some communities as much as 50 percent of the population was addicted. The imperial government tried repeatedly to stop this traffic by decree, but with little effect. In 1729, at the time of the first decree, importation was approximately 200 chests of pure opium per year. By 1830, this had grown to abut 19,000 chests, and by 1838 to 30,000. European persistence joined with ineffective decrees and corruption among Chinese officials to encourage growth of the drug trade.

The Opium War

The encounter of China with the West culminated in the Opium War in 1839, when a serious effort was finally made to halt the corrupt trade. A Chinese official named Lin Tse-hsu, commissioned to control the contraband, ringed the commercial enclave at Canton with troops, seized $11 million worth of opium, and drove the drug traffic out of Canton altogether. The British government, construing this as aggressive interference with freedom of international trade, promptly initiated a battle that resulted in the destruction of the Chinese forts at Canton and the signing of the Treaty of Nanking in 1842. In military terms China's losses were minor. But a handful of barbarians employing the mere gadgetry of their inferior civilizations had been able to humble the great Chinese empire. As one Chinese official said at the time to the British, "Except for your ships being solid, your gunfire fierce, and your rockets powerful, what other abilities have you?"[2]

The Opium War was the first in a long series of national defeats that lasted from 1840 to 1945, the Century of Humiliation. During this hundred years the power of the celestial throne was destroyed and China found itself increasingly the victim of external enemies—Europe and Japan—and internal dissolution—the warlords.

In the Treaty of Nanking (1842), China was forced to give Hong Kong to Britain "in perpetuity," to reopen Canton and the opium trade, to pay $21 million in reparations (a huge amount, equivalent to the American federal budget at the time), and most important of

2. Quoted in John Stoessinger, *Nations in Darkness* (New York: Random House, 1971), p. 14.

all in the long run, to give four more "treaty ports" to the Europeans. Treaty ports were put under the direct control of the Europeans; they were "extraterritorial," meaning that even civil laws were to be enforced by European courts. (In Cushing's Treaty of 1844, the United States was granted similar rights.) These "unequal treaties" led to many insults, including lax treatment of Europeans convicted of crimes against Chinese and even a sign in a park in Shanghai prohibiting Chinese and dogs.

China went into steady decline after the Opium War. In 1858, there was another skirmish in which British, French, American and Russian negotiators, backed by thirty gunboats and 3,000 troops, forced open eleven more ports to trade. Worse, they demanded for the first time access to the interior, meaning penetration from the coastal areas into the vast heartland. Now all of China would be open.

The T'aip'ing Rebellion

Another step in the decline was the T'aip'ing Rebellion, a civil war that occurred during the same years as the American Civil War, 1861 to 1865. In the American war about 400,000 died; in China the losses were closer to 20 million. The rebellion was a mass uprising led by a zealous Chinese Christian who had been converted by a missionary and believed that God whispered to him at night to redeem the nation. The T'aip'ings favored communal forms of social organization and production, a kind of peasant communism before Marx.

At first the Europeans looked with interest on the rebellion, thinking that its avowedly Christian leadership might have beneficial results. With European neutrality, the rebels almost succeeded in destroying the Manchu Dynasty. But late in the struggle, the Western governments concluded that the fanatical zeal of the T'aip'ings might make them more difficult to deal with than the corrupt officials of the imperial court, and they aided the emperor in putting down the rebels. The war ended with the imperial government weakened, the peasant movement destroyed and the Europeans strengthened. The very power of the Manchu Dynasty to survive thereafter depended directly on the Europeans.

Chinese society entered a period of self-criticism. How could China prevent total colonization by Europe? The policy of clinging to the great traditions and refusing to acknowledge the inevitability of change had failed. China had scorned Western technology, but a handful of foreigners had reduced China to submission. This point was driven home in 1894 when Japan, which had met the Western challenge by adopting Western economic and industrial values, seized the peninsula of Korea from China. In a mere quarter-century Japan had modernized its economic and military capacities while China had declined. The contrast was particularly humiliating.

Rebirth and Revolution: China Fights Back

Only with the victory of Chinese communism in 1949 can the control of China from the outside be said to have ended. But even during the latter half of the subjugation period there were significant attempts at national self-assertion.

The Boxer Rebellion

The first attempt at self-assertion was the Boxer Rebellion in 1900. The Japanese victory over China (1894–95), the spread of European commercial exploitation and the growth of Christianity outraged national sensibilities and some nationalists believed that the only recourse was a popular uprising against the "white devils." In 1900, large numbers of young patriots joined in a rebellion by the Society of Harmonious Fists, otherwise known as the Boxers. Attacks on converts to Christianity, on missionaries, and especially on European commercial and industrial interests aroused the Europeans to resistance. Here was a struggle between Chinese who felt that they were defending national independence and Europeans who thought they were defending the rights of free trade and protecting their citizens. The

This 5-yuan bill of the Kuomintang government, dated 1935, is printed in English on one side, demonstrating the dominant position of foreign business in the Chinese economy.

Chinese were enraged by the unceasing advances of foreign profiteers and missionaries. The Europeans were enraged by the assassination of the German minister and other wanton acts of violence against Western civilians and their Chinese friends. The United States demanded "speedy suppression of these rioters, the restoration of order, the punishment of the criminals and the derelict officials, and prompt compensation for the property destroyed."[3]

The Boxer Rebellion was counterproductive, stimulating foreign exploitation rather than stopping it. An eight-nation European force crushed the rebellion and looted the city of Peking. The collaboration of the Chinese government with the Boxers destroyed the remnants of foreign cooperation. Westerners now proposed the wholesale dismemberment of China into "spheres of influence" under the control of the various European powers. But the British and the Americans were opposed to the spheres of influence concept and insisted on the "open door," under which there would be freedom of trade in all parts of China—that is, everybody would share equally in the exploitation of China. Instead of outright colonization, France, Germany, Great Britain, Japan and the United States shared in the profits of carving up China and controlling many of its railroads, ports and mines, and of dominating its foreign trade.

Sun Yat-sen and the Republic of China

These external incursions combined with internal rebellion and corruption to produce a period of self-criticism in China toward the close of the nineteenth century. The rebellion of the Boxers failed, but the revolutionary spirit spread and deepened. In 1911 a nationalist rebellion by followers of Dr. Sun Yat-sen, the father of modern China, succeeded in overthrowing the Manchu Dynasty, which by then had become thoroughly discredited. But the revolutionaires had seized a rump government. Real power went to the warlords, who filled the vacuum created by a weak center. Sun Yat-sen was quickly replaced by the most powerful of the warlords, Yuan Shih-k'ai, who suppressed Sun's Nationalist Party, the Kuomintang (KMT). Sun fled the country, the party went underground, and the ideals of 1911 were temporarily defeated.

The Russian Revolution in 1917 revived the cause of Chinese nationalism. When European revolutions failed to materialize and Russia found itself an island in a hostile capitalist sea, the Soviet leaders looked

3. Quoted in Edmund Clubb, *Twentieth-Century China* (New York: Columbia University Press, 1964), p. 27.

with great interest to the possibility of a friendly China. In 1922, the Russians offered Sun Yat-sen substantial aid for his Kuomintang. The Russians conceded that "the conditions necessary for the establishment of either socialism or communism do not exist in China." In exchange, Sun admitted the Chinese Communist Party into the Kuomintang. Russian aid reawakened hopes of national rebirth.

Sun Yat-sen's death in 1925 occasioned the rise of a powerful new figure in the leadership of the Kuomintang: Chiang Kai-shek. Chiang was later to lead the most corrupt elements in China in their struggle to cling to power, but in this early period he was an important figure in the Chinese nationalist movement.

Chiang Kai-shek

Chiang organized and led a military campaign to break the power of the warlords in order to reunite China and to set it on a path to national development. In the Northern Expedition, Chiang's armies swept the country and destroyed or absorbed the power of the warlords. With the success of the Northern Expedition, a major step had been taken in the reunification of China.

Chiang rewarded the communists for their participation in a united front against the warlords by turning on them in the middle of one quiet night in 1927, having them dragged from their beds and shot in the streets. He did not want any competitors for power in the system of personal control he was to create. In one sweep, the membership of the Chinese Communist party was reduced from 50,000 to 10,000.

The Rise of Mao and the Communist Party

In 1928 a new figure emerged, a previously minor functionary named Mao Tse-tung. In five years of difficult organizing (1928–33), he built a party of 300,000 and a Red Army to oppose Chiang's Kuomintang. However, Mao's forces were no match for the huge Kuomintang, and in 1933 400,000 KMT troops killed 60,000 Red soldiers, still another defeat for revolution in China. The surviving elements of the Red Army made the famous Long March across China to sanctuary in the mountains.

No ordinary retreat, the Long March was a 6,000 mile forced march by 90,000 men and women, taking more than a year while they evaded KMT harassment on all sides. It is one of the great feats of military history and is celebrated in poems and operas throughout China today.

But successful evasion of KMT troops by the communists contributed little to expelling foreign influences. While the struggle between opposing Chinese forces unfolded, foreign interests continued their rape of China. In 1931, Japanese troops invaded Manchuria by way of Korea (which Japan controlled as a result of the Russo-Japanese War of 1904–05), and in so doing achieved a foothold for further expansion through the so-called "Greater East Asia Co-Prosperity Sphere," the Japanese term for their empire in Asia and the Pacific. Meanwhile, the Soviet Union, hostile to the peasant foundation of Chinese communism—pure Marxism preaches communism developing through the strength of the proletariat in industrial economies—doubted that the conditions for effective revolution existed in China. As a result, it was considered more important to limit the growth of Japanese interests in China than to influence the outcome of the Chinese civil war. Right up until World War II, therefore, Soviet aid, in the form of money, aircraft, advisors and provisions, was directed to the Nationalists.

The conclusion of the war meant little more than the removal of Japan as a threat to China, since disorder and administrative chaos followed the Japanese withdrawal. The Soviet Union, expecting the restoration of effective KMT control, lost no time in looting the industrial wealth of Manchuria abandoned by the Japanese. Whole factories were transported to Soviet territory. The Kremlin urged the Chinese communists to join a coalition with the KMT as the only available means of gaining access to a portion of political power. This coincided with the American view, as expressed in the mission of General George C. Marshall, that further struggle between the nationalist and communist parties would be useless and fratricidal, and that a coalition should be structured to speed national recovery.

By this time, however, the communists had hopes of an independent strategy. Mao knew that the administrative structure of the KMT had been shattered by the war, and that popular support for Chiang had evaporated. Over the course of the nearly half-century-long struggle to free China from foreign control, national society had in fact disintegrated.[4] Furthermore, the communists had emerged from the world war in many areas as heroes of the anti-Japanese resistance. The seeming selflessness and patriotism of the communist forces in wartime were contrasted in the public mind with the image of the Kuomintang as a self-seeking party of corrupt officials and landowners clinging to their own position in society. When the communists entered a village, they turned all land over to the peasants. When the KMT reentered, their initial act was often land repossession. The difference was not lost on the peasants.

4. James E. Sheridan, *China in Disintegration: The Republican Era in Chinese History, 1912–1949* (New York: The Free Press, 1975).

In the civil war that raged from 1945 to 1949, the position of the KMT steadily declined. Whole divisions of Chiang's soldiers, including officers, deserted to the Red Army. To the end, the Russians continued to write off the communist case as hopeless, and continued their relationship with Chiang. But the fierce determination of Mao's forces led to the final rout of the KMT in 1949. Chiang fled with the remnants of his army to the island of Taiwan (Formosa), subdued the people of that island when they resisted, and established a new but much reduced dominion behind the shield of the US Seventh Fleet, which since 1950 has protected the KMT from attack from the mainland. In the view of mainland Chinese, this United States act was an unjustified intervention denying the Chinese people the right to complete their own revolution and preserving the insulting fiction of a rump government in exile. Nevertheless, with the flight of the KMT the Century of Humiliation was concluded, and China was reborn as a free and self-determined nation.

The Chinese World Outlook

The world outlook of Communist China since 1949 has been deeply influenced by this history. Unlike the Soviet Union or the United States and its principal allies, China's soul has been seared by exploitation, humiliation and oppression. The last remnant of the seemingly endless waves of foreign conquerors passed through China within the memory of the current generation of leaders.[5] The difference between the sturdily independent and self-sufficient China of today and the previously pathetic and degenerate China is obvious even to its enemies. Without exaggeration, the absolutely overriding consideration of Chinese foreign and domestic policy has been the restoration and preservation of China as a powerful and independent nation invulnerable to external conquest and domination. This goal has required both objective and subjective changes, including the revival of self-confidence. But until the conclusion of the Vietnam War, and until the 1970s were nearly

5. It is interesting that no recent American president has felt compelled to learn the Russian language, let alone Chinese. Neither has any Soviet premier been known to speak either Chinese or English. But Chou En-lai, Chinese foreign minister through the era of Mao Tse-tung, was fluent in both Russian *and* English.

More generally, the isolation of China from world politics throughout these years, together with the hostile attitudes held of him by Americans and Russians alike, obscured Chou's potential contribution to world diplomacy. Dag Hammarskjöld, Secretary-General of the United Nations from 1953 until his death in 1961, said that Chou "to me appears as the most superior brain I have met in the field of foreign politics." Quoted in Brian Urquhart, *Hammarskjöld* (New York: Knopf, 1972), p. 117.

concluded, there was no disagreement among modern Chinese leaders concerning the paramount necessities of national defense and self-sufficiency. The enemies of China had to be kept at bay—and doing so meant deflecting the threats from the world's two most powerful and imperialistic countries: the United States and the Soviet Union.

In the ideological flexibility that followed Mao's death, the Chinese approach to world affairs changed substantially and evolved rapidly. In the period 1974–77, for example, China adopted a "three-world" theory of global politics in which the three worlds were defined differently than in the classic three-world concept of industrialized West, Soviet bloc and developing world. In the Chinese theory, the first world is the imperial world of the Soviet Union and the United States; the

FIGURE 4–1 *China and the Soviet Union, showing disputed territories.*

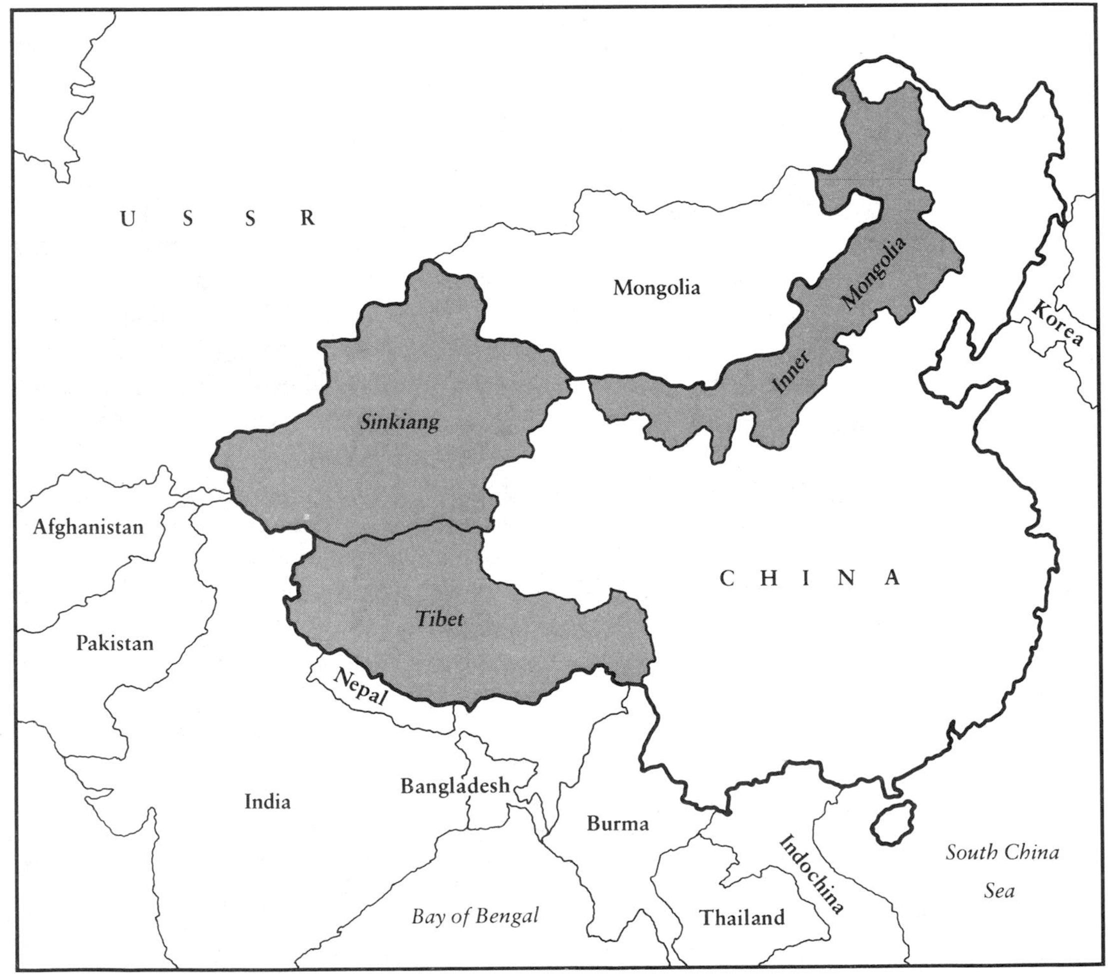

second is comprised of all other developed states; and the third world is the developing nations, with China as the inspirational leader. By 1978, however, as Sino-Soviet relations reached their lowest point and relations with the United States and the NATO countries developed at an extraordinarily fast pace, the Chinese world view became much more West-oriented. The objective of this shift was to unite with all anti-Soviet countries against the "social-imperialist," an ideological adaptation in which the Chinese accepted the notion that even some socialist countries can have imperial ways. The early 1980s, which brought signs of a Sino-Soviet thaw and increasingly strained Sino-American relations, also saw the Chinese world view becoming one of self-reliance and neutralism on East-West relations.[6]

This rapid evolution of the Chinese world view is a result of both domestic and international affairs. On the domestic front, three forces shape Chinese international attitudes. The first is that, in recent years, internal Chinese politics has taken a conservative turn which has resulted in the reshaping of domestic institutions along a traditional Soviet-type line. Some critics have gone so far as to refer to this development as the "Sovietization of Chinese politics," a reference to form rather than substance. The second force is a desire to avoid dependence upon the West, a possibility that appeared distinct at a time when the lure of Western technology seemed to be the correct answer to the Soviet military build-up in the Pacific. Third, relaxation of tensions with the Soviet Union is essential to the regional environment needed for China to succeed in its long-term "four modernizations" policy, a policy calling for the gradual modernization of agriculture, defense, science and technology.[7]

The international stimuli to a rapidly evolving world view are even more complex. They include the Chinese leadership of the Third World, at status that confronts China with disparate expectations; continued Soviet military expansion in Asia and the Pacific; an evolving economic and military relationship with Japan as well as with the United States and Western Europe; and anxieties over the political relationship with the United States, a relationship strained by the refusal of the United States to discontinue arms sales to Taiwan (discussed later in this chapter).

Under these combined internal and international circumstances, the

6. Herbert S. Yee, "The Three World Theory and Post-Mao China's Global Strategy," *International Affairs* (London), Spring 1983. One Chinese author ascribes the invention of this theory to Mao Tse-tung. See Huan Xiang, "On Sino-U.S. Relations," *Foreign Affairs,* Fall 1981, pp. 35–53 at pp. 35–36. The author is Vice President of the Chinese Academy of Social Sciences.

7. Edmund Lee (a pseudonym), "Beijing's Balancing Act," *Foreign Policy,* Summer 1983, pp. 27–46.

current Chinese leadership has chosen a path away from the pro-West, anti-Soviet coalition of the period between 1978–81. Instead, it has embarked upon one of balanced relations in which ideological imperatives are carefully mixed with pragmatic goals.[8]

Throughout this evolution, however, the intensely nationalistic outlook of the Chinese communist leadership has dictated an emphasis on defensive, China-centered priorities in international relations. We can infer the following hierarchy of priorities in the formulation of Chinese foreign policy since 1949:

1. Defense against external military attack or domination.
2. Reintegration of outlying and alienated territories (particularly Tibet, Sinkiang and Inner Mongolia).
3. Incorporation of Taiwan in the national administrative structure.
4. Prevention of foreign non-military interference in Chinese domestic affairs.
5. Reestablishment of international respect, and the achievement of a leading role in regional and international affairs.

Each of these principles requires brief elaboration.

National Defense

Defense of national territory and national values is, of course, the primary concern of any state. To the extent that a state feels that its territorial integrity is threatened, this concern becomes even greater. Since 1949, China has perceived itself as threatened by either the United States or the Soviet Union, and sometimes by both. Furthermore, China's geopolitical characteristics add to its concern about national defense. The seven thousand mile land border separating China and the Soviet Union (including Soviet-influenced Outer Mongolia) is the world's longest hostile border, and is considered indefensible mile by mile. On the east, the Chinese navy cannot defend the seaward approaches on the Yellow Sea, the East and South China Seas or the Straits of Taiwan. Even the Indian borders on the southwest demand extensive defensive preparations. Under these circumstances,

8. In addition to the preceding reference, see Donald S. Zagoria, "The Moscow-Beijing Détente," *Foreign Affairs,* Spring 1983, pp. 854–873; Robert A. Scalapino, "Uncertainties in Future Sino-U.S. Relations," *ORBIS,* Fall 1982, pp. 681–696; Allen S. Whiting, "Sino-American Relations: The Decade Ahead," *ORBIS,* Fall 1982, pp. 697–719; Herbert S. Yee, "The Three-World Theory and Post-Mao China's Global Strategy," *ORBIS,* Spring 1983; and Gerald Segal, "China's Strategic Posture and the Great-Power Triangle," *Pacific Affairs,* Winter 1981/82, pp. 682–697.

China must rely for its defense on primitive nuclear deterrence and on the reluctance of its opponents to undertake an invasion. It is not difficult to understand the obsession of China's leadership with security and defensive preparations.

The Chinese economy has made impressive strides since 1949, but they are inadequate to support simultaneously the technological demands of modern warfare (including significant nuclear and missile capability) and a rising standard of living. China has found it difficult even to sustain a major industrial effort, largely due to bottlenecks in supplies of energy and transportation. Wars abroad, limited as they were, had a devastating impact on the modernization plans of the late 1970s and early 1980s, as the February 1979 war against the Vietnamese ("to teach them a lesson") demonstrated. This test of the economic strength underlying China's military power has spotlighted its glaring weaknesses and its inability to sustain a major war effort.

Despite spending as large a fraction of its GNP on defense as does West Germany, China's defense capability lags behind. Its air force is small in comparison with those of the United States and the Soviet Union, and cannot begin to meet even the level of technological sophistication of hostile forces in Taiwan. The navy is insignificant by comparison; and the nuclear arsenal, while a real threat in regional combat and perhaps to some Soviet targets, is small in contrast to those of the US and USSR, and lacks the array of delivery methods upon which the latter two have built their deterrence policies.

China did test a submarine-launched ballistic missile in late 1982, one with a range appropriate to Soviet targets in Asia and the Pacific. The test enabled the Chinese to boast that they are now able "to enter the ranks of advanced nations in sophistication of national defense technology while being backward in economic modernization."[9] In fact, however, while it is the ultimate goal of the Chinese to be self-sufficient in military technology, at present it is dependent principally upon Western supply. By 1982 the United States alone had approved export licenses related to air defense radar equipment, transport helicopters, instrumentation for testing jet engines, communications systems, computing equipment, integrated circuits, submarine tracking systems, range-finding instruments and tank engines. Despite the Chinese boast, American estimates are that the Chinese military is fifteen years behind both the United States and the Soviet Union in military technology, and that the cost of closing the gap by the end

9. Beijing Radio as quoted in William T. Tow, "Sino-Japanese Security Cooperation: Evolution and Prospects," *Pacific Affairs,* Spring 1983, pp. 51–83 at p. 55.

of the century is between $41 billion and $63 billion for non-strategic goods (i.e., trucks, tanks, surface-to-air missile launchers, aircraft, etc.).[10]

The huge population and extensive territory of China, together with the resource potential of the territory, have not yet been marshalled into modern military and economic capabilities. China is looking to the West to compensate for some of these deficiencies, not only through military technology and equipment, but also through military relationships that some have been tempted to consider incipient alliances. In fact, however, while an arms-trade relationship has developed in the 1980s, the flexible Chinese world view makes such a relationship a temporary expedient. In 1983 the Chinese rejected Secretary of Defense Caspar Weinberger's proposal on the exchange of military missions; and in 1984, during his state visit to the United States, Premier Zhao Ziyang announced that China has no intention of entering into an alliance with Washington.

Reintegration of Outlying and Alienated Territories

During the Century of Humiliation, huge slices of Chinese territory were lost to hostile powers, as indicated in Table 4–1, through a series of "unequal treaties." Despite early renunciation of these treaties by the Mao government and demands for return of these territories, more modern Chinese territorial concern focuses on the outlying and alienated areas within the current Chinese territory. Of particular concern are Tibet, Sinkiang and Inner Mongolia.

The dynastic history of China and the longevity of its civilization conceal the fact that like most large nations, China has a number of national minorities within its population. These are particularly evident in the outlying and border areas of the territory where distance from the governmental and cultural centers of China has resulted in the preservation of diverse languages, cultures and national identities. Though small in numbers as part of the nation of a billion, these peoples occupy vast regions which could impose major new demands upon Chinese defense and economic development if their inhabitants were to achieve independence or incorporation into other nations. The increasing number of Soviet-oriented Uigurs in Sinkiang, the province in which China has its most important nuclear weapons facilities, poses

10. For a detailed account of Chinese arms-trade practices, see Douglas T. Stuart and William T. Tow, "Chinese Military Modernization: The Western Arms Connection," *China Quarterly,* June 1982, pp. 253–270. See also for more general comment, Douglas T. Stuart, "Prospects for Sino-European Security Cooperation," *ORBIS,* Fall 1982, pp. 721–747; and Thomas W. Robinson, "Chinese Military Modernization in the 1980s," *China Quarterly,* June 1982, pp. 231–252.

TABLE 4–1
Historic losses of Chinese territory.

Territory	*Recipient*	*Year*
1. Northeast Frontier Agency; Assam	Britain	after 1820
2. Left Bank of Amur River	Russia	1858
3. Maritime Territory	Russia	1860
4. Tashkent Region	Russia	1864
5. Bhutan	Britain	1865
6. Sakhalin	Russia-Japan	after 1875
7. Ryukyu Islands	Japan	1879
8. Indochina	France	1885
9. Siam	Independence	1885
10. Burma	Britain	1886
11. Sino-Burmese Frontier Region	Britain	1886
12. Sikkim	Britain	1889
13. Taiwan and the Pescadores	Japan	1895
14. Malaya	Britain	1895
15. Korea	Japan	1895 and 1905
16. Ladakh	Britain	1896
17. Nepal	Britain	1898

a constant threat to China's territorial integrity and defense modernization. Tibet, forcefully reincorporated in 1950, is subject to repeated rebellion in favor of national autonomy. For fully thirty years China has maintained a policy of intimidation, heavy-handedness and great-national chauvinism towards these minorities.

China has not yet succeeded in integrating all its diverse cultures into the dominant Han culture. This is no less true of the Soviet Union and the United States, but in China's case divergences of national identity have direct territorial corollaries, making the reintegration of these peoples and territories an urgent priority.

The Reincorporation of Taiwan

This is a special issue, different from all other territorial demands. In this case, both the People's Republic government and the Kuomintang government on Taiwan insist that the island is rightly a province of China (though some of the native Taiwanese, who comprise 85 percent of the island's population, demand national independence). The point at issue has been the larger one: Which party is the rightful ruler of China, of which Taiwan is a part? The Nationalists on Taiwan have refused to concede to demands for reincorporation, and for several years following the Korean War annually reaffirmed their intention

"Hey . . . talking about imperialism . . . "

Source © Behrendt (*Het Parool,* Amsterdam)/Rothco

to retake the mainland, by force if necessary. A combination of reason, dependence upon the guarantee against communist conquest provided by the US Navy and the futility of the mission all contributed to the emptiness of this threat. Nevertheless, despite the vast changes in the international politics of Asia in recent years, together with sharply changed Sino-American relations, Peking continues to regard the issue of Taiwan as one of the paramount challenges for Chinese policy in the future.

After the American withdrawal from Vietnam, the Taiwan issue continued to be one of the principal barriers to normal Sino-American relations. However, Peking's relations with Washington reveal a willingness to postpone demands for a permanent resolution of the matter in the interest of accelerating economic modernization and the reduction of the probability of hostilities at a time when the Soviet Union looms as the principal enemy. A series of major diplomatic episodes in Sino-American relations has demonstrated Chinese patience on the issue.

The first example is given in the Shanghai Communiqué, the official joint statement that concluded President Nixon's ice-breaking trip to China in 1972. In it, the Chinese government reaffirmed its insistent claim:

> The Taiwan question is the crucial question obstructing the normalization of relations between China and the United States; the Government of the People's Republic of China is the sole legal government of China; Taiwan is a province of China which has long been returned to the motherland; the liberation of Taiwan is China's internal affair in which no other country has the right to interfere; and all US forces and military installations must be withdrawn from Taiwan.

For its part, the United States declared that it

> acknowledges that all Chinese on either side of the Taiwan Strait maintain there is but one China and that Taiwan is a part of China. The United States Government does not challenge that position. It reaffirms its interest in a peaceful settlement of the Taiwan question by the Chinese themselves. With this prospect in mind it reaffirms the ultimate objective of the withdrawal of all US forces and military installations from Taiwan. In the meantime, it will progressively reduce its forces and military installations on Taiwan as the tension in the area diminishes.[11]

Inconclusive as these assertions may have been, they formed the critically important first step, enabling each side to reassess its approach to the Taiwan issue. To be sure, debate continued in the United States as to the ultimate Chinese motives, but the gradual thaw in Sino-American relations over the years following the communiqué gave to the debate a tone of staleness. With the passage of leadership in both China and Taiwan late in the 1970s, accompanied by decreased Sino-American tension and increased Sino-Soviet enmity, the issue also became less urgent in Asian politics as a whole.

The second diplomatic turning point occurred on January 1, 1979, when the United States and the Peoples Republic of China formally established diplomatic relations. The mutual recognition was preceded by a Normalization Communiqué two weeks earlier (December 15, 1978) in which the terms of recognition were elaborated as a sequel to the Shanghai Communiqué. In it, Washington accepted the Chinese insistence that the United States withdraw all of its forces from Taiwan gradually, that Washington sever its diplomatic relations with Taiwan, and that it unilaterally abrogate the Mutual Defense Treaty of 1954 with Taiwan (though China conceded that the break occur upon a formal notification of one year). In turn, the Chinese agreed to permit the continued sale of American defensive arms to Taiwan and to accept without denunciation a public statement of concern for the well-being of the people of Taiwan. China also agreed to a statement of intent

11. *Peking Review* 15, (March 3, 1972), pp. 4–5; and *United States Department of State Bulletin,* March 20, 1972, pp. 435–438.

to use peaceful means in dealing with Taiwan and with the reincorporation problem.[12]

When Congress reconvened early in January 1979, just days after the formal establishment of Sino-American relations, the leadership was concerned that the President had acted without prior consultation with the legislative branch, which continued to be concerned with the unresolved problem of relations with Taiwan. How was the nation to deal with a "derecognized" government which is a friend of long-standing, a major trading partner, and the site of billions of dollars in American foreign investments? The result was the Taiwan Relations Act of 1979, an act which the Chinese Government protested and attempted unsuccessfully to head off. The act not only declared Washington's intention "to make available to Taiwan such defense articles and defense services in such quantity as may be necessary to enable Taiwan to maintain a sufficient self-defense capability"; it went beyond military security and asserted American defense of "the social and economic system, of the people of Taiwan."[13] The Chinese regarded the act as virtual reestablishment of a defense arrangement in violation of the Normalization Communiqué.

As though the Constitutional separation of powers had not already imposed enough damage on Sino-American relations, there ensued the vagaries of American politics—the Presidential election campaign of 1980. As it became clear through public opinion polls that the Republican candidate, Ronald Reagan, would succeed the Democratic president who had recognized China, mixed signals came from the Republican party. Even while vice presidential candidate George Bush, who had been the first American liaison officer in Peking after the Nixon recognition of China, was visiting China in an attempt to clarify presidential candidate Ronald Reagan's position toward the Peoples' Republic, Reagan himself declared his intention to reestablish formal ties with Taiwan. Relations with China cooled as the new administration assumed office amid Chinese charges that the agreements of the Normalization Communiqué might not be secure. This uncertainty contributed considerably to the revision of the Chinese world perspective.

The second Reagan shoe dropped in late 1981 when it was an-

12. For a careful study of the implications of the Taiwan Normalization Communiqué upon American relations with both China and Taiwan, see John W. Carver, "Arms Sales, the Taiwan Question, and Sino-U.S. Relations," *ORBIS,* Winter 1983, pp. 999–1035.

13. For a brief history of the Taiwan Relations Act by one of its sponsors, see Jacob K. Javits, "Congress and Foreign Relations: The Taiwan Relations Act," *Foreign Affairs,* Fall 1981, pp. 54–62. Senator Javits was the senior Republican on the Senate Foreign Relations Committee at the time of passage of the act.

nounced that the United States would provide huge amounts of military spare parts to Taiwan. Later, it was announced that new fighter aircraft were added to the agreement. Under pressure from the right wing to reconstitute relations with Taiwan even if it meant a return to the foresaken concept of two independent Chinas, the Reagan administration engaged China in a nine-month negotiation over the arms sale crisis, often saying one thing and doing another, a form of duplicity unacceptable to China. The result was an August 1982 communiqué in which old ambiguities were resolved and new ones introduced. The United States was forced to concede that the question of arms sales to Taiwan "is a major issue affecting China's sovereignty," and that subsequent sales could be made only after consultation with the Chinese government. Taiwan was prevented from importing the aircraft it wanted (it got an older version), thus preventing it from having a craft superior to the one nearing deployment by China.

The struggle between Washington's wish to retain substantial though "unofficial" relations with Taiwan and China's campaign for eventual reunification continues from episode to episode.

Preventing External Nonmilitary Interference

Nonmilitary interference has been easier to achieve than the reincorporation of Taiwan. The traditional foreign interests were simply evicted after the revolution from their commercial and industrial positions. Foreign investments were expropriated, including, for example, $196 million in American holdings and larger amounts for other countries. Most remaining foreign residents were pressured to leave the country, and a deliberate policy of national isolation was adopted, a reaction in part to the isolation being imposed upon China by the West.

There were some important exceptions to this curtailment of external interference, particularly involving the Soviet Union and India. Soviet leaders took advantage of Chinese weakness immediately after the civil war to demand certain concessions in exchange for Soviet aid. These included the so-called "mixed companies" to develop Chinese oil and mineral resources, airlines, railroads and other facilities. These gave Soviet personnel direct influence over and access to internal Chinese affairs. One form of Soviet behavior particularly disturbing to the Chinese was covert support given to Uigur separatist elements in Sinkiang. After 1955 the joint stock companies were phased out, but subversive activities in remote regions have been more difficult to uproot, particularly as Sino-Soviet relations have worsened.

China perceives India to have interfered in Chinese internal affairs with regard to Tibet. One of the first acts of the People's Liberation Army after the revolution was the repossession of Tibet on October 7, 1950. India, part of whose territory abuts Tibet, refused to recognize Chinese suzerainty and gave various forms of covert aid to Tibetan autonomists. In April of 1954, the Indian government seemed to recognize the Chinese claim in an agreement referring to "the Tibet region of China," but this did not settle the issue. In 1958, Prime Minister Nehru of India announced, and then under Chinese pressure canceled, a visit to Tibet to symbolize support for Tibetan nationalists. This was one element sparking a Tibetan revolt against China in 1959, a revolt quickly suppressed by the Chinese authorities at a cost of 65,000 Tibetan lives. India is known to have allowed the shipment of supplies to the Tibetan guerrillas, and various dissident Tibetan elements fled to India after the revolt. In these ways, India has supported Tibet against China.

The issue of Indian interference is complicated by territorial issues on the remote Indo-Tibetan border in the lofty Himalayas. This region is so desolate that it might seem to be of little interest to anyone. But a Chinese arterial road in Tibet passes through a portion of the area that each claims. Indian claims rest on a Sino-Indian treaty of nineteenth-century vintage. China views this document as an unequal treaty of a bygone era, without legal or moral force today, and rests its own claims on historical boundaries. This dispute led to a brief but bitter Sino-Indian border war in 1962, which resulted in a reaffirmation of the Chinese claims. Despite the remoteness of the territory, however, the dispute continues.

China's Search for Renewed International Respect

The search for international respect has been substantially rewarded in recent years. Although the Chinese were eager to improve relations with the West, and interpreted the 1972 visit to China of President Richard Nixon, a confirmed anticommunist and rabid Sinophobe, as a sign that their country could no longer be ignored and isolated, and that their achievements had at last gained the acknowledgement and respect of the world. The seating of the Chinese delegation in the Security Council of the UN in place of the "Republic of China" delegation institutionalized the new great power image. Finally, the establishment of formal diplomatic relations with almost every major capitalist state, including the US—for fully thirty years the chief impediment to China's drive for international respect and often its open enemy—culminated a patient and persistent quest for acceptance in the international community.

China characterizes its own global role as that of the anti-imperialist supporter of Third World revolutionary movements. In this view, the world's subjugated peoples must go through two stages to free themselves from domination and oppression, the stages of national and social revolution. National revolution is the overthrow of colonialism and foreign control over territory and resources, including the economic mechanisms of neo-imperialism. Social revolution means a change in class ownership of the means of production, taking control from the landlords and capitalists and giving it to the workers and peasants.

Many countries have experienced a national revolution, but few have undergone a social revolution. China has experienced both. Yet China has rarely gone beyond supporting the national revolutions which have freed colonies from their motherlands. Its leaders, pragmatists in foreign policy, have ignored the internal political situation of various states and concentrated instead on establishing good relations with as many countries as are willing to recognize China on its own terms. Indeed, the 1970s witnessed China's establishment of diplomatic relations with a host of capitalist states and right-wing dictatorships.

This pragmatic assessment of the Third World's attitude toward large state intervention, as well as China's own lack of military and economic resources, make it unusual for China to intervene in the affairs of other states except through verbal exhortation. Indeed, the official position of the Chinese government on intervention, even in behalf of revolution, purports to be purely Marxist, while the Soviet turn to social imperialism is a dreaded departure from Marxism-Leninism. In the Chinese view,

> No Marxist would ever hesitate to state that communism will inevitably replace capitalism. . . . But Marxists also believe that it is entirely up to the people of a country to choose their own social system and it is futile for any outside force to try to do that on their behalf. Marxists always stand for peaceful coexistence among countries with different social systems; they do not stand for an "export of revolution." Particularly, they are opposed to any aggression or expansion carried out in the name of "revolution" or of "supporting revolution", and are opposed to the use of force or any attempt to use force as a means to settle differences arising from the difference of social systems and interests.[14]

14. Huan Xiang, "On Sino-U.S. Relations," *Foreign Affairs,* Fall 1981, pp. 38–39.

Relations with the United States

From the communist victory in 1949 through 1970, China and the United States regarded one another as implacable enemies. While Americans saw the triumph of the Red Army as the loss of China leading to a sweep of Red hordes across Asia, the revolution represented to the Chinese a rebirth. With the expectation that the political revolution would be followed by a comprehensive social and economic revolution, China saw an opportunity to rid the land of foreign influences (including nationalist influences, seen as foreign dominated), and a chance to build a vast modern society on pure socialist principles. America's aid to Chiang Kai-shek, both economic and military (the latter in the form of intervention by the Seventh Fleet), confirmed China's fears of the hostile intentions of the West. Why, except to defeat communism and to restore Chinese nationalism, would Americans want to support this corrupt vestige of the past?

Misperceptions and hostilities were magnified by the Korean War. While the United States considered the invasion of South Korea by North Korea in June 1950, an act of international aggression inspired and planned by Peking and Moscow, China played a minimal role even when American forces drove Northern forces out of the South and began the conquest of the North. As American troops approached the Yalu River and, therefore, Chinese Manchurian territory, China's restraint in face of America's anticommunist adventure gave way. In late November, with the American Seventh Division within striking distance of Manchuria and General Douglas MacArthur publicly advocating attack across the Yalu, China responded with 200,000 counterattacking troops, driving the Americans back and producing an eventual standoff. In return for this act of Chinese self-defense, the American government arranged for the United Nations to brand China an "aggressor against the United Nations." Continued threats of American attack, even with atomic weapons, drove home to Peking the urgency with which America wished to rid Asia of communism and China of its hard-won victory over the corrupt and aged KMT. Moreover, the Korean experience, both before and after the Chinese military response, underscored the extent to which the United Nations had become an instrument of American power rather than an independent and objective instrument for the regulation of international order.

American hostility was further confirmed to the Chinese by Washington's opposition to legitimate revolutionary aspirations in Indochina. As early as 1949, America had given financial aid to France in order to secure its colonial hold on Indochina, liberated in 1945 from

Japanese conquest, and to oppose the patriotic forces led by the Viet Minh. When the French effort collapsed at the bloody battle of Dienbienphu in 1954, the United States moved to replace France as the dominant foreign power in Indochina, even though this had not previously been an area of American interest or involvement. A puppet government of former French collaborators was devised, and American military and financial assistance was used to put a new face on colonialism in the region. Opposition to supposed Chinese influence in Hanoi provided the rationale for the new American policy, since China still labored under the label of "aggressor," and thus Indochina became another base for the American encirclement of China. From South Vietnam, a creature almost exclusively of American policy, anti-Chinese influences were extended to Thailand and Cambodia (now Kampuchea), with each of which China had previously enjoyed fairly good relations. Here again the United States demonstrated its hostile intentions by supporting corrupt and oppressive regimes which declared themselves to be the enemies of China.

By the mid-1950s, everywhere the Chinese looked they found the United States in alliance with anti-Chinese forces—Indonesia, Malaysia, the Philippines, Taiwan, Korea, Vietnam, Laos, Cambodia, Thailand and India, all far from the continental United States and clearly not traditional areas of American concern or deployment. In no manner could its security be construed to depend upon these distant activities. Yet the United States invested vast sums and spent scores of thousands of lives to secure political satellites on the Asian periphery, just as the British, Germans, Japanese and French had acted to subdue local populations in earlier periods.

From 1949 to the close of the Vietnam War, while Americans visualized hordes of aggressive, mindless and doctrinaire Chinese, Chinese publications depicted a China encircled by hostile American troops poised to strike at the heart of the Chinese homeland. While Washington intervened repeatedly (indeed, continuously) in Asian affairs remote from American interests but adjacent to those of China, Peking established no foreign military bases and undertook no aggression. Who, then, was truly the aggressor?

Despite this deeply troubled history, the Sino-American thaw which began in 1971 and progressed in earnest after 1976, has led to the near elimination of political invective between these two nations. Both have much to gain from the newer and warmer relationship, not least among the benefits the growth of trade (Chinese natural resources for American industrial and technological goods), peaceful participation in the regional and global balances, a common front against the threat of Soviet aggression, and the general stability of peaceful diplomatic relations. America's restrained reaction to China's invasion of Vietnam in 1979 gives some indication of the degree to which Washington is now willing to accept an independent Chinese role in the regional balance, yet it also indicated the limits beyond which it is not willing to permit China to roam. And from that attempt on the part of China to teach Vietnam a lesson, China learned something of itself: It lacks the military strength and the industrial power to extend its power even a few hundred miles beyond its own borders. China's power, then, is still limited by a variety of vital internal and external factors which peace with America and nuclear power status alone cannot overcome.

The political and social revolutions of China having been completed and old scores with Japan and the United States having been set aside, China has embarked upon an ambitious campaign of economic development. Despite recent advances, China remains underdeveloped, and the new national leadership is determined to accelerate the pace of modernization. To that end, the leadership announced in 1978 a national development plan to serve through 1985, calling for major advances in agriculture, industry, technology and defense. Apart from marked increases in agricultural output, the "Four-Modernizations Plan" called for $600 billion in capital investment for 128 major industrial projects. Vast increases in trade with Japan and the United States were anticipated as a stimulus to this development. Shortfalls in the availability of capital, together with inflationary consequences of rapid investment and the unfamiliarity of the Chinese leadership with economic reform (and particularly its capitalistic aspects), forced a first reassessment in 1979 and a second in 1980–81. The revised plan calls for emphasis upon agriculture, energy, transportation, communications, textiles and urban housing, and postpones massive industrial projects in such areas as steel and petrochemicals.[15]

Thus while asserting itself as a major regional power, China's principal interest for the 1980s is rapid economic modernization. Without this the pragmatic Chinese leadership might lose its power to those who have opposed rapid modernization and the resulting dependence upon capitalist countries. Already, frustrated economic aspirations have resulted in social unrest and in some economic confusion, since this is China's first massive experiment in planned modernization.[16] But the Soviet invasion of Afghanistan was a timely reminder to Peking of the reality of the Soviet threat, further requiring that China's modernization take place alongside a wary foreign policy which looks

15. Saburo Okita, "Japan, China and the United States," *Foreign Affairs,* Summer 1979, pp. 1090–110, especially pp. 1103–107; and *World Business Weekly,* December 22, 1980, pp. 24 and 64.

16. Ross Terrill, "China in the 1980s," *Foreign Affairs,* Spring 1980, pp. 920–35.

Source: Auth, © *The Philadelphia Inquirer/The Washington Post* Writer's Group

increasingly to the United States for the containment of Soviet power.

Recent disappointments in relations with Washington, however, such as the Taiwan arms-sale crisis, have forced a reassessment and a revised world view of flexible relations with the two superpowers. In any event, the fact that the Chinese leadership reduced the military budget in 1981 and again in 1982 and 1983 is a profound statement of national priorities: internal growth, not external defense (much less expansionism), rules Chinese public policy.

The Chinese image of the United States has changed from that of a mortal foe to a friend of whom to be wary. Ironically, the leadership is now concerned not that the presence of the United States in Asia is a threat to their country's security, but that the withdrawal of American forces from Asia and the Pacific enables the Soviet Union to expand its imperialist aims. Hence China now encourages Washington to continue its military presence in the area. Similarly, as China expands its trade and informal relations with the Soviet Union, it looks more and more to America and the West for military supply and commodities trade. The U.S. is China's third largest trading partner, ranking behind only Japan and Hong Kong.

American support for Taiwan persists in troubling the Chinese view of Washington's trustworthiness. An exchange of state visits between Premier Zhao Ziyang and President Reagan, planned for January and April 1984, was threatened (though not ultimately canceled) by what the Chinese Foreign Minister described as three "unpleasant incidents" at the end of 1983. The first was a resolution of the United States Senate that the reunification of Taiwan with China would have to be peaceful and that it would need the consent of the Taiwanese people. China regarded the second of these conditions as a violation of the Normalization Communiqué of 1979. Second, on a visit to Japan, President Reagan had declared that the United States will not abandon old friends while gaining new ones, and made a specific reference to Taiwan by use of the name "Republic of China," even after the Arms-Trade Communiqué of 1982 had recognized Chinese sovereignty over Taiwan. Third, in passing an appropriations bill for the International Monetary Fund, the Congress had declared its intention to defend Taiwan's (again called Republic of China) rights in the Asian Development Bank should China become a member and challenge Taiwan's rights to membership. This was regarded not only as an attack on China's sovereignty over Taiwan, but as a threatened return to a two-Chinas policy.[17]

Relations with the Soviet Union

Mao Tse-tung hoped that the final victory of the Red Army in 1949 would attract Soviet assistance, despite the skepticism with which the Kremlin viewed Chinese communism from its origins in the 1920s through the civil war and expulsion of the KMT. Even the Soviet raids upon Manchuria's industrial regions in the years immediately following the Japanese surrender did not dampen the expectation of Soviet aid. Indeed, a victorious Peking hoped that the Soviets might consider reparations for their part in the dismantling of Manchuria and for the other benefits that the Yalta Conference conceded to the Soviet Union at China's expense.

Accordingly, Mao made an unprecedented three-month visit to Moscow in December of 1949, immediately after his victory. In a prolonged and dramatic series of negotiations, he presented the Chinese case to the Soviet leadership. Surely this was an epic development in the history of the communist movement: there stood Mao Tse-tung and Joseph Stalin, at the pinnacle of power in two of the world's great nations, celebrating the greatest revolutionary achievement since 1917. Surely between them they could adjust the seemingly trivial issues dividing natural allies?

On the basis of what is now known, it can be said that the conflicts

17. For a summary and analysis, see *The Christian Science Monitor,* December 1, 1983, p. 1, by Takashi Oka.

between China and the Soviet Union were a great deal more profound than the Western world realized at the time, and that boundary conflicts were overlaid by substantial ideological disagreements. Stalin greeted Mao as an architect of revolution accepting the homage of a follower from a minor province. Khrushchev later revealed that Stalin had treated his guest in a domineering and demeaning manner, refusing to respond seriously to the rightfulness of Chinese demands.

Stalin took as given the primacy of the Soviet Communist Party in the world communist movement, and seemed to expect China to fall in faithfully behind the Soviet advance guard. He regarded loyalty to the Soviet party as the cardinal obligation of communists everywhere, since defense of revolution required first of all international solidarity and discipline. The requirements of the socialist bloc as a whole stood above the demands of individual countries. The Soviet Union was the source of all revolutionary inspiration, as well as the sword and shield against the threatening capitalist world. Furthermore, Mao was reminded of his great debt to the Soviet Union during the war. In Mao's view, this aid had gone principally to the KMT for use against the Communist Party.

Mao left Moscow with a very discouraging package. On only one territorial issue was there any concession by Stalin—a phased return of Port Arthur, acquired in 1945. On the issue of economic aid, the Russians pledged only $300 million for five years in high-interest loans, less than the United States gave to France to support the war in Indochina. Other assistance included joint Sino-Soviet companies for the exploitation of oil and mineral resources, with Soviet control of 51 percent of the stock. These terms were scarcely fraternal expressions of support.

This all must have been highly objectionable to the Chinese leader. The Soviet contribution to revolutionary success in China had been minimal—in fact, Soviet support flowed mainly to Chiang Kai-shek until the very end of the civil war. Had the Chinese party leadership accepted the advice of Stalin in 1945 to forgo revolutionary struggle during the years of Chiang's greatest weakness (after the Japanese collapse), there might never have been a communist victory. Now the Soviet Union demanded the right to dictate the future course of action for a regime that it did not create and, in fact, came very close to opposing. At the time, however, the Chinese leadership had little choice but to submit to the Soviet will, for the West had adopted a policy of isolating China. In spite of the tensions, which deepened over the years, the Chinese continue to acknowledge the support of the Soviets during the crucial early years of the People's Republic, even though the extent of Soviet assistance was disappointing at the time.

Sino-Soviet relations deteriorated during the 1950s as the Chinese pursued a course which, in their judgment, was more suitable to the culture and pre-industrial economy of the state, though it was inconsistent with Soviet wishes. The Chinese resented the reluctance of the Kremlin to supply more aid. Eventually, Chinese departures from the Soviet model of industrialization, which required extensive purchases of heavy machinery, became more pronounced. The sharp turn toward the Maoist model of economic development, which emphasized the role of human labor and agriculture, accentuated the ideological rift with the Kremlin. Mao perceived the Soviet reaction as evidence of a desire to oppose his Great Leap Forward and rapid communization, assuming that the Soviets feared that China would become too powerful a rival in the communist world. Twice Mao tested Soviet friendship, once by confrontation with the United States in the Taiwan Straits (1958), and once in a Sino-Indian border dispute (1962). In each case the Soviets declined to assist the Chinese. Withdrawing all of their technicians, leaving half-finished industrial plants, and taking home all spare parts for Soviet-built military and industrial equipment, the Soviets added fuel to the fire by tearing up the Sino-Soviet nuclear sharing agreement, and then by signing the Nuclear Test Ban Treaty of 1963. The latter of these two acts was interpreted by the Chinese as a Soviet effort to deny them membership in the coveted nuclear club of major powers. The tension between the two intensified steadily, and in 1963 erupted in open dispute. From that time to the present, their relationship has been one of bitter enmity. The Chinese looked on aghast as, in 1968, the Soviet Union invaded Czechoslovakia and declared in the Brezhnev Doctrine that the interests of the Socialist commonwealth are greater than those of any of its individual members. It was undoubtedly this event, coupled with border conflicts with the Soviet Union and the United States' reassessment of its Asian policy during the waning years of the Vietnam War, that led China to reconsider its relationship with the other old enemy, the United States.

Although the thaw with Washington and the increased animosity of relations with Moscow have made the view less popular than it has been in the past, some Western observers continue to expect that China's differences with the Soviet Union may adjust over time, and that the conflicts between capitalism and democracy and communism and revolution may outlast this quarrel between the two socialist giants. Issues of competing national interests and differing ideological interpretations might be forgotten if either of the communist powers were threatened from the capitalist world, for example, by Japan or the United States. However, if national interests rather than ideologies predominate in determining the actual behavior of states, the enduring problem of a contested border will prolong the Sino-Soviet dispute. After all, one-third of the Soviet armed forces are arrayed along the Chinese border, in addition to a considerable portion of Moscow's strategic and nuclear capabilities. If the Russians succeed in reaching a mutual force reduction agreement with the NATO powers in Europe, still more deployments would be freed from the European to the Asian sector. Who can be certain that the Soviets would not consider a preemptive nuclear attack on the Chinese atomic production facilities in Sinkiang, or not attempt to foster subversion among dissident populations? (China has a relatively homogeneous population—94 percent Han Chinese and only 6 percent minorities—but the minorities occupy a disproportionate share of territory, comprising over a third of the Chinese land mass.)

The possibility of war between China and the Soviet Union, long a subject of popular conjecture in the United States, withstood a critical test in early 1979 when China invaded Vietnam under a doctrine of punitive aggression, occasioned by Vietnam's earlier conquest of Kampuchea. It was an assertion of its determination to control the Asian continental balance, and only verbal protest from both Moscow and Washington greeted this act of force. However, in a show of belated solidarity with Vietnam, and in the interest of insinuating itself into the continental politics of China at the latter's southwestern flank, Moscow expanded its aid to Hanoi and moved vessels into the largest naval facility in the country, that at Cam Ranh Bay (built during the Vietnam War by and for the United States Navy). Thus, the uneasy peace between China and the Soviet Union is less likely to be one of ideological reconciliation than one of geopolitical strategy (the use of geographic placement for strategic competition) and balance of conventional forces.

Just as China's relations with the United States have profited from Soviet aggression in Afghanistan and expansion in the Pacific, so too have Sino-Soviet relations benefited from the perfidy of the American relationship. Since 1979, when China and the United States exchanged diplomatic recognitions, several disruptive events have occurred, most of them related to the wave of political conservativism which has swept the United States. These include arms sales to Taiwan in violation of the spirit of the Normalization Communiqué; growing American opposition to the Third World and to the New International Economic Order; and prolonged disagreements over textiles trade. These conditions, and the need to reduce tensions along the Sino-Soviet border in order to free resources for economic and industrial modernization, impel China to foster better relations with the Kremlin. As the result of an exchange of official visits in 1982 and 1983, trade between the two has now doubled and is expected to continue growing. Even while China regards the Soviet Union as social imperialist, a flexible policy with respect to the nuclear superpowers is a perceived necessity for a strengthened and independent China.

Relations with Japan

Japan is one of the powers that benefited most from China's subjugation during the Century of Humiliation. The invasions and conquests of 1894, 1931 and the Second World War brought to China the harshest consequences of Japanese militarism, and many living Chinese remember well the cruel behavior of the Japanese army. Chinese fears were not completely erased by the defeat of Japan in 1945. A prolonged boom has moved the Japanese economy to the third position among industrial powers, behind the United States and the USSR, but well ahead of China.

During most of the period when the United States isolated China, both the Beijing and Tokyo governments wished to establish normal trade relations. The Japanese need for raw materials, particularly fuels and ores, is historical and urgent (and was a major reason for Japanese militarism in the 1930s). For its part, China was in severe need of industrial goods to assist the Great Leap Forward, aid which came from the Soviet Union in too small volume and at too high a political price. Yet until the Sino-American thaw, Tokyo's military association with Washington was an ever-present threat of a resurgence of Japanese imperialism. More recently, as the Chinese have begun to appreciate the values of an American presence in Asia, the military alliance between Japan and the United States is viewed as an assurance that Japan will not undertake militaristic imperialism. The American nuclear umbrella, which enables Japan to honor the commitments of its post-war constitution to foresake a nuclear military capacity, helps ensure that a healthy trading relationship with Japan will not deteriorate into an imbalance which might invite conquest.

That Japan is the principal economic investor in China is regarded as almost entirely beneficial to the latter's economic development. Thus, in the Chinese view, Japan has moved from the position of imperial conqueror to one of natural and accessible trading partner, and part of the Western alliance which insures China against Soviet aggression.

In recent years, trade with Japan has increased dramatically. Japan now receives more than 21 percent of China's exports, and almost 35 percent of China's imports come from Japan. In absolute numbers the trade is still small: while Japan accounts for nearly 30 percent of China's external trade, China accounts for only a little more than 2 percent of Japan's. Nevertheless, the central position that economic development plays in China's plans for the decade, together with the peaceful but uncertain relationship of China and the U.S. and the wary improvements of Sino-Soviet relations, almost ensures that Japan and China will develop a gradual economic interdependence.

Conclusion

Perhaps the most abiding characteristic of the international political system is its dynamism—the constant change of relative positions, aims and national values and expectations. We have seen that in this century the Soviet Union has emerged from tsarism to vibrant socialism. The United States has risen from isolation to a position of world dominance, from which contemporary events and changes are forcing its reluctant retreat. America's principal allies (with the exception of Canada, which has grown steadily in international prominence even while holding off American economic encroachments) have gone through the turmoils of two global wars, near-total economic destruction and, in the cases of Germany and Japan, thorough rebuilding after military

Chinese Businessmen visit Kansas bottling plant in preparation for opening their own soft-drink and snack food industry, 1983.

Source: AP/Wide World Photos

occupation. They have by now established themselves as major competitors of the United States, though heavily dependent upon Washington for defense and national security.

The impact of the twentieth century upon China has been equally profound. Because of bitter memories of the Century of Humiliation and fears of hostile encirclement, the Chinese international perspective has, until recently, been entirely one of defense. Even today that perspective is largely defensive. To the Chinese, the international system seems to be fraught with dangers of imperialism, whether from capitalist nations hostile to the Chinese Revolution or from a Soviet government self-selected as the exclusive heir to Karl Marx's socialist doctrine, and embittered by China's notion of separate centers of socialism. Wherever practicable, China has promoted revolutionary trends elsewhere, and has supported anti-imperialist forces. But only with the opening of massive trade and diplomatic relations with Japan and the United States has China begun to extend itself into the international system, and it has done so in a new global environment in which complex political and economic forces have made it possible for the country to face the rest of the world less defensively.

Through all, China adheres closely to the view that each people must struggle for their own national and social liberation for the final defeat of imperialism and for global implementation of the Five Principles of Peaceful Coexistence. To play an effective part, China has reaffirmed its determination to undergo rapid and thorough economic modernization and to exert increasing influence over the power distribution of Asia, both among the Asian states and with respect to external superpower influence over Asian affairs. The irony in China's case is that her economic and military modernization has become remarkably dependent upon the capitalist world, particularly upon the wealth of the United States and Japan. Furthermore, for a brief period from 1976 through 1981, the course of modern Chinese foreign policy was based principally upon cultivating the friendship of the United States. Now, however, confident of the future and freed from a brief bout with anti-Soviet fever, Beijing has opted for a flexible policy with the superpowers, one that mixes fear with confidence, ideology with pragmatism, and a vision of the future with a keen awareness of the Century of Humiliation.

5

The Third World Perspective

Traditionally, the study of international relations has focused almost exclusively on those actors examined in the preceding chapters. As complex as diplomacy has always been, the criteria for selecting important international aspects of it for discussion, and for describing the structure dynamics of international policies, were few in number. Principal actors were those countries which participated in "high politics," those which contributed significantly to the world's military balance, those which were capable of bringing force to bear upon interstate relations, those which were part of critical communications flows throughout the world, and those which were most productive and deeply involved in world economic transactions. Other areas of the globe, most of them formerly colonized, were at the disposal of the major actors, who exploited their territories, their riches and their peoples in order to compete more effectively among the privileged few.

The realignment of world politics after the Second World War did not occur exclusively through ideological issues. Unmistakably, the postwar collapse of relations between the Soviet world and the West, though viewed by different parties as having been caused by different factors, led to an East-West confrontation which still threatens to erupt in nuclear war. But at the same time the emancipation of the formerly colonized peoples of Africa, Asia, the Middle East, South and Central America, the Caribbean and the South Pacific began to foretell a second major conflict of contemporary international relations: the North-South confrontation. In contrast to the ideological and military foundations of the East-West crisis, the North-South confrontation evolved principally over economic issues, and secondarily over political and human rights issues.

At the simplest level, the North-South crisis is a result of the imbalance between the wealthy industrialized countries of the northern hemisphere and the impoverished, underindustrialized peoples of the southern hemisphere. It developed during the early Cold War years, when newly independent countries wished to avoid embroilment in political controversy between the West ("first world") and the East ("second world"), and produced a loose coalition of economically deprived states, held together only by bonds of newness and poverty. The members of this group came to be known in the 1950s as the nonaligned states, or the less developed countries (LDCs). Although they comprise more than half of the global population and their populations increase at a rate considerably above those of the industrialized states, their composite industrial production is less than a third of America's or Western Europe's. Per capita incomes throughout the Third World (except in a few oil-rich countries) are a small fraction of those of the United States and Europe and are rising at slower rates. Moreover, the gap between the rich and the poor is not closing, but widening (see Figure 5–1).

When we speak of poverty in the Third World, it should be distinguished from deprivation in the industrialized nations. The poverty of American cities, for example, harsh though it is, is softened by many features not found in the slums of the developing countries: hot and cold running water, sewers and toilets, electrical appliances, a diversified diet including at least occasional meat, even automobiles. By way of contrast, hundreds of thousands of people in Calcutta, including whole families, live, sleep and die in the streets and doorways, literally competing with rats for food. Poverty in the United States is dramatic if we compare it to the wealth of the majority of Americans; but the American poor would be considered very fortunate by most of the peoples of the developing countries.

Although the common theme among the Third World countries is the struggle for development, within this unifying focus we must recognize broad differences among the more than 110 nations that comprise the group. First, although originally poverty was their most notable similarity, deep cleavages have occurred among the relations of Third World countries. No longer are all of them poor; indeed, Saudi Arabia holds the world's largest share of currency reserves, and the

FIGURE 5–1
The widening gap.

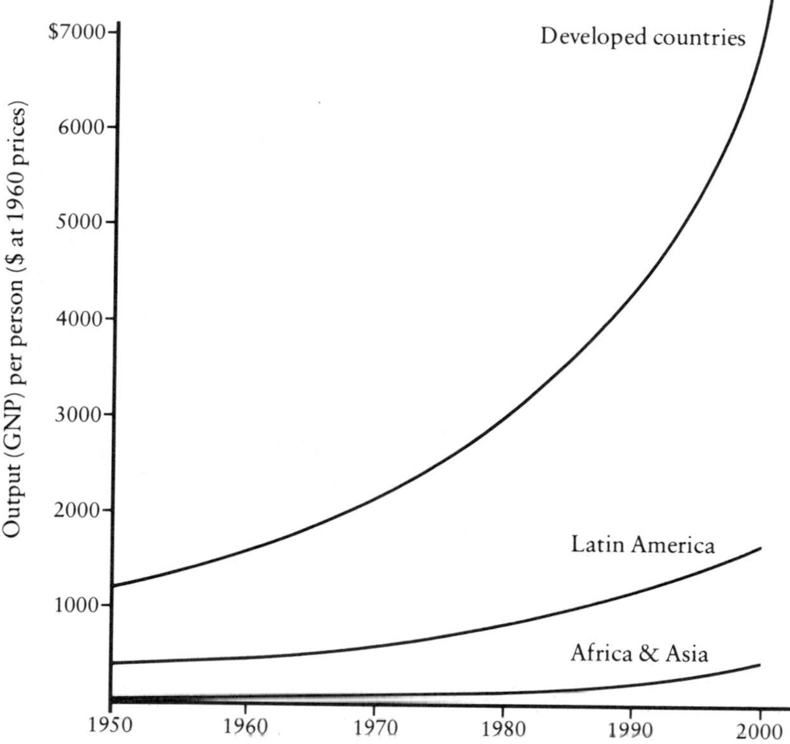

Source: From Barbara Ward, J. D. Runnalls and Lenore D'Anjou, eds., *The Widening Gap*. © 1971, Columbia University Press. Reprinted by permission of the publisher.

---

tiny country of Qatar has the world's highest per capita income. Kuwait and the United Arab Emirates follow closely. All of this is attributable to the huge international demand for oil and to the success of the Organization of Petroleum Exporting Countries (OPEC) in raising the world price sharply. Other oil-exporting countries of the Third World enjoy great national riches, too. Nevertheless, the "Third World" is understood to consist of countries ranging in national wealth from utter poverty and infant industrialization (such as Bangladesh, Pakistan, India and Sri Lanka) to substantial national wealth, still accompanied by underindustrialization (such as the OPEC nations).

Other useful distinctions in avoiding the misperception that Third World countries are all alike include the following:

Resources The poor countries vary greatly in the natural resources with which they are endowed. Some, like the Sudan, lack many raw materials and are hampered in their development by the relative barrenness of the earth itself. Others, like Nigeria, are richly endowed with the blessings of nature and need only to find the social and political means to utilize their gifts.

Population Less developed countries also vary in the concentration of their human populations. Some are teemingly overpopulated; tiny Java (Indonesia) has more than one-third the population of the United States. Others are sparsely populated; oil-rich Libya is almost empty; Tanzania cultivates only one-third of its arable land. Some are largely urban societies, concentrated in and dominated by the cities. Others are agricultural societies or even nomadic wandering cultures. Some are huge in territory, such as India and Brazil. Others are countries of postage-stamp dimensions, such as El Salvador, Lebanon and Gabon.

Ethnic Divisions Third World countries differ greatly in their ethnic composition and in the unity or diversity of their peoples. Some, like Chile, have relatively homogeneous populations. Others are sharply divided into two or three ethnic groups among whom there may be deep conflicts; for example, the struggle in Nigeria between the Ibo and the Hausa and Yoruba erupted into civil war in the late 1960s. Others are composed of a multiplicity of peoples held together by slender threads of common interest. An example is India, whose people speak the following languages: Hindi, Urdu, Bengali, Punjabi, Tamil, Kannada and Telugu, as well as many dialects. So incomprehensible are these to each other that the national tongue is English, the former colonial language. Thus, some Third World peoples are highly unified and ready to face national economic problems, while others face sharp ethnic divisions that consume much of the national energy.

Political Histories The nations of the Third World also have very different political histories. Some were colonies until recently (for example, Morocco, Kenya), while others have not been subjected to direct foreign control for many centuries (Thailand). Some are ancient countries that have existed as political entities longer than the United States (Iran), while others are new political creations recently formed by colonial masters for their own administrative convenience (Nigeria) or new federations of formerly separate peoples (Malaysia).

Modernizing and Traditional Cultures Some peoples hew closely to ancient traditions, have a low consciousness of nationalism, and are concerned mainly with age-old problems of village and religious life. In other societies, the traditional order is under challenge by a modernizing elite, some variety of participatory revolution is under way, and national identities are superseding antiquated principles of social organization. Literacy rates vary widely in developing countries.

Source: Hiroji Kubota/Magnum

Calcutta, India—one of the poorest and most crowded cities on earth.

Governments Governmental types include traditional ruling elites and monarchies, elected regimes on the Western democratic model, military juntas that have come to power by coup d'état and revolutionary movements.

Economies Economies vary from those highly dependent on imports and exports (Chile) to others for which foreign trade is relatively secondary (India); from societies in which income is distributed very unequally (Saudi Arabia) to highly egalitarian cases (Cuba); from primarily agrarian (Sri Lanka) to substantially industrial (Singapore); from stagnation (Afghanistan) to rapid growth (Brazil); from capitalist (Argentina) to socialist (Vietnam); and along many other dimensions.

These distinctions are overshadowed in significance, however, by the impact upon world politics found in the evolution of the Third World's collective diplomatic voice. Once only representative of a loose coalition of noncompetitive states dominated and exploited by the industrial powers, the voice of the Third World has grown in both volume and tone. Despite the differences that characterize the members, unity within diversity has enabled the LDCs to impose significant change upon the structure of international politics and upon the nonmilitary power relations of states (and more recently with the massive expenditure on armaments by some Third World states, such as Cuba and Syria, even the military relations of larger states). It is because of the awakening of the South to its political and economic potential and because of the inappropriateness of military solutions to North-South issues, that traditional measures of international power relations have deteriorated, that structural characteristics of the postwar world have changed, and that diplomatic practices of a power-oriented world have been found wanting in North-South relations.[1]

For almost twenty of its twenty-five years, the evolution of Third World politics was gradual, conservative and largely unrewarding, owing equally to disarray and the successful resistance of the industrial states. Despite major declarations of solidarity at Bandung (Indonesia) in 1955 and Cairo (Egypt) in 1962, and the first three meetings of the United Nations Conference on Trade and Development (UNCTAD) in 1964, 1968 and 1972, new inspiration came to the Third World movement only in 1973 when political and economic events converged. At a summit conference of nonaligned governments in Algiers, a concerted effort was launched to bring to fruition the economic agenda of the UNCTAD, and a specific program of action for developing a New International Economic Order was launched. Later in the year, renewed warfare between Israel and its Arab adversaries resulted in an oil embargo upon the Western supporters of Israel, dramatizing for the first time the potential economic and political powers of the Third World.

With the resulting control of world oil prices by the Organization of Petroleum Exporting Countries (OPEC), and more particularly by its Arab members, the Third World was able to force its economic agenda upon the United Nations in the form of the Sixth Special Session of the General Assembly, which formally launched the New International Economic Order. There followed two vacuous attempts by the industrialized states to wrest back the initiative, one the Seventh Special Session (1975) and the other the Conference on International Economic Cooperation, a two-year (1975–77) attempt to bring control to North-South economic relations while at the same time promoting

1. For a thorough and documented treatment of the revolutionary impact of the Third World upon international politics, see Roger D. Hansen, *Beyond the North-South Stalemate* (New York: McGraw-Hill, 1979), particularly Chapters 2 and 3. Elsewhere Hansen argues that " 'the South' is a label given meaning not by the degree to which those countries share economic characteristics but by the decision of those countries to act as a diplomatic unit coordinating a large measure of their international activity. Properly used, the label 'South' applies to a readily observable process in today's international politics, and not to an analytical categorization of countries based on relative levels of economic development." "North-South Policy: What's the Problem?" *Foreign Affairs,* Summer 1979, pp. 1104–28 at pp. 1105–6.

the rate of the South's development. The 1979 meeting of UNCTAD in Manila, at which the LDCs specifically requested action to restructure their international debts, to stabilize fluctuating world prices in a number of commodities that they exported and to reduce tariff barriers among the industrial states, resulted in little progress. In the half-decade following the 1973 petroleum crisis, the structural capacity to deal with North-South issues had changed markedly, but progress was infinitely slow. Nevertheless, it is broadly recognized that the 1973–75 phase of the Third World's evolution as a political force was typified by two dramatic changes: (1) the formulation of a unified position on international economic issues with respect to the industrial countries and (2) the determination to transform this united position and the perceived collective economic power of the Third World countries into an instrument of political pressure for the implementation of a New International Economic Order. Most important, the diplomacy of the Third World from the Algiers summit through the Sixth Special Session of the General Assembly is of crucial importance because it succeeded, for the first time, in politicizing the development issue.[2]

The North-South Dialogue

The reaction of the industrialized states to this new development in the Third World's status was one of resistance. The United States and many of its major Western trading partners initially refused to participate in preparations for the Sixth Special Session and, upon its conclusion, declared their intent not to participate in some of the outcomes. To the Third World this reaction was confirmation that the industrial powers had participated in the Sixth Special Session principally as a means of breaking the solidarity that OPEC had wrought, and their resolve was strengthened to benefit from OPEC politics and to forge other cartels that might add to the pressure on the wealthy states.

This mood, which dominated both the Sixth Special Session and the Paris planning sessions for the Seventh Special Session, was broken by a sharp reversal on the part of the United States. In an address prior to the Seventh Special Session, Secretary of State Henry Kissinger announced that the United States was "prepared to engage in a con-

2. Karl P. Sauvant, "Toward the New International Economic Order," in Karl P. Sauvant and Hajo Hasenpflug, *The New International Economic Order: Confrontation or Cooperation between North and South?* (Boulder, Co.: Westview, 1977), pp. 3–19.

structive dialogue and to work cooperatively" on issues pertaining to the New International Economic Order.[3] This new tone dominated opening statements at the Seventh Special Session, and the industrial states announced their intention to "turn away from confrontation" and approach the New International Economic Order with conciliation and in a mood of responsiveness to the initiatives of the Third World. The North-South Dialogue had commenced.

The Seventh Special Session, the first phase of the North-South Dialogue, concluded in a carefully negotiated agenda for action, principally addressing problems of international trade, and transfer of resources and technology. Since UNCTAD is the principal forum of the Third World, the responsibility fell to UNCTAD to transform that compromise into an agenda for economic action. As its first step UNCTAD prepared a summary statement on "Trade and Development Issues in the Context of a New International Economic Order," from which we summarize the content of the North-South Dialogue as follows:

1. *An Economic Security System for Developing Countries*
   a. Integrated Programme for Commodities—commodity market stabilization and price stabilization for the primary exports of the developing states.
   b. Improved Compensatory Financing Facilities—adaptation of the International Monetary Fund or establishment of a substitute organization to supervise stabilization agreements and provide compensatory export shortfalls due to international market instability.
   c. Debt Relief—improved mechanisms of channeling capital to the Third World and for reducing the indebtedness that hinders development.

2. *Changing the Structure of International Economic Relations*
   a. Reducing the Economic Dependence of the Developing Countries—expansion of trade in manufactures; strengthening the technological base of the Third World; and establishing a marketing and distribution system for primary commodities.

3. "Address by the Honorable Henry A. Kissinger, Secretary of State, before the Kansas City International Relations Council, Missouri, May 13, 1975" in *Issues at the Special Session of the 1975 U.N. General Assembly* (Washington, D.C.: Government Printing Office, 1975). A more detailed background can be found in Catherine B. Gwin, "The Seventh Special Session: Toward a New Phase of Relations between the Developed and the Developing States?" in Sauvant and Hasenpflug, *The New International Economic Order*, pp. 97–117.

b. Strengthening Trade and Economic Cooperation Among Developing Countries—reorientation of development strategy to one of collective self-reliance rather than dependence on the developed states, including thorough development of new international machinery.
c. Global Management of Resources—including the establishment of new rules of international trade, reform of the international monetary system and the development of strategies for the rational use of resources.[4]

UNCTAD, then, had by the end of the 1970s set an agenda designed to promote trade expansion, improve economic cooperation among developing states, restructure international debts, and promote economic integration among developing states in support of collective self-reliance.

The months and years that followed UNCTAD V (the Manila Conference), however, were among the most difficult in the history of the Third World. Deteriorating political relations between the United States and the Soviet Union had both political and economic repercussions in the Third World. China had set out on a new diplomatic course with a broader focus than just the Third World. Worldwide economic stagnation and recession resulted in deepening unemployment, a sharp drop in export prices and inflation of import costs. The need to assume additional debt added to the weight of the Third World's short-term and long-term burdens. And the continuing increase in oil prices widened the economic gap not only between the industrialized world and the developing world, but between the oil-producing and the oil-importing members of the Third World as well.

In some nations, the reversal of growth patterns were so serious that the question of survival was foremost. At the urging of the Third World, the United Nations marked the beginning of the third Development Decade with a Conference on the Least Developed Countries. At this conference, a program of action for the survival of thirty-one states totaling 220 million people (later increased to thirty-six countries) was established.[5] Special aid projects were designated for:

4. *Trade and Development Issues in the Context of a New International Economic Order* (UNCTAD/OSG/L/Rev.1), February 1976, pp. 8–33. Reprinted with minor adaptations from Sauvant and Hasenpflug, *The New International Economic Order,* pp. 39–62.

5. For a review of the conference, see Thomas G. Weiss, "The U.N. Conference on the Least Developed Nations," *International Affairs* (London), Autumn 1983; and Thomas G. Weiss and Anthony Jennings, *More for the Least?* (Lexington, Mass.: D. C. Heath, 1983).

Afghanistan	Lao People's Democratic Republic
Bangladesh	Lesotho
Benin	Malawi
Bhutan	Maldives
Botswana	Mali
Burundi	Nepal
Cape Verde	Niger
Central African Republic	Rwanda
Chad	Samoa
Cameroon	Sao Tome and Principe
Democratic Yemen	Sierra Leone
Djibouti	Somalia
Equatorial Guinea	Sudan
Ethiopia	Togo
Gambia	Uganda
Guinea	United Republic of Tanzania
Guinea-Bissau	Upper Volta
Haiti	Yemen Arab Republic

Only a year earlier an Independent Commission on International Development Issues, chaired by former West German Chancellor Willy Brandt, had issued a report entitled *North-South: A Program for Survival.* The report had noted that the conditions at the turn of the decade were such as to demand not simply more international aid, but ". . . new structures. What is now on the agenda is a rearrangement of international relations, the building of a new order and a new kind of comprehensive approach to the problems of development."[6]

But the deepening worldwide recession in the early 1980s resulted in a collapse in commodity prices for the Third World's exports. During the period 1980 through 1982, the total loss is estimated to have been approximately $21 billion. Furthermore, recession and unemployment in the industrialized West promoted demands of protectionism, that is, of governmental policies designed to protect domestic products from price competition with imported products. From the Third World's perspective, the entire post-war trend toward free trade was not only in jeopardy, but was being adjusted by the industrialized

6. *North-South: A Program for Survival,* The Report of the Independent Commission on International Development Issues under the Chairmanship of Willy Brandt (Cambridge: MIT Press, 1980), p. 18. In 1982 the Commission reconvened to review its findings and recommendations, and published a subsequent report, *Common Crisis—North-South: Cooperation for World Recovery* (Cambridge: MIT Press, 1983). The Commission found that since its first report, world economic conditions had worsened to the extent that emergency measures were needed to avoid such consequences as mass starvation.

world in violation of its own principles enunciated through the General Agreement on Tariffs and Trade, to the severe detriment of the Third World.

It was against this background that UNCTAD VI convened at Belgrade, Yugoslavia, in mid-1983. In preparation for the conference, the Third World held two preliminary meetings: the Group of Seventy-Seven, which speaks for 125 developing nations, met in Argentina; and the 101 politically non-aligned nations met in India. Together, these groups hoped that UNCTAD VI would produce guarantees against further protectionism among the developed countries; activate a number of commodity price agreements as well as a Commodity Fund to support sagging commodity prices on the world market; and double the aid of the developed countries to the thirty-six least developed. But opinion between the North and the South was sharply divided, and the Third World left the conference with little satisfaction. Particularly, they found that on many issues, while other industrialized countries abstained from voting, the United States cast the sole negative vote. UNCTAD IV produced little of value for the Third World.

Behind the politics of international economic development lies the key question in any analysis of the Third World: What are the causes and cures of underdevelopment? Why are some countries impoverished while others enjoy high standards of living? There are two sharply conflicting causal theories of underdevelopment. The *conventional* theory, favored in the Western countries and in the less developed countries closely associated with the West (such as Brazil or Indonesia), blames poverty on internal conditions within the poor countries that prevent them from achieving the advances accomplished by the developed countries. The *radical* theory, favored by revolutionary thinkers and the more militant voices in the Third World (such as Cuba and Libya), blames poverty on international conditions of exploitation of the poor countries by the developed nations. The conventional theory sees the rich countries trying to help the poor "lift themselves up by the bootstraps," while the radical theory sees the rich countries profiting at the expense of the poor through foreign investment and trade.

The Conventional Theory of Development

According to the conventional theory, the process of economic growth and development in the LDCs has been arrested because of low rates of productivity combined with high levels of social waste and inefficiency. The Western standard of living is high because the modern high-technology worker produces a great deal in eight hours. Conversely, the LDC worker produces less though he labors longer hours because he works inefficiently with primitive tools and methods. For example, the American farm laborer works on the average more than one hundred acres, while the LDC farmer averages less than three acres. Furthermore, the American squeezes two or three times as much annual yield out of each acre by using advanced methods of fertilization, irrigation and scientific farming. The result is that the American farmer is able to feed about fifty people, while the LDC farm worker feeds fewer than two. The higher rate of agricultural productivity in the Western countries allows a surplus to be invested in industrial development, while retarded agricultural production in less developed countries slows economic growth and drains the labor force.

The Western worker is more productive, not because of image or superior genes, but simply because he has machinery and automation to multiply the results of his labor. US production consumes about 22,000 pounds of coal equivalent energy annually per capita, while in India the comparable figure is 380 pounds per capita. Western productivity is based on using artificial means to multiply the efficiency of human workers.

The LDCs cannot match the mechanization of the West because of a shortage of capital. It is estimated that the average American worker is supported by $30,000 worth of capital equipment in addition to a substantial investment in education ("human capital") and economic infrastructure (roads, railroads, telephones, harbors and so on). The most basic question for the conventional theorists, then, is how and where the LDCs can raise the capital necessary to increase productivity to lift themselves from the cycle of poverty.

The basic source of capital for all economies is production itself. Capital is a surplus of production, a portion that is not exhausted by personal consumption but rather saved and invested. If 200 bushels of wheat are produced by a peasant family and only 100 are immediately needed to sustain the lives of the producers, the other 100 can be sold or traded for tools and tractors (capital goods) that would enable the family to increase its production, say to 300 bushels, the next year. The second year, perhaps 150 of the 300 bushels could be converted into "producer's goods"—that is, invested—to raise production still higher in the third year. Thus, the theory of *self-sustaining growth* holds that eventually a point is reached when productivity gains become normal as a result of constantly increasing investment. Under these circumstances, it becomes possible to achieve permanently expanding capitalization and also rising personal consumption.

The problem, according to the conventional theorist, is that economies reach this point of "takeoff" to self-sustaining growth only under conditions of rapid capital accumulation. But most of the LDCs have been able to achieve only modest rates of saving and investment because of poverty itself and various forms of waste and inefficiency. Even where surpluses might be generated, they tend to be squandered on unnecessary forms of consumption rather than on growth-oriented investment. Five kinds of waste significantly retard development: (1) runaway population growth; (2) excessive military expenditures; (3) needless luxury consumption; (4) official corruption; and (5) management inefficiency.

1. Population Growth

Population is growing much faster in the less developed countries than in the developed countries (see Table 5–1). Developed countries grow by about 1 percent per year. In contrast, Africa grows almost three times as fast—2.7 percent annually—and some populations are expanding even faster. Latin America will increase its population by 75 percent between 1970 and 2000, while Europe will grow by only 18 percent during these years.

The LDCs have twice as much of their population under ten years of age as the developed countries. Because infants and young children consume but do not produce, they act as a drain on economic growth. It is estimated that a country with a 3 percent population growth rate must invest 6 percent of its production each year just to keep up with the increase, without achieving any expansion of per capita income.

There is a tragic irony in the growth performance of the Third World. From 1960 through 1983, the total economies of the LDCs grew faster than those of the industrialized countries. (In the period

TABLE 5–1
Where population is growing fastest.

	Population (millions) 1950	1970	1977	*Projected Increase 1970–2000*	*Projected Population (millions)*
Latin America	162	283	342	75%	652
Africa	217	344	424	59%	818
Asia	1,355	2,056	3,355	52%	3,778
Oceania	13	19	22	46%	35
North America	166	228	242	37%	333
Soviet Union	180	243	260	35%	330
Europe	392	462	478	18%	568

Source: United Nations Statistical Yearbook, 1972, 1977 and 1979.

1960–73, for example, the combined rate of growth in the LDCs was 6.0 percent, while in the industrialized countries it was 5.1 percent. From 1973 to 1980, the comparison was 4.7 percent and 2.5 percent. During the recession years 1980–83, the growth rate of the developing world was 1.9 percent as against 0.4 percent. And in the recovery years 1982–85, the figures leveled off at 4.4 percent and 3.0 percent, respectively.) The wealthy countries of North America and Europe had population increases of only 30 percent during this time period, compared to a growth of over 85 percent for the combined populations of Africa, Latin America and Asia. As a result, the industrialized countries gained more in terms of per capita economic growth. In the developing world, then, population growth continues to outrun the benefits of economic expansion, with the result that the economic capability of the individual continues to slide even as national productivity improves. Thus excessive population growth among the LDCs retards their development and widens the gap between rich nations and poor.

Why is the population explosion occurring in the Third World? The cause is not, as many people believe, an increase in the birth rate; this has remained relatively stable. Rather, a decline in the death rate has been achieved by improved public health, medicine and nutrition. Historically, the richer countries have compensated for longer life expectancy by cutting the birth rate more or less correspondingly; and their average family size tends to be considerably smaller than the developing world's. The LDCs are caught in a difficult transition point: Life expectancy is rising rapidly and birth rates are dropping very slowly. As a result, their population growth is much more rapid than it once was, far exceeding the population growth of the industrialized countries. Pertinent comparisons are shown in Table 5–2.

Efforts by some LDCs to solve this problem through birth control and family planning have not, on the whole, made a great impact.

TABLE 5–2
Comparative population trends between industrialized and developing countries, 1965–2000.

	Average Size of Household			*Birth Rate (per 1000 population)*		
	1965	*1980*	*2000*	*1965*	*1980*	*2000*
Industrialized	3.5	3.1	2.6	17.9	15.6	14.9
Developing	5.2	5.0	4.1	38.4	29.4	24.3

Source: UN Chronicle, November 1982, p. 36.

Many peoples consider large families a blessing, or have religious objections to birth control or are culturally ill suited to the regular use of birth control methods. Some novel approaches have had a limited success. In India, payment of a small reward (less than $5) has induced men who already have several children to undergo voluntary sterilization. In China, the government has long urged young people to postpone marriage and child-bearing until they reach twenty-five or thirty years of age. More recently, however, the population control program in China has been combined with the ideology of heroic work effort, and has produced a national system in which cohabitation and personal sexual practices are matters of public interest.

Various medical innovations may achieve real breakthroughs in controlling the population growth of the Third World. Among these are oral contraception for men and chemical agents that prevent conception even if taken several hours after insemination. Meanwhile, in many countries population growth is not being arrested, and one result is continued economic stagnation and declining per capita GNP.

2. Excessive Military Expenditure

A second form of waste that erodes the small increases in production that the developing countries are able to achieve is military expenditure. Many developing countries spend large portions of their scarce resources on the maintenance of armed forces. From 1973 through 1982, for example, the oil-producing developing countries spent approximately $360 billion on military policy, while the non-oil group spent an additional $374 billion. Together, their total military bill for the decade was $734 billion. (Figure 5–2 demonstrates the spending trend for that period.)

This period was the first decade following the maturation of OPEC, a period when Western industrialized nations eagerly provided arms to the Third World, particularly to the oil-producing members, in return for steady supplies of petroleum. The major shift in arms supply occurred after the oil crisis in the West during the winter of 1973–74. While during the nine-year period 1965–73 the Third World purchased a total of $25 billion in arms from abroad, in the succeeding nine-year period (1974–82) the figure jumped to $76.2 billion, a threefold increase. Similarly, in the earlier period the greatest annual amount of arms purchased was $3.7 billion (in 1971 and again in 1973); in the latter period the highest was $11.2 billion (1978). Figure 5–3 reveals the principal suppliers of arms to the Third World. The figure demonstrates that four countries—the United States, the Soviet

FIGURE 5–2
Third World military expenditures, 1973–82, expressed in billions of US dollars at 1980 constant prices and value.

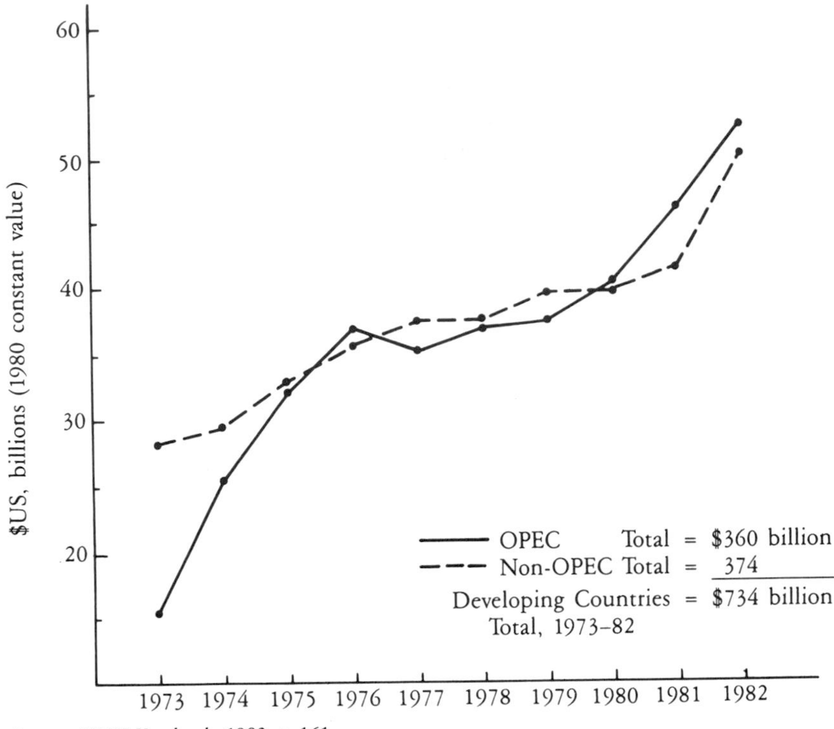

Source: SIPRI Yearbook, 1983, p. 161.

Union, France and Britain—provided 86 percent of the total. Most of the remainder was supplied by Italy and West Germany. The figure also demonstrates that the American commitment to arms supply policy reached its peak in 1976 through 1980, while the Soviet Union peak occured from 1978 through 1981.

The reasons for this huge increase in military expenditure in the Third World are many, and they go considerably beyond reasons of national grandeur. Perhaps most important is the degree to which the developing nations remain of interest to the superpowers. As Soviet advances and Cuban troop deployments in Africa have revealed, military opportunism in the Third World continues to be a foreign policy option of major powers interested in expansion. A second reason is that despite the apparent cohesion of the Third World on economic issues, it is in disarray politically, perhaps more now than at any other time. Important examples include:

1. War between China and Vietnam, causing the dislocation of a delicate balance in Asia.

FIGURE 5–3
Principal arms suppliers to the third world, 1973–82, expressed in billions of US dollars at 1975 constant values and prices.

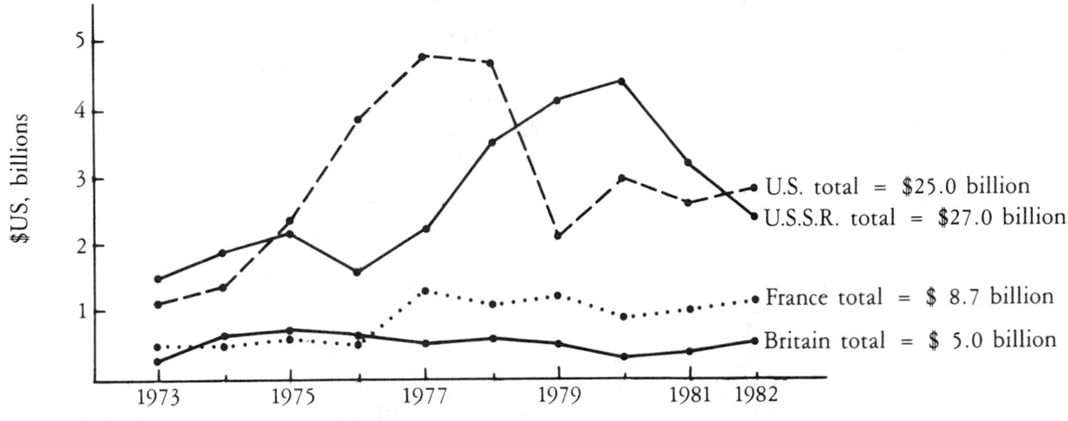

Source: SIPRI Yearbook, 1983, pp. 292–293.

2. The Arab isolation of Egypt after the Egyptian-Israeli peace, an indication of Third World discontinuity.
3. The withdrawal of Iran from familiar inter-Arab politics and development of solidarity following the right-wing revolution of the Ayatollah Khomeini.
4. War between Iran and Iraq.
5. Threat of Soviet expansion beyond Afghanistan.
6. Left-wing revolution in Central America.
7. War in Lebanon involving civil factions and both Israel and Syria.
8. Threat of war in southern Africa in face of South African commando raids on Lesotho, Somalia, Seychelles and Angola to wipe out sanctuaries of guerillas taking part in the fight for Namibian independence.

Regional conflict, then, is at the base of the huge military bill of the Third World, together with ideological competition, and sometimes revolution, between Western-oriented governments and Socialist movements. The largest single problem is the Middle East, where persistent Arab-Israeli difficulties threaten to erupt into major war; where Iran and Iraq are at war with great assistance from extra-regional countries including the United States, the Soviet Union and France; and where the military threat to maintain a free flow of oil to the West results in substantial expenditure. In the period from 1973 through 1982, the Middle East accounted for $380 billion of the Third World's entire military bill, representing 52 percent of the whole.

Military expenditures in the Third World have been increasing since 1974 more rapidly than general economic growth. The consequence is that an expanding share of national income is lavished on armaments, so that military costs are a severe drain on economic growth potential. In addition, Third World countries together expend two to three times as much for modern arms annually as they receive in foreign non-military assistance. Although many have attempted to recover some of the losses incurred by military expenditure by assigning troops to economic development projects, it is generally acknowledged that the excessive and costly arms build-up among developing countries is a luxurious indulgence undertaken at immense expense to social and economic development.

The cost of maintaining the Soviet-American strategic arms race so dominates thinking about world military expenditures that the cost of arming the Third World is often overlooked. But for advocates of the conventional theory of development, the military costs of the Third World are every bit as wasteful as the Balance of Terror. Critics of American arms expenditure are fond of reciting the number of hospitals, schools, modern farms, medical discoveries and social programs that could be supported by the money spent on a new generation of missiles. Those who subscribe to the conventional theory of development are equally quick to point out that were it not for the military investment in the Third World over the last decade—$730 billion—social and economic development could have been accelerated immeasurably. It seems ironic to these commentators that so much should be wasted on arms, only to have the same governments coming back to the Western capitals and to the United Nations and its aid agencies requesting still more funds for development.

3. Luxury Consumption

In many poor countries, the abysmal poverty of the masses contrasts sharply with the astronomical wealth of a handful of landlords, maharajas, princes or industrial barons. "Stratification" (unequal distribution) of wealth is much sharper in the LDCs than in the wealthy nations. For example, in Colombia the top 5 percent of the population gets 42 percent of the income. (In the USA, the top 5 percent of the population gets 16 percent of the income.) In more than half of developing countries, less than 10 percent of farms have over half the cultivable acreage. In general, the percentage distribution of income is less equitable in the LDCs.

It might be thought that concentrations of wealth could be invested in economic development. But the rich throw away much of this potential through luxury spending on automobiles and baronial estates, instead of putting it to developmental purposes. Wealthy classes in the Third World tend to emulate privileged Americans and Europeans. In addition some send sizable amounts abroad to avoid taxes and possible confiscation. The "Swiss-banks" factor is said to have drained more than $3 billion out of Latin America alone in unauthorized outflows during the 1960s. Keeping this money at home for useful investment could have replaced about one-third of foreign aid. One wonders what might have been done to modernize Iran had not much of the late Shah's wealth left the country, perhaps as much as $24 billion to the United States alone (as claimed by the Iranian government during the negotiations for release of American hostages in 1980–81). Clearly, luxury consumption by the rich and nearly rich is a serious drain on economic development.

4. Corruption

Another factor is the corruption of public officials, an especially acute problem in some developing countries. In the United States more than 90 percent of the taxes that are due (after loopholes) are successfully collected, but some LDCs have an actual collection rate below 50 percent. The state treasury—one of the main instruments of development—is depleted by tax evasion. In addition, allotments from the treasury are eroded by the corruption of project administrators at every level. A flood of resources put into the pipeline at one end can come out the other end reduced to a trickle. Sometimes corruption takes the form of "legitimate" expenditures such as luxury cars for officials and inflated expense accounts.

Another form of waste that we may list under corruption is lavish expenditure on prestige projects whose only function is to satisfy the needs of the ruling elites. Examples include opulent presidential palaces, ostentatious airports used only by the rich and other relatively private luxuries. Taken together, these various forms of corruption are a significant drain on the process of capital accumulation.

5. Management Inefficiency

The management of a thriving economy is an enormously complex affair both economically and politically. In addition to tax revenue, economic managers must arrange for finance, negotiate loans at tolerable interest rates, marshal human resources, establish priorities, create infrastructures, train personnel for industrial functions, make judgments about risks and probable profits, induce investments from internal and external sources, ensure economic efficiency and productivity and perform thousands of other integrated functions. Modern economies are far too complicated to be guided by an "invisible hand" or other self-regulator. Instead, countless well-trained specialists are needed both for creation and coordination. As the musician must know the scale before sight-reading Beethoven, so must a growing economy develop around trained and dedicated specialists. In realization of this, the developing countries have for the past three decades sent their most promising young scientists and managers to the industrialized world for education and training. Many of these have gone either to the United States or Western Europe for training in capitalist economics or to the Soviet Union for training in socialist economics. The objective is to improve the speed and efficiency of economic development without incurring additional dependence upon or interference by foreign interests.

The long-range costs of inefficient planning and economic implementation are illustrated dramatically in the spending binge carried on by the OPEC countries from 1974 through 1978. During that time they spent more than $400 billion on development projects, and Western observers estimate that more than half of it may have wasted.

> Immediate social and political consequences of rapid development were already evident: inflation, unsound organization, an excessive building boom, a large influx of foreigners, an adverse impact on agriculture and traditional industries and often a lopsided distribution of wealth. These problems, in turn, led to a weakening of established social and political values, accompanied by disappointment and resentment.[7]

Foreign Economic Assistance

As we have seen, the less developed countries are typically low-income agrarian societies that devote the greater portion of their economic activity to subsistence production. Industrial development and agricultural mechanization are the keys to economic expansion, but these are inhibited by a shortage of capital rooted in low productivity. The small capital surpluses that do accumulate are depleted by population growth, military expenditures, luxury consumption, corruption and inefficient management. The basic solution, in the conventional view,

7. Quoted from Robert Stobaugh and Daniel Yergin, "Energy: An Emergency Telescoped," *Foreign Affairs,* America and the World 1979 issue, pp. 562–95 at pp. 564–65.

is to find new sources of capital and to use more effectively the capital that is available.

While LDCs are suffering from a scarcity of capital and technology, these assets exist in surplus in the developed countries. Can the rich states, at reasonable cost to themselves, stimulate the systems of the poor states by injecting economic nutrients at critical points? Can we devise an effective means of capital transfer to "prime the pump" of development, without making unreasonable demands on the benevolence of the prosperous peoples? Four forms of assistance from the developed nations to the LDCs have dominated the theory and practice of the conventional view: (1) foreign aid; (2) foreign trade; (3) foreign direct investment; and (4) technical assistance.

1. Foreign Aid

Foreign aid is a transfer of publicly held or publicly guaranteed resources to one or more developing countries, either in the form of direct funding or in commodities and goods subsidized by the donor country. It can take the form of outright grants or of long-term, low-interest loans. It may come directly from a single country (called bilateral aid) or from an international organization or other funding consortium that has use of the funds of several donor states (called multilateral aid). When loans are involved, they may be made on a short-term basis (usually for not more than one year), or on an intermediate basis (usually for one to ten years), or for the long term (ten or more years, usually twenty-five but sometimes as long as forty years). Because of the length of time for repayment and the favorable interest rates, developing countries usually prefer long-term loans to others.

As evidence of the growth of long-term capital for use by the Third World, studies show that in 1970 the total amount of public and publicly guaranteed external capital that flowed to the Third World was $10.3 billion. By 1981, that amount had risen to $78.6 billion. This huge annual increase is attributed to a number of causes. One is that while the industrialized nations are not giving a larger share of their wealth to the Third World, their total wealth as measured in gross national product is increasing, so even a fixed percentage results in a larger total amount. More important, however, is the determination on the part of the Western world not to permit certain economies to collapse. This is particularly true of such nations as South Korea, Thailand, Egypt, Israel, Indonesia and the larger economies of Latin America.

Of the total amount of new public and publicly guaranteed capital that flowed to the Third World in 1981, $55.3 billion, or 70 percent, went to just fifteen countries. The amounts that they received ranged from $1.6 billion to $13.4 billion. Because of payments due on earlier loans, however, many of the recipients found that the value of their loans diminished instantly. In the case of Algeria, for example, a loan of $2.8 billion was used immediately to make payments of $2.4 billion on outstanding loans, leaving a net value of less than a half-billion dollars. And Mexico, which enjoyed the largest new flow of capital ($13.4 billion), received only $9.6 billion after paying installments on loans due. Table 5–3 shows the values of new capital to the fifteen largest Third World recipients for 1981.

Of the total contribution in 1981, 35 percent originated in the Western trading partners (including Japan) and 10 percent in the OPEC countries. Allowing for small contributions from the Soviet Union and China, public international organizations, principally the World Bank Group of the United Nations (The World Bank and the International Bank for Reconstruction and Development) provided slightly less than half. The principal national lenders are listed in Table 5–4.

TABLE 5–3
Fifteen principal Third World recipients of public and publicly guaranteed external capital, 1981, together with annual repayment debt and net value of new capital, expressed in billions of US dollars.

Recipient	*New Capital Flow*	*Payments Due*	*Net Value of New Capital*
Mexico	13.4	3.8	9.6
Brazil	9.0	3.6	5.4
Korea (So.)	6.1	1.8	4.3
Egypt	3.5	1.6	1.9
Algeria	2.8	2.4	0.4
Israel	2.5	1.4	1.1
Indonesia	2.4	1.0	1.4
Venezuela	2.1	1.4	0.7
India	2.0	0.6	1.4
Malaysia	1.9	0.2	1.7
Turkey	1.8	0.5	1.3
Greece	1.8	0.6	1.2
Argentina	1.8	1.1	0.7
Morocco	1.7	0.6	1.1
Portugal	1.6	0.6	1.0

Source: The World Bank, *World Development Report 1983*, Table 15, pp. 176–177.

TABLE 5–4
Principal national suppliers of public and publicly guaranteed external capital for the Third World, 1981, expressed in billions of US dollars.

Country	*Amount Loaned*	*Country*	*Amount Loaned*
1. Saudi Arabia	5.8	9. Sweden	0.9
2. United States	5.8	10. Norway	0.8
3. France	4.8	11. United Arab	0.8
4. W. Germany	3.2	Emirates	0.7
5. Japan	3.2	12. Kuwait	0.7
6. Britain	2.2	13. Italy	0.7
7. Netherlands	1.5	14. Australia	
8. Canada	1.2		

Source: The World Bank, *World Development Report 1983,* from Table 18, pp. 182–183.

When the United Nations initiated the first Development Decade (1960–70), it was hoped that the developed countries might eventually raise their international assistance to a level of 1 percent of gross national product per year. Later, when the United Nations Conference on Trade and Development (UNCTAD) became the major economic voice of the Third World, the goal was scaled down to a more modest 0.7 percent. Among the principal Western lenders, however, only the Netherlands had ever exceeded a full percentage of GNP through 1981, and only Denmark, Sweden and Norway had crossed the 0.7 percent mark for a single year. Table 5–5 shows the performances of several principal industrialized nations with respect to the internationally established goals.

By 1970, after having given more than $125 billion in bilateral economic and military assistance since the Second World War, plus substantial amounts of Food for Peace and multilateral aid, American willingness to contribute had declined. Increased awareness of unanswered social needs within the United States has led to demands by Congress and the public that resources be used to solve domestic problems first. Aid appropriations are a favorite target of the taxpayer revolt. In addition, some liberals have begun to oppose foreign assistance as a potential foot in the door for American interventionism, while conservatives are offended by hostility toward the United States among the more than seventy-five developing countries that have shared this largesse. Some US economists have come to see aid as a worn-out formula that doesn't work. Billions of dollars were poured into the Alliance for Progress in Latin America, for example, without achieving the decisive development breakthrough that had been prom-

TABLE 5–5
International aid by principal suppliers with respect to the original UNDP goal and the revised UNCTAD goal, expressed in percentage of GNP for maximum annual contribution and average annual contribution, 1971–81.

	Maximum Annual		*Ten-Year Average*	
United Arab Emirates	11.9			
Saudi Arabia	8.2			
Kuwait	8.2		6.8	United Arab Emirates
Netherlands	1.0		6.6	Saudi Arabia
Sweden	1.0	UNDP Goal (1%)	5.0	Kuwait
Norway	0.9		0.9	Netherlands
France	0.7		0.9	Sweden
		UNCTAD Goal	0.8	Norway
West Germany	0.5	(0.7%)	0.6	France
United Kingdom	0.5		0.5	Canada
Canada	0.5		0.5	Australia
Australia	0.5		0.4	West Germany
United States	0.3		0.4	United Kingdom
Japan	0.3		0.2	United States
Italy	0.2		0.2	Japan
			0.1	Italy

Source: World Bank, *World Development Report, 1983.*

ised by President Kennedy. In general, the American disillusionment with aid makes expansion of giving by the United States unlikely.

As the figures demonstrate, however, other industrialized countries and the oil exporting countries of the Third World have entered where the United States has tended to retreat. Some experts have argued that the OPEC countries have become lenders principally as a means of offsetting Western charges that OPEC's price increases throughout the period from 1973–1983 had a more devastating impact upon Third World development than did any Western policy, since the non-oil-producing Third World countries were faced with the same increases as were the industrial giants. Moreover, while the industrial trading partners had industrial produce with which to balance (at least partially balance) their international trade and capital accounts, the non-oil developing countries were driven further into debt by OPEC policies. Much of OPEC's lending policy was designed to ease this burden, and was in the form of petroleum subsidies.

Unfortunately, increases by all donors will not be sufficient to meet the capital needs of the less developed countries during the rest of this century. Some economists believe that the LDCs could usefully absorb five or ten times as much outside capital as will be available. The present prospect is a general decline in the significance of foreign aid, compared to population and growth needs.

2. Foreign Trade

It is for more than poetic reasons that foreign aid and foreign trade are considered by the conventional view of development to be the principal ingredients of modernization. Since self-sufficiency is impossible in most economies, the acquisition of foreign sources of goods (imports) and foreign sources of markets for the export of products are essential elements in economic expansion.

More specifically, foreign trade plays several important roles in a developing economy, one of which relates directly to foreign aid. Aid, which in effect is the temporary importation of money, brings new debt, both in the form of principal that must be repaid either gradually or at some distant point, and in the form of interest. Hence, every dollar borrowed represents a dollar plus in the debt column. Since domestic sources of public revenue are scarce in developing economies, profit from the export of products is the safest route to repayment of debt, or to "debt service." Export trade, then, is an important source of new capital. The certainty of export markets is also important in determining the volume of a product that will be produced, a factor that, in turn, determines the selling price of the item in both domestic and foreign markets. The price, for its part, helps to determine the ability of the product to compete in world markets. Finally, export trade is essential in maintaining the developing economy's trade balance. While accumulating a capital debt by borrowing foreign money, a developing economy cannot afford also to amass a trade deficit, a situation in which the value of its imports exceeds the value of its exports. Part of a development strategy, therefore, must be the manufacture of products for export in sufficient quantities and at competitive prices so that the sale of goods in world markets will at least equal in value goods that are imported.

Export performance, then, is a critical indicator of development progress in the conventional theory of development. Evidence shows that in the period 1965–73, the Third World's export performance parallelled that of the industrialized market economies at only a fraction of a percent lower. From 1973–85, however, as the export volume of the developed world continued to decline, the Third World's leveled off and exceeded both the industrialized market economies and the world. And after 1985, it is projected that while Third World exports will once again parallel those of the developed world, they will exceed the latter in volume. Figure 5–4 reveals these trends.

But what of import trade? Needless to say, one way to reduce the need to export (if one were not looking for profit) would be to reduce imports. But in a developing economy, this luxury is unavailable. Every development strategy attempts to convert reliance on exhaustable raw materials to manufactured or semimanufactured commodities. This conversion requires industrialization, thus introducing needs that are not common to the young economy: building materials (processed metals, cement), infrastructure (electricity generating plants, heavy transportation, importing and exporting facilities), machinery for production, etc. These are available only abroad, and although prices may be restrained by competition, they are very costly indeed. Thus, in order to prepare to manufacture goods for export, the economy must

Western aid—simple humanitarianism, or a worn-out formula that doesn't work?

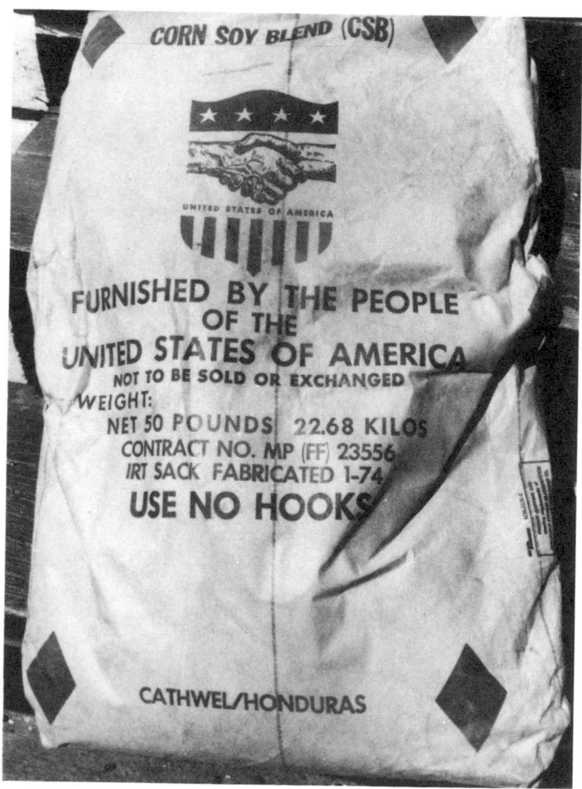

Source: Agency for International Development

FIGURE 5–4
Comparative changes in export rates past and projected, 1965–1995, for the world, the industrial market economies and developing countries.

Source: The World Bank, *World Development Report 1983,* adapted from Table 3.3, p. 31.

first import the wherewithal to produce. Import and export trade, accordingly, present a precarious problem of balance from the start, as do commodities with capital.

3. Foreign Direct Investment

Because the flow of governmental foreign aid is not on the recommended scale, conventional theorists look for other forms of capital transfers from developed to less developed states. Long-term private investment by profit-seeking firms offers the greatest possibility of expanded resource flow. Billions of dollars move through the money markets of the United States, Western Europe and Japan every day, and if even a fraction were directed to the Third World the effect would be substantial. But the share of global foreign investment going to developing countries has in fact been declining as the wealthy nations focus their trade and investment increasingly on each other. The problem for the conventional approach is to attract new interest from global business to invest in developing countries.

This positive attitude toward foreign capital, advocated by Western-oriented governments such as Indonesia, Brazil and Taiwan, is directly opposed to the radical ideology of states like Libya and Cuba, which depict foreign investment as a form of neocolonialism (see below). Even the Western-oriented states share some fear of the multinational giants like General Motors, whose $60 billion in annual sales dwarfs the GNPs of more than 110 countries. But conventional theorists argue that controlled foreign investment is a proven stimulus to rapid growth, as demonstrated in South Korea, Brazil, Nigeria and other countries. To attract more foreign investment, many countries maintain public relations offices and consulates in the major capital centers (New York, London, Paris and Tokyo, for instance) and publish advertisements and lavish inserts in the world financial press (such as *The Wall Street Journal, Fortune*) singing the praises of investment in their economies.

Advocates of increased foreign investment enumerate the following advantages of foreign capital.[8]

1. *Jobs* Most positions created by foreign firms go to indigenous workers. For example, US multinational enterprises operating in the developing countries employ more than three million locals as against only 25,000 American nationals located abroad.
2. *Technology* The foreign firm brings the most advanced methods and technologies, acting as an agent for the transfer of new knowledge. This spills over to local subcontractors as production is integrated in the local economy.
3. *Import substitution* Foreign investment often helps the balance of payments of the less developed country by enabling it to produce for itself what it once imported.
4. *Market access* The foreign firm brings international market connections conducive to a continued inflow of capital and the expansion of export opportunities.
5. *Efficiency* The profit incentive is keyed to cost reduction and maximal use of resources. The foreign investor has a natural motive and the managerial skills to organize local people and information in the most cost effective and productive way.
6. *Demonstration effect* Local enterprises may be induced to utilize the techniques and management ideas of the efficient foreign branch to maintain their competitive position.

8. Roberto Campos, "Economic Policy and Political Myths," in Paul E. Sigmund, editor, *The Ideologies of the Developing Nations* (New York: Praeger, 1967), pp. 418–24.

7. *Planning* The international investor is in an excellent position to assess the comparative advantages of local production in world markets, and he may aid in the identification of ideal lead sectors for planned national economic development.[9]

For all these reasons, the politically more conservative voices in the Third World reject the isolationist course of a closed door to Western capitalism.

4. Technical Assistance

A third form of international aid to the developing countries is technical assistance. Most of the world's research and development is conducted in the rich countries. If the results of technological advances are not to be confined to the privileged peoples and if the benefits of scientific discovery are to be shared by all of humanity, a means must be found to facilitate what has been called the transnational migration of knowledge. Examples of technical assistance include the Atoms for Peace Program, under which the United States has given small atomic reactors and fissionable materials to more than fifty countries to promote peaceful applications of nuclear technology; the arid zone research program, under which the United States supports research on desalinization of sea water by advanced means; and most significant of all, scientific advantages in agriculture known collectively as the Green Revolution, which brings to developing nations modern cultivation techniques and new seed strains that make possible a dramatic increase in farm productivity.

Using the new methods of the Green Revolution, the output of grain cereals (rice, corn, wheat) can be multiplied without any expansion of acreage or of the labor force. For example, high-yielding dwarf variety wheat, pioneered in Mexico, has a genetic potential double or triple that of the best yielders among older, tall-strawed varieties.[10] With American help, this advance has been introduced, along with necessary supporting improvements in fertilizer, insecticides, weed killers, irrigation and machinery on the Indian subcontinent.

The results have been spectacular. India increased its wheat production by 80 percent in four years, Pakistan by 60 percent in two. These two nations have long been known as major food-deficit suf-

9. Harry G. Johnson, "The Multinational Corporation as an Agency of Economic Development," in Barbara Ward, Lenore D'Anjou, and J. D. Runnalls, editors, *The Widening Gap* (New York: Columbia University Press, 1971), pp. 242–51.

10. Norman Borlaug, "The Green Revolution, Peace, and Humanity," *Population Research Bulletin*, selection no. 35, January 1971.

ferers, dependent on charitable imports. Now they are approaching not only self-sufficiency but even surplus and a capacity for export.

A similar advance in high-yielding dwarf variety rice, IR8, has ended the Philippines' historic dependence on rice imports. Transfer of the Philippine advances to Sri Lanka increased the latter's production by 26 percent in three years. Many other countries are benefiting from these hybrid grains, including Afghanistan, Burma, Indonesia, Iran, Laos, Malaysia, Morocco, Nepal, Tunisia, Turkey and Vietnam.[11] It is also known that the Green Revolution is finding its way into the Communist world.

These impressive achievements have vast political and economic consequences. A few years ago, leading demographers were predicting a global food crisis caused by population expansion. It is not clear whether this problem is now solved or only postponed, but the present trend seems to be toward food self-sufficiency. This trend will reduce external dependence and relieve balance-of-payments problems. Internally, productivity increases may support advances in industrialization. Many of the now advanced nations squeezed their surpluses out of agriculture to finance industrial development, and we can expect this pattern to be repeated in the LDCs. Thus, the Green Revolution may promote a more dynamic political and economic prospect for the developing countries.

There are, however, some costs that must be accounted for in the balance sheet of the Green Revolution. The intensive use of chemical fertilizers and insecticides raises ecological issues that are now familiar in the wealthier nations. Fish and wildlife are endangered, and the runoff carries excessive nutrients and poisons to the oceans, whose ability to sustain pollution is not infinite. The vulnerability of the new strains to disease requires increasing dosages of insecticide, with the long-term danger that new insect varieties will develop that are resistant to all known poisons.

There are also social problems associated with the Green Revolution. Advanced agriculture is based on the substitution of capital for labor to pay for machines, seeds, fertilizer, insecticides and irrigation systems. As agriculture becomes capital- rather than labor-intensive, small farmers are squeezed out. Agricultural employment may be reduced as productivity increases. Thus, the effect of the Green Revolution is to widen class disparities rather than to narrow them, increasing the characteristic problem noted earlier of stratification. The initial beneficiaries of the Green Revolution may be the already prosperous rather

11. Lester Brown, "The Social Impact of the Green Revolution," *International Conciliation,* no. 581, January 1971.

than the suffering poor. But advocates of the conventional theory argue that the flood of benefits will inevitably trickle down to the lower classes, and that the solution to maldistribution effects is rational planning by governments rather than forgoing the possibilities of the new approach.

The benefits of technical assistance are not limited, of course, to the agricultural sector. In industry, computers and advanced electronic equipment have been transferred to the developing countries to improve productivity and to expand industrial potential. Computers have also been introduced to improve managerial efficiency and education. Advances in chemical technology have enabled many of the oil-rich developing countries to improve their own refining capabilities, thus permitting them to deliver finished products rather than crude oil to industrial consumers.

Furthermore, both governments and international organizations such as the United Nations make technical experts available to the developing countries. Faced with technical problems in management, industry, finance or agriculture, developing countries can call upon foreign personnel from foreign agencies for assistance. These persons are part of the network by which technology is gradually transferred to the Third World from the industrialized centers of the world.

Summary

In broad outline, the conventional theory sees the root of underdevelopment as internal stagnation, and the solution as international aid from the advanced countries. The key forms of international help are foreign aid, foreign trade, foreign investment and technical assistance. Only with vigorous and benevolent intervention by the prosperous nations will the sharp international cleavage between rich and poor be reduced. Figure 5–5 demonstrates the successful consequences of three decades of aid, trade, investment and technical assistance from the industrialized world to the developing countries by comparing productivity in the industrialized economies with the Third World's aggregate productivity increase for the period 1973–83.

The Radical Theory of Development

The radical theory of development disagrees fundamentally with the foregoing view regarding both the causes and cures of underdevelopment. To the conventional theorist, the cause is internal inefficiency and the cure is outside help from the developed states. To the radical,

FIGURE 5–5
Comparative annual changes in production, 1973–83, in the non-oil developing countries and the industrialized countries.

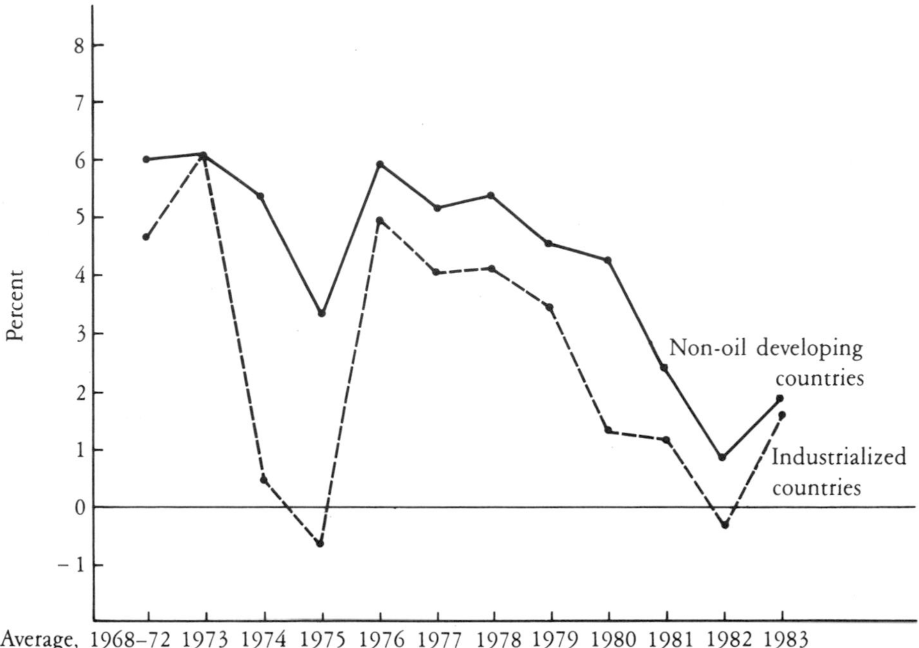

Source: International Monetary Fund, *World Economic Outlook,* May 1983. Adapted from Tables 1 and 2, pp. 170–71.

the cause is international exploitation by exactly these developed "friends," and the cure is a fundamental change of international relations between the poor and the rich. Indeed, the very medicine proposed by the conventional theorist—technical assistance, foreign investment, trade and aid—is considered the root of the disease by the radical, for whom investment, trade and aid are extractive mechanisms that systematically siphon away the wealth of the developing countries.

The two schools disagree on basic assumptions regarding the global inequality of life. To the conventional theorist, the rich are ahead of the poor because of dedicated effort and managerial skills. To the radical, the Western peoples achieved their advantage, "not by the laws of the market, but by a particular sequence of world conquest and land occupation."[12] It follows from the conventional view that

12. See Ward, D'Anjou and Runnalls, editors, *The Widening Gap,* pp. 152–164, where the two views are eloquently contrasted. For major expressions of the radical theory, see Samir Amin, *Unequal Development* (New York: Monthly Review Press, 1976); and Paul Baran and Paul Sweezy, *Monopoly Capital* (New York: Monthly Review

when the poor make up the gap in productive skills (with the help of foreign aid, and so on) the economic gap will close. It follows from the radical view that only cutting the international relationship will end the unjust division of the world's wealth.

The conventional view posits an essential similarity between the development problems of the poor today and the problems successfully mastered by the now rich states in earlier periods. It says in effect, "Just as the United States and Europe developed yesterday and Japan and Mexico are developing today, so will you, the late starters, develop tomorrow." Development is portrayed as a linear process in which every economy passes through certain known stages of economic growth.[13]

Radical analysis rejects this portrayal of the developing countries. The economies of the big capitalist states started as largely autonomous markets under domestic control, though international trade and investment were conducted within careful limits. The economies of the Third World, however, enter the modern development epoch as mere subsystems of global capitalism, having long ago been penetrated by foreign interests and been made economic satellites of the dominant states of the North. The global system consists of a "center"—Europe, America and Japan—and a "periphery"—the dependent economies of Latin America, Africa and Asia. The basic economic institutions of the dependencies were formed in response to the insistent demands of the industrial world, rather than in relation to local needs and interests. The typical dependency economy is geared to the export of commodities needed by the industrial center and the import of products from the center. This is known as the pattern of foreign-oriented development, in which external rather than domestic influences shape the society, economy and political structure.

What produced this lopsided and unnatural development, so heavily dependent on foreign interests? In the earliest period, it was caused by massive raw material hunger on the part of the industrial nations. The underdeveloped regions, subdued and controlled by the superior military force of the center, were reduced to cheap suppliers of raw materials, useful mainly for their wells or mines or tea or rubber. Cuba became a sugar plantation, Bolivia a tin mine, the Arab world an oil field, Southeast Asia a rubber plantation, Gabon (in Barbara Ward's

Ward, *The Radical Economic World View* (New York: Basic Books, 1979). Gunnar Myrdal, *Against the Stream: Critical Essays on Economics* (New York: Vintage, 1972), presents some challenging critiques of the conventional theory of development.

13. Walt W. Rostow, *The Stages of Economic Growth* (London: Cambridge University Press, 1960), is the standard source for this view.

phrase) "a faint appendage to a mineral deposit." In many cases, local impulses to produce industrial goods for home consumption were quelled by the dominant foreigners, as the dependency was needed as a secure market for exactly these products from the center. Thus foreign domination served to channel economic activity into a high degree of forced specialization.

In general, one main export item accounts for a much higher portion of foreign sales by poor nations than by rich nations—46 percent compared to 17 percent. Thus it is fair to say that the typical developing country is a one- or two-product exporter, while the typical developed nation has a diversified economy. Venezuela exports 90 percent oil; Colombia depends on coffee; Cuba has not escaped sugar dependence; two-thirds of Chilean exports are copper. Should the mineral be exhausted (as is happening in Bolivia) or a cheaper source be found for the national product (such as the seabed), or should changing consumer preferences reduce demand, dependent economies could be destroyed. In other words, highly specialized economies are dangerously subject to the vicissitudes of the world market.

The Terms-of-Trade Problem

The export commodities in which the LDCs specialize tend strongly to be "primary products"—minerals, fuels and crops taken more or less directly from the earth, with minimal processing. Approximately 80 percent of the exports of poor countries in 1973 were primary products, compared to about 20 percent for rich countries. Conversely, 80 percent of the exports of the rich countries were manufactures, compared to only 20 percent for the poor countries. The poor sell raw materials to the rich and from them buy finished goods.

This commodity composition of trade adversely affects developing economies. One reason is the tendency of primary product export prices to fluctuate substantially and sometimes extremely in the world market. Colombian coffee, for example, earned $7 in 1977, but fell to $3 in 1981. In the same interval, cocoa fell from over $5 to below $2. More significantly, while primary product export prices are dropping, industrial product import prices tend to rise rather steadily. In fact, a study done by the World Bank shows that when the export prices of a large sample of agricultural and mining (excluding oil) products are measured against the rising cost of industrial imports, the commodity prices of exports from the Third World were actually lower in 1982 than at any time since the end of the Second World War. Figure 5–6 demonstrates the trend that resulted in this circumstance. When large portions of an economic activity and a labor force

FIGURE 5–6
An index of Third World primary product export prices measured against industrial product import prices, 1950–82.

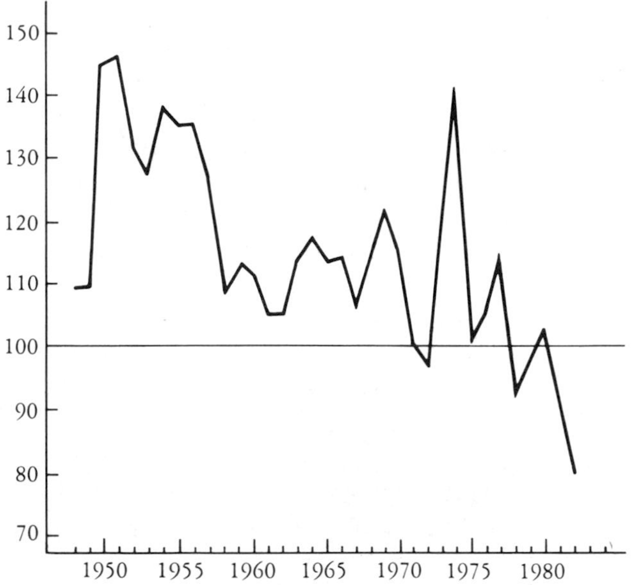

Source: The World Bank, *World Development Report 1983,* p. 11.

are tied to export products that are so unstable in the world market, wild boom-and-bust cycles may result that are socially hazardous and detrimental to orderly economic development. Furthermore, it is this kind of price decay with respect to industrial products that Third World economists consider an intrinsic inequality in trade between the industrialized world and the Third World.[14]

The relationship between world prices for primary products and those for industrial products is at the heart of the terms-of-trade problem for the developing economies. Defined as the ratio of export value divided by import value, terms of trade becomes a measure of the extent to which international trade assists in the development of a national economy. On balance, the developing countries conduct their most disadvantageous trade with the developed market economies because in the terms of that trade, Third World primary products are exported at unstable and declining world prices, while industrial pro-

14. Two classics developing this view from different perspectives are: the United Nations Conference on Trade and Development, *Towards a New Trade Policy for Development* (1964), universally known as the Prebisch Report, and Arghiri Emmanuel, *Unequal Exchange: The Imperialism of International Trade* (New York: Monthly Review Press, 1972).

duce is imported at stable and increasing prices. Nonetheless, trade with the developed market economies continues to be a larger part of the aggregate trade of the Third World, thus annually accentuating the terms-of-trade dilemma. As a consequence, billions of dollars have been drained out of the developing world simply by loss of value relative to industrial goods. It is significant that this drain results not from explicit imperialism or exploitation, but rather from the quiet operation of market laws seemingly beyond anyone's control—so-called objective world market prices.

One might reasonably expect that as industrialization increases in the Third World, dependence upon primary commodities would abate and terms of trade improve. In fact, however, despite the efforts made at industrializing the Third World, few of its members have increased by more than a few percent the portion of total production that is not related to primary products. The structure of production is such that only a handful of developing countries have industrial sectors which, as a percentage of total production, are equal to those of the fifteen largest industrialized market economies (greater than 24 percent of total production). They are listed in Table 5–6.

Elsewhere in the Third World, agricultural and mining products continue to be the principal focuses of economic development. And even in the countries listed, comparability of industrial sectors to those of the largest market economies is possible only in part because with the technological revolution and the growing service sectors in the West, industrial productivity is actually falling.

Productivity Increases The terms-of-trade factor puts the poor states in a position that cannot be compared to that of the rich states in an

TABLE 5–6
Principal industrialized nations of the Third World measured by manufacturing as a percentage of annual gross domestic product.

Argentina	Singapore
Brazil	South Africa
Egypt	South Korea
Israel	Syria
Nicaragua	Turkey
Peru	Uruguay
Philippines	Yugoslavia
Portugal	Zimbabwe

Source: The World Bank, *World Development Report 1983,* Table 3, pp. 152–53.

earlier period. The now advanced states achieved rapid increases in productivity during their "takeoff" stage, and these are regarded as the key to their success. But today, the primary price decay erodes productivity gains. Malaysia, for example, increased its rubber exports almost 25 percent from 1960 to 1968—from 850 to 1,100 thousand tons—while reducing its plantation labor force significantly. This is a notable gain in productivity. But its *income* from rubber sales *declined* by about 33 percent during these years as prices fell. In effect, productivity increases were passed along to foreign consumers in the form of lowered prices, rather than to Malaysian workers in the form of higher wages and living standards. The terms-of-trade problem can be a treadmill on which it is necessary to run faster and faster just to stand still.

Inelastic Demand Explanations of this phenomenon are based on disadvantages of primary products against finished goods. One is the relative "inelasticity of demand" for primary goods—only so many bananas will be consumed no matter how many are produced, tending to reduce prices after the market is saturated.

Unorganized Labor Another factor is the position of labor in the Third World compared to the industrial countries. Workers in the advanced states are relatively well organized into trade unions, and can command a share of the gains from productivity increases. The comparative weakness of labor organizations in the Third World, however, allows productivity gains to be taken by management in the form of profits or to be passed on to consumers in the form of lower prices. Productivity gains in the center are taken at home, but productivity gains in the periphery tend to flow away—to the center—in the form of lower prices or in profits remitted to foreign owners. The deck is stacked in favor of the already developed world, and mere productivity advances of the type advocated by the conventional theorists will not change the unfavorable rules.

The Radical View of Foreign Investment

While the conventional theorist views the multinational corporation as an agency for the transfer of capital and technology for the betterment of the developing countries, the radical theorist sees it as an instrument of foreign control extracting exorbitant profits. US investment, for example, increases its capital annually in both the developed and the developing worlds. However, the annual earnings yielded to American investors in the LDCs greatly exceeds in per-

TABLE 5–7
Annual American earnings as a percent of investment in developed and developing countries, 1970–79, expressed in billions of US dollars.

	American Investments in Industrialized Countries			American Investments in Developing Countries		
	Investment	Earnings	%Earnings/ Investments	Investments	Earnings	%Earnings/ Investments
1970	51.8	4.6	9	19.2	2.9	15
1974	82.9	10.4	13	19.5	7.9	40
1977	108.0	6.0	6	33.7	7.8	21
1979	137.9	24.4	18	47.8	12.7	27

Source: Statistical Abstract of the United States, 1980, Table 1529, p. 865.

centage the annual yield from investments in the developed world, as is demonstrated in Table 5–7. The ratio of earnings in developing economies as compared with industrial economies typically runs about 50–300 percent higher in the developing. Furthermore, taking 1979 as a typical year, American earnings on manufacturing investments in developed countries ran at 17 percent while similar investments in developing economies drew only 14 percent; but in petroleum investments, while the rate of return in developed countries was 21 percent, in the developing economies it was a sizzling 86 percent. So while Americans have complained that OPEC policies have destabilized the world oil market, American investors have profited handsomely. The result is an accelerated rate of economic penetration and exploitation, followed by the removal from the developing economies of those earnings which might be used as additional investment capital for the host economy. To this extent, American investors are actually *de*capitalizing the underdeveloped economies.

Multinational firms use several devices to evade legal restrictions on excess profits. For example, one foreign subsidiary of a multinational conglomerate typically buys some of its intermediate components from other branches of the same parent located in other countries. The internal "prices" of such sales may be manipulated by the parent for optimal bookkeeping results, taking losses in one subsidiary where profits are restricted and showing them in another where they are not. Other devices include the manipulation of royalties, management fees and other internally negotiated "costs." The multinational enterprise has a variety of options to remit profits without defying legal limits.

Another objection to foreign capital is its effect on the social and

Source: AP/Wide World Photo

Salvadoran guerilla denounces forthcoming presidential election in his country at La Palma, later site of peace talks between revolutionists and the elected government, 1984.

class structure of the host society. The foreign firm is at first typically an isolated enclave of modern economics in a sea of underdevelopment, but eventually a network of subcontractors extends the patterns of dependency outside the company gates. Often the multinational guest dwarfs all local enterprises—the sales revenue of the United Fruit Company, for example, exceeds the entire national budgets of countries such as Panama, Nicaragua, Honduras, Guatemala and El Salvador. The pure economic power of such an entity opens the doors of the middle and even the top strata of the official bureaucracy and creates at the same time a dependent class of local merchants and bankers. In addition, the foreign firm develops a special relationship with certain privileged sections of the labor force, sometimes by paying wages slightly above the depressed local rates. United States firms in northern Mexico, for example, are able to pay 75 cents an hour, which is more than three times the local average but at the same time less than a quarter of the rate in nearby southern Texas. Local workers are co-opted by the competition for these prized jobs. In effect, foreign capital creates satellite classes whose interests are tied to the *dependencia* syndrome.

Objections to Foreign Aid

It may seem surprising that even foreign aid is regarded with suspicion in the radical theory. If we concede that dependence on foreign capital and primary product exports is disadvantageous, wouldn't it seem to follow that aid as a form of capital transfer would give the recipient some relief?

There are several objections to this view. First, most foreign aid consists not of simple grants but of interest-bearing loans that must be repaid. The typical less developed country runs a chronic payments deficit because of the unfavorable balance of trade and the drain of excess profits to foreign firms. Borrowing foreign "aid" to make up the gap in current bills leads to mounting indebtedness and simply defers the day of reckoning, accumulating losses to be repaid in some future golden age. Borrowing from Peter to pay Paul (or "rolling over" the debt) does not break the pattern of dependency, but reinforces and perpetuates it. Foreign debt service cost the developing countries 11 percent of their export earnings in 1971 and 20 percent by 1980.

Figures abound on the total indebtedness of the Third World (see Figure 5–7). Generally, however, that debt can be expressed in three basic ways: (1) total dollar debt, (2) total debt as a percentage of either gross national product or total exports; and (3) accumulated interest liability on the cash debt.

By the beginning of 1984, the total medium and long-term debt of the Third World exceeded $575 billion; short-term debt (loans of five years or fewer) amounted to $90 billion more. Table 5–8 lists the largest debtor nations, together with total debt, debt as a percentage of gross national product, annual interest obligation, and annual debt obligation (payment due) as a percentage of GNP and as a percentage of total exports. All figures are those of the United Nations for 1981. (It is worth noting that three of these countries—Mexico, Indonesia and Venezuela—are petroleum exporters, so even the OPEC era did not save some oil producers from staggering debt.) By way of interpretation, read the table this way: Israel's total medium and long-range foreign debt for 1981 was $13.9 billion, equivalent to 23.4 percent of its gross national product for the same year; during that year it faced an interest payment of $700 million, and a total payment of interest and principal equivalent to 9.6 percent of its gross national product or 19.1 percent of its total exports for the year. Another way

FIGURE 5–7
Accumulating debt of the Third World, 1970–1983.

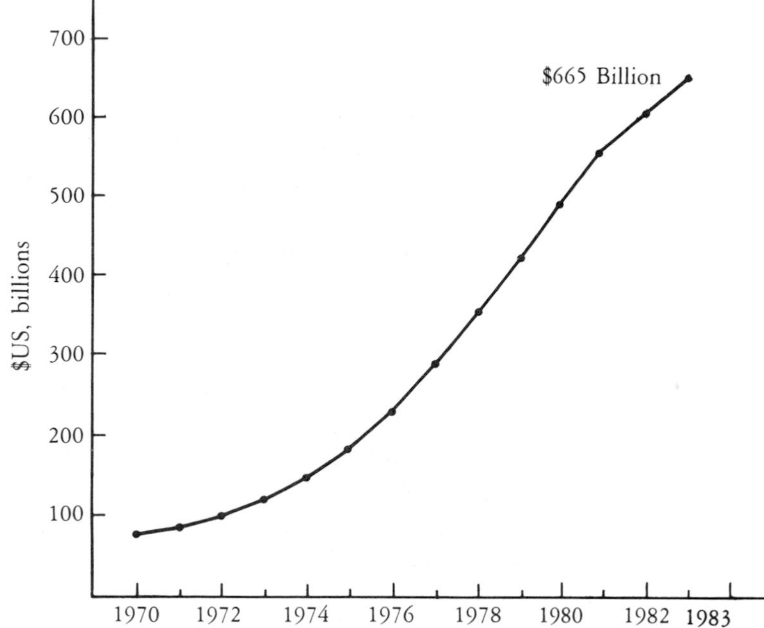

Source: For 1970–1981, The World Bank and Morgan Guaranty Trust as reported in *The Wall Street Journal,* January 29, 1981; for 1983, International Monetary Fund, *World Economic Outlook,* 1983, p. 201.

TABLE 5–8
International debt of eleven principal debtor countries for 1981, expressed in billions of US dollars.

Country	*Total Debt*	*Total as % of GNP*	*Annual Interest*	*Annual Obligation* — *As % of GNP*	*Annual Obligation* — *As % of Exports*
Brazil	$43.8	16.0	$5.0	3.1	31.9
Mexico	42.7	18.5	4.7	3.7	28.2
South Korea	20.0	32.0	1.8	5.8	13.1
India	18.0	10.8	0.4	0.6	20.9 (1970)
Indonesia	15.5	19.0	1.0	2.4	8.2
Algeria	14.4	35.2	1.5	9.5	24.9
Egypt	13.9	43.7	0.5	6.5	22.6
Israel	13.9	64.3	0.7	9.6	19.1
Turkey	13.8	23.4	0.7	2.0	15.0
Venezuela	11.4	16.9	1.7	4.4	12.4
Argentina	10.5	8.7	1.1	1.3	18.2

Source: The World Bank, *World Development Report 1983,* Table 16, pp. 178–179. (1970 is most recent figure available for India.)

to look at it is that 19.1 percent of all Israeli exports in 1981 did nothing more than cover the annual foreign debt; they contributed nothing in value to the country's economic development.

Still more alarming is the rate at which Third World debt is growing. Table 5–9 demonstrates the rate of debt growth for selected Third World countries for 1970, 1981 and 1983. These rapid increases in debt are alarming not only because of their size, but because the ability of governments to keep up with repayment schedules is in doubt. In many debtor Third World nations, debt is a multiple of total annual exports, the major source of revenue for repaying debt. In Argentina, for example, total 1983 debt was 4.24 times total exports of goods and services for the year. For Brazil the multiple for the same year was 3.59; for Chile, 2.9; for Mexico, 2.75; and for Venezuela, 1.96.[15] For all non-oil developing countries, total debt amounted to 145 percent of total exports in 1983.[16]

Under these pressing circumstances, it is not surprising that debtor nations are unable to meet their foreign obligations. Between 1974 and 1979, there were twenty-four agreements on rescheduling the payments of individual Third World countries. But in the period 1980 through 1983, the number grew to forty-one. In the years 1982 and 1983, there were as many rescheduling negotiations as there were for the entire period 1974–79.[17] And in 1983 alone, there were no fewer

TABLE 5–9
Growth in medium and long-term international debt for selected Third World countries, 1970–1983, expressed in billions of US dollars.

Country	*Debt 1970*	*Debt 1981*	*Debt 1983*
Brazil	$3.2	$43.8	$92
Mexico	3.2	42.7	87
Argentina	1.9	10.5	37
Venezuela	0.7	11.4	35
Chile	2.1	4.4	18
Peru	0.9	6.0	12
Nigeria	0.5	4.7	14

Source: For 1970 and 1981, The World Bank, *World Development Report 1983,* Table 16, pp. 178–179; for 1983, *The Washington Post,* September 25, 1983, page H1.

15. Sylvia Ostry, "The World Economy in 1983, Marking Time," *Foreign Affairs,* America and the World 1983 issue, pp. 533–560 at p. 551.
16. International Monetary Fund, *World Economic Outlook,* 1983, Table 33, p. 201.
17. The World Bank, *World Development Report 1983,* p. 23.

FIGURE 5–8
Relationship of debt to exports for all developing countries, 1970–95.

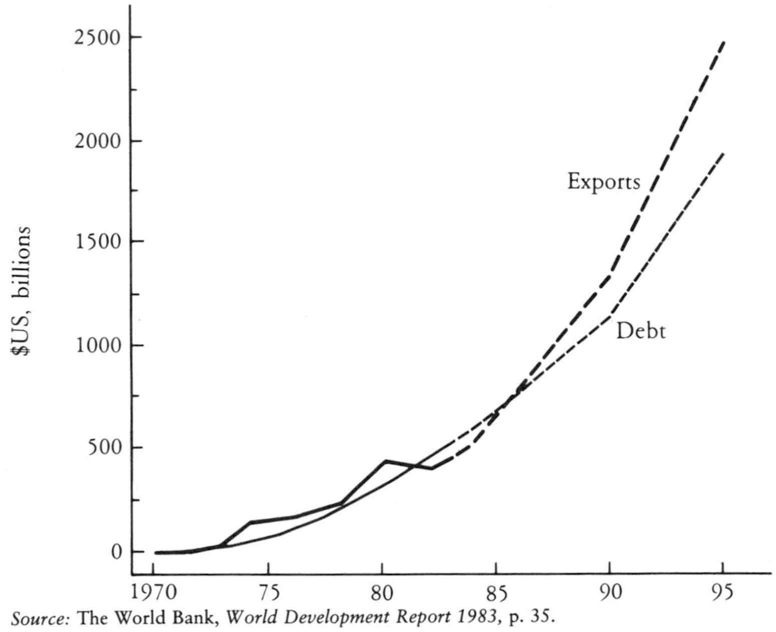

Source: The World Bank, *World Development Report 1983,* p. 35.

than fifteen international actions in which payments from Third World countries were rescheduled, suspended, postponed or subsidized with additional loans.[18] In the radical theory of international development, such events are predictable, and they have the consequence of deepening the dependence of the Third World upon the developed market economies. As Figure 5–8 shows, it is not expected that annual exports will exceed the aggregate debt of the Third World until at least 1986, when the total debt will have risen to over three-quarters of a trillion dollars.

Alternative Futures

Throughout the last quarter-century, the debate regarding international economic development has been conducted principally between the traditionalists (whose analyses focus on modernization strategies) and the radicals (who prefer to concentrate on the intrinsic charac-

18. For a chronological account listing the countries and the nature of each action, see *Foreign Affairs,* America and the World 1983 issue, pp. 778–781.

teristics of the international system that perpetuate dependency). More recently, however, a number of scholars have suggested new approaches to the problem. One, for example, has noted that neither of the two dominant theories can explain the late development of some countries because economic advancement is not necessarily tied exclusively to economic factors. This observation leads to the conclusion that disparate paths to development must consider such local sociological factors as traditions, motives, attitudes and religious influences upon traditionalism and modernism.[19]

A second effort at expanding the debate beyond the two dominant theories begins with the premise that in each developing state, class formation, capital formation and formalization of state authority take place at different times and at different paces. Furthermore, contemporary conditions render some of these states authoritarian, others nationalistic, and some dependent upon external economies or even in decline by now. The conclusion is that social interests and state policies influence dependency situations in order to multiply development possibilities and to create a variety of patterns of change explicable by neither the traditional theory nor the dependency theory.[20]

Still a third observation notes that in addition to the world's economic center and its periphery, there exists a "semi-periphery" of Third World states that are already fairly industrialized or are industrializing rapidly. For these states, development is led by exports rather than by agricultural or other primary export products. As a result, there are different paths to development that are not recognized by either of the dominant theories of economic development.[21]

Nonetheless, if reliance on foreign investment and aid is rejected as a solution to the development problem of the Third World, what are the alternatives? A majority of developing peoples now live under governments socialist in nature, but what does this mean in international relations beyond the symbolic hostility to capitalism?

A number of development models exist and some are examined below. It is important to point out, however, that as the ideological solidarity of the Third World begins to crack significantly, there is less

19. Ogura Mitsuo, "The Sociology of Development and Issues Surrounding Late Development," *International Studies Quarterly,* December 1982, pp. 596–625, translated from the Japanese by David Olson.
20. Michael Bratton, "Patterns of Development and Underdevelopment: Toward a Comparison," *International Studies Quarterly,* September 1982, pp. 333–72.
21. James A. Caporaso, "Industrialization in the Periphery: The Evolving Global Division of Labor," *International Studies Quarterly,* September 1981, pp. 347–84. The author emphasizes Argentina, Mexico, South Korea, Singapore, Portugal, Brazil, Hong Kong, the Philippines and Spain. Note similarity to text accompanying Table 5–6 in this chapter.

urge among the developing countries to emulate the growth principles of model countries. There has arisen a new individualism among the Third World countries that defies the adoption of existing models, and calls instead for individual development efforts that seem peculiar to the political cultures of the countries themselves. Nonetheless, certain models do appear still to contain a wealth of proven experience from which individual efforts might draw.

The Chinese Model

Some voices in the developing countries, such as the ruling party in Tanzania and the Maoist groups in Latin America, cite values in the Chinese experience for other poor countries. Before the communists took power, the industrial and commercial sectors of the Chinese economy were thoroughly penetrated by foreign influence, to the extent that paper and metal currency was printed in English on one side. As late as 1935, foreigners controlled 95 percent of China's iron, three-quarters of its coal, half its textile production and most of shipping, public utilities, banking, insurance and trade. Most industrial workers were employed by foreign firms, and the Chinese social structure showed many of the typical symptoms of what we now call the dependency syndrome. The corrective steps taken by the communists after 1949 were harsh, but they succeeded in cutting the ties of dependency and putting China on a self-reliant path of rapid development. China in effect virtually sealed its borders to capitalist trade and investment and adopted an economic policy of isolation and autarky for twenty years.

Could the Chinese example of the "closed door" and almost total self-reliance be imitated by other developing countries? Probably not. China is a world in itself, a nation of over a billion people providing a huge internal market with diversified resources and productive potentials. The thirty less developed countries of sub-Saharan Africa taken together have less than 25 percent of this population base; individually, most developing countries are much smaller. Most economists agree that the cost of isolationism to a small country would be a substantially reduced rate of growth, if not economic collapse.

Regional Integration

Another solution open to small nations is that of forming regional economic groups to consolidate the economies of several neighboring states into one larger entity. Present experiments in economic integration among developing countries include the East African Common

Market, the Arab Common Market, the Central American Common Market and the Latin American Free Trade Association. Degrees of integration range from the free trade area (where tariffs on trade among members are eliminated), through the customs union (where a common external tariff is added to the free trade area) to the common market (where labor and capital as well as goods and services are permitted to move freely). Later steps in economic integration may include monetary union (a common currency), the merger of tax systems and finally a single national budget including a shared defense budget. Each stage of economic integration has political costs as well as benefits, and inevitably some elites gain from a merger while others lose. The success of developing nations in achieving regional integration is partly a function of the relative strengths of these forces.

Another obstacle to regional economic integration is the fear that the costs and benefits of cooperation will be distributed unequally. Experience has shown that without special preferential measures favoring the less developed members of a group, the benefits of integration are likely to be concentrated in the more advanced countries, while a disproportionate share of the costs will be borne by the less advanced ones. In theory, this inequality could be relieved by asymmetrical tariff policies providing a higher degree of protection for a prolonged transition period for the less developed states, as well as directly subsidizing their development in key sectors. But in practice, even the more advanced members of a regional grouping tend to experience developmental strains, and national priorities rather than mutual interests tend to prevail. Moreover, the economic systems of neighboring states may have a limited potential for integration. States whose previous economic development was geared to the export of highly specialized products to the developed countries may find the expansion of trade with fellow developing countries difficult. The noncomplementarity of developing economies explains their tendency to concentrate the volume of trade on distant, more advanced partners rather than on their neighbors.

Another obstacle to integration is the national pride of newly independent countries and the mutual hostility of some adjoining states. Integration requires a sacrifice of unrestricted autonomy in favor of joint decision making, and this in turn requires mutual trust and a willingness to accept a shared fate.[22] Many developing countries, es-

22. D. C. Mead, "The Distribution of Gains in Customs Unions between Developing Countries," *Kyklos* 21, pp. 713–34; R. F. Mikesell, "The Theory of Common Market as Applied to Regional Arrangements among Developing Countries," in R. F. Harrod and D. C. Hague, editors, *International Trade Theory in a Developing World* (New York: Macmillan, 1963), pp. 205–29.

pecially those which gained independence within the past two decades, seem to prefer a go-it-alone strategy. Indeed, intra-African economic integration has declined rather than increased since the collapse of the colonial empires, and dependence on the center paradoxically has increased. During the colonial period, integration was forced on diverse neighbors by their European masters, such as the French-imposed West African Customs Union and the Equatorial African Customs Union. Britain established a common market, a common currency and common railways and other services in the East African colonies of Kenya, Uganda and Tanganyika. Since independence, these cooperative arrangements have been largely dismantled. The lines of commerce and communication from most developing nations flow not to their neighbors, but to the nations of the center, like spokes to a hub.[23]

Commodity Producer Cartels

In reality, many developing countries seem destined to play the role of primary product exporters for years to come, given all the obstacles to radical alternatives such as the closed door or regionalization. Means of stepping up the pace of economic development will have to be found within the present framework of commodity specialization. For this reason, some leaders of exporting countries are looking for progress in the formation of agreements among producers of primary products to regulate and improve the prices of their commodities.

The outstanding example of success for such producer groups is the Organization of Petroleum Exporting Countries (OPEC), which succeeded in raising the world price of crude oil more than 900 percent between 1973 and 1982 (see Figure 5–9). Petroleum exporters with large populations, such as Nigeria and Indonesia, suddenly had the capital resources to finance development at a greatly expanded pace. Exporters with small populations, such as Saudi Arabia, Kuwait and the United Arab Emirates, not only could afford rags-to-riches luxuries at home, but also were able to accumulate huge and unprecedented financial surpluses with which to influence other countries, even the great powers. The entire world watched as Saudi Arabia, once described as "rushing madly from the eleventh century into the twelfth," banked a $30 billion surplus in one year, while Great Britain, on whose empire the sun was never to set, was at its feet.

Oil is, of course, a very special commodity in international trade. It is the lifeblood of modern industrial society, and as the world be-

23. Dharam P. Ghai, "Perspectives on Future Economic Prospects and Problems in Africa," in Bhagwati, editor, *Economics and World Order* (New York: Macmillan, 1972), pp. 265–66.

FIGURE 5–9
World crude oil prices in current and constant prices, 1973–83, expressed in US dollars per barrel.

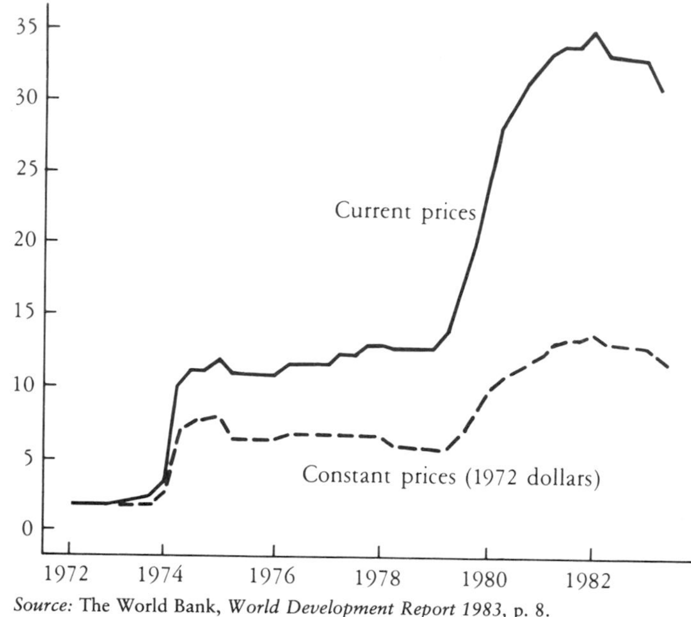

Source: The World Bank, *World Development Report 1983,* p. 8.

comes more wary of the dangers of nuclear substitutes, access to oil becomes a more precious foundation of economic growth than ever. Any substantial halt in oil flows could render prostrate the great industrial economies of the West, and particularly of Japan, which is almost totally dependent on imported oil. Western Europe and the United States are only relatively less dependent on international sources of oil. From 1973 to 1980, American dependence on OPEC alone increased nearly threefold, and the uncertainty of supply from Iran following the Iranian Revolution in 1978/79 increased American reliance on the more radical members of OPEC. By mid-1979 it was an open secret in Washington that achieving diplomatic leverage over OPEC had become the first priority of American foreign economic policy. More than ever before it was realized that a renewed oil embargo would be a uniquely potent weapon against the industrial West in forcing the North-South dialogue back to confrontation.

The monetary value of oil in international trade is a second noteworthy attribute of this unique resource. The revenue from trade in oil makes minuscule that of all other raw materials and fuels combined, and oil trade has a more profound impact upon the balances of payments of the industrial states than do all other forms of trade, industrial and agricultural. From the West's vantage point, the balance-of-trade issue is magnified by the small population bases of some of the OPEC states, which removes the necessity for large import volumes that might otherwise offset some of the surplus from oil exports. As a result, Saudi Arabia increased its international currency reserves 5,000 percent between 1970 and 1981 (and Kuwait and the United Arab Emirates had increases of 2,400 and 3,500 percent, respectively). For purposes of comparison, during the same period the American increase was 800 percent, the same as Japan's, and France and West Germany showed increases of 1000 and 600 percent, respectively. Meanwhile, the annual trade balances of the principal industrial oil consumers went into deeper deficit. In the United States, for example, oil imports alone added $10 billion to the trade deficit of 1979 and $14 billion more in 1980.

It is not necessary to expand upon these numerical evidences of OPEC's power to demonstrate that the pattern of dependency between the North and the South, at least insofar as fuel was concerned during the glory days of OPEC, was reversed with enormous significance for multilateral diplomacy and international relations in general. Furthermore, the OPEC experience seemed to demonstrate that a Third World cartel in a primary product badly needed by the industrial economies of the West and Japan would be a most advantageous route to economic development.

Yet despite the unique opportunity presented by oil for the formation of a cartel, it was never certain that even OPEC could sustain its strong position in the world economy. Historic ethnic and religious conflicts among the principal Arab members were the early challenges to unity. Later came disagreements on pricing and production policies, with the more radical members arguing for steep increases in price and reduction in production. Such a policy would have brought rapid capital accumulation and postponement of eventual exhaustion of supply. Meanwhile, the moderate members, conscious of the impact of pricing policies on the industrial economies and, therefore, upon the world economy, argued for modest price increases and careful controls over production in individual member states.

External crises mingled with internal conflict as the turn of the decade approached. Iranians held wholly new attitudes toward the world after their revolution. The war between Iran and Iraq threatened the security of the Middle East as well as the steady, peaceful oil export commerce out of the Persian Gulf through the Strait of Hormuz to the open sea. (A military closure of the Strait would prevent oil exports from Iran, Iraq, Katar, Bahrain, Kuwait and the United Arab Emirates, and force Saudi Arabia to transfer all of its export oil from the rich eastern fields to the Red Sea.) The Soviet invasion of Afghanistan added a dimension of insecurity and uncertainty, as did the constant threat of war among Lebanon, Syria, Israel and the Palestine Liberation Organization. Finally, the world economic recession, generally regarded as the worst in 50 years, upset international trade and the global flow of capital.

In the presence of all these external influences, matched internally by disagreement on price and production policies, OPEC lost control of the world petroleum market. Market gluts appeared where severe shortages had existed previously, and once again the price of oil began to drop. Although there was temporary stability during 1981 and 1982, the OPEC meeting of early 1983 was fraught with disagreement. The unity forged a decade earlier around the theme of common policy in the interest of rapid economic and social development had evaporated. As Figure 5–10 demonstrates, both production and external demand declined steadily from 1979 through 1983. But note also that Figure 5–9 shows the price increases in both current and constant dollars for the years 1979–82. Combining the two figures reveals that in the years 1979 through 1981, sharp reductions in OPEC exports were accompanied by markedly higher prices; but in 1982 and 1983,

FIGURE 5–10
Comparison of OPEC oil exports and oil imports by industrial economies, 1973–1983, expressed in millions of barrels per day.

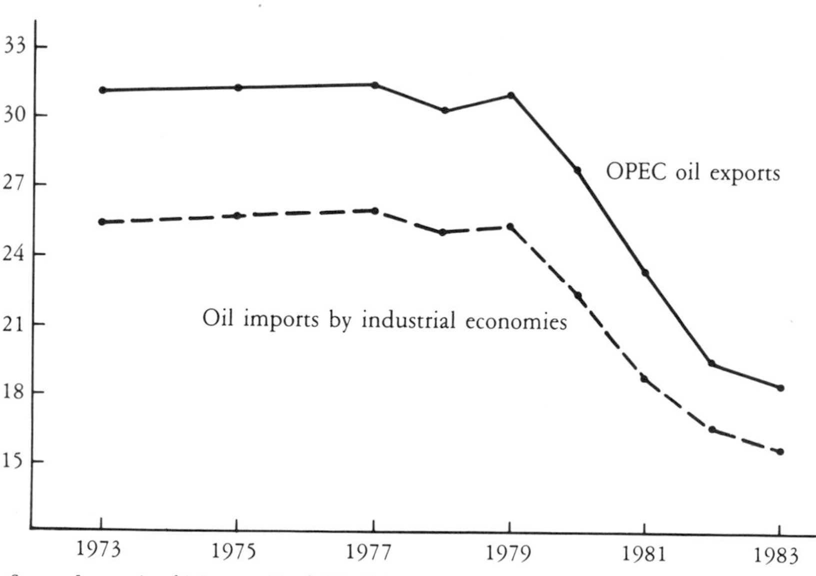

Source: International Monetary Fund, *World Economic Outlook*, 1983, from Table 67, p. 236.

the continued reduction in exports began to see a significant price decrease as well. The International Monetary Fund estimates that a price reduction of 10 percent would result in an annual loss to OPEC of $18 billion.[24] Hence with production down and prices declining, there is a severe reduction in development capital for the OPEC countries, and these combined factors represent a distinct reduction in the political power of the cartel.

Nevertheless, to the extent that OPEC has succeeded in advancing its goals, the question remains of whether or not the cartel experience can be duplicated by producer groups in other primary commodities. Members of the Intergovernmental Committee of Copper Exporting Countries, the Union of Banana Exporting Countries, the International Tin Council and at least a dozen other commodity groups hope so, but professional observers disagree on their prospects. Five conditions determine whether a cartel will be durable and effective.[25]

1. *Price Elasticity of Demand* Demand must be relatively unresponsive to price. If a commodity is important to consumers, and substitutes for it are not readily available, then price increases can be imposed without a severe loss of sales. This is the case with oil, and it is also believed to be true of minerals such as copper and aluminum and some foods such as coffee. Other products, such as natural rubber and bananas, have more elastic demand and cannot increase in price without also curtailing sales.

2. *Limited Number of Producers* A relatively small number of producers controlling a relatively large share of total world exports in a commodity is ideal for collusion. This condition is met by at least eight major commodities in which the top four LDC producers account for over half of world exports. Moreover, there must be high barriers to entry against new producers—that is, it must be difficult for new competitors to break into a market by underselling the cartel price. This also is true for many commodities, whether because of the limits of raw material sources, climatic and soil conditions, the start-up costs of production or other factors.

3. *Shared Experience of Producers* Producing states must be aware of their interdependence and be willing to cooperate and act as a limited economic coalition. This condition also is met by producers

24. International Monetary Fund, *World Economic Outlook,* 1983, from Table 69, p. 238.
25. Adapted from Steven D. Krasner, "Oil Is the Exception," *Foreign Policy,* Spring 1974, pp. 68–90.

of several commodities, though in other cases the necessary basis of shared values is less evident.

4. *Consumer Resistance* The probability that a cartel will be successful is reduced if consumers are organized for effective resistance. In the petroleum market, the position of the major oil companies is believed to have facilitated collusion among the exporting countries. Other commodity markets lack such middlemen, and the probability of resistance may be higher.

5. *Ability to Take a Long-Term Perspective* A cartel member must be prepared to accept short-term costs for long-term gains. The market may contract severely as buyers resist the inflated price and draw down their inventories. The oil-exporting states were in a good position to curtail production, as they could live for some time on substantial capital reserves previously accumulated. Also, the production of oil is not labor intensive, and relatively few workers were idled by the deliberate slowdown. Countries with small financial reserves and high proportions of the labor force dependent on export production are in a poor position to pay the short-term costs of cartelization. The temptation to cheat may be irresistible for poorer cartel members, who will be able to take advantage of the situation by price shaving. In no other commodity are producing countries in as strong a position to accept short-term costs as in oil.

Is cartelization of other primary commodities, then, probable or improbable? The evidence is ambiguous, but some Western observers believe that the developed world will face "one, two, many OPECs"[26] and some Third World leaders believe that this is the first opportunity for the developing countries truly to redress the global inequalities between rich and poor. Advanced states are being forced to consider a range of defensive measures to protect themselves from price gouging by cartels. Some have proposed expanding buffer stockpiles and diversifying sources of supply of primary commodities as measures to prepare for economic warfare. Consumer coalitions would be constructed to oppose the producer cartels. In the extreme case of economic strangulation of the industrial states by a hypothetical long-term oil embargo, some have raised the possibility of direct military

26. See especially C. Fred Bergsten, "The Threat from the Third World," *Foreign Policy*, Summer 1973, and his "The Threat Is Real," *Foreign Policy*, Spring 1974.

intervention to assure access to supplies and possibly to reduce prices if they were to reach dangerous levels.

Others reject this economic warfare model, and call for cooperation between producing and consuming states to raise the income of primary producers with minimum disruption to the international economy. Third World spokesmen particularly believe that the global redistribution of wealth is long overdue, and that increases in prices of exports of developing countries will be a principal means of achieving this. They reject the charge that the new price of oil is artificially high; rather, it is the old price that was artificially low. The rich countries have become used to a terms-of-trade structure that must be changed, and they are finding the transition painful. Americans have become accustomed to a situation in which their standard of living, measured in per capita GNP, is twenty-three times that of the developing countries. Now the developing world has an effective means of changing this balance of wealth, admittedly at some cost to the developed world, and they are unmoved by cries that "you're bankrupting us."

The Soviet Union may be expected to support the Third World on this issue. The USSR is the world's leading producer of petroleum, and is a fairly substantial exporter to East and West European countries as well. The change in the price of oil achieved by OPEC resulted in direct gains to the USSR of about $2 billion per year in export earnings, partly at the expense of the East European communist states. The Soviet Union is a major primary product exporter, and it would be strengthened by further revision in the terms of trade, while the NATO allies and Japan are the world's major raw materials importers.

The United States is in a less favorable position, but still is better situated than Europe or Japan. The US imports about 15 percent of the critical industrial materials it consumes, compared to about 75 percent for Europe and Japan. And while the absolute volume of imports is high, dependence is concentrated on other developed countries rather than on Third World sources. The leading suppliers of nonfuel raw materials to America are Canada, Australia, Rhodesia, South Africa and Brazil. As commodity power becomes more important in international relations, the US can be expected to upgrade its alliance with these states. In only a few minerals—notably bauxite (aluminum), manganese, tin and natural rubber—is supply significantly centered in the Third World, and for these, alternative sources of supply and substitute materials are available at some cost of transition. Moreover, the US is itself the leading exporter of another category of primary commodities: wheat and other grains. As "the world's breadbasket," the US has gained substantially from the inflation of world food prices. Indeed, increased agricultural export revenues almost canceled out the increased costs of imported oil in the US balance of payments for the first two years after the 1973 oil embargo. Since then, however, the more rapid increase in petroleum prices than in agricultural and industrial exports has contributed dramatically to American deficits in international trade and payments, revealing that, at least in the short run, America is no less vulnerable to resource warfare than are other industrial states.

Conclusion

This exploration of the radical and conventional theories of underdevelopment reveals some of the theoretical and practical issues that underlie the North-South dialogue and the perspective of Third World nations on the contemporary international system. Emancipated and free from imperialism, this huge portion of the earth's population remains enslaved by a poverty unimaginable in comparison with even the lowliest standards of the industrialized world. Though formal colonization may no longer exist, the economic control of the Third World by the economic tentacles of the developed world is everywhere true, and by their exploitation of Third World resources and populations they perpetuate the gap between wealthy and poor. Though international machinery and a generation of imaginative economic policy planning may have changed the characteristics and statistics of national subordination, the basic stratification of the world's nations and peoples is relatively unchanged.

But the demand for national emancipation that led to the coalition known as the Third World has been followed by a revolution of rising expectations—in economics, in human rights and in social development. Modern communications, rising levels of literacy and increased individual contacts of Third World individuals with the industrial world (through formal education and employment in multinational corporations, in particular) have stimulated an appetite for better standards of living and release from a system of international oppression. Neither socialism nor capitalism has provided an adequate formula for dealing with national economic issues or with international economic issues that so crucially affect the developing nation. And the governments of neither capitalist nor socialist nations have provided political initiatives to reverse the spiral of dependence, debt and subordination. Only the power of OPEC has risen from the Third World with a loud enough voice to have been heard as a challenge to the prevailing norms of the international political economy. From the viewpoint of the developing states, therefore, the North-South dialogue either will usher in a new era of cooperation between rich and poor for implementation of a new international economic order, or it will have been an interlude between two different eras of international politics. The first is characterized by dependence of the South upon the North; the second is marked by relentless economic warfare as the advanced industrial civilizations try desperately to obtain the primary products upon which their own well-being depends.

6

Perceptions in World Politics

We have reviewed the perceptual frames of five major actors in the international system today—the USSR, the USA, America's major allies, China and the Third World. The Soviet officials see the world divided into two innately hostile camps of capitalist and socialist states, itself the progenitor and protector of the socialist camp, and the United States the world headquarters of antirevolutionary reaction and imperialism. Americans see Soviet communism as an inherently expansionist totalitarian ideology threatening to engulf weaker nations of the Free World, which are protected only by the umbrella of American power; this gives the United States the responsibility of countering aggression. America's allies perceive themselves to be threatened less by communist menace than by subordination to the United States as modern economic colonies. Chinese see the US–Soviet Cold War as a thin disguise for two competing imperialisms, capitalist and socialist, both trying behind masks of protective benevolence to expand their domination of the world's peoples. China sees itself as the true home of peoples' revolutions and as a model for national development in a world of equals without superpowers. The Third World countries have little direct interest in these East/West conflicts and are as a group more concerned with the North/South conflict of colonialism, economic dependency and an international environment hostile to the development of the small powers.

Each of these perceptual systems supports itself with an array of data and historical analyses. Each seems to its proponents so well supported by facts that it needs no further substantiation. Each perceptual system regards the others as inaccurate and dishonest. Proponents of the other points of view are victims of misperception or are dissimulators who know the truth, but for ulterior motives pretend to have a different perception. In short, laymen and national policymakers believe their own perceptual systems to be true and those of opponents to be at least partly false.

How is it possible for each perceptual system to resist change when confronted with contradictory information? Why don't the nations of the world sit down and iron out their differences, work out each other's misperceptions, and resolve at least the portion of their conflicts that is rooted in misunderstanding? Why don't we get down to the facts and replace all this confusion with an understanding of reality?

To answer these questions, it will help to understand some of the propositions in the *theory of international perceptions*—propositions adapted from social psychology and applied to the study of international relations.

Facts

In everyday life, we generally assume that our understanding of reality flows directly from that reality itself. It is common sense that certain things are facts while the opposite assertions are not, and that if we can ascertain the facts, certain conclusions will follow. The purpose of information gathering, for both the scientist and the decision-maker, is to determine the facts, from which knowledge of reality can be drawn.

Perceptual theorists do not accept this simple conception of knowledge. To them, knowledge has a subjective as well as an objective component: the facts do not speak for themselves, but are given meaning by each interpreter from his own analytical point of view. The conclusion that follows from facts depends on the interpretation that is given to the facts.

Furthermore, facts do not spring from reality but are, rather, particular pieces of information from reality that are selected by an observer as having importance while other pieces of information are rejected as lacking importance. "Reality" consists of an infinite amount of potential information, from which only a tiny part is taken as a set of facts. For example, in writing the history of a particular war, the historian must select a small portion of available data to report. Millions of individuals are involved in billions and trillions of acts; billions of decisions are made by participants; the patterns of interaction are

The paranoias of East and West, as revealed in their political cartoons.

"SO THERE I WAS....TRYING TO DECIDE WHAT TO DO ABOUT THE TROUBLESOME PROBLEM OF HUMAN RIGHTS WHEN SUDDENLY IT CAME TO ME—BOOM! NO HUMANS, NO HUMAN RIGHTS!"

Source: Marlette *(The Charlotte Observer)* © King Features

Source: Pravda/World Press Review

beyond imagination. The historian must select from all this a few pieces of information that seem, summarily, to describe the interactions and succinctly explain their causes. Students of history and historiography know only too well that the facts do not speak for themselves.

Social science summarizes this view of facts in a terse definition: *A fact is but a peculiar ordering of reality according to a theoretic interest.*[1] That is, the facts themselves are imposed on "reality" by the observer, rather than the other way around; and the very nature of the "facts" themselves depends on the questions the observer chooses to ask. Since each perceptual system asks its own questions, observers of divergent viewpoints naturally arrive at different answers or facts.

To illustrate: from the Soviet point of view, data on the profit structure of American corporations is the body of facts that one must have to understand the international system; from the American point of view, it is off the point entirely. Someone given twenty minutes to explain the Cold War who spends fifteen on the nature of American investments will be regarded by a Soviet listener as having given "the facts," but by an American as having evaded them. To the American listener, the real facts have to do with Soviet aggression and American response, and examples of this kind of Soviet behavior will be pertinent. "Facts" are thus subjectively defined and are themselves a phenomenon of perceptions. Perceptions cannot be corrected when confronted with facts if the facts themselves are perceptions.

Values, Beliefs and Cognitions

Perceptual theorists distinguish among three components of perception: values, beliefs and cognitions. A value is a preference for one state of reality over another: health is better than illness, green is prettier than blue. Values do not specify what is but rather what ought to be. Values assign a relative worth to objects and conditions.

A belief is a conviction that a description of reality is true, proven or known. Often it is based on prior reception of information from the environment ("I have learned that . . .") but it is not the same as the data themselves. It is an analytical proposition that relates individual pieces of data into a "proven" pattern: democratic governments are less warlike than totalitarian governments; imperialism is the mature phase of monopoly capitalism. A belief is not the same as a value. One might believe that communism brings a higher rate of economic growth, and that capitalism has a better record of protecting

1. See David Easton, *The Political System* (New York: Knopf, 1953).

Source: Lurie *(Newsweek)*

individual freedoms. Given these beliefs, one must decide whether capitalism or communism is better according to one's own values. Which is worth more, economic growth or personal liberties?

A cognition is data or information received from the environment, for example, Russia is giving war planes to Syria. Cognitions are key elements in establishing perceptual systems and in changing those systems. The concept of changing national perceptions refers to introducing cognitions that will revise beliefs and values. If we held a conference between the major Cold War actors to iron out their differences and "misperceptions," our purpose would be to influence perceptions by introducing new information. We would try to change stubborn beliefs and values that cause conflict by confronting each side with new cognitive data.

Unfortunately, it has been found in a variety of studies that at all levels of human behavior, deeply held values and beliefs are highly resistant to change through new cognition. Social psychological research support a theory of "cognitive dissonance." Briefly stated, this theory holds that when a deeply held value or belief is contradicted by a new message from the environment (a "dissonant" cognition) the message (fact, cognition) will be rejected and the value or belief retained. This may not take the form of outright rejection of the discrepant message; it may take the alternate form of reinterpretation of the datum to make it consistent with existing belief. But the effect is the same: the individual's value and belief system protects itself from external alteration.[2]

We might relate this phenomenon to the idea of an "economy of thought." It is very "expensive" to carry about in one's head all the information supporting one view and its opposite. Mental economy requires that we have a filtering system to fit a single reality to our preconceptions so that we are not constantly revising our basic perceptual systems, with all the readaptation and adjustment that that would require. Political organizations choose as their leaders individuals with known points of view that concur reliably with those of the membership. If national leaders were relatively free to revise their perceptual frameworks, they would not be reliable. Hence, the rigidity and predictability of the leadership's perceptual system is an asset to the group. The leader should not be quicker to change than are his constituents.

The constituents, on the other side, must not be overly vulnerable to perceptual change from external influences. If foreign leaders could appeal over the head of a national leader to his own constituents, they might manipulate these persons to their own advantage. For this and other reasons, it is functional for each nation to have its own system of "authorities," public officials who determine the overall national interest with regard to other nations. These same public officials play a major role in channeling the cognitions that reach their "publics." Many studies have shown that individuals will accept or reject the same information depending on whether it comes from a positive or negative prestige source. Thus, constituents choose their leaders partly for the relative inflexibility of their perceptual systems, and the leaders process incoming information in such a way as to maintain the existing perceptual system of the constituents. The national belief system is thus stable and resistant to change.[3]

For all these reasons, we can safely assume that national perceptual frameworks will usually survive challenges from other nations and new experiences. They may make superficial or cosmetic improvements to adjust to new realities at times, but fundamental change is a long-

2. See Leon Festinger, *The Theory of Cognitive Dissonance* (Stanford: Stanford University Press, 1962).

3. Compare Herbert Kelman, editor, *International Behavior: A Social Psychological Analysis* (New York: Holt, Rinehart and Winston, 1965), especially "The Effects of Events on National and International Images" by Karl Deutsch and Richard Merritt; Ole Holsti, "The Belief System and National Images," *Journal of Conflict Resolution* 6 [(1962), 244–52] Kenneth Boulding, *The Image* (New York: Harper and Row, 1960); Robert Jervis, *The Logic of Images in International Relations* (Princeton, N.J.: Princeton University Press, 1971); and also by Jervis, *Perception and Misperception in International Politics* (Princeton, N.J.: Princeton University Press, 1976).

term process. The vehicle of national policy is steered by looking in the rearview mirror; nations are influenced more by where they have been than by where they are going. For over a quarter of a century the United States continued to respond to the failure of isolationism and the ill wisdom of Munich. Soviet policy continues to be obsessed with the territorial invasions of two world wars and with a threadbare theory of capitalism that is now over a century old. China's policy has, until very recently, been shaped by recollections of the Century of Humiliation. The Third World's concept of colonialism has scarcely evolved. Hardened perceptions, because of the conviction with which they are held and the information shaping for which they are used, are major obstacles to political progress.

Selective Perception in Big-Power Intervention

We have seen that international events are selectively perceived by key actors, and that every "reality" has multiple meanings depending on the nationality of the perceiver. This principle can be seen sharply in a comparison of two big-power interventions in the middle 1960s: American military intervention in the Dominican Republic and Soviet military intervention in Czechoslovakia.

The United States sent 25,000 Marines into the Dominican Republic in the spring of 1965 to prevent that country from shifting leftward; three years later the Soviet Union initiated a military invasion of Czechoslovakia to forestall that country's drift toward political liberalism. The Dominican Republic is in the traditional American "sphere of influence" in the Caribbean, while Czechoslovakia is a key element of the traditional Soviet sphere in Eastern Europe. Thus, to many outside observers the two events were a clear demonstration of the "dual-imperialisms" philosophy of the superpowers, dividing the world between them and intervening freely in the affairs of lesser states in their respective hegemonies. But to the superpowers themselves these events had very different meanings; each justified its own behavior as different in kind from the lawless intervention of the other. Perceptual analysis provides a key to understanding these two cases.

The Dominican Republic, 1965

The Dominican crisis arose from a conflict between a right-wing military government and a rebellion by supporters of ousted civilian president Juan Bosch. Bosch had been the first freely elected president in thirty-eight years following a long period of dictatorship, but he was evicted from office by a military coup after only nine months. The crisis of 1965 erupted when a "constitutionalist" movement attempted to restore him to office and to remove the generals. American officials on the scene and in Washington viewed the rebellion as a communist conspiracy using the good name of Bosch as a mere convenience, although this characterization was disputed by many observers. President Johnson felt obligated to dispatch the Marines to Santo Domingo to "prevent another Cuba" in the Caribbean.

By what right, we may ask, did the United States intervene in what were manifestly the internal affairs of the Dominican Republic, regardless of how American officials might have felt about events there? It was conceded that the rebellion itself was composed entirely of Dominican citizens, making the American action a foreign intervention in a civil war. This accusation had an important effect on America's self-image, because the United States considers itself a strict adherent to the principle of nonintervention in the internal affairs of other countries, as codified in the United Nations Charter, the Charter of

The USSR in Czechoslovakia, 1968.

Source: Wide World Photos

the Organization of American States and elsewhere in international law.

American officials responded that while the rebels were indeed all Dominican, the rebellion was nonetheless part of the international communist conspiracy and was, in the words of the legal adviser to the State Department, "an attempt by a conspiratorial group inspired from the outside to seize control by force" and was thus "an assault upon the independence and integrity" of the Dominican Republic.[4] It follows that American intervention was justified to "protect" the Dominican people.

The Soviet reaction to the American intervention was swift and indignant, and accorded with the strong reactions of many noncommunist governments. Soviet Ambassador N. T. Fedorenko said at the UN on May 1, 1965, "There can be no justification for the invasion of the territory of a sovereign state by the United States armed forces, . . . a cynical violation of the elementary norms of international law." Fedorenko specifically rejected one argument in defense of the American action: the assertion that intervention was justified by the principles of the Inter-American System as enunciated by the Organization of American States. This United States-dominated organization had passed several resolutions that affirmed and validated the American contention that communism was inherently a foreign threat to Western hemispheric nations, and on several occasions the OAS had endorsed American military interventions in Latin American countries to oppose developments believed to be communist inspired.

The Soviet spokesman objected that this American position amounted to a belief that

> the right to decide the fate of the Dominican Republic rests only partly with the people of that country and partly with their neighbors. . . . Such statements are incompatible with the obligations of the United States under the United Nations Charter, which prohibits any interference in the internal affairs of other countries. . . . The question of internal organization and regime is purely an internal affair of the Dominican people themselves and they alone . . . have the right to decide it without any pressure or interference from outside.

The United States, Fedorenko insisted, cannot act in Latin America "as if it was [*sic*] in its own private domain, . . . as if it were a

4. Statement of Leonard C. Meeker, "Legal Basis for United States Action in the Dominican Republic," reprinted in Abram Chayes, Thomas Ehrlich and Andreas F. Lowenfeld, *International Legal Process,* vol. 2 (Boston: Little, Brown, 1969), p. 1182.

question of Alabama or Mississippi."[5] Thus the United States had invoked certain regional principles that allegedly superseded the usual rule of noninterference, while the Soviet Union rejected these claims and stood firmly on traditional international law and standards of decent behavior. Three years later these positions were exactly reversed, and the statesmen of the two countries demonstrated an extraordinary rhetorical dexterity in reversing roles and taking opposite parts in the case of the Soviet invasion of Czechoslovakia. This time it was the Soviet Union that asserted a special regional right to intervene in the internal affairs of a sovereign country, and the United States that was outraged at the naked display of international gangsterism.

Czechoslovakia, 1968

The crisis in Czechoslovakia materialized when the government headed by Alexander Dubĉek began to move its domestic and foreign policies in directions that differed in basic orientation from the philosophy of the Soviet Union, leader of the Warsaw Pact nations. Just as the United States had feared "another Castro" in the Dominican Republic, the USSR came to fear "another Tito" in Czechoslovakia. (This is a reference to Marshall Josip Tito, the long-time maverick leader of communist Yugoslavia, who had advanced the notion of "separate roads to socialism," a theoretical threat to Soviet monopoly over the political philosophy of the Eastern bloc.) This might constitute an independent communist regime that could not be counted upon to contribute to "regional stability" and that might ally itself with hostile extraregional powers (that is, NATO). To prevent this, several hundred thousand troops of the Soviet Union and other Warsaw Pact nations entered Prague in August 1968 to dismantle and replace the Dubĉek government.

American officials, reflecting opinion in most of the world, labeled the Soviet action an outrage. Secretary of State Dean Rusk insisted that "a small country" is entitled to "live its own life" without having the will of a dominant neighbor forced upon it. American spokesmen portrayed the Czech events as a plain act of foreign interference, comparable to the Nazi invasion of Czechoslovakia in 1938.

The defense of the Soviet action began with the proposition that the Dubĉek government had become a conscious or unconscious agent of capitalist imperialism. Antisocialist forces were seeking to sever Czechoslovakia from the Socialist commonwealth. And while these

5. Fedorenko remarks as reprinted in Thomas M. Franck and Edward Weisband, *Word Politics* (New York: Oxford University Press, 1972), pp. 97–102.

antisocialist forces were Czechoslovak nationals, giving the conflict the appearance of an internal affair, Russia claimed to possess "irrefutable data concerning ties between the internal reaction in Czechoslovakia and the outside world," according to Soviet UN representative Jacob Malik.[6]

Furthermore, *Pravda* argued that the Czech government was responsible "not just to its own people, but also to all the socialist countries." Czechoslovakia occupies a crucial geopolitical position in the European balance of power, and "weakening of any of the links in the world system of socialism directly affects all the socialist countries, which cannot look indifferently upon this."[7] In effect the Soviet argument invoked the very same regional right to intervene that it had rejected in the Dominican case.

American spokesmen were equally inconsistent. Officials rejected most strenuously the assertion that there are special rules within the Socialist commonwealth that supersede the universal principle of noninterference, even though the United States had asserted precisely such a special relationship for the Organization of American States in the Dominican case. "No matter what the intimacy of one country with another," a United States delegate at the UN argued, "neither may claim a right to invade the territory of its friend."[8] And yet the American nations could, in this view, determine that no more communist governments would be tolerated in the western hemisphere, even if such governments were established by purely internal processes.

Thus the two superpowers sharply reversed their positions to accord with policy considerations. The Soviet Union rejected the idea that "the right to decide the fate of the Dominican Republic rests only partly with the people of that country and partly with their neighbors," but at the same time asserted that the Czech government "is responsible not just to its own people but to all the socialist countries." The United States asserted that the Organization of American States, as the institutional expression of the Inter-American system, could make determinations regarding the internal movement of members toward a communist government, but the Warsaw Pact bloc could not exercise the same rights in the name of the Socialist commonwealth.

6. UN Security Council, Doc. S/PV 1441, August 21, 1968, p. 32.
7. *Pravda* statement reprinted in the *New York Times,* September 27, 1968, p. 3.
8. Statement of the US representative to the UN Special Committee on the Principles of International Law on Legal Aspects of the Invasion and Occupation of Czechoslovakia, September 12, 1968, in *US Department of State Bulletin, 59,* October 14, 1968, p. 394.

Conflicting Perceptions

Underlying these disagreements of principle are critical differences in political perception. American officials see the inter-American system as a free association of self-determined nations, while the Socialist commonwealth is a mere collection of satellites and puppets of the USSR. Soviet officials, on the other hand, see the Organization of American States as a formal expression of the historical fact of American imperialism in Latin America, while the Socialist commonwealth is an alliance of progressive states under the leadership of the USSR. Thus, even if detailed cognitions of the two events were identical, interpretation would involve conflicting sets of prior contextual beliefs and values. To Americans, a shift toward communism would be a loss of freedom, while Soviets would see a progressive and even inevitable development. However, Americans regarded the liberal movement of the Prague regime away from Soviet-style orthodoxy as progressive and hopeful, while Soviet observers saw regression toward capitalism. Officials of the two countries would reject the contention that their positions in the two cases were contradictory.

Each side could also defend its actions by pointing to certain factual differences that favor a given perception. The Soviet intervention interrupted the otherwise peaceful evolution of Czechoslovakia, while the smaller United States force helped to end a fratricidal civil war that was already under way. The United States intervention was followed by reasonably free elections, while the Soviet intervention was followed by continued repression. On the other side, there is a pattern of United States economic domination in the Dominican Republic, while economic relations in Eastern Europe actually favor Czechoslovakia over the USSR. Also, Czechoslovakia is vital to the Soviet defense network, while the Dominican Republic is a minor matter for the United States—raising the argument that the Soviet intervention might have been the more justifiable in the name of necessity.

Facts of this sort can be raised to justify the rationalization of either side that "our case is different." Unflattering parallels can be rejected by either side, and the perceptual framework can remain invulnerable to empirical or logical refutation. This comparison of two cases shows that an intelligent perceptual structure is highly resistant to change, even in the face of direct contradiction.[9]

9. For an extended comparison of the Dominican and Czechoslovak interventions, including thorough documentary citations, see Thomas M. Franck and Edward Wiesband, *World Politics* (New York: Oxford University Press, 1972). For other comments, together with a comprehensive treatment of the roles of doctrines and perceptions in the management of international crisis, see Friedrich V. Kratochwil, *International Order and Foreign Policy: A Theoretical Sketch of Post-War International Politics* (Boulder, Co.: Westview Press, 1978).

These two examples, though twenty years old and somewhat remote contemporary events, are particularly illustrative of the problem of conflicting perceptions. Not only did the United States and the Soviet Union fail to understand one another in these instances, but each failed to recognize the contradictions of its own logic.

While not all such perceptual contradictions reveal themselves with such clarity as in these events, recent history is filled with evidences of perceptual confusion. In 1980, for example, while the Iranian Government was holding American hostages in retaliation for American support of the brutalities of the ousted Shah, that same government invoked international law against Iraq for behavior which contributed eventually to war between the two.

Soviet and American perceptions of the downing of Korean Airlines Flight 007 in 1983 constitute a similar example. From the American viewpoint, the craft was an easily identifiable civilian plane, characterized by its size, by the peculiar bulb superstructure of the Boeing 747 design, and by its commercial markings. To have shot it down with inadequate attempts to land it safely, even though it had strayed accidentally over Soviet territory in the Pacific, was a wanton act of disrespect for human life and unmistakable evidence of the savagery and barbarity of Soviet leaders. From the Soviet viewpoint, it was a craft that had crossed paths with a known American reconnaisance craft and then flown deliberately over Soviet territory on an act of espionage, conducted under cover of civilian markings. Any subsequent use of crowded civilian airliners to conduct intelligence missions in Soviet airspace would meet a similar fate. And any Soviet military personnel who might be reprimanded or punished as a result of the event would be singled out, not for having permitted firing upon the craft, but for having delayed firing until almost after the craft had escaped Soviet air space. If there were any savages or barbarians involved in the incident, they were the South Korean and American officials who had subjected hundreds of civilian passengers to the dangers of international intrigue.

Special Problems of the American Perception

Many Americans are sympathetic to the idea that leaders of other countries tend to look at the world through ideological lenses that create perceptual distortion, but reject the view that such an analysis can be applied with equal validity to the American case. Is it not true, they ask, that the United States has a free press in which diverse opinions and outlooks are represented? Virtually every point of view, no matter how silly or outrageous, has its own publication in the fantastic array of printed materials available. This contrasts sharply with the situation in the communist countries and in most of the Third World, where available information sources tend to be monopolized by the political party in power and only a single point of view is available. It would seem that the "free market of ideas" in the United States would make Americans less vulnerable to self-deceptions and rigid ideological distortions.

There is ample justification for this expectation, and it must be conceded that American policy mistakes are freely criticized at home as well as abroad, while dissent in some other countries is partially or completely suppressed. Alternative perceptions and policies are openly discussed within the domestic political structure of the United States, and misperceptions are quickly pointed out by domestic critics. Thus, the mechanisms of potential self-correction seem to operate much more effectively in America.

At the same time, it is undeniable that certain crucial American misperceptions have managed to persist over very long periods of time, despite their repeated "correction" by intelligent and responsible dis-

Afghanistan, 1980, government announcement: "The Presidium of the Revolutionary Council of the Democratic Republic of Afghanistan ratified the treaty between the government and that of the Soviet Union, on condition of the temporary stay of the limited contingent of Soviet troops on the Territory of Afghanistan."

Source: M. Olimov (Tass)/Sovfoto

senters. For example, the American image of China as a satellite of the Soviet Union dominated the ideas of foreign policy decision-makers until at least 1960, long after this misperception should have been adjusted by available information. Dissenters who questioned the orthodox point of view in the early years after the Chinese revolution had their patriotism and loyalty to "the American cause" seriously challenged; only the bravest voices were willing to continue their dissent from the official mythology. That other pictures of China could be obtained in small dissenting magazines and publications is interesting but not particularly meaningful: The dominant misperception was reinforced by all the major publications and the broadcast media—information that supported the official view. Thus, the "free market of ideas" is not a guarantee against false orthodoxies and misperceptions, though it does help to keep alive other points of view.

Another hazard of the American self-perception is the easy assumption made in this country that what Americans think is typical of "world opinion." The people of the United States, like people elsewhere, are prone to the delusion that when an opinion prevails among everyone they know, it is equally popular elsewhere. Americans are particularly subject to this error, because of their view of themselves as "the leaders of the Free World." Samplings of public opinion in different countries show, however, that the particular outlook of

"The other side!"

Source: Herblock's State of the Union (Simon and Schuster, 1972)

America is not universally popular, and that there are many issues on which American public opinion is inconsistent with opinion abroad. For example, the Gallup organization conducted an eleven-nation public-opinion poll in November of 1967 on United States policy in Vietnam (see Figure 6–1). It found that outside the United States the military escalation policy was almost universally unpopular, while within the United States the majority of opinion favored even greater escalation. In nine of the eleven Free World countries polled, American withdrawal was overwhelmingly the favored opinion, while in the United States 53 percent favored even greater escalation and only 31 percent favored withdrawal. On this issue, apparently, the American

FIGURE 6–1
Eleven-nation Gallup Poll on Vietnam

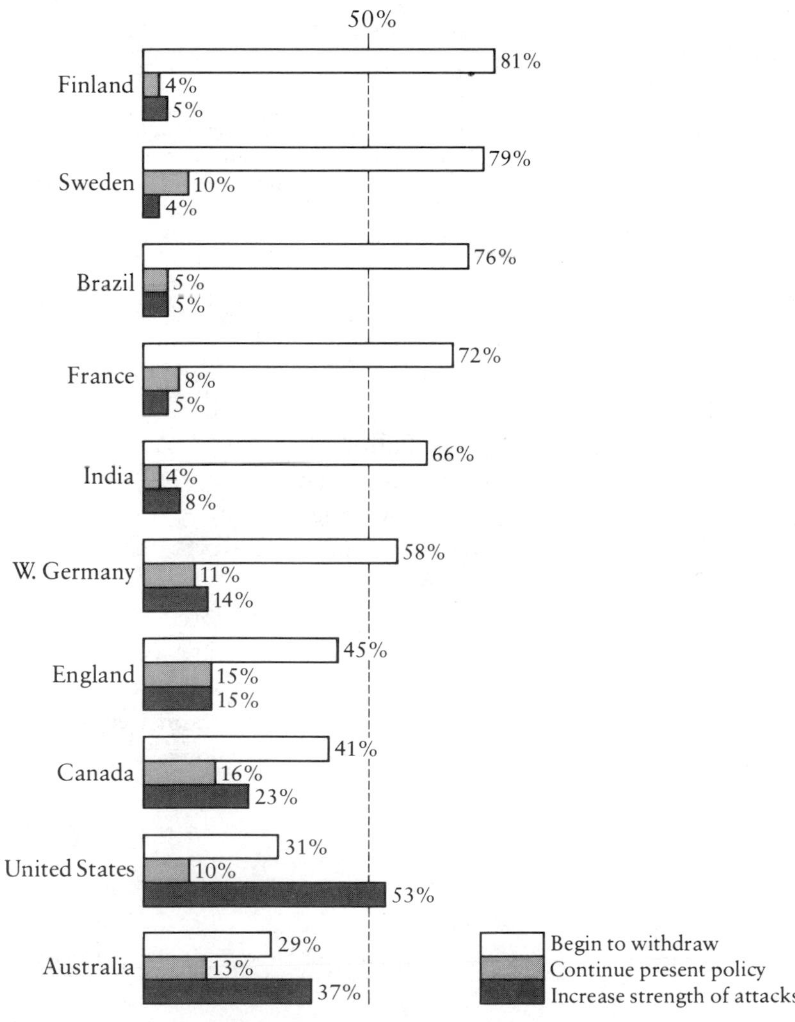

Source: Gallup Opinion Index no. 29, November 1967. Reprinted by permission.

people isolated themselves from world opinion and deluded themselves that they were the shield of the Free World. It is reasonable to conclude that Americans, despite a remarkably free press and apparent good intentions, are no less prone to errors and misperceptions than are other peoples, and that they as much as others should listen carefully to the opinions both of acknowledged friends and apparent enemies.

Moreover, while Americans regard other political cultures as ideological, they fail to recognize that much of the domestic backdrop of their own foreign policy is ideologically motivated. They consider their ideology simply as "democratic," and they dismiss skepticism concerning it. American foreign policy is virtuous, and dissent is "un-American." In such a context, periods of messianism are not uncommon. In his first detailed report to the American public on the two atomic bombings of Japan in 1945, for example, President Harry S Truman invoked heavenly authority.

> We must constitute ourselves trustees of this new force—to prevent its misuse, and to turn it into channels of service to mankind.
>
> It is an awful responsibility which has come to us.
>
> We thank God that it has come to us, instead of to our enemies; and we pray that He may guide us to use it in His ways and for His purposes.[10]

Nearly forty years later, President Ronald Reagan declared, "I have always believed that this anointed land was set apart in an uncommon way, that a divine plan placed this great continent between the oceans to be found by people from every corner of the earth who had a special love of faith and freedom." And, ". . .we are enjoined by scripture and the Lord Jesus to oppose [the evil empire of the Soviet Union] with all our might." Any American foreign policy, however ill-conceived or inhumane, however offensive to international law, is justified by heavenly decree.[11]

The consequences of foreign policy based on this assumption are themselves threats to stable world order, since it exempts American policy from the rule of self-restraint. The Constitutional guarantees of freedom of expression and free press are thus crucially important balances to official doxology.

10. "Radio Report to the American People on the Potsdam Conference," August 9, 1945. See *Public Papers of the Presidents of the United States: Harry S Truman, 1945,* pp. 203–214, at p. 213.
11. For a review of the contemporary consequences of this kind of foreign policy thinking, see Arthur Schlesinger, Jr., "Foreign Policy and the American Character," *Foreign Affairs,* Fall 1983, pp. 1–16.

Conclusion

We live in a world of nations created in response to revolutionary ideals that inspired the founders and continue to motivate subsequent generations. The Pilgrim Fathers, the early Bolsheviks, the Chinese Maoists and the various inspirational heroes of the Third World countries all bequeathed to their followers a special sense of creative mission and a feeling of obligation to carry foward the advances of their revolution. Today, like the missionaries of more religious times, each nation sends forth its young people into the outside world to convert the heathen and spread the gospel. This messianic spirit can be a constructive and energizing force, but when it is overlaid by misperceptions and self-delusions it can become a dangerous basis for international relations. In the incisive words of one observer, here is the image of ideological warfare in the modern world:

> The claim to universality which inspires the moral code of one particular group is incompatible with the identical claim of another group; the world has room for only one, and the other must yield or be destroyed. Thus, carrying their idols before them, the nationalistic masses of our time meet in the international arena, each group convinced that it executes the mandate of history, that it does for humanity what it seems to do for itself, and that it fulfills a sacred mission ordained by Providence, however defined.[12]

12. Hans Morgenthau, *Politics Among Nations,* 4th ed. (New York: Knopf, 1967), p. 249.

II

The Logic of Power

7

Power

The previous chapters have been concerned with values, perceptions and goals of key actors in the contemporary international system. This section focuses on the instruments of foreign policy and the ways that systems of international relations constrain states in their goals. We move from the level of actors to that of systems and interrelationships.

The Nature of Power

What is power in international relations? We may define it broadly as *the ability of an actor on the international stage to use tangible and intangible resources and assets in such a way as to influence the outcomes of international events to its own satisfaction.* This definition points out some of the important features in the relationship of influence among actors. First, power is the means by which international actors deal with one another. It implies possession, but specifically a collection of possessions to create an ability. Second, power is not a natural political attribute, but a product of material (tangible) and behavioral (intangible) resources, each of which has its unique place in the totality of the actor's power. Third, power is a means for achieving influence over other actors who are competing for outcomes favorable to their own objectives. And fourth, the rational use of power is an attempt to shape the outcome of international events in a way that will maintain or improve the actor's satisfaction with the international political environment. The derived satisfaction is normally a measure of the degree to which the influential policy-making elite of a nation perceive their needs and objectives to be served by the prevailing international norms.

These characteristics of power suggest others. It is important, for example, to think of power as having an *instrumental* character. Power is a means to an end, an instrument for achieving objectives. The possession of power is meaningless if its application is unable to bring about results that enhance the wielder's self-interest. Furthermore, one must consider the *relative* character of power. When two states compete over an international objective, their abilities to exert power may be roughly equal (a symmetrical power relationship) or severely unequal (an asymmetrical power relationship). Thus it is important when assessing power to ask, "Powerful relative to whom?" or "Powerful relative to what?" We know, for example, that in 1935 Italy was sufficiently powerful to overrun Ethiopia; its First World War weapons quickly subdued a primitive society. But the same Italian armed forces were virtually impotent in the face of the modern allied assault eight years later.

More modern military examples have dramatized still another peculiarity of power: the use of power may have diminishing returns. In South Vietnam, for example, the United States used virtually all military means short of nuclear warfare to bring about a North Vietnamese withdrawal. Yet for all its firepower it failed to achieve its objective. The North Vietnamese and Viet Cong, infinitely less powerful militarily, were able to seize upon national will and deteriorating support for the war in the United States and among Washington's allies to achieve politically what they could not achieve militarily: governmental self-determination and the expulsion of American force. The diminishing returns of American firepower, together with the superior intangible resources that the North Vietnamese were able to utilize, redressed the apparent asymmetry of their relationship. Some forms of power are impotent indeed!

But vivid as such military examples may be, not all power relationships are measured in armaments. In fact, it should be said categorically that power is not force, and the ability to exert power is not limited to forceful situations. Indeed, international actors exercise their power unceasingly; yet rarely, given the huge volume of international transactions, do they resort to force. Though the frequency of forceful operations may tempt us to think otherwise, the use of force in international relations is an aberration of the normal power relations between states. Force should be thought of as residing at the extreme end of a continuum of choices available to a nation when its agents want to manipulate the outcomes of events.

At the other exterme of that continuum is *persuasion,* or the achievement of influence by the power of reason. Regrettably, it is appropriate only in those international situations in which two actors have a close similarity of objective, or in which one asks but a small alteration in the policy of another in an event that is not crucial to the latter. Beyond this rare case, the achievement of influence depends on the relative availability of positive and negative *sanctions,* which may be extended to affect the behavior of the other party. When the sanctions are positive, they may be regarded as *rewards* or *inducements* to concur in a particular policy. One government, for example, may offer a major trading concession to another in exchange for its support on another issue. When such enticements fail, the same government may resort to negative sanctions, to *punishments* or *deprivations,* to alter the course of another state's policy. It may threaten to rupture diplomatic relations, to discontinue trade or to carry out any of countless other deprivations. Or in situations crucial to its satisfaction an actor can threaten or use *force.* Force, then, is the result of an escalation in the power relationship between actors.

The choice of any of these methods of power depends on several factors in the relationship of the parties. Foremost is the importance of the outcome. A government will not threaten nuclear war over small issues or issues of marginal importance. In addition, the choice of methods depends in part on the access that one actor has to another. Specifically, if the relationship is one in which there is a general agreement on the composition of international satisfaction, then persuasion and rewards will normally be adequate. Equally important, however, is the degree of similarity in the respective interpretations of the specific issue. For example, since the Second World War the United States and Britain have enjoyed an extraordinarily high degree of mutuality on general issues of international satisfaction. Yet they broke sharply over the British role in the Suez War of 1956, an occasion on which the United States resorted to diplomatic embarrassment—public withholding of concurrence—in order to alter the course of British policy. In some cases the problem has another dimension, one in which one government is simply unable to reach another. This was particularly true in the Cold War years when, in order to exert power over America's allies, the Soviet Union had to contend with American responses; and in trying to reach the governments of Eastern Europe the United States was faced with Soviet counteractions.

In all of these situations, it may be concluded that one actor has power over another when it enjoys the superior position in an asymmetrical power relationship. In all cases, diplomatic effectiveness is linked to the capabilities that underlie policy. In cases of ultimate confrontation, it is linked to the state's military capabilities.

The Ingredients of Power Potential

Studies of power in international relations recognize that power is a mixture of capabilities derived from both domestic sources and international activities. Furthermore, such studies recognize that power comes from three sources: *natural, socio-psychological* and *synthetic*. The importance of each varies according to the type of international transaction and to the choice of power exercise that has been selected as a matter of national policy. Needless to say, the greater the degree of conflict and more coercive the intentions, the more intricate will be the combination of power ingredients that have to be brought to bear.

Natural Sources of Power

Among the natural sources of power, *geography* is one of the more important. Decades ago geography was widely regarded as the most important single ingredient of power, though this theory has faded considerably in the era of jet and missile warfare. Nevertheless, geography and territorial position are among the most enduring determinants of national power. They determine the extent of the land mass, which affects both the ease (size) and the difficulty (length of hostile borders) of national defense. The vast extent of the Russian land mass frustrated and devoured invading armies throughout the history of that country, causing the defeat of Napoleon in 1812 and of Hitler nearly 150 years later. But just as sheer size can multiply the defensive capabilities of a state and reduce its vulnerability to enemies, so too can lengthy borders be detrimental to strategic planning and military costs. Both China and the Soviet Union, for example, which share the world's longest hostile border, are acutely aware of the additional costliness those borders present. Similarly Israel, surrounded by boundaries easily traversed by hostile tanks and infantry and further weakened by its tiny size, is severely hindered in national defense by the natural aspects of geography. In contrast, Switzerland is safeguarded against land invasion by mountain barriers; and the United States is protected by three thousand miles of ocean on the east and six thousand on the west, which separate it from major potential antagonists.

Tanker of Liberian registry after attack by Iranian missile, victim of war between Iran and Iraq in which each vowed to interrupt the imports and exports of the other, 1984.

Source: Wide World

It has been demonstrated that the frequency of wars correlates with the number of borders a nation shares, an observation that has led to the theory of geographic opportunity.[1] It was once fashionable in the study of international relations to search for simple geopolitical "laws" that delineated national power for all time. Three prominent examples:

1. Sir Halford Mackinder's "heartland" formula in 1904: "He who rules Eastern Europe commands the Heartland of Eurasia; who rules the Heartland commands the World Island of Europe, Asia, and Africa; and who rules the World Island commands the World."[2]
2. The dictum of Alfred T. Mahan, an American theorist of the late nineteenth century, that control of the seas is decisive in the global balance.[3]

1. James Paul Wesley, "Frequency of Wars and Geographical Opportunity," *Journal of Conflict Resolution* 6, no. 4, (December 1962), pp. 387–89.
2. Sir Halford Mackinder, *Democratic Ideals and Reality* (New York: Holt, 1919), p. 150.
3. Alfred T. Mahan, *The Influence of Sea Power upon History* (Boston: Little, Brown, 1890).

3. Attempts to explain the sweep of Russian imperialism as a search for warm-water ports open in winter.

While there can be no doubt of the importance of seapower, warm-water ports and control of Eastern Europe, efforts to derive immutable geopolitical laws from specific historical instances are prey to fallacy. No monocausal theory can account for the richness of military and political geography; this is not, however, to deny the critical importance of special geopolitical assets such as the Suez and Panama Canals, the Persian Gulf, the Straits of Gibraltar, the Dardanelles and the Straits of Malacca.

But even geographic features of power are not limited in their significance to security. Just as warm-water ports may house major naval facilities, so too do they facilitate international trade, support oceanic and suboceanic research and provide other services vital to national enrichment. By the same token, territorial size not only figures in the equation of national defense, but determines in part the resources that will sustain a population at peace, and that will contribute to the national economic well-being. Any of these factors may play a major role in national cohesiveness, the stature of the nation in the international community and, in general, the satisfaction of the population with international events and its ability to foster that satisfaction.

As suggested in the discussion of geography, a second critical component of power is *natural resources*. Relative endowments of natural resources and raw materials may affect the power of a nation significantly, though here again we should not assume an inflexible connection. There is no doubt that plentiful natural resources have helped to create the superpower status of the United States and the Soviet Union and may someday do the same for Brazil. Nations rich in raw materials are less dependent on the outside world and hence less vulnerable to negative sanctions (blockade, boycott and so on); at the same time they are better able to apply both positive and negative sanctions to opponents. The wealth conferred by natural resources may be held out as a reward, or it may be withheld as a form of persuasive deprivation. Ultimately, it may be used to expand the military potential of the state: the highest negative sanctioning (warmaking) capability.

An extraordinarily instructive example of the ability of natural resources to affect world politics, even to the point of altering its course, is found in the recent policies of the underindustrialized oil-producing states. Through rapid and very large increases in the price of crude petroleum, and by acting collectively through the Organization of Petroleum Exporting Countries (OPEC), most of them have accu-

Third world technology: the Saudi Arabian oil industry.

Source: Lochon/Gamma Liaison

mulated such huge trade surpluses and reserves of foreign currencies ("petro-dollars") that they are able to finance rapid development and to throw the international monetary system into upheaval, loosening its former imperialistic patterns. In addition, the coincidence of these events with exacerbation of Arab-Israeli tensions resulting in war in 1973 enabled the Arab members of OPEC to use the threat of oil embargo and the actual reduction of petroleum exports as an instrument to force many industrialized states to alter their political and economic policies in the region.

However, this should not obscure the fact that there are many poorly endowed nations that are powerful and richly endowed countries that are weak. Japan, for example, imports most of its critical raw materials and yet has been one of the most important economic and military powers of the twentieth century; Indonesia, with huge reserves of minerals, has played an insignificant role on the world stage. A nation that effectively mobilizes its economic and industrial capacities may adjust to a scarcity of raw materials by importing primary products and exporting finished goods. Critical strategic materials can be stockpiled against the possibility of wartime blockade, and natural and synthetic substitutes can be devised in case of shortages.

Quite aside from the warmaking capability that natural resources may impart, such richness is a vital part of national power. It is not because petroleum enables the OPEC members to wage war, for example, that they have been able to adjust the global power distribution by cooperative oil export policies. It is the need of the industrialized world for those riches that has led to the adjustment of international trading relations and the accelerated economic development. The sheer volume of international trade in raw materials dramatizes the amount of dependence that drives it. Also, it indicates the extent to which abundance in natural resources can enhance the ability of a state to influence other parties and, finally, to influence the outcomes of international events without overt force. Only in extreme cases for the need of sanctioning capability are natural resources correlated to military preparedness.

A third natural component of power is *population*.[4] In general, large populations are capable of a variety of social functions and services. They are able to promote industrial vitality, make maximum use of resources and support large military components. Yet there are major exceptions to the rule that size and power are directly correlated. Indonesia, for example, with 152 million people, cannot be ranked in modernity and power with West Germany (62 million), nor can India (676 million) be imagined above Japan (118 million). Table 7–1 reveals the disparity between population size and economic modernity as measure of power. The contribution of population to power depends not exclusively on size, but on the social, economic and psychological consequences of size as well. Among these qualitative factors are level of technical skill, productivity per capita, level of social and political development and effective coordination of human and material resources. Unskilled, starving and ineffectively governed populations such as that of India cannot marshal into effective power their other resources. China, where population size has traditionally been a barrier to modernization of power potential, has only now begun to coordinate its human resources to the point of turning them toward effective development of the state.[5]

Social and Psychological Components of Power

Just as national population size has significance for power, so too do the images, attitudes and expectations of peoples. Among the most critical is *national self-image*, which contributes acutely to the concept

4. For a good general theoretical background, see Katherine Organski and A. F. K. Organski, *Population and World Power* (New York: Oxford University Press, 1960).
5. Alexander Eckstein, *China's Economic Revolution* (New York: Cambridge University Press, 1977), particularly Chapter 6.

TABLE 7–1
Disparity between population and economic modernity as measure of power

Population			*Gross National Product*		
World Rank	*Population (millions)*		*World Rank*	*GNP (bill US $)*	*GNP/capita (US $)*
1	1,032	China	6	552	487
2	676	India	14	159	208
3	370	USSR	2	1,424	4,861
4	332	US	1	2,614	10,408
5	152	Indonesia	31	57	340
6	127	Brazil	9	248	1,846
7	118	Japan	3	1,153	8,946
8	93	Bangladesh	51	11	112
9	87	Pakistan	41	25	260
10	83	Nigeria	22	88	1,032
11	73	Mexico	16	142	1,901
12	62	W. Germany	4	848	12,485
13	56	Italy	8	368	5,855
14	56	United Kingd.	7	445	7,210
15	54	France	5	634	10,709
16	25	Canada	10	243	9,189

Source: For population, United Nations Statistical Papers, Series A, Vol. XXXV, No. 3, "Population and Vital Statistics Report," 1983. For gross national product, *Statistical Abstract of the United States, 1982–83,* p. 865. GNP is reported in current dollars for 1979; GNP/capita is in 1979 data using 1978 constant dollars.
Note: The *Statistical Abstract* lists only 63 countries, and excludes such countries as Saudi Arabia and Kuwait. Because of Saudi Arabia's high GNP, the world ranks here are approximate; and because of Kuwait's high GNP/capita (as with those of the United Arab Emirates, Bahrain and Oman) ranks for GNP/capita are not attempted here. Belgium, The Netherlands, Sweden, and Switzerland also have GNP/capita that either approximate or exceed that or West Germany.

of the role that the nation ought to play. Ideas, even when perverse, govern foreign policy in large measure. Such slogans, for example, as "White Man's Burden," "Manifest Destiny," "World Policeman" and others not only express a mood about national expectation, but form a social framework in which national policy is set. Such policies may be a manifestation more of mood than of rational choice.

Images of others are an equally important part of the policy-making framework. When national peoples hold the governments and peoples of other nation-states in high regard, their attitudes about foreign relations reflect tolerance and forbearance; when they view the second party with mistrust, suspicion and fear, their expectations about foreign policy are reactive at best. Social-psychological research has amply demonstrated that demands on foreign policy stem significantly from perception and from attitudes that peoples hold toward others.

All of these images are products of *political socialization,* the process by which the individual acquires political attitudes. And just as national peoples prepare through fear, affection and propaganda to trust some governments and distrust others, so too do they prepare themselves to measure the potential impacts of international events. Political information is also measured against these ingrained "mind sets" that socialization provides, giving rise to *images of situations*. Not all events are crises, and not all events evoke severe responses. The reaction to an event is a product of the immediacy of the event's consequences. If an event touches closely upon the interests of an individual and threatens to have some immediate impact, the reaction will be pronounced; if it and its probable consequences seem remote, the reaction will be muted. Clearly, when a salient event is initiated by a national actor whose intentions are feared or distrusted, the tendency of an opposing government to prepare a forceful response is understandable. Similarly, in such circumstances the sociopsychological mood of the body politic is elevated, with the result that great pressure is placed upon foreign policy. Tolerance for an adventurous response may result. This is all a result of the mental and emotional interpretation of information.

Political socialization is a continuous process, though ideas that are firmly fixed are difficult to erase or even alter. Nevertheless, it is not uncommon for events to change in significance. In the United States, for example, it seemed likely that the enmity toward China, firmly established in 1950, would take decades or even generations to reverse. Yet a single presidential visit to China unleashed a remarkable groundswell of reversed opinion, with the result that normalization of relations was able to commence in a matter of only months. In another familiar case, the American attitude to continued warfare in Southeast Asia turned around sharply between 1968 and 1972, to the point where there was public demand to discontinue the American involvement without even having achieved minimal objectives. Policymaking in Washington could not for long resist this new element in the opinion structure, and was forced to implement a policy of withdrawal, a policy that only a few months earlier had been officially regarded as defeatist and treacherous. It became clear to major decision-makers that the ability of the government to exert power was limited by the political consequences of resocialization, by the political meaning of a new national mood about the war.

All of these images of self and others contribute to yet another component of power: *public support and cohesion*. Support of government and popular unity are critical morale factors in national power. Internal divisions consume political and military resources needed to secure domestic cohesion, and they pose the danger of a "fifth column"—a domestic faction unifying itself with a foreign enemy. For example, some Ukrainian separatists joined the Nazi invaders

Source: Dennis Brack/Black Star
The power of population. . . . Public calisthenics are an integral part of the Chinese civil defense program.

of the Soviet Union in the hope of liberation from Russian domination. A relatively unified population such as Israel's, on the other hand, is capable of great exertions.

Unity does not necessarily indicate how "democratic" a government is. It is not consistently true that democratic regimes have enjoyed more popular support in foreign affairs than authoritarian governments. Germans rallied behind Hitler from 1936 to 1945, while the French were on the whole less unified in support of their democracy in the prewar years. The popularity of a government is difficult to measure from the outside—for example, the Castro government of Cuba is considered highly popular by some observers and highly unpopular by others. What counts in conflict is the effective disposition of the population to mobilize resources and undertake sacrifices proportionate to the perceived importance of the outcome. Thus, *unity* and *public will* are the indispensable catalysts for transforming potential power into useful power.

Final among the social determinants of power is *leadership*. The quality of leadership is the most unpredictable component of national power. Leadership orchestrates the other components, defines goals in a realizable manner and determines the path of strategy.[6]

China exemplifies the extent to which a change in leadership alone can mobilize the other latent energies and capacities of a nation, transforming it from the weak victim of a succession of international predators to a self-sufficient power able to exercise considerable influence in foreign affairs. The same population with the same territory and endowment of natural resources can be weak and disunited or strong and dynamic, depending on the quality of leadership.

Sometimes the rise of a unique individual at a particular moment catalyzes other historical forces to change the trend of events. Napoleon, Bismarck, Hitler, Franklin Roosevelt, de Gaulle, Lenin, Castro, Mao—these were visionary and sometimes charismatic leaders who changed the equation of international power and the course of international history. Some believe that the role of the individual "hero" in history has been falsely glamorized and overstated, and that events are decided more by systematic factors in national capability than by such idiosyncratic elements as individual personalities. And yet who does not believe that an incredible determination on the part of the British people to resist, in a bleak hour when Britain stood alone, was roused by Winston Churchill's defiance: "We shall fight on the beaches, we shall fight on the landing grounds, we shall fight in the fields and in the streets, we shall fight in the hills; we will never surrender." Leadership cannot create power out of air, but in can dip into untapped reserves of national creative energy. Sometimes a single statesman makes the difference.

The Synthetic Components of Power

In addition to the natural and sociopsychological determinants of power, there are some that are synthetic. These involve the skillful use of human and other resources in such a way as to coordinate, develop and ready the state to put its power into motion. Most important are *industrial capacity* and *military preparedness.*

Industrial capacity is virtually synonymous with major-power status in the twentieth century. Modern war requires both a sophisticated

6. Substantial scholarship exists on the extent to which leadership personality determines the selection of strategies (including war/no-war decisions). See particularly Harold D. Lasswell, *Psychopathology and Politics* (Chicago: University of Chicago Press, 1930) and *Power and Personality* (New York: Norton, 1948), and more recently a quantitative study by Lloyd S. Etheredge, *A World of Men: The Private Sources of American Foreign Policy* (Cambridge, Mass.: M.I.T. Press, 1978).

manufacturing capability and huge economic resources. The victory of the Allied powers in the Second World War, for example, may be traced to the ability of Soviet and American assembly lines to turn out artillery pieces, tanks and aircraft in greater numbers than the German and Japanese factories. The economic costs are staggering: the individual American soldier today is supported by annual equipment expenditures of almost $45 thousand; American outlays in Vietnam averaged several hundred thousand dollars for each communist soldier killed. Modern warfare is mechanized, expensive and technologically complex, and the ranking of nations by gross national product approximates closely their ranking in military power.[7] (See Table 7–2.)

Quantitative studies of power and capability have tended to confirm the importance of industrial capacity as the single most important determinant of power.[8] One found that the wealthier state or coalition won thirty-one of thirty-nine international wars from 1815 to 1945, suggesting that an advantage in industrial capacity brings victory in

TABLE 7–2
Ten principal military powers by expenditure, in US $ billions, 1981

	Military Expenditure	*Rank in GNP*
USA	170.0	1
USSR	135.5	2[a]
China	39.4	6[b]
UK	27.2	7
France	27.2	5
W. Germany	27.0	4
Saudi Arabia	25.8	>10
Japan	10.4	3
Italy	10.3	8
E. Germany	4.1	>10[a]

Source: SIPRI Yearbook, 1983, pp. 161–166. GNP rankings are expressed in constant prices and exchange rates based on 1980 values.

[a]Soviet and other WTO figures are estimates. US intelligence sources place the expenditures as much as 50 percent higher.
[b]Chinese figure as estimated by SIPRI.

7. Indeed, one study found that perceptions of laymen regarding the power rankings of nations correlate highly with GNP—people expect rich nations to be stronger. Norman Alcock and Alan Newcombe, "The Perception of National Power," *Journal of Conflict Resolution* 14, no. 3 (November 1970), pp. 335–43.
8. F. Clifford German, "A Tentative Evaluation of World Power," *Journal of Conflict Resolution* 4, no. 1 (March 1960), pp. 138–44; Rudolph Rummel, "Indicators of Cross-National and International Patterns," *American Political Science Review* 68, no. 1 (March 1969), pp. 127–47; Bruce Russett, *International Regions and the International System* (Chicago: Rand McNally, 1967); and Harvey Starr, *War Coalitions* (Lexington, Mass.: D. C. Heath, 1973).

four of five cases.[9] This reduces the warmaking function from heroic exploits of brave men to mundane statistical comparisons between the number of ironworkers, ballbearing output, efficiency of the airframe industry and so forth. Military might today depends as much on the managers as on the generals.

Power and the Ability to "Win" in War

We have identified several elements of national power potential: geography, natural resources, industrial capacity, population, governmental support and the quality of leadership. All are important, but industrial capacity is the outstanding *economic* variable and the quality of leadership is the most important *political* factor. Each state has a certain innate capacity to exercise influence on the world stage, and leadership determines the extent and purposes for which this capacity will be used.

The exercise of power takes many forms in international relations. Economic rewards and punishments may be used to elicit favorable responses from other nations. Cultural influence may be extended through the transfer of products, mass media, student exchanges and published materials. Public opinion in other countries can be influenced through direct propaganda efforts such as the Voice of America and the large foreign radio transmission programs of the Soviet Union, Egypt and other states. The international sale of armaments provides the exporter with a variety of positive and negative sanctioning powers, as shipments can be expanded or withheld. Power within international organizations and alliances may take the form of skillful lobbying and bargaining. Influence operates by various means, and it should not be assumed that the exercise of power most often involves the application of physical force. Most typically, force is used when one actor, unable to compromise on the outcome of an issue, perceives that it must deprive the opponent of alternative solutions.

Still, force tends to have overriding importance in international relations. Arab states may attempt to revise their borders with Israel through diplomatic persuasion, propaganda, economic sanctions and a host of other means, but in territorial conflicts, war is often the ultimate means. Especially in the international arena, where institutional means of conflict resolution are still at a low level of development and peace-enforcing authority is weak, the potential influence of an

9. Steven Rosen, "War Power and the Willingness to Suffer," in Bruce Russett, editor, *Peace, War, and Numbers* (Beverly Hills, Ca.: Sage Publishing Company, 1972), pp. 176–78.

actor is critically dependent on its capacity to wage war in the regions where its values are deeply engaged.

We may conceptualize war as a distribution mechanism making allocations of scarce goods to competing parties. The two sides make mutually exclusive claims to a given position or resource (such as a piece of territory or control of the instruments of state) and war decides who is to get what. The decision rule that operates in making a settlement is to award to each side a share of the disputed values that corresponds to its relative war power. War establishes a *ratio of power* between the contestants, and political bargaining allocates the prize according to this formula.

It is crucial, therefore, to understand the nature of power in war. The factors of power potential are translated into effective war power in terms of two specific warmaking capabilities: strength, meaning the ability to impose sanctions or to destroy the assets of the adversary, and cost tolerance, meaning the willingness to tolerate deprivation or the destruction that the enemy imposes on one's own assets. Our relative power in war is a function of my willingness to tolerate the harm that you are able to impose, versus your willingness to tolerate the harm that I am able to impose. Thus, the power to win wars is based on political as well as military factors.

The Importance of Cost Tolerance

The visible side of war is the mutual imposition of negative sanctions by two parties, tempting the observer to view the power relationship mainly as a function of relative strength. But the critical role of cost tolerance cannot be overlooked. A party inferior in strength and yet superior in cost tolerance may paradoxically be more powerful than a strong opponent less willing to suffer. This was precisely the case in Vietnam, where the physical might of the United States vastly exceeded that of the communists, yet the total power equation was nearly even or tilted to the weaker side. Ho Chi Minh predicted, "In the end the Americans will kill ten patriots for every American who dies, but it is they who will tire first." This was also the model in Algeria, where the deep commitment of the nationalists enabled them to withstand the immense power of France longer than the less committed French were willing to accept much lower costs delivered upon them by the Algerians. A study of forty wars found that almost half of them were won by the party that suffered more.[10]

10. Rosen, *ibid.*

Revolutionary strategists, who see themselves fighting the might of global imperialism, have put special emphasis on the idea that courageous hearts can compensate for the opponent's superior strength. The power of the anti-imperialists is their willingness to die; Arab commandos call themselves *fedayeen*—"the sacrificers." Chinese strategists, too, emphasize the military importance of revolutionary commitment and determination,[11] and an Irish revolutionist said, "It is a question which can last longer, the whip or the back."

This image of war is one of torture. The victim is on the table, and the question is whether his will can be broken by torment. Sometimes the resistance of the victim is actually stiffened by his suffering. German terror bombing of London had such a reverse effect—"the stimulus of blows."[12] A more recent example is the American bombing of North Vietnam:

The power of national determination . . . . These Afghan rebels share a horse and use outmoded weapons against the modern arms, helicopters and tanks of the Soviet forces occupying their country. Nevertheless, the number of guerrillas is growing, and their attacks increasing.

Source: UPI

11. See Robert North, *The Foreign Relations of China* (Belmont, Ca.: Dicksenson Publishing Company, 1969), pp. 34–35.
12. Arnold Toynbee, *A Study of History* (London: Oxford University Press, 1934), vol. 2, pp. 100–12.

> So far from terrorizing and disrupting the people the bombings seem to me to have stimulated and consolidated them. By the nature of the attacks so far, civilian casualities have not been very great, but they have been enough to provide the government of the Vietnam Republic with the most totally unchallengeable propaganda they could ever have dreamed of. A nation of peasants and manual workers who might have felt restive or dissatisfied under the stress of totalitarian conditions had been obliged to forget their differences in the common sense of resistance and self-defense. From the moment the US dropped its first bomb on the North of Vietnam, she welded the nation together unshakeably.[13]

The revolutionary's conviction that the will to resist can overcome immense disparities in material strength is often questioned by orthodox strategists. To a claim that communist cost tolerance in Vietnam was a bottomless pit, for example, Henry Kissinger is said to have replied, "Every pit has a bottom." While it is evident that in his devotion to a cause the revolutionary may survive overwhelming odds, it is clear that Kissinger is also right: more often than not, the weaker party will yield. The nation with a superior industrial capacity starts with a long lead in war power.

Measuring War Power

How do we determine which of two adversaries is the more powerful? How is it possible, given the complexities of the power relationship, to say that one nation is a "major power" and another weak? How can decision-makers reasonably estimate their national power potential in relation to a certain opponent, to chart a strategic course in the face of many uncertainties? One observer notes that in war "all action must . . . be planned in a mere twilight, which . . . like the effect of fog or moonshine, gives to things exaggerated dimensions and an unnatural appearance."[14] Systematic planning requires reasonably reliable bases on which to estimate the probabilities that a given course of action will have a predictable outcome. How can national leadership measure the balance of war power and plan accordingly?

There are many inherent uncertainties and difficulties in assigning specific weights to the various factors in war power, particularly in advance of actual fighting. The cost tolerance factor is wholly psychological and subjective, and there is no empirical referent simply visible to both parties by which the willingness to endure negative sanctions can be estimated reliably in advance.

13. James Cameron, *Here Is Your Enemy* (New York: Holt, Rinehart and Winston, 1966), p. 66.
14. Karl von Clausewitz, *On War* (Baltimore: Penguin, 1968), p. 189; originally published in 1832.

Even purely physical capabilities in war are exceedingly difficult to estimate. Simple magnitudes of hardware must be assessed. How many *X*-type tanks equal a *Y* piece of artillery, and under what conditions of development? Obviously, opinions will vary. Even the gross defense expenditures of an opponent may be difficult to estimate. It has been shown, for instance, that different methods of computation by "reliable" analysts yield estimates of Soviet defense expenditures as a percentage of US defense expenditures ranging from 28 percent to more than 100 percent for the same year.[15] Still more difficult to estimate is the skill a nation can show in the use of its available forces.

The age of the computer and the availability of quantitative techniques for measuring social and political phenomena have resulted in repeated efforts to give a precise answer to the question, "What is the probable outcome of a war between state *A* and state *B*?" Far more than a scholar's game, this quest has been a statesman's obsession; during the early years of involvement in Vietnam, Secretary of Defense Robert McNamara employed a battery of computer techniques and highly trained quantitative social scientists in an attempt to measure the probable outcomes of alternative strategies for victory in limited war. Although the attempts at prediction have all failed miserably, the drive for new and better answers continues.

The most common starting point in compiling measurable and comparable indices is the relative gross national products of the involved parties.[16] These give rough measures of the economic capacity of states to wage war, but careful scrutiny of results shows that economic data alone are not enough. Recently it has been argued that the measurement of probable outcomes must rest not only on a variety of economic data, but also on data expressing the level of political development of each participant, on the ground that economic and political development do not necessarily occur at the same pace. Hence a country with evidence of economic growth might still lack the political capability to organize its human and other resources for war. Thus, in addition to economic comparability, any prediction of probable outcomes must include a measure of the capacity of the political system of each combatant to fulfill the demands of its own constituents and the different and special demands that are imposed upon it by the international political environment.

The measurement of the internal factors involves quantitative evidence of governmental ability to exert as much control as possible on

15. Lynn Turgeon, "The Enigma of Soviet Defense Expenditures," *Journal of Conflict Resolution* 8, no. 2 (June 1964), pp. 116–20.
16. A standard example is J. David Singer, S. Bremer, and J. Stuckey, "Capability Distribution, Uncertainty and Major Power War, 1820–1965," in Bruce Russett, editor, *Peace, War and Numbers*.

the population in order to achieve international objectives. To give mathematical order to the relative strengths of enemies, the *internal component of power* must be tabulated. A suggested formula is:

$$\text{Internal component of power} = \left(\frac{\text{gross national product}}{\text{population}}\right) \times (\text{population}) \times (\text{tax effort})$$

where the tax effort is the computed relation of the tax capacity of the economy (based on GNP) and the willingness of the government to exert pressure to extract enough to wage war effectively. It is also suggested that the *external component of power* be expressed as:

$$(\text{foreign aid accumulated}) \times (\text{tax effort of the recipient})$$

The total measurable power of the state, then, should be the sum of these two formulae; and by tabulating these indices for two or more combatants, a rough measurement of probable outcome should emerge.[17]

Efforts to measure only the tangible frustrate attempts to measure power comprehensively, however, and undoubtedly explain the limitation of McNamara's efforts to measure comparability of the potential to win. Power, in addition to being relative, is situationally specific and cannot be divorced from purpose.[18] Thus, in addition to measuring tangible capability, any successful formula must include not only perceptions, but motivations as well.[19] Apparently with these warnings in mind, another researcher has attempted to measure both the physical and the motivational elements of power, this time using the formula

$$P_p = (C + E + M) \times (S + W)$$

where P_p is perceived power; C is the critical mass of population and territory; E and M are economic and military capabilities, respectively; S is strategic purposes; and W is the will to pursue national strategies.[20]

17. A. F. K. Organski and Jacek Kugler, "Davids and Goliaths: Predicting the Outcomes of International Wars," *Comparative Political Studies,* July 1978, pp. 141–80.
18. David A. Baldwin, "Power Analysis and World Politics: New Trends versus Old Tendencies," *World Politics,* January 1979, pp. 161–94. Baldwin summarizes recent studies on power comparability and critiques their weaknesses and identifies their valuable contributions.
19. Richard W. Cottam, *Foreign Policy Motivation: A General Theory and a Case Study* (Pittsburgh: University of Pittsburgh Press, 1977), particularly Part 1 ("Foreign Policy Motivation") and Part 3 ("Eliminating the Perceptual Basis of Conflict").
20. Ray S. Cline, *World Power Assessment: A Calculus of Strategic Drift* (Washington, D.C.: Georgetown University, The Center for Strategic and International Studies, 1975).

Note that in simplest form, this statement says that power is the product of physical capabilities and psychological capabilities. In Table 7–3, the ranking reflects this multiplication, thus departing from what might be called the conventional wisdom of measuring only the physical factors. For example, although the United States ranks considerably above the Soviet Union in physical measurements, the superior will of the Soviets to mobilize around national strategies gives them a much higher total than the United States. Note, however, that this study was completed in the years following the Vietnam War, when American resolve was low. A sweeping change in the notion of America serving as the world's democratic policeman followed the war. More recently, Cold War interventionist attitudes have enjoyed a resurgence, to the point where some now regard the folly of the Vietnam War not to have been American involvement, but to have taken the war as an illustration of the premise that intervention is undesirable. Were this study to be repeated today, the gap between the Soviet Union and the United States on the behavioral end of the formula undoubtedly would be narrower. Public tolerance of President Reagan's bellicose policies in Central America offers ample testimony.

Given the frequency of war by alliance, it is perhaps more useful to consider groups of nations. For example, the total for the United States and its major NATO allies is 147, while for the Soviet Union and its allies in Eastern Europe it is 102.5.

If the present power ratio between two parties is not easily measured, the projection of trends to predict probable future power relations is even more difficult to make. To assess present and future conditions, each party must make complex calculations based on arbitrary as-

TABLE 7–3
Power comparability by physical and psychological factors

Country	*Elements of Perceived Power*	*National Strategy/Will Coefficient*	*Total*
USSR	45	1.5	67.5
USA	50	0.7	35.0
West Germany	18	1.5	27.0
France	20	1.2	24.0
China	23	1.0	23.0
Brazil	16	1.3	20.8
Iran	14	1.4	19.6
UK	19	1.0	19.0
Canada	20	0.9	18.0
Japan	17	1.0	17.0

Source: Adapted from Ray S. Cline, *World Power Assessment* (Washington, D.C. Georgetown University, 1975), p. 125. Reprinted by permission. Note that the study occurred prior to Iran's destructive revolution of 1978–79, and its war with Iraq.

sumptions. Policy must be planned on the basis of perceptions of present factors and expectations of the future. The result is a highly conjectural process of reasoning in which it is necessary to rely on "guesstimates" at critical points to reach general and usable conclusions on which to base policy. How do you weigh the imponderables? Referring to the final decision to attack Pearl Harbor, the Japanese war minister said, "Once in a while it is necessary for one to close one's eyes and jump from the stage of the Kiyomizu Temple."[21] The Japanese

> went to war with a beautifully complex plan of attack but without a clear answer to the single question of how they were going to win. There was, to be sure, the expectation that the U.S. would shortly decide that the costs of defeating Japan were not worth the gains and would therefore seek a compromise peace. But the Japanese did not give this critical hypothesis any real analysis. It was a hope nourished from despair at the alternatives.[22]

Strategic Decisions Under Conditions of Risk

At each stage of strategic analysis, opinions diverge over whether optimistic or pessimistic assessments are warranted. Alternative pictures of any situation confront decision-makers with a range of power ratios from which they must choose. Should President Johnson have listened to the Joint Chiefs of Staff in 1965, for example, who told him that the communists could be defeated in Vietnam within two years, or to the CIA, which gave him a much gloomier prediction?

Research findings are highly contradictory about whether statesmen generally decide on optimistic estimates or darker ones. One study has found that social groups tend to overrate themselves and underrate their opponents,[23] but another found quite the opposite: that the "armed services inevitably overstate the military capabilities of the opponent."[24] Still a third study found that aggressors sometimes recognize the potential superiority of their opponents, perceiving this edge

21. Quoted in Stanford Studies in International Conflict and Integration, *Annual Report to the Ford Foundation* (Stanford, Ca.: Stanford University Press, 1961), p. 4.
22. Warner Schilling, "Surprise Attack, Death, and War," *Journal of Conflict Resolution* 9, no. 3 (September 1965), p. 389.
23. Bernard Bass and George Dunteman, "Biases in the Evaluation of One's Own Group, Its Allies, and Opponents," *Journal of Conflict Resolution* 7, no. 1 (March 1963), pp. 16–20.
24. Samuel Huntington, "Arms Races," in Carl Friedrich and Seymour Harris, editors, *Public Policy 1958* (Cambridge, Mass.: Harvard University Press, 1958). "In 1914, for instance, the Germans estimated the French Army to have 121,000 more men than the German Army, the French estimated the German Army to have 134,000 more men than the French Army, but both parties agreed in their estimates of the military forces of third parties."

more clearly than do the defenders, but take the risk that it will not be effective.[25] The inconclusiveness of this evidence underscores the subjective component in framing assumptions about going to war.

It is likely that a full study of strategic planning in past wars would show that decision-makers tended to use optimistic rather than pessimistic assumptions *if* both were based on equally plausible information. Effective leadership will concede critical objectives only when there is no reasonable hope of successful struggle. The rational strategy for mobilizing public will and forging national unity is to use the more optimistic estimates, provided that they are equiprobable with pessimistic alternatives.

Sometimes, of course, the use of hopeful estimates is mere grasping at straws. When the overwhelmingly superior Athenians demanded that the Melians surrender during the Peloponnesian War (431–404 B.C.), the Melians chose to resist.

> We know that the fortune of war is sometimes more impartial than the disproportion of numbers might lead one to suppose; to submit is to give ourselves over to despair, while action still preserves for us a hope that we may stand erect.[26]

It was an unfortunate decision. The Melians were easily defeated; the men all put to death, the women and children taken as slaves.

Another example of the grasping-at-straws syndrome was the reasoning of a Spanish commander about to sail with the Armada to its defeat at the hands of the British Navy, a defeat which destroyed Spain as a global power (1588).

> It is well known that we fight in God's cause. So when we meet the English, God will surely arrange matters so that we can grapple and board them, either by sending some strange freak of weather, or more likely, just by depriving the English of their wits. If we come to close quarters, Spanish valor and Spanish steel—and the great mass of soldiers we shall have on board—will make our victory certain. But unless God helps us by making a miracle, the English, who have faster guns and handier ships than ours, and many more long-range guns, and who know their advantage as well as we do, will never close with us at all, but stand aloof and blow us to pieces with their culverins, without our being able to do them any serious hurt. . . . So we are sailing against England in the confident hope of a miracle.[27]

Such was a very unfortunate line of thought.

25. Bruce Russett, "The Calculus of Deterrence," *Journal of Conflict Resolution* 7, no. 2 (June 1963), p. 97.
26. Thucydides, *The Peloponnesian War* (New York: Modern Library, 1951), pp. 330–37.
27. Quoted in Bernard and Fawn Brodie, *From Crossbow to H-bomb* (New York: Dell, 1962), pp. 67–68.

These are the extreme cases. Ordinarily, optimistic planning is based not on wild fancy but on seemingly reasonable estimates, such as the expectation of the Joint Chiefs in 1965 that the North Vietnamese could not withstand strategic bombing or the deployment of a half-million well-armed American troops. Doubters may offer gloomier projections, but they cannot prove their case over the optimists. The final decision is always in some measure a leap of faith. Hitler bet that the British and French would not intervene over Czechoslovakia; he was right. Acheson and Truman bet that the Chinese would not intervene in Korea; they were wrong. Certainty is much easier looking back than for the decision-maker forced to rely on advance projections!

How Wars Start and End

Overrating your own power means relatively underrating your opponent. In the First World War, for example, both the French and the Germans expected quick victories within a matter of weeks; both were disappointed. In Vietnam, each side long believed that the other would eventually yield, so that victory was purely a matter of time. The communists seemed to have in mind the example of Algeria or their own victory over the French in Vietnam, while the Americans based their policy on the model of postwar Greece and Malaya, where guerrillas had been defeated.

We noted earlier that the function of a war settlement is to allocate values in proportion to war power. Since the two parties have different pictures of the power ratio in advance of the fighting, they propose different settlements to each other. Each considers that the other is offering too little. The Americans reasoned in Vietnam, "Why should we accept a communist-dominated coalition government when they will be unable to force one on the battlefield?" The communists reasoned, "Why should we give up our political goals as the Americans demand when the trend of battle is sure to favor us?" The disparity in power perceptions ensures conflicting political demands.

Some theorists have argued that were it not for the disparity in power perceptions it would not be necessary to fight wars at all. Having a common assessment of the power ratio, the parties could simulate the war decision by making the same settlement in advance, without the bloodshed.[28] Both sides would be favored by avoiding violence if the same distribution could be achieved without it. Some parties might fight anyway without expecting victory, in despair at the alternatives

28. See for example, Raymond Mack and Richard Snyder, "An Analysis of Social Conflict," *Journal of Conflict Resolution* 1, no. 2 (June 1957), p. 217.

or in "confident hope of a miracle," or at least to make it expensive for the aggressor; but in most cases rational decision-makers would make the settlement without pointless violence.

The poverty of this theory is evident: it is seldom possible to predict the outcome with confidence. Opinions will differ about what resources the enemy has, what resources the enemy will use, how much outside help each side will get, whether the enemy will tolerate a given level of costs, exactly what the enemy intends to do, and which of several conflicting statistical estimates is correct.[29] It is undoubtedly true that "the most effective prerequisite for preventing struggle, the exact knowledge of the comparative strength of the two parties, is very often obtainable only by the actual fighting out of the conflict."[30] Unfortunately, "No medium of exchange [can] be devised which [will] bear the same relation to estimates of fighting power as monetary metals do to estimates of economic value."[31] War itself must sometimes resolve diverse perceptions of the power ratio.

Wars end when the parties arrive at a common picture of their relative power and a common assessment of appropriate settlement claims.[32] There is negotiating on these questions within each nation as well as between nations. Internal debate may split between "superpatriots," who want to fight on for national honor regardless of the odds, and "traitors," who are accused of being overly eager to throw in the towel and surrender. A leader making peace on less than perfect terms must sell both the settlement and his version of the battlefield situation to his own people.

One of the functions of international mediation is to help national leaders find domestic support for imperfect settlements. When a significant portion of the politically active population believes that the war situation is not as dire as claimed by the leadership, and/or that the leadership is making a needlessly unfavorable settlement, the basis may be molded for a later political reaction against the settlement. One of Hitler's main appeals was the claim that the nation had been sold out in 1918 and his demand that the Versailles treaty be repudiated as a document of shame. A stable settlement means that the agreement, however unfavorable, must be accepted as realistic.

Some kinds of conflict lend themselves to settlement more readily

29. Compare Fred Ikle, *Every War Must End* (New York: Columbia University Press, 1971), especially Chapter 2, "The Fog of Military Estimates."

30. Georg Simmel, "The Sociology of Conflict," *American Journal of Sociology* 9 (January 1904), pp. 490–525.

31. Harold D. Lasswell, "Compromise," in *Encyclopedia of the Social Sciences,* vol. 4 (New York: Macmillan, 1930), p. 148.

32. See William T. R. Fox, editor, *How Wars Are Ended,* the November 1970 issue of the *Annals of the American Academy of Political and Social Science.*

than others. In pre-Napoleonic wars, common symbols were available as manifestations of potency visible to both sides—for example, possession of a specific fortress or strategic position. When one side gained possession of these symbols, it was clear to leaders and followers on both sides that the issue was concluded.[33] In modern war, struggle engages whole societies, and victory and defeat are not so clearly marked. The victor is the side that wins the last battle, but which battle is the last is not so obvious. One exception to this problem might be a nuclear war, where the conclusion would be only too decisive.

Wars end when mutual rejection of claims is not worth the costs of continued fighting to either side, in light of the available strategic estimates.[34] As the power estimates of the two sides become congruent, their offers of settlement converge. In Vietnam, the United States at first offered the Vietcong a deal that amounted to its dissolution as a political force, while the Vietcong offered to preside over the dismemberment of the Saigon regime. As the two sides' optimistic hopes of decisive victory were frustrated, they came closer together.

The immediate function of war, then, is to provide empirical evidence to adjust divergent assessments of relative power in order to permit the parties to develop similar perceptions of reality upon which to base a settlement. The purpose of fighting is not ordinarily to destroy an opponent completely (the "Carthaginian peace"), or to deprive him of residual strength and render him helpless and defenseless. Wars seldom go this far. It is not usually necessary to destroy an opponent to change his opinion or values, or to cancel his objectives. The Second World War, which was fought to an unconditional surrender, is a notable exception.

Wars begin with a determination on the part of each group to convince the opponent of its version of the power ratio. The ideal strategic goal in war is to bring the enemy's power estimate to the point at which he will agree to the settlement that you seek. Full victory is obtained by one side if it can bring the other's perception all the way around to its view.[35] Typically, however, there is a process of mutual adjustment and compromise, where neither side can completely enforce its version of reality.

33. See Lewis Coser, "The Termination of Conflict," *Journal of Conflict Resolution* 5, no. 2 (December 1961), pp. 347–53. Many of the ideas in this chapter were developed in this seminal article. See also Anatol Rapoport's introduction to Karl von Clausewitz, *On War* (Baltimore: Penguin, 1968), p. 19.

34. Compare Paul Kecskemeti, *Strategic Surrender* (New York: Atheneum, 1964), especially pp. 5–30.

35. See Robert North, et al., "Capability, Threat, and the Outbreak of War," in James Rosenau, editor, *International Politics and Foreign Policy* (New York: Free Press, 1961).

Changes in Capability and the Outbreak of War

Wars occur during historical periods when there are major shifts in the balance of capabilities. New distributions of strength need to be tested to ascertain their limits. Spurts in industrial development, resource discovery, inventions and other developments in military power correlate with the frequency of international conflict.[36] Herman Kahn has estimated that fundamental advances in weaponry, which once occurred every five hundred years, now occur about every five years.[37] This accelerated development, coupled with the global diffusion of arms technology, may explain the frequency of wars in modern times (see Table 7–4), even though the Soviet-American strategic arms race has stabilized the relations of the superpowers.

Changes in the distribution of power will occur also after a war is settled. A good settlement should allocate values in such a fashion that future shifts in the power ratio between the two parties will not cause one side to reignite the struggle for a better distribution. In other words, the settlement should reflect not only the momentary balance of capabilities, but also reasonable estimates of future trends. A peace arranged by Jovian between Rome and Persia in A.D. 363, although not completely satisfactory to either party, so closely approximated the power relationship that it enabled the two sides to avoid further struggle for 150 years. Interestingly, the balance broke down when a minor border skirmish in A.D. 502 showed Persia to be stronger in relation to Rome than either of them had expected. Further fighting was then resorted to as a test of the new power ratio's limits.[38]

The Management of Power

In our discussion of power we have given primary emphasis to the threat or use of force as a means of influence. The dilemma is that nations continue to find military capabilities useful and necessary instruments of diplomatic action (as evidenced by constantly expanding defense budgets in many countries), even while technological changes make the use of violence ever more horrible and cataclysmic. In ancient and medieval warfare, a battle might rage all morning between two

36. See E. Chertok, "Source of International Tension," *3 Bulletin of the Research Exchange on the Prevention of War* no. 17, 1955, p. 20.
37. Herman Kahn, *On Thermonuclear War* (Princeton, N.J.: Princeton University Press, 1960).
38. Vern Bullough, "The Roman Empire vs. Persia, 363–502: A Study of Successful Deterrence," *Journal of Conflict Resolution 7,* no. 1 (March 1963), pp. 55–68.

TABLE 7–4
Ninety wars, 1945–83, with starting dates.

War	Year	War	Year
Syria-Lebanon	1945	India-Pakistan	1965
Indonesia	1945	Indonesia	1965
China	1945	Biafra	1966
Malaya	1945	Israel-Arab states	1967
Indochina	1946	Czechoslovakia	1968
Greece	1946	Malaysia	1969
Madagascar	1947	El Salvador	1969
India-Pakistan	1947	Chad	1969
Kashmir	1947	Northern Ireland	1969
Philippines	1948	Ethiopia (Eritrea)	1970
Israel-Arab states	1948	Cambodia	1971
Hyderabad	1948	Bangladesh/Kashmir	1971
Burma	1948	Burundi	1972
Korea	1950	Israel-Arab states	1973
Formosa	1950	Iraq (Kurdish)	1974
Tibet	1950	Cyprus	1974
Kenya	1952	Angola	1975
Guatemala	1954	Timor	1975
Algeria	1954	Lebanon	1975
Sudan	1955	Spanish Morocco	1976
Cyprus	1955	Somalia-Ethiopia	1977
Sinai	1956	Ethiopia (Eritrea)	1977
Hungary	1956	Syria-Lebanon	1977
Suez	1956	Libya-Egypt	1977
Lebanon	1958	Iran	1978
Cuba	1958	Nicaragua	1978
Vietnam	1959	Vietnam-Laos	1978
Himalayas	1959	Chad	1978
Rwanda	1959	Zaire	1978
Laos	1959	Rhodesia (Zimbabwe)	1978
Congo	1960	N. Yemen-S. Yemen	1979
Colombia	1960	Uganda-Tanzania	1979
Cuba (Bay of Pigs)	1961	China-Vietnam	1979
Goa	1961	Vietnam-Kampuchea	1979
Angola	1961	Nicaragua	1979
Yemen	1962	South Africa-Angola	1979
West New Guinea	1962	USSR-Afghanistan	1980
Portuguese Guinea	1962	Iran-Iraq	1980
Algeria-Morocco	1963	El Salvador	1980
Cyprus	1963	Britain-Argentina (Falkland Islands)	1982
Malaysia	1963	Israel-Syria-PLO (in Lebanon)	1982
Somalia-Kenya	1963	Kampuchea-Thailand	1983
Zanzibar	1964	Sri Lanka	1983
Thailand	1964	US-Grenada	1983
Mozambique	1964		
Dominican Republic	1965		

mercenary armies, pause, and then resume with equal ferocity in the afternoon, leaving at the end of the day losses of perhaps twenty men and a donkey. In trench warfare, on the other hand, the gain or loss of a few hundred yards may cost ten thousand lives. This form of fighting accounts for the dramatic increase in casualties in conventional warfare during the first quarter of the present century (see Figure 7–1). Modern nuclear warfare has the potential to tower above these numbers, as exemplified in the 100,000 deaths that resulted from the atomic bombings of Hiroshima and Nagasaki in 1945. Recent advances in both explosive might and delivery accuracy would enable a missile-launched thermonuclear war targeted to major population centers to kill millions of people instantly.

Clearly, controls must be established over the use of force, both to prevent the outbreak of war and to limit the scope and intensity of struggle once begun. International relations scholars look to three basic ideas for the control of power in the next hundred years:

1. War prevention through regional and global *balances of power* between quarreling states, so that resort to war is made unprofitable even though disagreements continue.

FIGURE 7–1
War casualties in Europe, 1500–1925

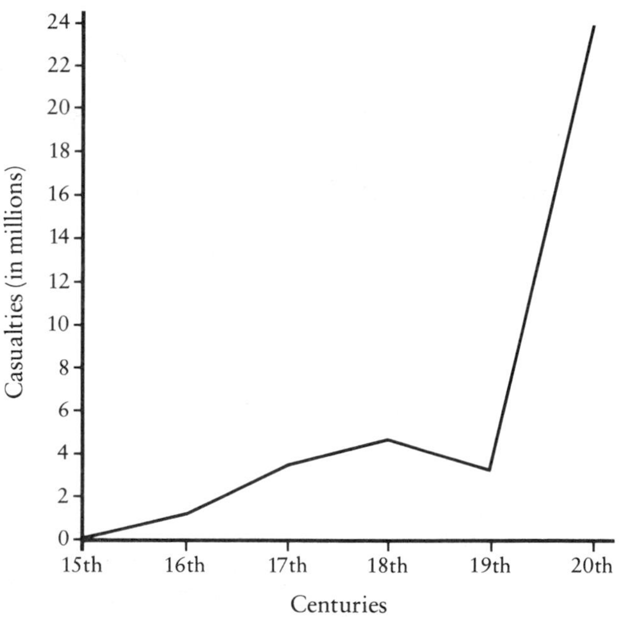

Source: Based on data from Pitirim Sorokin, *Social and Cultural Dynamics,* vol. 3 (New York: Bedminster Press, 1962); originally published in 1937.

2. War prevention by *balance of terror,* a variant of the balance-of-power concept, in which technologically developed adversaries have the capability for mutually assured destruction through finely targeted instantaneous warfare. Aggression is deterred by the certainty of intolerably destructive retaliation.
3. War prevention by further *institutionalization of mediation* and other means for the nonviolent resolution of international conflict, ultimately including a central peacekeeping authority and the disarming of nation-states.

Because the first two ideas address the practical problem of deterence in a world of heavily armed states acting autonomously in their respective interests, most contemporary scholars and statesmen consider them the most realistic options for the foreseeable future. Though inordinately expensive and consuming vast amounts of natural resources, these ideas respond to the decentralized and hostile environment in which political differences are acted out. Replacing this model

Army Medical Examiner: "At last a perfect soldier!"

Source: Antiwar cartoon by Robert Minor, 1915. Reproduced in Stephen Becker, *Comic Art in America* (New York: Simon and Schuster, 1959).

of international relations with one built upon intergovernmental institutions capable of establishing and enforcing an equitable distribution of values in the manner now served by war and deterrence is a process long held in infancy. To some observers it is an impossible dream. To others, who look beyond unstable peace to the survival of humankind and the betterment of its condition, it is the endurance of the nation-state system that is the impossible dream. The system of individual nation-states means precariously balancing fifty or more nuclear powers deeply divided by ideological, territorial and economic conflicts. If, since the Second World War, national governments have given us two wars per year, why must one presume that the costly pursuit of peace through competition is superior to the quest for peace through cooperation?

The remainder of this section explores war and peace through the balance-of-power and the balance-of-terror approaches. Part 4 of this book will consider the quest for peace and stability through political transformation of the international system.

8

The Balance of Power

Historians, statesmen and students of international relations often assert that the only way to keep peace is through a careful balance of power. What do we mean by this commonly used expression, *balance of power?* It connotes not only military and deterrent capabilities, but the entire structure of *power* and *influence* that governs the relations of states. Balance of power is concerned, therefore, not solely with the ability of states to threaten their neighbors or to dissuade others from planned policies; rather, it encompasses all of the political capabilities of states—coercive and pacific—by which the delicate balance of conflict without war is maintained.

Meanings of "Balance of Power"

Among laymen and scholars alike, the expression *balance of power* has many uses. Consider four uses in these sentences:

1. "There is a balance of power between India and Pakistan."
2. "The balance of power favors the United States."
3. "The balance of power has shifted in favor of Israel."
4. "Britain was the crucial actor in the nineteenth-century balance-of-power system."

Clearly, there are several different meanings here. The first statement implies that *equilibrium* exists between two parties. Further, the relations of the respective parties with outside states, particularly the nuclear superpowers, are nearly equal, thus preventing the occurrence of disequilibrium by the unilateral addition of external strength. In short, the equilibrium in the relations between India and Pakistan exists because neither has significantly more power or influence than the other; neither can distort the balance. Figure 8–1 (A) shows the situation that exists; (B) shows the maintenance of equilibrium by the equal use of influence upon outside states.

The second statement carries a sharply different implication. To say that the balance "favors" one party over the other is to introduce a *disequilibrium*. Though this meaning is most frequently used to describe the balance of military forces, in its broadest usage it says that the United States holds the upper hand over some other party, and is able to rely upon greater military, diplomatic and other resources. Throughout most of the Cold War, for example, the United States and the Soviet Union, while perhaps not absolutely equal in military potential (the USA probably always had superior military technology), had practical equivalence. Yet the United States had a vast edge in influence and in ability to work its will with economic resources. Hence, despite "mutual superiority" in arms and a balance of terror, the balance of power has traditionally favored the United States. "Balance of power" defined as disequilibrium is diagramed in Figure 8–2.

Now consider the third sentence: "The balance of power has shifted in favor of Israel." This sentence connotes either a shift from equilibrium to disequilibrium, or a shift in predominance from one party to the other. Acquisition of a new weapons system by Israel might have a major impact upon the Middle Eastern balance, as might a change in the country's stature by a diplomatic victory. Recognition by West Germany, for example, improved Israel's access to military and industrial goods, and gave it a new and powerful friend. Similarly, although the 1967 Israel-Arab War was preceded by regional equilibrium, Israel's victory significantly upset military and political relations

FIGURE 8–1
(A) Two-party equilibrium
(B) Equilibrium maintenance

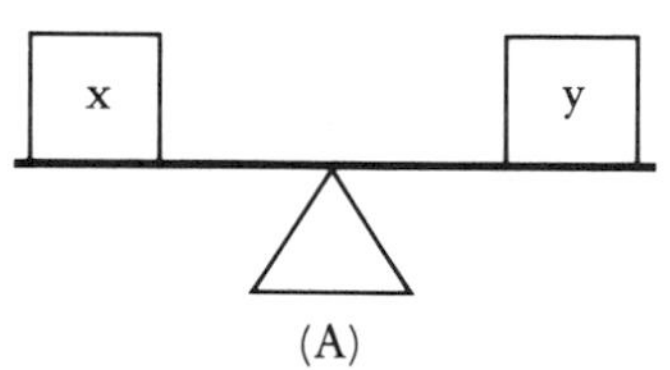

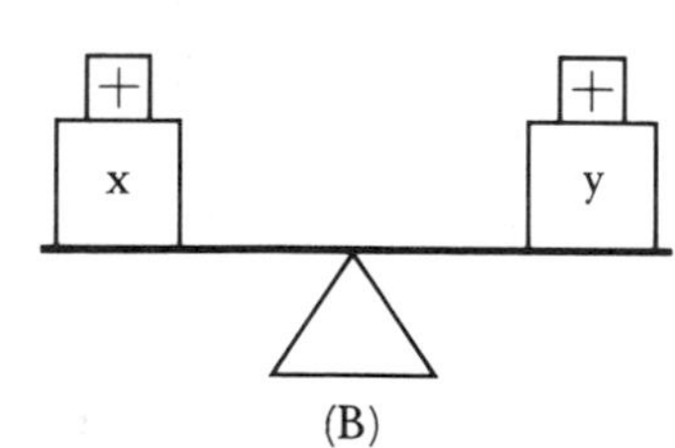

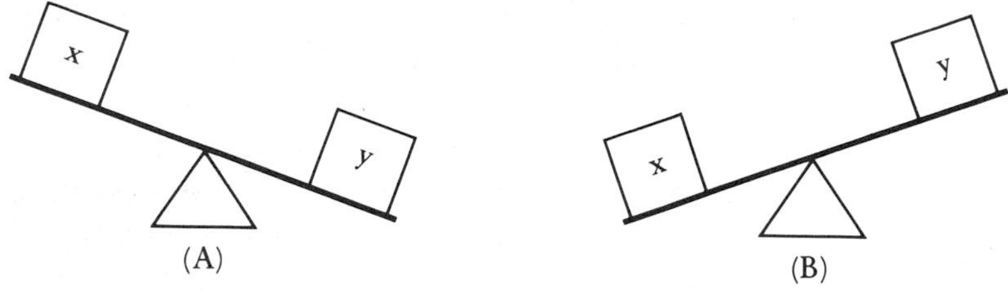

FIGURE 8–2
(A) Disequilibrium favoring y (B) Disequilibrium favoring x

both in the Middle East *and* among the major powers, who had to apply their influences anew to reestablish equilibrium. Figure 8–3 depicts the two patterns of a shift in balance.

The fourth statement implies still a different meaning, that cannot be illustrated by the simple balance beam. "The balance-of-power system" was a specific historical event in a Eurocentric world from the nineteenth century to the outbreak of the First World War. In that system, states behaved in certain ways (described below), with one state conserving its influence solely to maintain equilibrium.

In summary, then, in place of a concise definition of *balance of power,* we may say that it is a concept of many meanings, particularly equilibrium, disequilibrium and shifts in dominance, as well as a particular historical systemic principle. This chapter examines the various ideas behind the term. It is particularly concerned with balance as a system of keeping pace.[1]

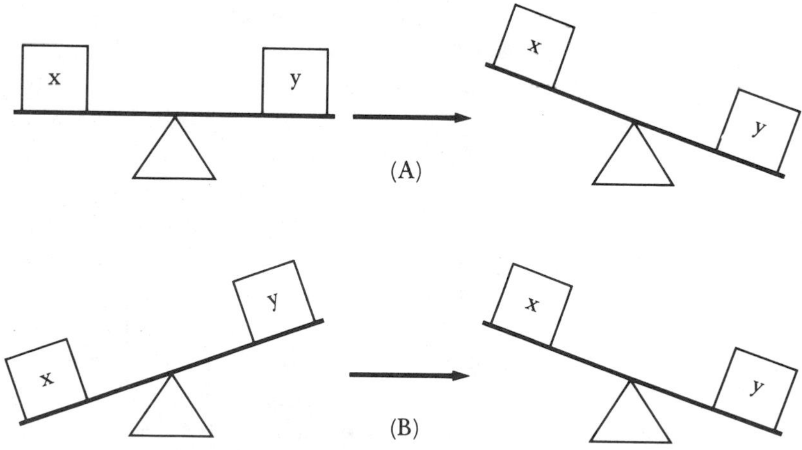

FIGURE 8–3
(A) Equilibrium shift to disequilibrium (B) Disequilibrium shift to opposite disequilibrium

1. For thorough discussions of the several, and often confusing, meanings of balance of power, see Inis L. Claude, Jr., *Power in International Relations* (New York: Random House, 1962), particularly Part 1; and Ernst B. Haas, "The Balance of Power: Prescription, Concept, or Propaganda?" *World Politics* 5, 1953, pp. 442–77. A third useful source is Hans J. Morgenthau, *Politics Among Nations,* 4th ed. (New York: Knopf, 1967), pp. 161–63.

Political Assumptions Underlying the Balance of Power

Before examining the components of the balance of power, it will be useful to clarify five features about the international system that apply regardless of historical era or structural form. First, as in all other relations of two or more parties, *the potential for conflict is permanent.* Throughout the history of the multistate system, governments and peoples have differed as to means and ends, their differences often resulting in crises. Even at the subwar level, divergent objectives and disputed means have perpetually threatened conflict. There is no justifiable reason to expect the potential for conflict to abate. Accordingly, the best we can do is to explore the elements of the balance of power to assess the capability for reducing the frequency and/or intensity of international conflict.

The second important feature of international politics is the *permanence of power,* and with it the ability of states to promote their external objectives. Since power is intrinsic to political relations, no international system is imaginable without it. The object of the balance of power, therefore, is not to eliminate power, but to *manage* or *control* it in such a way as to make it constructive rather than destructive, a stabilizing factor rather than a destabilizing one.

The third inherent feature of world politics is the *relativity of power.* Although a state may consider itself powerful, it cannot rely upon its power unless perceiving it to be great relative to that of an adversary.

A fourth fundamental feature about the international system is the *variety of sources of power.* Though in this nuclear world we seize upon military yardsticks, power still arises from several combined and coordinated sources. Some of these are natural (resources, population); others are social and psychological (social cohesion, mass perceptions); and still others are synthetic (governmental efficiency, military preparedness, economic vitality). To assess the balance of power and its practical effects upon the stability and instability of interstate relations, we must be able to assess the full power potentials of competing states, not merely their respective military capabilities. We must know something about their respective wills to use power, their determination to maintain peace at the expense of other interests and their willingness to risk war for national objectives.

Finally, except in abnormal circumstances, the *acquisition of power is designed as a means to subsequent objectives.* The measured and judicious use of power, therefore, is the currency by which governments influence others. This currency, said to be to politics as money is to economics, may be expended in many ways. Some of these are peaceful, such as persuasion or rewarding another party for acquiescing in policy. Others are coercive: deprivation of rewards (terminating trade or diplomatic relations, for example), threat of force, visible deployment of force (as in "gunboat diplomacy"), or the actual use of force in either limited or general warfare.

Balance of Power as an Analytical Device

In light of these observations, "balance of power" can be presented as an analytical concept for exploring the practical effects of equilibrium and disequilibrium in world politics, and for assessing the consequences of power shifts. It becomes an analytical device rather than a form of advocacy, prescribing no particular model(s) for world peace. Instead, it searches out the conditions of order and disorder in international relations, concentrating on the sources and consequences of balance and imbalance.

The role that a state plays in a global or regional balance of power is determined by its capabilities and intentions (see Chapter 7). In its external relations, a government makes what are presumably rational and calculated determinations of the costs and benefits of specific policies as related to specific objectives. From these formulae it sets the course of foreign policy, and by them it determines the state's role in the balance of power. "Will we attempt to enlarge our power, or are our present interests served in the international system by the power that we presently command?" "Do our relations with a neighbor require that we alter the existing balance?" or "Is our neighbor altering the balance to our detriment, and must we, therefore, increase our power potential?"

This distinction between "power" and "power potential" is an important one in the balance-of-power concept. Many states have considerable *potential* power, but have little effect upon global or regional balances. Thus, balance of power theory must take into account the *stages of power readiness.* The possession of adequate resources of power is *potential power.* When these are developed, coordinated and supplied with the will to use power, then the state possesses *mobilized power.* And when the developed resources are applied to actual situations, the state commands *active power* (or kinetic power).

The lowest stage of readiness (potential power) ensures a state little more than a passive role in the balance of power. More powerful states are only minimally moved by the actions of the potentially powerful. Such a state, in turn, must acquiesce in the prevailing norms of the international system (since it is ill prepared to alter them), must tie itself to the objectives and means of a more powerful state, or must mobilize its power to play an active part in the balance.

Command of mobilized power, in contrast, enables the state to be a major actor. Such a status compels other contestants to assess the relativity of power, the possibility of overbearing coalitions and the potential for sudden changes in the balance or redistribution of influence or major unilateral technological advances. The balance of power is concerned mainly with the balance of *mobilized* power.

Force—the extreme utilization of mobilized power—is used to alter the power balance drastically and rapidly. A state may wish to correct a disequilibrium by force, or to upset a power balance to the advantage of its own objectives. Perhaps the most illustrative use of active power in balance of power theory is the preemptive war. This is warfare in which state A anticipates attack by state B. Rather than waiting for an orderly escalation of hostilities, A destroys B's capability before B has a chance to start the fighting. A has preempted B, by an anticipatory attack depriving B of altering the balance of power, and in the course of affairs may have done so itself. Israel's purpose in attacking Arab military airfields in 1967 was preemptive. This means that Israel's intentions were not aggressive and not designed to aggrandize national territory, nor intended to alter the balance in Israel's favor. Rather, Israel wanted to strike at Egypt and Syria in a selective manner so as to destroy their capability to alter the balance at a moment when Israel anticipated attacks from the Arab states.

Preventive war has similar balance-of-power connotations. This is a type of selective attack undertaken against an enemy state considerably before that state has effective military potential. Long before China was a nuclear power, for example, people throughout the West, perhaps even in the Soviet Union, openly mused on the efficacy of preventive attacks upon Chinese installations to delay its nuclear development and prolong its weakness. Japan's attack upon Pearl Harbor in 1941 was a different type of preventive war, conducted to deprive the United States of retaliatory strength as Japan contemplated further territorial quests in Asia and the Pacific. Israel's attack on an Iraqi nuclear plant in 1981 was designed to prevent its Arab enemy from developing nuclear weapons. The only real difference between preemptive and preventive war is the time element; the effects for the balance of power are identical.

In the traditional study of international relations, it was assumed that the balance of power was determined exclusively by military relativities. More modern concepts of international relations, in contrast, recognize that relative military preparedness is not the sole determinant of the balance of power. The tendency now is to distinguish between military power, on the one hand, and the overall ability to command international influence, on the other. Thus a major component of the balance of power is economic potential.

Modern Japan is a case in point. Since the end of the Second World War, Japan has not been a significant military power. Its defense is firmly tied to American strategic policy, though in the Vietnam era that policy often offended Japan's sense of security. Despite this military inferiority, Japan has resumed major-power status by virtue of enormous economic revitalization. Even without military power its regional influence is growing apace, based on its bilaterial economic relations and on its ability to lead Asia and the Pacific in international development programs.

Western Europe is another illustrative case. The rapidly changing technology of war has outpaced the ability of even the most industrialized Western European states to compete alone. Economically, it is their collective activity and production that give the European states a major world role, rather than their individual efforts. Despite the continued European reliance on the transatlantic security arrangement, Western Europe has achieved major-power status through its ability to compete in world trade. Thus, one can go farther than to say that Western Europe plays a major role in the global power balance. One can conclude that through economic restoration, these states acquired a role in the global balance by using their resources to force change in it.

The Middle Eastern example of forced change in the global power balance through nonmilitary action is more recent and more striking, principally because its impact was registered in a much shorter time than in the case of either Japan or Western Europe. By deciding to profit from oil in the same way that Western commercial interests had done previously, and by tying their oil export policy to political objectives concerning Israel, the Arab oil-producing states were able to force changes in the foreign policies of virtually all Western industrialized countries and Japan. While still developing industrially, their vast petrodollar reserves have substantially affected economic relations throughout the nonsocialist world. And the threat of a petroleum boycott, which their new wealth affords them, is sufficiently menacing to Japan, Western Europe and the United States that it is potentially one of the most fruitful nonmilitary instruments of foreign policy available anywhere. As a result, this capability has forced a change in the global power balance as well as in that of the region.

Having now considered the fundamental issues of equilibrium, disequilibrium and change in balance of power theory, we turn to some alternative structural models.

Structural Models of Balance of Power

Although balance-of-power theory does not prescribe a preferred model of global or regional stability, it does facilitate description of the principal power configurations that have existed in the past 150 years. The theory also enables us to demonstrate graphically the power relations of major states and groups of states, whether their relation is global in interaction or limited to a region of the world.

These models are of no greater value than to depict roughly power configurations that have existed in the past. They attempt to freeze time in the sense of describing relations in fixed position, rather than explaining the dynamic flow of relations among international actors. In this sense, these models are static; and they are as artificial as a tinker-toy model of a molecule that demonstrates the ideal configuration of its major components while ignoring the dynamic flow of subnuclear particles that either maintain or change the basic shape.

The international system is as dynamic as such a molecule, and any attempt to reduce it to fixed form necessarily diminishes its vitality. Nevertheless, since such descriptive models are typically referred to as indicators of major-power configurations, they are instructive despite their static character.

1. The Nineteenth-Century Balance-of-Power System

In illustrating different meanings of balance of power at the outset of this chapter, we used the sentence, "Britain was the crucial actor in the nineteenth-century balance-of-power system." What distinguished that system from the balance of power as we know it now?

Historians of the balance-of-power system (dated from the end of the Napoleonic Wars in 1815 until the outbreak of the First World War in 1914) identify the underlying conditions. They note that it could exist only among several nation-states in a fairly well-defined territorial area. Though it was an interstate system, it was not global. The system could not have worked except among participants relatively homogeneous in political culture, who had rational means of estimating each other's power (wealth, military potential and so on).[2]

In retrospect, this international system seems to have been constructed on several basic assumptions. First, each state would attempt

2. Edward V. Gulick, *Europe's Classical Balance of Power* (Ithaca, N.Y.: Cornell University Press, 1955), Chapter 1.

to maximize its own power for its own purposes. Second, as a consequence, when states accumulated power and their interests (such as imperial interests) collided, there was potential for international conflict. Third, to enhance their respective power potentials, like-minded states entered into alliances, so that alliance competition rather than state competition characterized the system.

In these first three assumptions, the balance-of-power model sounds no different from any other international system. But the subsequent premises were unique. It is assumed, for example, that each participant placed a high value on equilibrium, and that in its alliance competition its objective was to achieve equilibrium rather than a disequilibrium, even one that would favor itself. To maintain equivalence, moreover, states were willing to switch alliances periodically to adjust the balance. Adjustment, therefore, can be said to have been automatic. Figure 8–4 diagrams the process of adjustment: (A) shows an existing equilibrium which is upset (B) by the addition of a new participant or by a major technical development that adds to the weight of one coalition. In (C), equilibrium is restored by the transfer of one state from one alliance to the other.

The concept of the adjustment function, and the notion of its automatic nature, have evoked criticism. As a result, supporters have offered several other means by which the classical balance was adjusted, apparently conceding that the process is, at best, semiautomatic. The means of adjustment are said to be vigilance, alliances, intervention, mobility of action, reciprocal compensation, preservation of participants, coalitions and war. Beyond this, however, supporters have introduced the concept of "holding the balance," which calls upon a specific state to change its allegiances expressly to maintain the balance. This state is referred to as the Balancer.[3] The introduction of this concept means that the adjustment process is less than semiautomatic; rather, it is manual.

The concept of the Balancer is an effective modernization of this model only if the Balancer State has special characteristics. If a weak

FIGURE 8–4
Adjusting the equilibrium

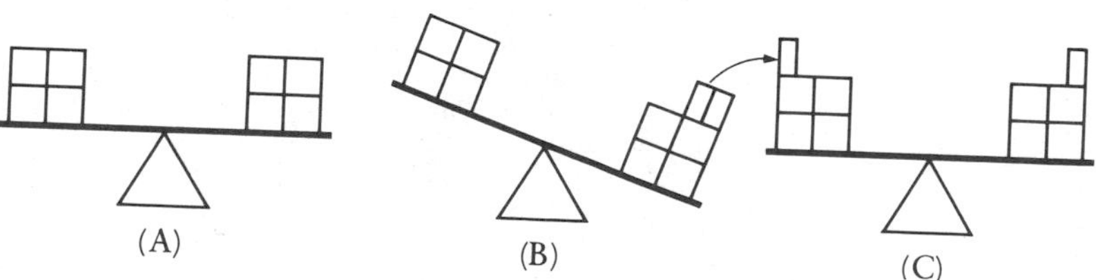

3. The means of balance are derived from Gulick, *ibid.*, Chapter 3.

state were to take on this role, or a state that favors disequilibrium, then the function of manual balanace would hardly be served. It follows that the Balancer must be an effectively powerful state, one whose strategic options enable it to have a major impact on the entire system. Moreover, it must be a state that favors equilibrium and, even more, one that demands for its own purposes that equilibrium be safeguarded. Of the Balancer one writer concludes:

> His task is difficult. A balancer is expected to be partial to no single national subject of the balance-of-power system but to direct his own mobile weight in such a way as to ensure the international object of an equipoise of power. He must be both at the focus of the system and outside it; otherwise he would not be free to withdraw and engage his weight in function of the system's requirements and thus manipulate the balance. An effective balancer must be both self-restrained and quick in imposing vigorous restraints on others. Only then can he frustrate and thus reduce the incentive to any one nation's quest for preponderance. A sufficiently powerful balancer of this kind might check the irrational drives and the miscalculations jeopardizing the balance of power and promote the realization of its objective norm.[4]

Among historians of this model, Britain is universally looked upon as having been the Balancer, though some also identify equilibrating functions in the policies of other states. Britain's virtues as the Balancer include its geographic location (which spared it from common boundaries with other powerful European states), its apparent interest in equilibrium as the most favorable climate for its imperial policies and its great mobility of action.[5]

Despite the modern refinements of this theory, skepticism continues to abound. One critic postulates that power is only one of the objectives of states, thus depreciating the assumption that power is the foremost national value. He also denies that nations are static and unchanging from within, insisting that through industrialization, marshaling of population resources, and improvements in governmental efficiency states increase their potential power. These changes are not adjustable

4. George Liska, *International Equilibrium* (Cambridge, Mass.: Harvard University Press, 1957), pp. 36–37.
5. This presentation follows the tradition of treating the entire balance-of-power century as having had a relatively unchanging political system. Recently, however, it has been shown that the period 1815 to 1914 actually consisted of three distinctly different balancing mechanisms, all governed by many of the same assumptions, but necessitated by different relationships and dominated by different parties and different balancers. They were: 1815–1878 (Britain the balancer; the most effective of the three experiments); 1878–1890 (Germany the balancer; ingenius but not inherently stable); and 1890–1914 (Britain the balancer; a desperate effort at maintaining order). See Gordon A. Craig and Alexander L. George, *Force and Statecraft: Diplomatic Problems of Our Time* (New York: Oxford University Press, 1983), Chapter 3, "Balance of Power, 1815–1914: Three Experiments."

through the presumed mechanics of the balance of power. Third, because states are often tied to one another through economic, political or psychological bonds, the freedom to switch alliances for no other purpose than balance is uncharacteristic of history. He interprets British policy as motivated by self-interest, not as fulfilling the self-appointed role of Balancer. In fact, he denies that *any* state in the nineteenth century preferred equilibrium to favorable disequilibrium. Finally, he concludes that imbalance of power is the characteristic pattern, particularly since the Industrial Revolution, with major states and their respective coalitions actually trying to maintain disequilibrium.[6]

Whether the classical mechanics of the balance-of-power model ever really operated is, therefore, in doubt. We may accept, nevertheless, the premise that in multiparty international systems favoring equilibrium, there must be some implicit rules of behavior. Based upon his studies of the nineteenth-century system, one theorist sets out the "operational rules" of a system of international balance as follows:

1. Participants will increase their capabilities, but they will accept the responsibility to negotiate their differences rather than to fight.
2. Since increase in capabilities is the prime motive of foreign policy, states must be willing to fight, if necessary, rather than to forego further development.
3. When at war, states will be prepared to terminate fighting rather than upset the foundations of equilibrium by eliminating a participant. This is important because the model is built upon the assumption of at least five major participants.
4. Every participant intent upon equilibrium will contest any tendency to dominance by any state or coalition.
5. Because the system is built upon the power of states, participants must constrain tendencies toward supranational organization or organizations that would alter the sovereign status of the system's participants.
6. Each participant must be willing to permit defeated major actors to restore their positions, and they must encourage lesser actors to achieve the status of full participants. All major parties must be treated equally as acceptable role partners.[7]

6. A. F. K. Organski, *World Politics*, 2nd ed. (New York: Knopf, 1968), pp. 282–99.
7. Morton A. Kaplan, *Systems and Process in International Relations* (New York: Wiley, 1957), p. 23; and also Kaplan's article "Balance of Power, Bipolarity and Other Methods of International Systems," *American Political Science Review* 51, 1957, pp. 684–95.

These rules have a pragmatic basis: if the system is to be viable, the participating states must be viable. We shall return subsequently to the question of whether multipartite systems such as this or limited-bloc systems (such as bipolarity) tend toward greater stability.

2. The Tight Bipolar Balance of Power

The nineteenth-century balance-of-power system involved political relationships that ended with the First World War. Thereafter, international stability was not governed by the factors we have discussed. Other systems of power balance emerged, particularly after the Second World War. It is necessary, therefore, to explore the military relations of other balance-of-power systems to understand the contemporary distribution of power.

The Second World War probably changed international politics more than any single modern occurrence. Statesmen in the postwar years were confronted with the unprecedented problems presented by atomic weaponry, and with the reduction of the number of effective major powers to two. Though the First World War had begun the process of restricting the number of major powers, the prostration of Western and Central Europe after the second ensured that for the foreseeable future world politics would center upon Washington and Moscow, rather than upon London and Paris. But there was also a third critical developement: the intense ideological hostility between the two principal powers, which opened an era of conflict, distrust, competition and misperception.

These three factors together—the two-part division of power, the advent of atomic warfare and unprecedented ideological rivalry—resulted in an international system of tight bipolarity, one in which virtually all of the world's effective power was encompassed in two competing blocs. The institutional structure was that of two formal alliance systems, dominated by the Soviet Union and the United States, respectively. For diplomatic or geopolitical reasons a few states did not participate (for example, Finland and Switzerland), but the fact remains that virtually all the measurable power in international relations was commanded through one or the other of these two structures.[8]

A tight bipolar international system may be said to have existed

8. This definition is only a slight adaptation of Kaplan's, which defines tight bipolarity as a system in which "non-bloc member actors and universal actors either disappear entirely or cease to be significant." ("Balance of Power, Bipolarity and Other Models of International Systems," *op. cit.* (1957), p. 693.) Kaplan denies, however, that a tight bipolar system has ever existed.

Source: Wide World Photos

The height of the Cold War, 1953. In the United Nations General Assembly, Ambassador Andrei Vishinsky of the USSR accuses the USA of acting like a "master race" in trying to push through a proposal on the makeup of the Korean Peace Conference. American ambassador Henry Cabot Lodge and British ambassador Sir Gladwyn Jebb listen resignedly to the familiar invective.

from 1945 to 1955, a decade that saw such momentous events as the combat use of atomic energy, the achievement of atomic capability by the Soviet Union, the establishment of NATO, SEATO and the Warsaw Pact, the Berlin Blockade, accession to power in China by Mao Tse-tung and the Korean War. In this era, the intense Soviet-American rivalry, particularly over Europe, resulted in the Cold War exchanges of threats and competing alliances. Technically, the Warsaw Pact did not come into existence until 1954 after the Western allies agreed to include West Germany in NATO membership; but long prior to this formal event the Soviet Union and Eastern Europe comprised a tacit alliance. Formal Sino-Soviet ties also existed. The American alliance structure was global (and remains so despite the collapse of SEATO after the Vietnam War), and developed as follows:

1947 Organization of American States (the Rio Pact, or the Inter-American Treaty of Reciprocal Assistance) (twenty-two members).

1949 North Atlantic Treaty (fifteen members).

1951 Security Treaty with Japan (bilateral).
1951 Security Treaty with Australia and New Zealand (trilateral).
1951 Mutual Defense Treaty with the Republic of the Philippines (bilateral).
1953 Mutual Defense Treaty with the Republic of (South) Korea (bilateral).
1954 Southeast Asia Collective Defense Treaty (eight members).
1954 Mutual Defense Treaty with the Republic of China (Taiwan) (bilateral).

Altogether, these treaties and the institutionalized alliances that they created encompassed some forty-four nations including the United States, with several states belonging to more than one alliance. In addition, the United States had bases agreements and status-of-forces agreements with Spain and Libya (the latter agreement no longer exists), so that the United States was involved in some level of military activity with no fewer than forty-six different governments on every continent in the world.[9] Solidarity was furthered by the alliances sponsored by London, including the Central Treaty Organization and its military prerogatives in its colonial areas, particularly in Asia and the Mediterranean (for instance, Malta). Combined, the Anglo-American alliances and the Soviet alliances involved in excess of sixty states and almost half again as many non-self-governing areas. Compare this with the 1955 membership of the United Nations, which was only seventy-six, sixteen of which were not admitted until 1955. Furthermore, of the original fifty-one signatories to the UN Charter, two—Byelorussia and the Ukraine—were not and are not sovereign states. Thus, at the start of 1955, while the UN had a membership of only fifty-nine distinctly different sovereign states, the United States and Britain, on the one hand, and the Soviet Union, on the other, were formally allied with over sixty states. The universality of the alliance systems should be self-evident.

Based on this survey of alliances, we can now diagram the tight bipolar system, noting also the existence of several scattered but relatively powerless nonparticipants. Figure 8–5 demonstrates that while a tight bipolar balance of power existed from 1945 to 1955, the US-oriented bloc commanded more influence when all power sources are considered. These included a superior number of allies, a larger supply of resources, and the global character of American alliances contrasted

9. For an extraordinarily useful description of these alliances, replete with texts, maps and comparative analysis, see the document *Collective Defense Treaties* (Washington, D.C.: US Government Printing Office, 1967), prepared by the Committee on Foreign Affairs of the House of Representatives.

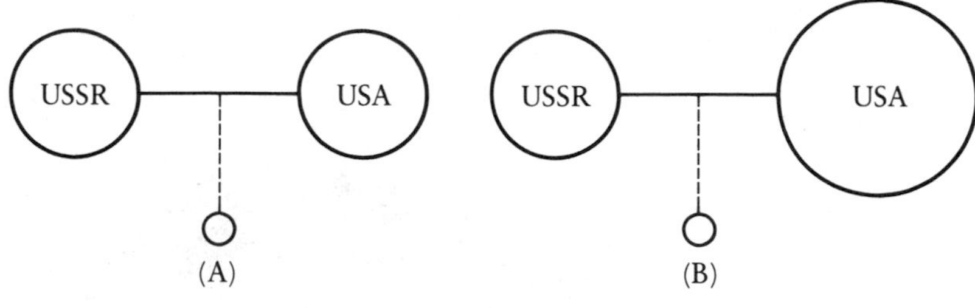

FIGURE 8–5
(A) Perfect tight bipolarity
(B) Actual tight bipolarity, 1945–55

with the regional reach of the Soviet. The point is that tight bipolarity need *not* imply equality of capability.[10]

Since power is always relative, it does not necessarily follow from lack of absolute equality that the political prerogatives of one bloc were less than those of the other in critical areas. In fact, in the tight bipolarity of 1945–55, the disparities operated outside of Europe, beyond the sphere in which the Kremlin generally wished to compete with Washington. Thus we may say that in the tight bipolar era there existed not European regional symmetry, but global asymmetry.

The operating characteristics of the tight bipolar balance of power differ markedly from those of the nineteenth-century system. The basic assumption here is that international equilibrium is a second-best objective; the principal aim of governments is to belong to the dominant coalition. Furthermore, the system is built on the premise that all effective power is included in the major blocs, or poles, with the result that there is no powerful state dangling free to play the role of Balancer. Indeed, the objective of this pattern of power is to anticipate the defeat of the other coalition should it breach the frontiers of one's own members. It is for this reason, rather than mere coincidence, that the ruling American political-military strategy of this era was massive nuclear retaliation, though it is doubtful that the threat was ever taken seriously. It is far more likely that the balanced conventional strengths of the European alliances ensured stability through this era. Nevertheless, the philosophy of tight bipolarity renders massive retaliation quite logical as a strategic foundation. It is safe to say that as a result of the conditions that dictated the emergence of bipolarity, and as a consequence of the strategies that it fostered, this model of international order is maximally hostile.

10. For a study suggesting that the power distribution be described in terms of symmetry and asymmetry regardless of number of major blocs, though especially in two-bloc systems, see Wolfram F. Hanreider, "The International System: Bipolar or Multibloc?" *Journal of Conflict Resolution* 9, 299–308. Hanreider provides alternative diagrams for depicting perfect and actual tight bipolarity.

Source: Gamma Liaison

The North Atlantic Treaty Organization commemorates D-Day: Fortieth anniversary of the landing at Normandy Beach which launched the drive to liberate Europe from Hitler's control, 1984.

3. The Loose Bipolar Balance of Power

In the mid-1950s a number of fundamental changes occurred in the international system. The two superpower alliance systems began to "loosen," with internal conflicts and losses of confidence appearing in each bloc; and dependencies began to dissipate. In the Soviet sphere events took several paths. Eastern European dissatisfaction with Soviet control, foreshadowed a few years earlier in East Germany, climaxed with the brief Hungarian revolt of 1956. Coupled with Nikita Khrushchev's campaign to "de-Stalinize" the Soviet Union and Eastern Europe, this event resulted in increasing demands for quasi-independence among the Soviet satellites, despite forceful suppression by Soviet troops. The politics of the Soviet sphere came increasingly to be identified as polycentric, suggesting reduced Soviet control over the states within its orbit.

If polycentrism characterized Eastern Europe, only the term "schism" describes Sino-Soviet relations in the same era. Though not yet a major power, after less than a decade of controlling the Chinese mainland the Mao government found itself disaffected from Moscow and in search of independent power status. Formal relations were broken in 1956, and Soviet technicians and aid were withdrawn, leaving China to develop alone. Gone was the Korean War-inspired American theory that all communist power and authority emanated from the Kremlin; the international communist movement could no longer be regarded as monolithic. The Soviet Union's influence in Asia was sharply curtailed, leaving Soviet-American relations more asymmetrical. More important, the Sino-Soviet split represented a major break in the solidarity of the Soviet world.

The American bloc began to crack also. Latin America, increasingly disenchanted with Washington's sporadic paternalism, began to consider itself a member of the Third World despite its formal military and economic ties with the United States. Fidel Castro's accession to power through armed rebellion, followed by his conversion to Marxism, brought the first serious challenge to the ideological solidarity of the western hemisphere.

Europe presented other problems. The enormous success of the Western European economies in reconstruction led to gradual resentment of American economic domination. Charles de Gaulle's demand that Europe be "de-Americanized" threatened to dilute the potential effectiveness of the United States in facing the Soviet Union across Europe. Strategic policy in NATO led to other resentments and suspicions, with some Europeans doubting the credibility of the American nuclear umbrella, while still others feared that impetuous behavior in Washington in response to Soviet threats might unnecessarily embroil Europe in war.

Worldwide interests and associations tend to present worldwide problems, and the United States found that troubles in Latin America and Western Europe were not the end of its problems. The cornerstone of American policy in Asia, the alliance with Japan, began to show signs of decay. In the years following the Korean War (1950–53), Japanese resentment at American security policy grew steadily, focused upon American nuclear strategy. Disharmony rose to the point of widespread rioting on the occasion of the renegotiation of the Security Agreement in 1960. The political climate in Japan grew so menacing that the Tokyo government successfully discouraged the planned state visit of President Dwight D. Eisenhower. The breakdown over security matters was compounded in Japanese minds by American efforts to prevent Japan from trading with China.

By 1960, then, it was clear that major shifts were occurring in the previous tight global bipolarity because of internal changes in the principal alliances. Another critical change was taking place, too. Beginning in 1957, though more markedly after 1960, the number of nation-states burgeoned. In 1960, seventeen states were admitted to United Nations membership, every one of them newly independent. A world that had been revolutionary in several respects now added a new dimension—a sudden and unprecedented increase in the number of national actors. These new states, bound only by poverty, underdevelopment and racial separation from the dominant white nations, were courted by both the United States and the Soviet Union, each one seeking new adherents to its ideology. Most of the new states, however, did not tie themselves to either giant, but accepted assistance from them with as little political cost as possible. Although they were not a solid bloc of states with coordinated behavior (except perhaps in voting patterns on economic matters at the UN), these states began to form a multistate group with potential collective impact.

In addition to the polycentrism of the Soviet sphere and the beginning of decentralization among American allies, the emergence of the Third World further loosened global polarity because it presented many "nonbloc actors." Figure 8–6 shows the resulting loose bipolarity. Diagrammatically, the differences between this and the tight bipolar model are the presence of nonbloc actors and the splintering in the two main blocs. Yet the structure is still basically bipolar with respect to effective power relations. Only two bloc actors are portrayed

FIGURE 8–6
Loose bipolarity, 1955–65

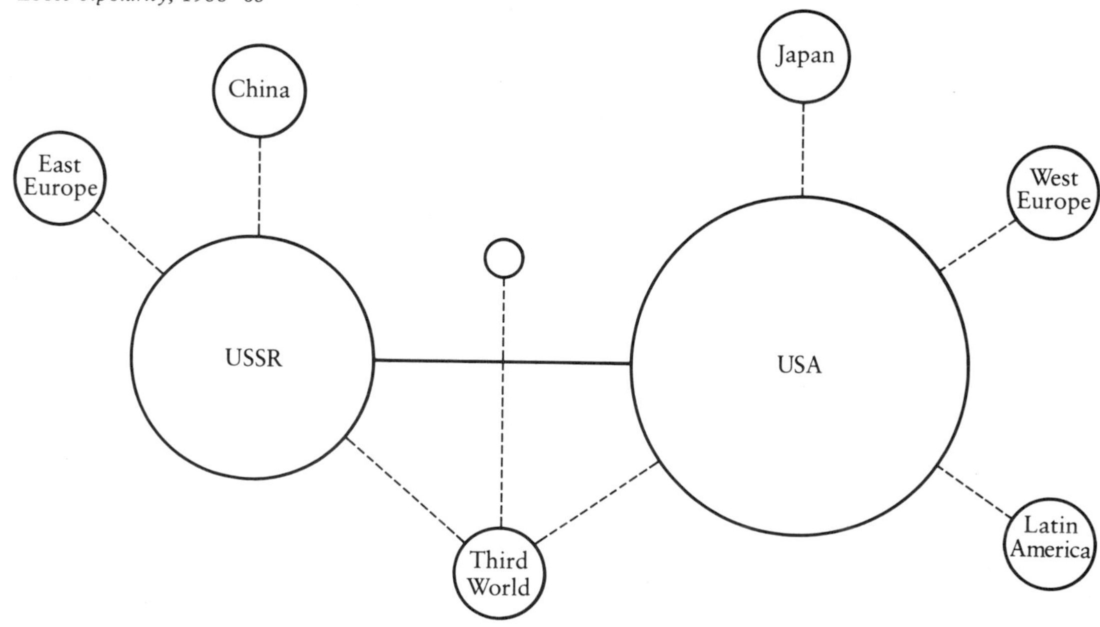

as relating directly to the fulcrum. Each of the others either arises from a major bloc or is tied to one for power purposes, though it may not be thoroughly allied.

For bloc members, the behavioral norms in tight and loose bipolar systems are essentially the same. Members are pledged to prepare to eliminate the opposing bloc, but prefer to fight small wars rather than large. Members agree to strengthen their own bloc internally, and to resolve differences by negotiation rather than open conflict. The threat of total destruction leads to a tacit agreement not to provoke war between the dominant members of opposing blocs.

But for the dominant members, the Soviet Union and the United States, there is an added objective in loose bipolarity—namely, to maintain optimum tightness under conditions that nurture fragmentation. The mechanisms for this function are like the normal rewards and punishments by which powerful states influence the less powerful: economic rewards and deprivations, offers and withdrawals of military supply beyond that needed for the state's contribution to bloc security, and so on. In extreme cases, strong states may use force, as the Soviet Union did in Hungary in 1956 and the United States did in Cuba in 1961 and in the Dominican Republic in 1965. In addition, especially when alliances are institutionalized, the polar states may use the alliance structure to prolong the perception of threat by playing to the self-aggrandizing behavior of pertinent elites, such as national military commands. In this sense threat perception becomes an important aspect of dominant-member political strategy in loose bipolar systems.

The norms of nonbloc actors are considerably different. Their basic role is as a ground for peaceful competition of the major powers and blocs, each intent primarily upon gaining the adherence of the nonbloc state, but secondarily on preventing it from going over to the other side. Their conflicts must be internalized (Nigeria-Biafra), carefully circumscribed (Rhodesia and Zambia) or submitted to global settlement (Congo). They must resist great-power intervention if it is likely to bring in the other major power or result in subordination.

In the normal course of events, it might be expected that loose bipolarity would give way to multipolarity, with the quasi-independent blocs becoming independent power poles. Some observers argue that such a situation has existed for as long as fifteen years.[11] However, while the loosening trend has carried us out of bipolarity, it does not appear that we have yet arrived at multipolarity. Hence an interim model is necessary.

11. See, for example, Cecil V. Crabb, Jr., *Nations in a Multipolar World* (New York: Harper and Row, 1968).

4. The Incipient Multipolar Balance of Power

During the early 1970s, the years in which American foreign policy was established by President Richard Nixon and Secretary of State Henry Kissinger, the basic assumption was that the world power distribution was evolving into a "pentapolar" model, one in which five major powers would dominate international politics. In addition to the United States and the Soviet Union, this view included China, Japan and Western Europe as critical participants in the power distribution. Events since 1973 have demonstrated that, in addition, the ability of the resource-rich Third World to force a transformation of the international economic system requires that that group be regarded as a serious and independent part of the global power structure, though its military influence is small. It should be kept in mind, however, that power consists of several important nonmilitary characteristics (see Chapter 7). Indeed, though Japan is a mighty nation economically, its ability to influence international events through military action is negligible.

The notion of incipient multipolarity suggests that the global power distribution is in a transitional stage between bipolarity, clearly a thing of the past, and true multipolarity, in which six states (or groups of states) are more or less equally capable of influencing the outcomes of major international events. The reader is cautioned against the conclusion that such a stage will automatically lead to multipolarity. In fact, while it was widely speculated a decade ago that full multipolarity was safely predictable, recent developments in both the physical and diplomatic characteristics of the world suggest that the transition stage may be prolonged. Among these developments have been the growing awareness that the Western industrial powers are not energy self-sufficient and are thus vulnerable in their capabilities; the modest pace of political integration in Western Europe; the resurgence of interest in the transatlantic defense structure as a response to rapid Soviet military build-up in Central Europe; and the tendency for Washington to shun direct intervention in the events of the Third World even while the Soviet Union has increased its willingness to participate in events greatly distant from its core interests. It has even been argued that the power imperatives of the 1980s are more nearly similar to those of the late 1940s than to the pre-Vietnam War 1960s.[12]

Nevertheless, if incipient multipolarity is a stage in which a fundamental realignment of world power is occurring, then we need to identify the principal political characteristics of a multipolar system

12. Robert W. Tucker, "The Purposes of American Power," *Foreign Affairs,* Winter 1980/81, pp. 241–274.

in order to have a standard by which to measure the progress of the main participants toward it. The characteristic suggested here is that a major participant in a multipolar system would have the capability to determine the outcome of a direct (though not necessarily cataclysmic) confrontation between two other major participants. Another standard, both more modest and more practical, is the ability to determine the outcome of a distant event despite Soviet or American intention to achieve some other outcome(s). To what extent have the major "poles" developed their international capabilities in these respects?

China

The government of Mao Tse-tung used the Korean War to announce that it would not permit the two great powers to divide the world, and especially Asia. For the quarter-century that followed, American respect for China grew as a result of China's cautious diplomacy, its decision to limit strategic activities to its immediate Asian and Soviet border areas, and its general restraint during the Vietnam War. There is little doubt that American behavior throughout that war was guided by a careful assessment of Chinese tolerance for American control close to its borders.

Soviet respect for China was growing during the same time because of the latter's willingness to challenge Soviet territorial control of certain border regions and because of the growth of China's nuclear capability. While both Washington and Moscow had considered China a bitter enemy and a clumsy diplomatic contestant through the 1960s, neither was concerned for China's strategic capability beyond the proximity of interests in Asia. Its nuclear capability was regional at most; its capacity to control external events by either military or economic means was meager; and its preference for self-imposed isolation from global politics was a tempting reassurance to both Washington and Moscow in the daily maneuvering of their worldwide interests.

But if little communication took place between China and either of the two giants between the end of the Korean War (1953) and the withdrawal of the United States from Southeast Asia (1972), in the years following the latter event there has been a startling change. The gradual normalization of relations with Washington resulted in formal diplomatic recognition in 1979, a rapid growth in Sino-American trade, and the conclusion of a Second World War peace agreement with Japan. With the deaths of both Mao and Foreign Secretary Chou En-lai, and the rise to power of Hua Kuo-feng, there was evidence of a new Chinese world perspective by the end of the decade. No longer interested in isolation and no longer fixed to the ideological notion of modernization that had resulted in the suffocation of education and a preindustrial rate of progress, China undertook to overhaul its educational system, to reawaken its scientific potential by welcoming foreign scientists as visitors and advisors, to stimulate diverse productivity (by, among other things, inviting the Coca-Cola Company to establish a production plant in China), and to enliven its cultural life.

More strikingly, however, in 1979 China signaled to the world its intention of controlling the regional power distribution of Asia by invading Vietnam. Under a doctrine of "punitive aggression," this was held to be payment for Vietnam's conquest of Cambodia (thereafter renamed Kampuchea) and persistent strikes against Laos. It may have been precisely this kind of expanded presence that the Soviet Union feared of post-Mao China, and the reason the Kremlin resisted multipolarity. The Soviet leaders may have considered multipolarity an abstract Western notion of world politics, pitting state against state and ignoring the fundamental power question of international politics: the contest between world capitalism and world socialism.[13]

For nearly a decade, while the United States viewed China's role as increasingly constructive in balancing regional power (save for Washington's displeasure at the Vietnam invasion), the Kremlin continued to view China as a deviant state capable of upsetting both Asian politics and world socialism. It viewed China as having seduced the United States into peaceful relations, military agreements and industrial trade with the attractiveness of China's large and impoverished markets, and with the richness of its natural resources, particularly petroleum. The Soviet Union deplored China's Westward leanings and collusion with capitalism, and considered China's ideological deviations to have been an encouragement to anti-Soviet influences in Poland. By 1982, however, Sino-Soviet relations began to thaw, a process symbolized by a visit of high-ranking Chinese officials to Moscow, the first such visit in a quarter century. Western observers began to write of a "Sino-Soviet détente."[14]

It is nonetheless true, despite the substantial changes in China's role which these events signal, that Peking's part in the power equation

13. Nils H. Wessell, "Soviet Views of Multipolarity and the Emerging Balance of Power," *ORBIS,* Winter 1979, pp. 785–813.

14. See, for example, Donald S. Zagoria, "The Moscow-Beijing Détente," *Foreign Affairs,* Spring 1983, pp. 853–873. Zagoria and others caution, however, that this détente is modest and limited because of the profound ideological differences of China and the Soviet Union, and because of recent Soviet adventurism in the Third World. In contrast, one Chinese scholar writing under the pseudonym Edmund Lee predicts that China will grow gradually closer to the Soviet Union and away from the United States. See "Beijing's Balancing Act," *Foreign Policy,* Summer 1983, pp. 27–46.

remains principally regional. Regardless of its nearly unlimited potential power and rapid advancement as a nuclear state, its capacity to determine the outcome of a direct confrontation between the Soviet Union and the United States is limited almost entirely to Asia. Furthermore, it is probable that with China's own power growing, the only area in Asia over which the two giants are likely to differ significantly—save possibly Korea—is China. Except as a matter of self-defense, therefore, it is difficult to imagine a situation in which China might be called to play a role in a Soviet-American confrontation in Asia. China's role in the brief war between India and Pakistan (1965) showed its willingness to take part in Asian politics outside of its direct sphere, but in that case any Soviet-American confrontation was merely diplomatic. At present, then, within its Asian regional sphere, the likelihood of a confrontation of two major powers calling for China to play a third power role is very small. One quantitative assessment of comparative power status suggests that China's "strategic reach" is two-thirds that of the Soviet Union and only 20 percent that of the United States. The study concludes that by this index, China is roughly comparable as a world power with West Germany and Israel.[15]

By the same token, because China's influence at its present stage of development has but regional reach, it is improbable that it will effectively control distant events in a manner undesirable to Washington and/or Moscow. On the whole, therefore, China may be said to play a major role in its Asian tripartite relations with the United States and the Soviet Union; but given the current limitations of its capabilities and those of its preference for regional politics, China has not yet achieved the status of a third global power. The decade-old rapprochement with the United States and the prospects for a serious effort at détente with the Soviet Union are less signals of a new global thrust for China than an indication of an evolving policy of expanding political and economic relations in order to accelerate domestic economic development. Although China shows increasing evidence of wishing to play on the global economic stage, her strategic reach remains regional.[16]

Western Europe

Years have passed since the states of Western Europe were wholly dependent upon the United States. Through their economic consolidation they have struggled against American economic domination,

15. Ray S. Cline, *World Power Assessment,* as reproduced in George T. Kurian, *The Book of World Rankings* (New York: Facts on File Publications, 1979), Table 49.
16. For a study of the strategic military implications of this observation, see Gerald Segal, "China's Strategic Posture and the Great-Power Triangle," *Pacific Affairs,* Winter 1981–82, pp. 682–697.

and they have labored to compete successfully with foreign goods in Europe and throughout the world. Declining apprehension of war has encouraged an awareness not only of Europeanness, but of pan-Europeanness, a desire for the economic and political reconciliation of all Europe as inaugurated in the *Ostpolitik* of West Germany.

Far from continuing the decline (brought on by the destruction of the Second World War and the postwar gap) between their own productivity and that of the United States, Western Europeans perceive themselves, in the era of economic integration, to be a competitive economic force during the technological revolution. Advantaged by the steady fall in the value of the American dollar from the mid–1960s through 1982 and by the ever-increasing American balance-of-trade deficit, the only external influences that the Western Europeans have not been able to control have been the instability in world fuel supplies and the uncertainty introduced in the world economy by huge annual American budget deficits. These problems notwithstanding, Western Europeans see themselves in the forefront of a world movement in which the status of the nation-state is changing. A gradual transfer of political loyalty from the national government to an integrated Europe, and to the transnational corporation with its worldwide connections is happening. The growth of Eurocommunism, signaling the apparent death of anticommunist hysteria in Western Europe, further divides Europe from Washington and Wall Street. In fact, if these trends should accelerate, in the view of at least one European observer, the Western alliance, in both its economic and military forms, could well disintegrate.[17]

Where strategic relations are concerned, conflicting attitudes abound in Western Europe. On the one hand, the economic slump of the worldwide recession from 1980 through 1983 resulted in the election of conservative governments in Britain and West Germany and of a socialist government in France. At the same time, the return of inflammatory rhetoric to Soviet-American relations led to the American strategic decision to deploy new intermediate-range missiles in Europe at the end of 1983, with the full support of the European NATO members. On the other hand, the prospect of new missiles revived peace and anti-nuclear movements throughout Western Europe. On an official level, then, the trans-Atlantic security system was more cohesive in early 1984 than it had been for a decade; but public opinion was not fully consistent with policy.

In the presence of these inconsistencies, European powers were reluctant to exert political or military influences elsewhere. The British

17. Mary Kaldor, *The Disintegrating West* (New York: Hill and Wang, 1978).

response to the Argentinian invasion of the Falkland Islands was the result of a long-standing commitment to hold the islands; and the limited French participation in the defense of Chad after the Libyan invasion in 1983 was a reluctant post-imperial attempt at preserving a special economic relationship.[18] Western Europe's strategic interests, to the extent that they are distinct from NATO policy, are limited to that of a regional deterrent capable not of waging nuclear war, but of inflicting unacceptable harm upon any attacker. Although Western Europe will continue to be a major economic power, its strategic interests are almost exclusively regional.

Japan

A third country that is regarded as a potentially effective third power is Japan, whose economic stature follows only that of the United States and the Soviet Union. Not only has Japan risen above American commercial domination; it has also proven its ability to compete in world markets and is preparing to be the dominant supplier of industrial goods throughout Asia, including China.

The growth pattern that Japan's economic power has followed alarms the West. During the 1960s Japan achieved world domination in a number of small electronics manufacturers; in the 1970s it dominated the international automobile trade; and in the 1980s it is in a race with the United States, France and Germany to introduce the first megacomputers equipped with artificial intelligence.[19] During each of these phases there have been charges that Japanese manufacturers have stolen Western designs rather than invent their own products. There have also been charges that Japanese export subsidy programs violate international free-trade laws and principles. Japan's international economic prominance has been accompanied, then, by substantial controversy and difficult diplomacy.

Despite its strong position, Japan is extraordinarily vulnerable to external pressures, so much so that even its economic productivity suffers significant external controls. Chapter 3 describes the susceptibility of Japan's economy to American economic policy, and its ex-

18. This intervention occurred only after a brief public disagreement between Paris and Washington on France's proper role and responsibility. President Ronald Reagan assured the American people in August 1983 that there was no anticipation of American intervention because Chad is in France's sphere of influence. This prompted one American observer to charge the President with attempting to revitalize an old European notion of power politics. See Chalmers M. Roberts, "The Old World Game," *The Washington Post,* Sunday, August 21, 1983, p. C7.
19. Edward W. Feigenbaum and Pamela McCorduck, *The Fifth Generation: Artificial Intelligence and Japan's Computer Challenge to the World* (Reading, Mass.: Addison-Wesley, 1983).

treme exposure to the demands of the fuel-producing states. Consequently, the economic foundation of Japan's claim to third-power status is a peculiar one: more than any other candidate for this global role, the greatness which Japan commands rests upon her extreme dependency on both external markets and foreign energy sources. Although its productivity continues to increase, new threats loom. The formalization of peace with both the Soviet Union and the People's Republic of China seems to offer new economic hope for Japan with respect to markets for industrial goods and acquisition of desperately needed petroleum. Nevertheless, much of this promise seems to depend on the continuation of good diplomatic relations between Peking and Washington, and is threatened by the general strain in relations between the Soviet Union and Western-oriented nations.

The security sector reveals similar weaknesses. Prohibited at present by the Atomic Energy Law from developing nuclear weapons or deploying troops outside of its home territory, and uncertain of the American security commitment at a time when the Asian power distribution is in disarray, Japan must rely on economic and political means to establish its regional and global role. Japan's role in Asia is constrained by the peculiarity of its being the indigenous economic giant without nuclear capability in a region that has two underindustrialized nuclear states (China and India). In Japan, opinion differs on the plan of controversial Prime Minister Nakasone to increase significantly the percentage of gross national product devoted to military build-up.

In spite of its apparent strength, then, Japan is a state struggling to adapt to regional and global power relativities. Like Western Europe, it has escaped from the perpetual subordination of a bipolar system, but because of its dependence on others, particularly the United States and OPEC members, it is unable to establish a self-determined third-power role.

The Third World

For more than a decade many observers have claimed that the Third World is, or is about to become, an effective third power in global relations. Because of its total population, its territorial vastness and its richness in natural resources, the potential development here is extreme. But until recently this potential has not been mobilized. Population, growing at alarming rates, has caused a decline in per capita wealth even while the gross national products of most of the Third World states have been climbing. New forms of dependency implanted by Western-based multinational corporations have been added to the burden of population. Furthermore, the recessionary markets of the early 1980s devastated export potentials in the Third World and increased the burden in international debt to the point where Western bankers feared the collapse of international capital markets.

The establishment of OPEC and the events of 1973–74, both of which enriched the fuel-producing countries and forced changes in the foreign policies of more powerful states including Japan and the United States, caused a reassessment of the long-range capabilities of the Third World. As described in Chapter 5, that reappraisal begins with a division of the Third World into the resource rich and the resource poor, and then turns to the role of the former. Because much of the West is dependent upon OPEC (and particularly upon the Arab OPEC states) for industrial fuel, the oil-rich nations have discovered an effective lever for dealing with large dependent states. Simultaneously, they have greatly improved their regional bargaining position.

Even more than the petroleum embargo of 1973–74, the collapse of the Iranian economy as the result of revolution in 1978 and 1979 and the devastation of both Iranian and Iraqi petroleum industries in fighting from 1980 through 1984 have demonstrated the extreme impact that Third World petroleum exporters can have upon the world economy. Japan, as we have discussed, is especially vulnerable. But in the United States, the discontinuation of Iranian oil occurred almost simultaneously with a serious nuclear accident at Three Mile Island in Pennsylvania. That near-miss tempered American interest in nuclear power as an alternative to foreign oil dependence, and at the same time brought an even greater awareness of the reversal of dependence and the potential power of Third World oil. Indeed, oil-exporting governments are fully aware that with this single commodity they have forced the world political economy into a transition. Nevertheless, their strength at present lies on a single asset, oil, making them vulnerable to a number of countermeasures, including the utilization of alternative sources of energy, depletion of the asset and military coercion. Only if Third World exporters of other natural resources are able to form equally effective cartels can the unique instrument be used for effective leverage in world politics.

Oil has not proved to be perfect magic for the Third World. It has long been known, for example, that the repeated increases in OPEC prices added substantially to the debt of the non-oil producers among the underindustrialized states. Furthermore, OPEC has experienced a reduction in political cohesion. In late 1982 OPEC meetings, bitter conflict arose over pricing policy, with radical members arguing for more increases and moderates calling for stabilization for a fixed period of time. The moderates prevailed, led by Saudi Arabia which had recently been the object of much wooing by the United States. (The Reagan Administration had announced its intention of courting moderate Arab states in an effort to stabilize the politics of the Middle East. Over sharp Israeli protests, it had provided Saudi Arabia with AWACS reconnaisance aircraft.) World petroleum prices dropped in face of a minor glut, and the rate of capital accumulation among the OPEC nations diminished for the first time in a decade.

The political value of oil for the long range is also in question, in part because it is an exhaustable resource. At current rates of extraction, the known OPEC reserves will be exhausted by approximately 2025. Meanwhile, world industry will change remarkably. Familiar "smokestack" industries, for almost a century the backbone of industrial economies, will diminish in number as the technological revolution progresses.[20] Furthermore, coal research may yet reveal clean methods of burning coal without producing acid rain. Finally, non-OPEC oil strikes are increasing in number as Western nations vow not to be subjected again to the types of policies that OPEC imposed after 1973.

The third-power aspirations of the Third World states are, therefore, but partially and precariously fulfilled. Because of their vast differences in wealth and in economic and political development, dependence continues to characterize their position in world affairs. Thus their influence is more sporadic than consistent, and their capacity to mediate continuously the compelling issues of world politics remains sparse.

Comment

These observations about China, Western Europe, Japan and the Third World demonstrate that while the world has outgrown the forms of subordination typical of loose bipolarity, it has not produced effective independent power centers that would usher in true multipolarity. Consequently, we conclude that the global balance of power is in a transitional phase of incipient multipolarity, in which the secondary power centers are still more attached to the primary than the independent poles. Figure 8–7 shows this configuration.

Prior to the 1973 revolution in oil politics, it appeared that this transitional phase was part of a linear trend from loose bipolarity to a multipolar balance of power. But those events revealed the weakest elements on which the aspirations of Japan—and to a lesser degree

20. Bruce Nussbaum, *The World After Oil: The Shifting Axis of Power and Wealth* (New York: Simon and Schuster, 1983).

FIGURE 8–7
Incipient global multipolarity, 1965 to the present

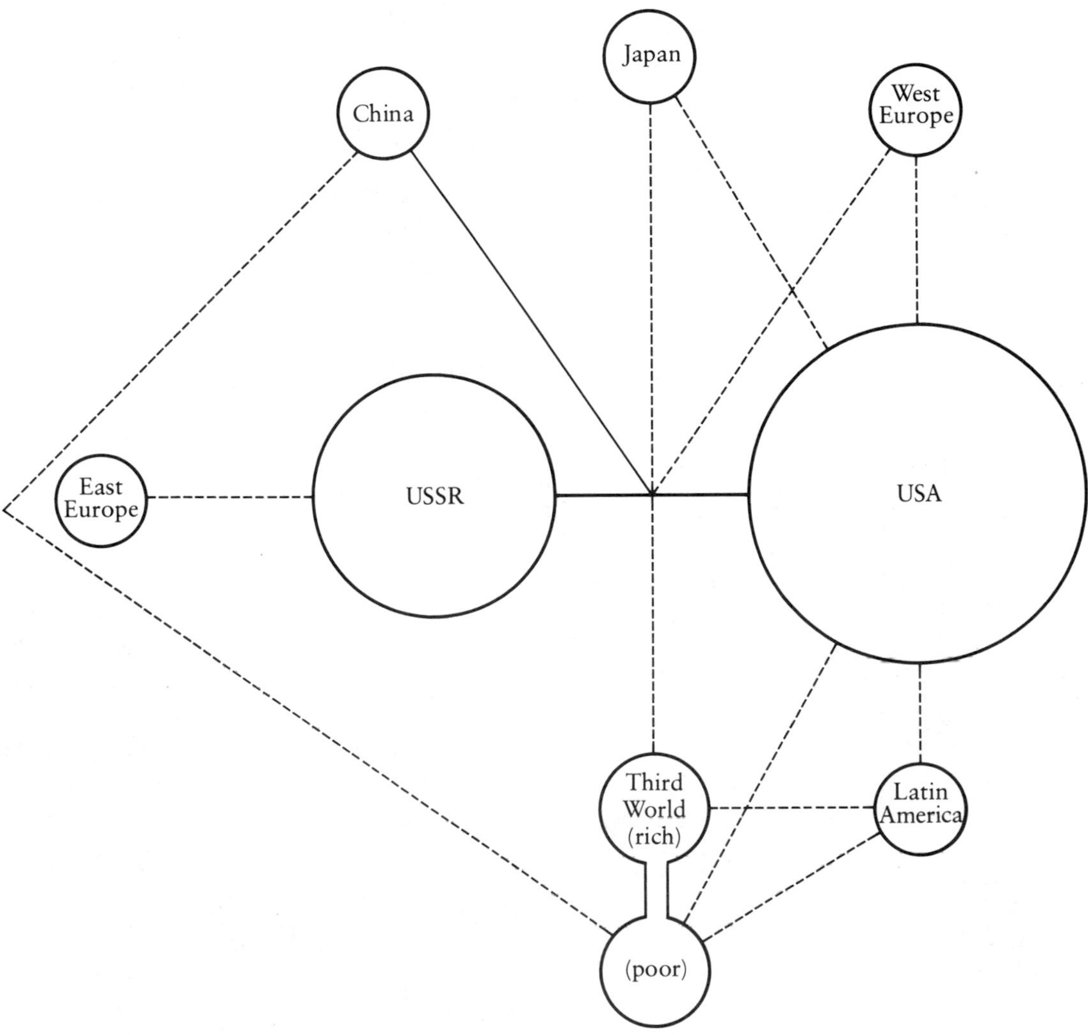

Western Europe—are constructed. Japan, joined by the Western European states except for France, has pleaded for common diplomatic and distribution policies, but this has only served to expose the previously hidden weaknesses of the industrial states among aspiring third-power candidates. The new dependences are so vivid as to warrant the conclusion that progress toward multipolarity is arrested, with resumption awaiting self-sufficiency in fuel among the industrialized states, and political-economic stabilization between the industrialized West and the resource-rich Third World.

5. The Multipolar Balance of Power

If significant power increases should occur in the Third World, China, Western Europe or Japan to the extent that two or more of these entities were able to challenge Soviet-American global interests, the international system could be defined as multipolar. Since the relative power capabilities need not be entirely equal, multipolarity might have either symmetrical or asymmetrical characteristics. The important issue is that several major power blocs would interact at virtually any place, without two-party domination. Such a system would appear as shown in Figure 8–8. As in the previous models, the important factor here is that each of these systems is depicted as affecting the fulcrum, rather than being derived from or dependent upon some other power unit.

A New Balance-of-Power Model?

It has occasionally been suggested that multipolarity might restore the conditions of the nineteenth-century balance of power. This argument has two bases. First, several independent power centers facilitate the switching of alliances and realignment of interests and power. Second, the same feature—multiple power centers—is necessary for the appearance of a Balancer, at the service of the international system to balance the system consciously (manually). Presuming that multipolarity was approximately symmetrical, any of several power centers

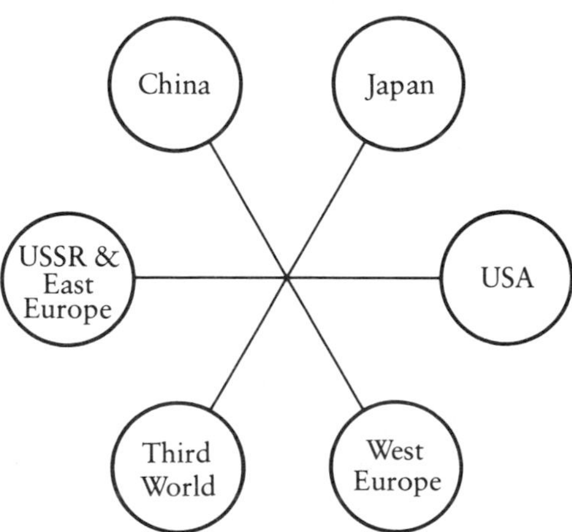

FIGURE 8–8
True global multipolarity, possible future

might serve in this capacity, and perhaps several would alternate in the role.

Because of its huge power potential, China is most likely the next effective independent power in global politics. If it is, then big-power confrontations calling for third-power intervention as a Balancer might take any of the following forms:

Contestants	*Balancer*
China—Soviet Union	United States
United States—China	Soviet Union
United States—Soviet Union	China

But there are several impediments to these relations. First, the power of each participant is so great that coalitions will necessarily overbalance. Hence the proper designation for these relations is not balance of power, but *mutual superiority* in noncoalition situations and *disequilibrium* in coalitions. Second, ideological barriers minimize the likelihood of each configuration. Third, balance-of-power theory assumes the dedication of each participant to the preservation of the others. Such devotion, whether out of strategy of sentiment, will be lacking for the foreseeable future. It follows that even the most probable form of global tripolarity is incompatible with a renewed balance of power on the nineteenth-century model.

Regional Balance of Power

Throughout this discussion of balance-of-power models, reference has been made to regional as well as global conditions. Although the concept has generally been applied to worldwide relations, the notion of a balance of power has critical interpretive meanings for regional conflict as well. This is true whether or not the major powers contribute significantly to the regional power equation.

Asia presents a highly complex power distribution. At the highest level, the two superpowers contribute directly because of their conflicting interests there. The Pacific Ocean, Taiwan and South Korea are at the American nuclear frontier. At the second level, China transforms Soviet-American relations in Asia into nuclear tripolarity. Beneath that, India pursues a nuclear policy to enjoy mutual deterrence with China, but in so doing tilts the scale in its own favor against Pakistan. It is precisely because as an economic power Japan must venture into all of these relations that its military inferiority confuses its role in the overall Asian balance of power.

The situation is made less clear by the military events of 1978–79, particularly the Vietnamese invasion of Cambodia (now Kampuchea) and the subsequent Chinese occupation of Vietnamese territory. When a partial Chinese withdrawal was followed by the stationing of Soviet naval vessels in Vietnamese bases (built and previously used by the United States Navy), the continental politics and power balance of Asia seemed once again to be thrown into disarray.

The balance-of-power question is less complex but equally crucial in the Middle East. There, Israel finds its tiny territory surrounded by a large coalition of hostile states, some of which are those same petroleum exporters who have amassed great wealth and used oil to manipulate the foreign policies of Western industrial states with respect to the regional conflict. Although the Israel-Arab War of 1973 was brief, it was indescribably destructive. Arabs, Israelis, Americans and Soviets were all dumbfounded by the amount of military hardware destroyed in such a short time by precision tactics. Inasmuch as both Israel and Egypt were within easy reach of nuclear technology at the time, the regional strategic balance seemed to be creeping toward one of mutual assured destruction. Quite apart from the competing interests of the superpowers, the regional balance as influenced exclusively by its participants seemed in desperate need of fine tuning.

Again, however, the dynamics of international politics offered its substitute of adjustment. As Israel and Egypt struggled through 1978 and into 1979 to establish a bilateral peace, two critical events occurred. First, Iran was torn by a revolution so significant for world politics that petroleum exports were discontinued. The Shah was forced into exile, and the religious leader Ayatollah Khomeini seized the reins of political power. Western influence was suddenly expunged, and the future of Iran's part in the regional balance thrown into question. At the same time, Israel's regional enemies announced their intention to boycott Egypt politically and economically should she enter into a unilateral peace. Suddenly, both Soviet and American naval presence in the area increased. The regional balance had undergone a fundamental change, but one of unspecific meaning. As has so often been the case, the superpowers were quickly on the spot to safeguard the balance; but *what* balance? When in 1980 the Soviet Union occupied Afghanistan and moved troops to within easy reach of the Iranian border, the loss of Iran from the American strategic circle (symbolized by Washington's inability even to secure the release of fifty-two Americans held hostage for a year) showed even more clearly the deterioration of the regional balance. The war between Iran and Iraq, which broke out late in 1980, raised the question of whether or not Iraq would achieve the position of the foremost power in the region with the approval of both the United States and the Soviet Union.

Factional liberators in the Lebanese Civil War, 1984.

Source: Bettmann/UPI

Further destabilization resulted from the 1982 war between Syria and the Palestine Liberation Organization, on the one hand, and Israel, fought on Lebanese soil by Syria and the Palestine Liberation Organization against Israel. The war resulted, among other things, in the repudiation by Middle Eastern states of United Nations peacekeeping forces, the lengthy occupation of Lebanon by both Israel and Syria, and civil warfare between rival factions of the PLO and between Druze and Christian factions. Before any of these issues were settled, Libya, Egypt's Mediterranean neighbor to the west, intervened militarily in the civil war in Chad, expanding its radical influence and raising a potential threat to Sudan.

Sudan forms the geographic link between the Middle East (with Egypt to its north) and Africa, where perhaps the most complex regional power balance exists. Africa is a continent torn between emancipation from bondage and interregional warring. While some observers worry that much of southern Africa is ripe for racial war, others are more concerned with the presence of the superpowers in areas rich in natural resources. At present Africa would seem to be the continent most vulnerable to external intervention, though in the wake of Vietnam the United States has been reluctant to do so. This was the case when the Soviet Union, with the assistance of Cuba, dominated the outcome of an internal struggle for governmental supremacy in Angola. Cuban presence seems to be especially prevalent, with a reported 54,000 soldiers and civilian advisors in fourteen African countries in April of 1978. Among these, nearly half were still in Angola and about 18,000 in Ethiopia.[21]

Chapter 9 is devoted to a detailed study of some of the world's most precarious regional balances.

Polarity and Stability: A Debate

The foregoing elucidation of past, present and possible future power distributions produces a critical question: Is international stability better ensured by fundamentally bipolar political patterns or by multipolar balance? Each has advantages, but each also suffers from disadvantages.

One advocate of bipolarity finds four specific benefits in that system. First, with two overbearing world powers there are no peripheries from which significant conflict beyond the control of the great powers can occur. Second, the tighter the bipolarity and the more intense the interbloc competition, the broader the range of the subject matter over which the great powers gain leverage and can control conflict. Third, pressure is constant, and crises recur at low levels rather than in major conflict. Finally, the combination of constant pressure within blocs and the superior power of the dominant members enables the blocs to tolerate potentially disruptive change, including revolution, which might otherwise lead to widespread conflict.[22]

The disadvantages and intrinsic dangers of bipolarity have also been elucidated. One is that bipolar systems accentuate antagonism because of the reactions of the blocs to one another, leading to a degenerative aspect. There is also skepticism over the maxim that peace is best ensured by a crisis atmosphere and mutual fear. As we have previously seen, the tighter a bipolar configuration, the more tense the relations of the blocs and of their respective dominant members.[23]

Others have investigated the stabilizing potential of multipolar systems and have concluded that the increased interaction of a multipolar model promotes stability. [24] In addition, increased interaction reduces obsession with any single one, thus enhancing the trend toward mod-

21. James Nelson Goodsell in *The Christian Science Monitor,* "Cuban Role in Africa Still Expanding," April 25, 1978, p. 3.
22. Kenneth N. Waltz, "The Stability of a Bipolar World," *Daedelus* 93 (Summer 1964), pp. 881–909.
23. R. N. Rosecrance, "Bipolarity, Multipolarity, and the Future," *Journal of Conflict Resolution* 10, 1966, pp. 315–17.
24. Karl W. Deutsch and J. David Singer, "Multipolar Power Systems and International Stability," *World Politics* 16, 1964, pp. 390–406.

eration. Though multipolarity cannot maintain stability interminably, it may be preferable in the shorter term.

In an empirical attempt to resolve the dispute over the stability of bipolar and multipolar systems, yet another scholar has studied the stratification and stability characteristics of twenty-one separate situations. He concludes that unipolar systems (single-nation domination), though historically rare, are the most stable. Bipolar systems, he finds, tend to produce less frequent but more prolonged wars than do multipolar. Multipolarity, in contrast, produces war among major actors more frequently and with more casualties. This argument thus leads to a choice, since neither configuration seems statistically to offer any guarantee against warfare.

> The choice between bipolar versus multipolar arrangements now seems clear. If a state or group of states is willing to accept long wars that are won by aggressor states, bipolarity provides an escape from the more war-prone character of historical multipolar subsystems. Multipolarity entails more violence, more countries at war and more casualties; bipolarity, fewer but longer wars.[25]

Conclusion

Equivalence or Nonequivalence of Power

"What is the balance of power between the United States and the Soviet Union?" "Describe the balance of power in the Far East." "Who holds the balance of power in the Cold War?" Expressions and questions of this sort are common in political discussion, and they suggest some of the ways in which the balance-of-power concept is applied to the direct relations of pairs or small groups of states. It is useful to think of "balance" for the moment not as a natural phenomenon, but as the familiar inanimate object. This permits us to recast the opening questions in this way: "In what position does the balance (scale) come to rest when the power of the United States is symbolically piled at one end, and that of the Soviet Union on the other?" For a tripartite situation (Sino-Soviet-American relations in Asia, for example), think of a perfectly balanced three-bulb chandelier hanging from a flexible chain. Now: "How does it hang when the power of the United States is symbolically plugged into one socket, that of the Soviet Union into a second and that of China in the third? Does it continue to hang on a perfect level, or does it tilt in the direction of one?" It should now be evident that the expression "balance of power" in small-group interstate relations refers to a rough measure of power equivalence or nonequivalence.

25. Michael Haas, "International Subsystems: Stability and Polarity," *American Political Science Review* 64, 1970, pp. 98–123.

Equilibrating Objectives

In the early part of this discussion on balance of power we noted that many analysts include among its many meanings that of a policy or a set of objectives. If we assume that states are power conscious, then in their external relations they may have any one of three power objectives: (1) to maintain equality with some object-state, (2) to achieve superiority over some other state(s), or (3) to decline to keep pace with some other state(s). Again, remember that power must always be determined and measured relative to the power of someone else: Italy is more powerful than Switzerland, but less powerful than France. The power choices that a government makes with respect to its neighbors or competitors comprise its equilibrating objectives.

Surprisingly perhaps, some states opt not to match the power of their neighbors. Finland cannot compete with the Soviet Union and does not care to compete with Sweden. Costa Rica has virtually no military forces. And Japan, despite its image as a powerful state, maintains but a small national defense force. The Republic of China (Taiwan), however, invests a disproportionate share of its public revenue in national defense, yet could not conceivably defend itself against aggression from China should it occur. In all of these cases, therefore, the potential adversaries of these countries "hold the balance" against them.

In other situations, particularly where the expectation of conflict is moderate to high, the contesting states will seek superiority, and may even abandon the traditional power balance in favor of the balance-of-terror variant. In contrast, where the probability of violence is perceived as low, states will seek no more than equivalence, or will arm themselves only up to the level of their alliance commitments (for instance, Canada). From the logic of these contrasting cases we may infer that in most bilateral situations, military allocations are governed by the quest for the safety of equivalence.

Balance of power, then, is an expression with many political meanings. In the global context it is useful as an analytical concept for assessing the overall power capabilities of states and coalitions, and it serves as a generic title for a host of specific power distributions. On the interstate level, in contrast, "balance of power" is a device for bilateral and small-group power relativities. It also expresses the equilibrating or disequilibrating objectives of national arms policies.

The bilateral and interbloc relations of the superpowers since the Second World War have been so intense as to have outgrown conventional balance of power logic. Instead, the dominant contemporary variant is the balance of terror. After studying some specific regional military balances in Chapter 9, we will discuss the balance of terror in Chapter 10.

9

Regional Military Balances

Maintaining international stability in a world of conflicting national values and perceptions depends on resolving or reconciling all conflicts, an objective that is in many cases unattainable, or on managing a world full of ideological, territorial, national, ethnic and other antagonisms in such a way as to prevent the outbreak of wars. Conflict management depends, in turn, either on the predominance of a single power center able to impose its will in contentious regions to maintain order, or on a network of regional balances of power that, taken as a whole, add up to a delicate global balance. In the contemporary world, in which there is neither a world government nor a single dominant imperial power able to maintain system-wide peace, stability depends largely on such regional balances. The great powers are often important, sometimes vital actors in the regional balances, but in most cases only insofar as they affect the capabilities of the local actors who are the dominant players in their own theaters.

Throughout this book the concept of power is considered to encompass more than military capability. Economic abilities as well as geographic, psychological and other factors of national strength constitute power. In this chapter, however, our concern is exclusively with military capability. Hence the chapter bears the title "Regional Military Balances" rather than "Regional Power Balances."

It is a sad fact that, for many regimes, maintaining an adequate military capability against external and internal enemies is a paramount objective to which many other needs must be subordinated. The net product of all these preparations is a global complex of antagonistic subsystems in the form of regional military balances. The preeminent fact of European life is the opposition of NATO and Warsaw Pact forces across the vast central European front; South Asian politics is conditioned by the hostility of India and Pakistan and their opposed military deployments; planning in the two Koreas is dominated by their preparations for war with each other; and Somalia and Ethiopia spend immense amounts on their opposed armed forces in spite of the crushing burden of underdevelopment that afflicts both. Table 9–1 lists additional examples and illustrates the great variety of regional balances which comprises the contemporary international system.

In many of these regional balances, the great powers play important roles by providing arms and military advisers, financial support and surrogate forces like the Cubans and East Germans to support or actually lead military operations and, in some cases, direct military intervention. While the great powers seldom control completely the elements of the local balance, what they do or do not do is often critical, as few of the local balances are fully autonomous. Local hostilities in Third World regions generally have local causes, and are not merely reflections of the overarching competition of the superpowers; but their outcomes are viewed by the great powers as important developments in the evolution of the larger international system. A pattern in which one side is supported by the Soviet Union and the other by the United States or another Western country is typical. The local

TABLE 9–1
The world as a collection of local military balances

Warsaw Pact vs. NATO
North vs. South Korea
Soviet Union vs. China
India vs. Pakistan
China vs. Taiwan
Soviet Afghanistan vs. Pakistan
Vietnam vs. ASEAN Nations
Arabs vs. Israel
Polisario/Algeria vs. Morocco
Libya vs. Egypt and Tunisia
South Yemen vs. Oman and Saudi Arabia
Iraq vs. Iran
Ethiopia vs. Somalia and Djibouti
Ethiopia vs. Eritrea
South Yeman vs. North Yemen
Kenya vs. Somalia
Christian Lebanese vs. Moslem Lebanese and Palestinians
South Africa vs. Angola, Mozambique, Zambia Zimbabwe and Seychelles
Yugoslavia vs. USSR

wars are therefore, in part, proxy wars between the two major power blocs.

The comparative involvements of the United States and the Soviet Union in the arms policies affecting regional balances varies greatly over time. From the onset of the Korean War in 1950 to the American withdrawal from Vietnam in 1972–73, Washington was directly involved in the establishment of arms programs in Europe, Asia, Latin America and parts of Africa. Following Vietnam, however, the American commitment to regional balances abated in many places, with only the European balance, the defense of South Korea and the arming of Israel against the threat of Arab aggression as major exceptions. During those years (1972–80), Soviet involvement in regional balances exceeded that of the United States. In 1979, for example, 25,600 Soviet tanks were in the inventories of Third World countries, compared to 11,000 American and European tanks (of which the U.S. accounted for 6,700). This disparity shows up in a more pronounced way in local comparisons of the high-intensity conflicts: Soviet-supported Ethiopia has 600 tanks compared to about 100 in Somalia (many of which also came from the Soviets when that country was on better terms with the USSR); North Korea has 2,600 compared to 1,360 in South Korea; Vietnam has 1,000 main battle tanks from the USSR compared to Thailand's 170 supplied by the United States; and Algeria has 500 Soviet-supplied tanks compared to the 100 provided to Morocco by the West. Even Israel has 550 "supplied" (i.e., captured) Soviet tanks in its active inventory, compared to 1,460 provided by the United States as of 1979; while Syria, Iraq, Libya and Egypt have 8,000 provided by the Soviet Union. Comparisons of supersonic combat aircraft in the Third World are not as extreme, but it is still the case that there are twice as many Soviet fighters and bombers in the inventories of these countries as there are American models.[1]

In the 1980s, however, the relative contributions of Washington and Moscow to regional balances have been approximately equal. This situation results in part from a general reduction of Soviet arms exports and a vast increase in American exports under the Reagan administration. The Soviet Union continues to provide arms for Libya and Syria in the Middle East, Cuba and Nicaragua in Central America, and Ethiopia and Angola in Africa, as well as to the Warsaw Pact countries and Afghanistan. But Washington has vastly increased its exports to Central America (particularly to Mexico, Honduras, El

1. For a reliable numerical report on comparative arms capabilities, see *SIPRI Yearbook* 1979, (Stockholm). Similar figures appear in subsequent annual editions and detail the arms export policies of the Soviet Union, the United States, Britain, Germany and France.

Salvador and right-wing insurgents in Nicaragua), to the NATO countries, to Israel, Egypt and Saudi Arabia, and to South Korea, Japan, India and Pakistan.[2]

Opinions differ as to the qualitative differences between Soviet and American weapons exported to specific regions. Generally, however, it is believed that the gap between the quality of Soviet and American supplies is closing rapidly, since Soviet weapons research efforts exceeded those of the United States for a period of years from approximately 1975–81. Furthermore, it is usually conceded that both Soviet and American arms exceed in quality the needs of the Third World, thus perhaps reducing the importance of the comparative quality issues.

Beyond the volume and quality of arms transferred to troubled regions by the Soviet Union and the United States, the Soviet bloc has demonstrated a superior willingness to arrange deliveries on schedules that could not be matched by the West, thus enabling it to influence events in regional hotspots at critical junctures, while Western arms have generally been much slower to arrive. And beyond the arms transfer process, the Soviet effort to influence local balances has often been superior in the use of other levers of influence. The Soviet bloc has mounted a more systematic and sustained effort to influence, and sometimes exploit, nationalist and ethnic minority movements; it has organized mobile and flexible interventionary forces of surrogates like the Cubans and East Germans able to affect events in diverse locations at critical times; and it has achieved considerable freedom of action in the direct invasion of Afghanistan by the Soviet Union and Cambodia by Vietnam. Since the end of American involvement in the Vietnam War, Soviet bloc presence in regional flashpoints has been substantially greater and more tangible than that of the Western powers.

Much of current international history is dominated by these regional tensions and military balances, and detailed examination of the many regional cases is an essential part of the study of international relations. It is not possible to consider all the tension areas here, but it may be worthwhile to review briefly three cases of particular contemporary importance: the European military balance, the Arab-Israeli case and the conflict between the two Koreas. Although every region has its own "personality," these three cases may exemplify some of the major trends that are seen also in other areas, and they are of course worthy of study in themselves.

2. For a detailed list of military supplies ordered by and delivered to Third World countries in 1982, see *SIPRI Yearbook, 1983* (Stockholm), pp. 306–337.

The European Military Balance

Any consideration of the European military balance in the 1980s should begin with the simple but dramatic fact that forty years after the conclusion of the Second World War, and after many efforts to achieve a relaxation of tensions in this area and a reduction of mobilized forces, large communist and Western armies at comparatively high levels of readiness still face each other across the same lines of military demarcation that existed when the world war ended. Fifteen years ago, when major East-West treaties settling postwar territorial changes were finally signed, many observers hailed the spirit of détente and predicted a scaling down of military preparations as political conflicts lessened. The Soviet Union, it was said, was wearying of the burden of maintaining these oversized forces in Europe, needed to turn its attention to domestic social and economic needs, and in any case would have had to divert some divisions from the European theater, now less critical, to the Chinese border, where conflicts were intensifying. While few observers fully believed that the Cold War in Europe was over, there was, at the dawn of the 1970s, some hope that a major reduction of standing armies in Europe would soon occur.

It is now clear, in retrospect, that the era of détente did not produce this result. While some reductions on the Western side did occur, Soviet forces in Europe expanded significantly in spite of détente and simultaneously with an increase of twenty-five divisions on the Chinese border. American land, sea and air forces in Europe were reduced from 430,000 to around 300,000, but Soviet forces in Europe increased from twenty-six divisions in 1967 to thirty in 1980. Moreover, these divisions are now larger in size and vastly improved in equipment and logistics. The European military balance is therefore a matter of continued and even heightened concern, in spite of the progress that has been achieved in resolving some of the political issues left unsettled after the Second World War.

Ordinary citizens no longer think of Europe as a major theater of military confrontation. But to professional military analysts, Europe remains the central territorial stage of the global competition. Far larger and more capable forces face each other in Europe than in any Third World hotspot; military expenditures in the conflict between NATO and the Warsaw Pact greatly exceed those of all other regional arms races combined; and its political and economic importance, as well as its geographic position, still makes Europe the most important area of contention.

What, then is the balance of forces in Europe? Before exploring the facts, some background information is necessary. First, a study of the

European military balance is not merely a comparison of Soviet and American strengths in the region, but of the combined strength of the Soviet Union and its Warsaw Pact allies, on the one hand, and the United States and its NATO allies, on the other. Second, while most statistical information about American and Western European military efforts is public, similar information for the Soviet Union and its allies is not. Hence the best information available of Warsaw Pact military strength is a product of American (or other Western) intelligence. Third, when estimating military capability for the purpose of planning national or regional defense, analysts tend to underestimate their own strength and overestimate those of the potential adversary. Consequently, intelligence estimates are rarely accurate and equally unreliable for scholarly purposes. And, finally, it is useful to divide the study of military comparison in Europe into (a) strategic (nuclear) capabilities, (b) conventional (non-nuclear) strengths and (c) the small but critically important component of a regional arsenal known as tactical nuclear strength, a body of weapons that fire nuclear-tipped devices either from small, mobile vehicles such as jeeps or small trucks, or from shoulder-mounted launchers.

The Strategic Balance

In Chapter 10, "The Balance of Terror," we will discuss the capabilities of the United States and the Soviet Union to wage intercontinental nuclear warfare with the use of ICBMs. Our concern here, though, is slightly different: it is not with the vehicle capable of delivering weapons of huge megatonage over distances of several thousand miles, but with that capable of delivering moderate yields over the dimensions of the European theater only. This class of vehicle is technically referred to as the Long-Range Intermediate-Range Nuclear Force, meaning that it is on the long end of the intermediate-range class. For purposes of simplicity, it is usually referred to as the Intermediate-Range Nuclear Force, or INF.

During the last five years, most of the controversy over the defense of Western Europe has centered on the INF component of the arsenal. This debate resulted in part from a large and rapid increase in Soviet INF weapons from 1979 forward, and in part from the NATO decision to deploy two new INF weapons (the ground-launched Cruise missile and the Pershing II) beginning in late 1983. Among other consequences, the arrival of the first new missiles touched off huge anti-nuclear popular sentiment, forced a reconsideration of policy in the West German government, drove Soviet statesmen from all arms ne-

Source: Urraca/Sygma

American military maneuvers in Honduras, 1983.

gotiations then in progress, and prompted Moscow to increase its own INF deployment along the European dividing line.

Prior to the beginning deployment of the Pershing II and Cruise missiles in the European theater in 1983, the Soviet Union had, for five years, been deploying three classes of INF missiles. In early 1983 these consisted of 248 older SS-4 and SS-5 missiles, each with a single warhead, and 330 of the new SS-20 rockets, each capable of mounting three independently-targeted reentry vehicles. American intelligence estimates the range of the SS-4 to be 2,000 miles, that of the SS-5 to be 4,100 miles, and that of the SS-20 to be 5,000 miles. With the deployment of the SS-20, many of the older weapons were being dismantled or moved to Asia; so even though the actual number of rockets declined in 1982 and 1983, the total nuclear striking capability of the Warsaw Pact forces increased considerably. In addition, the accuracy of the SS-20 is far superior to that of its predecessors, thus raising the threat of successful strike.[3]

3. Force estimates are taken from U.S. Department of Defense, *Soviet Military Power, 1983,* pp. 34–35. *SIPRI Yearbook, 1983,* p. 6 reports the ranges of SS-4 and SS-5 as 1800 and 3500 miles, respectively.

During this period, the United States had no INF weapons in Western Europe. When the NATO decisions was made in 1979 to install 542 of the new weapons beginning 1983, the Soviet Union responded by agreeing not to deploy the SS-20 in replacement of older missiles if the United States would cancel the decision to deploy Pershing IIs and Cruise missiles. The Soviet Union continues to claim that it was the 1979 NATO decision and the subsequent determination to execute the decision that led to rapid installation of SS-20s. The Reagan administration, which had come to power partly on its repudiation of of the SALT II draft treaty, withdrew the SALT II draft from the Senate, terminated all negotiations relating to it, and called for the beginning of Soviet-American talks (the START negotiations) to reduce rather than simply to limit nuclear weapons. But when the controversy over theater nuclear weapons threatened the START conversations, President Reagan elected to separate theater from global negotiations, and the Soviet Union agreed to conduct START negotiations on worldwide strategic issues and INF talks on theater issues simultaneously.[4]

The controversy surrounding the INF competition goes far beyond a mere counting of missiles or warheads. The main problems are the speed of delivery (about six minutes in either direction, thus considerably increasing the threat of unnecessary war from a decision to strike on warning of incoming missiles), and accuracy. The new generation of missiles on both sides is believed capable of reducing to within two hundred yards the probability of direct hit on target by 50 percent of missiles fired. To both sides, this raises the threat of instantaneous destruction of command, control and communications (C^3) systems, thus rendering defenses useless. That all of these new missile systems are mobile (truck-launched) results in increased intelligence problems. Despite these considerations, the Soviet Union continued to add about fifty additional per year to its 330 SS-20s, as the United States began in late 1983 the plan to deploy 108 Pershing II (range: 1,800 miles) and 464 Cruise missiles (range: 2,500 miles). More striking than the numbers is the fact that these missiles are said to have controllable accuracy to within forty and fifty meters of target, respectively.

Negotiations over this competition are complicated by differing perceptions of actual strengths. The Soviet Union, for instance, insists that all NATO weapons be included in negotiations and in strength

4. For a brief but excellent review of the diplomatic and strategic considerations behind START, see David Holloway, *The Soviet Union and the Arms Race* (New Haven: Yale, 1983), particularly Chapter IV.

counts, while the United States, which has no direct control over French and British arms policies, argues that only American weapons should be included. Furthermore, the Kremlin is interested in discussing only missiles that are now deployed in Eastern Europe, while the United States, fearful of the degree to which the balance can be disrupted by new mobile missiles, wants to consider all new generations of Soviet missiles east of the Urals. Moreover, the sides cannot agree on a means for considering theater nuclear forces deliverable from aircraft or from submarines. The United States is particularly concerned about the capabilities of the new Soviet *Backfire* bomber.

With all of these factors yet to be sifted, it is not surprising that the Kremlin and the Pentagon have vastly different assessments of the current balance. The breadth of the assessment gap is revealed in Table 9–2 and Table 9–3. The reader should note that based on its own

TABLE 9–2
American assessment of the strategic balance of the European theater.

	USA	*USSR*
INF missiles	0	330 SS-20
		350 other SS generations
Submarine-launched	0	30
Bombers	164 in Europe	45 Backfire
	63 in US for European deployment	350 strategic bombers
		2,700 attack fighter-bombers
	333 within range	
	560 total	3,715 total

Source: Soviet SS-20 and other SS generations from several sources; all others adapted from David Holloway, *The Soviet Union and the Arms Race* (New Haven: Yale, 1983), p. 74.

TABLE 9–3
Soviet assessment of the strategic balance of the European theater.

	USA and NATO	*USSR*
INF missiles	18 French	243 SS-20
		253 other SS generations
Submarine-launched	80 French	18
	64 British	
Bombers	723 American	461
	46 French	
	55 British	
	986 total	975 total

Source: David Holloway, *The Soviet Union and the Arms Race* (New Haven: Yale, 1983), p. 74.
Note: These figures are all American intelligence estimates of Soviet strength. The SS-20 figures are for early 1983; all others for 1981.

estimates, the United States accuses the Soviet Union of having a six-to-one advantage in strategic weapons in the European theater. Thus Soviet opposition to the deployment of new American missiles in Europe is viewed as an attempt to retain numerical superiority and, with the replacement of old SS-4 and SS-5 rockets by new SS-20s, to secure qualitative superiority. From its vantage point, the Soviet Union considers a balance to exist, with the result that any new American weapons constitute an effort to upset the balance in favor of NATO. Western European governments, parties to the 1979 NATO agreement, stand behind the American position; massive anti-nuclear sentiments in the West do not.[5]

The Conventional Balance

In an era when military observers are preoccupied with nuclear warheads, new generations of missiles, accuracy and megatonnage, the fact remains that nuclear weapons are only part of a superpower's strategy. Except for the American bombings of Nagasaki and Hiroshima in 1945, weapons of mass destruction have not been used at all. Though the costs of technological devices for the delivery of nuclear weapons dominate budgetary planning, all principally for deterrence rather than combat, governments continue to put billions of dollars annually into non-nuclear forces and weapons development as well. The probability of a war starting as a nuclear war is still relatively slight; but the probability of one or another government with nuclear capability resorting to nuclear weapons because its conventional forces are unable to stand a battlefield challenge is frighteningly great. Thus conventional forces remain the first line of defense even for the nuclear powers. Furthermore, the ability of conventional forces to deter aggression is every bit as important as a stable nuclear balance. If conventional forces among nuclear powers are sufficiently unbalanced to invite aggression and a probability of victory rather than impasse, the likelihood of nuclear war as a desparate strategy increases.

As in the case with nuclear forces, the United States claims that the Soviet Union and the Warsaw Pact enjoy a two-to-one advantage in virtually every category. The Soviet Union argues that there is parity. The differences result from disparities of intelligence estimates, disagreements as to what should be counted, insistence by one party that

5. For a variety of European comments on the political-strategic conflict, see as examples Christopher Bertram, "Implications of Theater Nuclear Weapons in Europe," *Foreign Affairs,* Winter 1981/82, pp. 305–326; Pierre Lellouche, "France and the Euromissiles," *Foreign Affairs,* Winter 1983/84, pp. 318–334; and Paul Buteux, "Theatre-Nuclear Forces," *The Yearbook of International Affairs, 1983,* pp. 113–128.

TABLE 9–4
Warsaw Pact and NATO conventional force comparisons.

	USSR/WTO	*USA/NATO*
Military personnel	4.0 mill.	2.6 mill.
Divisions	173	84
Tanks	42,500	13,000
Anti-tank launchers	24,300	8,100
Artillery and mortars	31,500	10,750
Transport vehicles	78,800	30,000
Transport and support helicopters	1,000	1,800
Attack helicopters	700	400

Source: U.S. Department of Defense, *Soviet Military Power, 1983,* p. 63.

only deployed forces should be included while the adversary concentrates on the total deployed and deployable, the geographic range within which forces should be counted, etc. Table 9–4 provides American estimates for forces in place in 1981 (limited to ground forces).

Air force comparisons for non-strategic craft show a sharp Soviet advantage in all classes except fighter-bombers for ground attack, as shown in Table 9–5.

Finally, although much attention is focused on the development of nuclear submarines capable of delivering nuclear weapons over great distances, naval surface weapons continue to be one of the most rapidly developing sectors of Soviet-American competition, particularly in the vicinity of Western Europe. Table 9–6 indicates the status of that competition.

NATO has, in the past, attempted to offset the Soviet advantage in quantity through Western advantages in quality, but these efforts, never fully satisfactory in the past, have become more difficult over time. The Soviet Union outspends the West in military research and development by a considerable margin. There are inefficiencies in Soviet science and engineering and in the management of the Soviet military production effort; excessive bureaucratization seems particularly to plague the pace of development. But these are offset—at least partly—by Western inefficiencies, such as the frequent cancellation of

TABLE 9–5
Conventional air capabilities of the European theatre.

	Fighter-Bomber	*Interceptor*	*Reconnaissance*
USA/NATO	1,950	740	285
USSR/WTO	1,920	4,370	600

Source: U.S. Department of Defense, *Soviet Military Power, 1983,* p. 62.

TABLE 9–6
Conventional naval force comparison of the European theatre.

	USA/NATO	USSR/WTO
Attack carriers	7	2
Helicopter carriers	2	2
Cruisers	15	21
Destroyers/frigates	274	182
Coastal escorts and fast patrol boats	167	551
Amphibious ships		
Ocean-going	41	16
Independent coastal craft	69	155
Mine warfare ships	257	360
Total submarines	190	258
Ballistic missile submarines	35	52
Long-range attack submarines	60	149
Other types	95	57
% NATO submarines nuclear powered	49%	45%
Sea-based, tactical and support aircraft including helicopters	712	146
Land-based tactical and support aircraft	180	719
Land-based anti-submarine warfare fixed-wing aircraft and helicopters	450	179

Source: U.S. Department of Defense, *Soviet Military Power, 1983,* p. 62.

programs after expenditure of large sums of research and development money. In addition, the continuity of Soviet leadership has an advantage in military development which the United States does not have. During the Carter administration, for example, it was decided to cancel a new bomber program even while the Soviets proceeded with theirs. After this long delay in modernizing the air force, the Reagan administration gave high priority to a new bomber.

Western observers are especially concerned that the Soviets are compounding their advantage in quantity of arms by reducing the quality gap. In some areas, such as surface-to-air missiles and armored personnel carriers, the Kremlin is achieving qualitative superiority on some performance criteria. Furthermore, there are signs of accelerated independent development in modern electronics, computer science and computer applications for, among other purposes, military development. Until recently it was believed that Soviet computer science was five to ten years behind that of the United States, but Soviet-designed materials now at the disposal of Western scientists testify that the gap is more like three years.

By and large, then, the Soviet advantages seem to be expanding. In most scenarios, the Soviet bloc would enjoy the advantages of first strike, possibly including large elements of strategic and tactical surprise. Soviet divisions in the central theater are organized well for an offensive against weakly held positions of the NATO defense structure, and are trained and configured for a rapid blitzkrieg offensive. Critical elements of the NATO defense plan depend on adequate warning to permit time for mobilization, while a considerable portion of the Pact's armies are ready to fight from a standing start. NATO also depends critically on forward operating airbases, which could be vulnerable to a well-planned attack by new Soviet systems. Pact forces also use standardized Soviet equipment, while NATO armies employ a wide variety of systems from different countries. This advantage in standardization and interoperability greatly simplifies problems of deployment, command and control, and logistics, and is part of the greater technical integration enjoyed by the Pact forces.

NATO does, however, enjoy significant advantages of its own. Foremost among these is the fact that, to penetrate fortified and prepared defenses, the attacker, presumed to be the Warsaw Pact, must have a considerable numerical advantage, believed by many observers to be at least three to one. The Soviet-bloc numerical advantage, while substantial, falls short of this criterion theater-wide. Although wider margins of advantage might be achieved in local sectors of the front, it would be difficult for a Pact commander to initiate an attack with a high degree of confidence.

Moreover, aggression in Europe, although undertaken by conventional means, would, in the opinion of most observers, lead inexorably to nuclear escalation. While the Soviet bloc is numerically superior at the nuclear level as well, the devastating costs of an atomic war, even for the "winner," are expected to dissuade adventurism at the subnuclear level in Europe. It should, be noted, however, that not all specialists are convinced that nuclear deterrence will succeed if a conventional war-fighting capability is lacking. Some argue that if the Soviets are superior at all levels, they may believe themselves capable of initiating a conventional attack without risking a NATO nuclear response, or may even, through a devastating nuclear first-strike, so reduce NATO's retaliatory capability as to reduce the costs of a nuclear exchange to a level that they might find tolerable. While the majority of analysts do not share these views, there is general agreement that conventional defense in Europe must be adequate in itself, and not necessarily depend on a link to the nuclear deterrent.

This assessment has led to a search for technological and organizational solutions that would cancel the Soviet numerical advantages and secure the Western defense without a massive increase in expenditures and forces. Foremost among these technical fixes is the search for anti-tank weapons that exploit precision-guidance technologies, such as smart missiles, bombs and shells, to knock out expensive Soviet tanks with cheap Western countersystems. If, ideally, the West had a $10,000 missile that could reliably destroy a $500,000 Soviet tank on a one shot/one kill basis, for example, it could, at a given expenditure on both sides, deploy many more of these defensive systems than there are tanks and thereby cancel the value of the massive Soviet investment in armor. In actuality, the countersystems are sometimes as expensive as the tanks themselves; their reliability is not nearly 1:1; and a wide variety of countermeasures can be employed to foil them and restore the offensive capability of the tank. Still, the current state of the art in military technology gives certain advantages to the defense, and the communist commanders would have to consider this as well as the compounded uncertainties of initiating an offensive engaging opposed systems whose battlefield capabilities in the European environment cannot be known in advance. Some believe that this uncertainty factor is the greatest deterrent of all, because communist planning is based on the scientific approach and not on the roll of the dice.

A final NATO advantage is the political weakness of the Warsaw Pact, and especially what must be doubts in the minds of Soviet leaders as to the reliability of Polish, Czech and other East European divisions assigned to the Pact. Would these armies fight alongside the Russians, or would they seize the occasion to break the Soviet hold on their countries? In a real crisis, the Soviet Union might feel compelled to divert significant portions of its own forces to secure the rear of the empire. Even in a well-run colonial system, there must come a point where overexpansion stretches the resources of the imperial center so thin that control over the entire system is lost, and a robust offensive in Western Europe would under the best of circumstances demand a great deal.

In summary, then, the Soviet bloc enjoys a wide margin of numerical superiority in Central Europe; it has in recent years compounded this with qualitative improvements, modernizing more rapidly than NATO; and the general pattern has been one of a military balance moving steadily against the West. However, there is disagreement among experts whether the Soviet advantages are sufficient to defeat NATO's defenses, particularly as augmented by modern anti-tank technologies, and there are additional doubts about the practicality of a conventional attack on Europe without nuclear escalation. The Soviets have achieved a superior position, at great expense; the questions for the future are what they can do with it, and what NATO can do about it.

The Korean Military Balance

The Korean conflict is essentially a struggle between the two halves of a divided nation, one of which came under communist rule in the aftermath of the Second World War, while the other has been influenced by the West. As is often the case when one people have been separated into two states pursuing different courses in their domestic and foreign policies (other examples include the two Germanys, China and Taiwan, North and South Yemen and the former two Vietnams), reintegration of the nation is impeded by deep and often bitter differences between the rival regimes and social systems, yet each side is greatly affected by actions taken by the other. This combination makes conflicts of divided nations particularly bitter and difficult to resolve.

The Korean problem is a matter of global interest because of the strategic location of the divided nation: the Korean peninsula is a kind of bridge or strategic corridor between the Chinese mainland and Japan, and is adjacent to the critical industrial region of Manchuria (now part of China), which has long been a theater of strategic competition among China, Japan, and Russia. At least three times during modern history (in 1592, 1894 and 1935), Japanese forces have used Korea as the principal corridor and axis to provide lines of communication for influence in China and Manchuria.

Indeed, the modern period of conflict over Korea began not after World War Two, but in 1895, when the forces of newly resurgent Japan defeated Chinese armies to gain control of Korea. Subsequently, and for the next seven years, Japan was opposed in Korea by Russia as Tokyo struggled to consolidate its hold over the peninsula. In 1905, in one of the climactic events of the Russo-Japanese war that figured importantly in modern Russian history, Japan defeated the Czarist forces, and subsequently annexed Korea in August 1910.

Japanese influence in Korea continued until the end of the Second World War in 1945; indeed, the progressive waves of Japanese invasions of Manchuria and China from 1931 to 1945 moved primarily through Korea, enhancing the peninsula's importance. Japan's collapse in August 1945 brought an end to its control of Korea. When the Soviet Union joined in the fighting in Asia in the final days of the Second World War, its troops swept down into the northern portion of the Korean peninsula; and in the crucial General Order Number One setting the initial conditions of peace, President Truman established a demarcation line at thirty-eight degress of latitude as the line above which the Soviet Union would be responsible for the Japanese surrender and below which the United States would be responsible.

As in Europe, the establishment of a line of liberation and occupation was to prove portentous.

Washington and the Kremlin had declared the independence and freedom of Korea to be an objective in their struggle against the Axis powers, but after the victory they were unable to agree on political measures to bring this about. Instead, postwar political developments were guided differently by the superpowers in their respective occupation zones. Soviet forces constructed a communist regime in the North, while the Americans attempted to organize a constitutional political order for the South. While these separate movements proceeded, the two sides engaged in rancorous negotiations, both in Korea itself and at the United Nations. Finally, when the Soviet Union announced its intention of preventing United Nations officials from entering the North to supervise elections designed to reunite the two halves of the country under a single constitutional rule, the United States encouraged the UN to proceed with elections in the South, an event which led to the permanent division of the two Koreas. While some looked upon the event as the first step toward reunification, others saw it as the final step of separation. In 1949, having established the independent and militarily secure state of South Korea, the United States withdrew its occupation forces. Meanwhile, the civil war in China was progressing toward a communist victory and, with the threat of war persisting in Europe, NATO was about to be established. In Japan, where the occupation had progressed toward its objectives with unanticipated speed, preparations for self-government were in motion, and the early removal of the American occupation forces was anticipated.

The withdrawal of American troops from South Korea seemed to signal, therefore, that this newly independent state would be outside of the American strategic sphere. But within a year the pace of events quickened. Chinese Communist forces had driven the Nationalist government from the mainland to the island of Taiwan and, on June 25, 1950, North Korea mounted a massive invasion of the South by well-trained and experienced forces employing Soviet armor and artillery and supported by tactical aircraft. Overwhelmed by the vastly superior forces, the small and unprepared South Korean army was forced to retreat southward, surrendering the capital city of Seoul, and facing the possibility of total collapse.

Within a day of the surprise attack the Security Council of the United Nations met in emergency session. In the absence of the Soviet Union, which had been boycotting the Council over the refusal of the Western members to seat a Chinese Communist delegation in place of the Nationalist, the Council condemned North Korea for a breach of the peace and called for a cease-fire and withdrawal of North Korean troops to points above the thirty-eighth parallel. Two days later, in an effort to enforce their position, the Western powers were able to persuade the Council to call upon member states to assist South Korea in repelling the aggressor. Under this act of legitimization, the United States transferred troop contingents from Japan, and these, together with troops and materials from some forty countries, comprised the eventual United Nations Command. The communist victory in China had forced a revision of American policy in Asia. Now, contrary to its former policy, it intended to defend South Korea and, indeed, attempt to reunify the two Koreas by force. At the same time, it would now support the French in their struggle against communism in Southeast Asia (a decision which ultimately led to American involvement in Vietnam); and it would transform Japan not into the pastoral state envisioned by the occupation, but into a powerful ally in the crusade against Asian communism. Other than the Berlin Blockade, then, the invasion of South Korea in 1950 was the most dramatic event in shaping America's Cold War strategy.

By October 1 the international force, composed largely of Americans but including major contingents from Australia, Great Britain and elsewhere, succeeded in reversing the tide, recapturing Seoul and pressing the drive north to clear South Korea of communist forces. Under cover of an October 7 resolution of the General Assembly (the Soviet Union had returned to the Security Council, so this organ was no longer an effective instrument of Western policy with respect to Korea), the Western forces crossed the thirty-eighth parallel in an effort not only to repel, but to defeat totally the communist forces, and to establish a single Korea. Within six weeks, the North Korean army faced extinction.

Now, however, as Western forces neared the Korean border of Manchuria and as the American Commander, General Douglas MacArthur, began to speak openly about attacking Chinese territory (even with atomic bombs), Chinese "volunteers" swept down out of Manchuria on behalf of the tiring North Koreans. Through the bitter cold of the winter of 1950–51 small-scale territorial struggles occurred, but the failure of either side to advance further led to the beginning of negotiations which were to last more than two years. The armistice of 1953, which has never been concluded in a formal peace agreement, preserved two Koreas along a border near, but no longer precisely at, the thirty-eighth parallel.

Because the armistice was a military rather than a political settlement, the military balance between the two Koreas is one of the world's most crucial, even three decades later. From 1953 to the present, each side has mounted a force-building campaign against the possibility of another round of fighting. Though there is neither peace nor war in Korea, there is a continuing arms race stabilized only by a precarious military balance. The balance has proven reliable to date, despite the occasional uncertainty of the United States' commitment to the South. The Nixon Doctrine, which declared America's intention of helping allies in Asia to forestall communist aggression without direct intervention, shook the confidence of the Seoul government, and the general American distaste for intervention after the Vietnam War was another test of South Korea's resolve. The massive military build-up undertaken by the Reagan administration, and the firmly anti-communist stance accompanying it, have resulted in closer ties between the two allies, in a Presidential visit to Korea, and in Operation Team Spirit 84, joint Korean-American naval and military maneuvers held in 1984. (During those exercises, an American carrier was struck from below by a Soviet submarine, with no severe damage to either and without nuclear spill.) In any event, the absence of political peace and of steady economic relations between the two Koreas ensures that the military balance will continue to be the principal, if not the only, foundation of stability between these two bitter adversaries. Despite occasional reunification talks, enmity prevails; in 1983, when a terrorist attack on South Korean officials visiting Burma resulted in nearly a dozen deaths, including those of four cabinet members, the government of South Korea condemned the government of North Korea for the assassinations. Amid these events, however, the military balance promoted stability, as the South Korean government refrained from aggressive response.

What, then, is the status of the military balance in Korea? SIPRI reports that North Korea dedicates between 8 and 9 percent of its gross domestic product to military expenditures, and that South Korea commits about 6 percent.[6] American military sources, in contrast, acknowledge the same figure for South Korea ($4.4 billion in 1983, or 32.8 percent of the national budget), but claim that the North spends approximately 25 percent of its gross national product on the military.[7] In either case, the annual dollar commitments of the two governments are about the same, as Figure 9–1 reveals, and the growth rates are approximately equal. The large spike in the South Korean military expenditure in 1982 is a reflection of the Reagan defense build-up in Europe and Asia.

6. *SIPRI Yearbook, 1983,* p. 172.
7. General Robert W. Sennenwald, U.S. Army, Commander of U.S. Forces in Korea, to House Appropriations Committee on the Defense Department Authorization Hearings, March 8, 1983, pp. 1119–1253.

FIGURE 9–1
Comparison of North Korean and South Korean military expenditures, 1976–82, expressed in US$ billion at constant 1980 prices and exchange rates.

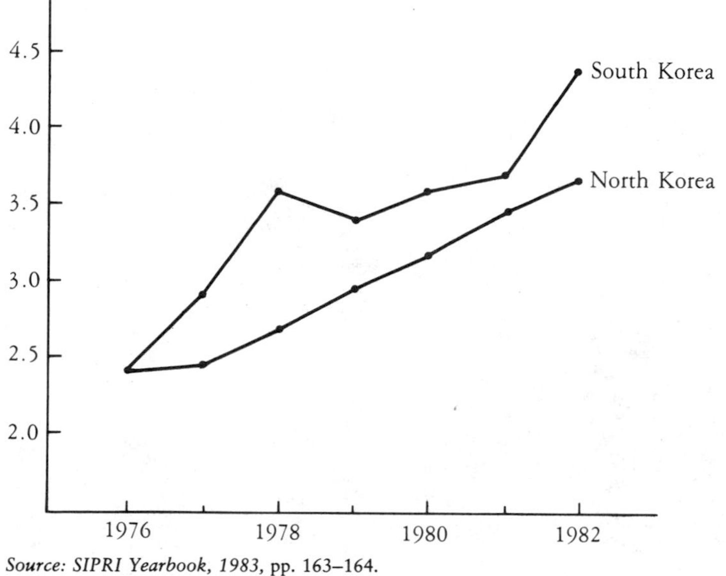

Source: SIPRI Yearbook, 1983, pp. 163–164.

In more specific terms, North Korea outnumbers the South in most categories, even when the American presence is added. For example, the North Korean Army alone, half of which is deployed along the Demilitarized Zone separating the two, numbers 750,000, while the combined air, sea and land forces of the United States and South Korea total only 650,000. Of this number, about 38,000 are American ground forces. (Note: These figures are not solid, since the air and naval forces throughout the North Pacific, particularly in the waters from the Philippines to Japan, are available for deployment to South Korea. The same is true of air defenses.) In equipment, the North enjoys an advantage of approximately two to one in divisions and tanks, even with American contributions counted, and an advantage of approximately three to two in artillery and combat jet aircraft. Only in armored personnel carriers does combined American and South Korean equipment approximate that of the North. In many instances, however, the South has qualitative superiority, such as in aircraft. Although North Korea has between twenty-five and fifty F-7 fighter aircraft (old Chinese copies of the Soviet MIG-21), the South Korean Air Force is adding new American F-16 and A-10 fighter and attack craft. This offsets the numerical superiority of North Korea's 700 combat aircraft.[8]

Even though the Korean military balance is currently stable, a number of specific concerns bother the West. The greatest concern is that the fastest growing aspect of North Korean forces is the coastal craft

President Reagan views the demilitarized zone between North Korea and South Korea two months after the Soviet downing of a civilian Korean airliner, 1983.

Source: Wide World Photos

capable of delivering shipborne surface-to-surface missiles. Given the long, slender geography of Korea and the dependence of South Korea upon its ports for military and other imports, this capability is a major threat. The second concern is that while much of the recent development in North Korean military equipment is designed as defensive, the vehicles that comprise the largest increase make it apparent that North Korea is equipping for rapid, mobile attack capability. For this reason, South Korean forces are on constant alert for attack without warning.

Beyond the disparity of numbers, the communist forces enjoy another cardinal advantage: Seoul, the South Korean capital, which is also the hub of the South's communications, industry and culture and the heartland of the nation, lies only twenty-five miles south of the northern border. The defense of Seoul is the sine qua non of the South's security, and its capture or destruction is presumed to be the principal

8. Defense estimates and strategic comments derived from General Robert W. Sennenwald, *ibid.*, and from U.S. Department of Defense, Joint Chiefs of Staff, *U.S. Military Posture for Fiscal Year 1983*, pp. 43–44.

immediate military objective of the North. Reflecting this logic, the North's forces are arrayed and deployed in offensive postures along the main axis of military advance toward this objective, and the South's forces are deployed in defensive positions along the presumed lines of advance.

American analysts disagree deeply as to the stability of the military balance and the viability of the South's defenses. The US Second Division is maintained in Korea at the request of the South, and the need for it to remain there has been a matter of controversy in the United States. Those who favor its removal argue that the South, outnumbered but favored by technological advantages, can defend itself without the US presence. Those who believe the Second Division to be essential to stability on the peninsula argue that the North's wide advantage in numbers might comprise a temptation to aggression without the US presence. Some believe that the North could win even with the US presence, if it could consolidate control of the peninsula before American reinforcements arrived.

It is appropriate, then, to close this brief discussion of the Korean case with a question: Will the Korean balance continue to be stable, eventually to evolve in the direction of a political settlement? Or does the momentum of the North Korean build-up point to renewed conflict on the peninsula, possibly in the form of a war launched during a crisis in the South while that nation is still militarily weak compared to its rival?

The Middle Eastern Balance

The most complex, and quite probably the most unstable, of the world's critical regions is the Middle East. It is complex because (1) it contains a number of subordinate balances, (2) the relationships among the regional parties change over time, and (3) the roles of the major powers change with international conditions and domestic politics. It is unstable because (1) the historic roots of conflict are so invasive as to defy political resolution, (2) much of the potential international conflict results from the regionally destabilizing consequences of domestic violence, (3) the worldwide economic changes ushered in by OPEC's power led to uncontrolled arms sales to the area, and (4) the degree to which local governments serve as proxy forces of the major powers is substantial. Each of these characteristics of the regional balance merits a brief comment.

Although the Middle East military balance usually brings to mind the Arab-Israeli conflict, there are several other influential forces in the region. At present the most visible of them is the war between Iran and Iraq, a war fought with modern weapons but primative tactics. Because of the complete rupture in Iranian-American relations after the rise to power of the Ayatollah Khomeini, Washington has quietly urged an Iraqi victory; and the Soviet Union, determined to seal one of its flanks by controlling both Afghanistan and its southern borders, seeks Iraqi victory as a means of preventing Iran from intruding in Afghanistan on grounds of religious unification with a major faction. Early in 1984, however, it was learned that China had quietly provided arms to Iran, including Chinese-made copies of Soviet MIG-21 aircraft.

Another subordinate balance within the region exists between Libya, on the one hand, and Egypt on behalf of the Sudan, on the other. In late 1983 and early 1984, threat of a Libyan invasion of the Sudan mounted, and Egypt announced its willingness to assist the Sudanese cause. The United States entered the picture by offering to assist Egypt with military equipment, and made available an AWACS early-warning aircraft, a sophisticated communications craft previously provided only to Saudi Arabia in the region. Indeed, Saudi Arabia and Egypt are regarded by the United States as the Middle Eastern powers most moderate in both economic and military policy, and most capable of providing stability to the region as a whole.

Changing relations among the regional parties is a second characteristic of the balance. After more than thirty years of alternating between declared and undeclared war, the most dramatic change was the Israeli-Egyptian peace treaty (1979), a peace that stabilized a major determinant of regional conditions and divorced Egypt from more radical Arab politics. Similarly, the fall of the Shah of Iran and the rise of Ayatollahs introduced a reactionary theocracy determined to change the entire basis of both regional relations and the region's interplay with the major military and industrial powers.

Volatile relations among the region's nations precipitated the third characteristic of the region's complexity: the changing roles of the major powers in the Middle East. In the years between the two world wars, British and French influences dominated the Middle East. Later, because of the decline of Anglo-French interests, American oil aspirations and the American commitment to defend Israel as the long-sought (since 1917) Zionist homeland, America's presence rose to preeminence. Yet the role of the United States has been less than consistent. In 1956, for example, when Britain and France attempted to assist Israel in war against Egypt, the United States condemned the intervention of two of its closest allies. The successive policies of the Nixon, Ford, Carter and Reagan administrations have varied so much that the foundations of the Israeli-American partnership are generally considered an unpredictable element in the Middle Eastern military equation.

All of these complexities are accompanied by a number of factors that render the region persistently unstable. The most important among these is the depth of emotion, engendered by centuries of animosity, which is a constant strain on stability. Since the Middle East is the historic center for several of the world's principal religions, contemporary events are colored by the legacies of religious conflict dating back over more than twenty centuries. To these roots must be added the consequences of modern imperialistic events, which intertwined traditional loyalties with growing ties to the nineteenth century's competing empires in the region, principally the French and British.

In the last fifteen years, it has been necessary to add the regional consequences of the maturation of OPEC with its political and economic implications of worldwide power. Some of the region's members, particularly those that export petroleum, have modernized more rapidly than others. Iran, ten years ago the richest and most powerful militarily as the region's major non-Israeli recipient of American arms, has set aside its economic revolution in favor of fulfilling ancient spiritual aspirations. So while some Middle Eastern nations are busily modernizing, others are more concerned with perpetuating historic enmities. As Egypt and Saudi Arabia forge ahead, Libya and Syria long to settle old scores. Meanwhile Israel plans and fights for survival, sometimes by territorial activity regarded by its adversaries (as well as by neutral Egypt) as imperialistic and aggressive. And the Palestinians, still homeless, continue acts of terrorism and war.

Domestic violence is an additional threat to the region's stability. The most outstanding example of this occurs in Lebanon, a republic of fewer than 4,000 square miles (twice the size of Delaware, smaller than Connecticut) with a population under three million, coastally located at the eastern-most edge of the Mediterranean Sea. Its civic life is torn by hostility among Christians and Shiite and Sunni Moslem factions. Its strategic location in the unresolved conflict between Israel to its south and Syria to its east and north makes Lebanon's internal control of vital interest to both countries. Throughout 1983, to cite a year of particularly complex relations in Lebanon, all of the following occurred: civil war among Christian and Moslem groups; civil war among factions of Palestinians; war between Syria and Israel, each with the assistance of one or more of the preceding factions; Palestinian and Lebanese Moslem attacks on positions of American, French and Italian "peacekeeping" forces. A full-scale American intervention was probably averted only by the fact that the Soviet role is limited to its support of Syria. Had similarly complex events occurred in another place, such as in Iran, Soviet and American interventions would have been a more serious threat, and the possibility of a major power war in the region greatly expanded.

All of these complex factors notwithstanding, the most explosive aspect of the Middle East balance is the so-called Arab-Israeli balance. The Arab-Israeli conflict is, basically, a case of two national movements emerging from long years of suppression at the same time, but making conflicting claims to the same piece of land. It is one of the perceptual analysts' favorite cases, because both sides have moving and persuasive stories, and the answer to the question "Who is right?" depends more on the particular question the observer himself happens to ask than on any inherent superiority of the claims of one side or the other. No settlement could be devised that would fully satisfy the legitimate aspirations of both peoples at the same time, and, while compromise solutions may someday be arranged, there is no way to slice the pie fairly for everyone.

While the Arab-Israeli conflict is probably more familiar to many students than other regional tensions, it is worthwhile to review briefly the roots of the problem from the two perspectives. From the Arab point of view, the problem began when centuries of foreign rule—first by the Ottomans (Turks), and then by the European colonial powers—finally ended after World War Two. Most of the Arab peoples gained independence and sovereignty, but in the case of the territory formerly known as Palestine, a new form of alien infringement on Arab sovereignty emerged—the creation of a Jewish state in the Arab heartland by people whom the Arabs regard as European settlers. Israel is, in this perspective, a vestige of the colonial era—a colonial settler state, in a phrase borrowed from Marxist parlance—and its presence in the Middle East is a symbol of the indignities inflicted upon the Arabs during their age of weakness. Now that the Arab nation is resurgent, the continued existence of this foreign body unnaturally grafted onto the Arabs' land is, at best, an insult to be tolerated. Moreover, the burden of the Israeli presence has fallen most heavily on the Arab people most directly affected—the Palestinians—and no solution will be possible without the agreement of the organization regarded as their spokesman, the Palestine Liberation Organization (PLO).

The Israeli point of view begins with roots still further back in history—the expulsion of the Jews from their homes in the Holy Land by the Romans and other conquerors, and their forced migration to many distant lands where they lived at the mercy of often hostile peoples and suffered unspeakable degradations. Throughout this long history of *Diaspora* (the Greek term meaning scattering or dispersion), the dream of returning to the homeland and gathering in the exiles was never forgotten.

The rebirth of Jewish nationalism in the modern period coincides with the Arab awakening, both stimulated by European nationalist thought in the late nineteenth and early twentieth centuries. But the main impetus to Zionism, the name of the national liberation movement of the Jewish people, came later when, in a genocidal campaign unprecedented in scope and scientific brutality, Adolph Hitler murdered six million Jews in ovens and gas chambers as part of the so-called final solution to the "Jewish question."

Germany had been considered by many before the war as the most civilized of nations and as the European state in which Jews had been permitted to live with the least harassment. The fact that evil on so massive and organized a scale could occur there convinced other Jews all over the world that the Jews who had escaped the slaughter, including the handful of shocked survivors of the European Holocaust, would never be safe and free without a Jewish state. In the many upheavals following the war the plight of the Jewish survivors continued, as many other nations refused to take the desperate refugees.

At the same time, Britain was preparing to relinquish its control over Palestine, but was willing, for the moment, to tolerate stepped-up Jewish immigration to Palestine. From the Arab point of view this may have been a case of dumping Europe's unwanted people on the Middle East, but from the West's point of view it was the least that could be done for the pathetic survivors of this terrible experience.

Thus the stage was set for the Arab-Israeli conflict: a vacuum of power created by the British withdrawal; an Arab expectation that now, at last, they would have independence and sovereignty in Palestine as throughout the Middle East; and a Jewish flight to safety led by men and women who, understandably, would fight to death for a haven.

Intercommunal fighting broke out between Arab and Jewish mobs and armies, and the surrounding Arab states sent expeditionary forces to support the Palestinians. In the war that ensued in 1948–49, the Jews prevailed in the coastal areas, but the Arabs were able to retain the hills, including the Old City of Jerusalem. This was a bitter outcome for both sides. The Jews had a foothold, but not their goal of goals—Jerusalem—and the Arabs controlled commanding hills overlooking the Jewish flatlands below. The Arabs held major parts of the land, including Jerusalem, but had lost territory in which many of their brothers fell under Jewish rule. Also, several hundred thousand Palestinian Arabs felt compelled to flee the zones of Jewish control, creating a Palestinian refugee problem that has not been solved to this day. The outcome was satisfactory to neither side, and was particularly unstable due to the lack of geographical separation and terrain obstacles between the two sides. The 1949 armistice line was easily penetrable by both conventional military forces and terrorist infiltrators, and did not lend itself to a stable military balance.

A second round of fighting occurred in 1956, but this left the basic situation essentially unchanged. However, the third round, the 1967 Six Day War, significantly altered the subsequent military and political terms of the conflict. It resulted in Israeli capture of the Sinai desert on the Egyptian front, the commanding hills of the Golan Heights on the Syrian front, and, most important, Jerusalem and the hills of the West Bank on the Jordanian front. This had several basic effects: (1) The borders were moved from some of the least defensible lines in the world (for Israel) to the strongest positions in the region. This would make future Israeli defense much easier. (2) Jerusalem, the holiest place of the Jews but also the third holiest of the Moslems, and Hebron, the second holiest place of the Jews but a city inhabited today almost entirely by Arabs, fell under Jewish control. (3) One million additional Palestinian Arabs fell under Israeli rule, creating a situation where there are now half as many Arabs as Jews under the administration of the Jewish state. (4) Israel, which had previously been in an entirely defensive position, was now a military occupying power ruling over a large number of Arab civilians. Whereas the Jewish state had enjoyed considerable foreign sympathy before, this military occupation created a morally ambiguous situation for many in the West who sympathized with the Jewish state's right to exist and were alarmed by Arab efforts to destroy it, but who could not condone Israel's extension of its authority over additional territory containing so many Palestinian Arabs.

The most important military result of the Six Day War was the creation of more secure borders. The most important political result was the transformation of the conflict from one over the very existence of Israel to one over the future disposition of the territories captured in 1967. While some of the Arabs continue to press for the final elimination of Israel, others are moving to the view that a compromise solution is possible: recognition and acceptance of Israel in exchange for the return of the 1967 territories.

However, turning this principle of "territory for peace" into a reality is impeded by several obstacles on both sides. On the Arab side, it is not clear whether all the parties in the coalition, particularly the so-called Steadfastness front and the more militant elements of the PLO, are prepared fully to recognize and accept the existence of Israel on a permanent basis. Some appear ready to accept back the territories, but only as a launching point for continued struggle against Israel.

On the Israeli side, there are several problems. First, Israel is being asked to retreat from lines that are relatively secure in a military sense, but unrecognized politically, to lines that might be recognized but will never be secure and defensible. This would make Israeli security dependent on the faithfulness of the Arabs to the agreement, and many Israelis are not willing to take this chance. Compromise regarding the Sinai was possible in order to achieve peace with Egypt, but the Sinai desert is different from the other fronts in that, because of the wide separation it puts between the former adversaries, the element of risk was relatively small. By contrast, the West Bank hills and the Golan Heights are immediately adjacent to Israeli population centers, and the opposing parties are locked in a bear hug. The element of risk is inherently greater, and the adversaries on these fronts have so far been less compromising than the Egyptians. Indeed, Egypt's reward for peace, while other Arab states continue to call for a Holy War to eradicate Israel, has been diplomatic and partial economic isolation from the other Arab countries.

Second, while the Sinai had no essential historic or religious importance to Israel, Jerusalem and the West Bank, which Israelis call by the biblical names Judea and Samaria, contain many places of great symbolic importance. The overwhelming majority of Israelis are opposed to returning the Old City to Arab rule, and many favor establishing the national capital there. An influential minority is opposed to the surrender of any other part of the historic lands of Judea and Samaria. The majority of Israelis favors a territorial compromise in which Israel would give up most but not all of the West Bank, but there is at the present time almost no Arab interest in anything but every last inch, so territorial compromise is not yet feasible.

It appears that while solutions can be conceived abstractly and may, over an extended period of time, come to be accepted, the conflict will not be resolved soon. This means that a positive peace of political compromise and reconciliation is unlikely. However, it is conceivable that a "negative" peace can be achieved, in which there is no complete solution but there is a military balance to dissuade aggression and thereby prevent war. From the point of view of the United States, there are four possible conditions. In descending order of preference, they are: (1) a comprehensive political settlement and an end to the state of tension; (2) no settlement, but a stable military balance that prevents war; (3) a military balance that does not prevent war, but does permit Israel to defend itself and bring about an acceptable military result in as short a round of fighting as possible; and (4) a military imbalance that leads to the destruction of Israel which presumably would not go down before taking very drastic actions against the Arab states as well.

All four, including the political solution, relate to the state of the military balance—the political solution because it is generally believed that the Arabs will settle with Israel only if they see that it is impossible to win completely on the battlefield. For this reason, in the Arab-Israeli conflict, as in Korea, the military balance has special importance for political and strategic stability.

What, then, is the balance in this case? Statistical comparisons are difficult, because the Arab side consists of a constantly changing coalition. Do we count Egypt, or will it stay out? Will Iraq be allied to Syria at the time of a war, or will it be in conflict with this sometimes ally/sometimes rival? Will Jordan commit all its forces, or just token units in Syria rather than the home front? Will Saudi Arabia fight or stay out?

If past wars are any guide, the Arab coalition will greatly outnumber Israel in tanks, aircraft, artillery and other categories of equipment as well as manpower. Moreover, the Arabs will be able to depend on a standing army ready to fight almost at once from their peacetime condition. By contrast, Israel will have to depend on the mobilization of civilian reserves—a process that takes twenty-four to seventy-two hours. This time gap will give the Arabs great advantages in the opening hours—particularly if they can successfully organize a surprise attack and catch Israel unprepared. The Arabs, who draw on a much larger population base, can also tolerate higher casualty rates.

Different sources vary strikingly on actual military expenditures in the Arab-Israeli balance. Most figures are, indeed, little more than estimates, since not all governments publicize their military costs in order to conceal their efforts. Ideally, there would be figures for annual expenditures in constant dollars, actual dollars, and percent of either gross national product or gross domestic product. What exists, however, is a series of conflicting estimates. Nonetheless, the two major turning points in expenditure patterns are the peace treaty between Israel and Egypt which brought a sharp drop in Egyptian military spending, and the fall of the Shah of Iran which had similar effects in Iran. (The Iranian military costs in the war with Iraq are not reported anywhere.) Table 9–7 attempts, with all these caveats considered, to present an approximation of spending in the military balance.

Beyond these operational facts, there is a fundamental strategic difference in favor of the Arab side. Israel can win one round after another, but the Arabs can return to fight another day. If the Arabs ever fully won, on the other hand, Israel would cease to exist as a state. Also, Israel, drawing on a much smaller economic base and enjoying far less international support, cannot bear the economic and social costs of repeated rounds of fighting as well as the Arabs.

TABLE 9–7
Israeli average annual military expenditure, 1973–82, in percent of gross domestic product and constant 1980 US$ billion, compared with those of proximate Arab states and more distant potential adversaries.

	Before Egyptian-Israeli Peace (1979)		*After Egyptian-Israeli Peace (1979)*	
	Cost in US$, bill.	*Percent of GDP*	*Cost in US$, bill.*	*Percent of GDP*
Israel	4.3	26.1	3.9	18.6
Inner regional ring				
Egypt	4.1	30.3	1.9	8.7
Jordan	0.4	20.5	0.5	15.4
Lebanon	0.1	3.6	0.3	6.1
Syria	1.0	14.5	2.0	16.5
Outer regional ring				
Iran	11.1	10.9	5.8[a]	6.6
Iraq	2.1	11.5	3.3[a]	n.a.
Libya	1.3	6.5	2.5	11.4
Saudi Arabia	6.6	10.3	19.2	15.6

[a]For Iran and Iraq, cost references are for the period beginning with the fall of the Shah and ending with the eruption of war between the two.

Source: SIPRI Yearbook, 1983, pp. 163–164 and 172–173.

But there are other asymmetries that favor Israel. The post-1967 boundaries, while offering no absolute protection, do make offensive operations against Israel very difficult. In general, the terrain lends itself to effective defense by an outnumbered force able to take advantage of topographical obstacles and prepared fortifications. Another great advantage for Israel is its wide margin of technological and managerial superiority. This is manifested most dramatically in past air battles, in which Israeli pilots have destroyed twenty to sixty Arab aircraft for every Israeli fighter downed in air-to-air combat. On the ground, the results are similar though with less extreme disparities. For example, in 1973, the average Israeli tank engaged in combat killed five times as many Arab tanks as Arab tanks killed Israeli. These advantages in competence have enabled the Israelis generally to prevail in spite of the Arab numerical superiority.

It is difficult, then, to quantify the Arab-Israeli balance, because, over time, Israeli qualitative superiority has been more important than Arab quantitative superiority. This fact also makes it difficult to predict the future with certainty, because the balance will depend on the ability of the Arabs to close the gap in terms of quality of men and equipment.

In general, experts believe that the Israeli margin of superiority continues to be wide. According to some, it has a greater margin today than in the past. But Israelis believe that qualitative factors alone are not enough: a certain quantitative ratio must also be maintained, lest the Arab superiority in numbers grow to the point where it swamps the Israeli qualitative advantage. This creates a demanding and stressful situation for Israel, because it must compete with a coalition vastly larger and incomparably better financed.

Overall, Israel's strategy is progressively to convince its Arab adversaries, if necessary one at a time, that military action will not yield positive results and that the costs of resort to force will greatly exceed the benefits. The most powerful member of the Arab coalition—Egypt—has already shifted from a military to a diplomatic strategy, resulting in the peace treaty between Israel and Egypt. The most significant remaining military challenge is Syria. Many Israelis are convinced that the Syrians have not given up the military option exactly because, in past wars, they suffered less than Egypt. This perception could lead Israel to adopt a punitive strategy in the event of another round of fighting, inflicting heavy damage on the Syrian armed forces to convince Damascus of the futility of continued confrontation. If Syria and Jordan gave up the military option, the war threat would, for practical purposes, be ended, because no combination of outer-ring Arab states, however militant, could pose a credible threat without the front-line states adjacent to Israel. The purpose of a strong military balance, then, is both defensive and political—to create the preconditions for an eventual settlement that will require a greater spirit of willingness to compromise and make concessions than has been evident in the past.

Conclusion

This brief overview of three regional balances suggests several conclusions. (1) In high-tension areas, positive peace based on political solutions is difficult to obtain, and stability often depends on carefully calibrated military balances to prevent cold wars from becoming hot ones. (2) Allies of the Soviet bloc, such as the Warsaw Pact, North Korea and many of the Arab confrontation states, tend to enjoy a numerical superiority deriving from the much higher levels of arms production sustained in the Soviet Union. Western and Western-associated states, such as South Korea and Israel, depend on qualitative advantages of technically superior equipment to offset their disadvantage in number. If, in fact, the current massive Soviet investment in military research and development closes the quality gap, the communist states may compound their advantage in quantity with equal or superior quality. This will upset the delicate regional balances. (3)

Many of the regional balances are less stable, and more subject to decay, than is widely understood. Significant changes in both the relative number and the comparative quality of equipment held by rivals continually occur. And the management of regional tensions through military balances requires eternal vigilance.

10

The Balance of Terror

Think, for a moment, about the unthinkable. Imagine a nuclear attack. Somehow, by accident or design, nuclear war has erupted. What would it be like?

The US Atomic Energy Commission's "Nuclear Bomb Effects Computer" gives us some horrifying estimates.[1] Let's say, first, that you are about four miles from the center of an important military installation, an industrial area or a densely populated metropolis. Second, let's assume a nuclear "surface blast," the bomb having detonated at ground level rather than in the atmosphere (an "air blast"). Third, to have a measure of the explosive potential of the weapon, we set the computer "yield" adjustment at one megaton, or the explosive equivalent of one million tons of TNT. That much TNT would comprise a stack reaching almost the height of the Empire State Building! One

1. Atomic Energy Commission, *The Effects of Nuclear Weapons* (Washington, D.C.: US Government Printing Office, 1962). For a more technical study, see Samuel Gladstone and Philip J. Dolan, editors, *The Effects of Nuclear Weapons,* 3rd ed. (Washington, D.C.: US Department of Defense and Department of Energy, 1977). *The Effects of Nuclear War* (US Congress Office of Technology Assessment, 1979) conducts several well-designed test simulations varying in assumptions, and attempts to assess the physical, economic and social consequences in each case.

megaton is fifty times as great as the bombs used in 1945 at Hiroshima and Nagasaki (twenty kilotons each, or 20,000 tons of TNT equivalent, each kiloton having the punch of 1,000 tons of TNT).

The effects of such an attack will be catastrophic. It will gouge out a crater half a mile across and three hundred feet deep. Virtually everything in this area, pulverized by the blast and altered by its heat, will be engulfed in a fireball with a 1.5-mile diameter. The surface temperature of this fireball will be greater than that of the sun. A huge mushroom-shaped cloud will form, carrying up and away the particles that remain of former life and structure.

Though the effects upon you, four miles away, will not be quite as bad, they will be severe. Everything combustible in your area will be ignited; and things normally resistant to heat will be melted and misshapen. If you survive, you will be burned badly. (More than half of the people who died in the twenty-kiloton attacks upon Hiroshima and Nagasaki died of fire and heat.) If you survive skin burns, the heat of the air may destroy your lungs. Moreover, the supply of oxygen in your area will have been reduced by the nearby fireblast.

Percussion effects will also be devastating. Buildings around you will crumble from the shock waves of the blast. Glass and other torn materials will catapult through the air at a speed of two hundred feet per second. The misery of your burns will be compounded by injuries sustained in collisions; and your eardrums will have been shattered by violent soundwaves, and by the eighty-miles-per-hour windstorm set off by the blast. If you survive the initial dangers at four miles distance, you will be among fewer than half who do.

Radiation effects are your next hazard. If you have not been severely injured by immediate irradiation, if your vital organs have not been damaged by its unique penetrating power, you will have a lengthy bout with radioactive fallout. All of the particles vaporized and sucked up into the atmosphere in the mushroom cloud will carry radioactivity. As they precipitate back to earth they will contaminate everything in their path. Once again the air you breathe will be hazardous; your skin will be exposed once again to potentially lethal radiation; and exposed water and food supplies will carry certain death. Even if you are alive and mobile, you will be confined to your location. The danger is not over when the fires have subsided and the rubble has been removed, either. Radiation sickness may strike at any subsequent point in life, or may torment its victims for decades. In 1982, fully thirty-seven years after the atomic bombings of Hiroshima and Nagasaki, ten thousand people died of radiation-related diseases attributed directly to exposure in August 1945. And the genetic effects upon subsequent generations are unknown.[2]

All of this destruction has been brought on by a single one-megaton bomb. Yet in actual nuclear attack it is unlikely that a single bomb would be used or that yield would be limited to one megaton. Warheads of three and five megatons are now common in the stockpiles of the Soviet Union and the United States, and the Soviet Union is known to have tested a device of fifty-megaton yield. Altogether, the strategic operational nuclear forces of the United States are equipped with approximately 9,000 warheads capable of delivering about 3.5 trillion tons of TNT equivalent; comparable figures for the Soviet Union are 5,000 warheads bearing roughly six trillion tons of TNT equivalent. Add to this the tens of thousands of nuclear weapons mounted for tactical use and then add the deliverable nuclear power of the other nuclear states, and the total global nuclear capability amounts to about thirteen trillion tons of deliverable TNT equivalents. This is equal to over one million of the bombs dropped in 1945.[3] Thus a yield of one megaton in our imaginary attack is conservative. But when compared with conventional weapons, this blast exceeds all the explosives used against Germany and Japan in the Second World War, and equals the total of all bombing in the Vietnam War.

Every year the picture of nuclear destruction grows more frightening. By 1983, the United States had a nuclear stockpile of approximately 28,000 weapons and the Soviet Union about 20,000. US plans at that time called for an increase to about 32,000 in 1990, equaling the record number of 1967. The Soviet plans were assumed to be roughly the same. According to one authoritative source, at the rate of production between 1946 and 1983, the United States and the Soviet Union had each added to its arsenel about one new weapon every thirty minutes, day and night, for thirty-six years.[4] The total yield of these weapons is estimated to be eighteen trillion tons of TNT equivalent.

To return to our nuclear attack scenario, the attack on your area need not have been an isolated one. Suppose it were part of general nuclear war with an enemy seeking to destroy 50 percent of your nation's industry and 25 percent of its population. This would mean hitting several major cities in a matter of minutes, perhaps some of them with several warheads, in order to gain the advantage. In the

2. Studies conducted fifteen years after the bombings suggested extensive genetic consequences for subsequent generations. More recent evidence, collected over a period of thirty-five years, suggests that there are trends toward genetic damage to the fetuses and children of those exposed, but does not lead to statistically significant results. See William J. Schull, Masanori Otake and James V. Neel, "Genetic Effects of the Atomic Bombs: A Reappraisal," *Science,* 11 September 1981, pp. 1220–1227.
3. *SIPRI Yearbook, 1979.*
4. *SIPRI Yearbook, 1983,* pp. LII–LIV. Figures include both strategic and tactical weapons.

TABLE 10–1
Principal American industrial and population centers: likely targets of Soviet countervalue attack. Populations are for metropolitan areas (primary metropolitan statistical areas) rather than for individual cities. Note that in 1980 the total American population was approximately 230,000,000, with the result that the sixteen largest metropolitan areas accounted for over 28 percent of the national population.

Rank	*Metropolitan Area (PSMA)*	*Population (1980)*
1	New York City	8,275,000
2	Los Angelos–Long Beach	7,478,000
3	Chicago	6,060,000
4	Philadelphia	4,717,000
5	Detroit	4,488,000
6	San Francisco–Oakland	4,073,000
7	District of Columbia	3,251,000
8	Dallas–Fort Worth	2,931,000
9	Cleveland	2,834,000
10	Boston	2,806,000
11	Houston	2,736,000
12	Nassau-Suffolk Counties (N.Y.)	2,606,000
13	Pittsburgh	2,219,000
14	Baltimore	2,200,000
15	Atlanta	2,138,000
16	Minneapolis–St. Paul.	2,137,000

Source: 1980 census data reported in *Statistical Abstract of the United States, 1984,* pp. 20–25.

United States, for example, almost one-third of the total national industrial might and one-fourth of the total national population is concentrated in the twelve largest metropolitan areas. These are, therefore, the areas with the highest concentration of defense industry and trained personnel; they also house some of the major military and governmental installations. Table 10–1 lists these concentrations. If the enemy prefers countervalue targeting, these areas are all vulnerable. If he chooses instead to knock out retaliatory forces (counterforce strategy), these areas might be spared.

The effect of total warfare on national survival and the human future is unmeasurable. Yet there are still subjects for speculation. Optimistic observers speculate that with intelligent planning, consequences of a nuclear attack could be limited to losses of not more than 25 percent of national population, with recovery of the gross national product within as few as ten years. Others take quite a different view, arguing that the damage would be considerably greater and consequences for human survival incalculable. The Department of Defense estimated in 1974 that a massive Soviet strike would result in 95 to 100 million American fatalities; a strike limited to missile sites and strategic submarine and bomber bases would take 5 to 6 million lives; and a strike limited to SAC (Strategic Air Command) bases or ICBM (Intercontinental Ballistic Missile) sites would result in 0.5 to 1 million deaths.[5] Such estimates are sensitive to assumptions about enemy intentions and targeting, the number of independently targeted warheads, delivery vehicle accuracy and other variables.

This speculation only accounts for immediate devastation. Recently a number of scientific simulations have been conducted to estimate the long-range consequences of nuclear war. They deal with human and genetic consequences as well as with environmental, agricultural, biotic, and behavioral results. One simulation, conducted by a group of scientists and endorsed by a broader group of American and Soviet scientists and strategists, predicts a "climatic catastrophe and cascading biological devastation" complicated by smoke and dust obscuring the troposphere and the stratosphere, radioactive fallout and partial destruction of the protective ozone layer, all producing a prolonged nuclear midnight and severe low temperatures.[6] Figure 10–1 outlines the long-term predictions of the various effects over time, and the resulting dangers for populations in the United States and the Soviet Union, and for the Northern and Southern hemispheres.

The Balance of Terror

Despite this horrifying potential, nuclear weapons development has become such a common part of our lives that we seem almost unmoved by each new advance. Can it be that we have learned to live with the Bomb? Presumably we have, though an estimate of the true economic magnitude of the nuclear arms race and its cost might disrupt our complacency. The United States and the Soviet Union alone have spent over $4 trillion on defense since the Second World War (though certainly not all of it on nuclear development) and they continue to develop and staff their armories at an annual rate of almost $200 billion each. In 1982, the world's total military bill was $700–750 billion; the combined expenditures of the North Atlantic Treaty Organization and the Warsaw Pact (NATO's Soviet/Eastern European counterpart) comprised over 70 percent of the world total. Alarmingly, while in the period 1974–1978 the world's military expenditures rose at a rate of 2.2 percent per year, the figure rose to 3.8 percent between 1978 and 1982, and then jumped to nearly 7 percent in 1982.[7] This

5. Herman Kahn, *On Thermonuclear War* (Princeton, N.J.: Princeton University Press, 1960); Kahn, *Thinking About the Unthinkable* (New York: Horizon, 1962), the title of which inspired the opening sentence of this chapter; Linus Pauling, *No More War!* (New York: Dodd, Mead, 1958); and James R. Schlesinger, "Briefing on Counterforce Attacks," Senate Committee on Foreign Relations Hearing, September 11, 1974.
6. Carl Sagan, "Nuclear War and Climatic Catastrophe: Some Policy Implications," *Foreign Affairs,* Winter 1983–84, pp. 257–292. See also Jeannie Peterson, Editor for AMBIO, *The Aftermath: The Human and Ecological Consequences of Nuclear War* (New York: Pantheon Books, 1983).
7. *SIPRI Yearbook,* 1983, pp. 129–130.

FIGURE 10–1
Ten-year natural consequences of nuclear war and the accompanying hazards for populations in the United States and the Soviet Union, and in the Northern and Southern Hemispheres. H = high risk; M = medium risk; L = low risk.

Effect	Time after Nuclear War (1 hr, 1 day, 1 wk, 1 mo, 3 mo, 6 mo, 1 yr, 2 yr, 5 yr, 10 yr)	U.S./S.U. Population at Risk	N.H. Population at Risk	S.H. Population at Risk	Casualty Rate of Those at Risk	Potential Global Deaths
Blast		H	M	L	H	M–H
Thermal radiation		H	M	L	M	M–H
Prompt ionizing radiation		L	L	L	H	L–M
Fires		M	M	L	M	M
Toxic gases		M	M	L	L	L
Dark		H	H	M	L	L
Cold		H	H	H	H	M–H
Frozen water supplies		H	H	M	M	M
Fallout ionizing radiation		H	H	L–M	M	M–H
Food shortages		H	H	H	H	H
Medical system collapse		H	H	M	M	M
Contagious diseases		M	M	L	H	M
Epidemics and pandemics		H	H	M	M	M
Psychiatric disorders		H	H	L	L	L–M
Increased surface ultraviolet light		H	H	M	L	L
Synergisms	?	?	?	?	?	?

Source: From Carl Sagan, "Nuclear War and Climatic Catastrophe," *Foreign Affairs,* Winter 1983–84. p. 231. Copyright © 1983 by Carl Sagan. Reprinted by permission of the author and the author's agents. Scott Meredith Literary Agency, Inc., 845 Third Avenue, New York, New York 10022.

is attributed in part to increased arms importation by the Third World, to the continued Soviet build-up, and to the decision made by NATO in 1979 to request all of its members to increase their arms expenditures to 7 percent of gross national product by 1984. Only the United States and Britain were approaching that figure in 1983, with the United States' military expenditures rising to over 6 percent of GNP.

On what grounds are such huge expenditures and such an astonishing potential for "overkill" justified? The unanimous response of nuclear strategists who are satisfied that a strong nuclear deterrent is the key to national security is that the nuclear arms race is not lunacy at all—that it is a carefully balanced system designed not to threaten peace, but to guarantee it. This outlook assumes that the greater the capability of two or more parties to destroy one another, the less likely they are to engage in combat. This *mutual deterrence,* which some strategists regard as the sole guarantor of peace, is based on an uncomplicated message to any potential adversary: "Before you strike me, you had better consider that I will strike you back, and I will do more damage to you than will justify your attack on me." Hence mutual deterrence is built upon the twin abilities of first attack, and of surviving first attack to be able to launch a retaliatory attack of insufferable proportions. This system of keeping the peace by mutual threat of destruction was labeled by Winston Churchill the *balance of*

The scene is the attempted assassination of President Reagan in Washington in March 1981. Police, secret servicemen and bystanders are jumping on the suspect; the president has been thrust into his car. Sprawled at the feet of the agent on the left, still gripping an attache case, is the president's air force aide. In the case is the device which, by unleashing the nuclear arsenal of the United States, can signal the destruction of half the world. This aide travels everywhere with the president, and was even in the operating theater during the emergency four-hour operation that followed the shooting.

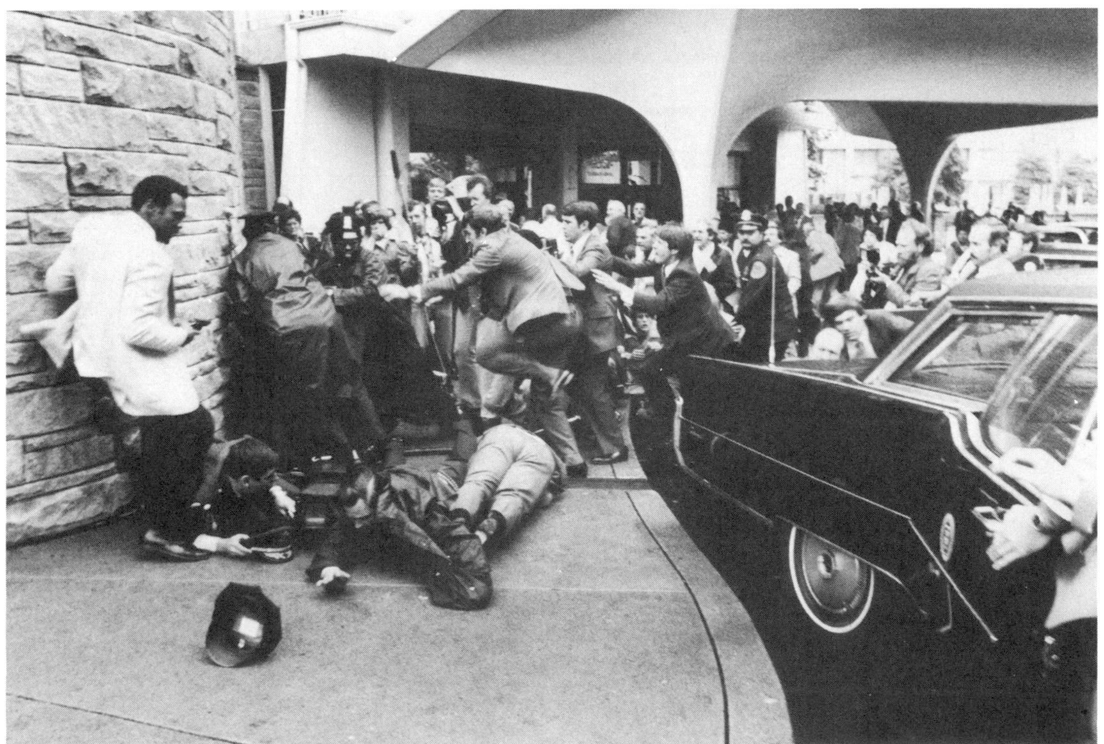

Source: Michael Evans (The White House)/Contact

terror. With time, it has been renamed *mutual superiority*, or, with greater irony, *mutually assured destruction* (MAD)!

Despite the simple logic of this prescription for avoiding nuclear war, the theory of mutual deterrence has been reexamined in recent years and found wanting. Critics argue, first, that deterrence strategy is derived too much from anticipated behavior and too little based on actual study of decision making during conflict, whether nuclear or nonnuclear. They also find a contradiction in the basic logic: on the one hand, the theory of deterrence emphasizes the strategic value of showing a willingness to increase the risks of military policy, while on the other hand the objective of the policy is to make situations safer. Third, critics attack the theory for its stress upon punishment, and of directing too little attention to the potential value of compromise. Fourth, they charge the policy with being excessively rigid in the sense that nuclear weapons might be used in anticipation of an attack from the other party when, in actuality, policymakers have misunderstood or misinterpreted the intentions of the adversary. Finally, the policy has been attacked because of its absoluteness, in the sense that a commitment to nuclear deterrence implies an all-or-nothing response to international crisis above an uncertain, but nonetheless intolerable threshold. In the view of the critics, this absoluteness is another potential cause for misunderstanding intentions, for ignoring the context of a crisis, for incorrectly evaluating deterrent capability because of domestic or bureaucratic politics, or for failing to recognize opportunities for compromise or alternative policies.[8]

First- and Second-Strike Capabilities

Despite these criticisms, however, the conventional wisdom of nuclear strategy continues to dominate the policy establishments of both Washington and Moscow. According to that wisdom, mutual deterrence requires not only the possession of nuclear arms by two opposed parties, but also the ability of each to absorb a first strike by the other without losing the capacity to retaliate. Atomic stability depends on a belief in the mind of the potential aggressor that he will suffer retaliation at an unacceptable cost (the essence of deterrence). This means above all that a considerable portion of the defending state's strike force must survive the initial assault. If either or both parties can achieve a first-strike capability—a capacity to destroy the adver-

8. For a thorough review of the critical literature see Robert Jervis, "Deterrence Theory Revisited" *World Politics*, January 1979, pp. 289–324. Criticisms of deterrence are not new; see, for example, Fred Ikle, "Will Nuclear Deterrence Last Out the Century?" *Foreign Affairs*, January 1973.

sary's strategic arsenal by surprise attack—mutual deterrence does not exist. Stable deterrence requires that both parties possess secure second-strike forces capable of surviving surprise attack.

Those who advocate mutual assured destruction argue that it is in the interests of both parties that their adversaries have secure second-strike potential. Without it the retaliatory response, to be effective, would need to be launched before the arrival of the opponent's incoming attack forces. Intercontinental ballistic missiles travel at speeds that reduce warning times to fifteen to thirty minutes. Thus, without second-strike security, a retaliatory force would need to be on hair-trigger alert during periods of political tension and ready for instant launch. Such a time-urgent system would be prone to catastrophe in the event of misinformation or miscalculation. Stable deterrence depends on a less sensitized system, one that permits time to verify the existence of an attack, and even to receive it, before taking irreversible counteractions.

On the American side, however, there is a contradiction between this goal of second-strike stability and the imperatives of defense in the European theater. It is the declared policy of the United States that if NATO forces could not turn back a Soviet attack at the conventional weapons level, tactical and strategic nuclear forces would be used. This nuclear umbrella is the heart of the Atlantic alliance. But it implies that the United States might be placed in the position of making first use of strategic nuclear weapons. To reduce retaliatory damage to the American homeland, and to make the threat of an American nuclear attack credible, the USA has an incentive to develop the capability to destroy the largest number of Soviet strategic forces on the ground before they can be used against American targets. Thus, the logic of the NATO alliance presses Washington toward the development of a first-strike force—one declared to be defensive in intent, but one sure to be perceived in Moscow as threatening an offensive potential. Indeed, President Carter announced in 1979 that American strategic targeting henceforth would be based on first-strike logic: American weapons would be aimed at the nuclear delivery vehicles of the Soviet Union. The Kremlin greeted this with a charge that the United States was planning nuclear war by designing a strategy for destroying the Soviet Union's second-strike capability, thus eliminating the careful balance of retaliatory forces that assures peace in a nuclear world.

The American commitment to Western Europe poses a dilemma between the objective of second-strike stability and the requirements of a first-strike force. The reality of this dilemma is the precise reason why the conventional wisdom of nuclear strategy (the assumption of mutual deterrence and mutual assured destruction) fails to stand up to the necessities of strategic policy. As a result, a new school of thought has developed, comprised of nuclear utilization theorists (NUTs as contrasted with MADvocates!), who hold that a doctrine built upon second-strike capability is inferior to one constructed upon the concept of first-strike advantage. This view derives only in small degree from the fear that a sufficiently destructive first strike will destroy weapons intended for second strike. It is founded more on the notion that the satisfaction of having scored a second-strike victory over the aggressor hardly compensates for the carnage inflicted by the original attack. In brief, fearing that the nuclear future is subject to unforeseen imbalances, deterrence is an unreliable policy; and if deterrence fails and second-strike weapons are destroyed (or if a society is destroyed), then a doctrine that relies on second-strike technology or second-strike psychology may fail. As a result, in recent years both in Washington and in Moscow, a quiet transformation of strategic doctrine has occurred, one that continues to stress deterrence, but that is equipped increasingly to invoke nuclear weapons as a first-strike strategy. In a sense, then, the contemporary doctrine of both parties is a compromise between MADvocates and NUTs.

The on-going debate between advocates of first-strike capability and those of second-strike retaliatory strategy blossomed into a major contest within NATO on the eve of deploying 572 new intermediate-range theater nuclear weapons in 1983, as a purported response to the Soviet deployment of SS-20 theatre weapons over the preceding three years. Second-strike traditionalists argued that a mutual Soviet-American guarantee not to take first resort to the use of nuclear weapons is crucial to stable deterrence. Others, including the European advocates of first-strike thinking, argued that first-strike is an option that cannot be removed from the doctrine of flexible response to potential aggression, particularly in the European theatre where Soviet and Warsaw Pact conventional weapons greatly outnumber NATO's.[9]

Nuclear utilization theory results from a rethinking of both the psychological and technological aspects of nuclear arms competition. Its advocates are aware that second-strike strategy depends not only on the will to deploy strategic forces in a certain way, but also on the technical capacity to protect a retaliatory force from destruction. Up to now, this has been achieved by the so-called triad of delivery ve-

9. For a spirited written debate of these two positions, see McGeorge Bundy, George F. Kennan, Robert S. McNamara and Gerard Smith, "Nuclear Weapons and the Atlantic Alliance," *Foreign Affairs,* Spring 1982, pp. 753–768, advocating the no-first-use principle; and a German response arguing for the inclusion of first-use in a flexible response doctrine by Karl Kaiser, Georg Leber, Alois Mertes and Franz-Josef Schulze, "Nuclear Weapons and the Preservation of Peace: A German Response to No First Use," *Foreign Affairs,* Summer 1982, pp. 1157–1170.

hicles: land-based ICBMs protected in underground silos; submarine missile launchers protected from detection (and therefore destruction) by thousands of miles of ocean in which they prowl; and long-range heavy bombers kept in the air on routine alert to prevent their destruction on the ground. This triad has provided a considerable degree of security to second-strike forces.

Both the United States and the Soviet Union maintain strategic triads, but for a number of reasons, their respective compositions differ. The Soviet Union, severely lacking in year-long, warm-water ports except in staging bases far from home (*e.g.*, Cuba), has a smaller percentage of its deliverable nuclear warheads on submarines than does the United States. Similarly, because of its long hostile borders in Asia as well as in Europe, the Soviet Union has concentrated its launcher development on large, land-based missiles. Weapons deliverable by aircraft are far fewer than those of the United States. While the United States bases 27 percent of its deliverable warheads in the air, the Soviet Union bases 3 percent; Washington has 51 percent of its warheads based on submarines, and the Soviet Union 32 percent; but while the United States places only 22 percent of total warheds on ground-based missiles, the Soviet Union bases 65 percent of its warheads on the ground.[10] Table 10–2 depicts the deployment patterns of the two countries by missiles and total warheads.

One of the elements of the Soviet triad that is most disturbing to American defense planners is the rapid increase in the number of deliverable warheads atop intercontinental ballistic missiles (ICBMs). As Table 10–2 indicates, the United States maintains 1051 deployed ICBMs and the Soviet Union 1398 (many of which are targeted at Chinese objectives). But since multiple, independently-targetable reentry vehicles (MIRVs) were first deployed in 1974, the total number of warheads atop Soviet missiles has grown to 5481. (The US Department of Defense reports the number at approximately 6000.) Figure 10–2 illustrates this growth from 1968 to 1983.

To the extent that the nuclear triad of either the United States or the Soviet Union is a deterrent and, therefore, a defensive complex, it should be noted that new military technologies raise the possibility that the margin of safety will be reduced substantially in the future, and even that one or the other contestent may have the option to develop a first-strike force able to overcome all existing defenses. A hardened silo, for example, the underground well where ICBMs hide, effectively defends its missile against all but very near hits by enemy warheads, and is designed to withstand the fairly wide circular error

10. *SIPRI Yearbook, 1983*, p. 46.

TABLE 10–2
Force comparisons of American and Soviet Strategic Nuclear Triad Defense Systems.

	Number Delivery Vehicles	*Number Warheads Each*	*Total Warheads*	*Total Delivery (megatons)*
Land-based				
US	1051	1–3	2151	1429
USSR	1398	1–10	5678	5481
Sea-based				
US	644	8–10	4960	314
USSR	937	1–10	2813	885
Air-based				
US	316	4–12	2570	1745
USSR	145	2	290	290
Total				
US	2011		9681	3488
USSR	2480		8781	6656

Source: SIPRI Yearbook, 1983, pp. 48–49. Where SIPRI data differ from those reported in *Soviet Military Power, 1983* (United States Department of Defense), SIPRI data have been used.

FIGURE 10–2
US and Soviet ICBM Launcher and Reentry Vehicle (RV) Deployment Comparisons, 1968–1983.

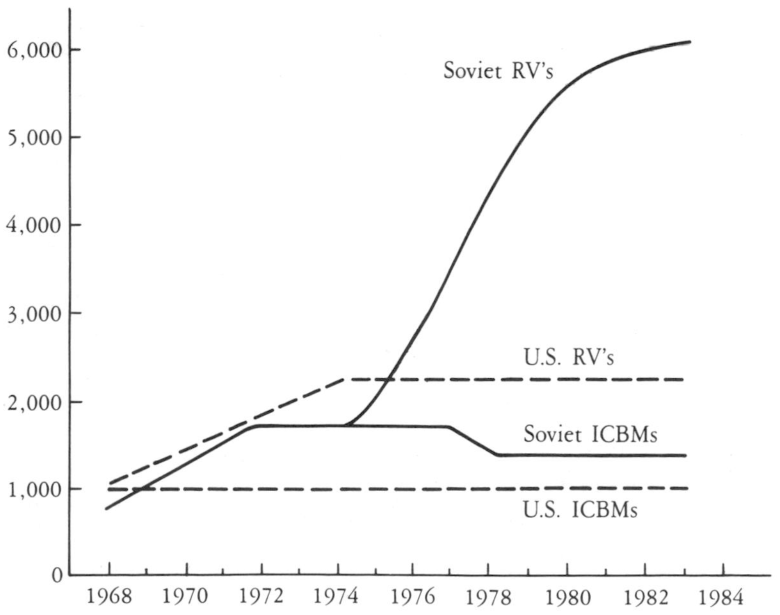

Source: Soviet Military Power, 1983 (US Department of Defense), p. 19.

probabilities (CEPs) of available long-range missiles. (The CEP is a measure of the probability that at least one-half of the warheads targeted at an object will fall within a predicted radius of that object.) But recent advances in microelectronics have made possible offensive weapons with highly accurate terminal guidance, vastly reducing the CEPs (or increasing the probability of one half of the warheads falling within the predicted radius) and possibly opening a new era of silo-busting techniques. For the newest generation of American intermediate-range missiles (Pershing II and ground-launched Cruise missiles), for example, the CEP is 300 feet, meaning that one-half of the warheads fired at a single target will fall within a radius of 300 feet of the target from a distance of over a thousand miles.[11] Figure 10–3 reveals a sliding scale of CEPs for warheads of differing megatonage and the probability of a missile surviving.

Similarly, the margin of security for submarines and strategic bombers is eroding. The submarine is protected by the physical properties of seawater, which impede the passage of detection impulses. But advances in antisubmarine warfare technology are vastly extending the ranges over which detection is possible. Strategic bombers are vulnerable to precision-guided surface-to-air and air-to-air missiles, if radars are developed to respond to their characteristic low-level flight patterns. In general, and without overstating the point, it is fair to conclude that the new technologies will render obsolete many of the familiar means of protecting second-strike forces.[12] The probability that offensive weapons will modernize more quickly than defensive ones gives an edge to nuclear utilization theory, thus providing an added impetus to develop first-strike capability.

11. The value of the CEP in predicting the attack's effectiveness is not without detractors. Some argue that while the theory is mathematically sound, it fails to take into account a number of uncontrollable "bias" factors. Even if the CEP is demonstrated by firing repeated shots at a single target over a known test course, with the advantage of being able to correct the targeting on the basis of experience, it does not necessarily follow that the CEP will hold up when firing over an untested course. The detractors hold that the CEP may be a meaningless figure when missiles are fired between the United States and the Soviet Union over the north pole because the "bias" factors peculiar to this untested course are unknown. See, for example, "A Question of Accuracy," *Science,* 11 September 1981, pp. 1230–2131.
12. Authors differ on the effectiveness of nuclear defenses. One view holds that a "deterrent is deterred" because of the vulnerability of cities to retaliatory attack, while the other holds that the foremost weakness of American strategic policy has been to concentrate on offensive capability, leaving defenses weak, while the Soviets improve their defenses considerably. See, respectively, Robert Jervis, "Why Nuclear Superiority Doesn't Matter," *Political Science Quarterly,* Winter 1979/80, pp. 617–33; and Daniel Gouré and Gordon H. McCormick, "Soviet Strategic Defense: The Neglected Dimension of the U.S.-Soviet Balance," *ORBIS,* Spring 1980, pp. 103–27.

FIGURE 10–3
Probablity of a missile surviving nuclear attack as a function of the explosion's megatonnage and the hit's accuracy (CEP)

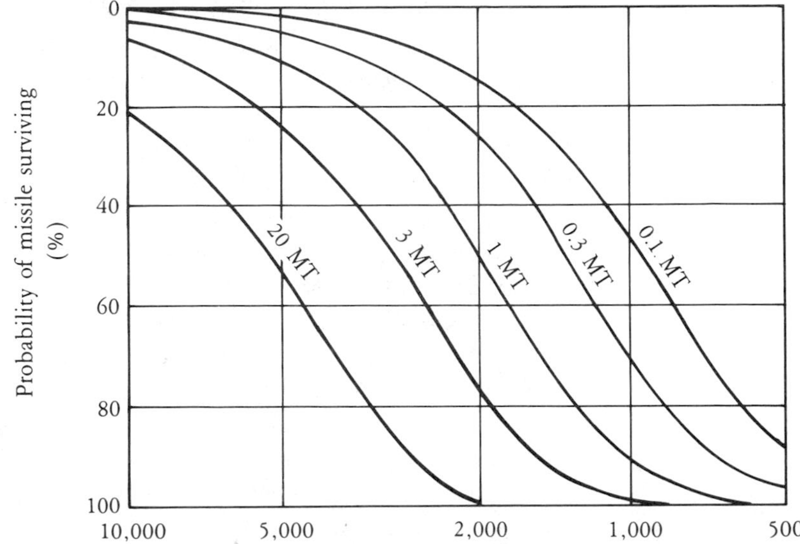

Source: Sidney D. Drell, "L + RV: A Formula for Arms Control," *Bulletin of the Atomic Scientists*, April 1982, p. 28–34, reprinted with permission of the *Bulletin of the Atomic Scientists*, a magazine of science and public affairs. Copyright © 1982 by the Educational Foundation for Nuclear Science, Chicago, IL 60637. Example for reading the graph: A missile in a hardened silo has an 80 percent chance of surviving attack by a 20 megaton nuclear device carried by a missile with a CEP of 2000 feet.

In the race between offense and defense, it can be safely predicted that new methods will be developed to protect nuclear strike forces. Suggestions include superhardening to give missile silos extremely high levels of blast resistance; camouflage and dummies, so the enemy wastes his force on fake targets and misses the real ones; land mobile systems rather than fixed sites; electronic countermeasures to jam the sensitive guidance systems of the attacking force; high energy laser beams to destroy missiles or their warheads in flight; and, in the case of submarines, increased ranges and improved electronic warfare equipment to provide more cover against detection.

Behind all of this competition, not only between governments but between proponents of offensive and defensive strategies as well, lies the logic of the nuclear arms race. No doubt the uncertainties of strategy and intent will force the competition to greater effort, higher cost, heightened technology and greater probable loss. It seems that the arms race has gained so much momentum that it is unstoppable. Nevertheless, there are nuclear strategists who continue to insist that the race has reached the point of diminishing returns for both parties; that is, that the current strategic balance, with respect to both deterrent capability and destructive potential, is durable and safe, so that increasing the cost of weapons development provides ever smaller measures of security.

Credibility of Intent

Deterrence, as has been noted, is more than simply the possession of weapons of mass destruction. There is a reciprocal psychological factor through which the parties signal one another as to their intentions and the depth of their commitments. The possession of power is not an effective deterrent unless accompanied by the will to use it in defined situations. Thus the threat of nuclear retaliation must not only be horrifying; it must also be credible. The probability of nuclear attack is the product of capability and intent: if intent equals zero, then the probability is zero.[13]

Credibility is also determined in part by the object of conflict. There is an obvious difference in expectation when (1) one's home territory is threatened, or (2) one's vital allies are intimidated or (3) conflict brews over some remote areas or some remote interest. In the first case, there is little cause to doubt the credibility of deterrence. Doubt begins to spring up, however, in the second case. While the United States would surely launch a counterattack if New York City were subjected to nuclear attack, would it do likewise if the object of the first strike were a Western European city? If the United States does respond with nuclear weapons, does it invite an attack upon its own cities and its own defenses from the other side, after having already expended some of its deployed weapons? The European fear that for these reasons the American nuclear umbrella lacks credibility has greatly motivated the development of British and French nuclear forces. In the third case of remote areas and interests, of course, nuclear deterrence has little credibility whatever.[14]

Object of conflict is closely tied to commitment. While there is no doubt of self-defense credibility, commitment may become obscured as the issue in question wanders farther from home. This is the case

13. J. David Singer, "Threat Perception and National Decision-Makers," *Journal of Conflict Resolution,* 1958, pp. 90–105; also J. David Singer, *Deterrence, Arms Control and Disarmament* (Columbus: Ohio State University Press, 1962); and Dean G. Pruitt, "Definition of the Situation as a Determinant of International Action," in Herbert C. Kelman, editor, *International Behavior* (New York: Holt, Rinehart and Winston, 1966), pp. 393–432.
14. Kahn, *Thinking About the Unthinkable,* pp. 110–25, suggests three types of deterrence pertinent to three distinctly different levels of interest.

with the American pledge to defend West Berlin, a small island of the Western world surrounded entirely by Eastern Germany in the Soviet world. Its size and location make it indefensible. The pledge to defend it seems impossible in the face of overbearing power from the Warsaw Pact nations. But the American pledge was boldly underscored by President Kennedy in 1961 when he declared in German to a cheering throng in West Berlin, "I am a Berliner!" A few years later President Nixon told a similar audience that "All the world's free peoples are Berliners." Some politicians have gone so far as to say that even God may be a Berliner! The point is to dramatize to the Soviet Union the American commitment to defend what appears to be tactically indefensible.

But how is this commitment made credible? Among the NATO forces in West Berlin there are many thousands of Americans who, in the event of invasion, would be killed or captured. Their deaths or detention would commit the United States to retaliatory action (not necessarily nuclear), and the Soviets know this. Hence the commitment of the United States to the defense of a most unlikely piece of territory is made credible by the "trip wire" character of the American forces there. It is based on mutual knowledge that a Soviet attack might force the United States to do something that it does not want to do. This process of voluntarily tying one's own hands is generally called the process of commitment and posits this rule: Credibility is assured when you deprive yourself of the option of not honoring your own threat. Among other things, this process signals to the other side that the burden is on it to prevent a clash.

Thomas Schelling has proposed the game of "Chicken" as a model of communicating to an enemy that a situation is out of control and that you are powerless to restore control because of the depth of your commitment. He likens international conflict to two hotrodders on a deliberate collision course, each expecting the other to "chicken out." If neither does, each is the loser in a bloody conclusion. Schelling suggests a strategy in which one participant becomes conspicuously drunk before the start. As the vehicles approach each other, the inebriated driver throws his steering wheel out of the car so as to signal to the other his inability to restore control. The burden is now on the other, because one is irrevocably committed. The major liability, of course, is that two may play at the same strategy, and instead of having one participant out of control, there may be two.

In the jargon of the nuclear era, this danger of uncontrolled escalation of commitments is called "brinkmanship," or the process of proceeding stepwise to the brink of thermonuclear war. In this process, called by the late Herman Kahn "the rationality of irrationality," each side attempts to convince the other that its commitment is irrevocable, and that it is the other's responsibility to defuse the situation. Irrevocability is communicated by tying it to larger values or to constituents who will not be satisfied with any other course. Language involving ideological necessity has been common in Soviet brinkmanship, especially in the Cuban missile crisis of 1962. By the same token, the specter of abandonment of allies and references to a determined Congress or electorate have accompanied American nuclear diplomacy. The danger is that if both sides play at the same tactics, issues and threats become magnified. The sole full threat of bilateral nuclear confrontation—the Cuban crisis—was defused only when the Soviet Union agreed to remove its offensive missiles as a quid pro quo condition for an American pledge not to sponsor further invasions like that at the Bay of Pigs in 1961.

Fortunately, that crisis and all others between nuclear powers up till now have been resolved short of the type of runaway commitment envisaged by Kahn. His image of a Doomsday Machine portrays a device running on computers that could not be drawn off the course of total destruction if an adversary were to undertake any of certain selected policies; it would be capable of universal destruction. Presumably it would be a totally credible deterrent, because it would be irreversible, and able to compute events without human interference.

Counterforce and Countervalue Strategies

Some strategists have argued that deterrence may operate even during a nuclear exchange. Both sides have assets of greater and lesser value, and there may be a mutual interest or a tacit understanding to limit targeting in order to minimize the loss of human life. Former Secretary of Defense Robert S. McNamara suggested in 1962 that American planners seek not only the avoidance of nuclear war, but also its limitation through a counterforce strategy. This calls for the targeting of delivery vehicles on the forces of the adversary, rather than on its population, and for destruction of weapons rather than people. While we ought to maintain a strike force targeted to cities and population centers to deter attack upon our own civilian population, we should positively avoid striking cities. In this way, a level of deterrence could still operate even within a nuclear war.

Proponents of the counterforce strategy argue that any nuclear attacker realizes his advantage comes not in killing people, but in debilitating the enemy's forces. This is an especially acute consideration in warfare that will have a duration of only hours, in which no government would be able to utilize its population for manufacturing or any other purpose.[15]

But a counterforce strategy implies the ability to destroy missiles in silos, submarines in their hidden sanctuaries, and long-range bombers on the ground, at sea or in the air. If this can be achieved against most or all of the enemy force, then the nation with such a capability will also have achieved a preemptive first-strike potential, whether or not this capability is intended. The opponents of counterforce argue, therefore, that the McNamara strategy which was reaffirmed in 1980 by President Carter and later by President Reagan as official American nuclear strategy, is a threat to the concept of stable mutual deterrence based on secure second-strike capabilities.

Although modern nuclear strategy is based on second-strike thinking, the original nuclear strategy was based on the countervalue concept, the notion of striking population and industrial centers. This notion was a natural extention of the saturation bombing strategy of the United States during World War II. But as the Soviet Union achieved nuclear strategic capability, newer considerations for deterrence entered the picture, and American strategy turned to counterforce coupled with notions of mutual deterrence and mutual retaliation.[16] Current strategy involves actual targeting at a combination of military and civilian targets, with the combined objectives of knocking out Soviet retaliatory forces, reducing the capability of the Soviet Union to recover from retaliatory attack, and eliminating the Soviet military and political leadership.[17] This may be interpreted as a strat-

15. See, for example, Kahn, *Thinking About the Unthinkable,* p. 66, and *On Thermonuclear War,* p. 115.
16. For the evolution of the counterforce strategy, see: Fred Kaplan, *The Wizards of Armageddon* (New York: Simon and Schuster, 1983), particularly Chapter 13, "Counterforce."
17. Although counterforce dominates current American strategy, countervalue planning (or "economic targeting") continues. See Benjamin S. Lambeth and Kevin N. Lewis, "Economic Targeting in Nuclear War: U.S. and Soviet Approaches," *ORBIS,* Spring 1983, pp. 127–49.

    One account claims that the United States has 40,000 targets in the Soviet Union: 20,000 military targets (among the nuclear: ballistic missile launch facilities, nuclear weapons storage sites, airfields with nuclear-capable aircraft and bases with nuclear missile carrying submarines; among the conventional: supply depots, marshaling points, conventional air fields, ammunition storage facilties, tank and vehicle storage yards); 2000 urban targets to kill leadership of state and military forces; and 15,000 economic-industrial targets (divided between sites of war-supporting industry and industry capable of contributing to economic recovery). See AMBIO Advisory Group, "Reference Scenario: How a Nuclear War Might Be Fought," in Jeannie Peterson, Editor for AMBIO, *The Aftermath* (New York: Pantheon Books, 1983), pp. 38–48 at p. 40. The paper cites as its authority an unspecified report of the US Department of Defense in 1980 and a subsequent analysis by Desmond J. Ball, also unspecified.

    Contrary to these reports, Defense Secretary Caspar Weinberger denied the use of contervalue planning as "neither moral nor prudent, neither necessary nor sufficient for deterrence," and as a strategy that would "invite the destruction of our own population." See *Annual Report to the Congress, Fiscal Year 1984,* p. 55.

egy in which the basic planning is counterforce, but the targeting is a combination of counterforce and countervalue.

Matter of Muscle?

When Richard N. Perle, Assistant Secretary of Defense for International Security Policy, and other arms control hardliners in the Pentagon talk about "throw weights," they are not commenting on recent Olympic feats. A major issue in United States arms control policy is how persistently to press the Russians to agree to steps that would lead to equivalent ballistic missile "throw weights," that is, the amount of weight, exclusive of the missile rocket, that the boosters can lift into ballistic space trajectory.

It would be difficult for the Russians to comply, even if they wanted to do so, because they took a different design path than the United States and built very large missiles with lots of throw weight. But the issue has become an obsession of Mr. Perle and some of his arms control colleagues in the Pentagon.

However, arms control specialists in the State Department generally seek other avenues to reduce any disparity in nuclear strength. One State Department office has on prominent display a handmade poster that reads: "Real Men Don't Need Throw Weight."

In an age of nuclear weapons, do the relative strengths of the United States and the Soviet Union in the number of missiles, bombers and warheads make any difference? Each of the superpowers has an arsenal equivalent to several tons of TNT for every person. In 1974, Henry Kissinger offered the hypothesis that "when two nations are already capable of destroying each other, an upper limit exists beyond which additional weapons lose their political significance." Speaking in Moscow, he professed not to know what strategic superiority is, nor to understand its significance, nor to be able to imagine what to do with it. Winston Churchill put it succinctly: after a certain point, more bombs will only make the rubble bounce.

But in practice, statesmen and strategists take a different view, and regard any change in the quantitative or qualitiative balance of nuclear forces as a matter for the closest scrutiny. Does a new deployment signal a change of intentions by the other side? Is there a technological breakthrough that will confer an advantage to the adversary and upset the basis of the existing balance? Is he achieving a first-strike option, or gaining a local superiority in a particular region or theater? What political and strategic opportunities does he have under the new balance of forces, and how will our own policy alternatives be constrained? The major governments operate under the assumption that to ignore the strategic nuclear balance that underlies the panoply of relationships in the modern world system would entail great peril.

These questions give rise to two important distinctions. First, one must learn to distinguish between the implications of compiling more nuclear weapons, on the one hand, and the implications of improving the ability to deliver those weapons, on the other. Clearly, the emphasis in strategic decision making is on the latter; for it is the ability of the adversary to penetrate defenses, together with one's own ability to overcome the defenses of the adversary, that really drives the strategic debate and the pace of advancement in weapons technology. Second, and in contrast to conventional weapons, literal *parity* in nuclear forces is meaningless. It is unimportant that one side's nuclear arsenal is as big as that of the other side. The critical issue is whether one's own side possesses *sufficiency* or *practical equivalence*. It is only that one have enough capability to meet the maximum strategic (both first-strike and second-strike) need, not that one side be able to match the other in a count of weapons. It is for this reason that comparisons of weapons arsenals, such as that shown in Table 10–2, are of limited value; it is also important to have measure of the quality of defenses, the respective rates of developments in weapons technology, the efficiency of weapons as measured in distance and accuracy, etc.

TABLE 10–3
*US military expenditure 1980–1987, real or projected, depending upon year. *Indicates first Reagan budget.*

Fiscal Year	*Defense Outlay ($Billions)*	*Percent of Total Government Outlay*
1980	135.9	23.6
1981	159.8	24.3
1982*	187.5	25.9
1983	221.1	29.2
1984	253.0	31.4
1985	292.1	33.6
1986	331.7	35.8
1987	364.2	37.2

Source: Office of Management and Budget, *The Budget of the United States Government, Fiscal Year 1983.*

Needless to say, it is hazardous in the extreme to draw major conclusions about international politics from crude numerical comparisons of weapons capabilities. Furthermore, such comparisons, imperfect and inconclusive as they may be, are turned to a vast array of political uses. In the presidential and congressional campaigns of 1980, for instance, there were few candidates who did not concede the superiority of the Soviet Union, and just as few who denied that a major new weapons development era is needed in the United States. Before he departed from office, President Carter submitted a budget for the fiscal year 1982 calling for an increase of 20 percent in defense spending; within four weeks President Reagan had announced that he would call for still 25 percent more. Debate began afresh about the status of the MX missile system; the B-1 treetop bomber (the B-52 had been at the core of strategic defenses for over twenty years and the youngest one was over ten years old); and the neutron bomb, which President Carter had decided not to manufacture and deploy in Europe. Table 10–3 indicates the anticipated growth in military expenditure from 1980 through 1987 for the United States. In that time, expenditure is expected to grow by a factor of 2.7, with military costs rising from 23.6 percent of total government expenditures to 37.2 percent. In 1982, American defense spending amounted to 6.6 percent of the gross national product. Intelligence estimates put Soviet expenditures at 15 percent of gross national product.[18] Figure 10–4 demonstrates comparative American and Soviet investment in new military technology

FIGURE 10–4
Comparative Soviet and American (with and without costs of Vietnam War) investment costs for new military technology, 1960–1981.

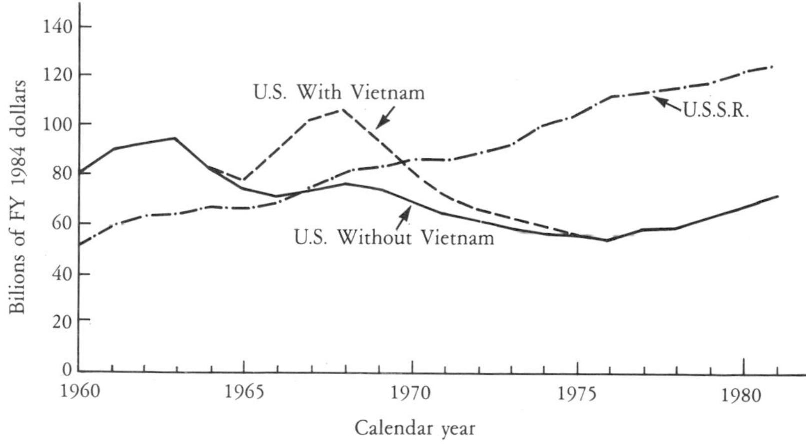

Source: U.S. Department of Defense, *Annual Report to the Congress, Fiscal Year 1984*, p. 22.

18. U.S. Department of Defense, *Annual Report to the Congress, Fiscal Year 1984*, p. 20.

for a twenty-one year period, as estimated by the United States Department of Defense (Fig. 10–4).

It should also be noted that strategic arms comparisons address total capabilities worldwide for the two principal contestants, and overlook both the important regional strategic balances and the delicate balance of combined strategic, tactical and conventional weapons in the areas of greatest interest. In the European theatre, for example, the Warsaw Treaty Organization and the North Atlantic Treaty Organization glare at one another not only with MIRVs, but with hundreds of thousands of troops, conventional (nonnuclear) weapons and billions of megatons in TNT equivalents atop tactical (short-range, relatively low-yield) nuclear weapons capable of being launched from the battlefield.

The Spread of Nuclear Weapons

Up to this point, all references to nuclear politics have assumed the simplest of political configurations: a "binuclear world," or one in which only two states possess combat nuclear capability. In fact, this is a false situation, for at present, in addition to the United States and the Soviet Union, nuclear capability can be deployed by Britain, France and China, and India has successfully detonated at least one nuclear device. Several other governments are within easy reach of nuclear capability should their policies call for it (though to develop it, many would have to renounce their ratification of the 1970 Nuclear Non-Proliferation Treaty). Among these are Japan, Taiwan, South Korea, Australia, virtually all of the Western European and Eastern European states, Israel, Egypt, Pakistan, Canada, Brazil and Mexico. In all there are perhaps twenty-five states that might in the foreseeable future opt for nuclear weapons, and there is evidence that South Africa tested one in 1983.

One needs to look briefly at the reasons for which the present nuclear powers opted for such weapons. The United States did so in order to bring the Second World War to a fast and sudden conclusion and, in pre–Cold War spirit, to demonstrate its incomparable weapons strength to the Kremlin.[19] The Soviet Union was moved to nuclear capability by the rapid breakdown and polarization of world politics after the war. Britain and France undertook nuclear development both for reasons of prestige and in order to prepare European defenses that would not be dependent upon the United States. China undertook the

19. Gar Alperovitz, *Atomic Diplomacy: Hiroshima and Potsdam* (New York: Vintage, 1965).

nuclear course for reasons of global prestige, regional political-military supremacy and the dissolution of peaceful security relations with the Soviet Union. India, the newest (1974) of the nuclear partners, undoubtedly chose to enter the club principally for reasons of prestige (especially in relation to nuclear China and nonnuclear Pakistan), Asian balance and appearances of modernity.

On balance, then, there appear to be four discernible reasons for nuclear weapons development: security, prestige, regional dominance or equilibrium and reification of modern scientific development. Even though most citizens regard nuclear development as unreasonably costly, potentially aggressive and generally without use, the competition among governments for security and recognition makes the nuclear option enticing. Quite possibly, were it not for the twin facts (1) that many states are protected by nuclear umbrellas through alliances (Western Europe and Canada by the United States through NATO and Eastern Europe by the Soviet Union through the Warsaw Pact) and (2) that despite public denunciation, nuclear equilibrium has contributed to East-West peace for three decades, there would be many more nuclear powers at present than there are. Basic nuclear weapons technology is known virtually throughout the world, and the cost of production is relatively low. In the hands of terrorists, a small, concealed weapon could have immense political effect; but for most governments attempting to base national strategic defense policies on nuclear deterrence, the cost of delivery technology will remain a barrier to entry for the foreseeable future.

It should not be assumed, however, that the other countries have progressed as far as the Soviet Union and the United States in weapons development. The distribution by country of 1375 nuclear test explosions conducted between 1945 and the end of 1982 is shown in Table 10–4. During the 1970s, the average number of tests conducted annually was forty-two; in the first three years of the 1980s it was fifty-one. As both the Soviet Union and the United States prepare new warheads for new delivery systems for the remainder of the century, the annual number of test firings is expected to increase.

The relative ease by which nuclear weapons are acquired, either from allied governments or through independent scientific development, has raised a number of crucial questions about their spread or *proliferation*. In early nuclear jargon the problem was expressed as the "*n*th power problem," referring to the possibility that an indeterminable number of states might undertake nuclear weapons development. Was the world better off with only two (or a few) nuclear powers which fully understood the rules of the nuclear game in such a way as to establish a peace by threat? Or would the world benefit

TABLE 10–4
Atomic and Nuclear Test Explosions, 1945–82.

	Before Sept. 1, 1963[a]	After Sept. 1, 1963[a]	Country Total
US	293	407	700
USSR	164	336	500
France	23	105	128
UK	8	12	20
China	0	26	26
India	0	1	1
Total	488	887	1375

Source: SIPRI Yearbook, 1983, p. 100.

[a]*The Partial Nuclear Test Ban Treaty was concluded in August 1963, yet the number of tests conducted since that time is double the pre-treaty era. France and China have not joined the treaty, with the result that while all others restrict testing to underground sites, forty-one French tests and twenty-two Chinese tests have been above ground.*

by being "multinuclear," that is, by having several nuclear states, each capable of adjusting its own security without reliance on fragile alliances? Was a binuclear status anything more than a device of the two greatest powers to manipulate everyone else's security, and to manipulate world politics in general to their conflicting outlooks? The modern problem, needless to say, places renewed emphasis on these questions, given that scientific knowledge enables the nuclear membership to multiply by five in a matter of a few years. Urgency is heightened by the fact that there are several critically important regional balances in the world where the Soviet Union and the United States play external roles, such as in the Middle East and continental Asia. Are the imperatives of regional balances and the demands for prestige sufficient to justify the rapid growth in number of nuclear states?

Most scholars and statesmen prefer to think of a world in which the management of nuclear power is kept in as few hands as possible. Controlling the spread of nuclear weapons has been an agreed goal of most of the leading powers. Efforts to stem proliferation of these weapons achieved a major success with the Non-Proliferation Treaty (NPT), which took effect in 1970. In this treaty, the nuclear members pledged not to transfer to nonnuclear states any form of nuclear explosive, and not to assist in its development. Likewise, the nonnuclear members agreed not to accept such weapons or assistance. But, like most treaties, signature is wholly voluntary, and compliance with the terms is left to self-restraint. Furthermore, Article 10 of the treaty provides that any state may withdraw from the treaty's obligations upon three-month notification by merely informing the other parties and the United Nations Security Council. The notification must be accompanied by a statement of the "extraordinary events it regards as having jeopardized its supreme interests."

Although almost one hundred governments have ratified the NPT, it does not enjoy universal popularity. Nonnuclear states have often objected that the treaty is a luxury of the nuclear states, designed to freeze the international distribution for maintenance of special superpower privileges. Others have been reluctant to enter into the treaty without guarantees of deterrence assistance from one or another of the nuclear powers. We have already seen that such guarantees are without practical benefit, since the level of commitment embodied in them leaves much slack in credibility.[20]

The nonnuclear states have not been alone in their objections. Among those who enjoy nuclear status, both China and France have vigorously opposed membership in the NPT. Each argues that it is a Soviet-American device to subordinate others, and to profit from their unique ability to offer and then withdraw the nuclear umbrella. France, especially, insists that the possession of even minimal nuclear capability is a political and strategic equalizer.[21] China adds the view that nuclear status promotes decay of imperialism, and is therefore a progressive international trend. The opponents of the NPT are not necessarily reckless, since their arguments are intended not to destabilize the international system but to challenge the political superiority of a few nuclear states. While the United States pledges its aid against "nuclear blackmail," France, China and India refuse in turn to be "blackmailed" by the United States and the Soviet Union.

The fragility of the NPT as a safeguard against the spread of nuclear weapons is, however, becoming more a matter for concern, due less to traditional reasons of security and prestige than to the global crisis of natural resources. Commencing with the petroleum embargo of 1973/74, governments have been increasingly aware of the need to develop nonpetroleum energy reserves. A method particularly favored has been nuclear fuel. The ease of acquiring nuclear fuels in international trade has raised the issue of "innocent progress toward the Bomb," or the acquisition of nuclear capability for peaceful industrial reasons, only to succumb to the temptation to transform fuel for energy into fuel for combat potential. Not only does this possibility greatly increase the number of states that might in the foreseeable future have the nuclear military option; it also raises grave questions about the wisdom of nuclear fuel transfers, the management of nuclear policy internationally and anticipatory controls over regional nuclear arms

20. Joseph I. Coffey, "Nuclear Guarantees and Nonproliferation," *International Organization* 25, 1971, pp. 836–44.
21. Raymond Aron, "The Spread of Nuclear Weapons," *Atlantic Monthly*, January 1965.

races. Indeed, India's single nuclear explosion resulted from nuclear fuel provided by the United States for peaceful purposes. The American charge that India violated the terms of the transfer agreement in using the material to develop a prototype nuclear weapon caused a serious rift in relations between the two governments. Israel's 1981 preventative attack on a French-built reactor in Iraq was undertaken because of evidence that the reactor was going to be used to produce weapons-grade nuclear fuel.

The problem is especially acute with respect to fast breeder reactors which produce plutonium, a manmade element, as nuclear fuel. In the view of the United States and other governments, the recycling of nuclear fuels threatens to close too rapidly the gap between nuclear energy technology and nuclear weapons technology, a threat both to the stability of international politics and to the control of terrorism. The threat is so severe that it is now estimated that by the turn of the century there will be enough breeder reactors in use to produce sufficient plutonium to build as many as thirty thousand bombs as powerful as the one dropped on Nagasaki.[22]

In an effort to bring this under control, Washington has sought to preserve time with the Nuclear Non-Proliferation Act of 1978, which purports to give the United States the authority to prevent the international transfer of plutonium in conjunction with its membership in the Nuclear Suppliers' Group, founded in 1975. In addition, the United States has succeeded in establishing the International Nuclear Fuel Cycle Evaluation, a project of some forty governments, charged with exploring the international need, control and storage of spent nuclear fuels. It is hoped in Washington and other capitals that these efforts will delay the excessive recycling of nuclear fuels long enough to develop reprocessing technologies that do not simplify the creation of weapons-usable material.[23] The Nuclear Non-Proliferation Act provides strict controls upon the uses of fuel provided by the United States, but states that are not members of the Non-Proliferation Treaty and that have wanted to embark upon nuclear generation of electricity have been able to turn to other suppliers, most notably France, for nuclear fuels.[24]

22. Frank Barnaby, "World Arsenals in 1980," *Bulletin of the Atomic Scientists,* September 1980, reporting on the findings of the *SIPRI Yearbook,* 1980.
23. Joseph S. Nye, "Non-Proliferation: A Long-term Strategy," *Foreign Affairs,* April 1978, pp. 601–23. See also Victor Gilinsky, "Plutonium, Proliferation and the Process of Reprocessing," *Foreign Affairs,* Winter 1978/79, pp. 374–86. For a study of alternative policies together with pertinent technical information, see Ted Greenwood, George W. Rathjens and Jack Ruina, *Adelphi Paper no. 130,* Winter 1976 (London: International Institute for Strategic Studies).
24. For an evaluation of the American policy, see Gerard Smith and George Rathjens, "Reassessing Nuclear Nonproliferation Policy," *Foreign Affairs,* Spring 1981, pp. 875–894.

Other Hazards of the Nuclear Arms Race

Popular literature throughout the nuclear era has given much attention to the possibility of *unintended* nuclear war ignited by accident, human error, nervous impulse or unauthorized behavior. Occasionally, these horrors have been brought to life by close scrapes with nuclear disaster. On some occasions errant radar signals have indicated the possibility of incoming missiles over the North Pole. Soviet behavior in Germany, especially in the Berlin air corridors, has sometimes raised fears of nuclear war out of sheer nervousness. The projected "surgical strikes" on Soviet missile encampments in Cuba in 1962 might have brought Soviet nuclear response. And the use of tactical nuclear weapons, and even low-yield strategic nuclear weapons, has been advocated by the political right in both Korean and Vietnam wars.

A vivid example of the possibility of accidental nuclear warfare occurred when a bomb-laden American Stratofortress crashed off the Spanish coast in the mid-1960s. Though its cargo did not detonate, two nuclear devices were temporarily lost, one on land and one in shallow waters. With nuclear bombs in the air at all times, and with knowledge that reconnaissance craft have been shot down in the Pacific and the Caribbean, do such incidents suggest that misunderstanding and coincidental happenings in international crises could touch off holocaust?

American strategists are convinced that the risk of Soviet-American nuclear war through technical accident is negligible. The risk may be increased, however, by proliferation of "cheap" thermonuclear systems in the hands of states with inferior scientific development whose economies force dangerous shortcuts in safeguard systems. While the giants invest heavily in careful electronic and mechanical shielding devices that make unintended detonation quite unlikely, similar protective devices may be either technically or economically beyond the reach of smaller states. It is believed that the bombs of the big powers are less accident prone than those of small future atomic powers might be.

American strategists are also confident that an accidental detonation would be unlikely to ignite a world conflagration. The superpowers depend upon careful systems of bureaucratic checks and controls designed in part for exactly such a contingency. The maintenance of secure second-strike capabilities permits methodical inquiry rather than impulsive reaction. Here again, smaller powers, lacking protected capabilities and intricate verification devices, might be forced to react more hastily. The Moscow–Washington "hotline" was instituted after the Cuban missile crisis for the respective heads of government to communicate their intentions during times of tension. The hope was that an accident might not be taken as open hostility, and that a single firing might not burgeon into global destruction.

Despite faith in "fail-safe" systems, strategists continue to acknowledge the remote possibility of accidental nuclear launchings. For that reason Moscow and Washington have joined in an Agreement on Measures to Reduce the Risk of Outbreak of Nuclear War. Effective in 1971, this bilateral treaty calls upon the parties "to notify each other immediately in the event of an accidental, unauthorized or any other unexplained incident involving a possible detonation of a nuclear weapon which could create a risk of outbreak of nuclear war." They agree in such cases to take measures to render the weapons harmless. They also pledge to communicate with one another upon sighting unidentified incoming vehicles, and to notify one another in advance of missile tests that will extend beyond home territory in the direction of the other. To ease such communications, they entered into executive agreement to update the hotline by adding communications links through two or more telecommunications satellites.

These arrangements have not succeeded, however, in resolving the question of whether or not each new generation of delivery vehicles raises the prospects of unintended nuclear war. While some observers retain the faith that fail-safe measures are adequate, others are concerned that the speed with which missiles can round the globe leaves inadequate time for rational decisions about response. Furthermore, according to the skeptics, command and communications systems are imperfect and not wholly defensible. According to the Senate Armed Services Committee, for example, in an eighteen-month period from early 1979 through June 1980, American nuclear forces received no fewer than 3,703 alarms of in-coming nuclear attack, of which 147 were serious enough to require immediate evaluation. In addition, on the American side alone, there have been thirty-two accidents involving nuclear weapons, none of which resulted in a detonation. Some analysts argue, therefore, that the fail-safe measures are adequate, but others expect that the hair trigger alert required by new missile technologies and the probability of subsequent accidents steadily increase the probability of accidental or unintended nuclear war.[25]

Another popular fear is the Dr. Strangelove syndrome, or the fear of a perverse individual who, for reasons known only to himself, uses

25. For a recapitulation of these events and for a skeptical view of fail-safe systems, see particularly Arthur Macy Cox, *Russian Roulette: The Superpower Game* (New York: Time Books, 1982), Chapter I, "Accidental Nuclear War." Jonathan Schell, *The Fate of the Earth* (New York: Knopf, 1982), pp. 26–27, raises the possibility that one human, mechanical or electronic error could lead by chain of errors to unintended war.

military rank to launch an unauthorized attack on the enemy. Even the most careful psychological testing and training cannot, of course, guarantee that an anticommunist paranoiac on the American side, or an overzealous Soviet anti-imperalist, could not somehow gain access to the buttons. As a safeguard, the superpowers have installed elaborate multiple control systems, which require the coordinated acts of two or more persons at separate centers of decision to unshield nuclear weapons. Only a small group of people knows who operates the other button to the same weapon. In this way, unauthorized use of weapons of mass destruction would require a conspiracy of people who do not know one another's identities. Short of an all-out conspiracy, achievable probably only through a coup of the entire armed forces, the two-key system prevents unauthorized firings.

Still another danger is that of catalytic war, or unwanted war between superpowers, provoked by a calculating third party. This concept arose in popular literature in the early days of the atomic race, especially from the book (and later movie) *On the Beach,* in which a nervous third party prompted nuclear war between two superpowers. In the days of America's policy of massive retaliation, many Americans feared that a nervous European decision-maker might deliberately provoke war with the Soviet Union and force the United States to demonstrate the credibility of its defense doctrine. All in all, however, the vast increase in destructive potential makes it unlikely that any third party would provoke a war from which no nation could entirely escape.

But there is one type of nuclear threat over which governments have virtually no control: nuclear attack launched by terrorist or other nongovernmental actors. In recent years there has been growing concern that the basic science of nuclear weaponry is so well known that terrorist organizations might fall upon someone with the right background to provide them with crude nuclear devices. In addition, fears regarding the possible weapons-related consequences of reprocessing spent nuclear fuels are multiplied by the prospect of their falling into the hands of terrorists or revolutionaries. When the first known act of sabotage against a nuclear reactor occurred in France in early 1979, fears of clandestine access to nuclear fuel raised grave security questions about nuclear development.

Chemical and Biological Warfare

In addition to nuclear devices, missiles and weapons for land, sea and air warfare, arms designers have created a variety of weapons less well known but equally horrifying.

Chemical warfare consists of several methods of using chemical agents to poison, burn, blind, expose and otherwise incapacitate enemy troops. It has a long, and often colorful, history. The first known use was by Solon of Athens, who defeated the army of Kirrha in 600 B.C. by throwing bundles of hellebore roots into the enemy's water supply. While the enemy attempted to contend with the resulting diarrhea, Athenian troops marched in for the conquest. Other ancient uses involved leaving poisoned wine in evacuated camps, tossing venomous snakes into enemy ships and the use of poison for arrows and wells. Fire was used by Sparta as early as 429 B.C. in a mixture of pitch and sulphur used to ignite enemy cities. "Greek fire," first used in A.D. 350, acted as a primitive flame thrower by spurting burning liquid from a siphon. Smoke has been used since early times to seclude troop movements and naval maneuvers.

Chemicals have played a role in twentieth century wars, too. Teargas grenades were introduced by France during the First Wold War, and Germany responded by the full-scale use of lethal chlorine gas (contemplated, but not used, by the Union Army during the American Civil War). The United States fielded a Gas Regiment in the First World War, which launched as many as 2,000 cannisters in a single battle. In 1936 mustard gas was dropped from Italian planes onto Abyssinian troops in the conquest of Ethiopia, causing incapacitating burns to bare feet. Only a year later, Japan used toxic gases against Chinese troops. During the Second World War, in the battle against Japan, the United States advanced modern incendiary warfare with napalm—a soap-thickened petroleum that cannot be extinguished, capable of igniting human torches. In the Vietnam War, American troops experimented with induced forest firestorms using the same principle.

Though toxic gases were not used during the Second World War, German researchers happened upon discovery of the deadly "nerve gases," which cause paralysis of the motor nervous system. Through captured documents, the United States acquired the secret of sarin, while the Soviets seized a tabun plant. Either of these gases is lethal to a man if only a drop penetrates the skin. Contact causes instant nausea, vomiting, diarrhea, convulsions, respiratory paralysis and death in a few moments. These agents would be most effective in local warfare for population attrition. Like other gases, their battlefield use is limited by the liabilities of windshift and the possibilities of self-infliction.

A new category of non-lethal chemical methods is called the incapacitating agent, designed to cause temporary paralysis, blindness, dizziness and narcosis. The psychochemicals are a special category that have incapacitating mental effects such as paranoia, confusion, delirium, hallucinations, disorientation, giddiness or maniacal behavior. These can seriously alter any army's fighting capacity, its will, its speed of movement, its reaction time and other variables of ground warfare. General William M. Creasy, former chief chemical officer of the US Army, suggests that the future of warfare may lie in the psychochemicals.

The future of chemical agents for combat purposes is still under debate. There is strong sentiment for their uncategorical elimination, but others consider incapacitation preferable to slaughter. Proponents of their prohibition insist that the greatest danger is from the thought-controlling potentiality of the psychochemicals, opening new and incalculable opportunities for tyranny. But fire, incapacitating agents and defoliants have become so important to modern land armies that they are unlikely to be given up, especially when, with nuclear arms limitations, conventional arms are being restored to first priority. The flexibility, mobility and visibility of flame, defoliants and "incaps" are likely to give them the stature of conventional machine guns, especially in guerrilla and counterguerrilla warfare. They are not apt to vanish from the conventional arsenals of major powers.[26]

Biological warfare has horrors of its own. Often called germ warfare, it utilizes infectious agents. It is the deliberate inducement of disease, either by spreading bacteria or viral microbes, or by using their organic toxins. Though efforts have been undertaken sporadically since 1925 to outlaw these methods, not until 1972 was a multilateral treaty signed by states to that effect. Again, however, compliance is left to self-restraint and the possibility of investigation by the UN Security Council of alleged violations. Moreover, the Convention on the Prohibition of the Development, Production and Stockpiling of Bacteriological (Bacterial) and Toxin Weapons and their Destruction permits any state to withdraw from its obligations by three-month notification accompanied by a statement of the jeopardy to national interests that motivates the withdrawal. The same treaty defers chemical elimination to a future "objective," and stipulates only that outlawing biological weapons may also be a step toward prohibition of chemical weapons.

For much of the post-World War II period, the use of chemical agents in warfare has been rare, and of biological, non-existent. A major exception was the American use of defoliants in Vietnam, a process of spraying thick vegetation from above in order to kill the

26. United States Senate Subcommittee on Disarmament, *CBR Warfare* (Washington, D.C.: 1960); *Chemical Warfare of Special Significance to Civil Defense*, Civil Defense Technical Bulletin, TB-11-28; J. Leiberman, "Psychochemicals as Weapons," *Bulletin of the Atomic Scientists*, January 1962; "Biological and Chemical Warfare: An International Symposium," *Bulletin of the Atomic Scientists*, January 1960; Marcel Fetizon and Michel Magat, "The Toxic Arsenal," in Nigel Howard, editor, *Unless Peace Comes* (New York: Viking, 1968).

leaves and thus deprive the North Vietnamese of the ability to move men and materiel behind their camouflage. More recently, the United States has reported "unequivocal evidence" of the Soviet use of chemical and toxic weapons in Afghanistan and Southeast Asia.[27]

Other Developments

The focus upon developments in the nuclear field ought not to obscure other parallel advances in the conventional arsenals. The Vietnam War, like all others, refined the human ability to destroy. The United States, for example, applied electronic science to conventional war, especially for automated air warfare. Other innovations included weather modification to disrupt movement of enemy troops and goods, and "smart bombs," which are able to seek out specific targets and aim themselves by reciprocating signals. Fragmentation bombs were used to inject painful fishhooks into the skin so as to demoralize troops and strain the enemy's medical facilities. Bomb targeting devices were developed that detected humans in the dark of night, thus depriving the North Vietnamese of the cover of darkness.

The major powers have exchanged charges that they have encouraged small wars as a means of combat testing new military devices. For several months prior to the 1982 Israeli-Syrian war in Lebanon it was charged by Western sources that the Soviet Union was encouraging Syria to provoke a war in order to observe the combat effectiveness of new Soviet equipment. Similarly, Soviet sources claimed that the military suppliers of Argentina, particularly France, encouraged the invasion of the Falkland Islands in 1982 in order to test certain anti-ship weapons against the Royal Navy. Whether or not there were such conscious motives in these two cases is debatable; that new warring devices were unveiled is not.

The prospects for future arms seem limitless. Nuclear weapons may be miniaturized for movement by saboteurs, as plastic bombs are now used. Robot tanks will have multiple tactical uses, as will "kamikaze" bombers on suicide missions. Some writers envisage the use of anthropomorphic robots on the ground, within this century, to replace shock troops; and possibly even two-sided robot warfare. The robot may be the soldier of the future.

In addition, greater efforts at weather modification may have a role in future tactical warfare, both to slow the enemy through natural disaster and bad visibility, and to facilitate one's own tactics by clearing

27. *Science,* 9 April 1982, pp. 154–155.

techniques. Growing seismological understanding suggests that eventually it will also be possible to induce earthquakes in some regions.

Underwater and outer space zones will become more important. Undersea operatons are ideal because the physical properties of salt water impede the passage of detection impulses. If downward-pointing antiaircraft devices are circulated in space, the role of supra-atmospheric space may increase. Control of interplanetary space may determine control of airspace, even national airspace. Despite the fact that the United States and the Soviet Union have entered into treaties prohibiting the orbiting of nuclear devices in space (1967) and the placement of such weapons in or on the ocean floor beyond a twelve-mile national limit (1972), the military importance of both sea and space is steadily increasing, and is likely to continue to do so.[28]

Early in 1983, President Ronald Reagan instructed the Pentagon to begin immediately an investigation into the electronic weapons potential of American armed forces for the turn of the century. By the mid-1980s, plans were being readied to alter the foundations of the American defense system in a manner that would reduce reliance on nuclear deterrence and transfer it to laser and electronic technology. Observers around the world agreed on certain conclusions: (1) that although it sounds like science fiction, the probability of making such a transformation is high; (2) that success in this new effort would so alter strategic thinking and preparedness as to destabilize international tensions maximally; and (3) that because of American superiority in technological research, the transformation would measurably improve the position of the United States, perhaps at the risk of provoking the Soviet Union to arms prior to the deployment of new generations of American weapons.

The first solid evidence of America's preparedness to initiate the space-war generation occurred in mid–1983 with public disclosure of Pentagon plans to destroy a satellite in space. According to published reports, the plan was to arm an F-15 fighter craft with an explosive cylinder called a miniature homing device (MHV), and to fire the device at the upper reaches of the atmosphere. By electronic command, the MHV would seek out the target satellite and destroy it.[29] With knowledge that the Soviets were also working on advanced anti-satellite weapons (ASAT), the United States Air Force had already declared its intention of achieving superiority in space.[30]

28. For a scientific forecast of future weapons, see Howard, editor, *Unless Peace Comes.*

29. Fred Kaplan, "We're About to Launch a Costly and Crazy Arms Race in Space," *The Washington Post,* October 16, 1983, p. B1.

30. The first successful test of a Soviet ASAT occurred in June 1982, a test in which a killer missile was placed in a corrected orbit to seek and destroy a target satellite. See *SIPRI Yearbook, 1983,* pp. 437–439.

At about the same time, it became generally known that the United States was beginning electronics research, to be funded in 1985, for the invention and deployment of laser techniques such as anti-missile devices in space. These weapons would seek out and destroy missiles actually launched and in flight. Beyond being just another difficult-to-imagine advance in weapons technology, such weapons raise anew the strategy questions pertaining to first-strike capability and second-strike retaliation capability. While the stability of the nuclear arms race is founded on the principal that neither party will strike the other because of fear of retaliation, anti-missile weapons make a first strike more attractive to the initiating party. Such an attack against an adversary that does not have anti-missile instruments would enable the initiator to undertake a first strike and knock out much of the second party's retaliatory ability. Then the attacker could intercept and destroy those second-strike missiles that might be launched. Such a new generation of weapons, estimated in 1983 to cost about $27 billion for research and development, might potentially destabilize the nuclear arms race, make arms reduction impossible in the interim and possibly provoke military action.

War, Peace and the Arms Race

Thermonuclear war, deterrence, brinkmanship, ABM, MIRV, tactical nuclear weapons, committal strategy, counterforce, nuclear proliferation, finite deterrence, accidental war, catalytic war, incendiary weapons, nerve gas, incapacitating agents, psychochemicals, robot warfare—to many people, all this sounds like Dr. Strangelove's inventory of madness. To the ordinary person, these preparations add up to *less* security rather than more. What chance of peace is there when every nation is armed to the teeth, when a dozen different arms races of differing proportions are conducted simultaneously, when the best of science is turned to killing? Many people share Kant's view in *Perpetual Peace* that standing armies and arms races are inextricably linked to war, and that high levels of armament guarantee war rather than ensure against it.

But to statesmen, nuclear strategists and students of war the belief that nations fight because they have arms reverses history. Nations arm because they have conflicts with other states: conflicts over mutually exclusive goals cause war, not the maintenance of arms. The Cold War caused the arms race, since the incompatibility of potential objectives of the United States and the Soviet Union requires military preparedness. Only stable competition in arms prevents existing conflicts from erupting into war.

This conclustion does not, however, deny the wastefulness of arms races as measured both in economic cost and in nonproductive absorption of resources. "National strength," a nearly universal slogan, is easily sold to frightened populations. In addition, professional military elites want the most modern equipment available, in some cases if only for personal or service aggrandizement. As a result, a generous share of national resources is given by most countries to national defense, ranging from a low of less than 1 percent in Iceland to a high of over 20 percent of GNP in Israel and North Korea. These figures exclude many costs such as veterans' benefits and pensions. In total, the world devotes over 7 percent of total annual production to military expenditures.

Contrasted with critical social indicators, these amounts loom even larger. While most of the southern hemisphere seeks to modernize, and while most of the industrialized world searches for remedies to the social problems created by technology, the world's governments go on spending billions of dollars per year more on military expenditures than on such things as public health, foreign economic assistance and international peacekeeping. In 1974, world expenditures on education exceeded the cost of the arms race by a slight margin, and for only the first time. They do no longer.

The human cost of this proliferation of arms is staggering. A single modern jet fighter, such as the McDonnell Douglas F15, costs as much as a community hospital. A single second-generation nuclear submarine of the Trident class costs the equivalent of five hundred schools. One modern nuclear-powered aircraft carrier equals four years' budget of the United Nations! American ABMs, if deployed in the numbers originally planned, would equal the cost of 2.5 million small homes. These costs are increasingly unacceptable in industrialized economies with constant growth in public revenue; but they are wholly unbearable in the poor countries which, ironically, are now increasing their military budgets the most rapidly.

Arms Control and Disarmament

Should arms races be controlled? If so, how? The answers to these questions may be critical to the human future. With respect to the nuclear race, have we reached the point of diminishing returns? At this point, each new increment of power is not only vastly more expensive than its predecessor, but buys relatively less security than previous developments. If so, what is the sense of undergoing the expense and the potential destabilization generated by further enlargement of nuclear stockpiles and development of more sophisticated vehicles? Does the respectability of membership in the nuclear club portend proliferation despite treaties to the contrary? Does the temptation among nonnuclear powers to enter into the club because of lingering regional disputes raise the prospect of future nuclear blackmail and, with it, increased regional instability? In short, does the continuation of arms races, and the strategic nuclear arms race in particular, absorb more human and material resources than is now justified? Do arms contests prevent or delay peaceful transformation of the international system?

There is scarcely a student of public affairs who does not fault the logic of arms races on one or more of these bases. For those who find such competition important enough to exceed even treatment of social problems, the fear of nuclear proliferation is a major concern. Others lament the massive expenditures for small gains in security which thus serve to postpone correction of social inequities. Still others fear that the price of nonproliferation may be increased nuclear protection of many states by a few; and to ensure credibility of these defenses, there may be a greater impetus to brinkmanship. To reduce arms, a particular party must first build more in order to have negotiating advantages, though this increase may itself delay political agreement until the other party catches up, thus prompting yet another turn of the upward spiral. However, regardless of what position one may take on the value of arms and their costs relative to other needs, arms control and disarmament are on everyone's mind—save, perhaps, for a few unthinking profiteers.

From the earliest attempts at disarmament at the beginning of this century, three principal motives for limiting arms races have been recognized: (1) the desire to reduce the likelihood of war; (2) the desire to decrease the amount of destruction that would occur if war were to break out; and (3) the desire to reduce the economic cost of defense. Secondary objectives include attempts to adjust the international power distribution by establishing permanent military relativities, and adjusting the number of effective military powers and the number of alliance systems. Each of these objectives is directly related to the structural characteristics of the international system. Finally, behind all other reasons for arms control is the desire of governments to maintain nothing less than military equality with adversaries and, where possible, a slight advantage.

If "disarmament" is thought of in grand terms—as the dismantling of all weapons, the stilling of munitions industries and the total forswearing of the sovereign right to arm for national defense—then it is, indeed, a radical concept designed to alter the basic nature of the international system. In practical fact, however, twentieth-century attempts at arms control have never been this ambitious. Their objective has been the more conservative goal of managing arms races in such a way as to provide stability at the lowest possible price. Some have emphasized qualitative aspects of armaments (attempting to limit progress in the technological level and total destructive capability), while others have concentrated on quantitative measures (the number of weapons deployed). Among the latter, some agreements have anticipated future arms deployment and have set limits for the future, while others have tried to reduce the number already in place. For the most part, strategic arms limitation has emphasized quantitative controls of future deployments.

The first Strategic Arms Limitation Treaty (SALT I) is illustrative. Through this instrument, the United States and the Soviet Union agreed in 1972 to absolute ceiling numbers of ICBMs, deployed nuclear warheads and multiple independently targeted reentry vehicles, or MIRVs. They also agreed to limit antiballistic missile sites to two each, a frank recognition of their faith in second-strike strategy at that time.[31] Quite obviously, the effort here is to prevent the strategic arms race from becoming still more threatening, still more horrifying and still more expensive. Rather than reduce their respective arsenals, the two parties agreed only to limit the upward spiral.

Proportional reduction of nuclear weapons is far more complex. The variety of weaponry, the distances over which warheads can be delivered, the inaccessibility of some weapons to detection and surveillance—these problems and others vastly complicate mutual reduction. To make matters worse, neither side is eager to enter into negotiations while substantially ahead. Thus parity seems to be the ideal negotiating posture, but it probably has never existed. The result has been to approach nuclear arms limitation item by item, or on the basis of direct tradeoffs. It was formerly believed, for example, that the United States might decline to deploy ABMs if the Soviets would not proceed with MIRV. As timing and strategies dashed hopes for such an agreement, each party proceeded to deploy both ABMs and MIRVs. The SALT I agreements are the result.

Together, changes in strategic thinking (such as renewed interest in first-strike strategy) and development of weapons technology since SALT I made SALT II an even more difficult undertaking. The technological gap between the United States and the Soviet Union has narrowed considerably, and both sides are emphasizing offensive strat-

31. This faith has been reiterated several times. For example, former Secretary of Defense Harold Brown: ". . .the absence of a widely deployed ABM system makes for stability." *The New York Times,* January 18, 1981.

Anti-nuclear demonstration in New York, 1979.

Source Robert Gumpert/© 1979 Black Star

egy in planning for new developments. The increased MIRV potential of each side, the launching of the new generation of Trident nuclear submarines by the United States, the availability of cruise missiles to the United States, and the confusion of whether or not a new Soviet-American strategic agreement will negatively affect the security of Western Europe (theater balances are not addressed in SALT I) all contribute to a new negotiating and political environment. Furthermore, American relations with Turkey and Iran have fluctuated to the point where access to tracking facilities to monitor Soviet missile development is in constant jeopardy. A further complication is added by an apparent intelligence coup by the Soviet Union in acquiring copies of the design by which the United States intends to survey Soviet compliance with any new agreement.

The détente atmosphere which enabled the Nixon administration to negotiate SALT I and the Carter administration to negotiate SALT II had vanished by the time Ronald Reagan assumed the United States presidency. Furthermore, Soviet adventures in Afghanistan, the imposition of martial law in Poland, and American conservative dislike of SALT II (Reagan and others thought it advantageous to the Soviet Union and disadvantageous to the West) all combined to terminate the SALT II process. Never ratified by the Senate, Reagan withdrew it from consideration and announced a new arms limitation policy. When arms limitation talks resumed in 1981, they did so under the name START, or Strategic Arms Reduction Talks. This was more than a mere change in name, for the aim of the talks from the American viewpoint was not only to limit the upward spiral, but to begin the process of reducing the number of deployed strategic arms. Later, by Senate inspiration, a new gambit was offered: the so-called "build-down," a system of arms reduction in which two missiles would be dismantled for each new one put in place.[32] The eventual goal of American negotiations is the "zero-zero option," the phased and eventual mutual reduction to no nuclear weapons. The Soviet Union views the American position as one designed to undo the balance created by SALT I, and a disguise for an American superiority.

Central to the Reagan strategy, however, was the prior Soviet-American agreement to separate the START negotiations from those regarding intermediate-range nuclear forces (INF) in the European theater. The MIRV discussions, in turn, were based on the supposition that the United States would be prepared to deploy in Europe more than 500 new-generation Cruise and Pershing II missiles, either to counter the Soviet deployment of SS-20 rockets or to achieve their removal in return for a promise not to deploy Pershing II and Cruise missiles. The Soviets, in turn, refused to proceed with the START negotiations until the theatre weapons question had been resolved. Thus by the end of 1983, three sets of talks had commenced—START on global strategic issues, INF on European theatre weapons, and MIRV on the mutual and balanced reduction of conventional forces—and progress in START and MIRV awaited events at INF, although officially START and MIRV were to be conducted simultaneously.

32. Alton Frye, "Strategic Build-Down: A Context for Restraint," *Foreign Affairs*, Winter 1983-84, pp. 293–317.

Verification of Compliance

Even though governments might enter into arms-control agreements in good faith, the need to *verify* compliance with such agreements is a paramount problem. If obligations are carried out by only one state, the other state's opportunity for blackmail is unlimited. This is regarded as a problem unique to the nuclear era, but it is not. Unilateral failure in convention reduction might produce such instability as to tempt the stronger. There is considerable likelihood that the threat here is greater than in noncompliance with nuclear control or reduction agreements, since both the USA and the USSR have sufficient deterrent capability to tolerate even sizable imbalances in strategic potential. But if the two should arrange an agreement on mutual and balanced (conventional) force reductions for Europe, and only one party were to comply, the danger of war through temptation might be increased.

On the nuclear side, the problem of verification is even more difficult. Ships, tanks, troops, air bases and so on are more accessible to counting than are strategic submarines and hardened missile sites. In addition, even though exposed delivery vehicles may be counted with some accuracy, the problem of counting warheads and estimating their megatonnage remains. How many missiles does a submarine carry? How many warheads does each bear? What is their total explosive potential? Similar problems arise with respect to hardened missiles.

Diplomats and scientists have shared the problem of perfecting verification systems. Early in the atomic age, the United States and the Soviet Union exchanged ideas for detecting atomic tests. These included on-site inspection plans involving neutral personnel and the use of "black boxes," or seismographic stations, which could be monitored for explosions and estimates of yield. Other plans included "open skies," in which the nuclear states would permit one another to enter national airspace for photoreconnaissance flights. None of these proposals ever materialized.

Modern technology has resolved much of the verification problem. The participants in the nuclear arms race have tracked one another's missiles firings, and have been able to estimate rocket thrust. From this information each has been able to estimate the amount of nuclear power capable of being delivered by specific missiles systems. The United States knows, for example, that the successful testing and deployment of the giant SS-9 rocket by the Soviet Union represented MIRV potential. By the same token, the Soviet Union knows the lift potential of the Minuteman II and the Poseidon II. Furthermore, by orbiting reconnaissance satellites, each party is able to monitor the construction of missile sites, and to determine satisfactorily the number of missiles poised for firing. ABMs are easily detectable from above because of the huge radar complexes that they require. About the only important thing technology is unable to determine is the momentary location of nuclear submarines.

What is it, technically, that verification seeks? There are four general objectives. First, each party wishes to be satisfied with the other's compliance with immediate obligations of the treaty, such as dismantling, termination of site construction or closing of bases. Second, each party needs to know that the other is not undertaking to replace what has been removed. Third, each wants satisfaction that the other has not merely moved certain instruments to other places and concealed them from surveillance. Finally, each wants demonstrated assurance that remaining forces are what they are said to be. Therefore, verification of four objectives must be achieved: *initial obligation, nonreplacement, nonconcealment* and *remainders.*[33]

The problem of *enforcement* of arms control and arms limitation agreements is even more difficult politically than that of verification. If two states agree to limit their arms and only one complies, then it is difficult for the weaker to enforce the agreement against the stronger. Ideally, therefore, enforcement ought to be left to some neutral agent that has both the political capability to enforce agreements and the military wherewithal. Yet imagine states giving over to some other party or institution authority greater than their own, and military power superior to their own even though they are capable of creating more and better! To expect the United States and the Soviet Union to vest the UN, for example, with both the political power to order sanctions against a great power and independent nuclear capability, is politically naïve. Hence international arms agreements have traditionally left to states the privilege of "national means of enforcement." Often implicit in reluctance to negotiate reduction of arms is the argument that such reduction would minimize ability to enforce compliance against a treaty partner that violates its obligations.

Since every arms race is tied to a political context, arms reduction and political thaw are interdependent. Where favorable political opportunity is lacking, most progress toward arms reduction is dictated by cost factors. In 1899, Tsar Nicholas of Russia convened the First Hague Conference, not to negotiate a new political order for Europe, but because he felt economically incapable of competing in arms development with Germany. Likewise, the American "return to nor-

33. Hedley Bull, *The Control of the Arms Race,* 2nd ed. (New York: Praeger, 1965), p. xix. For verification problems under SALT, see Stuart A. Cohen, "SALT Verification: the Evolution of Soviet Views and Their Meaning for the Future," *ORBIS,* Fall 1980, pp. 657–83.

malcy" after the First World War was motivated largely by budgetary fatigue, coupled with the desire to retreat from power politics. The SALT I agreements arose from mutual Soviet-American desire to control the costs of yet another spiral in the race between offensive and defensive missiles. The abortive SALT II was likewise inspired in part by economic considerations, but was complicated by the question of whether or not it would provide sufficient safeguards for Western security. The European anxiety over this issue was political: given the Soviet build-up, were the circumstances of the political context such as to justify marginal changes, through a treaty of self-denial, in the strategic balance of the theater? Western European endorsement of the START and INF negotiations faces the same question, and rests upon the assumption that if the talks fail, Pershing II and Cruise missiles will provide deterrence against the Soviet Union for the remainder of the century.

The United States and the Soviet Union seem caught in a policy dilemma. While they negotiate arms limitation agreements, they forge ahead with ever-advancing weapons technology and, at the same time, transfer modern arms to other governments in an effort to use the threat of force as a rationale for regional military stability. So far as the strategic arms race is concerned, weapons development becomes both the cause and the consequence of agreement. For while each new weapons system on one side may promote further development on the other, it also signals the need to bring the upward spiral under control. But this is to look at arms limitation as nothing more than a technical problem. Indeed, the technical problems probably lend themselves to resolution more readily than do the political and diplomatic problems. Just as Albert Einstein once remarked that scientific problems are easier to solve than are social scientific problems, so too effective control of arms development depends upon the evolution of an East-West political context congenial to arms reduction. This serves to accentuate the dilemma of arms races and arms limitation: as strategic arms limitation depends in part upon cordial political contexts, so too is it hoped that temporary management of the technical aspects of arms control will contribute to the evolution of such an environment.

National Perceptions of the Balance of Terror

The American Perception

Popular opinion about the balance of terror in the United States is sharply divided. Those who object to American participation insist that the arms race is unjustifiably costly, both absolutely and in relation to other needs. Each new generation of arms is more expensive than is justified by the minimal gains in security; and each new upward spiral may accentuate insecurity. Furthermore, the critics ask, are official assessments of need built on misperceptions? Are the nation's legitimate interests so vitally challenged as to require such exorbitant extremes to preserve them? Critics farther to the left wonder if such levels of arms are not maintained simply to safeguard less legitimate interests.

The official view is markedly different. It holds that in addition to the need for strategic balance, military threats to U.S. interests are ever-present. American foreign interests have been targets of China and the Soviet Union, which sought to divide the Western allies, to undermine confidence in American leadership and the American economy and to seize territories and governments not vigorously defended by the United States. Only the defense of Berlin and the resolute interventions in the Korean and Vietnam wars taught these foes that Washington will not tolerate encroachments on its interests. Establishment of the North Atlantic Treaty Organization, the Truman Doctrine (determination to prevent the spread of Soviet influence), and incorporation of Japan and West Germany in defense alliances were the types of actions that signaled to the Kremlin an intent to resist challenge to American interests.

But there was another lesson as well. Soviet threats dramatized the need not only for intense political relations and institution building among allies, but for impressive arming. Only the ability to signal the Soviet Union, with credible threat, that the use of their arms would bring about massive retaliation, could insure the Allies against impediments to the founding or restoration of democratic political institutions. Arms policy was coupled with the "export of democracy," and provided the umbrella under which the US could "help others to help themselves." If the Soviet Union proceeded to greater threats with improved weapons, the the US would improve its weapons. Each new Soviet development demanded American response: the Soviet Union was responsible for fueling the strategic arms race, through its combined political threats and strategic capability.

The interpretation of Soviet intentions as villainous abated only slightly with the death of Joseph Stalin, and Khrushchev's new policy of peaceful coexistence and de-Stalinization. But the tone did change. With the exception of rare direct confrontations (such as the Cuban missile crisis), the Soviet-American arms race began to yield to the need for rational policies of stable deterrence. The lessening of political tension did not result, however, in bilateral willingness to reduce stockpiles. Before such events could take place, a new factor arose: the prospect of China, with its immense potential power, as a nuclear state in enmity with both Washington and Moscow. The US was finally obliged to acknowledge that there did not exist a communist monolith, that the threats of Moscow and of Peking were politically and strategically distinct.

By the end of the 1970s, some of the uncertainties that dominated American strategic thinking had been better illuminated, while others seemed even move vexing. The sudden accord with China and the friendly Chinese attitude toward NATO substantially reduced American strategic concern with the nuclear capability of the Asian partner. In contrast to the preceding three decades, China now encouraged a strong American presence in Asia, in part for reasons of regional stability, in part as a deterrent to Soviet political offensives and in part to reduce the probability of Japan developing nuclear weapons.

But if the China puzzle in American nuclear strategy seemed to have abated, the Soviet build-up in Europe and its greatly improved weapons technology revewed the challenge to American strategic thinkers. European opposition to SALT II (which never became a ratified treaty) owing to the potential effect of a global strategic arms agreement upon the balance of the European theater, led to division regarding new weapons systems. To be sure, since SALT I the United States had improved its MIRV potential and its accumulated nuclear warheads, and it had constructed cruise missiles and begun the Trident program. In all of this, the cost of defense was skyrocketing, and those political forces that regarded the strategic balance as stable and durable were calling for reduced defense spending. On the other hand, competing voices argued that Soviet military modernization presented a grave challenge to American security as well as European, and that new weapons were called for urgently. Only on the issue of proliferation of nuclear weapons to additional nations was there solidarity, and the president and congress together attempted to take global leadership in preventing such proliferation. Meanwhile, America's arms transfers to Third World countries continued, both in order to maintain regional balances and to force restraint upon the Soviet Union's client states throughout the world.

With the resumption of the Cold War in the 1980s, Washington abandoned all détente-related notions of coexistence with the Soviet Union without still more modernization of its armed forces and, more specifically, its strategic forces. Furthermore, in face of an uncertain Sino-Soviet détente, fears grew that Soviet missiles pointed at Asia might be retargeted at Japan. This fear resulted in a Western declaration of intent to defend Japan against Soviet aggression. The declaration was the most important outcome of the 1983 Williamsburg,

Virginia economic summit meeting of the Western trading partners. Soviet deployment to Syria of SS-21 missiles, potentially nuclear-tipped, also raised the threat of nuclear war in the Middle East in 1983.

The global circumstances under which the START negotiations commenced were, accordingly, severely strained. And the situation was further complicated by the imminence of anti-satellite techniques that threatened intelligence systems and potential devices for mutual verification of arms reduction agreements. Finally, both the United States and the Soviet Union were aware of the vulnerability of their communications, control and command systems, known in the United States as C^3. Washington was aware that the speed and probable accuracy of new Soviet weapons exceeded the capabilities of C^3 to ensure safe and secure responses; the Pentagon was aware that even a single nuclear explosion could destroy the delicate electronic and computer-programmed basis of American defenses and retaliatory capability.[34]

Given these immense problems, the White House chose to pursue two lines of arms negotiations. The first was START, designed to replace the scrapped SALT II, dealing with global strategic issues. The second, called the INF talks, addressed the immediate security questions related to the balance of intermediate-range nuclear forces within Europe. With the demise of détente, the Soviet Union had commenced the deployment of SS-20 intermediate range, nuclear-tipped missiles targeted at Western Europe. The United States intended either to counter this deployment with 572 of its own Cruise and Pershing II missiles, or to secure the dismantling of the SS-20s in return for an agreement not to deploy Cruise and Pershing IIs. From the viewpoint of the Reagan administration, this strategy was necessitated by Soviet refusal to discontinue the deployment of SS-20s. Washington would negotiate only when its military technology put it in a position of either parity with, or superiority over, the Soviet Union.

Contrary to its professed interest in a peaceful balance resulting in mutual deterrence, the Soviet Union has shown no sustained evidence that its strategic policy is based on anything but Khrushchev's 1960 declaration that the world would eventually know that "capitalism is the source that breeds wars and would no longer tolerate that system, which brings sufferings and disasters to mankind." The goal of the Kremlin, in the official American view, is not peace or mutual deterrence; it is a strategic military superiority for the purpose of world

34. See, for example, Jonathan B. Tucker, "Strategic Command and Control Vulnerabilities: Dangers and Remedies," ORBIS, Winter 1983, pp. 941–963.

enslavement. Military build-up in the last decade has not only expanded Soviet influence in areas contiguous to the USSR's borders; it has given Soviet forces virtual worldwide basing capability in many areas previously allied to the West: Cuba, Central America, Ethiopia, Yemen, Vietnam, etc.[35] Today's Soviet Union is not the country of Lenin and Marxist-Leninist ideologists; it is a nation of imperialists ruthlessly directing economic potential to a war machine with global reach.[36] The American role in the balance of terror is a necessary corollary to this threat.

The Soviet Perception

Far from accepting the role of antagonist in world politics and in the strategic arms race, the Kremlin seeks to defend its island of socialism from capitalist encirclement. Bolstering their traditional fears of exposed borders, the Soviets have experienced overt attempts by Japan and the West to bring down their power. Japanese and American landings in Siberia at the close of the First World War, shortly after the Bolshevik Revolution of 1917, were historic signals of the need to maintain rigorous defense against the capitalist industrialized states. More recently, American efforts after the Second World War to influence Soviet policy in Eastern Europe through atomic monopoly have accentuated the need for vigilance. NATO in particular, and the string of anti-Soviet alliances in general, added further to the need. Incorporation of West Germany into NATO in apparent violation of the Potsdam Agreement of 1945 was the ultimate sign of American intentions of maintaining anti-Soviet tension throughout Europe; the Kremlin responded by forming the Warsaw Pact. Soviet arms policy, far from being the cause of the balance of terror, is a response to the capitalist (specifically American) political and strategic threats.

The Soviet view is confused by questions pertaining to the current status of basic assumptions underlying both SALT I and SALT II. During these talks, each party assumed that the other would continue to build its strategy based upon the second-strike philosophy, *i.e.*, that neither would build systems principally for first surprise nuclear strike, but would base its strategy, instead, upon a plan of retaliation against a first strike. But late in the Carter administration and during the Reagan administration, it appeared that the nuclear utilization theo-

35. See two publications of the US Department of Defense: *Annual Report to the Congress, Fiscal Year 1984*, pp. 27–28, and *Soviet Military Power, 1983,* Chapter VI, "Soviet Power Projection."
36. Edward N. Luttwak, *The Grand Strategy of the Soviet Union* (New York: St. Martin's Press, 1983).

rists (NUTs) had gained ascendency over the second-strike philosophers, the advocates of mutually assured destruction (MADs). Evidence is obvious in several ways: (1) the Carter and Reagan administrations' belief that nuclear war is survivable, hence the risk of second-strike retaliation against an effective first strike may be worth taking; (2) American plans to test and deploy anti-satellite weapons might indicate American intent to prevent the Soviet Union from verifying American claims of retaining the second-strike philosophy; (3) the new generation of medium-range American weapons were sufficiently swift and accurate over intermediate distances to provide an effective first strike, at least within the European theater; and (4) open discussion in the United States about deploying anti-missile lasers in space constituted a break with the SALT notion of a bilateral restriction on anti-missile instruments as a means of stabilizing the nuclear arms race on second-strike premises.

In the mid-1980s' Soviet perception, these evidences belie American protestations about the desire for peace through a stable arms race. In practice, these protestations are a cloak for bringing fundamental change to the arms race by using new weapons technologies to shift from the trusted second-strike basis to the suspect first-strike strategy. This, in Moscow's view, is deliberate destabilization of the nuclear arms race for purposes of superiority and domination.

From the Soviet perspective, the failure of détente occurred simultaneously with the growth of anti-Americanism in the Third World. In Central America and the Caribbean, in Asia and the Middle East, Third World reaction to American imperialism and to capitalism has demonstrated the failure of *pax Americana* and called for Soviet protection against forceful American colonialism. What America calls Soviet aggression, then, is no more than world socialism coming to the aid of those who are determined never again to be colonized by capitalist exploiters. While Washington claims to want peace through mutual deterrence, the American negotiating position in START and at INF is one of demanding unilateral Soviet reductions as a contribution to eventual American superiority. Given the speed and accuracy of American strategic weapons, particularly in the intermediate range of the European theater, Soviet diligence is required in maintaining a stable balance.

The role of China in the Soviet perception is a changing one. After twenty-five years of hostility and threat of war, during which the Soviet Union partially protected its Asian borders with long-range missiles pointed at Chinese targets, there is now a move toward détente. Ironically, while during the Soviet-American détente the principal strategic preoccupation was with China, the new prospect of a Sino-Soviet détente, together with a new fear of American strategic intentions, results in a renewed preoccupation with the European borders. However, while there is a serious possibility of direct NATO security co-operation with China, the two-continents problem continues to burden Soviet defense planning.

American motives were never more evident than in the months following the Soviet destruction of a Korean airliner, which had entered militarily sensitive Soviet air space on an American intelligence mission conducted under the cover of commercial aviation. Washington, President Reagan in particular, used the occasion to brand the Soviet leadership as savages and as an excuse for destroying the atmosphere in which START was to have resumed and INF negotiations were to have commenced. In Washington, where madness had taken over, a new effort to achieve an imbalance of terror hazardous to the Soviet Union had been initiated behind a campaign to discredit the Soviet Union as a diplomatic partner, at a time when the imminent deployment of a new generation of missiles called, as never before, for guarantees of strategic stability.

The Perceptions of America's Major Allies

Caught between the need for security and the desire to liberate themselves from American domination, Washington's principal allies have an ambivalent outlook on the balance of terror. Yet there are considerable differences in their attitudes, owing particularly to their geographic locations, the external imperatives that guide their foreign policies and the coincidence of their interests with those of the United States.

Japan Throughout the history of the nuclear arms race, Japan has played the paradoxical role of being one of the most intensely interested states but one of the least involved. Its interest results in part from having been the only country to have been victimized by atomic bombs, and in part because it is located in close proximity to Korea, China, the Soviet Pacific possessions including Sakhalin Island, and Southeast Asia. The superpower dispute, the Korean War and the Vietnam War, together with the long containment of China by the United States, all threatened the possibility of nuclear action. Japan's vulnerability resulted both from geographic location and from the use of Japanese territory as staging bases for military activity and materiel. Yet because of its close ties to the American security system, Japan has not been a principal participant in international military politics; and because of constitutional prohibitions, it does not participate at all in the nuclear balance of terror. Despite its anxieties regarding superpower strategies in Asia, Japan has, for the most part, profited from the Soviet-American arms race and from global bipolarity.

More recently, however, the Japanese outlook has shifted. American withdrawal from the mainland of Asia after the Vietnam War, together with the uncertainties introduced to national security by the Nixon Doctrine, necessitates a larger measure of self-dependence. Furthermore, since Japan has enjoyed a commanding role in international industrial trade, the United States has insisted that it cannot continue indefinitely to provide Japan's protection. On the other hand, the Sino-American détente has enabled Japan to enter into a belated World War II peace agreement with China that was followed by a treaty of friendship and commerce, both diminishing the security concern for China and opening new economic opportunities for both import (raw materials and fuels) and exports (industrial goods). Despite closer economic ties with the Soviet Union, the growing Soviet military presence in Asia imposes new security imperatives. Given all these circumstances, including the uncertain reliability of the nuclear umbrella, Japan has agreed to undertake a three-fold increase in its military expenditures exclusively for use in domestic territories and territorial waters.

Nonetheless, Japan is not a participant in the strategic nuclear race and is unlikely to become one.[37] Because it is limited to conventional armed forces, it sees the strategic race as wasteful; and because it must rely upon a potentially unreliable American nuclear deterrent, it regards the race as threatening in the extreme.

Western Europe Proximity to the Warsaw Pact nations, the degree of American security and economic domination, and progressive reestablishment of Western Europe as a vital world center all contribute to the maturation of the attitude concerning the global balance of terror. Through the years following the Second World War, American responses to what Europe perceived as a Soviet military threat were a welcome instrument of stabilization, one that permitted the gradual resurgence of economic activity and the integration of Western Europe.

During the détente period of the 1970s, however, Western Europeans found themselves Cold War weary and resistant to additional increases in military spending. They were happy to have more American security support and less American economic interference. But

37. For a view that accepts the possibility of an eventual Japanese entrance into the nuclear arms business, see Michael Pillsbury, "A Japan Card?", *Foreign Policy*, Winter 1978/79.

with the resurgence of the Soviet-American Cold War in the 1980s, attitudes changed markedly, though they are still divided. In face of Soviet deployment of SS-20 theater (intermediate range) missiles, the Western European governments all endorsed a decision made by NATO in 1979 to deploy 572 new-generation American missiles starting at the end of 1983. This endorsement resulted in part from the election of conservative governments in Britain and Germany, the two countries where the initial deployments were to occur; but it was also endorsed by socialist governments in France and Italy, for which subsequent missiles are destined. Throughout Europe this decision encountered resistence from anti-nuclear organizations, but the governments remained resolute.

The perceived new threat also forced a change of position in France, which previously wanted to build a joint Anglo-French nuclear deterrent in order to become nuclear-independent of Washington. Soviet aggression in Afghanistan, manipulation of politics in Poland and deployment of intermediate range nuclear devices in Europe stilled this movement. In Socialist Italy, where fully half of the initial Cruise missiles were to be deployed, there was steadfast resolve to move forward as planned. The smaller Western European states, particularly Belgium and the Netherlands, are able to bear such a small portion of the cost of defense that the American nuclear umbrella became more important than at any time in fifteen years. Western European governments uniformly endorsed the MIRV and START talks only on the supposition that SS-20 missiles would either be eliminated as a result of the talks, or would be balanced by American Pershing II and Cruise missiles.

But if the Western European governments were solidly behind NATO's deployment strategy regarding theater weapons, public support was not. As the time for deployment neared at the end of 1983, massive peace and anti-nuclear rallies occurred throughout Western Europe, particularly near the sites of deployment in Germany and Britain. Activists viewed the deployment of new generations of theater weapons to be a vast escalation of the possibility that Western Europe would eventually become a nuclear battleground. Advocates of deployment charged the activists with having been duped by Soviet propaganda, a charge that sounded particularly hollow when worldwide revulsion at the Soviet firing on a Korean civilian airliner failed to reduce the intensity of resistance to deployment. More influential, it seemed, was Western European reaction, in this instance both governmental and public, to the American invasion of Grenada. In the eyes of many Europeans, this action equated American foreign policy tactics with Soviet, thus redoubling the demand that new missiles not raise the threat of nuclear confrontation in Europe.

There is one common attitude between the governments and people in Western Europe regarding the nuclear arms race. The arms race has enabled the United States to enjoy unequaled scientific and technological advances, improving the American standard of living and enabling American manufacturers and the American defense establishment to perpetuate Western Europe's dependence upon America. Therefore, it is fitting and proper that the United States should carry the principal expense burden of NATO's side of the balance of terror.

Canada In contrast to Japan and Western Europe, Canada has been relatively removed from the balance of terror. Though it participated in the Korean War and is a member of NATO, it has avoided major military commitments and has chosen instead to be a significant participant in United Nations peacekeeping efforts. While maintaining a small but relatively modern defense force, Canada has avoided the nuclear option and has chosen to divert funds that might normally have gone to defense into economic development.

In part the Canadian position is a fortuitous result of proximity to the United States. Even disregarding for the moment Ottawa's efforts to maintain friendly relations with Moscow and its relatively early recognition of China, it remains true that the closeness of Canada to the United States, and particularly to its industrial heartland, has lent a strategic immunity to Canadian policy. But this proximity is a double-edged sword. For like Western Europe, Canada has felt the penetrating effects of American industries, and of the technological and industrial superiority that the balance of terror has enabled American manufacturers to develop. Thus, while Canada has remained aloof from the balance of terror as an active participant, it has quietly deplored its wastefulness and with increasing vigor resisted its domestic economic consequences. In particular, the wastefulness that the balance of terror imposes upon North American natural resources now threatens to force upon Canada a continental allocation policy, one that will further erode national sovereignty. To Canada, then, while the balance of terror may have produced coincidental security, it has resulted in economic relations with its continental neighbor that have been injurious to national self-esteem and integrity. Thus while intact territorially, Canada perceives itself to have been a casualty of the balance of terror through indirect and continental economic exploitation.

The Chinese Perception

Until recently, the Century of Humiliation and the growth of power under Mao Tse-tung shaped the Chinese view of the balance of terror. Hemmed in by the Soviet Union to the north and America and its allies to the west and south, China experienced a modern history of containment. The achievement of nuclear combat potential was the sole means by which Peking was able to demand recognition from both Washington and Moscow. If political advantage is a product of equality in arms, China must compete to gain full political potential in the international system. In this age of military technology, the ability to field millions of combat troops is no match in global security issues for strategic capabilities.

Both domestic and international events began to erode this viewpoint. At home, the death of Mao, the conclusion of the Cultural Revolution and the implementation of a careful diplomatic and economic plan for the modernization of the state resulted in a new view of relations with both the Soviet Union and the West. The international scene, too, changed. The conclusion of the Vietnam War and the withdrawal of the United States from the Asian mainland as a military power; the Sino-American normalization; China's participation in NATO military affairs; the growing prospects of a Sino-Soviet détente—all of these international events have combined with new internal perspectives to alter virtually all vital Chinese interests. The emphasis now is on economic development, industrialization, improved education, international trade and cooperation, and diplomatic leadership of the Third World. While Peking and Moscow warily test the feasibility of their new cooperation, China's closeness to NATO makes it an informal party to a global strategy of nuclear defense against the Soviet Union.

Despite its status as a nuclear state, China feels strongly that responsibility for global arms control lies principally with the United States and the Soviet Union. At the Special Session of the United Nations General Assembly on disarmament in 1978, China held firmly to the view that the lesser nuclear powers are forced by the Soviet-American arms race to make an effort to keep up, hopeless though that effort might be, in order to prevent a division of the world by threat and nuclear blackmail.

The uncertainty surrounding President Reagan's policy regarding Taiwan has introduced new anxieties to China's attitude about the balance of terror. Never happy with America's continued arms sales to Taiwan, indications by Reagan that an effort would be made to conduct normal diplomatic relations simultaneously with China and

Taiwan were met in China with protest. Fears were deepened early in 1981 when the Dutch government announced its intention of selling advanced conventional submarines to Taiwan. This action prompted China to announce sanctions against the Netherlands, including a boycott of the port of Rotterdam, to which nearly 300 Chinese ships sail annually, and a discontinuation of Dutch oil explorations on Chinese territory.[38] Should the Reagan Taiwan policy interrupt the growth of Chinese-American relations, new arms policies might result in Peking, despite the clear preference of the Chinese government that the decade of the 1980s be one of domestic economic modernization.

The Third World Perception

Faced with the costly and difficult problems of modernization in a world where the rich get richer and the poor get poorer, the Third World nations deplore the unproductive squandering of natural, human and economic resources. The balance of terror fits especially into this vision, inasmuch as it has absorbed a trillion dollars during the past quarter century.

But it is not merely the cost of the strategic arms race that is objectionable. Added to it is the unjustifiable vigor with which the United States and the Soviet Union deny their economic capability to assist fledgling governments, or even to aid old and trusted, though impoverished, friends. The Third World has been a casualty of the nuclear era in still another way. At the height of the Cold War, when both the United States and the Soviet Union sought the allegiance of newly independent nations, their aid programs were considerably larger than at the present time. Since then, the strategic race has stabilized and the expensive quest for friends among the ideologically uncommitted nations has become less competitive. As a result, development assistance from the superpowers has diminished, and the two wealthiest and most powerful governments have only reluctantly participated in enlarged multinational aid programs through international institutions.

But if this be the outspoken attitude of the Third World regarding the balance of terror, then contradiction abounds. In the past decade, while decrying the nuclear arms race and the reluctance of the superpowers to sponsor more rapid economic and social development in the Third World, the governments of the developing states have been

38. *World Business Weekly,* February 9, 1981, pp. 28–29.

importing arms at record expense. In fact, most of the regional fighting in recent years has been in the Third World, principally in Africa, the Middle East, Southeast Asia, and Central America.

Conclusion

With or without arms races the world will continue, for as long as the nation-state remains the dominant actor, to face problems of power, competition and potential conflict. Disparities of wealth, ideological distrust, conflicts of interests, confrontation of objectives, perceptions and misperceptions—these and other aspects of international relations will continue to ensure that states will apply their power in pursuit of their interests and of their needs. And, regrettably, they will also continue to ensure that humans will expend their scientific skill and their technological achievement as much to destructive purposes as to the betterment of the human condition.

11

Principal Causes of War

One of the most pressing matters in the field of international relations is the causes of war. Why are international political controversies so often violent? The pages of international history are saturated with blood; and the moralist may fairly ask why people condone in war behavior that they would not tolerate in peace. Is war an international disease of the human social system, a collective insanity, a malfunction like falling down the stairs? Is it the product of conspiratorial behavior by certain interests and groups? Or is war a rational and functional, if horrible, component of the international system? In this chapter, we shall review fourteen theories of the causes of war that have emerged from the growing field of conflict and peace research.

War is one of the most carefully studied human activities, and literally tens of thousands of books and tracts have been written about it. Many universities have established research centers and teaching programs focused on conflict and violence, and several major journals are devoted exclusively to the subject (*Journal of Conflict Resolution*, US; *Journal of Peace Research*, Norway; *Peace Research Reviews*, Canada). Findings by conflict researchers in various disciplines are exchanged at dozens of national and international conferences annually. Peace research has by now generated many scientific findings and spawned several distinct schools of thought. The theories of the causes of war reviewed in this chapter represent some of the most important propositions and findings that have emerged.

In studying the fourteen theories of the origins of war which follow, the reader will discover that while war is typically regarded as a political phenomenon, it springs not only from political events, but from economic motives, from ethnic and racial conflict, from cultural and anthropological differences, from individual personalities and sometimes from psychopathology. A comprehensive study of the causes of war necessarily carries one into the literatures of politics, economics, history, philosophy, psychiatry, social psychology, anthropology, psychology and other pertinent fields of study. In keeping with the central concept of this book, then, this chapter seeks not to present a single comprehensive theory of the causes of war, but a comparative and comprehensive review of the several principal theories.

Scientific research on war is based on a critical assumption: *there are patterns and regularities in conflict behavior that can be identified systematically.* If this assumption is not true—that is, if war behavior is random, idiosyncratic or unique from case to case—then research of this kind will be unproductive. But historians and statesmen tend to agree with the conflict researchers that orderly principles *do* underlie the complexities of warlike behavior. It follows that war is a serious question for social inquiry.

In reviewing the fourteen principal causes of war listed in Table 11–1, we define war as *the organized conduct of major armed hostilities between social groups and nations.* This definition enables us to con-

TABLE 11–1
Fourteen theories of the causes of war.

1. Power asymmetries
2. Power transitions
3. Nationalism, separatism and irridentism
4. International Social Darwinism
5. Communications failure
6. Arms races
7. Internal cohesion through external conflict
8. International conflict through internal strife
9. Relative deprivation
10. Instinctual aggression
11. Economic and scientific stimulation
12. The military-industrial complex
13. Population limitation
14. Conflict resolution by force

sider internationally significant civil wars as well as international conflict, the distinction between the two having been eroded in recent years. Varying length of discussion of the individual causes should not be interpreted as implying greater or lesser importance.[1]

1. Power Asymmetries

The condition most feared among governments as a cause of war is the power asymmetry—that is, an unfavorable tilt in the distribution of power. There is widespread conviction that whatever other impetuses to war may be present, a careful equilibration of power between antagonists will tend to prevent war, while a disequilibrium will invite aggression. The maintenance of international peace requires that technological and other gains on each of two sides be matched and kept relatively even. A "vacuum" of power, such as that created by unilateral disarmament, destabilizes international relations and encourages military ventures. Proponents of this *Realpolitik* believe that occasions and issues for conflict always exist, and that the immediate cause of warfare is usually a failure to balance power symmetrically. The operating principle of this doctrine is: "If peace is your goal, prepare for war." Hence the United States Air Force boasts that "peace is our profession," and the MX missile is sold to the American people with its thirty billion dollar price tag as the "Peacekeeper missile."

In conflicts in which one side seeks a major redistribution of values while the other wishes to preserve the status quo—that is, when there is a clear distinction between the offense and the defense—peace may be preserved by a certain kind of asymmetry. An advantage to the defensive party will more reliably deter aggression than a close balance. Conversely, an overbalance in favor of the offensive party will make war more likely. Thus, in the clear offense/defense case, peace is more nearly ensured by superiority of the nonrevolutionary antagonist. For example, Winston Churchill argued in his "iron curtain" speech at Fulton, Missouri, in March 1946, that Soviet aggression would be stopped only by Western military superiority: "The old doctrine of a balance of power is unsound. We cannot afford, if we can help it, to work on narrow margins, offering temptations to a trial of strength." However, power asymmetries are inherently dangerous and tend to

1. For a penetrating analysis of several key theories, see Kenneth Waltz, *Man, the State, and War* (New York: Columbia University Press, 1965); also, Quincy Wright's classic, *The Study of War* (Chicago: University of Chicago Press, 1965), 2nd ed.; and Karl von Clausewitz, *On War* (Washington, D.C.: Infantry Journal Press, 1950), reprint.

produce aggressive policies even when the favored state was previously peace loving and defensive.

Asymmetries pertain not only to different levels of industrial capacity, population and other physical elements of war potential (see the preceding four chapters), but also to the more variable and volatile political elements. Of special importance is the ability to attract and retain allies willing to pool resources for mutual security. Only two states in the modern world, the USA and the USSR, are able to act alone in most contingencies, and even for them there are many political and strategic advantages in joint action. For lesser powers, it is vitally important to cement alliances to prevent asymmetries. For example, Israel depends on the United States while Syria relies on the Soviet Union.

Another important factor is will. Even very good capabilities and solid alliances can result in asymmetries if a party declines to fight. Conversely, a state with limited resources and support may be able to prevent asymmetry by showing a resolute determination to utilize its capacities fully. To prevent power asymmetries, it is not necessary that all possible pairs of states be balanced perfectly, but only that potential aggressors know in advance that the costs of overcoming resistance will outweight the benefits. Thus, the asymmetry of power is one cause of war that can be controlled.

2. Power Transitions

One special adaptation of the theory that power asymmetries produce international conflict is the power-transition theory of war. Its unique feature is that it concentrates not on existing asymmetries, but on evolving asymmetries, upsets in the international balance produced by rapid advantageous development among states inclined to challenge the international status quo established and protected by dominant states.

This theory postulates that states are differentiated by their relative power capabilities *and* by their satisfaction or dissatisfaction with the prevailing international system. Thus, in addition to the dominant states (United States, Soviet Union), some are powerful and satisfied (Britain, Germany, France, Japan, Canada), others are powerful and dissatisfied (China), still others powerless and satisfied, and others both powerless and dissatisfied. Similar relationships exist within regional settings. In the Middle East, for example, Israel and Egypt are powerful and satisfied, Syria and Lybia are powerful and dissatisfied, Jordan is relatively powerless but satisfied, and Lebanon is powerless and dissatisfied.

The power transition is characterized by sudden and significant challenges to the status quo that result from rapid internal development in power capabilities. Whether they are a result of rapid social mobilization or of sharp advances in national economic capability, the roots of the challenge are in internal national development. Should the events occur in a state satisfied with the prevailing international or regional system, they are unlikely to be disruptive. But should they occur in a state that was not a party to the establishment of the prevailing norms and prefers to replace them, the development will be viewed by the dominant states as a challenge. Conflict results and war may follow. By the same token, if the development occurs gradually, the prospect of accommodating it to the existing system is brighter than if it occurs at revolutionary speed.[2]

Although the United States and the Soviet Union have not fought war directly, the Cold War is an ideal example of the power-transition theory. At the close of World War II, many of the satisfied nations (e.g., Britain and France) were in ruins, and the dissatisfied nations that had attempted through global war to replace the pre-war system (Germany, Japan and Italy) were occupied by conquering powers. The United States was the sole surviving dominant nation, determined to restore the political and economic systems of the pre-war international system. The Soviet Union, socialist rather than capitalist, used its post-war geographic advantage and rapid economic and thermonuclear development to challenge Washington's exclusive right to restore the system. It was this rapid development, filled with economic, military and geographic credibility, which led to the measures and counter-measures later labeled the Cold War.

There are many other examples, though not all have culminated in war. The mobilization of China's economic capabilities in the 1960s enabled Peking to challenge the Soviet and American dominance of the Third World; and the rapid reversal in the flow of wealth generated by the politics of OPEC in the 1970s enabled its members to confront the international economic system and to influence the military balance in the Middle East.

2. The most influential work on the power-transition theory has been done by A. F. K. Organski and his collaborators. See particularly A. F. K. Organski, *World Politics,* 2nd edition (New York: Alfred A. Knopf, 1968), Chapters 7 and 8, and *Stages of Political Growth* (New York: Alfred A. Knopf, 1965); also A. F. K. Organski and Jacek Kugler, *The War Ledger* (Chicago: The University of Chicago Press, 1980). For related works on the subject of internal development and international power redistribution as causes of war, see Nazli Choucri and Robert North, *Nations in Conflict* (San Francisco: W. H. Freeman, 1974); Nazli Choucri and Dennis Meadows, *International Implications of Technological Development and Population Growth* (Cambridge, Mass: MIT Press, 1971); and Michael D. Wallace, *War and Rank Among Nations* (Lexington, Mass: D. C. Heath, 1973). The Wallace work deals with quantitative studies of international status and status redistribution as causes of war.

3. Nationalism, Separatism and Irredentism

Nationalism is a collective group identity that passionately binds diverse individuals into "a people." The nation becomes the highest affiliation and obligation of the individual, and it is in terms of the national "*we*-group" that personal identity is formed: "I am a Canadian." From Hitler's celebration of the *Volk* to de Gaulle's near-mystical belief in the French, the most powerful elements of the political spectrum seem to agree that the ethnic nation is the highest form of identity.

This curious and compelling identification with one group tends to produce conflicts with others. A 1969 research team enumerated 160 disputes having a significant likelihood of resulting in large-scale violence within fifteen years. This large inventory fell broadly into the following classifications:

1. *Nationalist* conflicts, including disputes between ethnic, racial, religious and linguistic identity groups perceiving themselves as "peoples"
2. *Class* conflicts, including issues of economic exploitation
3. *Other* conflicts not characterized primarily by clashes between identity groups or classes

Significantly, nationalist and ethnic conflict accounted for about 70 percent of the cases, while class and other conflicts divided the balance. Indeed, nationalism appears to be a potent factor in the causal chain to war, accounting for more bloodshed than any other cause.[3]

A review of the disputes identified in 1969 fifteen years later in 1984 reveals that serious civil strife occurred in more than thirty cases at least once, and international conflict with significant damage and death occurred in twenty-three.[4]

In recent years, the main link between nationalism and war has been the survival of separate identities among populations whose geographical distribution differs from the international boundary lines. "Peoples" who do not have "countries" tend to feel an infringement

3. Steven Rosen, editor, *A Survey of World Conflicts* (Pittsburgh, Pa.: University of Pittsburgh Center of International Studies Preliminary Paper, March 1969).
4. The reader is cautioned that a study of this kind is fraught with pitfalls, principally about definition and threshold conditions. How much destruction does it take to make an insurrection or terrorism a war? Are isolated instances of severe violence individual or continuous events? Is foreign occupation tantamount to war even if death and destruction do not occur? For these and other reasons, a count of the actual "wars" that occurred in a fifteen-year period is necessarily general. In the review of the original predictions, civil or international war has occurred only when conflict and violence have been sustained, when death has been substantial and when violent events have been continuous or repeated with considerable frequency.

of basic human rights in a world of *nation*-states. Populations submerged in other peoples' countries (Lithuanians), populations divided among two or more countries (Kurds) and populations denied the control of the governments of their own countries (black South Africans) tend to rebel against these denials. But territorial and political rearrangements often cannot be achieved without armed conflict between the deprived or oppressed groups and other interests. Thus, the link between nationalism and war today operates most importantly through militant territorial and political demands organized around certain principles of ethnic, linguistic, religious and racial we-group identities.

Two key forms of nationalist militancy predominate in modern war. These are the *separatist* form and the *irredentist* form. In the separatist form, a nationalist group attempts to secede from an existing state to form a new one. In the irredentist form, an existing state lays claim to a territory and population group presently subsumed within another state. These forms are illustrated in Figure 11–1.

Separatism and War

Most of the world's approximately 170 nation-states incorporate substantial minority populations. Even after prolonged periods of apparent assimilation among other groups, many minorities continue to

Steve Biko, popular leader of South African blacks, died in police detention. The resulting government investigation was widely considered to be a cover-up of the truth.

"It's my favorite color!"

Source: Marlette *(Charlotte Observer)*/© *King Features*

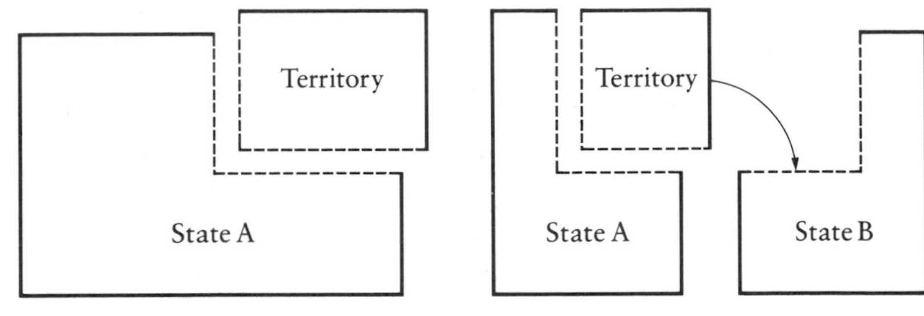

FIGURE 11–1
Left: The separatist model. Territory X secedes from State A to form new State X. Right: The irredentist model. State B claims Territory X from State A.

think of themselves as separate and distinct. (See Table 11–2). This feeling of distinctness becomes a separatist movement when a formal demand is made for territorial secession to form a state or, short of this extreme, for a considerable measure of internal autonomy from control by the existing political order. These separatist demands usually are resisted by the incumbent authorities because of the threat perceived to the state's political and territorial integrity. In this way, conflicts over separatist demands become common causes of war.

Minority movements take on added significance for the study of international relations when outside powers intervene. Often, one comes to the aid of the threatened government, while another lends its support to the restive minority. The various factions in the internal dispute become clients of outside sponsors motivated by their own interests. Foreign intervention is particularly important when a neighboring state allows its territory to be used as a sancturary and staging area for guerrilla forays and political organization by the dissident population. This is seen by the threatened government as subversion and tends to lead to intergovernmental conflict.

Irredentism and War

Nationalist and ethnic disputes have still greater significance for international relations in their *irredentist* form. Virtually all the world's populated land surfaces are by now identified with the delineated territory of particular nation-states. But in many cases the historic demarcation of boundaries (mainly through war and conquest) ignored "natural" lines of division between different peoples. Thus, political lines often are not congruent with ethnogeographic regions, and in many places one "people" straddles a border between two states. Irredentism is the struggle of such a people for reunification,[5] and the

5. The term referred originally to the late nineteenth-century struggle of Italian patriots to redeem or reincorporate into Italy certain neighboring territories having a predominantly Italian population. As the term is used here, the impetus for reunification can come from the separated population *(irredenta)*, the main body or from both.

TABLE 11–2
Some separatist and autonomist movements.

Recent wars of secession
1. Nigeria: struggle by Ibos for a separate Biafra; unsuccessful
2. Pakistan: secession of East Pakistan to form Bangladesh; successful
3. Sudan: black secessionists vs. Arab state; unsuccessful
4. Chad: Arab secessionists vs. black state; unsuccessful
5. Iraq: Kurds; unsuccessful
6. Ethiopia: Arabs of Eritrea, supported by Arab states; unsuccessful
7. Oman: Dhofar region; unsuccessful

Other separatist movements
1. Spain: Basques; Catalans
2. Yugoslavia: Croatians; Albanians
3. Uganda: Bugandans
4. India: Sikhs
5. Puerto Rico: Independista movement
6. France: Brittany; potentially Basques
7. United Kingdom: Ulster Catholics; Welsh; Scots
8. Indonesia: minorities in Moluccas, Sumatra, Celebes
9. Russia: Latvians; Estonians; Lithuanians; Ukrainians
10. Sri Lanka: Tamils
11. Switzerland: Jura
12. Canada: French of Quebec
13. China: Sinkiang; Tibet
14. Burma: Karens; Kachins; Shans; Chins; Mons; Arkanese
15. Pakistan: Baluchis
16. South Africa: Namibia (Southwest Africa)

Multiple secession movements
1. Kurds from Iraq, Iran, Turkey and USSR
2. Bakongos from Zaïre, Congo, Cabinda and Angola

Strained federations
1. Lebanon: Moslems vs. Christians
2. Yugoslavia: Serbs, Croatians and others
3. Guyana: Blacks, East Indians and others
4. Ghana: northern vs. coastal tribes
5. Czechoslovakia: Slav minority
6. Mauritius: Hindu, Creole, Moslem
7. Surinam: Creole, East Indian, Japanese
8. Rwanda and Burundi: Wa-Tutsi vs. Bahutu
9. Belgium: Flemings and Walloons
10. India: many minorities

irredenta is a territory where a portion of the ethnic nation resides that is regarded as lost or stolen.

The irredentist territorial claim normally evokes resistance from the state, since its territory would be reduced in the event of a successful claim. The challenged state often can base its own claim on historic ties and treaties regarded as legally binding. There is a fog of claims and counterclaims, and the stirring patriotic call of one side is a threat to the other. Even the most barren piece of territory is regarded as a sacred part of the national patrimony, and seldom does a border move a hundred yards in any direction without the spilling of human blood.

Resistance to irredentist claims occurs when

1. an existing state would cease to exist as an independent entity
2. one or more states would lose territory. (Both India and Pakistan lost territory in the establishment of Bangladesh)
3. irridentism would reunify two halves with different political ideologies (The post-war reunification of the two Vietnams; the possible reunification of the two Koreas or the two Germanies)
4. one population occupying the irridenta fears that it would be a disadvantaged minority in the case of reunification (Protestants in Northern Ireland; Turks in Cyprus)

In all of these cases, some group stands to lose in the event of successful irridentism.

Issues in Separatist and Irredentist Conflicts

Economic Consequences Although territorial issues of separatism and irredentism begin as ethnic questions, they also entail profound economic and natural resource issues. When Hitler seized the Sudetenland from Czechoslovakia in the name of three million Sudeten Germans, he also seized 70 percent of Czechoslovakia's iron and steel, 86 percent of its chemicals and 70 percent of its electrical generating capacity. Similarly, British support for the self-determination movement in Kuwait and Brunei is related to their oil wealth; and Belgian support for the Katanga secession attempt in the Congo was keyed to the copper deposits of that region. The secession of Biafra would have taken from Nigeria not just the Ibo people, but also much of the national resource base and industrial capacity. Thus, nationalist disputes are also international economic issues.

The Moral Dilemma Aside from economic issues, separatist and irredentist movements pose a moral dilemma for the international system. National self-determination is a cardinal value, and many concerned observers support struggling peoples seeking their own places in the sun. But the immense complexity of ethnogeography means that the world cannot possibly accommodate each splinter group with its own territory. All African states, for example, include members of tribes that straddle international borders. If each national group were given its own country, thousands of economically nonviable units would result. The fifty states of Africa, with a total population less than half that of India, are already too fragmented. When the Ibos sought secession from Nigeria, they were supported by only a few outside states (notably Tanzania, Zambia, Gabon and Ivory Coast), despite the moral appeal of their position. Pan-Africanists hold that the real future of the continent is in regional amalgamation and federation, not further "Balkanization." In addition, wholesale border revisions probably could not be achieved without an unacceptable amount of conflict and warfare among interested states.

Colonial Boundaries Many frustrated minorities blame their problems on past imperialism. Borders violate ethnic lines primarily because they reflect the points at which advancing armies stopped, or where "deals" between big powers were reached. They rarely reflect "natural" lines of human settlement. In many underdeveloped regions,

Quebec's campaign for independence from Canada is one close-to-home example of the many nationalist and separatist movements that exist around the globe.

Source: Jean-Pierre Lafont/Sygma

precolonial societies simply did not have officially drawn boundaries. When the Europeans came, they drew lines that seemed administratively, economically and politically convenient in Paris, London, Lisbon and Brussels, but that often ignored tribal and ethnic lines. Unified peoples were splintered, and incompatible tribes and groups were often lumped together. This was not just chance, but a calculated policy of divide and conquer. Many peoples have permanent problems as a consequence of past colonialism.

Unresolved and unresolvable irredentist and separatist issues are threats to the territorial interest of many nations (see Table 11–3).

TABLE 11–3
Some irredentist movements.

Claims to whole states

1. Tibet was reincorporated by China.
2. Togo has been claimed by Ghana on grounds of Ewe reunification.
3. Mauritania is regarded by some as part of Morocco.
4. French Somaliland (now Afar-Issa or Djibouti) has been claimed by Somalia.
5. Israel is regarded by Arab nationalists as a land stolen from the Arab nation.
6. Kuwait has been claimed by Iraq.
7. Gambia was carved artificially out of Senegal by the colonial power.
8. Cyprus is regarded as part of Greece by Greek Cypriots.
9. Taiwan is claimed as part of China.

Divided states with different political orientations

1. North and South Korea
2. East and West Germany
3. The two Yemens
4. The two Vietnams, now undergoing reunification

Claims to parts of states

1. United Kingdom is threatened by IRA demands that Northern Ireland (Ulster) be reunited with Ireland.
2. Algeria is threatened by Moroccan claims in Spanish Sahara, rich in phosphates, and Tindouf, rich in oil.
3. India is threatened by Pakistan's claim to Kashmir.
4. Kenya is threatened by Somali nationalist claims to the Northern Frontier District.
5. Guyana faces territorial claims by Venezuela and Surinam.
6. Italy has negotiated territorial claims by Austria and Yugoslavia.
7. China has extensive claims against the Soviet Union, Mongolia and other states.
8. Malaysia has resisted Indonesian and Philippine claims to Sabah.
9. Germany, under Hitler, laid claim to regions of Czechoslovakia, Poland and Austria on grounds of Aryan reunification.

Nationalist conflicts may be latent and seemingly forgotten for prolonged periods, suddenly to emerge with renewed vigor as group identity reawakens. Recollections of lost territory tend to simmer beneath the political surface, and it is a simple matter for a jingoist leader or a demagogue to stir them up and ride to power on a nationalist tide. A latent irredentist or separatist feeling is a potent chemical reaction waiting for the right catalyst and is always, therefore, a potential cause of war.

4. International Social Darwinism

International social Darwinsim is the belief that societies, like biological species, evolve and advance through competition, resulting in the survival of the fittest and the elimination of the weak. The social Darwinist sees the war of each against all as a cruel necessity for the progressive advancement of civilization. International relations is, in this perspective, the arena of combat between whole peoples where the global destiny of humanity is determined. The role of war is to pass the reins of power from the weak and decaying to the strong and dynamic.

In recent years, this philosophy has most often been associated with *fascism.* In advancing war as a positive aspect of fascism, Benito Mussolini declared: "Fascism sees in the imperialistic spirit—i.e., in the tendency of nations to expand—a manifestation of their vitality. In the opposite tendency, which would limit their interests to the home country, it sees a symptom of decadence."[6] Moreover, "fascism above all does not believe either in the possibility or the utility of universal peace. It therefore rejects the pacifism which masks surrender and cowardice." And "war alone brings all human energies to their highest tension and sets a seal of nobility upon the peoples who have the virtue to face it."[7]

Carried to its logical conclusion in *Nazism,* the fascist philosophy views societies as biological entities united by blood ties. Two principles link Nazism with war: the principle of race and the principle of territory. Nazism, according to Adolph Hitler, "by no means believes in equality of the races, but along with their difference it recognizes their higher or lesser value. . . . Thus, in principle, it serves the basic aristocratic ideas of Nature." Moreover, because population

6. Quoted in S. William Halperin, *Mussolini and Italian Fascism* (Princeton, N.J.: Van Nostrand, 1964), p. 152.
7. Benito Mussolini, quoted in Reo M. Christensen et al., *Ideologies and Modern Politics* (New York: Dodd, Mead, 1971), p. 70.

Source: Jerome Chatin/Gamma

Desecration of a memorial to Jewish victims of the Holocaust in France, 1981. A reminder, if any were needed, that racism is symptomatic in even the most "civilized" of countries.

expands but living space *(Lebensraum)* is limited, races must compete for territory. "Nature knows no political boundaries. First she puts living creatures on this globe and watches the free play of forces. She then confers the master's right on her favorite child, the strongest." The higher races must not agree "in their pacifistic blindness to renounce new acquisitions of soil" or they will leave mastery of the world to "the culturally inferior but more brutal and more natural peoples." Hitler was deeply suspicious of international law and diplomacy—"a cozy mutual swindling match"—and frankly set out "to promote the victory of the better and stronger, and demand the subordination of the inferior and weaker in accordance with the eternal will that dominates this universe."[8]

As these passages suggest, international social Darwinsim glorifies conflict and focuses on incompatibilities among groups. It offers an appealing and simplistic account of history, providing a perfect ra-

8. Adolph Hitler, *Mein Kampf* (Boston: Houghton Mifflin, 1943), pp. 134–57.

tionalization for aggression. And, of course, it raises many questions for social theory.

Is race the basic human unit, or only a biological accident that is promoted and distorted by corrupt politics? Is competition the "basic law of nature," or are the most important human achievements attained mainly by cooperation and mutual effort? Do nations in fact face a shortage of "living space," or are the most densely populated nations (for example, Japan) often the most prosperous? (It is interesting to note here that of the estimated twenty-five million square miles of arable land in the world, only about one-sixth is under cultivation.) Are people pressing outward from overcrowded population centers, or is the trend toward urbanization and concentration increasing while rural population is declining? Is the creative height of civilization reached in war or in peace?

Whatever the answers to these questions may be, and despite the fact that Nazism is now nearly dead, the philosophy of international social Darwinism is alive and well. Its sharpest critics are the Marxist-Leninist theorists who build their theory on dialectical materialism and believe that all war is a social phenomenon rooted in class differentiation across national boundaries. So to them, international social Darwinism is one of many attempts on the part of bourgeois theoreticians to substitute biological, psychological and other factors for the social-class basis of war.[9]

5. Communications Failure

Another cause of war treated extensively in the conflict literature is the theory of communications failure. Nations perceive each other through ideological lenses and with stereotypical images,[10] as we showed in discussing the Cold War conflicts. These perceptual distortions result in selective reception of messages and signals and in mutual misperception of intentions.[11] For example, potentially threat-

9. For a collection of papers by Soviet authors see *Problems of War and Peace: A Critical Analysis of Bourgeois Theories* (Moscow: Progress Publishers, 1972), translated from the Russian by Bryan Bean, particularly Part II, "The Origins and Essence of War."

10. See, for example, H. C. J. Duijker and N. H. Frijda, *National Character and National Stereotypes* (Amsterdam: North Holland Publishing, 1960), and O. Klineberg, *Tensions Affecting International Understanding* (New York: Social Science Research Council, 1950), Bulletin 62.

11. See Anatol Rapoport, "Perceiving the Cold War," in Robert Fisher, editor, *International Conflict and Behavioral Science* (New York: Basic Books, 1964); also Kenneth Boulding, *The Image* (Ann Arbor, Mich.: University of Michigan Press, 1956); and Karl W. Deutsch and Richard L. Merritt, "Effects of Events on National and International Images," in Herbert Kelman, editor, *International Political Behavior* (New York: Holt, Rinehart and Winston, 1965).

ening messages from another government may be more salient or perceptually prominent than cooperative or concilatory statements. The listener hears what he expects to hear, as in the theory of cognitive dissonance. The images that nations have of each other not only fail to match the realities they are supposed to represent, but these images are also highly resistant to change—even when evidence and experience contradict fixed expectations. (See Chapter 6 for a more detailed treatment of this process.) Communications failure and exaggerated fear contribute to escalatory processes by multiplying the consequences of international tensions.

As the speed and precision of modern weapons have increased the need for improved communications, so too should the communications revolution have assisted government leaders throughout the world in communicating their intentions better. There is no shortage of technical devices for these purposes: hot-line telephone connections between the White House and the Kremlin; communications satellites that transmit information around the world in seconds; computers that communicate with one another over great distances; etc. The difficulty, of course, is that as technical aids have become more sophisticated, leaders have become more rather than less wary of the spoken intentions of one another. Furthermore, international communications tend to be public statements secluded in political messages. It is not uncommon, for example, for the President of the United States to deliver a message to the Soviet Communist Party Chief in a State-of-the-Union speech, but in a politically popular way that risks distorting the message to the Kremlin.

While the technical aspects of international communication have become modernized, the strategic aspects have become more complicated. This is particularly true about the language of escalation. Only in its final stages does the escalation of international events involve such things as deploying troops, making decisions regarding tactical nuclear weapons, or mobilizing alliances. The earlier, equally critical phases are largely verbal and symbolic. Often their form, designed as much for domestic political consumption as for international communication, may make de-escalation all but impossible. Threats, deliberate distortion of images, propaganda, public rejection of settlement proposals, legislative condemnation, domestic mobilization, economic restructuring, political positioning among the loyal opposition—these and hundreds of other events, all of which carry messages of intractability to the adversary, precede actual preparation for combat. As patriotism begins to run high in public opinion polls, the difficulty of conducting more informative and accurate communications through diplomatic channels increases. Governments may simply lose the ability to communicate effectively to the adversary, or to place strategic trust in the messages that are being received from abroad.[12] Instead they head straight at one another as two drivers playing chicken, each determined to force the other off the road by sheer resolve of purpose. But unlike the two drivers, neither can remove its steering wheel and throw it onto the highway to signal its inability to change courses. Lacking a last-minute communications display, the two collide in combat.

There is a great irony in the contemporary communications revolution with respect to international relations: Rather than improving communications between adversary governments, the revolution has been used to introduce precision warfare, to transform global powers into planetary powers by giving them military strength without occupation in distant lands, and to introduce new methods of concealing one's own strengths while improving the ability to detect another's. Together with sensing devices and computers, communications advances have produced a "transparency revolution" in which the competition for arms superiority is between the visible and the hidden. Thus rather than enhance international communication for peace, the revolution has brought strategic competition to an unstable and dangerous condition. Whether or not the next generation of advances will emphasize mutual detection and verification rather then further competition in invisibility remains to be seen.[13]

Unquestionably the most tragic example of failed communications in recent international relations was the Soviet destruction of a civilian Korean airliner over the sea of Japan in September 1983. Apart from unanswered questions of why the plane was off course and over Soviet territory, the inability of the United States, the Soviet Union and Japan (all of whom were monitoring conversations between the Soviet pilot and his command base) to avoid tragedy astonished the world. The Soviet Union claimed that because the plane had previously intersected paths with an American intelligence craft, they were unable to determine whether the intruding plane was the American spy craft or the civilian liner. (Later they claimed that they knew it was the Korean plane, but that they had evidence it was conducting a spy mission over Sakhalin Island under the cover of civilian aviation.)

Whatever may have been the real Soviet motive in firing an air-to-

12. For a general treatment of escalation and its role in political communications, see Herman Kahn, *On Escalation* (New York: Praeger, 1965).
13. For a systematic review of communications in world politics, see Andrew M. Scott, *The Functioning of the International Political System* (New York: Macmillan, 1967), pp. 68–70. For a pioneering discussion of the transparency revolution and its impact upon international communications, see Daniel Deudney, *Whole Earth Security: A Geopolitics of Peace,* Worldwatch Paper 55 (Washington: Worldwatch Institute, 1983), particularly pp. 20–32.

air missile, however, we know that several communications opportunities were missed.

1. The plane was nearly out of Soviet air space when fired upon, and had thus been followed for sufficient time to have enabled either Japanese or American officials to intervene by communication with the Soviet Union, or for Soviet officials to have made international inquiries about the known locations of civilian craft in the vicinity of Sakhalin.
2. Translation difficulties between Japanese intelligence and the National Security Agency of the United States delayed a real understanding of the pending crisis longer than tolerable under the speed-of-sound flight of the Soviet intercepters.
3. There is no evidence that the Korean pilot was contacted by accepted international signals with the message that he was off course and in forbidden air space.
4. There is speculation, though no hard evidence, that the plane was off course precisely because of an error in operating a navigational computer or because of an electronic failure within the computer.
5. The communications hot line between the White House and the Kremlin was never activated.

All of these failures of communication, and failures to use to best advantage the most sophisticated communications electronics ever known, demonstrate the precarious condition of international relations when military or intelligence events occur at speeds greater than the speed of the human link in a communications chain. In this case, inefficient use of intelligence data resulted from (1) the onset of the new Cold War; (2) the unexplained location of the Korean flight; (3) the earlier intersection of the civilian craft with an intelligence plane; (4) the Soviet eagerness to make a fire or no-fire decision before the plane left Soviet air space and entered international air space; and (5) delays caused by slowness in translating Soviet air-to-ground communications first into Japanese and then into English. Despite the speed-of-light communications capability among the three parties, it was actually the speed-of-sound chase seven miles above ground which determined that 269 persons would die as targets of a Soviet missile.

6. Arms Races

Another theory links the outbreak of war to the build-up of runaway arms that becomes unstable and uncontrolled. Here, hostile nations lock into a cycle of mutual fear (a process called hostility reaction formation), in which each side believes itself to be threatened by the other. The defensive preparations of one are taken as evidence of offensive intentions by the other, who then arms in response. Each seeks a margin of superiority, leading to qualitative and quantitative competition in armaments and organized forces. The assumption that such arms races tend to erupt into active conflict after a certain critical point in the reaction process is passed was the basis of a pioneering mathematical study of war.[14]

Many thoughtful people on the liberal end of the American political spectrum agree that excessive military preparations and armaments accumulation are a cause of war. On the other side, conservatives tend to favor the adage *Si vis pacem, para bellum* ("If you want peace, prepare for war"). Do armaments cause wars or prevent them? Norman Cousins once invented a completely imaginary computer study of all the arms races in history to determine whether arms races were a cause of war or a guarantee of peace. He "found" that since 650 B.C., there had been 1,956 arms races, of which only sixteen did not end in war, and that most of the exceptional cases ended in economic collapse.[15]

More authentic studies have been much more equivocal and ambiguous in their findings. One well-known study found that arms races may be either a prelude to war or a substitute for it, depending on other conditions.[16] Even if a significant correlation were discovered between arms races and the outbreak of war, it could not be inferred that the former caused the latter. It is plausible that profound political disputes cause both arms races and wars, so correlation in this case would not prove causation. *A* might correlate with *B* because both are caused by *C*.

The role of arms races in international conflict is closely linked to the issue of power symmetries or asymmetries. If an arms race has a stabilizing effect because it results more in symmetry than in asymmetry, then it is not likely to be an immediate cause of war. If, on the other hand, the race tends toward asymmetry because of superior acceleration on one side, then war-related temptations may be irresistible. Hence it is not mere existence of the race that influences the outcome, but its comparative characteristics.

For three and a half decades, the strategic arms race between the

14. Lewis Richardson, *Arms and Insecurity* (Pittsburgh: Boxwood, 1960).
15. See Norman Cousins, *In Place of Folly* (New York: Harper and Row, 1961); also, Brownlee Hayden, *The Great Statistics of War Hoax* (Santa Monica, Ca.: Rand Corporation, 1962).
16. Samuel P. Huntington, "Arms Races: Prerequisites and Results," in Robert J. Art and Kenneth N. Waltz, editors, *The Use of Force* (Boston: Little, Brown, 1971), pp. 365–401.

United States and the Soviet Union has tended distinctly toward stabilization. While one party may have had a momentary advantage in one sector, the other has enjoyed superiority in another. Neither has been tempted to a first strike, well aware of the second-strike (retaliatory) capabilities of the other. Not only has this prevented direct military conflict, it has also kept alive a glimmering hope of mutual arms reduction. But some observers fear that new military technologies may upset the effective balance in the near future, thus reducing the prospects for significant arms limitation, accelerating the arms race and multiplying its cost on both sides, or rekindling thoughts of preventive or anticipatory war. Opponents of the MX missile, for example, have argued that its deployment is more than an escalation of the race; it represents the introduction of an entirely new weapons system that will place the Soviet Union at a strategic disadvantage of inestimable duration, thus reducing prospects for successful arms control agreements and generally destabilizing the race. Similarly, American superiority in the application of computer and electronic techniques to military preparedness may result in a major divergence of strategic plans and capabilities at the end of the century. President Ronald Reagan's call in early 1983 for a comprehensive study of the weapons of the future, built not on nuclear stockpiles but on weapons and delivery systems that are futuristic, may result in severe destabilization in the future.

It is not exclusively in Soviet-American relations, however, that these destabilizations may have consequences. In the many regional arms races to which Washington and the Kremlin contribute—from the Arab-Israeli arena to the two Koreas and the upheaved nations of Central America—the unbalanced introduction of new weapons systems could have revolutionary consequences. This underscores the conclusion that arms races alone do not determine outcomes; it is the stabilizing or destabilizing characteristics of those races that are the critical factors.

Arms races, like communication failures, are seldom the root cause of conflict. The decision to maintain extremely high military expenditures most often reflects a prior condition of discord and conflict with an opponent. Arms races and exaggerated fears may inflame an existing conflict, but seldom create one that does not otherwise exist. The distinction should be underscored, however, between arms races as causes of conflict and arms races as causes of armed conflict (war). Arms, after all, expand the alternatives for dealing with conflict as a result of either rational or irrational decision making. In particular, perceptions of armed strength between adversaries may result in preventive war (armed conflict to prevent another party from expanding his decisional alternatives or his armed might) or preemptive war (armed aggression undertaken in anticipation of aggression from the other party, and launched in order "to beat him to it").

7. Internal Cohesion Through External Conflict

Another theory sees war as the product of policies designed to promote internal group cohesion through the unifying effects of outside conflict—the process of drawing together to face a common enemy. Bismarck's calculated provocation of three external wars from 1866 to 1871 to integrate the German states is the classic example of wars fought purposely. Secretary of State William Henry Seward's fruitless proposal to President Lincoln that the United States precipitate international warfare to reunite the nation and to avoid civil war exemplifies the same tactic. There exists an extensive literature that demonstrates the relationship of external conflict to internal cohesion at all levels of social interaction.[17] In international relations the implication of this theory is that resort to international warfare may be preferable to internal dissolution.

Despite the apparent weight of this theory, however, most scientific studies conclude quite differently. If internal conflict tended to be externalized in foreign wars, it is hypothesized that there should be a statistical relationship between the frequency of internal and external conflict. But in the most careful quantitative research, no clear and consistent relationship has been found.[18]

Among the scientific studies, only one has substantiated the theory that the quest for domestic cohesion is a cause of war, and that one finds only a slight relation.[19] Whatever may be the merits of these

17. Anthony de Reuck and Julie Knight, *Conflict in Society* (Boston: Little, Brown, 1966), p. 32; D. Kahn-Freund, "Intergroup Conflicts and Their Settlement," *British Journal of Sociology* 5, 1954, p. 201; Georg Simmel, *Conflict and the Web of Group Affiliations* (Glencoe, Ill.: The Free Press, 1955); Lewis Coser, *The Functions of Social Conflict* (Glencoe, Ill.: The Free Press, 1957); pp. 104–6 and 92–93. For a thorough review and synthesis of the literature up to about 1959, see Robert North, Howard Koch, Jr. and Dina Zinnes, "The Integrative Functions of Conflict," *Journal of Conflict Resolution* 3, September 1960, pp. 355–74.
18. Rudolph Rummel, "Testing Some Possible Predictors of Conflict Behavior Within and Between Nations," *Peace Research Society (International) Papers* 3, 1963, p. 17; Rudolph Rummel, "The Relationship Between National Attributes and Foreign Conflict Behavior," in J. David Singer, editor, *Quantitative International Politics* (New York: The Free Press of Glencoe, 1968); Michael Haas, "Social Change and National Aggressiveness: 1900–1960," in Singer, p. 213; Raymond Tanter, "Dimensions of Conflict Behavior Within and Between Nations, 1958–1960," *Journal of Conflict Resolution* 10, no. 1, March 1966, p. 46; and Samuel P. Huntington, "Patterns of Violence in World Politics," in Huntington, editor, *Changing Patterns of Military Politics* (New York: The Free Press of Glencoe, 1962), pp. 40–41.
19. Jonathan Wilkenfeld, "Domestic and Foreign Conflict Behavior of Nations," *Journal of Peace Research* 1, 1968, pp. 55–59.

conflicting findings, it must be conceded that most studies have not found the relationship that was predicted between internal unity and external conflict.

8. International Conflict Through Internal Strife

In contrast to the preceding theory of the causes of war, one may observe that in the twentieth century many international military encounters have resulted from domestic dissolution. To a very large extent, in fact, the distinction between civil and international war has been blurred, particularly as a result of frequent external intervention. While the superpowers manage by a symmetrical arms race to avoid direct military conflict, civil wars around the world result in international conflict.

Illustrations abound. At the close of World War I, when Russia was destabilized by the Bolshevik Revolution and the civil war which followed, American troops landed in Russia to assist the White Russian Army in defeating the Bolsheviks and returning the government to non-Marxist-Leninist elements more sympathetic to the West and to capitalism. The Vietnam War, fought almost continuously from 1950 to 1973, first involved French intervention (supplied in large measure by the United States as part of the Asian anti-Communist strategy which led to American intervention in Korea) and later American. In 1984, the United States intervened indirectly in Nicaragua to bring down the Cuban-oriented leftist Sandanista government there, and in El Salvador to protect the pro-American government from falling to leftist insurrectionists. In each of these civil wars, direct American or Cuban intervention is possible at any time.

Governments often claim that they are forced to intervene militarily in their client states because of destabilization caused by adversaries. The Soviet Union, for example, justified interventions in Czechoslovakia (1968) and Poland (1981, with martial law rather than invasion), in part on the allegation that the United States and its NATO allies had, through propaganda and economic relations, created domestic instability which threatened the solidarity of the Socialist commonwealth. In the case of Czechoslovakia, intervention resulted in the Brezhnev Doctrine, which proclaimed that the Warsaw Pact would not permit any political or economic change in an individual Eastern European state that would threaten the cohesion of the alliance. This does not differ greatly from the Theodore Roosevelt Corollary to the Monroe Doctrine which dominated inter-American relations from 1907 through 1932. Roosevelt's Corollary attempted to stabilize South America, Central America and the Caribbean under American influence by simply declaring Washington's willingness to use force if necessary to prevent the further establishment of European influence in the hemisphere. This led to American interventions in Venezuela, Colombia, and Mexico, to name only a few major examples.

Many twentieth-century interventions have resulted from revolt against imperialism and colonialism. Not only is this a major theme of Marxist international relations theory, but it is observable in a number of concrete instances. The Boer War, for example (1898–1900) was a British imperial action designed to consolidate its rule in South Africa, which was mineral rich and strategically important to British shipping lanes from the south Atlantic to the Indian Ocean. At the same time, as China was being divided into sectors for Western and Japanese economic dominance, military occupations and forceful defeat of local opposition became common.

It has been argued that foreign intervention occurs when domestic strife threatens to establish governments hostile to the economic aspirations of specific external countries. For example, it has been claimed that the motive for American intervention in Vietnam was not simply ideological or geopolitical, but economic and neo-imperialist as well. This thesis claims that by 1960 the United States had determined to protect from Soviet-oriented or Chinese-oriented influence all Third World territories that have significant deposits of minerals and other raw materials critical to America's economic dominance in an era when history moved from the industrial age to the technological age.

The preceding examples vary in kind, but they all illustrate that external intervention in the domestic strife of nations, particularly economically underdeveloped ones, has become so common and frequent for a variety of reasons as to have eliminated the distinction between civil and international war in current history. While the thesis that external war results in part from an effort to preserve domestic cohesion is precarious, the idea that civil strife often results in international war is abundantly demonstrated.

9. Relative Deprivation

The concept of relative deprivation is especially useful in describing the origins of internal wars. It maintains that political rebellion and insurrection are most likely when people believe that they are receiving less than their due. To achieve greater benefits or to relieve the frustration of denial, groups may turn to aggression and political violence.[20]

This differs from simple common sense in one important respect: the objective or absolute conditions of poverty and oppression do not lead directly to rebellion, but rather the subjective or psychological response to these conditions is determinant. To illustrate, studies of rebellion and revolution find that violence most often occurs when conditions are beginning to improve rather than when they are at their worst point. The beginnings of improvement after a long period of deprivation trigger a "revolution of rising expectations." Hopes rise more rapidly than realities, and an "aspiration gap" results, as shown in Figure 11–2. Careful statistical studies have found that violence has tended to increase during the transitional period from traditional to modern society, as predicted by the theory of relative deprivation. Figure 11–3 shows the general relationship between violence and level of economic development.

Since 1945, civil wars have been more frequent in the developing

FIGURE 11–2
Level of economic development: the aspiration gap.

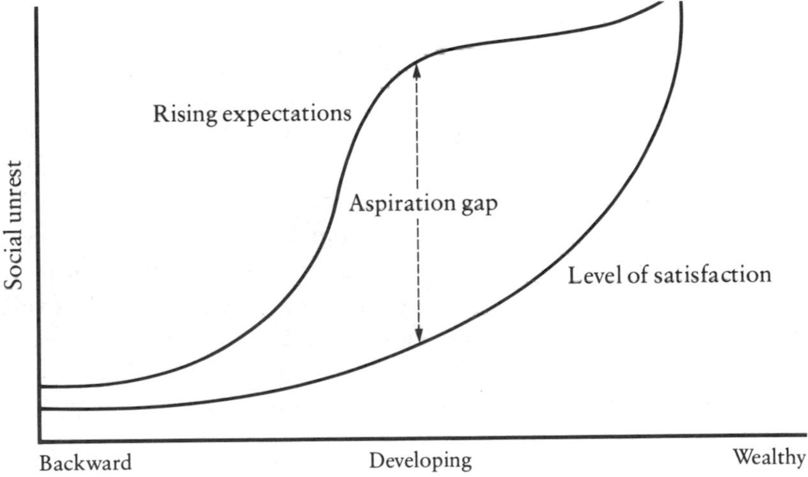

20. See especially Ted Gurr, *Why Men Rebel* (Princeton, N.J.: Princeton University Press, 1970). Also, Crane Brinton, *The Anatomy of Revolution* (New York: Vintage, 1965), and James Davies, "Toward a Theory of Revolution," *American Sociological Review* 27, no. 1, February 1962; Peter A. Lupsha, "Explanation of Political Violence: Some Psychological Theories Versus Indignation," *Politics and Society,* 2, no. 1, Fall 1971; John Dollard, Leonard Doob and Neal E. Miller, *Frustration and Aggression* (New Haven, Conn.: Yale University Press, 1939); and Ivo and Rosalind Frierabend, "Aggressive Behavior Within Politics, 1948–62," *Journal of Conflict Resolution* 10, no. 3, September 1966, pp. 249–71.

FIGURE 11–3
Economic improvement and rebellion.

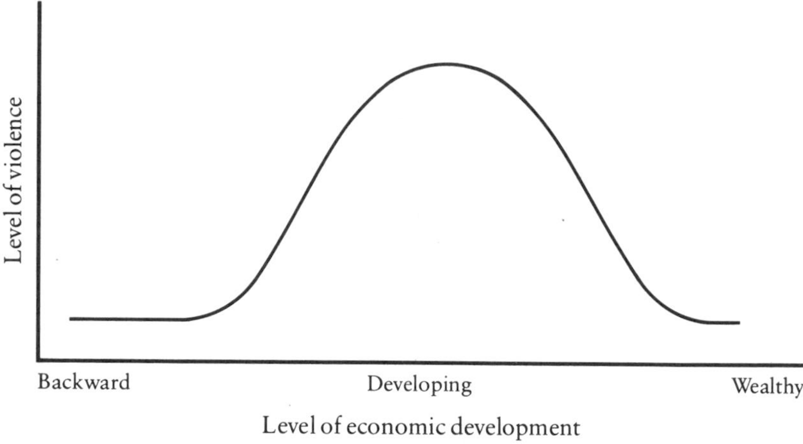

world than in already developed states. While there were more than eighty-five wars of varying magnitude in the Third World between 1945 and 1984, some quite substantial, the developed countries experienced only sporadic incidents of riot-scale violence on their own territories. In Korea, Vietnam, Nigeria, Bangladesh, Indonesia, Colombia, Algeria, Kampuchea, Laos, Zaïre, Angola, Mozambique, Guinea-Bissau, Chad, Sri Lanka, Lebanon, Nicaragua, El Salvador, Uganda, China, Sudan, Yemen, Iran, Iraq and India, the dead numbered in the tens and hundreds of thousands and even in the millions. But in the highly publicized violent events in the developed countries, the dead have numbered only in the tens of hundreds: in the United States (the black revolution), Northern Ireland, French Canada, Belgium, Portugal and Czechoslovakia. To explain this disparity between rates of violence in developed and less-developed countries, the theory of relative deprivation and the aspiration gap is attractive.[21]

However, several objections arise. Rich countries have engaged in

21. One of the overlooked facts of contemporary life is that many governments have increased expenditures for the use of force against internal upheaval much more dramatically than they have for international stability or war. From 1966–75, for example, police expenditures in Africa rose by 144 percent, while appropriations for armies rose 40 percent. See Morris Janowitz, *Military Institutions and Coercion in the Developing Nations* (Chicago: University of Chicago Press, 1977). For a study of "macroparasitism" since the year 1000 AD, see William H. McNeill, *The Pursuit of Power* (Chicago: University of Chicago Press, 1977). This is a study of the interaction of technology, armed force and society, in which macroparasites are defined as "other men who, by specializing in violence, are able to secure a living without themselves producing the food and other commodities they consume. Hence a study of macroparasitism among human populations turns into a study of the organization of armed force with special attention to changes in the kinds of equipment warriors used" (p. vii).

many hostile confrontations outside their own borders, usually in the territory of dependent Third World client states. This *displacement of violence* to the developing countries may be a privilege conferred by the unequal distribution of influence in the international system. Also, Marxist critics have argued that there is an essential unity in the global revolutionary movement, and that even revolutions in remote parts of the world are challenges to the worldwide system of imperialism. Today's struggles occur in the periphery rather than in the center because of the relatively weaker hold of the imperialists in outlying regions. The overbalance of violence in the developing nations is, in the Marxist view, a transient historical phenomenon from which causal inferences cannot be drawn too hastily.

Another objection to this theory of political violence concerns the separation of physical bloodshed from other forms of abuse. The isolation of violence as the dependent variable in many studies ignores the fact that physical conflict exists on a continuum with other forms of harm, such as systematic oppression, imprisonment and political denial. Such "institutional violence" can be quite as painful as physical abuse, and it can continue over much longer periods of time. Singling out rebellious violence alone as a social disease ignores the everyday suffering of millions of people and may result in false theories and vacuous remedies.

10. Instinctual Aggression

One of the most popular theories of war among laymen is the idea of an instinct of aggression—the blood lust that is depicted in so many lurid movies and magazines. In the aggression theory, the root of war is seen as a vestigial instinct of pugnacity or bellicosity that has survived from our animal roots. Many observers have concluded that people like to fight, and that at least in part, international conflict has its basis in male competitiveness *(machismo)* and even direct sadism. The outbreak of war is traced to biological proclivities and to individual and collective psychopathology.[22]

22. William McDougall, "The Instinct of Pugnacity," in Leon Bramson and George Goethals, *War: Studies from Psychology, Sociology and Anthropology* (New York: Basic Books, 1964), pp. 33–44; Edward Glover, *War, Sadism, and Pacifism* (London: Allen and Unwin, 1933); Elton McNeil: "Psychology and Aggression," *Journal of Conflict Resolution* 3, no. 3, September 1959, pp. 195–293; "Personal Hostility and International Aggression," *Journal of Conflict Resolution* 5, no. 3, September 1961, pp. 279–90; "The Nature of Aggression," in Elton McNeil, editor, *The Nature of Human Conflict* (Englewood Cliffs, N.J.: Prentice-Hall, 1965), pp. 14–44.

It is quite evident that people enjoy violence; otherwise television and the movies would not be so full of it. But there is much controversy concerning the relationship between aggressive impulses and the decision to go to war. One major study of twenty-five wars found that the decision to go to war was "in no case . . . precipitated by emotional tensions, sentimentality, crowd behavior, or other irrational motivations."[23] As organizations become more bureaucratic, controls are put on personal impulsiveness and deviance; studies have found that decisions made by groups are more likely to approximate rational choices than decisions made in similar situations by individuals.[24]

On the other side, several theorists view aggression as a dominant impulse triggered by political disputes that provide the necessary rationalization for violence. As Albert Einstein said, "Man has within him a lust for hatred and destruction. . . . It is a comparatively easy task to call this into play and raise it to the level of a collective psychosis."[25] Bertrand Russell claimed: "War is accepted by men . . . with a readiness, an acquiescence in untrue and inadequate reasons."[26] Naturally, this opinion is more convincing to those who reject the official rationale but must account for the persistence of their opponents in adhering to it.

Systematic studies distinguish between realistic and nonrealistic conflicts.[27] In a realistic conflict, the cause of struggle is rational disagreement over goals. In a nonrealistic conflict, the immediate issues are merely a pretext for fighting, and the real purpose of the combatants is violence itself. When we have both an instinct of combativeness and a disagreement over political issues, we have a chicken-and-egg problem, of deciding which is the real cause. Are the political issues only rationalizations to justify violence and to permit the relaxation of normal inhibitions against bloodshed that are applied unless "reasons of state" are involved? Or is it the reverse—leaders facing realistic disagreements with opponents take advantage of the aggressiveness of

23. Theodore Abel, "The Element of Decision in the Pattern of War," *American Sociological Review* 6, 1941, p. 855.
24. See O. G. Brim, editor, *Personality and Decision Processes* (Stanford, Ca.: Stanford University Press, 1962). For an important view on the other side, see Harold Lasswell, *Psychopathology and Politics,* 2nd ed. (New York: Viking, 1960). Lasswell found a tendency for psychopathological individuals to go into public life out of proportion to their numbers in a group, displacing and rationalizing private disturbances in terms of the "public interest." For a review of literature on this question, see Brent Rutherford, "Psychopathology, Decision-Making, and Political Involvement," *Journal of Conflict Resolution* 10, no. 4, December 1966, pp. 387–407.
25. From a letter to Sigmund Freud in James Strachey, editor, *The Standard Edition of the Complete Psychological Works of Sigmund Freud* (London: Hogarth, 1964), vol. 22, pp. 199–202.
26. Bertrand Russell, *Why Men Fight* (New York: Bonibooks, 1930), pp. 5–6.
27. Lewis Coser, *The Functions of Social Conflict* (New York: The Free Press of Glencoe, 1957).

their followers to arouse a spirit of national struggle? Is aggressiveness a cause of war or only a consequence of it?

No final answer to this question has emerged from conflict research, but it is a reliable maxim that the aggressive urge is important only insofar as it is translated into ideology. Sheer blood lust plays a relatively minor role, but aggressive and demanding definitions of the political situation are commonly behind warlike disputes. If the aggressive urge distorts perceptions and magnifies perceived threats (Cold War, for instance), it is a causal contributor to war. Thus, serious researchers tend to reject the crudest forms of the aggression theory and to accept the more complex and subtle formulation.

If an aggressive instinct is the cause of war, what is the cure? Some theorists have argued that the solution to the problem of aggression is not to attempt to eradicate the instinct, but to channel it into constructive forms. Freud believed that if the aggressive urge were not released in socially functional expression, it would turn inward as a death force and destroy the individual.[28] Even Gandhi, the apostle of nonviolence, said that he would rather "risk violence a thousand times than [risk] the emasculation of a whole race."[29] The classic advocate of this view was the philosopher William James, who argued in 1912 that a warless world with "no scorn, no hardness, no valor any more" would be "a cattleyard of a planet." War elicits from men and women the highest ideals of self-sacrifice and personal striving for excellence. The goal, according to James, should not be to eliminate the aggressive urge, but to develop a "moral equivalent of war" as an alternative constructive outlet for the same capacities. He proposed a cooperative struggle to tame nature for human betterment, with workers organized in paramilitary units.[30]

There is now a substantial research literature on the nature and function of the aggressive urge and its relation to political violence. Much of it focuses on animal behavior for clues to human aggression. In the best known of these reports, Konrad Lorenz examines the logic and functions of aggression in a variety of animal species. He finds that aggression is useful in many ways: for self-defense and protection of the young for forcing territorial spacing over the available food area, preventing depletion in one location; or for mate selection through male rivalry, leading to the upward evolution of species. He

28. Reply to Einstein in Strachey, editor, *Complete . . . Works of Sigmund Freud,* pp. 209–11.
29. See Norman Bose, editor, *Selections from Gandhi* (Ahmedabad, India: Navajivan Publishing House, 1957), pp. 159–63.
30. See *The Moral Equivalent of War* (Cabot, Vt.: International Voluntary Service, 1960); reprinted from William James, *Memories and Studies* (London: Longmans, 1912). Elsewhere, Seymour Melman proposed to replace the arms race with a "peace race"; see *The Peace Race* (New York: Ballantine, 1961).

then asks, What keeps aggressive behavior within tolerable and useful limits and prevents it from destroying the species altogether?

This question leads him to his key finding: that a second, previously unknown factor exists alongside the aggressive urge. This is a built-in inhibition *against* the use of violence, which is present in every species whenever aggression occurs. The inhibition is biologically triggered when the victim of an attack gives an appropriate signal of submission; the signal is different for each species. Most important, the strength of the inhibition in each species is proportional to the innate "lethality" of the species—the stronger the natural weapons of the species, the firmer the inhibition. The supposedly vicious wolf, for example, is quite incapable of continuing an attack on another wolf once the victim signals submission by exposing a vulnerable section of its neck. The dove, on the other hand, supposedly as peaceful as the wolf is warlike, is actually quite vicious. Having poor equipment for aggression, it has little inhibition against aggression and has been known to pluck apart another dove ruthlessly over a forty-eight-hour period of torment, disregarding signals of submission.

Lorenz extends this theory to an explanation of human aggression. He reasons that man lacks teeth, claws, poison and other natural weapons of great power. Hence, the corresponding level of his inhibition is relatively moderate, but he has used his brain to develop artificial weapons which greatly enhance his lethality. His programmed inhibitions are exceeded by his unprogrammed potential for destruction, and he is able to release his aggression with relatively little restraint. Aerial bombardment, long-range artillery and other remote-control weapons interfere with the passing of signals that would restrain the attacker. Thus man, according to Lorenz, has upset nature's balanced design, and the aggressive urge threatens to destroy him.[31]

If aggression, in fact, does underlie violent political ideologies, political controls against the outbreak of wars will be difficult to institute. Some have proposed that candidates for national leadership in all countries be subjected to psychiatric examination. Utopian thought in the science fiction literature has even raised the possibility that hostility-suppressing drugs be given routinely to heads of state to control their bellicose drives. Another idea is to change the psychological environment of international conferences to remind statesmen of the potential consequences of their acts. One creative suggestion is to place a child maimed in war in the middle of the conference table, and to have windows of the conference room open onto a playground. Still another idea is to keep the families of national leaders in rival capitals

31. Konrad Lorenz, *On Aggression* (New York: Harcourt Brace Jovanovich, 1966); see also Robert Ardrey, *The Territorial Imperative* (New York: Atheneum, 1966).

Source: *Greensboro Daily News*/Gamma

The face of hatred. These men, members of the Ku Klux Klan, are pulling guns from the trunk of a car, and are about to start shooting at a small group of communists holding a rally in Greensboro, North Carolina, in November 1979. Five members of the Worker's Viewpoint Organization were slain.

as hostages against bombardment and surprise attack. These measures would strengthen the weak inhibitions postulated by Lorenz.

Unfortunately, these colorful suggestions overlook the subtle process by which aggressive drives are translated into depersonalized ideologies. Once this translation is made, national policy becomes a matter of high principle, and controls on purely personal impulses are quite beside the point. If the national belief system itself incorporates a biological tendency into a highly rationalized form, biological and psychological solutions will be less important than political controls (such as the balance of power) that check aggressive policies. While the problem of war may have in part a biological cause, the solution must be political.

Cultural Differences and Aggression

Are some countries and cultures more aggressive than others? Many historians and social scientists have attempted to match degrees of aggressiveness with different national characters. Germany, for example, has been identified as a country with a cultural background particularly conducive to authoritarianism and the use of force, as reflected in prevailing child-rearing practices, the martial quality of German music and other cultural attributes.

Nineteen hundred years ago Tacitus gave this classic account of the German propensity to war:

> Many noble youths, if the land of their birth is stagnating in a protracted peace, deliberately seek out other tribes, where some war is afoot. The Germans have no taste for peace; renown is easier won among perils, and you cannot maintain a large body of companions except by violence and war. . . . You will find it harder to persuade a German to plough the land and to await its annual produce with patience than to challenge a foe and earn the prize of wounds. . . . When not engaged in warfare, they spend some little time in hunting, but more in idling, abandoned to sleep and gluttony. All the heroes and grim warriors dawdle their time away, while the care of the house, hearth, and fields is left to the women, old men and weaklings of the family. The warriors themselves lose their edge. They are so strangely inconsistent. They love indolence but they hate peace.[32]

This opinion accords with the views of many observers of German behavior during the present century.

But is there a scientific basis for the opinion that different cultures have varying propensities to political violence? Careful studies disagree on the answer. Some relate various cultural attributes to the occurrence of aggressive behavior, taking the frequency of violence as an indicator of the cultural propensity for war.[33] But others doubt that the frequency of violence and war is attributable to culture. A more important factor may be the number of common borders that a country shares with other nations. This is the theory of "geographical opportunity"—the more borders, the more war.[34] Another factor unrelated to aggression is the territorial distribution of ethnic groups. As we have seen, multiethnic countries have more opportunity for conflict than homogeneous populations. Against these and other factors, purely cultural variations in aggressiveness may be a weak explanation for warlike behavior. At least one study concludes that there is no good evidence for a cultural propensity to aggressiveness:

> Although culture patterns may be fruitfully compared in terms of their ways of handling and expressing hostility/aggression, it is essentially

32. Tacitus, *On Britain and Germany* (Baltimore: Penguin, 1948), pp. 112–13.
33. For example, Tom Broch and Johan Galtung, "Belligerence Among the Primitives," *Journal of Peace Research,* 1966, pp. 33–45; and Quincy Wright, *The Study of War,* appendices 9, 10 and 20.
34. James Paul Wesley, "Frequency of Wars and Geographical Opportunity," *Journal of Conflict Resolution* 4, December 1962, pp. 387–89.

> meaningless to describe one culture as more or less hostile/aggressive than another in any absolute terms, since no external criterion exists that is not in some sense arbitrary.[35]

In general, one may say that the present evidence for cultural propensities to aggressiveness (in the sense of warlike violence) is inconclusive.

War–Peace Cycles

Another strand of aggression research is the search for cycles of violent behavior. Does the amount of violence in human society ebb and flow in patterns? Is there a "war curve"? Such research is generally based on the aggression view of war, but sometimes the aggression theory is left implicit.

Early quantitative research into this matter varied in its conclusions, with some researchers rejecting the cycle theory, some demurring from it by finding certain trends, and others accepting it.[36] Most recent studies point more conclusively toward validating the war-cycle theory. One finds a trend of an upswing in the level of violence about every twenty-five years, with a twenty-year cycle prior to 1680 and thirty years the apparent cycle after that. Another hypothesizes that the observed cycle of war is caused by patterns in social psychology. After a war, memories of suffering are vivid and further fighting is avoided. As time passes, unpleasant memories fade or are repressed, and "the themes employed in the descriptions of the last great war shift from 'horror'-dominant to 'glory'-dominant." War is then romanticized again until a new opportunity arises to satisfy violent needs. There is a parallel rotation of decision-makers every twenty to twenty-five years, and the new leaders, it would appear, need to have their "own" war. This seems to assume that "the opportunities for employing violence are always present."[37]

With these exceptions, most researchers have not found a uniform pattern in the temporal spacing of wars. There does not appear to be a reliable war/peace cycle. This suggests that aggressive war is not a

35. R. T. Green and G. Santori, "A Cross Cultural Study of Hostility and Aggression," *Journal of Peace Research* 1, 1969, p. 22.
36. See, respectively, Pitirim Sorokin, *Social and Cultural Dynamics* (New York: Bedminster, 1962), vol. 3, p. 357; Lewis Richardson, *Statistics of Deadly Quarrels* (Pittsburgh, Pa.: Boxwood, 1960), pp. 137–41; and J. E. Moval, "The Distribution of Wars in Time," *Journal of the Royal Statistical Society* 112, 1949, pp. 446–58.
37. Frank Denton and Warren Phillips, "Some Patterns in the History of Violence," *Journal of Conflict Resolution* 1, no. 2, June 1968, p. 193. A similar conclusion positing fifty-year cycles is found in Oswald Spengler, *Decline of the West* (New York: Knopf, 1926), vol. 1, pp. 109–10.

simple instinctual need, since instinctual desires, by nature, require periodic satisfaction. The frequency of wars is not primarily a function of culture or time, but of political conflicts. War cannot be understood apart from politics.

11. Economic and Scientific Stimulation

Another theory of war concerns its economic functions. War has promoted the acceleration of scientific discovery, technical innovation and industrial development. It might be said that a major "external economy" of war is this great industrial spinoff. Sluggish economies may be stimulated by the creation of "artificial demand": "The attacks that have since the time of Samuel's criticism of King Saul been leveled against military expenditures as waste may well have concealed or misunderstood the point that some kinds of waste may have a larger social utility."[38] There is little doubt, for example, that the Great Depression of the 1930s ended for America only with the onset of the Second World War. Military demands put Americans back to work and primed the pump of economic recovery. Today, with economic pump priming managed principally through manipulation of the public sector, military spending is a crucial factor in most industrialized nation-states.

Again, empirical studies challenge intuitive logic. Some argue that, on the whole, the economy would prosper with substantial cuts in defense spending. However, some industries would feel harsh effects, while the gainers would profit only slightly.[39] Supporters of military spending are therefore better organized than opponents.

Nevertheless, even if high levels of military spending can be shown to be good for the corporate economy, it does not follow that war is

38. Arthur Waskow, *Toward the Unarmed Forces of the United States* (Washington, D.C.: Institute for Policy Studies, 1966), p. 9. Also, David Bazelon, "The Politics of the Paper Economy," *Commentary*, November 1962, p. 409; and Michael Reich, "Military Spending and the US Economy," in Steven Rosen, editor, *Testing the Theory of the Military-Industrial Complex* (Lexington, Mass.: D. C. Heath, 1973), pp. 85–86. See also John Nef, *War and Human Progress* (Cambridge, Mass.: Harvard University Press, 1950).

39. Stanley Lieberson, "An Empirical Study of Military-Industrial Linkages," in Steven Rosen, editor, *Testing the Theory of the Military-Industrial Complex*. For more general issues, see especially Robert G. Kokat, "Some Implications of the Economic Impact of Disarmament on the Structure of American Industry," in US Congress, Joint Economic Committee, *Economic Effects of Vietnam Spending* (Washington, D.C., 1967); Wassily Leontief, et al., "The Economic Impact of an Arms Cut," in Wassily Leontief, editor, *Input-Output Economics* (New York: Oxford University Press, 1966). See also Emile Benoit and Kenneth Boulding, editors, *Disarmament and the Economy* (New York: Harper and Row, 1963).

good for business. Major wars tend to produce side-effects such as inflation, the tightening of credit, and the interruption of international trade and financial flows—all of which harm the largest corporations. The New York Stock Exchange averages *declined* in response to escalation in Vietnam and Kampuchea (formerly Cambodia) and recovered their losses only with the deescalation of the war.[40] Even firms specializing in the production of military hardware did not flourish during the Vietnam years. US defense profits ran at substantially higher rates from 1961 to 1964 than from 1965 to 1972. Thus, we are led to the paradoxical conclusion that defense spending might be good for the capitalist economy, but war definitely is not. Perhaps the perfect combination from a profit viewpoint is a prolonged state of controlled international tensions (such as the Cold War) with high military spending but without the actual outbreak of war.

Even if warlike policies were clearly and unambiguously favorable to business, it would not automatically follow that governments would act in these interests. It was shown in 1935 that financial and industrial elites had played a relatively secondary role in the expansionist policies of the imperialist states. Investors supported governments interested in expansion for other reasons, but the political elite used the business groups rather than the reverse.[41] Another study found that economic causes figured directly in less than a third of wars from 1820 to 1949, and that they have been more important in small wars than in large wars.[42] The results in studies like these often depend on the way that the question is posed and the measures that are used for key variables.

12. The Military-Industrial Complex

One issue of special interest in the debate over causes of war is that of the military-industrial complex. Powerful domestic groups within the major states that have vested interests in military spending and international tension use their influence to promote antagonistic relations between nations, according to this theory. These domestic groups that comprise the military-industrial complex include (1)

40. See Betty Hanson and Bruce Russett, "Testing Some Economic Interpretations of American Intervention," in Rosen, editor, *Testing the Theory of the Military-Industrial Complex.*
41. Eugene Staley, *War and the Private Investor* (Garden City, N.Y.: Doubleday, 1935). See also Kenneth Boulding and Tapan Mukerjee, editors, *Economic Imperialism* (Ann Arbor, Mich.: University of Michigan Press, 1962), and Steven Rosen and James Kurth, editors, *Testing the Theory of Economic Imperialism* (Lexington, Mass.: D. C. Heath, Lexington Books, 1974).
42. Richardson, *Statistics of Deadly Quarrels* (Pittsburgh, Pa.: Boxwood, 1960). Contrast John Bakeless, *The Economic Causes of Modern War* (London: Yard, 1921).

professional soldiers, (2) managers and, in the capitalist states, owners of industries deeply engaged in military supply, (3) high government officials whose careers and interests are tied to military expenditure, and (4) legislators whose districts benefit from defense projects.

These core members of the military-industrial complex are supported by associated and lesser groups such as the veterans and military service associations who do defense-related research. These groups occupy powerful positions in the political structures of the major states, and they exercise their influence in a coordinated and mutually supportive way to maintain optimal levels of war preparation and to direct national security policy. According to proponents of this theory, the influence of the military-industrial complex exceeds that of any opposing coalitions or interests.

This complex rationalizes high levels of military spending with an ideology of conflict, such as the mythology of the Cold War. This ideology may be a deliberately manufactured deception to mislead the public, or it may be a militaristic false consciousness that arises spontaneously with high military spending. Whether or not the complex is a conscious conspiracy, it requires an ideology of international conflict to guarantee its position within the political and economic structure of the society. To the conventional theorist, arms races are caused by realistic conflicts and a cycle of mutual fear between opposing states. To the military-industrial-complex theorist, the external threat is merely a necessary projection for the self-aggrandizing activities of domestic military-industrial complexes.

In its classic formulation, this theory applies to both capitalist and socialist states.[43] In the latter, the professional military combines with managers of state defense industries and with related functionaries within the Communist party apparatus and the ministries and bureaucracies. There is a natural and effective alliance of interests between Soviet heavy industry, the armed forces and the conservative wing of the Communist party, forged upon "their understanding of the interdependency that exists between security, heavy industry, and ideological orthodoxy." Without it, harm would befall the career interests and social positions of both the professional military elite and some of the most highly paid civilian personnel in the country. Thus, despite state ownership of productive facilities, the USSR also has a military-industrial complex interested in the continuation of international conflict.[44]

43. C. Wright Mills, *The Causes of World War III* (New York: Ballantine, 1958) and *The Power Elite* (New York: Oxford University Press, 1956).
44. Vernon Aspaturian, "The Soviet Military-Industrial Complex: Does It Exist?" in Rosen, editor, *Testing the Theory of the Military-Industrial Complex*.

The theory of the military-industrial complex is far from flawless. It fails to account for the decline in percentage of national production devoted to defense in both the United States and the Soviet Union in the early 1970s. The US defense budget in constant dollars (that is, discounting inflation) declined in 1973 to a level comparable to the 1950s, and the decline in both constant dollars and percentage of the GNP continued throughout the decade. This occurred even as the cost of designing and building military technology increased, though some of the cost was offset by the decrease in the military population after the Vietnam War. Several congressional battles over military procurement have resulted in the elimination of entire weapons systems. For a brief period several aerospace industries faced bankruptcy, one of which (Lockheed) had to be rescued by the government. In many ways, then, the defense sector shows signs of decline and weakness rather than the omnipotence attributed to it by military-industrial-complex theorists, at least in the United States (which alone accounts for about 40 percent of the entire world's military expenditures).

Until recently, a similar trend seemed to be under way in the Soviet Union. But by 1977 it was apparent that the Kremlin was in the midst of a substantial commitment to expanded military capability, and an increase of as much as 50 percent in the share of gross national product devoted to military procurement was estimated by Western observers. Similarly, by 1979/80 there were increases in the American military budget in constant dollars, due both to expansion of American capability and to the construction of arms and military hardware for international trade. During the presidential and congressional election campaigns of 1980 it became clear that the United States was headed toward a major new military build-up. Both President Carter and challenger Ronald Reagan called for increases in defense spending, as did most candidates for congressional seats, in part based on the Soviet declaration of 1980 that it would never again rank second to the United States as a military power. With the Reagan victory, the stock market soared, particularly in the defense industries.

There followed, however, the deepest and most prolonged recession since World War II, which did not break until the early months of 1983. The break was dramatic, raising the stock market to record heights and an increase of almost five hundred points in five months. Among the stimulants was the President's wish to increase defense spending by ten percent; defense contractors were happy with the actual increase of five percent approved by Congress, since it represented approximately a ten billion-dollar increase over the preceding year.

But even when the defense sector expands rather than shrinks, other doubts still apply. The theory of the military-industrial complex assumes that political behavior is motivated essentially by private interest rather than public good or national interest. At the core of the theory, critics charge, is a crude and simplistic economic determinism. Careful studies of international events generally find a much more complex pattern of motivation behind national policies. Particularly in warlike conflicts, where the highest values of life and death and national survival are at issue, behavior tends to be guided by principled conviction rather than crude self-interest.

The theory of the military-industrial complex gains plausibility if ideology is considered alongside self-interest and conflict behavior. Behavior may be determined by convictions, but where do these come from? Perhaps self-interest sets the frame for broader values and perceptions. If so, military-industrial dependency might produce a conflict-filled world view.

This analysis is similar to the view taken earlier of the relationship between the aggressive instinct and warlike behavior. War decisions are guided by rational calculations, but the conscious values and perceptions themselves may conceal an underlying aggressiveness. Similarly, values and perceptions may sublimate private interests into the supposed national interest. Social scientists are only now beginning to inquire where political ideologies, convictions and beliefs come from. More research on this question will be needed before we can arrive at a definitive analysis of the role of the military-industrial complex and the aggressive instinct.

13. Population Limitation

One of the precursors of Hitler's theory of *Lebensraum* is the theory of population expansion and war suggested by Sir Thomas Malthus. In his *Essay on the Principle of Population* (1798), Malthus argued that there is an innate tendency for population to expand geometrically while food resources expand only arithmetically. Thus, "the power of population is infinitely greater than the power in the earth to produce subsistence for man." Since population must be proportioned to food supply, there must be controls on population growth. One of these is war.

This theory of war as a control on surplus population growth still remains attractive to laymen, though not to conflict researchers. The rate of global population expansion is much greater now than in Malthus's time. Indeed, more people have lived on the earth since 1900 than in the sum of human history before that date! And this number is expected to double and redouble in the next one hundred years. Some observers, echoing Malthus, predict cataclysmic wars and famines in the future to dispose of surplus population.

This theory, however, does not accord with the facts. Wars have in general taken very few lives when measured as a percentage of populations, even when the deaths have been in the millions. Only the most exceptional wars have taken more than 5 percent of the populations of the warring parties; more than half of all wars end with battle losses under one-half of 1 percent (see Figure 11–4). Even during the Second World War, the loss rate did not significantly depress populations. The losses of the North and South Vietnamese, staggering as they were, were lower than the birth rate, so the population continued to grow.[45] These figures do not agree with the Malthusian view of war as a significant population-limiting device. In addition, the technology of the Green Revolution now promises to multiply the capacity of the earth to produce food geometrically—finally putting to rest the theory of Malthus, unless, of course, we include nuclear war in the analysis. But an atomic cataclysm would destroy arable land as well as population.

FIGURE 11–4
Percentage population lost in battle death in major international wars.

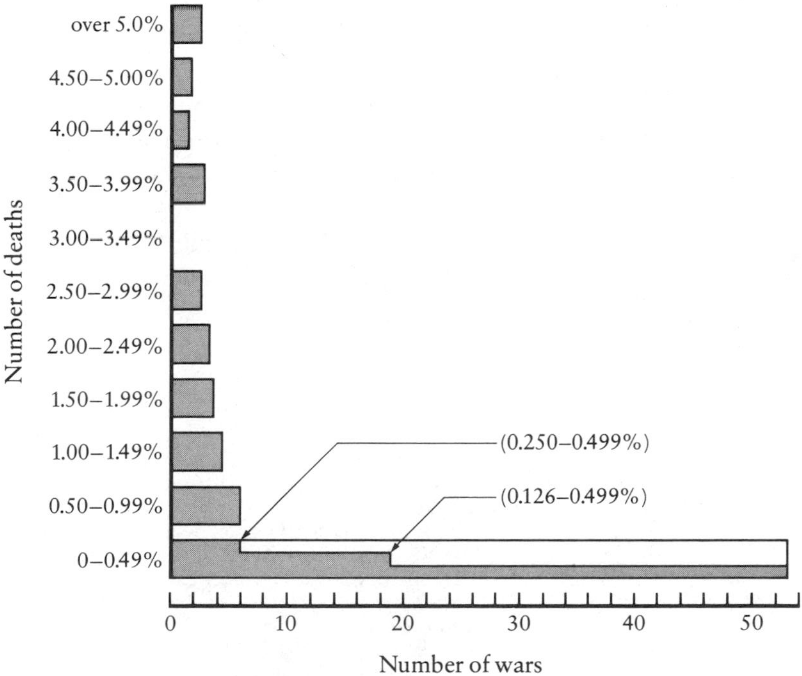

45. See Steven Rosen, "War Power and the Willingness to Suffer," in Bruce Russett, editor, *Peace, War, and Numbers* (Beverly Hills, Ca.: Sage Publications, 1972).

14. Conflict Resolution by Force

We have saved for last the most general and comprehensive theory: war as a device for conflict resolution. In the general theory, conflict exists when two or more groups make mutually exclusive claims to the same resources or positions, and war is a means of allocating scarce values to resolve the conflict. War, in this view, is a rational instrument of decision, and war policies are decided by a logical computation of costs and benefits.

The claim of rationality is controversial. Conflicts can be decided by arbitration, elections, courts and tribunals, administrative decisions, direct negotiation and compromise—even the flip of a coin. How is it rational to spill blood when nonviolent means are available?[46]

The answer lies in the importance of the issues typically involved in warlike disputes. Every nation or movement has a few "core" values that cannot be compromised and many "shell" values that it would also like to satisfy but are not vital. Secondary interests can be compromised with an opponent, but leadership is obligated to defend core values by all available means—including, if necessary, violent defense. War is the *ultima ratio*—the last resort. In the words of Walter Lippmann, war is "the way in which the great human decisions are made."[47]

In recent years, the image of the armed forces and military policy has been depreciated in the United States and other countries, partly as a consequence of the unpopular Vietnam War. At the same time, most people reject absolute pacifism and retain a belief in the "just war." For example, on May 24, 1969, the World Council of Churches resolved that, "All else failing, the church and churches would support resistance movements, including revolutions, aimed at elimination of political or economic tyranny which makes racism possible." While most people value nonviolence, they evidently value other things even

46. Just as war may be used to resolve differences among nations, so too may the escalation of war be used to bring about fast results. The theory of applying maximum force, even to levels that have previously been regarded as disproportionate to the conflict and to the objectives of the parties, was labeled the "madman theory" during the Vietnam War. President Nixon is reported to have suggested massive bombings of North Vietnam and the mining of Haiphong Harbor (at risk of destroying Soviet and other Eastern-bloc ships) as a means of forcing a conclusion to the war prior to the elections of 1972. Henry Kissinger is reported to have endorsed the "madman theory." See Seymour M. Hersh, *The Price of Power: Kissinger in the Nixon White House* (New York: Summit Books, 1983); refer to index for several references.
47. Walter Lippmann, "The Political Equivalent of War," *Atlantic Monthly,* August 1928, pp. 181–87.

more and are willing to pay the exorbitant price of human lives in their pursuit of core value objects.

Conclusion

Many of the theories that we have reviewed imply that the cause of war can be found in conspiracies, irrationality, hidden motives and the influence of certain elites. One is attracted to the conclusion that calm and thoughtful people who are not involved in the munitions industry or the military high command, and who are not particularly aggressive or greedy or sinister, and who neither hate the enemy unreasonably nor willfully misunderstand him, and who detest the idea of war as a waste of life and treasure do not make wars, but are led or duped into them.

But most wars involve very real incompatibilities between the basic moral objectives of the two sides, and it is historical fact that ordinarily the population of each side deliberately and without any element of crowd irrationality supports the carefully formulated policy of the leadership. In their zeal to eradicate war, political scientists cannot ignore the nonconspiratorial and quite rational processes in social life that turn the peace loving into warriors. It is the behavior of these people that is at the core of the theory of war as a rational instrument of conflict resolution.

III

The Logic of International Trade and Exchange

12

International Trade

Even though most international relations transactions appear to relate to power and military preparedness, the principal interactions of peoples and governments concern economics. One of the most important aspects of the international system is the international political economy, defined simply as the area of interaction between politics and economics. Some describe it as the study of the impact of politics upon economics and the impact of economics upon politics. Economic relations may be a cause of peace and friendship, or a cause of hostility and war. But of paramount importance is the fact that as measured by frequency of occurrence, economic transactions are the most important and fundamental in the international system.

Economic aspects of the international system have been a dominant force since the Industrial Revolution. As distances have beome shorter and competition keener, the need for markets and for inexpensive skilled labor, not to mention such other driving forces as raw materials and sources of energy, has stimulated volumes of international political implications. The quest for development in the post–World War II era has added another impetus, as has the central political-economic antipathy between the capitalist West and the socialist East. Though all of these problems stem from economic issues, they nevertheless fuel the international political system. In order to regulate these relations, the world has created an elaborate international economic system, much of which has become institutionalized (that is, it is organized around formal intergovernmental institutions) since the United Nations was formed. Such agencies as the International Monetary Fund, the International Bank for Reconstruction and Development, the General Agreement on Tariffs and Trade, the Organization of Petroleum Exporting Countries, the Organization for Economic Cooperation and Development and dozens of others contribute to the orderly regulation of the international political economy. Yet other aspects remain conspicuously unorganized: East-West economic relations, economic intervention in the developing world and political-economic subversion, to mention only a few. Because of the extent to which trade accounts for international activity, this chapter examines the logic behind it.

Goods pass daily between nations, and payments are adjusted through systems of international credit. But international trade is a source of more than profit; for as nations compete with one another for natural resources, labor, capital and world markets, they collide with each other's interests. We have seen, for example, that despite the closeness of Japanese-American relations since the Second World War, the great success of Japan's technological growth has threatened American sales throughout the world, has eroded profits within the United States because Japanese imports are less expensive than similar American products, and has made Japan so nearly self-sufficient industrially as to need fewer and fewer American goods. The result is that two friends are engaged in a constant effort to adjust their economic relations so that severe conflict might not develop over economic competition. Their respective abilities in international trade, generally looked upon as two independent capabilities for enrichment, in fact become a source of tension.

Economic relations between states are strained by more than trade. East-West trade, for example, is hampered by ideological differences, and the great difficulties of establishing meaningful price comparisons between capitalist and socialist economies. Even within the capitalist world, however, price comparisons and currency values impose severe strains on international activity. Domestic inflation, international trade volume and the numerical ratio of a state's exports and imports all affect the value of that state's currency. For twenty years after the Second World War, the American dollar and gold were regarded as the most precious media of exchange. Now, however, the decontrolled value of gold (which went from $35 per ounce to as high as $900 per ounce in a five-year period, only thereafter to drop again to $300) provides little stability to international business; and the value of the American dollar has slipped, despite two official devaluations, to the point where, until recently, central banks outside the United States have preferred to hold German marks or Japanese yen. For all of these reasons and more, a comprehensive understanding of international relations requires that not only economics, but also international trade and the international organization of money be considered as sources of international conflict.[1]

The logic of international trade has not in the past been considered part of the normal curriculum of international relations, and until recently political scientists have been content to leave what they regarded as an arcane subject to economists. Yet it is now universally agreed that contemporary international relations cannot be understood without at least a rudimentary comprehension of political economy—the impact of politics upon economics, and the impact of economics upon politics. As the great power conflicts of the postwar world have receded from the brink of war, the normal peacetime issues of commerce and trade have played a larger role in foreign policy and international interaction. The spread of industrial capability, the onset of the technological era, the huge increase in international trade volume, fluctuation of national currency values, foreign aid, the desire to protect national economies from foreign-made goods, the domination of international economic activity by transnational corporations—these and other characteristics of contemporary international political economy ensure that economic topics often dominate front-page political news. Theoretical refinements, counterarguments and mathematical treatments important to the economist are left aside in our discussion in favor of concentration on a few essential principles particularly important to the student of politics, many of which have been touched upon elsewhere without having been flagged as uniquely economic topics. The reader is reminded, for example, of the extent to which the Cold War resulted from conflicting world views attributable to fundamentally opposed economic philosophies; of the discussion of capitalist imperialism in the opening two chapters; of economic comparisons of China with the United States, the Soviet Union and Japan; of the economic causes of tension in Japanese-American relations; and of the economic objectives of Western Europe as a unitary actor with its resulting conflicts in European-American relations.

1. For a comprehensive introduction to history and theory, see Benjamin J. Cohen, *Organizing the World's Money* (New York: Basic Books, 1977).

International Trade

At the simplest level, a nation will import a commodity that it does not produce, and export one that it produces beyond the needs of the domestic market. For example, a nation that lacks fuel will import oil and gas, while another nation, which produces more automobiles than it needs (because they are cheaper individually when produced in large numbers), will export the excess. If all nations imported and exported different items, if there were a perfect international division of labor in the production of goods such that competition were absent, and if all participants kept constant both their need (demand) for imported goods and their production (supply) for export, then perfect natural regulation of international trade would result. But with modern innovation and demands for improved standards of living worldwide, such circumstances are as unlikely as a single, rigidly regulated and centrally directed world economy. In fact, most nations engage in international trade in a vast array of goods even while their domestic corporations attempt both to control domestic markets and to produce goods at prices that will compete in international export markets.

Furthermore, many nations import goods that they themselves also produce in large numbers; some goods might be both imported and exported! A standard example is the United States, which is the world's largest producer of cars and trucks, but which is also the largest export market for Japanese cars and the German Volkswagen. In the latter case, the German producer was in danger of falling behind the American demand and of losing its share of American market to Japan, so it purchased an abandoned automobile production facility in Pennsylvania, modernized it and commenced to produce VW Rabbits actually in the United States. Meanwhile, American manufacturers were finding production costs in the United States so high that they were producing automobiles abroad and selling them in the home market as American goods: Fords made in Canada and England, Buicks made in Italy, Mercurys made in Germany and Dodges made in Japan. (The 1975 Mercury Capri, which was sold to Americans as an American product, calls attention to the need for unleaded gasoline by the command "Achtung!" on a sticker over the tank cap.) Now American Motors and Renault, a French corporation, jointly produce the AMC/Renault Alliance in the United States; Honda produces automobiles in Tennessee; and Ford and Toyota will soon join forces to produce a new small car in California.

If all of this seems comical, it is nonetheless vitally important for international relations. For when VW produces in the United States, German workers lose jobs while Americans gain them; and the establishment and management of the production facility represent huge financial transactions for Germany, which must export funds (probably from the surplus of American dollars within its currency reserves) to the United States. On the other hand, external production of autos by American manufacturers represents a loss of jobs for Americans, as well as a large capital export. In addition, when producing overseas, American manufacturers spend capital and production costs abroad (thus producing no tax revenues at home) and bring home (repatriate) only their profits.

Obviously, the real circumstances of international trade are unlike the simple example with which we started. In the modern context, then, the theory of international trade begins with a question: Why, if a nation can produce a given product at home, should it import from abroad? Imports, after all, cut into domestic jobs and demand for domestic produce. Beyond a certain point the growth of imports might even lead to the collapse of domestic firms and the loss of employment for an entire labor sector. It is well known, for example, that production of color television sets in the United States has halted almost entirely, with the loss of thousands of jobs. Similarly, imported shoes, steel and other products have flooded the American market, devastating whole industries and geographic regions. It is not uncommon in the United States or elsewhere to encounter occasional demands that the government protect domestic industries by stopping or controlling imports of selected items, or that it apply such high tariffs (import charges) as to make imported goods significantly more expensive than similar domestic goods. Why, it is often asked, should a nation expose its products and workers to competition from abroad and to the perils of international competition? Everyone would agree that we should buy from abroad what cannot be produced at home, but why allow imports of those same commodities to threaten domestic production and employment? Even for nations that espouse the philosophy of free trade (trade without political restraint), what justification can there be for the potentially calamitous effects of imports, even if free trade does enhance international cooperation?

The answer to these vexing questions is found actually at the heart of this familiar argument. What should strike us immediately about it is the exclusive focus on imports and the lack of reference to exports. If indeed imported goods do substitute for domestic products, and do replace domestic jobs, it is equally the case that exports represent jobs performed and goods produced at home. A thorough comparison of the gains and losses in employment from international trade would be complicated, and would have to involve actual volume and composition of import and export flows, the labor intensity (the degree to which the cost of production represents the contributions of labor rather than capital) of production in pertinent industries, economic multiplier effects, economic and scientific spinoffs and several other critical details. Nonetheless, it is quite possible that a large volume of imports and exports will lead to a net gain in total employment, even if the dollar value or volume of imports were greater than the value and volume of exports.

It would seem that imports are inherently dangerous, and exports of extreme value. In fact, there is a popular myth that a few overproducers are madly flooding foreign markets with goods, while the recipients import with equal vigor and produce little or nothing. The myth relies on the assumption that the world's major producers will accept worthless currency in return for imported goods—that importers need only print more and more of their respective currencies to meet the import demand. In fact, however, money has value only insofar as it is able to pay for a subsequent claim, and that ability is determined in part by the vitality of the economy that produces it. In order to maintain the promise of the currency, a nation must maintain a steady flow of imports and exports. Such a policy ensures (1) that the value of exports will to some degree offset (and may even exceed) the cost of imports, and (2) that the vigor of the economy will enable the national currency to maintain its position relative to others.

Before looking at the notion of an international trade balance, it is instructive to return with this new perspective to a question posed earlier: Why do nations trade at all? Part of the answer is found in the comparative prices of goods in two countries. If the price of autos produced in country *A* is significantly lower than for those produced in country *B*, and if the cost of transporting them from *A* to *B* is less than the production cost difference, it is sensible for *B* to import automobiles from *A* because of the lower price. But given the impact on employment in *B*, it is of far greater advantage to *B* to import *A*'s autos if in return *B* is able to produce and transport some other commodity, such as computers, at a lower price than *B* can build them. This is the beginning of a rational exchange between the two: *A*'s autos for *B*'s computers.

Although this situation is considerably more complex than the primal circumstances used earlier, it is still atypical of international trade. Such reciprocal advantage is quite rare, especially given the broad array of goods that nations produce and demand. Moreover, it is common that one country in a trading partnership may be more productive and more cost efficient in several, or even all, of the goods that might be exchanged. Even under these circumstances it may be rational for them to maintain a bilateral trading relation. To explain this paradox, and to lay the foundation for a deeper understanding of international trade, it is necessary to go beyond isolated examples and to introduce the basic theory of comparative advantage that underlies the global exchange of goods and services.

The Theory of Comparative Advantage

The Ricardian theory of comparative advantage, named for the eighteenth-century classical economist David Ricardo, holds that the general welfare of two or more countries will be higher for all if free trade among them is permitted than if each attempts a policy of restricting trade and producing only for itself. Moreover, the theory holds that this will be true even if some countries are absolutely more efficient in the production of all goods than others and even if, in theory, each country could produce everything for itself.

To explain this essential principle, let us imagine a two-country, two-commodity world in which we have only the United States and Taiwan and only two products, automobiles and wheat. Let us further assume that American labor is absolutely more efficient in the production of both items: it takes an average of one person-year to produce a car in the US compared to two person-years in Taiwan, and one person-year to produce a thousand tons of wheat in the US compared to four person-years in Taiwan. We will make the simplifying assumption that these direct labor costs represent all factors of production in each country, and for the moment assume a world without money in which there is a direct barter exchange of goods.

At first glance, it might—incorrectly—appear that the United States will be in a better market position as a producer. But this impression is immediately corrected when we consider the *comparative* production advantages in the two countries, as reflected in their internal barter rates of exchange.

In the United States, if we assume that labor is the only cost of production and that all workers are paid equally within the country, an automobile, which represents one person-year of labor, will be worth exactly one thousand tons of wheat, since each thousand tons also contains one person-year. However, in Taiwan the internal barter rate of exchange will be different. There, it will take two automobiles to buy one ton of wheat, since the two person-years contained in a Taiwanese automobile is only half of the four person-years it takes to produce a ton of Taiwanese wheat.

The comparative advantage of each country is inherent in this difference of the barter rates of exchange—one car equals one thousand tons in the US compared to five hundred tons in Taiwan. Both sides will gain if there is a trade of American wheat for Taiwanese cars. For example, if the American wheat producer offers the Taiwanese car producer 750 tons for an automobile, the American will be spending less wheat than would be needed to buy an American car—750 compared to 1,000 tons—and the Taiwanese will be receiving more wheat for a car than he would in a home trade—750 compared to 500 tons. Clearly there is a mutual advantage in the trade.

Note that the opposite exchange does not work. The American car producer wants at least one thousand tons of wheat per automobile, since this is the price at home. But the Taiwanese producer of wheat will not be willing to accept such an exorbitant price, since one thousand tons at home will net two cars. Therefore, the exchange of American cars for Taiwanese wheat does not work. Only the exchange of American wheat for Taiwanese cars is sensible.

In this example, there is likely to be a thriving trade in American wheat for Taiwanese autos at 750 tons of wheat per car because this barter rate of exchange is advantageous for both sides. Is there a loser? As trade grows, the short-term loser will be American producers of cars and Taiwanese wheat farmers. Neither will be able to export, and it is to be expected that both will also lose shares in their domestic markets as their products are undersold by foreign competition. The American producer was, for example, able to buy 1,000 tons of wheat for each automobile before international trade, but in the changed market a car brings no more than the Taiwanese price in wheat: 750 tons. The industrialist might profit, in fact, from leaving the car business to produce wheat instead, because one person-year of labor will produce 1,000 tons, with which to buy a Taiwanese car and still have 250 tons of wheat. By remaining in the automobile business our industrialist produces one car per year and has no wheat at all.

The advantage of free trade will be clearer after considering two economies as a whole. Imagine that there are one hundred workers in each country, and that workers are freely transferable between industry and agriculture. Assume further that in each country workers are in the pretrade situation, evenly distributed between the two production sectors. We have, then, the picture as presented in Table 12–1.

Now, to compare the situation that might result after the introduction of trade, assume that a certain volume of American wheat is exchanged for Taiwanese autos at the barter rate of 750 tons of wheat per auto—an exchange rate that we have already indicated is advantageous to both sides. Assume also that as a result of the trade, there is a growth in US wheat production, which now produces for both the home and foreign markets, and a reduction in the size of the US

TABLE 12–1
Total output without trade.

	Number of Workers (A)	Output per Worker/ Year (B)	Total Production (A × B)
US wheat	50	1,000 tons	50,000 tons
US autos	50	1 auto	50 autos
Taiwan wheat	50	250 tons	12,500 tons
Taiwan autos	50	0.5 auto	25 autos

auto industry, which loses part of the home market and is unable to export competitively to Taiwan. Similarly, there is a decline of the Taiwan wheat sector and a growth in the Taiwan auto sector. These changes will be reflected in a reallocation of the work force in the two countries away from the declining industries and into the growing ones. Table 12–2 represents the result.

We see that with the same number of workers and the same output per worker/year (labor productivity rate), total world production of both products increases significantly when each country specializes in the line of production in which it is *comparatively* more efficient (even though the US is in our example *absolutely* more efficient in both production sectors). Before trade (Table 12–1), combined production of wheat was 62,500 tons and combined production of autos 75 units. With trade and its accompanying reallocation of the work forces,

TABLE 12–2
The gains of free trade.

	col. A	col. B	col. C	col. D[a]	col. E[a]	col. F	col. G	col. H
	No. of Wkrs.	Output per Wkr/Yr	Total Prod. (A × B)	Minus Exports	Plus Imports	Net Supply (C − D + E)	Supply before Trade from Table 1	Gains of Trade (G − F)
US wheat	65	1000	65,000	12,750		52,250	50,000	+4.5%
US autos	35	1	35		17	52	50	+4%
Taiwan wheat	10	250	2,500		12,750	15,250	12,500	+22%
Taiwan autos	90	0.5	45	17		28	25	+12%

[a]Assumes trade at the barter rate of 750 tons wheat = 1 auto

combined production is 67,500 tons of wheat and 80 autos. By having each country concentrate in the area of its comparative advantage, and permitting free trade between the two at the mutually advantageous rate of 750 tons = 1 car, the final supply of goods in *both* countries is significantly higher in every area than before trade. That is, the result of free trade increases the aggregate standard of living for both partners, and, conversely, a refusal to trade would result in a lower standard of living for both.

This is the powerful economic principle behind the call for free trade. With all its problems and dislocations, a free flow of goods, under normal conditions, has the potential to enhance the welfare of all countries. The results illustrated by Tables 12–1 and 12–2 could be extrapolated to apply to any number of countries and any number of products, though such a demonstration would require complex examples and calculations beyond the requirements of our analysis.

The Problems of Free Trade

In spite of the attractiveness of the free trade argument as set forth in Ricardian theory, free trade is not without its practical problems. It is generally acknowledged that international trade raises a variety of conflicting interests that must be reconciled in order for the international political economy to function smoothly and profitably. Some of these difficulties can be managed within the framework of a free trade regime, such as that established by the United Nations—consisting principally of the International Monetary Fund, The World Bank Group and the General Agreement on Tariffs and Trade—while others are considered sufficiently important to merit restrictions on trade. It is important to differentiate, therefore, between world trade problems that are sensibly resolved or regulated by a free trade program and those for which such a program might be counterproductive. Keep in mind also that the extension or withdrawal of free trade can be used as an instrument of power in world politics. Governments may use free trade as a means of strengthening friendly governments, and may discontinue trade individually or through collective sanctions in order to weaken hostile governments. Clearly, the philosophy of free trade is not entirely divorced from higher political principles and objectives in international relations.

The most frequent objection to free trade arises from workers, managers and owners in industries adversely affected by imports, who quite naturally wish to protect their jobs and investments by reducing the price advantages of imports or banishing them altogether. In recent American experience, loud calls upon Congress and the White House for such protection have come from the shoe industry, fishing interests, steel, automobile manufacturing, textiles, petrochemicals and electronics, to mention just a few representative sectors in which domestic productivity and market dominance are severely threatened by import competition. Typically, advocates of protection call for some or all of the following instruments.

1. *Tariffs, Import Surcharges or Other Import Taxes* All of these are designed to increase the selling price of imported goods relative to the prices of domestically produced goods. If a compact Japanese car normally sells in the American market for $200 less than a comparatively equipped American-made car, then an import tax of $300 on the Japanese car should result in increased sales of the American product and decreased sales of the import. But discriminated governments do not take lightly to changes in tariff policy, and are likely to threaten or even to undertake tariff retaliation. Such action and reaction can result in trade warfare or tariff warfare, which is antithetical to the concept of free trade. In order to prevent this, the major capitalist nations have engaged in intermittent multilateral trade negotiations in order to regulate as much as possible the character of tariffs and import taxes among them, both as a stimulus to world trade and as a means of preventing disruption in trade relations. In addition, the establishment after the Second World War of the General Agreement of Tariffs and Trade (GATT) as an integral part of the United Nations system provided the international machinery for dealing with the same problems.

2. *Preferential Tax Treatment for Domestic Producers* One of the major reasons imports become a threat to domestic producers is differences in the rate of investment for modernization in different countries. If an industry in country *A* continues to produce a commodity by out-of-date means, it is possible that it will keep its price unnecessarily high. If at the same time the same industry in country *B* has adopted innovative means of production, it may be able to bring the world price of the item down and therefore to invade the domestic market of country *A* at a lower price than that of domestic production. One rational response in country *A* would be to invest heavily in modern production techniques and attempt once again to surpass the efficiency of country *B*'s producer. But if investment erodes stockholders' profits while sales fall to imports, investment may require an incentive. Often the incentive industries call for is preferential tax treatment for producers in selected sectors, specifically in order to permit them to divert dollars to production that would otherwise go

to taxes. The threat of import underselling is a common cause for preferential tax treatment in capitalist economies. In economies where the government controls all means of production, such preferences are always present, but more as a matter of public policy and economic philosophy than as an exception under duress.

3. *Import Restrictions Including Prohibition* Whatever combination of remedies might be sought, import restrictions almost invariably are included. This mechanism, a device that simply prevents or limits subsequent importation of the threatening commodity, can scarcely be undertaken without severe disruption in the other relations of trading partners. It is a unilateral act without compromise, and reasonable as it might seem in light of urgent domestic circumstances, it is highly destructive of international relations. Its impact on employment, investment and fiscal policies in the target countries is immediate and profound, and it runs the risk of provoking economic retaliation and subsequent escalation.

4. *Licensing and Advertising Restrictions* These more subtle means of alleviating perceived threat from import competition work against the foreign competitor within the domestic setting. Domestic importers may be prohibited from importing certain goods from some or all countries; and domestic exporters may be denied licenses to export their goods to certain places as a retaliation for trade practices in the target country. Similarly, though foreign goods may be permitted to enter the country, advertising restrictions may prevent their effective sale.

5. *Product Regulation* This is a deterrent to sales competition that involves strict stipulation of standards of production and product that may and may not be sold in the import market. This is commonly applied to food imports, generally using public health safety standards as the ostensible rational. In the automobile industry, protection was given temporarily to American manufacturers in the United States by suddenly raising the environmental control standards, an act that rendered thousands of imports unsellable, and required redesign and retooling abroad. Among other things this policy required that Japanese and European automobile manufacturers increase investment in their plants, a cost that was reflected in the price of cars imported to the United States.

The student is cautioned that these instruments of protection apply only in the bilateral economic relations of countries, and that they have little application to relations among groups of states. Two caveats are appropriate, however. First, though protection is usually an act of a single country, the multilateral trade negotiations and the General Agreement on Tariffs and Trade are both collective means of regulating trade-restraint decisions by individual governments. Second, when states enter into agreements to combine their economies in order to compete more effectively in world markets, they adopt group trading policies that may run counter to the prevailing principles of the international political economy. This "customs union" arrangement is typical of international economic integration and results in the elimination of trade restraints among the participants and common trade policies by all of the participants in their trade relations with nonmembers. These arrangements are central to the concept of the European Economic Community and other economic integration agreements.

To assess the merit of a protectionist case, it is necessary to consider whether the advantage of the foreign producers grows out of their real comparative efficiency or is an artifact of unfair and unnatural advantages conferred by their own governments. If there is a real comparative advantage enjoyed by the foreign producer, it is not generally considered wise to restrict imports solely because they are of lower cost. Indeed, it is the very fact that the imported good is cheaper that provides the rationale and advantage of free trade, and denying cheaper goods to one's own people solely because they are produced abroad is a hidden form of taxing the majority to protect an inefficient minority. In such a case, the more rational response is to allow the foreign goods in, and to devise compensatory measures to divert some of the gains of trade to the expansion of export industries. For example, advocates of free trade often propose governmental assistance to workers in adversely affected industries, to train them in new skills better suited to areas of production where the home country has a comparative advantage. In our example, this might take the form of a tax on the savings from importation of foreign autos to retrain American auto workers for the booming electronics industry.

As this example implies, the real world problems of transferring workers from one industry to another, particularly if the two production sectors are widely separated by geography and work patterns, can be substantial. The dislocation may be unacceptable to the affected workers, particularly if large-scale changes in the market take place in a compressed period of time. In a democracy, the adversely affected workers will use their political influence, through the legislative process and the electoral system, to soften the impact of changes on them.

Realistically, it is unlikely that the perfectly logical model of free trade, unfettered by restrictions and protectionism, can be consummated. Instead, the potential gains of unrestricted trade act as an inducement to liberal exchange, while the adverse effects of free trade act as a counterbalance. Thus, there is a tug-of-war, both nationally and internationally, between those who stand to gain and those who stand to lose from free trade, and the overall trade regime that exists at any moment represents the balance of power between these two forces. This controversy is well known to students of American economic history, who have observed wide fluctuations between periods of liberal trade and periods of protectionism.

The arguments for protection are stronger when the foreign products enjoy their advantages not because of inherent efficiencies and inefficiencies, but because of unfair advantages enjoyed by the foreign producers. For example, it is sometimes the case that American tax treatment of home products is prejudicial, compared to the tax systems of foreign countries. If the total effect of American taxes is to double the price of an American automobile, while Taiwanese automobiles produced for export are effectively exempt from taxation, the final price difference between the two goods may have less to do with production efficiencies than with government policy. In such a case, it is reasonable to expect that the workers in the US auto industry will call upon the US government either to reduce taxes or make representations to the foreign government to equalize the difference. If neither of these approaches proves effective, the demand for tariff protection will grow. Such issues are often lively subjects of international trade negotiation.

Beyond these considerations, there are several special classes of protectionist argument that are worthy of note. One is the problem of an *infant industry,* one that has just started in a country and must face competition with the imports of a mature firm in the same industry of another country. For example, in the first years or automobile manufacture, a new firm in a developing country cannot be expected to match the efficiency, quality and cost-effectiveness of a huge foreign producer that has been in the business for years and has established firm markets abroad, even perhaps in the country in which the new firm is being established. The new firm will not have achieved the scale of production at which large savings can be realized (economies of scale); it will not have developed a competitive network of sales and service facilities; and it will not have solved all of the problems of engineering, design, manufacture, finance and marketing necessary to achieve its eventual level of efficiency. During this period of infancy it may be rational and consistent with the national interest to restrict imports to assist the fledgling producer. If it does not have to compete with cheaper foreign products in the early years, it may eventually realize its own comparative advantage as a domestic producer and even as an exporter competing in world markets with the older foreign producer.

This is a rational approach, but two dangers should be recognized. First, the new industry may never become fully competitive, and may demand to be treated preferentially long beyond infancy. In such a case, indefinite restrictions on imports can no longer be justified strictly on economic terms, with respect either to the domestic economy or any sensible regime of free international trade. Second, once an industry is created it becomes a political fact and possesses a reality of its own. In effect, an inefficient industry may bear the seeds of its own perpetuation even if it never realizes a comparative advantage. For these reasons the infant industry argument, properly applied, should pertain only to those lines of production in which there is a reasonable expectation that a comparative advantage will eventually accrue. It is not rational to apply this argument for protection to any and every industrial endeavor. Too often, particularly in developing countries and those in the second industrial rank, new projects are undertaken for reason of national pride or in the absence of adequate business judgment, rather than because of reasonable anticipation of long-term comparative advantage.

Another special class of protectionist argument applies to *strategic industries*. These are industries in which there may be recognition that domestic suppliers have a permanent comparative *dis*advantage relative to foreign producers, but in which that disadvantage is offset by the decision that higher national interest precludes dependence on foreign supply. If it is judged that the supply of a vital product could be interrupted by international conflict, or that the long-range commitment of the external supplier is uncertain, or that political relations between the government of the country in need and that of the supplier are either untrustworthy or adversely affected by overdependence, then the country in need may wish to be self-sufficient even at a higher economic cost.

Strategic self-sufficiency is often a compelling argument in this world of conflict, but it is an argument that lends itself to gross overextension in practice. For example, radio manufacturers have been known to demand protection on the grounds that military applications of their products must be protected; watchmakers produce chronographic instruments for the army; and agricultural interests point out that an army marches on its belly. It behooves the policy-maker to raise a skeptical eyebrow when every interest group wraps its self-interest in the sacrament of the national flag. Even in the area of arms production, it is by no means self-evident that dependence on foreign producers is ipso facto against the national interest. The strategic value of self-sufficiency must be weighed against the larger interests of the economy, which are also strategic concerns. If a country sacrifices all other interests to pursue absolute strategic autarky, it may weaken rather than strengthen its international position. Conversely, a nation like Japan, which accepts dependence on foreign producers of many strategic goods, may enjoy a favorable international position. Moreover, defense is not the only criterion; at some point, an obsession with strategic needs may unduly sacrifice other needs of the people, including their aspiration to an improved standard of living that often comes with freer trade. Whether or not protection of a particular strategic industry is a rational choice will depend on sober consideration of all these factors.

A third class of special protectionist argument applies particularly to the Third World countries struggling to escape the shackles of underdevelopment. It concerns the effort to diversify production so that the country's development pattern need not rely on only one or two primary products that may comprise the whole economic system as inherited from colonial days. Diversification is aimed at a more healthy balance of production and of export potential, which both diminishes reliance on too few commodities and enables the developing economy to adapt to fluctuations of international demand. The older, prediversification pattern of single- or dual-commodity dependence in exports while importing an array of goods from industrialized nations, often termed foreign-oriented development, is now recognized as pernicious in most cases, and adverse to the long-range interests of most developing countries, however powerful the short-run economic logic might have seemed. For this reason many developing countries seek to nurture a limited number of domestic industries through protection against import competition, irrespective of the normal calculations of comparative advantage.

But while diversification contains a number of obvious symbolic attractions, it may not always correspond to the real enlightened self-interest of a country. It is unlikely that many of the world's poorest countries can achieve competitive production efficiencies in the thousands of product lines that they consume, and in which they rely on imports at present. Some infant industries may be deserving of protection, but attempts to replicate in small populations industrial miniatures of a world economy are not rational. (Some of the world's poorest one hundred countries have populations of less than five million, and a few have populations of less than one million.) Most will either fail miserably or will be forced by economic inefficiencies to charge their domestic customers far higher prices than would be required by imports. The result of such uncontrolled diversification will be to lower rather than raise the aggregate economic level. *Selective diversification,* on the other hand, will carefully apply the infant industry argument to protection of a few especially promising sectors.

The final class of protectionist argument applies to countries that suffer *chronic trade imbalances.* This is a situation in which, year after year, a country's imports have a higher monetary value than its exports, resulting in a form of chronic debt from trade. Typically this type of debt leads to unemployment, as jobs lost to imports are not made up by employment created by exporting industries. Moreover, such a situation weakens a nation's currency relative to those of countries with stronger trade positions. Here protection against imports may be seized as a partial corrective, but it is not the principal solution. The principles of international monetary exchange, discussed in the next chapter, take over where simple barter fails.

Trade Balances and Contemporary Strain in Western Trade

Because export trade is so vital to a nation's economy, competition among trading partners frequently becomes acrimonious. Moreover, since the trading activities of the principal Western industrialized nations are so intricately interwoven, multilateral trade negotiations have virtually replaced bilateral economic diplomacy. Four times since World War II those partners have engaged in long, elaborate efforts to reduce barriers to trade. Conducted under the auspices of the General Agreement on Tariffs and Trade (GATT), these several rounds of negotiations have gradually, but not entirely, reduced the tension that results from unilateral efforts to secure advantage. The most recent round, the so-called Tokyo Round (also known as the Multilateral Trade Talks) was conducted over a period of ten years, from 1973 through 1982.

By 1980, Western trade was troubled by significant events. The first was that the economic law of the European Economic Community (also called the European Common Market) permitted financing subsidies for export industries at interest rates of 4 percent to 6 percent below prevailing rates in the Western world. In the view of the United States and others, these rates gave an artificial advantage to Western European producers, enabling them to sell products on world markets at prices that reflected lower capital and production costs. The European resistance to change on this issue led to predictions of a trade war against them.[2]

The more severe cause of disruption, however, was the enormous success of the Japanese automobile industry in world trade. In 1980, Japan became the world's largest producer of automobiles (though the United States continued to lead all others in the production of cars and trucks combined). At the same time, the American auto industry was suffering its worst single-year loss in history (approximately $5 billion). European producers, particularly in Italy, France and Germany, were also failing to keep pace with Japan's exports. To make matters worse, while Japan was courting foreign investment into the Japanese economy because so much of its capital was flowing out to places of less expensive production in Asia and Australia, the automobile industry remained under the sole control of Japanese investors. And since it was clear that the majority of the autos produced were for export (about 6.5 million of the 11 million produced in 1980), it was also clear that the Japanese denial of stockholder influence on production and marketing policy indicated an aggressive attitude toward world markets.

The Japanese view was, of course, very different. In response to the United States the Japanese claim that their domination of the American market results not from marginal international practices but from wiser production policies, superior technological applications and better marketing strategies. Most especially, Tokyo argued, the United States auto manufacturers failed to recognize in time the impact of the 1973–74 petroleum embargo upon consumer tastes. Rather than adjust production to small, fuel-efficient models, American manufacturers treated the slump in big-car sales as an anomaly, and returned to old production habits. Had they recognized the permanence of the OPEC phenomenon and shifted production to smaller and more efficient cars, the Japanese producers would not have secured such a dramatic advantage.[3]

Whatever might be the accurate argument regarding the imbalance of Japanese-American trade, the fact remains that such imbalances invariably result in cries for the protection of domestic industries. In this case, the demands were heightened by growing American awareness of the Japanese intention of dominating the electronics market

2. For a summary of the problem, see "Is Trade War with Europe Inevitable?" *World Business Weekly,* December 15, 1980, p. 6.
3. For details on the auto issue and more generally on the issue of Japanese management innovations, see *World Business Weekly,* December 1 and December 15, 1980 and January 19, 1981, and *Forbes,* September 1, 1980.

worldwide, and of the tangible and less tangible means being used by the Japanese to restrict imports. These included metallurgical coal and natural gas, pharmaceuticals, cigarettes, telecommunications equipment and certain agricultural goods, principal among them beef and citrus fruits.[4] As Congress began officially to consider protectionist measures, the President headed off an embarrassment to the United States—the embarrassment of the principal champion of free trade engaging in official protectionism—by negotiating agreements with Japan. These resulted in 1981 through 1983 in both increased American exports to Japan (the United States' largest customer in agricultural goods) and in a freeze on the number of Japanese automobiles imported into the United States. In 1983, however, the Japanese government announced that it would not extend the auto agreement, which originated in 1981, beyond 1984.

But the Japanese auto dominance is only a single symptom of the trade imbalance problem. As the American economy is transformed from heavy industry styles of production to modern electronic applications (including robotics manufacturing), it has faced demands for protectionism in other areas. Steel is a major example. The steel trade between the United States and the European Economic Community was regulated in 1983 after exchanges of trade war threats. In areas of lighter manufacturing, too, the demand for protectionism has risen: shoes, textiles, rubber goods, electronic appliances, etc.

From the point of view of a single nation, the ideal goal of international trade is to secure wealth. From a global perspective, however, it is better for each state to achieve a balance between the value of its exports and that of its imports, so that, through trade, no nation becomes a significant debtor unless it is able to make up its trade debt by international exchange of services or capital. Chapter 13 deals with monetary exchange; here we are concerned only with the global consequences of international commodity trade.

Among the major market economies of the world, only West Germany and the OPEC countries have been able, over the last decade, to retain consistent balance-of-trade surpluses, though Japan and Canada have done so with a few annual exceptions. The United States and the remainder of the EEC members have become chronic debtors. There are several reasons for this. First, structural changes in the world economy have had a marked impact upon international industrial trade, and the long period of adjustment has not yet ended. Second, particularly since 1982, some countries have emerged from recession faster than others, with faster growth in earnings and greater import

4. *The Economic Report of the President, 1984,* pp. 64–71.

demand as results. Third, exchange rates have not yet adjusted to world economic conditions, resulting in artificial pricing structures. Fourth, the debt-laden nations, particularly of the Third World, are using so much of their earnings from productivity development to service debt that they are unable to afford imports, thus reducing worldwide demand for the industrial products of the developed market economies. Fifth, the terms of trade for the products of the Third World are both unfavorable and deteriorating at a rapid rate, reducing the international trade earnings used to purchase industrial goods.

Together, these five factors result in the trade balances shown in Table 12–3. All figures in parentheses represent trade deficits, that is, the country's import value exceeds its export value (or it buys more than it sells), resulting in a negative balance. Note that the United States, the United Kingdom, France and Italy are among the principal chronic debtors who must use other resources to balance their trade deficits. Note also that in 1983, the United States accounted for fully 70 percent of the entire trade deficit of the developed economies, while Japan and the OPEC countries combined (and particularly Saudi Arabia, Kuwait and the United Arab Emirates) offset slightly more than half of the total deficit of the developed economies. The OPEC role and the world market for petroleum is another major determinant of the current imbalances of trade worldwide.

The Special Case of Petroleum Trade

While the world's fossil fuel reserves are dwindling, industrialized nations find themselves in need of greater and greater amounts of energy resources to run factories, to power transportation systems, to generate electricity, and so on. At the same time, with the advent of OPEC and its escalating pricing policy, they find themselves more and more dependent upon expensive oil from the Middle East. From 1974 through 1982, OPEC increased the price of crude petroleum an average of twice a year, eventually raising the price of a barrel from slightly over $3 to about $34. Not until early 1983 did OPEC unity begin to crumble, with the ensuing dispute between moderate demands for stable prices and controlled productivity, on the one hand, and radical demands for continued price increases and uncontrolled production, on the other, resulting in the first modest price decreases in a decade. (Note in Table 12–3 the performance of the OPEC trade balance beginning in 1975, the year after the maturation of OPEC, and then the drop in 1983.)

TABLE 12–3
World trade balances, 1970–1983, expressed in billions of US dollars.

		OPEC 1973–1974			
	1970	*1975*	*1979*	*1981*	*1983*
Developed Economies	(10.0)	(29.7)	(93.4)	(97.2)	(100.8)
US	0.5	2.2	(40.2)	(39.7)	(69.7)
Canada	2.4	(2.1)	1.3	2.4	12.9
Japan	0.4	(2.1)	(7.5)	8.6	22.6
France	(1.0)	(0.9)	(6.3)	(14.6)	(11.3)
W. Germany	4.3	15.3	12.2	12.2	14.5
Italy	(1.8)	(3.7)	(5.7)	(15.8)	(7.4)
UK	(2.5)	(9.9)	(13.2)	(0.5)	(9.1)
All EEC	(5.2)	(9.9)	(33.9)	(32.9)	(21.6)
Other	(8.2)	(20.7)	(13.1)	(35.7)	(45.0)
Developing Economies	(2.3)	20.2	55.2	(6.0)	(36.8)
OPEC	6.9	61.4	113.9	119.6	29.9
Other	(9.2)	(41.2)	(58.7)	(125.6)	(66.8)
Non-Market Economies	0.8	(10.3)	(0.9)	5.2	20.0

Source: Economic Report of the President, 1984, p. 339.

Note: For 1983, figures are preliminary estimates derived by extrapolation from known third-quarter results. Numbers in parentheses are deficits.

TABLE 12–4
Oil as a percentage of total American imports, 1979–1983, expressed in billions of US dollars.

	Total Value of Imports	*Value of Petroleum Imports*	*% Petroleum of the Whole*
1970	39.9	2.9	7.3
1973	70.5	8.4	11.9
1974	103.7	26.6	25.6
1976	124.0	34.6	27.9
1978	176.0	42.3	24.0
1980	249.8	79.3	31.7
1982	247.6	61.2	24.7
1983	254.3	53.5	21.0

Source: Economic Report of the President, 1980, p. 318, and *1984,* p. 334.

For most industrialized countries, oil represents the largest single portion of a trade deficit. Table 12–4 shows the extent to which petroleum dominates American imports, though it should be pointed out that not all oil is imported from OPEC countries (Canada is a major exception). Nonetheless, the volume figures for all sources of oil are significant since virtually all international petroleum trade has occurred at OPEC prices.

In addition to these observations, it is useful to demonstrate the cost of United States' petroleum imports for the same approximate period. This is shown in Figure 12–1. Again, remember that the muscle of OPEC was first felt in 1974. The cost decreases in 1981 and 1982 are due principally to decreased import volume; the decline in 1983 is a combination of sustained reduced demand and a modest reduction in price at the OPEC ministerial meetings early in the year. As in Tables 12–3 and 12–4, the figure for 1983 is a preliminary estimate based on real performance through three quarters.

Oil importation does not occur in a vacuum but in the context of trade in other commodities. Indeed, as we have seen elsewhere, the price of OPEC oil and the volume available might have been much more unfavorable to the developed economies had it not been for three things: (1) vast increases in agricultural exports to the oil producing states, from which the United States profited most in controlling its

FIGURE 12–1
US import costs for petroleum and petroleum products, 1973–1983, expressed in billions of US dollars.

Source: Economic Report of the President, 1984, p. 334. Figure for 1983 is a preliminary estimate based on real performance through three quarters.

petroleum-caused deficit; (2) huge increases in arms sales to the entire Third World, but particularly to the oil-producing members, from which the United States, France and West Germany took the greatest advantage; and (3) the so-called oil-for-technology agreements, by which oil was kept flowing at a partially controlled price in return for technology transfer in arms and other goods. All developed Western countries took advantage of these oil-for-technology arrangements, but Japan profited most.

Because Japan is nearly total reliant on other nations for fuel to support the manufacturing productivity on which its world stature depends, the OPEC maturation was particularly threatening to Tokyo. Contrary to common opinion and to its government's own prediction, the Japanese consumption of imported energy did not skyrocket from 1974 to 1981. In fact, the total consumption in 1974 and 1981 was almost identical, though in 1979 the demand grew to a level of approximately 111 percent of the base year.[5] But given the huge price increases during those years, the cost of maintaining even a steady supply of OPEC fuel was staggering, as Figure 12–2 demonstrates. The statistics include only Iran, Iraq, Kuwait, Oman, Qatar, Saudi

FIGURE 12–2
Japan's trade with OPEC, 1973–1981, in billions of US dollars.

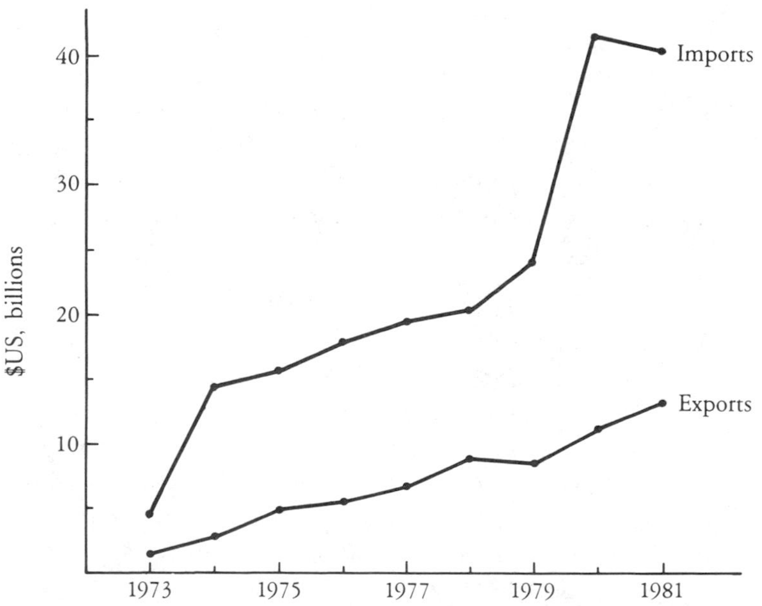

Source: International Monetary Fund, *International Financial Statistics,* as reproduced in and compiled from *Europa Yearbook, 1979* and *1983.*

5. *U.N. Statistical Yearbook, 1981.*

TABLE 12–5
Japan's trade deficit with OPEC, 1973–1981, in billions of US dollars.

1973	(3.4)	1978	(11.3)
1974	(11.9)	1979	(20.5)
1975	(10.8)	1980	(31.9)
1976	(12.5)	1981	(26.8)
1977	(12.9)		

Source: International Monetary Fund, *International Financial Statistics,* as reproduced in and compiled from *Europa Yearbook, 1979* and *1981.*

Arabia and the United Arab Emirates, since they are the principal OPEC suppliers to Japan. Note that the statistics do not include non-Arab OPEC members (such as Venezuela or Nigeria), nor do they include non-OPEC members (such as Mexico and Canada).

Clearly, the cost of petroleum, not increase in volume, resulted in the burden for Japan's trade balance. Even a tenfold increase in the value of exports to OPEC could not offset the ravages of OPEC's price increases, which also increased by a factor of ten, but from a higher starting point. Table 12–5 shows the annual Japanese deficit incurred as a result of this badly balanced trade. Though it is of no particular significance for the global economy since adjustments are made annually, it is nonetheless shocking to discover that for the nine-year period, Japan suffered a cumulative deficit in its trade with the OPEC states of $142 billion.

Meanwhile, in their trade with Japan and other oil-consuming customers, Saudi Arabia, Kuwait and the United Arab Emirates (UAE), in particular, were piling up trade surpluses even while multiplying their industrial imports. Figure 12–3 shows the impacts upon the Saudi Arabian and UAE economies, respectively. They are expressed in local currencies, but the trend is nonetheless revealing.

East-West Trade

If trade among friendly nations committed to the same economic philosophy is prone to such hostilities, it is easy to imagine the difficulties of establishing reliable and well-regulated trade between the capitalist economies and the socialist world. Strained in the first place by political differences severe enough to appear irreconcilable, the economic relations of these countries are complicated by differences in methods of assigning value to goods, and by the deeply troubling question of whether one should trade with one's potential adversary and, in so doing, strengthen him and improve his advantages.

During the age of containment, a basic Cold War political maxim was that Western industrialized states should not trade with the Soviet

FIGURE 12–3
Sample trade balances for two OPEC countries, 1972–1981.

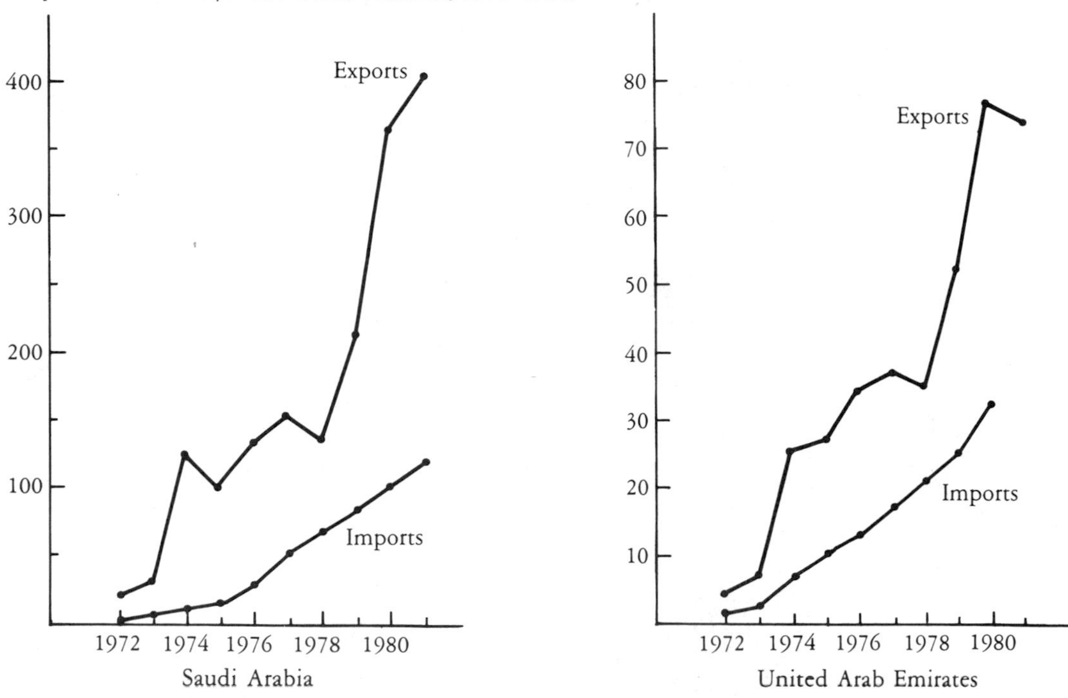

Source: International Monetary Fund, *International Financial Statistics,* as reproduced in and compiled from *Europa Yearbook, 1983.*

Union or China and their respective friends. Certain exceptions (mostly of food and consumer goods) were made for Eastern European countries, particularly by the Western Europeans. But it was not until the era of détente that the idea of using trade deprivation as a political instrument was replaced by the one that mutual trade is a potential route for intercultural understanding and improved international tolerance. In essence, this view interpreted trade as a functional instrument, one with which to build trust and confidence. This general revision of thinking was accentuated by the growing Western European tolerance of socialism and communism, and by the growth of Eurocommunism. Moreover, the trans-European policies of Germany, commencing with Conrad Adenauer, and of French Gaullism became a suitable rationale for trade between East and West Europe—though more with the smaller satellite states than with the Soviet Union itself. Finally, in addition to détente and pan-Europeanism, the Sino-American political thaw of the 1970s was accompanied by vigorous Western and Japanese overtures to China in order to trade industrial products for natural resources.

By the mid-1970s, then, East-West trade was growing quickly, and it continues to grow. The East has maintained a positive trade balance

Ideologies and economics . . .

Source: © Vadillo (Mexico)/Rothco

(surplus of export value over import value) over the Western industrialized economies. Japan has taken the lead role in trade with the Asian centrally planned economies, including China; and in trade with the Soviet Union and Eastern Europe, the European community has an overwhelming lead over other Western traders. American trade with the socialist economies of Asia is all with China.

Among the several large Eastern trading targets, the Eastern European states have proved the most steady. Washington has wavered in its interest in trade with the Soviet Union because, with the deterioration of détente, increased trade has been linked conditionally to Soviet political behavior. At the same time, China's dramatic economic development plan has been set back by a variety of domestic factors, with the result that many lucrative service and trading contracts have been terminated or postponed.[6]

6. *World Business Weekly,* March 2, 1981, p. 6.

The Soviet invasion of Afghanistan, the single most disrupting event in the demise of détente, led to an American economic boycott of the Soviet Union. An immediate embargo was placed on grain shipments (despite a long-range contract), and several licenses for transfers of technological goods were canceled or suspended. As a matter of official policy, the president adopted a report of the President's Export Council which recommended as follows:

> As to the Soviet Union, the Council recommends that the process of normalizing trade relations, which was broken off by the Soviet invasion of Afghanistan, be resumed only if and when there is significant improvement in U.S.-U.S.S.R. relations. Meanwhile, the U.S. should continue non-sensitive trade as circumstances make appropriate, while indicating a willingness to increase trade and resume normalization steps if and when the Soviet Union changes its policies to a peaceful cooperative course.
>
> As to other Eastern European non-market [Socialist] economies, the Council recommends that the U.S. continue its present policy that differentiates these countries from the U.S.S.R. so long as they do not engage in unwanted diversion of U.S. goods to the Soviet Union. Trade normalization steps (including Most-Favored-Nation treatment for Poland, Romania, Yugoslavia, and Hungary) should be continued with these countries as appropriate, except if cases develop that show diversion.[7]

Mutual verbal provocations between the Reagan administration and the governments of Brezhnev, Andropov and Chernenko have made it unlikely that the requisite conditions for implementation of a more extensive trade relationship between the United States and the Soviet Union will evolve rapidly, even though a new grain deal was made in 1982.

Conclusion

In the Western market economies, international trade is a vital component of economic, and therefore political, stability. Though the trading partners have attempted rather elaborately to organize international trade and to regulate it, imperfections inherent in competition have prevented the system from being entirely harmonious, though multilateral negotiations are now a common part of the international political economy. Trade between the market economies of the West and the socialist economies of the East has improved in recent years because of détente, the Sino-Western thaw and the advent of Eurocommunism, though the recent deterioration of détente has resulted in a reduction in Soviet-American trade in an age when the United

7. The President's Export Council, *The Export Imperative,* December 1980, vol. 1, p. 104.

States has made the improvement of trade contingent upon the international political behavior of the Kremlin. Finally, OPEC's rise and decline has had deep consequences for international trade and for the international economy, even as the terms of trade for the non-oil developing countries have continued to deteriorate.

But for the major Western developed economies, the most pressing problem of international trade is the chronic deficits incurred by the United States and the Western European countries. These imbalances introduce serious difficulties among friends as well as dangerous trends such as increased arms sales to the developing nations. Furthermore, a trade deficit is a form of debt, and the debt must be addressed through means and transactions other than trade. Those adjustment mechanisms are the subject of the next chapter.

13

International Monetary Exchange

While it is handy to discuss international trade in terms of a steady flow of imports and exports that offset one another in value, such perfect reciprocity rarely exists. Even in the uncommon case where one nation's trade with a single partner is in perfect balance, it would not follow that that country's world trade for the same period would be in perfect balance. More typically, a nation may have an export surplus with respect to some trading partners and an import surplus with respect to others, putting its total trade in surplus (higher total export value than import value), deficit (higher import value than export value) or balance (equal import and export values). A nation's annual trade performance and its performance trend over a period of a few years is a crucially important indicator of its economic condition, irrespective of its standard of living.

But note that the discussion of international trade in Chapter 12 emphasized the importance of trade value rather than trade volume. (Although volume units were used in the hypothetical example of wheat and autos in Taiwanese-American trade, certain assumptions were made in advance with regard to the value of labor and produce.) Needless to say, given the complexities of international trade, simple barter is rarely if ever used. Value is measured in monetary units; and

French foreign exchange market in action at Paris on the day on which the US dollar rose to a record high with respect to the French franc, 1984.

Source: Wide World

because of social and economic differences among countries, national currency units have different absolute values. As a result, their values have to be compared with one another. To an American, for example, a dollar is worth a dollar (though with inflation, it purchases less even in the domestic market than it did at any earlier time). To an Italian a hundred lira is worth a hundred lira, and to a Briton a pound is worth a pound. But when an American dollar is offered in Canada, it may bring anywhere from ninety Canadian cents to a dollar and ten cents Canadian. In London, it will draw about two-fifths of a pound sterling, and in Rome, a cascade of lira. Hence, while a dollar is worth a dollar, it is also worth a specified amount in foreign currencies. The same is true of all national currencies: A national unit has a price in international exchange, and the price may vary frequently, perhaps even daily, and sometimes violently. Goods are traded internationally according to the prevailing relative values of the currencies of the importing country and exporting country. Table 13–1 provides sample exchange rates for eight capitalist countries on a given date.

Note that in this table only capitalist currencies are considered.

TABLE 13–1
Sample currency exchange rates in the capitalist world.

January 8, 1981 Middle rate for:	*US Dollar*	*Belgian Franc*	*British Pound*	*Canadian Dollar*	*French Franc*	*German Mark*	*Italian Lira*	*Japanese Yen*
1 US dollar	1	31.57	0.416	1.188	4.537	1.963	932.4	201.5
100 Belgian francs	3.168	100	1.318	3.763	14.37	6.219	2954	638.3
1 British pound	2.405	75.90	1	2.856	10.91	4.720	2242	484.5
1 Canadian dollar	0.842	26.58	0.350	1	3.820	1.653	785.0	169.6
110 French francs	2.204	69.57	0.917	2.618	10	4.326	2055	444.1
1 German mark	0.509	16.08	0.212	0.605	2.311	1	475.0	102.6
1000 Italian lira	1.072	33.85	0.446	1.274	4.866	2.105	1000	216.1
1000 Japanese yen	4.963	156.7	2.064	5.895	22.52	9.742	4627	1000

Source: World Business Weekly, January 19, 1981, p. 56. Adapted and published with permission.

Comparing values of currencies in the capitalist world with those of the socialist is extremely difficult, because of the different way in which these two fundamentally different economic philosophies attach value to goods. This is one factor that hinders the growth of East-West trade, and one reason why trade between, say, the United States and the Soviet Union usually takes place in massive, celebrated, long-range contracts rather than through a consistent flow of traded goods that are constantly repriced according to market value. Virtually any licensed American corporation can trade with a British counterpart in a legal commodity, but the exchange of grain between the United States and the Soviet Union calls for a vast long-range contract at permanent terms that are worked out in advance.

Also note that the figures in Table 13–1 are for a specified date. This suggests, correctly, that currency values change constantly. In a stable and unchanging relationship, currency values fluctuate in only small amounts. But in a dynamic complex of trading relations among nations, fluctuations can be extreme and divergences of value can be dramatic. These changes will be influenced by such factors as volume activity, different rates of capital investment, different degrees of productivity, variations in incentives, domestic inflation or deflation, etc. Until recently, for example, the American dollar had become steadily less valuable in international finance, while the German mark and the Japanese yen have increased in value. In each instance, it took gradually more American dollars to buy a unit of currency; and as a result, it took more American dollars to purchase German and Japanese goods. As one currency deteriorates in value, goods purchased from the economy of the other currency become more expensive. These trends reversed in 1983 and 1984.

To illustrate, consider the following questions: Does it pay for an

American to buy an Italian car priced at 1 million lira rather than an American car priced at $5,000, assuming the quality of the two products to be identical? Or does it pay for the Italian consumer to buy the American car at these prices? The questions cannot be answered without knowing the exchange rates between the two currencies. Americans do not ordinarily carry lira to the market, and Italians to not ordinarily carry dollars. The exchange rate is therefore the instrument through which the price system of one country is related to the price system of the other. Pegged at one level, the exchange rate might stimulate American interest in Italian products and discourage Italian interest in American products. Pegged at a different level, the exchange rate might reduce American interest in Italian goods and increase Italian receptivity to American products. At some intermediate point, the exchange rate might result in mutual trade: Some Italian goods would be less expensive for buyers in both countries, while other American products would be advantaged in both markets. The exchange rate determines the price of each country's goods in the other's markets.

Now take another example. Suppose that on some hypothetical Day One the German mark and the American dollar are exchangeable one for one. Suppose also that identical automobiles are made in the two countries such that the American model will sell in Germany for $5,000 and the German model will sell in the United States for $5,000. Now suppose that at some subsequent Day Two, because of a variety of national and international factors, the mark has become twice as valuable as the dollar; it would now take two dollars to buy one mark. It follows that it will now take two of the American models to purchase (or trade for) one German model. If one is exchanged for one, Germany will be owed the cash value of a second in order to get its full value from the trade, since trade is measured in value. Without such a payment, Germany will have suffered a trade deficit in the transaction; but in order to compensate Germany's trade balance by making a payment of $5,000, the United States must incur a payments deficit of $5,000.

National Accounts

This second illustration reveals that international monetary balance consists of two factors: trade balance and payments balance. In the preceding chapter we were concerned almost exclusively with the former; in this chapter we look at the two combined.

It is important to understand at the outset that the overall balance is a product of the import and export of goods and services, and the import and export of funds, both public and private. The export of a load of tractors means a financial earning, so that transaction contributes positively to a trade balance. An import of a similar load contributes negatively. The use of domestic funds to support an undertaking overseas, on the other hand, means that the domestic economy is deprived of those funds, so the export of funds contributes negatively to a payments balance. When those funds are returned to the domestic economy, however, they contribute positively to the domestic payments balance. Table 13–2 summarizes the positive and negative contributions to a national balance. From it a rule of thumb emerges: goods going out contribute positively, but funds going out contribute negatively; goods coming in contribute negatively, but funds coming in contribute positively.

It is possible, of course, for a nation to have a deficit in one account and a surplus in another. From 1945 into the 1960s, for example, the United States had huge annual trade surpluses because of the vigor of its export markets prior to the economic recoveries of Japan and Western Europe. At the same time, however, it was exporting public funds in the form of recovery and development aid, and private funds were leaving the country in large amounts as invested capital overseas. Thus, while the economy was typified in those years by a large trade surplus (greater total value of goods and services exported than imported), it had at the same time a large payments deficit (greater value of public funds and private capital leaving the economy than entering). In order to bring control to the combined payments problems, both presidents Johnson and Nixon attempted to persuade corporations to reduce their capital exports. Again, however, this was due to the close relationship of monetary balance to trade balance: The United States did not become alarmed over the payments deficit until after the re-

TABLE 13–2
Factors contributing to a national balance.

	Positive Contributions	*Negative Contributions*
Balance of trade	Export of goods	Import of goods
	Export of services	Import of services
Balance of payments	Collection of fees	Payment of fees
	Import of capital	Export of capital
	Collection of debt	Payment of debt
	Repatriation of capital	Return of capital to abroad
	Collection of interest on debt	Payment of interest on debt

coveries of Japan and Western Europe, for by the mid-1960s the trade account was also in deepening deficit.

Interest rates are noted in Table 13–2 as having an impact upon national accounts. This is particularly true for the less developed countries, which are caught in a cycle of paying interest rates in addition to repayment of loans that they have taken out over a period of more than twenty years. Some of the underindustrialized countries pay as much as 20 percent of public revenues in such debt service. In addition, whereas new loans ten years ago carried average interest rates of 3 percent, new ones in 1981 carried interest rates in the vicinity of 10 percent. It is not uncommon for the annual debt service obligation of an underindustrialized country to equal or even exceed the total annual increase in export value.[1] In such cases, an increase in international exporting contributes positively to the trade balance, but the revenue goes immediately to debt service, thus deepening the capital deficit. Many observers consider this an inescapable spiral unless radically new principles of development aid are implemented. In fact, this is a characteristic of international development aid that the radical theory of development, explored in Chapter 5, criticizes. That theory argues that the debt cycles imposed by financial assistance to the developing countries are one of the principal means by which dependency is perpetuated and real economic freedom prevented.

In addition to interest payments and debt service as causes for the international flow of money, capital flow for purposes of investment is a major source of such movement. In the developing countries, capital flow is almost entirely inward, while for the industrialized countries some capital will flow out and other capital money will flow in. Thus it is the net capital flow which determines the impact of investment upon the national account. Table 13–3 demonstrates the net capital position of the United States for the period 1970 through 1980. Note that each figure is a total rather than an annual increment. The increment is calculated easily, however. Between 1978 and 1980, for example, the increase in US foreign direct investment was $50.8 billion (representing capital outflow) and the increase in foreign investment in the United States was $13 billion (representing capital inflow), for a net deterioration of $37.8 billion.

Earnings on investment also figure into the capital account. The value of a portfolio abroad may be enlarged not only by additional capital transfer, but by reinvestment of earnings. In the period 1978–80, for example, some of the additional $50.8 billion of American investment abroad may be attributed to reinvested earnings. In cal-

1. For general comments on this subject see "LDC Debts: The End of the 'Cheap Money' Era," in *World Business Weekly*, January 19, 1981, p. 51.

TABLE 13–3
Net US capital position, 1970–1982, expressed in billions of US dollars.

	US Direct Investment Abroad	*Foreign Direct Investment in US*	*US Net Capital Position*
1970	75.5	13.3	(62.2)
1972	89.9	14.9	(84.0)
1974	110.1	25.1	(85.0)
1976	136.8	30.8	(106.0)
1978	162.7	42.5	(120.2)
1980	213.5	65.5	(148.0)
1982	221.3	101.8	(119.5)

Source: Economic Report of the President, 1982, p. 351. For 1982, *Survey of Current Business,* August, 1983, p. 14.

culating the net capital position of the United States for that period, therefore, earnings abroad should be discounted, since they did not represent additional money leaving the United States.

But not all earnings on investment are put back into the capital account. A large share is withdrawn from the capital market of the host country and returned home, or repatriated, for payments to stockholders, savings or subsequent investment in the home country. Unlike reinvested earnings, repatriated earnings count positively in a nation's capital account, for they represent capital returned to the country. In 1982, earnings on $221.3 billion in foreign investments earned a total of $22.9 billion for American investors, some of which was reinvested and some of which was repatriated. These investments earned approximately 13.5 percent in developed economies, and 8.6 percent in the underindustrialized countries. In North America, US investments in Canada in 1981 earned 9.4 percent and in 1982, a year of deep global recession, 5.0 percent. Meanwhile, Canadian investments in the United States earned 1.4 percent and 2.1 percent, respectively.[2]

National Payments

1. Changes in Currency Value

Because value rather than volume measures the effectiveness of a nation's international trade, and because that value is tied to fluctuating relative currency values, one way of correcting a trade imbalance is

2. For a comprehensive study, see *Survey of Current Business,* August 1983, p. 14.

to alter the exchange rate, that is, alter the values of the two currencies with respect to one another (having in mind, of course, the consequences for the changes on the value of trade performance of both countries with third parties). This process is termed *revaluation*. Normally only one of the currency's values would be altered. It might be altered so as to increase its value (up-valuation) or to decrease it (devaluation). In the case of an Italian-American proceeding, a reduction in the number of lira demanded for one American dollar (an up-valuation of the lira respective to the dollar) would result in an across-the-board price cut for Italians looking at all American goods and, at the same time, an across-the-board increase in the prices of Italian goods in the United States. The net impact of the revaluation would be for Italy to stimulate American exports to Italy and reduce Italian exports to the United States, thus reducing an American balance-of-trade deficit with respect to Italy.

Departing now from hypothetical examples, let us look at the trade performances of Germany and Japan in recent years. Each has been in the position of exporting far more industrial products than it imports, with the result that each has maintained a balance-of-trade surplus in their total world trade. (Because of its complete dependence on external sources for energy to fuel its industries, Japan's balance has been subject to the conditions of the international petroleum market, and has actually run deficits in the two major crises of 1974–75 and 1979–80. As a result, her deficit has run as deep as $10.9 billion in 1980 and her surplus as high as $18.4 billion in 1978.) From the point of view of the deficit countries like the United States, this is seen as a chronic surplus, one that ought to be remedied by currency revaluations. The deficit governments request that Germany and Japan charge more for marks and yen and pay fewer marks or yen of given numbers of their own national currencies. This would raise the price of German and Japanese goods exported (thus decreasing their exports) and lower the price of foreign goods imported into Germany and Japan (thus stimulating the exports of the deficit countries). The result, it is presumed, would be a more nearly realistic trading performance of Germany and Japan with respect to the rest of the world.[3]

The contemporary international monetary analyst must, of course, look at the world as a whole. (At least, it must look at the non-Soviet world as a whole, since the socialist countries of Eastern Europe play no part in the formal structure of the system, viewing it suspiciously as a device used by the international wealthy classes to exploit the

3. For a study on currency revaluation to regulate Japanese-American trade, see C. Fred Bergsten, "The US-Japan Economic Conflict," *Foreign Affairs,* Summer 1982, pp. 1059–1075.

proletariat without respect for national borders.) It is assumed theoretically that there is a perfect set of exchange rates among all participating countries at which every country, over time, will have an import-export balance. If currencies are allowed to float to their natural levels, all of their exchange rates would tend to equilibrate. (This does not imply that all exchange rates would be 1:1.) Under the circumstance of equilibrium, if a country were to charge too much for its currency, its goods would become unattractive to the rest of the world, and neither its currency nor its goods would be bought. Similarly, the overvalued country would be unable to buy foreign currencies, and thus would be unable to purchase foreign goods. It would then be excluded from international trade until it devalued its currency exchange rate to a level profitable to foreigners.

But this invisible hand of international exchange rates persistently fails to work. This is due principally to the fact that exchange rates are powerful statements of national economic prosperity and of world economic status. Furthermore, exchange rates have a major impact upon national politics and upon national fiscal policies, with the result that nations with strong exchange rate positions are reluctant to allow rates to be adjusted exclusively by market factors. Consequently, far from being an esoteric aspect of international economic relations holding little interest for students of global politics, exchange rates are a topic of vigorous negotiation, and are one of the principal means by which the capitalist governments adjust their relations with one another.[4]

2. National Reserves

Currency and exchange rates, it is now clear, are vitally important elements of international trade. But the picture is not yet complete. A nation that suffers a trade deficit must somehow resolve its debt to each country that holds that debt; that is, it must make up in money what it has not made up in commodity value of its exports. The easiest solution, or so it seems, would simply be to print and transfer to another country more of its own currency. But here the effects of declining trade balance become intertwined. A flood of new currency to make up a trade deficit signals a declining economy. What value is there for a vigorous economy in collecting the currency of a declining economy? For example, what value is there to the Japanese in collecting American dollars as payment of a trade deficit (a form of debt), when

4. The view of the directors of the International Monetary Fund on this subject is found in *The Role of Exchange Rates in the Adjustment of International Payments: A Report by the Executive Directors* (Washington: IMF, 1970).

the international position of the dollar is falling and that of the Japanese yen rising? In times of crisis, friendly nations will accept such payments, and they will do all they can to raise the value of an ally's currency. But in a time of economic competition, it is not in the interest of a vigorous economy to accept in payment the currency of a declining economy. How do governments resolve this dilemma?

In the long run, the answer of course is to stimulate declining economies. Transient economic declines may have little long-run effect upon international relations, but sustained declines are indicative of major shifts in the world's economic capability. Even revaluing currencies with respect to one another may be little more than a short-term response to long-term problems, and cannot long substitute for fundamental changes in fiscal policy or national industrial policy. But the latter may have such profound effects domestically that the short-term substitutes are more politically appealing, even though they are less effective.

Short of major economic realignment, governments have at their disposal three other devices for compensating the holders of their trade deficits. The first is gold transfer, a method that was popular for the half-century before World War I during which many major trading economies were on the gold standard. At that time, all national currencies were valued using gold as a standard, and the value of gold was fixed at $35 per ounce. (After the Second World War, the capitalist world went to a gold-dollar standard, in which gold and the American dollar were equally used as standards for valuation.) Gold transfers among governments became a common instrument for settling international deficits. Today, however, the value of gold has been decontrolled and it is subject to wild fluctuation. Under circumstances in which gold is of less reliable value than strong currencies, governments are hesitant to accept it in payment, particularly in cases where bilateral trade deficits may reach into the billions of dollars annually. Furthermore, in most capitalist economies, circulating currency is backed by gold at a fixed percentage of currency value, with the result that governments are extremely reluctant to use gold for international settlements. Except when there are major increases in the world's gold supply, therefore, as there have occasionally been when South Africa or China has announced a major gold discovery, gold is not an effective means of international payments settlement.

The second method is thus of greater value to governments: national currency reserves. As governments adjust their balances, they deal in many currencies. First among them, of course, is their own. The others are the currencies of the countries with which they trade, and particularly those with whom they enjoy trade surpluses, since those other governments will be settling their debts principally in their own currencies. Suppose, for example, that the United States has a trade surplus with Britain. It may carry that surplus as a paper debt or it may request cash payment, much of which will be made in British pounds sterling. In that way the American currency reserve comes to contain a larger fraction of pounds than, for example, of German marks, most of which the United States has transferred back to Germany as compensation for its trade deficit there. Meanwhile, the United States continues to adjust its surpluses and deficits with other countries, thus changing the various national currency fractions in the total American supply of foreign currencies. These holdings of other national currencies, which may be used in payment of international settlements if recipients are willing to receive them, are termed the country's currency reserves.

"The dollar fell today on European exchanges, but rose slightly in Tokyo." This has become a common headline in the economic news. In addition to indicating that money, like all else, is for sale in international markets, the statement illustrates that the practical value of a currency may change from one day to the next (as American travelers abroad have discovered). As is the case with economic indicators,

Inside Fort Knox.

Source: Conrad/Sygma

short-term fluctuations have little impact upon international political economy, but long-term trends may impact significantly. One fraction of a nation's currency reserves may have a high value one month and a relatively lower value the next; or the value of another currency may rise. For this reason, governments establish as part of their foreign policies specified currencies that they will attempt to hold in specified minimum amounts. Naturally, they will attempt to maintain substantial reserves in those currencies most valued internationally, and smaller amounts in those least acceptable. This simplifies international adjustments and ensures flexibility in payments as exchange rates vary and trading partners threaten to decline certain currencies in payment.[5]

The composition of a country's currency reserves depends upon several factors. Most commonly it is determined by the basic trading habits of the country: the countries (and therefore the currencies) with which it trades and those from which it has accepted cash payment in redress of trade imbalance. In addition, however, reserves will be influenced by the willingness to accept payment in the currency of a third country. For example, in an effort to reduce its holdings in dollars, Japan might refuse to accept payment in dollars from the United States, and insist instead that a specified fraction of the American debt be paid in other currencies. By the same token, a country that has compiled a debt to one country but has also collected large sums of some third-party currency may wish to pay its debt in the stockpiled currency. Japan might wish, for instance, to pay for Saudi Arabian oil with American dollars. The willingness of a state to accept a third-party currency and the insistence of another state upon using it are parts of the international confidence level in those currencies. That one country is trying to rid itself of excess holdings in American dollars and another is reluctant to accept those dollars is a statement of declining confidence in the dollar as an international medium of exchange. The reluctance, on the other hand, of governments to part with their marks and yen, while other governments are demanding these currencies in settlement of debts, is an indication of the extreme confidence in these currencies and the economies from which they are generated. Currencies that are in short supply internationally are said to be shortage currencies, while markets that are oversupplied with less desirable currencies are said to be glutted with them. Until recently there was a shortage of yen and marks, and a glut of dollars.

In recent history the dollar has gone from a shortage currency to

5. For a thorough treatment see Robert Triffin, *The World Money Maze: National Currencies in International Payments* (New Haven, Conn.: Yale University Press, 1966).

one of oversupply. At the close of World War II, dollars were the most desirable currency for reconstruction and revitalization of the European and Asian economies. American private capital flowed throughout the capitalist world, and governmental foreign aid left the United States in scores of billions of dollars. But as the partners recovered and began to become vigorous competitors, and as American dollars became so abundant as to exceed demand for them, the former shortage was transformed into a glut. Central banks were no longer eager to accumulate dollars for capital spending and international settlements, but to control the dollar portions of their national reserves. Particularly, in Europe, the recovery of the mark and the French franc, together with the other, less voluminous currencies, overshadowed the dollar and its value. Dollars of declining value held in huge amounts by European central banks thus became known, somewhat disparagingly, as *Eurodollars*. This phenomenon has spread to places wherever the United States has a significant trade deficit.

A second, and similar, phenomenon occurred in the decade following the advent of OPEC and the world's first petroleum crisis in 1973–74. The increased American dependence upon Middle Eastern oil, together with the rapid increases in OPEC petroleum prices since 1973, has led to a huge deficit in American trade with the OPEC nations and, therefore, to an equally huge dollar payment. The OPEC central banks accumulate foreign currencies, among them the dollar, at a rate of millions of dollars per day. Dollars compiled as a result of oil trade have been labeled *Petrodollars*, again a somewhat demeaning term because it indicates a reversal in traditional patterns of dependence and because it underscores the international inflation of the dollar and, with it, diminished value.

Until late 1983 the American currency was most welcomed in the United States, where foreign holders began to spend it at unprecedented rates. While throughout this book there has been emphasis upon American capital expenditures abroad as a measure of influence over the international political economy, it is equally important to point out that foreign investors are now using stockpiled dollars to invade the American capital scene. In 1982, while American private investments abroad totaled $221.3 billion, foreign investment in the United States had grown to fully 46 percent of that amount, $101.8 billion (See Table 13–3).

Because OPEC has had a dramatic impact upon all Western industrialized countries, the dollar is not alone in its current plight. To be sure, the vastness of the American dependence ensures that the dollar will lead the flow to OPEC central banks, but other currencies, including particularly the yen, are facing the same difficulty, as even

TABLE 13–4
Comparative trends in national currency reserves, 1970–1981, expressed in US$ billions. For Iran, the final figure is for 1979; thereafter, figures were unavailable due to the revolution.

	1970	*1976*	*1980*	*1981*	*Maximum Multiple*
Industrialized Nations					
US	0.6	0.3	10.1	9.8	16.8
Canada	3.0	3.5	2.1	3.0	Negligible
France	1.3	4.4	25.3	20.0	15.4
W. Germany	8.5	25.5	43.9	39.6	5.2
Japan	3.2	13.9	21.6	24.7	7.7
OPEC Nations					
Kuwait	00.0	0.9	3.4	3.6	36.0
Saudi Arabia	0.5	24.3	20.7	28.0	56.0
Venezuela	0.5	6.9	5.6	7.1	14.2
Iran	0.1	7.5	14.6	N.A.	146.0
United Arab Emirates	0.0	1.8	1.9	3.0	30.0

Source: Statistical Abstract of the United States, 1981, p. 898 and *1982/83,* p. 888.

unprecedented trade in food and arms has not been able to offset the rising cost of importing OPEC crude oil. Table 13–4 reveals the extent to which the OPEC phenomenon has affected the world's distribution of currency reserves. It shows a sample distribution for the industrialized world and a similar sample for the OPEC nations, contrasting the status of their respective reserves before and after the first actions of OPEC, and after the 1979–80 crisis in the international petroleum market. While the industrialized economies continue to increase their reserves, the rate at which they do so is modest in comparison with all OPEC countries except Venezuela, in which the rate is comparable to the fastest national rates among the industrialized countries. Were it not for technology transfer and the rapid increase of arms sales to the Middle East during the OPEC era, the statistics would lean dramatically more toward the OPEC states. (In Table 13–4, the "maximum multiple" is calculated from 1970, the base year, to the highest reserve recorded in the eleven-year period, not necessarily to 1981.)

Recall that this discussion pertains only to reserves of convertible currencies. Total national reserves include these currencies, gold, regular drawing rights at the International Monetary Fund (IMF) and Special Drawing Rights at the IMF. The regular drawing rights result from depositing with the IMF an amount established by agreement. These reserves are used by all participating governments, including the donor, for the adjustment of international deficits. The next section deals with the Special Drawing Rights.

3. Special Drawing Rights

A third device available to governments in settlement of trade debts was created in 1968 through the International Monetary Fund, which from its inception in 1945 has held a number of monetary adjustment responsibilities. By vote of the membership, the IMF was authorized in 1968 to create Special Drawing Rights (SDRs), a form of international monetary paper that has become known popularly as paper gold. When a participating government shows a chronic balance-of-payments deficit (trade balance is, together with capital balance, a major component of payments balance), it may request that it be granted permission to use some of its allocated share of SDRs to exchange with the central banks of other participating countries for convertible currencies. The value of an SDR is based on the values of a "basket" of the five principal Western convertible currencies: the American dollar, the German mark, the French franc, the British pound and the Japanese yen. Thus, as is the case with individual currencies, the value of the SDR is subject to fluctuation, but since it is based on several currencies simultaneously, the values of which change with respect to each other, these fluctuations are small compared with those experienced by the individual currencies.

Once voted, each participating country is required to accept SDRs

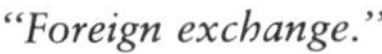

"Foreign exchange."

Source: Herblock on All Fronts (New American Library, 1980)

in exchange for convertible currencies up to a level of twice its own SDR allocation. Although SDRs are not literally currency and cannot be spent for commodities, they have the effect of expanding governmental payment capabilities by making convertible currency reserves available. This right is subject at all times to the voting procedures of the IMF, which are complex and weighted in favor of the most important currencies, including the American dollar. Nevertheless, their creation has been regarded as "a genuine breakthrough in monetary thinking,"[6] and has contributed considerably to easing the currency reserve problem of countries with chronic trade deficits.

The World Debt Crisis

Although a discussion of global payments mechanisms reveals certain trends in the world's flow of wealth, the period 1980–84 was one of marked disruption in the world economy. Several events or series of events contributed to the darkest years in the global economy in a half century. While it is impossible to place them in order of importance, it is nonetheless useful to outline them briefly.

1. *Worldwide recession of the industrialized market economies* Throughout the West and Japan, productivity fell sharply, unemployment rose to near-record levels, interest costs rose to the point at which borrowing for business growth became impossible, and the total value of world trade diminished. In several places in this book we have noted that the economic trends of the 1970s were partly interrupted in 1980. The trade deficit of the United States reached its record.

2. *Deterioration of OPEC's control of the world oil market* From 1979 onward, the ability of OPEC to control world oil prices diminished consistently, largely because of a dispute among members. The more radical members called for rapid increases in price and freedom among members to determine output, while the more moderate members wished to control total output on a quota basis while also controlling prices. War between Iran and Iraq, together with the continuing uncertainty of the international consequences of the Iranian Revolution, led not only to disruption of supply, but to fears that the Strait of Hormuz would be closed as a military measure, and oil would no longer be able to leave the Persian Gulf by ship.

6. Fritz Machlup, *Remaking the International Monetary System* (Baltimore: Johns Hopkins University Press, 1968), p. 34.

3. *Political instability and loss of confidence in investment* The increasing political instability of Latin America and the Caribbean, as well as of the Middle East, North Africa and southernmost Africa, disturbed the climate for international investment. Heated rhetoric between the two Koreas and continuing conflict among China, Kampuchea, Thailand and Vietnam threatened the destabilization of Asia. The mounting strategic arms race, the West's reaction to the Soviet attack upon a civilian Korean aircraft, Soviet occupation of Afghanistan and oppression of Poland all interrupted dialogue between East and West, not only on arms reduction, but on economic cooperation as well.

4. *Rescheduling of debt payment by Poland and the Third World* The Falkland Islands War and the imposition of martial law on Poland were the first two events that illuminated the pending inability of Poland and the Third World to keep abreast of their debt payments. It is an error, however, to consider that these events themselves caused financial prostration. They can be understood only in the context of a sluggish global economy, the economic consequences of political instability both regionally and between the superpowers, deteriorating terms of trade for Third World exports (including oil), demand by over-committed lending institutions for repayment and exhaustion of the IMF's reserves as a source of rescue.

Many of the consequences of these problems have been considered elsewhere in this book, particularly in Chapter 5, which dealt with the global perspective of the Third World. In this chapter, therefore, we shall address the problem only as it relates to the global economy, having dealt already with its impact upon the Third World.

Table 3–5 outlines the current debt problem of the developing world by showing the 1983 indebtedness of the fourteen leading debtor nations. In gross terms, by the end of 1983 the total debt was approximately $680 billion. Alarmingly, nearly half of the debt was in

TABLE 13–5
Principal debtor nations, 1983, expressed in billions of US dollars.

Brazil	92	Philippines	21
Mexico	87	Yugoslavia	19
Argentina	39	Chile	18
So. Korea	37	Algeria	15
Venezuela	35	Nigeria	14
Poland	27	Peru	12
Indonesia	22	Romania	10

Source: Compiled from Pedro-Pablo Kuczynski, "Latin American Debt: Act II," *Foreign Affairs,* Fall 1983, pp. 17–38 at p. 19, and *The Washington Post,* September 25, 1983, p. H1.

Latin America, with six countries owing $283 billion of the region's total of $330 billion. And in Asia, three of the most rapidly developing countries owed fully $80 billion of the total remaining debt of $350 billion. Moreover, total debt by the end of 1983 had grown by almost $40 billion in a year.[7]

The debt was owed to a number of lenders, including national governments, international organizations and a variety of private sources including banks, insurance companies and bondholders in the developed countries. Approximately 80 percent of the total was owed to private lenders, many of whom were threatened with collapse in the face of non-repayment.[8] More than a dozen major banks in the United States, Germany, France, Britain and Japan had extended themselves up to $20 billion each, and the threat of default meant the possibility of the largest bank failures in history.

Amid substantial ideological disarray, the non-socialist world sought to stabilize the threatening situation. The International Monetary Fund sought additional reserve contributions from the developed nations in order to provide more drawing power for the indebteded. In the United States, President Reagan's request to Congress for additional funds led to bitter rangling among liberals who regarded this as a mechanism for deepening still further the Third World's dependence upon large banks. These forces considered the request a bail-out for America's largest lending institutions. More conservative elements supported the request, but attached language that would have prevented the IMF from making the American contribution available to communist governments. Liberals who opposed this language (successfully) were then branded communists themselves. The successful increase in the IMF's reserves restored confidence sufficiently to result in another round of lending by the banks.

Another attack on the world debt crisis was a case-by-case treatment. In some instances, debt repayment was rescheduled; in others, variable interest rates were adjusted. In still other cases, carry-over loans were made available short-term to cover interest for postponement of payment.

But in the long run, such temporary measures will not resolve the vicious cycle of debt in the Third World. Debt has now risen to the point that the average Third World debtor owes annual interest payments equal to approximately 33 percent of its annual export value

7. Compare Samuel Brittan, "A Very Painful World Adjustment," *Foreign Affairs,* America and the World 1982 issue, pp. 541–568 at p. 549 with Pedro-Pablo Kuczynski, "Latin-American Debt: Act Two," *Foreign Affairs,* Fall 1983, pp. 17–38 at p. 19.

8. The figure is adapted from Samuel Brittan, "World Adjustment," p. 549.

(50 percent for the largest Latin American debtors). Furthermore, total debt may now be as high as three times the total annual value of exports and almost 50 percent of gross national product for a year.[9] All of these observations make it clear that the solution to international debt is not more lending, but revision of the global trade regime with improved terms of trade for Third World products, solutions which will add further to the trade deficit woes of some of the chronic deficit nations such as the United States.

Conclusion

Like most economic matters, the content of the international political economy is extraordinarily complex. Concerns of volume, value and reciprocity abound, since the failure of exports to match the value of imports has extreme consequences for payments, currency values and subsequent international (and even domestic) economic interaction. This chapter has addressed the monetary aspects of international trade and the processes by which governments, through their central banks and international organizations, redress imbalances. We have been concerned with the political as well as the regulatory aspects of international exchange, and with the recent history of monetary trends, particularly as they have affected the American dollar in the international market and as they have contributed to the fitful development of the Third World. As in the preceding chapter on international trade, we have looked at the impact of OPEC upon the distribution of currency reserves as an indicator of the changing character of the international political economy.

9. Adapted and estimated from Pedro-Pablo Kuczynski, "Latin American Debt," *Foreign Affairs,* Winter 1982/83, pp. 344–364 at p. 349.

IV

The Logic of World Order

14

International Law

As the preceding section has stressed, certain economic mechanisms accompany day-to-day international transactions. These are intended to adjust the relations among states as they compete for natural resources, for markets, for development opportunity and for national enrichment. These adjustments contribute to the pacification of international practice, and do their part to bring order to a global political system that in their absence would tend to be characterized by self-assertion and disruption for national purposes.

But other relations among nation-states are not subject to such mechanisms. Adjustment of payment balances has little bearing on the ability of the nuclear powers to destroy the planet; and currency revaluations, though a great help in the stabilization of relations among nations, are of little assistance in offsetting nuclear arms races, or aggressive intervention or border clashes. Specifically, since power is a relative concept (power with respect to what?), some international actors will always be able to threaten others with coercion, enslavement or destruction. Whenever states are unwilling to exercise self-restraint (or *autolimitation*), there are but two alternatives for ensuring international stability: holding the future of other states in ransom by threat of superior force, or submitting to collective means for making international decisions and for enforcing compliance. This chapter deals with the second of these alternatives by exploring one specific method that has been practiced by governments with varying amounts of enthusiasm and varying degrees of performance for over three centuries: international law. The chapters which follow in this section continue that examination by looking at other practical methods: international organization, international integration and transnational participation. How do legal and organizational processes in the international system promote a more stable world order?

The Nature of International Law

In a well-ordered domestic society, there is a complex legal system with specific organs for making, adjudicating and enforcing laws. The state has the authority to call individuals to account for their behavior relative to the law. Laws are made on their behalf, they can be called to court against their will, and legal regulations are enforced whether an individual likes them or not.

The international system is not so well ordered. Since only the nation-state is sovereign, it is not subject to the decisions of external institutions in the way citizens are to the institutions of their societies. No legislative body exists above the state, no international court has the capacity to compel its behavior, and there are few organs to execute international regulations. If a parallel between the domestic legal system and the legal attributes of the international system is lacking, just what is international law? If it is not by nature a formal system of regulations made by a supreme legislature, judged by supreme courts and enforced by a supreme executive agency, what is it?

No student need feel alone in skepticism about the existence or the nature of international law. It is a matter which scholars and governments have been debating for centuries. The debate among scholars is in the realm of *jurisprudence* (science of law), within which countless interpretations have been offered. It will be useful to look into two theoretical interpretations that differ vastly: *positivism* and *neorealism*.

Positivism

Positivist theory is based on an analogy between domestic law, with its rules and institutions, and the international setting. It understands the law to be a *system of rules* (norms) that specify the rights and obligations governing the external behavior of states. Positivist theory holds law to have a *consensual basis*—that is, states become subject to rules only by voluntary consent. These two concepts are summarized in an opinion of the Permanent Court of International Justice, to which France and Turkey voluntarily submitted the *Lotus* case for decision in 1927.

> International law governs relations between independent States. *The rules of law binding upon States therefore emanate from their own free will* as expressed in conventions [treaties] or by usages generally accepted as expressing principles of law and established in order to regulate the relations between these co-existing independent communities or with a view to the achievement of common aims. *Restrictions upon the independence of States cannot therefore be presumed.*[1]

The progressive development of an international legal order depends, accordingly, upon convincing governments that their relations are best protected by mutually arranged norms with which they will comply consistently and voluntarily.

Neorealism

At the other end of the theoretical spectrum is the neorealist school. This interpretation denies that rules are at the center of a legal order, and argues instead that policy and values are the foci. This theory is said, therefore, to be *policy oriented* and *value oriented.* Since international relations are in constant change, regulatory law must be a process of decision making in which all states and international agencies participate, with the content of the law changing at every moment. There are no fixed rules that can be relied upon tomorrow as they are today. Thus international law is not a system of rules, but *a constitutive process of authoritative decision.* The law is what the policies of the contributors make it, and it is imposed on the world by power of the actors in accordance with the values that they wish the law to promote and defend. When major actors dispute the outcomes of the constitutive process, or when they disagree on the values to be promoted, then international law is identified with the foreign policy of that state whose value objectives most nearly approximate the pursuit of human dignity. The highly subjective standard is a product of the Cold War.[2]

1. PCIJ Series A, no. 10. The emphasis has been added to illuminate the twin positivist principles of *rule orientation* and *consent.*
2. For statements of the neorealist theory, see Harold D. Lasswell and Myres S. McDougal, "Jurisprudence in Policy-Oriented Perspective," *Florida Law Journal* 19, 1967, pp. 486–513; Myres S. McDougal, "The Comparative Study of Law for Policy Purposes: Value Clarification as an Instrument of Democratic World Order," *Yale Law Journal* 61, 1952, pp. 915–46; Myres S. McDougal, "International Law, Power and Policy," *Recueil des Cours* 82 (The Hague: Academy of International Law,

The political uses to which these two theories can be put by governments are as different as the doctrines themselves. If a government accepts the positivist definition, it will presumably regulate its behavior by existing treaties and other agreements, and it will expect other governments to regulate their actions by formal norms as well. In this way governments will be able to predict one another's actions and will have solid ground on which to question one another's motives. Compliance or noncompliance with formal agreements communicates the intentions of governments.

If, however, a government prefers the neorealist interpretation of international law, it will shun the reliability of formal agreements and justify its behavior on the claim that its value objectives are superior to those of its adversary, that its foreign policies more nearly approximate the goals of human dignity than do those of someone else. In this way declarations of foreign policy become international law. One neorealist author, for example, argues that the Truman Doctrine "has gradually evolved . . . into a kind of common law of international order, a prudent rule of reciprocal safety."[3] The doctrine was announced in 1947 as a unilateral policy of the United States for restraining the growth of international communism. It was an instrument of containment undertaken by the United States against the Soviet Union.

No government accepts either view of the law exclusively. In fact, for most powerful states, the choice of legal interpretations depends on the facts at hand. A safe rule of thumb emerges: Governments will seek to maximize their rights (neorealist interpretation) and minimize their obligations (positivism); but they will attempt to minimize their adversaries' rights (positivism) and maximize their adversaries' obligations (neorealism). When governments have genuine concerns for legal interaction, they will speak as positivist; but when they have politicized concerns for the law, they will come forth as neorealists.

1953), pp. 133–259; and Harold D. Lasswell, Myres S. McDougal and W. Michael Reisman, "The World Constitutive Process of Authoritative Decision," *Journal of Legal Education* 19, 1967, pp. 253–300 and 403–37, in two parts.

For critiques, see particularly Stanley V. Anderson, "A Critique of Myres S. McDougal's Doctrine of Interpretation by Major Purposes," *American Journal of International Law* 57, 1963, pp. 378–83; and Rosalyn Higgins, "Policy and Impartiality: The Uneasy Relation in International Law," *International Organization* 23, 1969, pp. 914–931.

3. Eugene V. Rostow, *Law, Power and the Pursuit of Peace* (Lincoln, Nebr.: University of Nebraska Press, 1968), p. 43. (Also published in paperback edition by Frederick A. Praeger.)

The Sources of International Law

Think again about the analogy of international law to domestic law. Rules arise from constitutions, formal legislation, custom and the decisions of formally constituted courts. Such institutionalization exists in the international system to a far less authoritative degree. From where, then, do the norms of international law come? What are its sources?

The authoritative statement of the sources of international law is found in Article 38 of the Statute of the International Court of Justice, the permanent judicial organ of the United Nations. The statute lists the sources as (1) international conventions (treaties) in force between parties, (2) international customary rules, (3) general principles of international law and (4) such subsidiary sources as prior judicial decisions and the writings of the highly qualified publicists.

Treaties, bilateral and multilateral, are the most logical primary source. Whether a convention be one of *codification* (merely formalizing in codes practices already accepted through custom) or of a *legislative* character (creating new rights and obligations), it represents the maximum explicit consent of signatories. Much of the business of twentieth-century intergovernmental organizations has been the codification of existing principles and customs. Only in the last few years has the bulk of international law come to be treaty law.

Custom, until recently the largest component of positive law, is the practice of states. It is generally held that usage becomes an international legal norm when it has been repeated over a period of time by several states, when they have generally acquiesced in such behavior by one another, and when governments begin to act in certain ways out of a sense of legal obligation. In this manner most of the international laws of the high seas originated, as did the laws of diplomatic and consular privileges and immunities, and the rules governing neutrality and international commerce, to mention only a few.

General principles of international law are less clearly defined, partly because it is difficult to demonstrate widespread acceptance, and partly because the distinction between a firm principle and a customary rule is an obscure one. Nevertheless, there are general principles that can be readily identified. Many of the amenities of international relations are general principles that arise out of the theory of sovereignty. Other general principles emerge from the necessity for sovereign equality, including the principle of legal equality and the expectation of fair treatment of one another's nationals.

Subsidiary sources are still less specific, and merit last place among the sources of international law. In judicial tests of legal rules, the rules themselves must undergo interpretation. The business of courts is to interpret the law and to apply it. In international adjudication, rules may be interpreted by national courts, standing international tribunals, panels established to deal with specific problems or by international courts, among them the International Court of Justice. In most national systems, courts are bound by the rule of *stare decisis,* meaning that what the court has previously decided *is* the law, and is precedent binding upon courts. International tribunals generally subscribe to the same principle, and the decisions of such courts contain references to former cases just as the decisions of American courts do in domestic cases. The International Court of Justice, however, while availing itself of its prior decisions and of those of other courts, does not feel itself so firmly bound by precedent. Unlike other tribunals, the ICJ may interpret the legal significance of declarations and resolutions of the political organs of the United Nations. This is especially the case in its advisory jurisdiction, which enables the ICJ, upon request from the UN organs, to render "constitutional" interpretations that may have political effects upon member states.

Viewed from a big-power standpoint, the most significant example of this action was embodied in the advisory opinion *Certain Expenses of the United Nations* (1962).[4] Because the Soviet Union and other governments had refused to pay their apportioned shares of financing UN peacekeeping operations in the Middle East and in the Congo, the General Assembly requested clarification of its authority under the Charter to bill members for such expenses against their will. The Court dealt with the legitimacy of the operations themselves, rendering a "constitutional" interpretation on the limits of UN authority. It favored an expansive view. Out of this controversial decision, an argument has arisen that the Charter contains implied powers of UN organs over and above the explicit ones.[5] The contrary view holds that the most effective contribution that the ICJ might make to the progressive development of international law is through the cautious use of advisory jurisdiction—that the Court might thus earn the trust of states, which might then be more willing to submit to it their bilateral disputes.[6] Whichever of these positions may carry the greater

4. International Court of Justice, advisory opinion of July 20, 1962, found in *ICJ Reports,* 1962, pp. 151–80.
5. Rahmattullah Khan, *Implied Powers of the United Nations* (Bombay: Vikas Publications, 1970).
6. Leo Gross, "The International Court of Justice and the United Nations," *Recueil des Cours* 120 (The Hague: Academy of International Law, 1967), 313–30.

hope of eventual judicial contributions to a more stable international order is for the moment less important than that the *Expenses* case reveals the potential political impact of international judicial activity.

The Sanctions of International Law

How is international law enforced without international government or police? Merely to posit the existence of a body of international law is not to claim that the international system is capable of legal regulation. We must demonstrate the extent of states' willingness to *comply* with legal norms. What, then, is the compelling force of international law, and by what mechanisms is it presumably enforced? Is international law "law, properly so called," or is it merely "positive international morality" which lacks the enforceability necessary to make it law?[7]

Any form of law has as its incentives a variety of *normative, utilitarian* and *coercive* sanctions. An individual may drive his automobile lawfully because he fears the consequences of wrongdoing (fear of coercive sanction), or as a matter of personal safety (utilitarian sanction) or as a contribution to orderly social coexistence (normative sanction). Likewise among states, compliance with rules of law is rather consistent, and is grounded in normative and utilitarian motives. Governments do generally regard reciprocal behavior as mutually beneficial, and are often sensitive to international pressures. They wish to avoid reprisals and embarrassing declarations and resolutions brought on by improper behavior, except when perceived needs exceed the risk of external criticism. Furthermore, states rarely enter into formal international agreements unless they intend to benefit, and unless they intend to comply with them. Nor do they acquiesce in custom over the long run without anticipating benefits. Accordingly, it is not at all extraordinary that states should normally comply with their voluntary obligations.

Coercive sanction takes over where all else fails. Indeed, the necessity for coercion occurs only when a state departs from its normal pattern of behavior under existing rules, when a behavior pattern is devoid

7. This is the classic distinction made by the English positivist John Austin. For American expressions and discussions of the argument, see particularly Westel W. Willoughby, *Fundamental Concepts of Public Law* (New York: Macmillan, 1924), p. 224ff., and "The Legal Nature of International Law," *American Journal of International Law* 2, 1908, pp. 357–65; and Hans Kelsen, "The Pure Theory of Law and Analytical Jurisprudence," *Harvard Law Review 55,* 1941 pp. 44–70.

of legal restraint, or when a state does not participate in what is considered by other nations to be law. All of this is just another way of saying that when a state is not party to formal normative or utilitarian sanctions generally applicable, its behavior with respect to others may be controllable only through the threat of coercion.

Coercive theories of law abound, especially of international law. Some claim that norms are not *legal* norms unless they are capable of coercive enforcement by some political entity juridically superior to the actor. Hence, unless international law is enforceable by some power above the sovereign state, it is not really law. Others go so far as to define law in terms of its enforceability: Only if violation of a norm elicits a coercive response can that norm be interpreted as a legal rule.[8] It is the response that defines the character of a norm, rather than the mere content. Law is a statement of coercibility.[9]

Among the coercive measures that states utilize are a vast array of forceful and nonforceful acts. Nonforceful acts are referred to as *retorsions,* which are reciprocal punitive acts, and often referred to as nonforceful acts of retaliation. If one state should take steps to restrict the imports of another, the victimized state may respond by freezing the assets of the first state held in the banks of the second. In general, such acts are proportionate, so as to minimize the likelihood of escalation.

Retaliatory acts that are responses to forceful violations and that themselves involve actions that would otherwise be considered illegal are called *reprisals.* Because such acts involve use of military material, it is difficult to measure and to maintain proportion. Yet it is normally held that reprisals ought to be equivalent to the original violation. Familiar recent acts of reprisal are the American bombing raids of North Vietnam as a response to the alleged attacks upon American destroyers in the Tonkin Gulf in the summer of 1964, and Israeli air strikes on guerrilla sites in Lebanon after that country's government failed to prevent terrorist activities.

The ultimate sanction in international relations is war. War is a political instrument, not always undertaken to destroy, but to deprive the target state of the ability and will further to violate normal behavior. The threat of war, then, may deter states from aberrant be-

8. See Hans Kelsen, "The Pure Theory of Law and Analytical Jurisprudence," p. 58; "The Pure Theory of Law," *Law Quarterly Review 50,* 1934, pp. 474–98; and *General Theory of Law and State* (Cambridge, Mass.: Harvard University Press, 1949), pp. 51–58.

9. The coercive theory of law is not, however, universally accepted. For major exceptions, see Gerhart Niemeyer, *Law Without Force: The Function of Politics in International Law* (Princeton, NJ: Princeton University Press, 1941) and Michael Barkun, *Law Without Sanctions: Order in Primitive Societies and the World Community* (New Haven, Conn.: Yale University Press, 1968).

havior; and the use of war as a response to prior actions is punitive. But in either case, the major intention of a state undertaking responsive warfare is to force political submission.

Traditionally, responses to illegal behavior have been left to aggrieved states. Indeed, international law includes a doctrine of *self-help,* which permits each state to launch punitive responses to illegal or other noxious acts. Although the doctrine of self-help (a by-product of absolute sovereignty) tries to provide international politics with formal and legal means for sanction, it is apparent that abuses or excesses actually contribute to international anarchy. Primarily for this reason, twentieth-century international organizations have striven to replace unilateral sanctions by *collective sanctions.*[10] This process was begun by the League of Nations Covenant (Article 11), which inscribed the principle that "Any war or threat of war . . . is hereby declared a matter of concern to the whole League." This concern was to be activated through Article 16:

> Should any Member of the League resort to war . . . it shall *ipso facto* be deemed to have committed an act of war against all other Members of the League, which hereby undertake immediately to subject it to the severance of all trade or financial relations, the prohibition of all intercourse between the nationals of the Covenant-breaking State and the State, and the prevention of all financial, commercial or personal intercourse between the nationals of the Covenant-breaking and the nationals of any other State, whether a Member of the League or not.

The Covenant further authorized the Council to recommend to states what military forces they should contribute for the implementation of Article 16.

These principles of the League of Nations were greatly expanded in the Charter of the United Nations. Chapter 7 of the Charter, entitled "Action with Respect to Threats to the Peace, Breaches of the Peace, and Acts of Aggression," authorizes the Security Council to determine the existence of a threat to international stability and to recommend either peaceful measures for its resolution or coercive acts short of force. Ultimately, however, in Article 42, the Security Council is authorized to call upon states to use armed force in behalf of the organization.

> Should the Security Council consider that measures provided for in Article 41 would be inadequate or have proved inadequate, it may take such action by air, sea, or land forces as may be necessary to maintain or restore international peace and security. Such action may include dem-

10. For a systematic study of Security Council responses to unilateral reprisals, especially in the Middle East, see Derek Bowett, "Reprisals Involving Resort to Armed Force," *American Journal of International Law* 66, 1972, pp. 1–36.

> onstrations, blockade, and other operations by air, sea, or land forces of Members of the United Nations.

This principle of "all against one"—the entire world against the aggressor—is termed *collective security*. This differs both from self-help, which is a doctrine of unilateral action, and from collective self-defense, which is an alliance arrangement by which a few states agree that an attack upon one shall be considered an attack upon all.

Since the United Nations is not a government and must depend upon separate nation-states for military forces, much of Chapter 7 is devoted to the means by which such forces are to be placed at the disposal of the Security Council. Since the Military Staff Committee has been wholly unable to create a stand-by force, the ability of the Security Council to act still rests upon states' willingness to be the Council's agents. To this end, Article 48 provides that "the action required to carry out the decisions of the Security Council for the maintenance of international peace and security shall be taken by all the Members of the United Nations or by some of them, as the Security Council may determine."

Despite the apparent limitlessness of Security Council authority on enforcement action, the Council has never undertaken an act of enforcement within the full meaning of the expression and of the Charter's provisions. Demands for action have been highly politicized, and have failed to achieve the concurrence of a majority of the Security Council members—including the permanent members, which are the United States, the Soviet Union, Britain, France and China (until 1971 the last of these having been represented by an envoy of the government of the Republic of China in Taiwan). Among the great impediments to Security Council action is that, when the United Nations was created, the great powers sought to prevent action against their own interests by including in the Charter the principle of great power unanimity. Article 27 requires that matters of substance be decided by a majority of nine of the fifteen members "including the concurring votes of the permanent members." Only in the case of the UN response to the invasion of South Korea in 1950 has the Security Council been able to transcend its internal politics to vote enforcement; but since the Soviet delegation did not participate in the decision (because of its boycott after UN refusal to seat the Peking representative), it cannot be said that collective security was involved within the full meaning of the Charter even in the Korean situation.

Enforcement measures are not the sole means of United Nations sanction. Indeed, skeptics of the coercive theory of international law note that forceful sanctions through the United Nations are limited to situations involving threats to the peace, breaches of the peace and acts of aggression. In all other instances of non-compliance with international law, the Charter's own general provisions outlawing the threat or use of force actually prevent forceful sanction. Those same skeptics regard this as an appropriate paradox in a decentralized state system of international politics.[11]

Nonetheless, other means of collective sanction through the United Nations involve diplomatic intervention, economic sanctions and peacekeeping operations. In the forty years of the United Nations, over one hundred disputes have been submitted for collective consideration. While none has resulted in enforcement except for the peculiar Korean decision, troops have been dispatched in more than a dozen cases for truce observation purposes or for interposition between combatants.

In its economic sanctions, the UN has followed in the path of the League of Nations, which undertook economic sanctions against Italy in 1935–36 for its attack upon Ethiopia. In the UN period, the most celebrated sanctions have been those voted against China by the General Assembly in 1951 as a result of Chinese intervention in the Korean War, and the 1967 decision of the Security Council to isolate Southern Rhodesia (now Zimbabwe) for its policy of racial separation following its unilateral declaration of independence from Britain.

As in other cases of economic sanctions, effectiveness in the Rhodesian situation was limited by the twin problems of (1) achieving universal participation and (2) the resistance of national elites to external coercion, especially when the issue was one of prominent internal concern. With respect to universal participation, even states usually sympathetic to Britain's policy demonstrated weak compliance.[12] For example, by executive order, the United States imposed restraints upon imports originating in Rhodesia,

> *Provided,* however, that the prohibition against dealing in commodities or products exported from Southern Rhodesia shall not apply to any such commodities or products which, prior to the date of this Order, had been lawfully imported into the United States.[13]

11. See, for example, J. A. Watson, "A Realistic Jurisprudence of International Law," *The Yearbook of World Affaris* (London), 1980, pp. 265–285.
12. Report of the Committee Established in Pursuance of Resolution 352 (1968) of May 29, 1968 (New York: UN Publications S/8954, dated December 30, 1968); also, Johan Galtung, "On the Effects of Economic Sanctions, with Examples from the Case of Rhodesia," *World Politics* 19, no. 3, April 1967, pp. 378–416; Frederick Hoffmann, "The Functions of Economic Sanctions," *Journal of Peace Research,* no. 2, 1967, pp. 140–60; and Ronald Segal, editor, *Sanctions Against South Africa* (London: Penguin, 1964).
13. United States Department of State Release no. 176, July 29, 1968; in *US Department of State Bulletin 59,* 1968, p. 199, and as reprinted in *American Journal of International Law* 63, 1969, pp. 128–30, in the section entitled "Comtemporary Practice of the United States Relating to International Law."

As a matter of international interest, the United States sought formally to implement the Security Council sanctions. But as a matter of self-interest, the US government demurred from full implementation by interpreting the sanctions to affect only commodities in which trade had not customarily occurred between the two nations. The reason was that Southern Rhodesia was a prime supplier of chromium to the United States, and continued flow of this resource was necessary for production of steel alloys needed in, among other things, military hardware.

This decentralization of sanctions remains one of the major weaknesses of international law. While international bodies sometimes make decisions in the implementation of sanctions, member states must implement them. The states are the importers and exporters in the international system. They command industrial economies and the passage of goods across national boundaries. Just as Stalin once remarked that the Pope has no military divisions, so too does the United Nations have no troops of its own, no industries to produce the coveted commodities which, if withheld, might alter the external or internal policies of states. The UN has no chromium deposits to withhold from the United States! Furthermore, the United Nations is wholly dependent upon its members for operating funds, so no matter what decisional authority its members give it, its ability to take action depends not only upon decision, but upon means. Without the support, the wealth and the material assistance of national governments, the United Nations is incapable of effective sanctions. The resistance of governments to a financially independent UN arises principally from their insistence upon maintaining control over sanctioning processes in international politics.

In the absence of a reliable system of collective sanctions, individual and group sanctions must be accepted as legitimate within current international law. Until states can achieve their demands through collective actions, governments and their close allies will invoke coercive self-help. As a result, the imposition of individual sanctions is common.

Some cases in which sanctions are threatened see no actual implementation. The United States, for example, did not impose measures upon those Latin American states which nationalized privately-owned American property, despite legislation that authorizes the president to discontinue aid in the absence of adequate compensation.

A most interesting case of sanctions between major powers was raised by the Soviet Union's refusal to permit Jews to emigrate, and later its consent to do so only after payment of an exorbitant "education tax." This became an issue of public debate when hopes for expanded Soviet-American trade brightened (1972–74). Several interest groups demanded withholding agreement until after relaxation of Moscow's emigration policy. These pressures were expressed in the Jackson-Brock Amendment, which imposed restraints upon American trade with the Soviet Union until the latter recognized the open right of its citizens to emigrate. Because Moscow regarded these restraints as interventionary and politically exorbitant, it declined to enter into a commercial agreement offering it most-favored-nation status (tariffs no higher than those required of other major trading partners of the United States). Later, in 1980, when Soviet troops invaded and occupied Afghanistan, the United States responded with a number of sanctions, including unilateral discontinuation of treaty-regulated grain trade with the Soviet Union.

Other acts of unilateral sanction may also be noted. In the fall of 1975, after the United States suffered several embarrassing defeats at the United Nations, including the majority declaration equating Zionism with racism, it became American policy to threaten with economic sanction those of its friends who contributed to the continuing embarrassment. In another instance, as a potential recipient of sanctions, the United States was informed by Britain and France early in 1976 that if it refused limited landing rights in American airports to the supersonic plane Concorde, they would initiate economic sanctions against the US.

The frequent resort to individual sanctions leads some to conclude that international law is incapable of restraining states. Yet we know beyond doubt that much of the conduct of states *is* regulated, and that it is regulated by legal means. We know, for example, that the law of the high seas is highly developed, though laden with modern complications; that under all but the most peculiar political circumstances such as those in Iran in 1979 and 1980 in which dozens of American diplomatic personnel were held hostage for more than a year, diplomatic and consular personnel may rely upon foreign governments for specified treatment; that there exist developed principles for international exchange of fugitives through extradition; and that a host of relatively nonpolitical functions is regulated by international conventions.

We know equally well, however, that the power relations of governments are but sparsely regulated, and even then imperfectly. The General Pact for the Renunciation of War (the Kellogg-Briand Pact, 1928) was considered inapplicable in cases of self-defense, and each state retained the right to determine the conditions and needs of its defense. Article 51 of the UN Charter continues to permit "individual or collective self-defense" prior to Security Council assumption of responsibility. By the same token, neither France nor China has entered into the Nuclear Non-Proliferation Treaty, nor is either likely to do so until after having achieved its desired level of deterrent capability. And while the United States, the Soviet Union and Britain have forsworn nuclear testing at sea and in the atmosphere, they have reserved the right to continue nuclear competition by underground testing.

The Effectiveness of International Law

If we are to conclude that international law provides effective restraints upon states, then we must demonstrate not merely the existence of legal principles, but also the willingness of states to comply with them. Compliance is a function of several factors, among them: (1) the subject matter that law seeks to regulate; (2) changes in the motives and needs of governments; (3) the ability of states to violate the law without serious threat of sanctions; and (4) the importance of the outcome of an event. So while we are concerned here with international law, each of these elements is subjected to the political judgment of the state. The decision as to whether one will be "law-abiding" is a decision for the state's political apparatus. A state's compliance with legal obligations is a function of (1) the degree to which issues are politicized and (2) the state's ability to behave in a lawless manner without serious threat of adverse consequences.

International law consists of norms of varying political levels.[14] On some subjects states readily recognize the utility of collective regulation, especially where the subject matter is relatively mechanical and depoliticized. This level of law, referred to as *the law of reciprocity,* is a network of treaties and customs through which governments acknowledge reciprocal benefit. Compliance with these norms is predictable.

As the subject matter of the law becomes more politicized, however, states are less willing to enter into formal regulation, or do so only with loopholes for escape from apparent constraints. In this area, called *the law of community,* governments are generally less willing to sacrifice their sovereign liberties. In a revolutionary international system where change is rapid and direction unclear, the integrity of the law of community is weak, and compliance with its often flaccid norms is correspondingly uncertain.

The law of the political framework resides above these other two levels, and consists of the legal norms governing the ultimate power

14. Although this concept has been expressed by several legal scholars, this analysis follows most closely that of Stanley Hoffmann, "International Systems and International Law," *World Politics* 14, 1961, pp. 205–237.

relations of states. This is the most politicized level of international relations; hence, pertinent law is extremely primitive. Those legal norms that do exist suffer from all of the political machinations that one might expect. States have taken care to see that their behavior is only minimally constrained; the few international legal norms they have created always provide avenues of escape such as the big-power veto in the UN Security Council.

The question of states' compliance with international law and, therefore, the effectiveness and credibility of international law, has been crucial throughout interstate system history. While some theorists base effectiveness exclusively on the built-in sanctions of the law, more modern studies tend to emphasize the behavioral aspects of political decision making related to law, such as domestic political considerations or profit-maximization strategies of foreign policy.[15] A third school finds problems of compliance rooted particularly in global cultural and ideological diversity, a condition that makes it difficult to frame a cohesive world order without attempting simultaneously to bring about fundamental changes in political relations.[16] A fourth view concerns the diversity of ethical standards.[17] One scholar has examined these several literatures and found no fewer than thirteen explanations of compliance and noncompliance with international law.[18]

Uncontrollably rapid changes in the current international political system have multiplied the need for a sound world order built on the rule of law. Some of those changes involve military technology, speed and stealth of military delivery, command and control communications, international intervention and economic coercion. Others, however, involve the social and legislative foundations of the law itself. One scholar summarized the patterns of contemporary change related to international law in this way:

1. the emergence of the quasi-legislative functions (see Chapter 15) of the United Nations and other international institutions that purport to prescribe conduct without any formal legal codification

15. Oran Young, *Compliance and Public Authority* (Baltimore: The Johns Hopkins University Press, 1979).
16. George Schwarzenberger, "The Credibility of International Law," *The Year Book of World Affairs* (London), 1983, pp. 292–301.
17. Schwarzenberger; and Stanley Hoffmann, *Duties Beyond Borders: On the Limits and Possibilities of Ethical International Politics* (Syracuse: Syracuse University Press, 1981).
18. Oscar Schachter, "Towards a Theory of International Obligation," in Stephen M. Schwebel, editor, *The Effectiveness of International Decisions* (Dobbs Ferry, NY: Oceana Publications, 1971), pp. 9–31. Schachter identifies these explanations as: consent, customary practice, juridical conscience, natural law or natural reason, social necessity, international concensus, direct intuition, common purposes of governments, effectiveness, fear of sanctions, systemic goals, shared expectations and rules of recognition.

2. evolution of informal international "rules" regarding apparent understandings or unilateral actions and acquiescence
3. the frequency with which social revolutions have overturned traditional order and challenged assumptions on which authority was previously based
4. cooperation and reciprocal behavior resulting from global interdependence, but not yet institutionalized in traditional forms of law
5. the increased permeability of states by technology and economic interdependence, which blurs traditional distinctions between matters of domestic concern and those of international concern
6. scientific and technological expansions that have led to informal means of setting standards and exercising supervision without formal legal instruments[19]

Considering these circumstances, the normative basis of international law is, in the opinion of some, deteriorating just as the probability of major international conflicts is rising; and the deterioration is not accompanied by a strong will to return to the difficult act of codifying a legal order acceptable to the majority of states. Those who hold this view have also concluded that there is a direct relation between the threat to world order and the deterioration of the normative basis of international law.[20]

If law attempts to depoliticize international relations, then what exists today in one level of law may tomorrow reside in another. International conditions may change, or domestic politics may alter a government's willingness to depoliticize an external issue. Thus the predictability of compliance may be determined not merely by the level of the subject matter, but by a state's determination to affect certain outcomes of international events. Compliance, then, and the overall effectiveness of positive international law, may be viewed as a horizontal problem as well as a vertical one, and may be represented as in Figure 14–1. Behind these indicators of compliance are social and political motives. It is the intent of this book to demonstrate that the sociopolitical motivation is attributable primarily to the respective perceptions that the major actors hold of the international system. Therefore, after noting briefly some of the areas in which effective international law is most urgently needed at present, we will turn to an exploration of the views that the principal world actors hold of international law, in order further to reveal some of the sources of cooperation and resistance.

19. Schachter, pp. 9–31.
20. See, for example, Richard A. Falk, *The Year Book of World Affairs* (London), 1982, pp. 3–16.

FIGURE 14–1
Levels of compliance and political salience.

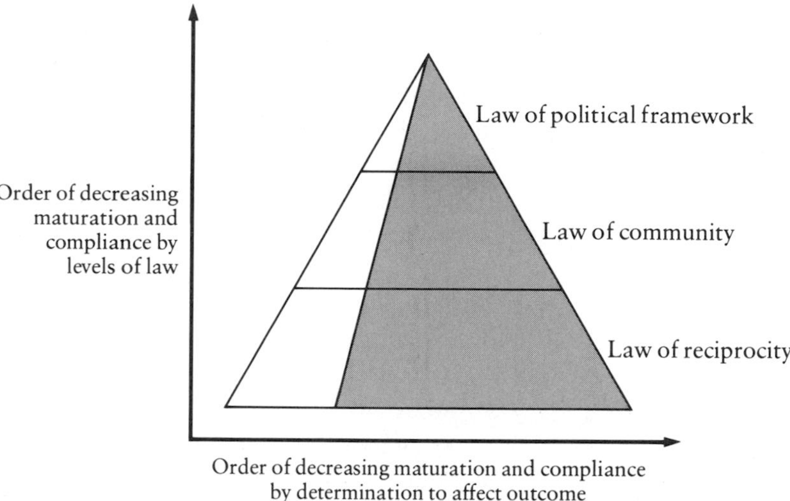

Areas of Urgency in International Law

Each observer of the international scene has his or her own priorities as to the areas most urgently requiring the attention of international law. By the same token, each views differently the probability of achieving effective legal control in these respective areas, and the matter of national or multinational primacy in undertaking to achieve legal control. All of these differences notwithstanding, there are a few areas of political activity where the effective control of law is visibly insufficient. Some of these are outlined below as a primitive agenda of legal issues.

Prevention and Control of Aggression

No issue is more vital to the global political context than prevention of aggression, serious disruption of important international transactions, and massive destruction and death. Once preventive measures have failed, control of the level and territorial scope of aggression is the next most crucial issue, as is the restriction on the number of participants, particularly in instances that may involve the crucial interests of the most powerful and nuclear-armed states.

Given the degree of contemporary international economic interdependence and the far-flung interests of governments, there is scarcely a corner of the earth where aggression would not be a major threat to the security and survival of most nations. Although the scope of the Vietnam War was ultimately contained, the degree to which it touched upon the political and geopolitical interests of three nuclear powers carried civilization to the danger point and beyond. War between Iran and Iraq not only adds to the instability of the Middle East, already fraught with threats of war between Arab and Israeli interests (and ultimately Soviet and American interests), but threatens the entire Western industrialized world with fuel depletion should the area of the Persian Gulf become fully embroiled or should the straits through which petroleum is shipped to the high seas be closed. Similarly, the transformation of Lebanon into a battleground, first between Israel and Syria, then by a combination of local factions and, simultaneously, by factions of the Palestine Liberation Organization with Syrian participation, threatens major power confrontation and territorial expansion of fighting.

As we have seen, the United Nations Charter addresses matters that constitute "Threats to the Peace, Breaches of the Peace, and Acts of Aggression." But in United Nations law as in all international law, effective action begins with agreement on definitions, and it was not until 1974 that the General Assembly adopted, without balloting, a "consensus" definition of aggression: "the use of armed force by a State against the sovereignty, territorial integrity or political independence of another State, or in any other manner inconsistent with the Charter of the United Nations."

But even in the presence of general agreement on a definition, collective security is not likely to serve as an effective deterrent or remedy. Individual or multinational responses are much more likely for the foreseeable future to be the act of choice. In rare instances when the political and geopolitical interests of the involved states have been uniquely suited, United Nations peacekeeping has been substituted for unilateral response. For the most part, however, only self-restraint and fears of escalation and nuclear consequences have deterred would-be aggressors or restricted the expansion of wars. As sophisticated weaponry overspreads the world through arms transfers, particularly as a form of trade to secure Middle East petroleum, the threat of regional wars may increase and the impulse of third parties to intervene may grow. The simultaneous rapid change in the international economy, with its uncertain direction, adds to these threats.

Meanwhile, where aggression is not checked it is rewarded. For whatever reasons the Soviet Union may have decided to invade and occupy Afghanistan in 1980, it is certain that its objectives were simplified by the unwillingness of the Western alliance to respond with force. Therein lies the dilemma of an international legal order that lacks effective collective sanctions: it is unable to deter aggression under some circumstances, and having allowed it to occur, it can respond only with silent acquiescence or with military force, which risks enlarging beyond control the intensity, geographic scope and number of participants.

Arms Control and Disarmament

As with the case of legal controls of aggression, arms control and disarmament are matters that touch directly upon the political context and are therefore so sensitive to national governments as to be submitted rarely and only partially to effective legal control. Furthermore, in eras of instability and of vastly changed economic relations, modern weaponry becomes not only a coveted prize of governments, but a major instrument of international trade. As a result, while the superpowers negotiate limitations on strategic nuclear arms, they are busily and enthusiastically supplying other governments, many of them unstable, with conventional arms at the same level of sophistication as those with which their own forces are equipped. Control of resort to arms is made more difficult in an international legal order where there is no control of access to arms.

The New International Economic Order

Until the past decade, international economic law was restricted largely to trade and currency agreements, international economic aid, and agreements between (or among) imperial states dealing with forms of competition in colonized territories. The formation of the European Economic Community and other regional customs unions expanded the scope of interest to investment controls within protected areas. But the commencement of the New International Economic Order called for a comprehensive legal order.

Views about what the prospective content of that law should be depend upon national perspectives. The industrializing countries call for a legal order that limits the political activities of the transnational corporations, ensures the transfer of technology, protects agricultural and semifinished products from dangerous variations in international prices, protects natural resources from foreign exploitation, removes political strings from intergovernmental aid and places restrictions on foreign direct investment. For their part, the industrialized states call for protections against nationalization of property by host governments, assurances of controlled increases in the price of natural resources, guarantees against repudiation of contracts to purchase industrial produce and guarantees of a steady export flow of raw materials. The concern of the latter group is directed especially to the oil-exporting countries of the Third World which, since 1973, have demonstrated their ability to influence the industrial productivity of the West and Japan by controlling the export and price of oil, and which in the meanwhile have disrupted the international currency exchange system by amassing nearly $100 billion annually in reserve currencies.

The vast and sudden change in world economics, which occurred over a span of barely five years, calls for legal control not only because of its economic aspects but because of its immense impact upon political and social conditions both globally and within the industrialized world. Because modern arms are a major instrument of trade from the industrialized side of the equation, the uncertain directions of world commerce gain an additional destabilizing characteristic. Without an effective, comprehensive legal order, the new economics will continue to be regulated by hazardous self-help.

Law of the Sea

While this may have the sound of a maritime problem, it is an intensely economic one. Not only does the sea provide a large share of the world's nutrition (all of it in some societies); it also contains a treasure of minerals and proteins. The floor of the sea at great depths beyond the continental shelf and beyond national territorial waters is strewn with metal deposits, and the suboceanic floor may contain fossil fuel supplies that today's technology cannot reach.

It is for these economic reasons that the members of the United Nations struggled for more than a decade to arrange a comprehensive legal regime for the seas. National positions are often incompatible because the value of the sea's resources is determined roughly by the technology necessary to exploit them, thus giving the advantage clearly to a handful of states, an event that the rest of the world vows to avoid. Furthermore, not all of the world's nation-states have coastal territories; nearly 20 percent are wholly landlocked. What rights to the oceans' resources do they have?

As the world's accessible and known resources are depleted at an accelerating pace, and by more and more competitors, ownership of rights to the riches of the seas becomes one of the most vital issues in international economic law. Conclusion of a treaty on the law of the sea in 1983, which will not enter into force until ratified by the required number of governments, still leaves many important issues inadequately addressed.

During rescue operations an HH-3F helicopter from Coast Guard Air Station, Cape Cod, Massachusetts hovers over the 644-foot Liberian-registered tanker SS Argo Merchant *after she ran aground 28 miles southeast of Nantucket Island in international waters on December 15, 1976.*

Source: Official United States Coast Guard Photo

Terrorism and Skyjacking

Aggression is not the exclusive province of national governments. In recent years the frequency of terrorist violence by national and transnational extremist groups have become a common element in political activity. While most of it occurs internally and is therefore solely within the domestic jurisdiction of the state, there are a number of international considerations. First, many acts of terrorism have occurred against foreign nationals, as in the many cases in which foreign businessmen have been shot by Italian and Latin American terrorists. Prevention, apprehension and conviction are the responsibilities of national governments, and international substitutes for ineffectual national actions do not yet exist. Furthermore, some terrorist acts have occurred on the territories of third parties, the most notably the massacre of Israeli athletes by Arab terrorists at the 1972 Olympic Games in Germany. Although this fell within the responsibility of the West German government, the international implications are evident.

Yet another aspect eagerly awaits international legal supervision.

Many terrorists have sought protective refuge in countries where they are aliens, but which fail to prosecute them under domestic jurisdiction or to return them to their national governments or to the governments of territories from which they have fled. In the absence of extradition treaties or of formal international obligations to do otherwise, these governments are free from all pressure save moral suasion to bring law to bear upon terrorists.

A special case in point is the form of terrorism called *skyjacking,* in which a commercial aircraft crew is commanded by armed terrorists to divert the craft to an unintended destination, usually a foreign one where the individuals will be free from prosecution. Many such acts are not directly linked to international terrorism, but many have been, as is evidenced by the common occurence of a negotiated political demand in return for release of the craft and its crew and passengers. Once again, the absence of established international norms compelling national governments to act in behalf of the international community in the legal prosecution of such terrorists contributes to the frequency of the act. Despite the many differences between Cuba and the United States, they have entered into an agreement regarding strict Cuban treatment of skyjackers who land in Cuba. As a result of this agreement, incidents of skyjacking with Cuban destinations have diminished sharply.

Questions of Jurisdiction

One of the frequently debated topics among theorists of international law is the relationship of domestic law and jurisdiction to international law and jurisdiction. Although most theories and judicial findings subordinate domestic law to international law, there are several that endorse the superiority of national law and jurisdiction. In drafting the Statute of the Permanent Court of International Justice and later of the International Court of Justice, negotiators debated this relationship in connection with the obligation of states to submit international disputes to the jurisdiction of the Court. Still today, international organs and international jurisdiction extend into the state only on the rarest of occasions.

Until states agree on the extent to which national jurisdiction is subordinated to or defined by international law, there will be little opportunity for international organs to pursue international criminals into protective jurisdictions. Furthermore, only under certain regional codes of law (such as the agreements attendant to the European Court of Human Rights) does international jurisdiction address itself to individuals rather than to governments. These twin problems of jurisdiction, the place of the individual in international law and the relationship of international jurisdiction to national jurisdiction, are major obstacles to a more effective international legal order.

The American View of International Law

The view that the United States takes of international law originates with America's European origins and from the fact that the United States is heir to the central political position previously held by Great Britain. The United States is a by-product of Western European culture and civilization, and is the first offspring of the British Empire. Despite its revolutionary separation from Britain, in its legal traditions and international outlook the United States behaves as the progeny of Europe.

International law evolved in a Eurocentric world, its norms originally serving the reciprocal convenience of European monarchs. But as the trade of the European states became global, and as European empires swelled, the European view of international law became imprinted upon much of the inhabited world. Law came to protect and serve capitalist economic interests; the doctrine of noninterference in the policies of other states was used in part to foster imperialism; the law of the seas facilitated the commercial and military shipping of the richest and most powerful. Many of these laws were oblivious—and occasionally hostile—to the interests of competing economic systems and to colonized populations. Yet they enjoyed a high degree of integrity, since they had the political protection of the states whose interests they served. Thus the United States, reared in the cultural, economic and legal traditions of Britain and Europe, inherited dominance of a Euro-American world prior to the Second World War in which existing international law was much to its advantage. In the interwar period the United States took a major role in expanding this legal system along the same lines, seeking, for example, to sponsor a vast network of treaties for peaceful settlement of international disputes. It also participated in the functional activities of the League of Nations, and sought international economic regulation through bilateral and limited multilateral pacts.

The postwar world presented different conditions, as the Euro-American domination of international politics began to dissolve. The security of Western-oriented concepts of international law fell under stern challenge. The breakup of colonial empires strained legal norms, as did the rapid proliferation of new states. The bellicose unwillingness of the Soviet government to comply with formal norms threatened

American interests throughout the world. Soviet refusal to permit self-determination in the countries of Eastern Europe, the brutal absorption of Latvia, Lithuania and Estonia, the Soviet-inspired Czechoslovakian coup d'état in 1948, the launching of the Korean War, guerrilla fighting in Greece, Turkey and Iran, and the invasion and occupation of Afghanistan—all these events and more underscored the law-breaking character of Soviet foreign objectives.

Besides codifying customary law to formalize the international legal order, the USA turned to the UN as a focal point of international political and ideological struggles. It relied upon the General Assembly to pass quasi-legislation designed to foster peaceful change. At the time of the Korean War (1950) it utilized the Security Council in calling for defense of the aggrieved South Koreans. The refusal of the Soviet Union to participate in this collective deliberation gave further testimony to the Kremlin's refusal to cooperate in the legal order. The military intervention of Korea by China accentuated the law-breaking character of international communism, but the General Assembly joined with the United States in labeling China an aggressor and retaliating with economic sanctions.

Flags of the 152 member states fly at the United Nations Headquarters in New York City. At left is the General Assembly building topped with a shallow dome.

Source: United Nations/John Isaac.

But the revolutionary international system in the years following the Second World War was not always receptive to the positivist concept of international law. Soviet and Chinese behavior often threatened global norms, and just as often made compliance with them quite dangerous for the United States. As new forms of politics appeared, they escaped from positivist regulation. Finally the United States was forced by Soviet policies to adopt neorealistic attitudes toward the law. Hence the Truman Doctrine occurred outside the UN, and the occupation of Japan was replaced by a close Japanese-American security arrangement for the Far East. Whenever possible, then, Washington pursued a policy of enhancing the positivist approach to international law; but whenever Soviet foreign policy prevented this, the United States was forced to resort to the broader standards of neorealism.

The View of America's Major Allies

Because of the Cold War, rapid rates of industrialization and the westernization of Japan after 1945, Washington's principal allies have had similar attitudes toward positive international law in all three categories: community, reciprocity and the political context. Indeed, because of their social and economic origins, the United States and Canada derived much of their perception of international law from Europe. Japan, earlier a victim of such a legal order, after 1950 came to enjoy its fruits, and thus adopted a Western-sympathetic attitude.

Recent events have forced changes in the attitudes of these industrialized states, however. The burgeoning resource scarcity in Europe and Japan, in particular, has resulted in a call for new systems of allocation; but more specifically, it has given rise to new attitudes concerning economic coercion. While industrial states have always appreciated the coercive capability of resource boycott, they have only recently felt the negative effects of such boycotts themselves. Now at last, although they hardly share with the resource-rich Third World the same objectives concerning international economic law, they are prepared to clarify economic rights and duties on a reciprocal basis. Thus necessity has forced upon them a reassessment of the economic portion of the law of community. Canada, itself richly endowed in natural resources, is driven to the same sense of reciprocal adjustment not out of fear of boycott, but out of sympathy for the Third World's sovereign compromises in asymmetrical economic relations, a sympathy engendered by Canada's own asymmetrical relation to the American economy.

The Soviet View of International Law

In contrast to the United States, the Soviet Union gained major-power status in a world fundamentally hostile to its political, ideological and economic principles. Its view of international law arose from the writings of Karl Marx, who had seen the state as an instrument through which one class oppresses others. To Marxist jurists, law is the formal instrument of such oppression. They looked upon the law of nations, therefore, as a body of rules and principles through which powerful classes in several societies undertake jointly to promote class exploitation in the international system. International law, like all other law, is of class origins.

Yet Soviet leaders have found reason to cooperate with prevailing international law. Their principal justification is the Stalinist premise that the withering away of states must await the universal socialist revolution; and meanwhile, Soviet politics is partly motivated by the fear of capitalist encirclement. It is necessary to participate at least minimally in capitalist international law to escape this encirclement. In later years, after Nikita Khrushchev introduced his notion of peaceful coexistence, it became the fashion of Soviet international legal science to promote cooperation with the institutions of interstate law as a means to achieve peaceful coexistence.

Although it is officially denied by Soviet spokesmen, the contemporary view, for practical purposes, is founded upon the notion that three bodies of international law exist concurrently. The first is that body of law which regulates the class interests of the capitalist nations. The second pertains to the relations between the capitalist and socialist worlds. Finally, they posit a totally separate body of communist-bloc law.

The second body is the law of peaceful coexistence. The Soviets agree that a body of rules and principles exist that govern diplomatic and economic relations between East and West. While they take a positivistic view of its content, they nevertheless insist upon distinguishing between textbook law and political reality. While they opt for treaties, particularly bilateral treaties, as the source of choice, they nevertheless hold that politically outmoded rules have lost the quality of law. Probably because of their political minority status in international organizations, they are more sensitive than the United States to political controls of international law.

Intrabloc law is another area in which Soviet outlooks appear more forthright than those of the United States. While the United States purports to respect the self-determination of its friends and allies, it has not always demurred from commanding domestic politics abroad.

Recent examples are the American manipulation of the government of South Vietnam especially from the mid-1950s to the mid-1960s, and American intervention in the Dominican Republic in 1965. In broader terms, the Monroe Doctrine was more a doctrine of unilateral intervention than one of hemispheric self-determination.

Soviet policy, at least recently, has been more forthright in its treatment of intrabloc law. The climax occurred in the invasion and occupation of Czechoslovakia in the summer of 1968. The legal rationale for this act, called the Brezhnev Doctrine, holds that among socialist states, sovereign liberties are subordinate to the needs of all the states collectively. The Czech government is free to establish internal policy, but not to the detriment of the overall interests of socialist states. Presumably, the Brezhnev Doctrine is as much a part of the international law of the socialist states as the Monroe Doctrine and its remnants have been of inter-American relations. In addition, while Marxist theory requires that nonsocialist law be of *class* origins, that of the group members is based upon collective social need as centrally determined.[21]

Although at the time of writing the Soviet government has yet to offer ideological explanations, two events of 1980 presumably represent extensions of the Brezhnev Doctrine. The major interbloc event of the year was the Polish Workers' strike and the official recognition, in declaration if not in practice, of independent labor unions. The Polish government's capitulation to the workers' demands resulted in a Soviet-directed change of governments. Until a doctrinal explanation is offered, one may interpret the Soviet action as consistent with the view that the member states of the socialist commonwealth are politically independent up to the point where their actions or policies countervene the basic ideological foundations of interbloc law.

The second event was the Soviet invasion and occupation of Afghanistan, an act for which there is no direct explanation in the precepts of either interbloc law or the law of coexistence. One may expect that an official doctrinal explanation will cite the necessity of protecting that flank of the contiguous socialist territory from imperialist aggression in view of the possibility of an American intervention in

21. For interpretations of the Soviet science of international law, see especially Kazimierz Grzybowski, *Soviet Public International Law* (Leyden, the Netherlands: A. W. Sijthoff, 1970). Good Western commentaries may be found in James L. Hildebrand, *Soviet International Law* (Buffalo, NY: William S. Hein, 1969); Edward McWhinney, *"Peaceful Coexistence" and Soviet-Western International Law* (Leyden, the Netherlands: A. W. Sijthoff, 1964); and Bernard A. Ramundo, *Peaceful Coexistence: International Law in the Building of Communism* (Baltimore: Johns Hopkins Press 1967). A useful collection of papers by authors of several nationalities appears in Hans W. Baade, ed., *The Soviet Impact on International Law* (Dobbs Ferry, NY: Oceana, 1965.)

the Iranian Revolution either to avenge the taking of American governmental personnel as hostages or to stabilize the flow of oil from Iran and the Persian Gulf to the United States and its industrial allies.

To summarize briefly, Soviet jurists understand general international law to be rules and principles that govern the relations of socioeconomically different states, based upon the necessity of peaceful coexistence. Socialist international law, however, which regulates the relations of the socialist countries, emerges from the principle of socialist internationalism, a doctrine that goes directly to the heart of sovereign theory. According to G. I. Tunkin, at present the most authoritative spokesman among Soviet jurists, this new principle is "the result of the application of the principle of proletarian internationalism to relations between states of the socialist type."[22]

The Chinese View of International Law

Though the Chinese share with the Soviet Union the notion of the class origins of international law, they face the additional problem of having been a major victim of Western treaty law. During the Century of Humiliation, China was subjected to treaty relations based on Western power superiority and the ability of other states to imperialize its territory and its commerce. More recent events, such as exclusion of the People's Republic of China from the Japanese Peace Treaty (1951), have accentuated the Chinese alienation from prevailing international legal norms. Although all Chinese governments of the present century have deplored the "unequal treaties" and have shared the determination to repossess territory granted to other state, none has coupled these determinations with other diplomatic grievances more vigorously than did the government that ruled China from 1950 through 1977.[23] It looked upon Western-oriented international law as vacuous humanistic platitudes designed to attract China's support and participation on Western grounds. The concept of President Wilson's Fourteen Points as the gospel of the First World War and the Atlantic Charter of the Second World War, with its stress upon fundamental freedoms, seem to the Chinese to have been withdrawn in time of peace, and the actual destiny of China cynically given over to other "legal" agreements. Most vexatious among these is the Soviet-Amer-

22. As quoted in Chris Osakwe, "Socialist International Law Revisited," *American Journal of International Law* 66, 1972, pp. 596–600, at 598.
23. For a general treatment of the unequal treaties, see William L. Tung, *China and the Foreign Powers: The Impact of and Reaction to Unequal Treaties* (Dobbs Ferry, NY: Oceana, 1970).

ican Yalta Protocol (1945), which enlisted Soviet military assistance against Japan at the cost of Chinese political and territorial integrity.[24]

As much as these perceptions persist justifiably, the Chinese view of Western-dominated international law is thawing considerably due to its newfound diplomatic, economic and military relations with the United States, relations that not only accelerate China's economic development, but also diminish the likelihood of Soviet aggression upon Chinese territory. For the first time, then, save for a brief period of Western support to the Chinese Nationalist government between 1939 and 1949 (much of which was designed to assist the Nationalists in defeating the domestic communist forces), China has begun to profit from the Western content of international law.

The contemporary Chinese view of international law, then, is shaped by three factors: (1) the historical perception that Western-oriented law has aided Western growth at the expense of China, and that the Soviet Union increasingly benefits from the same; (2) that international law has class origins that make it a peculiar instrument of transnational class struggle through economic oppression and intervention; and (3) that as an industrializing socialist state, China's sympathies on the restraints and licenses of law lie more with the Third World nations than with the Soviet Union.

Although the Chinese understanding of international law shares with the Soviet view the notion that law has class origins, the Chinese view rejects the idea that there are several types of international law in operation simultaneously. The Chinese accept the notion of a single *general international law* which represents the will of the ruling classes in any particular agreement. With respect to the *theoretical* basis of international law, however, the Chinese strike a difference between a bourgeois theory founded upon assumptions derived to preserve the capitalist world order, and a proletarian theory founded upon assumptions designed for a socialist world order uniting classes across national boundaries. The first emphasizes the state and the ruling class, the second stresses the liberation of the working class (proletariat). This view concludes that "only the proletarian science of international law established on the base of Marxism-Leninism is genuine science."[25]

Unlike the highly industrialized states, whose interests are world-wide, China's growth phase dictates that its interests be regional and,

24. Ishwer C. Ojha, *Chinese Foreign Policy in an Age of Tradition: The Diplomacy of Cultural Despair* (Boston: Beacon Press, 1969), particularly Chapter 3, "China and the Western World Order."

25. For a Chinese statement on the basis of international law see Ho Wu-shaung and Ma Chun as reprinted in Jerome Alan Cohen and Hungdah Chiu, *People's Republic of China and International Law: A Documentary Study* (Princeton: Princeton University Press, 1974, two volumes), vol. I, pp. 33–36.

for the most part, defensive. Except for attempts to repossess former territories lost under duress, and except for its intervention in Korea when its borders seemed threatened, modern China has not behaved as an aggressive or expansionist state. Even her invasion of Vietnam in 1979 was explained in legal terms: China's was a punitive attack, designed to punish Vietnam for its earlier aggression against Cambodia. But in broader terms, since China's interest in international law and in the international power distribution is principally regional, the attack may be looked upon as a device for punishing Vietnam for forcefully altering the balance of forces among the Asian states.

China's interest is not so much in expanding its rights as in attempting to restrict the rights, and formalize the obligations, of other major powers that have interests in Asia. Thus China argues for the sanctity of treaties, though it acknowledges membership in few. As its fundamental statement on international law, it has accepted the content of a Sino-Indian declaration of 1954, which encompasses the five Primary Principles of Peaceful Coexistence:

1. Mutual respect for sovereignty and territorial integrity
2. Mutual nonaggression
3. Mutual noninterference in internal affairs
4. Sovereign equality and mutual advantage (or benefit)
5. Peaceful coexistence

(Unlike the Soviet formulation enunciated by Khrushchev in 1961, "peaceful coexistence" in Chinese terms does not mean peaceful *competition.*)

Although most of these principles do not depart substantially from the classical notions of Western international law, the Chinese formulation stresses mutual advantage more than others do. Imbued with an historical sense of inequality in treaty relations, the Chinese argue that unless a treaty exists for mutual benefit, it is not binding regardless of the apparent formalities of consent. Chinese jurists argue explicitly that treaties need not be renegotiated or formally terminated if their obligations were imperialistically imposed. It is held, rather, that in these cases the victim state may simply renounce obligations.[26] Despite ideological origins similar to the Soviet Union, the Chinese view of international law is tempered more by history and policy imperatives than by ideology.[27]

26. Hungdah Chiu, *The People's Republic of China and the Law of Treaties* (Cambridge, Mass.: Harvard University Press, 1971), especially Chapter 6, "Suspension and Termination of Treaties."
27. James Chieh Hsiung, *Law and Policy in China's Foreign Relations: A Study of Attitudes and Practices* (New York: Columbia University Press, 1972). For general

The Third World View of International Law

The Third World nations share China's perception of having been victimized by the Western international order, and view much of its legal content as designed to facilitate Euro-American growth at their expense. New states of revolutionary birth sympathize, furthermore, with the Chinese view that the law of nations still is pitted against their interests. But even old Third World states, and those which became independent through peaceful means and with formal preparation for self-government under UN surveillance, have found that much existing international law is inimical to their needs and politics.

The element of succession that distresses these states most is *devolution.* Upon achieving independence, many states have found themselves left with debts and commitments that they are expected to honor. Certain obligations have devolved upon new governments, some informally and others through the formal device of the *inheritance agreement.* Some of these may be bilateral obligations easily renegotiated into modified arrangements called *novations.* In other cases, however, the other partner may be unwilling to change the agreement. Here the new state is likely to adopt the Chinese view that, conditions having changed, the obligation no longer holds. Some new states have taken up the *clean slate doctrine,* which insists on the nullity of all prearrangements.

Multilateral treaties present a more complex problem, since renegotiation with multiple partners is more difficult. The pressure to accept responsibility may be heightened by the former controlling capital on behalf of third parties. Furthermore, upon entry into international organizations the new state assumes obligations that it did not create. Certain unwanted restraints may have to be undertaken as the price of membership benefits.

Customary law creates larger problems, too. The Third World countries are expected to partake virtually without consent; and it is here

studies of the Chinese attitude not previously cited, see Hungdah Chiu, "Communist China's Attitude Toward International Law," *American Journal of International Law* 60, 1966, pp. 245–67; Jerome Alan Cohen, "China's Attitude Toward International Law—and Our Own," *Proceedings of the American Society of International Law* 1967, pp. 108–16; Luke T. Lee, "Treaty Relations of the Peoples Republic of China: A Study of Compliance," *University of Pennyslvania Law Review* 111, 1967, p. 271; and Suzanne Ogden, "Sovereignty and International Law: The Perspective of the People's Republic of China," *New York University Journal of International Law and Politics* 7, 1974, pp. 1–32. For a thorough study of China's attitude regarding international law, particularly in the United Nations context, see also Samuel S. Kim, *China, the United Nations and World Order* (Princeton, NJ: Princeton University Press, 1979), particularly Chapter 8, "China and International Legal Order," and Chapter 9, "Chinese Image and Strategy of World Order," based almost exclusively on evidence taken from China's pre-1979 participation at the United Nations.

that they find themselves most disadvantaged by the legal rules and principles created by, and in the interests of, the more powerful states. This is especially true in the economic sphere, where the desperate need for investment capital and favorable terms of trade may be held in ransom by externally imposed trade principles, liquidity agreements and tariff regulations.[28] In this regard, the Third World has combined efforts to develop a more advantageous structure of positive international law designed to overcome some of the collective economic strength of the industrialized states. Their principal mechanism has been the creation of the United Nations Conference on Trade and Development (UNCTAD), and its use to press their common needs upon the wealthier countries in the United Nations. More recently, the voting majority that the Third World has achieved at the UN has enabled it to pass the Declaration of the Establishment of a New International Economic Order and its companion Programme for Action, as well as the Charter of Economic Rights and Duties of States. It is now clear that the efforts of the underindustrialized world toward the establishment of an international legal order will turn principally upon effective law for economic self-determination. Accordingly, it will applaud the efforts of both the Organization for Economic Cooperation and Development and the United Nations Task Force on Multinational Corporations to conclude codes of conduct for international business, with the hope of reducing by law some of the neoimperialistic patterns justified under existing Western-oriented international law. So too will it welcome the recent efforts of the International Criminal Law Commission to define international economic crimes.

To the Third World, and especially to its newly independent members, the main objection to international law combines the notion of sovereignty with the philosophical understanding of self-determination. The achievement of independence illuminates a bold fact of international life—that in the face of disparate power, sovereignty is an abstraction; while formal self-determination may have been achieved, it does not confer all the latitudes of an economically powerful state. The destiny of the state is in large measure determined from without, both because it is expected to comply with certain established rules and because relations with more powerful states and corporations may limit economic and political prerogatives. In place of formal colonialism, the economically less developed states find that international law provides few, if any, defenses against the neoimperialistic trend by which the developed states encroach upon their economics.

28. An exhaustive study of the problems of succession is found in D. P. O'Connell, *State Succession in Municipal Law and International Law*, two vols. (New York: Cambridge University Press, 1967).

Source: Wide World Photos

International terrorism: Officials inspect scene of bombing in which seven horses of the Queen's guard were killed in London, 1982.

Conclusion

The diverse outlooks toward contemporary international law exist because four fundamental bases of the Western legal order no longer enjoy universal validity. First, it is no longer accepted that there is a fundamental distinction between law on the one hand, and ideology and politics on the other. Second, there has been a breakdown in the practical distinction between war and peace, and the mere conviction of the desirability of peace. Third, our revolutionary international system does not accept the sanctity of the coexistence of independent, territorially discrete states. And finally, it is no longer universally held that governments are able to undertake mutually binding obligations through consent and voluntary compliance.[29] These premises have deteriorated primarily because we live in a multicultural world which the West no longer dominates.

The future of international law, however, is not bleak. Though multiculturism will continue to mark the international system, there is encouraging evidence that material interdependence, especially

29. Adda B. Bozeman, *The Future of Law in a Multicultural World* (Princeton, N.J.: Princeton University Press, 1971), pp. 35–48 and 180–86.

among states of equivalent power, fosters the growth of positive legal principles. In addition, as friendships and enmities change, some bilateral law may cease to be observed among new enemies; but new law may arise among new friends who have newfound mutual interests. In the meanwhile, some multilateral law may have developed. Finally, research suggests that the social effects of industrialization are universal, and that they result in intersocietal tolerances that did not exist during periods of disparate economic capability.[30] On social, political and economic grounds, therefore, international law is intrinsic to transformation and modernization of the international system, even though the "law of the political context" has remained primitive so far. To what extent does modern international organization help here?

30. Edward L. Morse, "The Transformation of Foreign Policies: Modernization, Interdependence, and Externalization," *World Politics* 22, 1970, pp. 371–92.

15

International Organization

In the discussion of international law in the preceding chapter, the point is made repeatedly that the development of an effective international legal order is impeded both by the sovereign equality of states and by the lack of authoritative international institutions competent to "govern" the international system. Since 1648, and more especially since 1815, creative statesmen have sought to remedy this institutional defect by founding a network of international agencies for international decision making. While there is little expectation that these will replace nation-states as principal actors, there is considerable evidence that their presence contributes to settlement of disputes, prevents the occurrence of disputes and facilitates decision making on a broad spectrum of problems.

But the notion of collective decision making should not be interpreted to excess. Only in rare cases are international institutions authorized to impose their decisions upon members. *Inter*national organizations conduct their business among states, and do not exist separately from them. *Supra*national organizations, in contrast, have authority above the state and are capable of dictating to it, within carefully defined limits. International organizations, as presently constituted, do not pretend to supplant the nation-state or its authority over internal or external policies.

In a world of hostilities and power politics, students of international relations have traditionally focused their attention upon public international organizations (also called intergovernmental organizations or IGOs). Recently, on the heels of communications and travel revolutions, and recognizing that business and other interests often transcend international boundaries, attention has been directed to private international organizations (also called nongovernmental organizations, or NGOs). These facilitate transactions by means other than governments, and they are the vehicles of transnational participation. Governments become involved in their business only indirectly or secondarily. Their principal subjects are individuals and organized social groups, corporations and so on. While the IGO is a government-to-government institution, the NGO deals people to people. They are, respectively, intergovernmental and intersocietal.

Throughout the last century there has been a steady growth in the number of both intergovernmental organizations and nongovernmental organizations. At present there are approximately three hundred IGOs and something in excess of two thousand NGOs.[1] Moreover, even among the IGOs the variety of content and intent is so wide that further subdivision is needed. That the North Atlantic Treaty Organization and the International Court of Justice are both IGOs ought not to imply that they have very much in common, except that each has several member governments! The following typology (breakdown of types) suggests some of the important classifications and provides familiar examples.

I. Global Organizations
   A. Multipurpose (United Nations)
   B. Single purpose or functional
      1. Economic (Economic and Social Council)
      2. Security (Security Council)
      3. Anti-imperial (Trusteeship Council)
      4. Nutrition (Food and Agricultural Organization)
      5. Transportation—sea (International Maritime Consultative Organization), air (International Civil Aviation Organization)

1. These numbers are offered as approximations only, since there is no agreement as to the precise numbers. Different counts have used different criteria, such as the number of members required to constitute an actual organization. More difficult is the determination of which entities are independent organizations and which are appendages of larger organizations. As a result, all counts on this matter are approximations. For a discussion of this problem, see Harold K. Jacobson, *Networks of Interdependence: International Organizations and the Global Political System* (New York: Knopf, 1979), pp. 425–439.

6. Communications—mail (Universal Postal Union), telegraph (International Telegraphic Organization)
7. Judicial (International Court of Justice)

II. Sub-Global Organizations
  A. Intrabloc organizations
    1. Economic (International Monetary Fund)
    2. Security (North Atlantic Treaty Organization)
  B. Regional Organizations
    1. Economic (European Economic Community)
    2. Security (Organization of American States: Rio Pact aspects)
    3. Sociocultural and economic (Organization of American States: Bogotá Pact aspects)
  C. Integrating Organizations
    1. Economic (European Coal and Steel Community)
    2. Judicial (European Court of Human Rights)

International Organization and World Politics

The expression "international organization" has two related but different meanings. The expression can be considered synonymous with international *institution.* The United Nations, for instance, may be labeled an international organization or an international institution (or group of institutions). In another context "international organization" refers to a major international political *process,* one in which member states are attempting through collective measures and diplomatic experimentation to facilitate their transactions, particularly when the subject matter is deemed to be handled more efficiently collectively than competitively.

Whatever form an IGO may take, states enter into it because of anticipated benefits. But in determining the effectiveness of such institutions from a collective viewpoint, it is not mere service to governments that matters. There are three critical measurements of organizational ability to draw states into collective policies and therefore to overcome the potentially anarchical charactristics of the nation-state system.

Association or Disassociation?

The first of these is the *associating* or *disassociating* character of the organization. Does the activity of membership tend to draw states closer together, or does it accentuate their differences and drive them farther from collective decision making? Does parliamentary diplomacy facilitate the discovery of workable common denominators, or does it magnify the differences among states? Does it help to remove the clouded images that states hold of one another, or does it further distort them?[2] From a global perspective, even associating organizations have a paradoxical component: the more associating they may be with respect to members, the more disassociating they may be in relation to outside states. The North Atlantic Treaty Organization is a case in point. Though it intends to be associating among the members, its existence maintains the disassociation of Europe. But it exemplifies also a second phenomenon: As Europe has embarked upon other paths of association, NATO has come to have internal disassociating effects.

Contribution to Future Improvements

The second test of organizational capability is its contribution to change in the international system. While institutions are often imprisoned by the will and power of their members (which, as sovereign states, safeguard their supreme decision-making capability), they may make independent contributions to world politics, often by helping members to clarify obscured possibilities in their relations. But they may also contribute through a more complex mechanism. Dag Hammarskjöld, second Secretary-General of the United Nations, visualized two distinctly different models of UN effectiveness. The organization might be either a "static conference machinery" or a "dynamic instrument of governments" for introducing a new world order. Far from prescribing a supranational role, Hammarskjöld hoped only that a politically immune international civil service, together with quasi-legislative competence of the deliberative body, might help states overcome their immediate and narrow interests.[3] The extent to which an international organization is able to emulate the second model may be taken as one of the criteria of its effectiveness in stabilizing the international system.

Most studies of international organization suggest that regional organizations are understandably more effective than global organizations. The usual explanation is that regional states share historical understandings, have had a long history of diplomatic and international relations, and have built an informal sense of understanding among themselves due to the frequency of their transactions. Although the Western European experience with international integration partially vindicates this outlook (see Chapter 16), at least one quantitative

2. Bruce Russat, *International Regions and the International System* (Chicago: Rand McNally and Company, 1967).
3. Dag Hammarskjöld, "Two Differing Concepts of United Nations Assayed," *United Nations Review* 8, no. 9, September 1961, pp 12–17.

study suggests that global organizations are actually more effective in improving the relations of members than are regional institutions. Based on comparative data, the study concludes that through international institutions states may find solutions to problems that they are unable to resolve through bilateral diplomacy; that the degree of cooperation in international institutions is determined more by the expanse of the organization's mandate than by the characteristics of the member states (ideological, economic, etc.); and that, on balance, global institutions are more effective than their regional counterparts.[4] One plausible interpretation of these findings is that in multipurpose global institutions, competing states are able to isolate their conflicts, so that while they undertake bilateral diplomacy on those issues, they are free in the multinational forum to cooperate on other issues.

Constraints on Member States

The third criterion is closely related to both of the preceding. It is taken for granted (1) that states enter IGOs in anticipation of benefits to their individual interests and (2) that institutions become the instruments of their members' foreign policies. Under these circumstances, are such institutions ever capable of bringing restraint upon states' behavior? True, they serve definite purposes for specific governments; but in the long run, are they able to constrain governmental behavior?

If the principal objective of international organization is to overcome some of the anarchical characteristics of a decentralized, state-centered global system, then the capacities of any institution to be associative, to contribute to future improvement in the system's transactions, and to constrain the behavior of member governments become important measures of effectiveness. Since we are concerned here with the global system, the discussion that follows addresses only global organizational efforts; and because of space limitations the discussion centers entirely upon the components of the United Nations organizational system.

The United Nations System

The United Nations consists of six permanent organs, and a vast array of specialized agencies, conferences, funds and commissions. Table 15–1 categorizes some of these. Each body has different objectives

4. James M. McCormick, "Intergovernmental Organizations and Cooperation Among Nations," *International Studies Quarterly,* March 1980, pp. 75–98.

TABLE 15–1
The United Nations system.

All Permanent Organs	*All Specialized Agencies*	*Some Commissions, Funds and Institutionalized Programs*
General Assembly	World Health Organization	Conference on Trade and Development
Security Council	Food and Agricultural Organization	Children's Fund
Trusteeship Council	Intergovernmental Maritime Consultative Organization	Special Fund
Economic and Social Council	International Civil Aviation Organization	Peacekeeping and Observer Forces
Secretariat	Universal Postal Union	Disarmament Commission
International Court of Justice	International Telecommunications Union	High Commission for Refugees
	World Meteorological Organization	Institute for Training and Research
	International Labor Organization	Development Program
	Educational, Scientific and Cultural Organization	Industrial Development Organization
	International Atomic Energy Agency	Environment Program and Earth Watch
	International Monetary Fund	
	World Bank Group[a]	
	General Agreement on Tariffs and Trade	
	World Intellectual Property Organization	

[a]The World Bank Group consists of the International Bank for Reconstruction and Development, the International Development Association and the International Finance Corporation.

and capabilities. As a result, each relates differently to the sovereignty of the state, and each has a different potential impact upon the international system and change therein.

The General Assembly

If modern IGOs attempt to emulate the American doctrine of separation of powers, then the General Assembly may be said to be the legislative branch of the UN system. Yet such a claim does not hold up much beyond form. The work of the Assembly is done through

Source: United Nations

The founding of the United Nations, San Francisco, June 1945. US President Harry Truman stands on the speaker's right, in front of the assembled delegates.

parliamentary diplomacy, which combines the techniques of legislation and negotiation.[5] Yet while the General Assembly has broad competence to consider virtually any subject so long as it does not intrude upon the domestic jurisdiction of states, it has little authority to make binding decisions. Except for final decision-making authority on certain matters internal to the organization (budget, membership, temporary members of the Security Council), its conclusions are expressed in three forms, none of which is decisive.

Declaration The first of these is the declaration, which is a pronouncement of principle. Such pronouncements do not have binding capacity, though they may result in subsequent treaties and may have customary or moral impact. One of the declarations of the General Assembly that has been most celebrated but least observed is the famous Universal Declaration of Human Rights (1948). Its principles

5. Philip C. Jessup, "Parliamentary Diplomacy," *Recueil des Cours* 89 (The Hague: Academy of International Law, 1956), pp. 181–320.

have found their way into several constitutions, and it has become the substance of two international covenants on human rights. But the declaration itself lacks the force of law, despite adoption without a dissenting vote. Since lawmaking is a highly political process, states are not generally willing to subordinate their sovereign controls to the General Assembly.

Other declarations of the United Nations' General Assembly, while also lacking the binding force of law, have resulted in "programmes of action" which have gained substantial effectiveness by the voluntary support, both political and financial, of states. A major example is the Declaration of the Establishment of a New International Economic Order (1975) and its Programme of Action. Together they formed the framework for a new approach to North-South relations and to international economic development.

Resolution The General Assembly's second decision-making instrument is the resolution, around which there swirls a controversy. Is it or is it not a source of international law binding upon states? If a resolution encompasses a previously accepted law, then the resolution does little more than illuminate existing law. But what is the effect of a resolution that imposes some new standard? Presumably, until many states acquiesce, law cannot be said to have been generated.[6]

But may it not be that policy has been implemented through the subsequent actions of states? If a resolution is of a recommendatory nature, calling upon states to act as agents of the General Assembly, then perhaps the General Assembly has transcended the will of some states in bringing about collectively determined policy. The *recommendatory resolution,* then, may not be legally binding, yet its execution by eager states may nevertheless place the imprimatur of the General Assembly upon their policy.[7] This distinction between legally binding norms and nonbinding norms engenders the notion of quasi-legislative competence of the General Assembly.[8]

But all of this assumes the willingness of states to act on behalf of the organ, usually indicating prior intention to act. As a result, the recommendatory resolution may have less of a policy-making function than a *legitimizing* function—one of the major activities of the United Nations.[9] In some instances when states have flocked to the support

6. Leo Gross, "The United Nations and the Role of Law," *International Organization* 19, 1965, pp. 537–61.
7. Jorge Castaneda, *Legal Effects of United Nations Resolutions* (New York: Columbia University Press, 1969).
8. For example, Richard A. Falk, "On the Quasi-Legislative Competence of the General Assembly," *American Journal of International Law* 60, 1966, pp. 782–91.
9. Inis L. Claude, "Collective Legitimization as a Political Function of the United Nations," *International Organization* 20, 1966, pp. 367–79. This article does not deal specifically with the General Assembly.

of the General Assembly's legitimizing resolutions, the result has been profound both in impact upon international events, and in the evolution of the United Nations. The most outstanding example of this was the Uniting for Peace Resolution (1950), passed by the General Assembly during the early months of the Korean War. With the Soviet Union's return to the Security Council after a lengthy boycott, the United States was unable to use the Council for legitimization of its policy in Korea. In face of Soviet vetoes of American-sponsored resolutions, Washington moved its policy to the General Assembly. The Uniting for Peace Resolution expanded the Assembly's legitimizing capability to the area of international peace and security, a province originally reserved for the Security Council. Under the resolution, the United States and other Western powers continued their military actions in Korea and, at the same time, opened a debate not yet resolved regarding the relative constitutional positions of the Security Council and the General Assembly on matters pertaining to international peace and security.

Convention The third mechanism by which the General Assembly expresses its will is the convention, or multilateral treaty. Although we have previously noted the primacy of the treaty as a source of international law, the treaty-making power of the General Assembly is more qualified. In fact, the expression "United Nations treaty" has two meanings. The first refers to treaties signed by a state and by an organ of the UN, such as the General Assembly. These treaties, envisioned by the Charter, concern relations not between states, but between a state and the IGO. As a rule, these do little to alter the behavior of the state with respect to other states, though there are exceptions. When, in 1956, the Egyptian government agreed with the United Nations to permit the dispatch of peacekeeping troops to Egyptian soil, that agreement resulted in a major temporary change in the area's political events.[10]

The more common meaning of "United Nations treaty" concerns conventions generally applicable among members. Such treaties are debated on the floor of the Assembly and then put to votes. With passage, the treaty is carried back to member governments for domestic ratification. Ultimate decision making, therefore, lies not with the membership collectively, but with individual governments. No government is bound until it has given formal constitutional assent, or until the treaty is formally in effect, conditions of which are determined by the treaty itself. Thus, despite the favorable position that treaties

10. Rosalyn Higgins, *The Development of International Law Through the Political Organs of the United Nations* (London: Oxford University Press, 1963), especially Part 5, "The Laws of Treaties: United Nations Practice."

hold as sources of international law, treaties arranged by the General Assembly represent minimal concession to collective decision making; and the process is not so centralized as the title indicates.[11]

The strictures placed upon the General Assembly by the Charter suggest that it is rare that the Assembly makes authoritative decisions regarding the vital interests of states. Yet through its legitimizing role, the Assembly has occasionally made significant contributions to the theory and practice of international stability. The Uniting for Peace Resolution, for all its political aftershocks, is one such example. Another, much more original in form and reusable in content, was an action of the General Assembly pursuant to an initiative of the Secretary-General in 1956. Because of their participation in Middle East combat (Suez), Britain and France had immobilized the Security Council. When the issue was shifted to the General Assembly, it was suggested that Britain and France remove their forces in favor of a United Nations presence. The result was an Assembly mandate to Secretary-General Hammarskjöld to formulate the principles of a new system that came to be known as "peacekeeping"—a specific way of keeping peace. The idea was not to enforce a political objective of one party against that of another, but to interpose a lightly armed force between belligerents to gain time for diplomacy. This was, then, preventive deployment of troops made available to the Assembly by states. Not only was its concept a departure from UN standards, its implementation was as well. Most remarkably, the membership accepted Hammarskjöld's suggestion that the great powers be excluded from the action, on the ground that their presence would tend to expand, rather than contract, the scope of conflict.

The Soviet Union's reaction to this step was both consistent and predictable: The General Assembly had exceeded its powers and once again eroded the exclusive authority of the Security Council to take action on security matters. Furthermore, though the same principles were invoked by the Security Council in the handling of the Congo crisis of 1960, the Soviet Union objected to the Western-oriented manner in which the Secretary-General executed his mandate. Hence, by 1962 the Soviet Union, along with France and other governments, refused to pay their apportioned shares of the operations. They objected to the General Assembly's role in the Emergency Force for the Middle East, and they protested the Secretary-General's handling of the Congo operation. A major financial crisis ensued, with the Soviet Union and many other states never paying their apportioned shares

11. For a comprehensive treatment, see Henry H. Han, *International Legislation by the United Nations* (New York: Exposition Press, 1971).

of the two operations. The crisis was legally, but not politically or financially, resolved by the International Court of Justice in the *Certain Expenses* Case, which elucidated constitutional principles, derived from the Chapter, applicable to financial obligations.

The details of these situations are presented here only as illustrations of the informal manner in which General Assembly resolutions may change the course of multilateral relations, sometimes with the added authority of the International Court of Justice. Although the Assembly's ability to make final decisions is severely limited to relatively non-political issues, the strength of its majority may, either through authorization or legitimization, give it a capacity to influence international events and behavior beyond what the great powers envisioned when they attempt to balance the roles of the General Assembly and the Security Council through the Charter. Not all issues fall within the scope of international peace and security. Examples include the expulsion of the delegation from the Republic of China and the seating of the delegation from the People's Republic of China, an event that had profound consequences for great-power relations and Asian politics; the labeling of Zionism as racist, raising the call to the Third World countries to support Palestinian and other Arab enemies of Israel; and the establishment of the New International Economic Order, an event which both formalized and fueled a major redistribution of wealth and influence during the 1970s.

Although government viewpoints on the effectiveness of the General Assembly may differ from one event to the next (with their differing evaluations resulting from the incompatability of their objectives), scholars have concluded that the General Assembly's effectiveness is greater than public opinion and conventional wisdom will admit. One study, for example, which attempts to correlate effectiveness of action with the willingness of states to comply with Assembly resolutions, concludes that in twenty-nine resolutions concerning international political situations between 1946 and 1962, effectiveness of action reached 87 percent among those resolutions complied with by states. Where compliance was not forthcoming, the level of effectiveness was a scant 21 percent. The study also substantiates that in matters dealing with threats to the peace, breaches of the peace and acts of aggression, the level of compliance and effectiveness was higher than in less dangerous and nonmilitary situations.[12] But these data pertain only to compliance with, and effectiveness of, General

12. Gabriella Rosner Lande, "An Inquiry into the Success and Failures of the United Nations General Assembly," in Leon Gordenker, ed., *The United Nations in International Politics* (Princeton, NJ: Princeton University Press, 1971), pp. 106–29.

Assembly resolutions, which often deal only with parts of disputes. To this extent, and except for specified situations, the General Assembly shares other international agencies' failure to prevent war situations, as detailed in the empirical data of yet another study.[13]

This discussion of the General Assembly's role has been confined largely to matters of international peace and security. But given the broad competence of the body, it is unjustifiable to write off its successes on social and economic issues. These, however, are left to later discussion of functional activities.

The Security Council

In comparison with the General Assembly, the Security Council of the UN is both more complex and more simple. It is more complex because it is the forum not only of general world politics but of great-power politics more intensively than is the General Assembly, with the result that clashes of opinion tend to wound the international system more deeply. Complexity is added by the type of subject matter dealt with by the Council. Yet it is less complex because the veto power of the permanent members is able to prevent effective decision making. Even more than the General Assembly, the Security Council suffers from the inability to pass meaningful resolutions—a problem that logically precedes that of seeking compliance and effective implementation.

The Security Council grew out of the so-called "grand design" or "grand alliance" of the Second World War. During the war, despite the mutual suspicions and antipathies between the West and the Soviet Union, the necessity of alliance against the fascist menace resulted in cooperation which led some to believe that the victorious great powers, including the Soviet Union, could continue through the United Nations to ensure international peace and security by collective means. But the lingering suspicions, coupled with the historic American fear of being dragged unwillingly into foreign warfare, are expressed in the Security Council's complex voting formula. On matters of substance, decisions of the Council are made by a majority of nine votes "including the concurring votes of the permanent members." The final phrase is the veto power of the permanent members. Abstentions are not counted as negative votes, and over time all of the permanent members have chosen to abstain from voting with the understanding that their abstentions will not affect the outcomes of decisions. Earlier, however, a controversy raged over the meaning and political impact of abstentions, since it was during the Soviet absence in June and July of 1950

13. J. David Singer and Michael Wallace, "Preservation of Peace, 1816–1964: Some Bivariate Relationships," *International Organization* 24, 1970, pp. 520–47.

that American Korean War policy was legitimized by the Security Council. At that time, many observers (including Soviet) held that in the absence of one of the five permanent members, the votes of the Council had no binding effect upon the organization.[14] More recently, the issue has ceased to have meaning, and often votes are recorded as "in favor," "opposed," "abstaining" and either "absent" or "not participating."

The main impediment to effective Security Council action is great-power dominance. Though the Council is composed of fifteen members, only five of them (the Soviet Union, the United States, the United Kingdom, France, and China) are permanent members and have the veto power. The result is that while decision making is relatively centralized for ten members, the ability of any single permanent member to prevent action means that ultimately the Security Council is highly decentralized. It is true that if all five permanent members abstain and nine of the others constitute a majority, then a decision can be reached. But what is the likely effectiveness of Security Council resolutions in which the great powers take no part? Is there an obligation to comply? As in the General Assembly, the making of formal norms by majority voting can be deceptive; unless states are willing to put their power behind decisions, no effective impact upon the international system will occur.[15]

Even the membership of the Security Council fails to reflect international political reality. True, the belated seating in 1971 of the delegation from the Chinese People's Republic erased a long-standing misrepresentation. But the changing global power distribution complicates the situation in other ways. West Germany, one of the most powerful economic competitors in the world, is probably permanently denied membership on the Security Council because of Germany's East-West division. Likewise Japan, now restored to full power except for its nonnuclear status, and beginning to work out its relations with the Soviet Union and China as it rejects American paternalism, may eventually seek a permanent seat on the Security Council, but not without prior Charter amendment, an amendment which the Soviet Union is certain to block.

14. For starkly contrasted interpretations of this matter, see the works of a positivist and of a neorealist, respectively: Leo Gross, "Voting in the Security Council: Abstention from Voting and Absence from Meetings," *Yale Law Journal* 60, 1951, pp. 210–57; and Myres S. McDougal and Richard N. Gardner, "The Veto and the Charter: An Interpretation for Survival," *Yale Law Journal* 60, 1951, pp. 258–92.

15. Leo Gross, "Voting in the Security Council: Abstention in the Post-1965 Amendment Phase and its Impact upon Article 25 of the Charter," *American Journal of International Law* 62, 1968, pp. 315–34.

But the expansion of Security Council membership would not of itself generate greater effectiveness. In fact, the opposite is more probable. The more the Council reflects conflicting policies and outlooks, the less likely it is to achieve its objectives. Indeed, granting the veto power to more states by charter amendment would decrease the likelihood of Security Council effectiveness. It is regrettable but nonetheless true that despite the "grand design," the major powers consciously created such a situation by insisting upon veto power.

Again, however, all is not hopeless, though Security Council performance has been less than fully encouraging. While it has occasionally achieved peaceful settlement of incipient crises, it has instituted enforcement measures in the sole case of Korea; and since the Soviet delegation took no part in those decisions, it must be concluded that the Council's actions in that case constituted legitimization rather than collective security. Now, however, as attention turns from collective security toward peacekeeping, the Security Council may find a less politically charged method by which to exercise its responsibility. Logically, the Security Council is the proper organ for the uses of peacekeeping, though politically it is a most difficult forum from which to get action.

The logical argument stems from the historical anticipation that the great powers should make the critical decisions regarding international peace and security. Yet politically, the hope of their electing enforcement procedures against their own interests is unrealistic. Because peacekeeping is intended to be *preventative* rather than enforcing, *neutral* rather than carrying the stamp of great power and *impartial* rather than serving the will of one party against another, it is not so inimical to the interests of Great Powers as is collective security. War (and the implementation of collective security *is* war) is intended to erase political alternatives. Peacekeeping is intended only to prevent warfare while political wrangling proceeds.

The International Court of Justice

The International Court of Justice (ICJ), or World Court, enjoys a dual role in the international system. It is simultaneously the constitutional court of the United Nations and the court of law among states. In its relation to the UN, the Court has the authority to render *advisory opinions* upon formal request from official bodies of the UN. As we have seen in the *Certain Expenses* case concerning the funding of United Nations peacekeeping actions in the Congo and the Middle East, these opinions may lend to the strength and operating scope of the organization. At the same time, however, the opinions are unenforceable, so that their effectiveness is determined by the voluntary willingness of member states to comply with any organizational policy that results from an advisory opinion of the Court.

In its role among states, the World Court is authorized to hear contentious cases, or cases involving disputes between or among states, and to render judgments. But unlike domestic courts, the International Court of Justice is limited in this activity by the wilingness of states to bring their disputes before it. Domestic courts possess *compulsory jurisdiction,* which means that they determine their own jurisdiction according to law, and that subjects of the legal system are bound to appear when called. In the United States, for example, individuals can be summoned into court; corporations can be sued against their will; and governmental officials can be enjoined from certain acts. In the international system, such authority does not exist. While all members of the UN are members of the International Court of Justice, their obligation to utilize the Court is restricted by the Court's own Statute.

The Statute was created by a Committee of Jurists in 1921 for the establishment of the Permanent Court of International Justice, a court affiliated with (but not a permanent organ of) the League of Nations. The Committee recognized both the desirability and the political impracticability of imposing compulsory jurisdiction upon states, knowing from the outset that inclusion of compulsory jurisdiction in the Statute would prevent many states from joining the Court's membership. They sought, therefore, to establish an interim arrangement by which states could accept limited compulsory jurisdiction with respect to certain matters, with or without reservation, and on condition of reciprocity. These conditions comprise the Optional Clause of the Statute.

When the International Court of Justice was established as a permanent organ of the United Nations, the Statute was adopted virtually unchanged. The critically important passages regarding the obligations of member states to use the United Nations' "principal judicial organ" are found in Article 36.

> Article 36.—1. The jurisdiction of the court comprises all cases which the parties refer to it and all matters specially provided for in the Charter of the United Nations or in treaties and conventions in force.
>
> 2. The states party to the present Statute may at any time declare that they recognize as compulsory *ipso facto* and without special agreement, in relation to any other state accepting the same obligation, the jurisdiction of the Court on all legal disputes concerning:
>
> a. the interpretation of a treaty;
> b. any question of international law;
> c. the existence of any fact which, if established, would constitute a breach of an international obligation;

d. The nature or extent of the reparation to be made for the breach of an international obligation.

3. The declarations referred to above may be made unconditionally or on condition of reciprocity on the part of several or certain states, or for a certain time.

• • •

6. In the event of a dispute as to whether the Court has jurisdiction, the matter shall be settled by the decision of the Court.

Since the Court is a permanent organ of the UN, all UN members are automatically its members. Yet, as Article 36.2 indicates, recognition of the Court's limited compulsory jurisdiction requires an act separate from joining the organization. By the end of 1983, only 47 of the UN's 157 members had such declarations in force, only 6 of these without some form of reservation. Reservations typically excuse the state from use of the Court on matters that lie within the domestic jurisdiction of the state or that are classified as matters of vital national interest. Some national reservations, including those of the United States, effectively nullify Article 36.6 by declaring that the state alone shall determine whether or not an issue lies within its domestic jurisdiction.[16] Given all these protections against compulsory jurisdiction of the World Court, final judgments by the Court in contentious cases have been rare.

Under the conditions of membership, then, there is little obligation to use the Court; thus a decision to use the World Court is a political rather than a legal decision. Studies have considered why nations use the Court. The most recent study involved comparison of the decision processes on each side of four suits brought to Court: the *Nuclear Test* case in which Australia and New Zealand sued to prevent France from conducting nuclear tests in the South Pacific; the *Fisheries Jurisdiction* case in which Britain and Germany brought suit against Iceland to determine the territorial limits of exclusive fishing rights; the *North Sea Continental Shelf* case in which Germany sued both Denmark and the Netherlands on division of the North Sea continental shelf for purposes of fishing and mining rights; and the *Prisoners of War* case between Pakistan and India. The study determined that six motives lead plaintiffs to invoke the authority of the World Court. First, such a decision may be a tactical move to speed up negotiations. Second, it provides the suing party an opportunity to save face in

16. One of the four reservations included in the American acceptance reads: "Provided, that this declaration shall not apply to . . . [d]isputes with regard to matters which are essentially within the domestic jurisdiction of the United States of America *as determined by the United States of America*" (emphasis added). The emphasized final clause is referred to as the Connally Amendment, after the senator who sponsored it.

domestic politics. Third, such a suit may focus worldwide critical attention upon the opponent and its international policy. Fourth, while the parties may not be equally powerful and influential in world politics, the judicial environment tends to equalize them and to remove disparities. Fifth, the acting state may wish to use the Court in order to establish or clarify a norm or rule of international law. And sixth, in cases of suits between states that have generally friendly relations, utilization of the Court permits isolation of the dispute from the full body of their relations, thus preventing contamination of other issues between them. [17]

If the decision to bring suit in the World Court is political, then a decision to be sued is doubly political. When threatened with action in the World Court, states generally react by claiming that they have exempted themselves from the Court's jurisdiction. In the cases examined in the same study, the respondent states also felt that it is politically preferable to seek a partial solution by agreement or compromise than to await an absolute solution based on Court procedure and a potentially embarrassing decision. In other words, states prefer to avoid suit than to face outcomes that they are politically unwilling to execute. Finally, states attempt to avoid the jurisdiction of the Court because of the vagueness, uncertainty or absence of the law to be applied, all circumstances which make it more difficult for respondents to assess the probable outcome.

In rare cases when both parties agree to a Court decree and the Court renders a final judgment, the international legal system is faced with its second problem: *compliance.* It is commonly thought that states ignore or violate the Court's decisions. In fact, however, that is not so. A high degree of compliance exists, for two reasons. First, the ICJ is capable of rendering either *declaratory* or *executory* judgments. In declaratory judgments, it declares itself on a point of law, and may in effect advise states as to their rights, or may limit behavior by clarification of existing law. These judgments are not intended to favor one state over another in a specific issue and neither contestant need make restitution to another. Executory judgments are quite a different matter. These arise when the court finds for one contestant rather than for another, and orders one to undertake remedial or compensatory action. Much misinformation has circulated about these judgments leading to the impression that states have rarely carried out judicial awards made against them. In fact, however, such cases are exceptional.

17. Dana D. Fischer, "Decisions to Use the International Court of Justice: Four Recent Cases," *International Studies Quarterly,* June 1982, pp. 251–77.

The second reason is closely akin to an argument used in earlier discussion of states' compliance with treaties. Since, in the absence of compulsory jurisdiction, use of the Court is almost wholly voluntary, it stands to reason that a government will not make the political decision to seek a judicial settlement without having assessed possible outcomes, and without having accepted the obligation to carry out an award in case of an adverse decision.

What remedies exist when states refuse compliance? As the traditional standards of sanctions suggest, a judicial award gives a state an *actionable right.* This may be exercised through general IGOs, functional organizations or regional organizations. Conceivably, even the Security Council might be called upon to enforce compliance, as provided by Article 94 of the UN Charter. Such actions, however, may serve merely to repoliticize a dispute previously depoliticized by having been taken to the Court in the first place. The other alternative is to rely upon self-help, with all its potential anarchical and escalatory effects.

Social, Economic and Humanitarian Functions

Although media attention usually focuses upon the contribution of the United Nations to global security, the organization engages in a vast array of social, economic and humanitarian activities which receive far less attention or acclaim. These activities are consistent with the *functional theory* of international relations introduced in the early 1930s. The theory of functionalism posits that, in the long run, peace is preserved by growing international trust and reciprocity constructed around specific common objectives of states. It assumes, not entirely accurately, that as trust builds around relatively nonpolitical interests, it will spill over to the crucial political interests of governments. Its first practical verification occurred in 1936 when, even while the African and Asian conflicts of the Second World War were already in progress with little lingering hope of effective action on the part of the League of Nations, a major evaluation of the non-security activities of the League found them to be still healthy and productive.

The post-war endorsement of functionalism was signaled by inclusion of the Economic and Social Council and of the Trusteeship Council among the permanent organs of the United Nations. Thereafter, specialized agencies were created on the basis of perceived international needs with respect to health, refugees, economic development, children, educational, social and cultural activities, labor, trade, etc. At the same time, two venerable functional organizations, the Universal Postal Union and the International Telecommunications Union, were incorporated into the United Nations system. Special programs, commissions and funds continue even now to be added as world attention is focused upon new humanitarian needs: the environment program, the development program, the population program, etc. Today, a survey of the activities of the United Nations in areas not directly related to international peace and security is a virtual tour of world political, social, economic and humanitarian concerns. While the world has stumbled into nearly one hundred wars since the World War II armistice, functionalism through the United Nations (and elsewhere) has flourished and has been a major force of change.

Many of these functional activities are discussed elsewhere in this book, particularly those related to international economic development. One that merits specific mention here, however, is the progress made through the United Nations toward self-government of formerly colonized peoples. The UN shares with the League of Nations formal commitment to the self-determination of national peoples, largely on the ground that competitive imperialism is a cause of war. To deal with this problem, the League created a system of *mandates* by which established states undertook formally to prepare colonized peoples for self-government in the League's behalf. The UN has provided a dual system, consisting of a Trusteeship System and a Declaration Regarding Non–Self-Governing Territories.

The *Trusteeship System* was arranged (Chapters 12 and 13 of the Charter) for international surveillance of progress toward self-government. To colonized peoples, the trusteeship was a desirable mechanism, for it included formal terminal dates and the promise of international pressure to enforce major power compliance with the terms of the agreement. But to the major states, trusteeship agreements involve too much obligation and exposure. As a result, trusteeship has not been the main route to independence.

But out of this gap between plan and performance emerged one of the great success stories of UN history. In Chapter II of the Charter, the framers had arranged a Declaration Regarding Non–Self-Governing Territories. Though it was initially assumed merely to inscribe principles rather than legal obligations, this Declaration became the prime peaceful mechanism through which sovereign status has been achieved in the postwar era. The focal point of this development has been the evolution of Article 73(e). Here UN members who control non-self-governing territories accept as a "sacred trust" the responsibility to achieve well-being for the inhabitants, and in pursuit of this goal they consent:

> to transmit regularly to the Secretary-General for information purposes, subject to such limitation as security and constitutional considerations may require, statistical and other information of a technical nature relating to economic, social and educational conditions in the territories for which they are respectively responsible.

By evolution, this hope has been transformed into an obligation. Article 73(e) became a source of international scrutiny (it would be excessive to say "surveillance"). It shares significant responsibility for the huge increase in the total number of states and in the membership of the United Nations. More than half of the UN member nations have become independent in the last quarter-century. Even more remarkable as the result of this emancipation, between 1945 and 1982 the number of people living in dependent territories has been reduced from 750 million to 4 million.[18] This reduction has occurred while the world's total population has increased by 50 percent, with a disproportionate amount of that increase in the newly independent, underindustrialized areas of the world.

To a large extent, these newly emancipated peoples make up the Third World; and for the United Nations as well as for the major powers, they have created huge new problems. Although sovereign equality enables them to control much of the decision making in the General Assembly and in the Economic and Social Council, more than ninety of them declared themselves underdeveloped economically. Thus while they make a small dollar contribution to the UN system, they profit mightily from its grants and other programs. Yet it has been shown that relative to gross national product, and in comparison to national expenditures on armaments, the two poorest categories of states have had better UN financial records that the two richest.[19] In the political realm these new states present other problems. Foremost among them is the "mini-state problem"—the difficulty of equal voting when many of these states are very small, ranging even below 100,000 inhabitants.

Can the United Nations Keep Peace?

Few questions in international relations are so frequently asked. The ability of the UN to safeguard international stability rests on three issues: (1) the fostering of peace, (2) the making of peace and (3) the

18. United Nations, *Report on the World Social Situation,* 1982.
19. Edward T. Rowe, "Financial Support for the United Nations: The Evolution of Member Contributions 1946–1969," *International Organization* 26, 1972, pp. 619–57.

keeping of peace. Can it improve international perceptions so that the impulse to war will be less frequent? When conflict does occur, can the UN rise above some of the political muddle and restore order? And once a conflict has been extinguished, can the UN provide a consistent influence to maintain the peaceful status quo?

While in the long run the prevention of aggression is the objective of international organization in the security realm, the more immediate issue for the United Nations is the control and termination of war once in progress. The framers of the Charter chose as the primary method of controlling aggression a concept derived from the Covenant of the League of Nations: collective security. This doctrine claims that a war against one member is a war against all, and that the world's governments should be prepared collectively to meet aggression anywhere in the world. In the United Nations Charter, the concept resides in Chapter 7, entitled "Action with Respect to Threats to the Peace, Breaches of the Peace and Acts of Aggression." This chapter authorizes the fifteen-member Security Council to determine the existence of a threat and, thereafter, to prescribe non-military sanctions or military sanctions. Since the only source of military action is its member states, the United Nations calls upon states to make troops available to the Security Council and provides that the decisions of the Security Council will be carried out "by all the members of the United Nations or by some of them, as the Security Council may determine" (Article 48). All decisions are subject to the formal voting arrangements of the

Source: © Liederman/Rothco

Security Council and, therefore, to the possibility of veto by any permanent member (United States, Soviet Union, United Kingdom, France and China). Given the disparate interests and global objectives of these states, the likelihood of Security Council action under Chapter 7 is hopelessly low.

The international security system envisaged under Chapter 7 has had only one partial test, the Western response to aggression in Korea in 1950. But the Council acted only in the early phases, during which the Soviet Union maintained a boycott of the Council over the question of seating a delegate from the People's Republic of China in place of one from the Republic of China (Taiwan). The use of the veto at one time or another by every permanent member has prevented a full test of the collective security scheme.

An early test occurred in 1956 when Britain and France joined with Israel in war against Egypt, but because of British and French participation and veto power, the Security Council was unable to influence the situation. Secretary-General Dag Hammarskjöld, in one of the boldest initiatives in the UN's history, proposed to the General Assembly that it establish, consistent with the Uniting for Peace Resolution, a lightly armed, multilateral force (deliberately excluding the superpowers, lest the scope of the conflict widen). This force would interpose itself between the combatants, not to enter into the fighting, but to create a neutral zone that would separate the parties while diplomatic efforts at ending the conflict were conducted. Over the objections of the Soviet Union, France and a handful of other governments, the first United Nations *peacekeeping* operation was conducted under the principles enunciated by the Secretary-General. The United Nations Emergency Force (UNEF, 1956) thus became the first attempt by the United Nations to formulate a substitute for the failed notion of collective security. Summaries of the principal uses of the new method follow.[20]

Egypt

Although Egypt expected the United States to finance construction of the Aswan High Dam, Secretary of State John Foster Dulles announced in 1956 that Washington would not do so. In disgust over this an-

20. For a synopsis of all UN interventions and peace observer groups, see Larry L. Fabian, *Soldiers Without Enemies* (Washington: The Brookings Institution, 1971), pp. 261–68. An exhaustive treatment of military, logistical and budgetary details is found in David Wainhouse, *International Peacekeeping at the Crossroads* (Baltimore: Johns Hopkins University Press, 1973). At the time of writing, thorough treatments of the current Middle East and Lebanon operations are not available.

nouncement Colonel Gamal Abdel Nasser, Egyptian head of state, seized the Suez Canal, despite a treaty ensuring its international ownership. This seizure affected Israeli imports, threatened the flow of Middle Eastern oil, upset the British and infuriated the French, who were beset by problems in Algeria. Jointly, these three nations drove Egyptian troops away from the Suez region and reestablished control.

At the United Nations, Britain and France prevented the Security Council from assuming responsibility for order in the area, voting against everything from censure to action. During the voting, a most unusual event occurred: the United States and the Soviet Union voted together against two of Washington's most prestigious allies. This American reaction ought not to have surprised its friends, since President Eisenhower had warned that he would not support their operations. Yet not until faced with the American vote did the British will begin to subside. France was more deeply committed, but British second thoughts sent Paris scurrying for an alternative policy. Thus when the issue arrived in the General Assembly, the point of contention was not a superpower confrontation, but the embarrassment of two second-rank powers who by then were amenable to collective decision. The atmosphere was receptive to the new principles of peacekeeping, which resulted in the stationing in Egypt of a multinational interventionary force (the United Nations Emergency Force) from 1956 to 1967.

The Congo

The situation in the Congo in 1960 was wholly different. There, stability had been upset by the secession of Katanga Province, with a resulting civil war. In the view of third parties, widespread fighting in the Congo was a threat to the stability of the entire African continent, especially in the small and struggling new states south of the Sahara. But the Congolese situation did not rival the Middle East or Cyprus in the interests of the Soviet Union or the United States, with the result that major-power demands were not a barrier to effective management. Thus, partly liberated from the normal constraints upon its politics, the Security Council was able to adapt the peacekeeping principles used by the General Assembly in the Middle East. Though there were serious (and at one point almost disastrous) Soviet-American differences over execution of the principles, the convergence of their interests in settlement permitted the Security Council to restore stability by dispatching a peacekeeping force (the United Nations Operation in the Congo) from 1960 to 1964.

Cyprus

Cyprus was still a different problem. A small insular state in the eastern Mediterranean, its domestic politics suffered from a power struggle between the majority Greek population (about 80 percent) and the smaller Turkish population. As far back as 1931 there had been moves by the Greek population to merge Cyprus with Greece. In the years immediately prior to independence in 1960 there was sporadic violence. Fed up with responsibility and under pressure to divest itself of colonial holdings, Britain agreed to the formation of a Republic of Cyprus in 1960, with guarantees that the president would be elected by Greek Cypriots and the vice-president by Turkish Cypriots. The former were also to hold 70 percent control of the national legislature.

But independence was only a palliative for the social and ethnic problems of the tiny republic. By 1963 Turkish Cypriots were charging the Greek majority with denial of rights. Open hostilities began. In March 1964, amidst crises, the Security Council voted a peacekeeping operation, which it still maintains, despite Turkey's seizure of much of Cyprus in a brief war in 1974.

Again, the objectives of the great powers are a critical consideration in the successful utilization of peacekeeping principles. Since both Greece and Turkey are formal allies of the United States, Washington saw the crisis as a threat of intra-alliance warfare. Though Britain had retained two small military posts on the island, it wanted collective responsibility lest anyone accuse the British government of resort to imperial tactics. France, by then extricated from both Algeria and Indochina, was receptive to any plan for stability in the Mediterranean. And the Soviet Union, though always ready to profit from disruption among the Western security allies, wanted peace in the Mediterranean. Most particularly, Moscow wished to court the favor of Turkey, since Turkey controls the Bosporus and the Dardanelles through which Soviet ships must move from the Black Sea to the Mediterranean. With plans for a major naval build-up, the stability of Turkish foreign policy was critical to Moscow. The conditions were optimal for interventionary peacekeeping. The Security Council continues periodically to extend the mandate of the United Nations Force in Cyprus (UNFICYP) despite the Turkish sector's 1983 declaration of an independent republic.

The Middle East, 1973

The resumption of war in the Middle East in 1973 threatened once again to plunge that area into catastrophe. This time, the interests of the United States and the Soviet Union were more directly touched. The US strongly supported Israel, and the USSR was determined to support its Arab friends and to maintain a naval balance in the Mediterranean. A written Soviet threat to intervene militarily in the fighting, reported to the American people without detail as "a brutal note," resulted in a temporary worldwide alert of American forces, including mobilization of some reserve units. In withdrawing from this potential superpower crisis, the Soviet Union proposed a joint Soviet-American peacekeeping operation for the region—a proposal vigorously rejected by Washington on the traditional ground that such an operation would threaten larger crisis. As an alternative, the Security Council agreed to establish a multimember peacekeeping force consisting of the troops of smaller powers, to be commanded by a Finnish general. The initial troop contingents were ferried to the area from Cyprus. The command assumed the functions of interposition, administration of prisoner repatriation, exchange of checkpoints and logistical facilitation of truce talks in the desert.

The Council's decision to establish this force signaled the growth of a Soviet-American consensus on the utility and political acceptability of peacekeeping as a means of ensuring regional security. This promising characteristic was partly offset by Chinese refusal to take part. Though the force was established without a negative vote, the Chinese were recorded as "not participating." They repeated their view that such operations are instruments by which the two largest powers use the UN as a tool for perpetuating their control of world events and regional conflicts. That China did not veto the proposal, however, restores expectation that the major powers may now have come to accept peacekeeping as the most appropriate means of maintaining regional stability. The Security Council's willingness and political ability to reaffirm the mandate of UN functions both in the Sinai (where American diplomacy had arranged for Egypt-Israeli agreement) and for the Golan Heights (where no Syrian-Israeli agreement applies) adds encouragement to peacekeeping as a means of ensuring regional tranquility. Indeed, although we must await memoirs to confirm the possibility, the quiet success of the 1973 UN Emergency Force operation in the Sinai may well have contributed to the healthy environment leading to the long-awaited Egyptian-Israeli peace in 1979, after which the Security Council dissolved the United Nations Emergency Force (UNEF) in the Sinai. It continues, however to extend the mandate of the United Nations Disengagement Observation Force (UNDOF) in the Golan Heights.

Lebanon

Throughout the hostilities between Israel and its Arab neighbors, the Israeli government has repeatedly reaffirmed its intention of striking against Palestine Liberation Organization positions in southern Lebanon from which terrorist attacks have been launched frequently. The interests of Israel were closely touched by the Lebanese Civil War, which resulted in the arrival of a Syrian interventionary force charged with establishing peace in an environment in which Lebanon would be oriented to Arab views of regional politics. To help neutralize Lebanon in the regional struggle, Israel threw its weight behind the Lebanese Christians.

In 1978 the frequency of terrorist attacks launched from southern Lebanon increased, and Israeli air and ground forces retaliated with attacks against suspected positions, even briefly occupying Lebanese territory. Both Lebanon and Israel called the issue to the attention of the Secretary-General of the UN. Lebanon considered itself to have been occupied, and Israel wanted to bring world public pressure to bear on the Palestinian terrorists. Not only did immediate events cause discomfort, but they seemed also to jeopardize the delicate Egyptian-Israeli peace talks.

After studying the situation, the Security Council voted (without dissent) to establish a United Nations Interim Force in (southern)

UN forces in Beirut, 1983.

Source: © Time Magazine

Lebanon (UNIFIL). The Soviet Union and Czechoslovakia both abstained, in part because of larger considerations of foreign policy in the area and because the Security Council had not declared Israel an aggressor. Interestingly, the Security Council resolution establishing UNIFIL also established a system of financing the operation by which the General Assembly would bill the organization's members. This was based on a formula of size, wealth and dues to the UN, a method disliked by the Soviet delegation but not ultimately rejected by it. China, in keeping with its suspicion of peacekeeping, was recorded as "not participating." Again, however, it was gratifying to peacekeeping advocates that China did not exercise the option to veto the establishment of UNIFIL, lending further evidence to the cooperative spirit of China in such multilateral efforts to maintain international peace and security.

UNIFIL was charged with the responsibility of supervising the withdrawal of Israeli forces, of restoring peace and security in the area and of assisting the government of Lebanon in reestablishing effective control over southern Lebanon. This was a far more complicated mission than had originally been envisioned for peacekeeping forces. Far from merely interposing a lightly armed force between two combatants who had accepted the general principle that such a force would be beneficial to both, UNIFIL was introduced into a conflict involving multiple interests. These included Syria, Israel, Palestinians and both the Christian and Arab forces within Lebanon. Boundaries and lines of demarcation were thus absent and as a consequence of the complex situation, UNIFIL was as much a political force as a military operation. Success in its mission demanded that its leaders arbitrate virtually every move among the competing domestic and international interests.

In the spring of 1983, the situation in Lebanon changed dramatically when several wars erupted simultaneously. Rival Lebanese factions resumed civil war, and Syrian and Israeli troops engaged one another. In the midst of conflict, UNIFIL positions in southern Lebanon were overrun by Israeli troops, but the Security Council continued its periodic extension of the UNIFIL mandate to try to moderate the situation in the south and to provide humanitarian aid to refugees and local victims of occasional shelling. By summer, the Palestine Liberation Organization agreed to vacate the Beirut area under the protective cover (from Israeli shelling) of a multinational force consisting of American, French and Italian troops. The United Nations did not take a direct part in this exodus. Subsequently, the United States, France, Italy and Britain agreed to station a few thousand troops in different areas of Beirut as a multinational peacekeeping force, separate in mission and command from UNIFIL in the south.

As factional fighting continued, and as terrorist attacks on both American and French positions increased in number and intensity (with nearly 300 deaths and hundreds of injuries in a six-month period), the PLO slipped back into the Beirut area and conducted its own civil war. At the end of 1983, the PLO loyalist faction led by Yasir Arafat was evacuated from Lebanon once again, this time in rented Greek vessels flying the protective flag of the United Nations. The Security Council had agreed to this extraordinary condition to help reduce the carnage in Beirut, a city near total destruction. During the evacuation, the presence of the French navy prevented Israeli gunboats from firing on the fleeing Palestinians, their mortal enemy.

Meanwhile, under political pressure at home, increasing criticism of the role and indefensibility of Marine positions in Beirut, President Reagan first "redeployed" the Marines to vessels off Lebanon's coast and then removed them from the zone altogether. American efforts to secure the consent of fifteen non-aligned governments to form a new multilateral force outside of United Nations command failed. During this entire period, there was no formal discussion of a United Nations peacekeeping role in the Beirut area, though the UNIFIL mandate in the south of Lebanon was renewed once again at the end of 1983. Even there, however, the role of the United Nations was diminished by the withdrawal of the Nigerian contingent.

Evaluation of Peacekeeping

These brief histories are provided less in an attempt to detail international events than to demonstrate the evolution of peacekeeping as a substitute for collective security, and to demonstrate the benefits and liabilities of this method as well as the way it fits into great-power politics.

It is widely agreed today that except in matters touching directly upon the interests of the superpowers, peacekeeping is a promising method for restoring regional stability. Though it began as a General Assembly decision, thus calling into question the relative roles of the Assembly and the Security Council in matters pertaining to international peace and security, since the United Nations Emergency Force of 1956, it has been used exclusively by the Security Council. The UN Operation in the Congo was a Security Council operation, and it was threatened not by matters of initiation, but by the Soviet Union's objection to the West-leaning manner in which the Secretary-General carried it out. Even though the United States and the Soviet Union have grave disagreements over the uses and execution of peacekeeping operations, they have cooperated on all recent decisions regarding the

Middle East and Cyprus. Even China, which originally believed that peacekeeping was a form of organized aggression, abstained rather than vetoed peacekeeping decisions until 1981. In a 1981 vote on one of the several periodic extentions of the UNFICYP mandates, China voted affirmatively for the first time. Scholars and statesmen seem now to agree that in the hands of the Security Council, where peacekeeping can be subject to great-power unanimity and where issues affecting international peace rightfully belong under the original intentions of the Charter's framers, peacekeeping is a major hope for stability. One distinguished scholar of international relations provides this assessment:

> Perhaps the most significant development in the thinking of scholars and statesmen about international organization in the postwar period has been their gradual emancipation from the collective security fixation, their breaking out of the intellectual rut in which it was taken for granted that the suppression of aggression was so crucial a function of general international organizations that if this function could not be exercised, the only issue worth thinking about was how to make its exercise possible. Dag Hammarskjöld gave dramatic and forceful expression to the new and less constricted approach to international organization when he put the question of how the United Nations could contribute directly to keeping the peace when it could not enforce the peace and answered the question by formulating the theory of preventive diplomacy, now generally known as peacekeeping.[21]

Even in the hands of the Security Council, however, peacekeeping's role in the international system is not assured. Foremost among the difficulties is that it can be used only in very special circumstances. First, there must be relative equivalence of power among the local forces, since the UN can usefully interpose a force only if neither party can gain a quick military advantage; second, unless the Security Council is willing to use its special privileges under Chapter 7 to bypass host-state rejection of forces, it is able to operate only with the consent of one or more of the local disputants; third, either the General Assembly or the Security Council must be able politically to agree on the mandate and organization of the emergency force. This is a lengthy catalogue of politically sensitive conditions, and it cannot be expected that many local disputes will fit it. Only under special and peculiar circumstances will political and military conditions permit a United Nations peacekeeping role.[22]

21. Inis L. Claude, "The United Nations, the United States, and the Maintenance of Peace," *International Organization* 23, 1969, pp. 621–36.
22. James Stegenga, "United Nations Peace-Keeping Patterns and Prospects," in Robert Wood, editor, *The Process of International Organization* (New York: Random House, 1971), pp. 299–316. For a study of proposed methods of overcoming both

Given the special positions and prerogatives of the major powers, however, agreement in principle on the conditions and scope of peacekeeping is a required precondition for reliable utilization. The manner in which peacekeeping originated, over the Soviet protest of a General Assembly action, means that even today peacekeeping is accompanied by substantial residual distrust. To help resolve this underlying difficulty, in 1965 the General Assembly established a United Nations Special Committee on Peacekeeping Operations, charged to enunciate general principles. This committee, also referred to as the Committee of Thirty-Three, worked amicably but unsuccessfully through its session of 1983, when it reported that it had been unable to resolve problems related to the financing of peacekeeping operations, the creation of a Ready Force (although Canada, Norway, Iceland, Sweden and Denmark already have stand-by agreements with the UN) and on the extension of its own mandate. It is the General Assembly's decision whether or not it should continue its work, and at the time of writing, the General Assembly had not taken up the question.

The financial matter has always been at the center of the problem. The Soviet Union and others originally objected to being billed for peacekeeping because they had opposed it. Proposals have been exchanged ranging from supporting the operations with voluntary contributions, billing only the participating nations, billing only the governments that voted affirmatively on the establishment of an operation, and billing the combatants whose activities resulted in peacekeeping operations. In the midst of it all, while reimbursing those governments that supply troops to the UN at a rate of only $950 per soldier per month, the UN has run up an unpaid bill of $300 million exclusive of the unmet costs of the operations in the Middle East and of the Congo in 1956 and 1964! Moreover, at least $195 million is currently regarded as a permanently uncollectible bad debt.[23]

With collective security virtually an historic vestige of international organization, and with peacekeeping still hostage to the geographic and political interests of the permanent members of the Security Coun-

national and international barriers to peacekeeping, see Indar Jit Rikhye, Michael Harbottle and Bjorn Egge, *The Thin Blue Line: International Peacekeeping and Its Future* (New Haven, Conn.: Yale University Press, 1974). See also Lincoln Bloomfield, "The United States, the Soviet Union, and the Prospects for Peacekeeping," *International Organization* 24, 1970, pp. 548–65; Larry L. Fabian, *Soldiers Without Enemies* (Washington: The Brookings Institution, 1971), especially chapters 5–8. For another general discussion of the future, see Arthur M. Cox, *Prospects for Peacekeeping* (Washington: The Brookings Institution, 1967).

23. For a thorough review of the history of financing UN peacekeeping operations, see James Jonah, "Funding United Nations Peacekeeping," *UN Chronicle*, May 1982, pp. 65–70.

cil, it is still an unanswered question whether or not the United Nations is able effectively and consistently to maintain international peace and security. One study has shown that even though the veto has been used in the Security Council in forty-six of the armed conflicts since the Second World War, the UN had a great impact in twelve cases, some impact in twelve others and virtually none in twenty-two cases.[24] The potential ability of the United Nations to maintain peace, therefore, is not subject only to the use of the veto by the great powers, but to the willingness of states to permit third-party interests to enter into diplomacy, a decision closely tied to domestic politics and regional histories.

Evaluation of United Nations Performance

The United Nations is not a political system acting in a vacuum; nor does it operate above the international system. Its effectiveness depends on the quality of world politics and the degree of community among members. In a revolutionary system, community is at best fictitious, with the United Nations representing victories for legal authorization but only modest advances in the political impact. While it presents a picture of utmost institutionalization, its structure contributes only intermittently to change in the international order. As recently as a decade ago it was predicted that with the termination of the Vietnam War and the quickening pace toward multipolarity the sense of global community might intensify and collective decision making through international institutions might be more acceptable to states.[25] But since that time the North-South confrontation has replaced the Vietnam War as the obstacle to progress, and the upsurge of political activity in the Third World has produced new uneasiness. The principal difference, of course, is that while the Vietnam War was not fought diplomatically at the United Nations, the North-South controversy is acted out principally in the UN's organs.

Just as the international system undergoes change, so too does the United Nations, and change in the UN may alter national attitudes about its effectiveness. In American public opinion, for example, the United Nations has declined in popularity in recent years, principally because the UN has not consistently endorsed or legitimized American

24. Ernst B. Haas, "Regime Decay: Conflict Management and International Organizations, 1945–1981," *International Organization,* Spring 1983, pp. 189–256.
25. Stanley Hoffmann, "An Evaluation of the United Nations," *Ohio Law Review* 22, 1961, pp. 474–94, and "International Organization and the International System," *International Organization* 24, 1970, pp. 389–413.

foreign policy. Disapproval has occurred partly because of the character of American overseas operations, and partly because the UN has seen a fundamental change in its membership that has resulted in an automatic majority for the Third World members and with it a new policy orientation, one which seems threatening to American economic stature.

When the UN was founded in 1945 it had fifty-one members, each represented in the General Assembly. Today the total membership is 153. Virtually all of the states admitted after 1956 were newly independent states. Before 1957, the membership of the Assembly was such that the United States could count on being in the majority on virtually every issue. But the new membership deprived the United States of that certainty. Not willing to align themselves with American foreign policy and not willing to be taken into the vituperative politics of Soviet-American relations, these new states have taken a highly independent course. Sometimes neutral to American objectives and sometimes critical, the attitudes of the Assembly have eroded American confidence in the UN, and the new voting patterns rarely support American policy. This has been especially true about issues concerning

Economic development and social action: Honduran women learn new bee-farming methods in a program sponsored by the United Nations Development program designed to give women access to financial credit for the first time, 1983.

Source: United Nations/John Isaac

the international economy and the Middle East. On each of these the US has suffered major diplomatic setbacks at the hands of the automatic majority.[26]

Changing voting patterns in the UN have had even more profound effects. The Third World voting majority had made advancement of industrialization the UN's first concern. But within that goal there has taken root a Third World ideology, sympathetic to neither the Soviet Union nor the United States. Instead, it is an ideology of independent leftism, scornful of industrial states but covetous of industrialization. To the West it is ill conceived and petulant; to the Soviet Union it is useful as a constraint on American control of UN decision making. But in any event, it has diverted the UN, and particularly the General Assembly, from its old obsessions with security as an East-West problem. The UN is now more typically a forum for the war of wits and dollars between the industrial North and the maturing South.

As Figure 15–1 indicates, one study links the declining effectiveness of the UN to the decreased American satisfaction with the organization and with the declining American hegemony in the world. The study, however, deals exclusively with matters directly related to international peace and security.

Whether or not the United Nations is an effective organization depends foremost upon one's perspective, as the following section illustrates. It also depends upon recognition of major changes in world politics which have had significant impacts upon the United Nations system: the global redistribution of power and wealth which has diminished American satisfaction with the UN, the rise of the Third World to where it controls the voting majority at the UN on all issues pertaining to global economics, the Chinese competition with the Soviet Union for the allegiance of the Third World, etc. It depends also upon a careful study of different functions of the UN organs, since they function at different levels of effectiveness.

We have already looked at the UN's record of keeping and restoring peace. Elsewhere in this book we look at the UN's success in specific functional areas. In general, however, it is important to point out that

26. Robert E. Riggs, "The United States and Diffusion of Power in the Security Council," *International Studies Quarterly,* December 1979, pp. 513–44, discusses and analyzes American public opinion regarding the Security Council and the General Assembly, respectively. He concludes that since the "automatic majority" of the Third World was consolidated in 1972, American faith in that body has deteriorated steadily. In contrast, while the Assembly was once held in high esteem by Americans and the Security Council low because of Soviet-American confrontations there, since 1972 American opinion has swung back in favor of the Security Council because it gives the United States "an institutional foundation for maintaining a tolerable political position within the U.N."

FIGURE 15–1
UN success in influencing action on disputes referred to it compared with US opinion of those actions and with general US dissatisfaction with the UN as measured by the decline of frequency of US voting with the majority on all issues, 1945–1978.

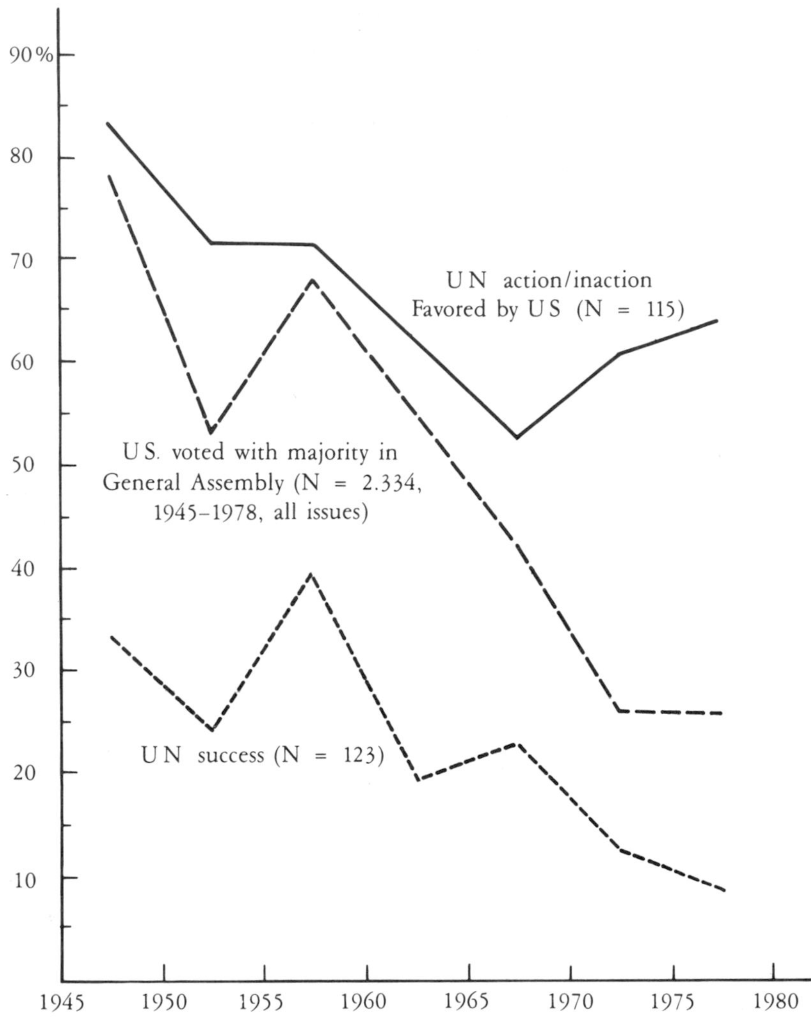

Source: Reprinted from Ernst B. Haas, "Regime Decay: Conflict Management and International Organizations, 1945–1981," *International Organization*, Spring 1983, pp. 189–256 at p. 231, by permission of the MIT Press, Cambridge, Massachusetts. © 1983 by the World Peace Foundation and the Massachusetts Institute of Technlogy.

while public opinion condemns the UN for its relative inability to maintain regional peace in several areas of the world and to reduce arms trade between the developed world and the underdeveloped world (not to mention its failure to slow down the strategic arms race between the Soviet Union and the United States), many of the UN's functions proceed with remarkable effectiveness.

One of the UN's restrictions is its total dependence upon the member governments for financial support. For the two-year period 1983 and 1984, the formal UN budget was barely $1.5 billion, an amount apportioned to the member states according to an elaborate formula. In addition, however, while in 1950 the specialized agencies received only

$40 million in additional voluntary contributions, the corresponding amount in 1983 was over $1.0 billion. Similarly, voluntary contributions for the United Nations Development Program exceed $2.0 billion (up from $8.0 million in 1950); and World Bank Group commitments have increased from $0.5 billion in 1960 to over $12.0 billion in 1983. These increased contributions result from a broad recognition of the growing functional needs of the world, particularly in the economically less-developed regions. Through improving coordination among the functional agencies and gradually reducing the vulnerability of the programs to political fighting, particularly between the industrialized North and the developing South, the functional activities of the UN will be increasingly productive.[27]

Organic Growth and Humanitarian World Politics

In addition to changes in political patterns at the UN brought on by the maturation of the Third World, events of the age have also refocused the concerns of the world organization. In the past decade the world has undergone the crisis of recognizing that humanity is imperiled by its own excesses, that the catastrophes that one may safely predict will result not from natural forces, but from peoples' overzealous efforts to conquer those forces. In the search for a better life we have contaminated our biosphere, polluted our environment and offended all our senses. Through the battles against disease, old age and premature death, we have created a global population boom that now threatens to exceed food supplies even as nonreplaceable resources are consumed at an increasing pace. These three crises—ecocide, excess population and agricultural limitation—have forced a reassessment of the trend toward undifferentiated growth, and have called forth an attempt at balanced, planned development the world over. This latter concept, often labeled *organic growth,* is at the center of the UN's new concern for humanistic world politics.[28] It is treated in the final chapter of this book as an issue of future world order.

27. Evan Luard, "Functionalism Revisited: The UN Family in the 1980s," *International Affairs* (London), Autumn 1983, pp. 677–92.
28. Mihajlo Mesarovic and Eduard Pestel, *Mankind at the Turning Point* (New York: New American Library, 1974). This is the Second Report to the Club of Rome, in which the authors report computerized projections about the human condition and reflect on the consequences of delaying action toward resolving the principal human crises. The references to "undifferentiated" and "organic" growth are biological analogies, the former representing growth for the sake of growth (as cells dividing without changes of function) and the latter coordinated growth (as cells dividing into organized units for interdependent activity).

    For a less specialized but equally informative treatment of these issues, see Ronald Higgins, *The Seventh Enemy : The Human Factor in the Global Crisis* (New York: McGraw-Hill, 1978). Higgins lists the first six enemies as the population explosion,

The American View of the UN System

The American record of participation in international institutions has been erratic. To avoid involvement in European war after 1918, the Senate rejected American membership in the League of Nations in a fascinating and tragic struggle with President Wilson. Despite only rare participation in the League's political activities, the United States was an active contributor to its functional activities. Most American policy between the world wars, however, was conducted with little regard for the League. Furthermore, despite the efforts of the European states to enlist the United States in the Permanent Court of International Justice (going as far as offering to alter the statute and to limit the advisory jurisdiction of the Court if the United States should wish), Washington steadfastly declined membership.

Relations between Washington and the United Nations have been quite another story. Finally convinced during the Second World War that global international organization and collective security were indispensable to future world stability, the United States played a leading role in the creation of the UN. Virtually throughout the war, planning groups—at first quite secret—worked on drafts of the Charter. The major political parties declared their support for a renewed outlook upon international organization. In September of 1943, the House of Representatives resolved, with the Senate concurring,

> That the Congress hereby expresses itself as favoring the creation of appropriate international machinery with power adequate to establish and to maintain a just and lasting peace among the nations of the world, and as favoring participation by the United States therein through its constitutional processes.[29]

Not to be outdone in its influence upon the foreign-policy process, the Senate resolved two months later,

the food crisis, resource scarcity, environmental degradation, nuclear abuse and science and technology unleashed. The seventh enemy is the "human factor," consisting of the political inactivity that prevents dealing with the global crisis and the blindness of individuals to the need to contribute through self-restraint to solving the global crisis.

Since "science and technology unleashed" is a unique problem of the technological (or postindustrial) age, attention is beginning to be given to it as a political problem of the future. See particularly Langdon Winner, *Autonomous Technology: Technics Out-of-Control As a Theme in Political Theory* (Cambridge, Mass.: sachusetts Institute of Technology Press, 1977).

29. House Concurrent Resolution no. 25, 78th Congress, first session; sponsored by Congressman J. William Fulbright of Arkansas, passed by the House September 21, 1943. *Congressional Record,* vol. 89, p. 7729. As reprinted and footnoted in Ruhl J. Bartlett, editor. *The Record of American Diplomacy,* 4th ed. (New York: Knopf, 1964), p.675.

> That the United States, acting through its constitutional processes, join with free and sovereign nations in the establishment and maintenance of an international authority with power to prevent aggression and to preserve the peace of the world.
>
> That the Senate recognizes the necessity of there being established at the earliest practicable date a general international organization, based on the principle of sovereign equality of all peace-loving states, and open to membership by all such states, large and small, for the maintenance of international peace and security.[30]

American interest in establishing the United Nations was portrayed most vividly by its sponsorship of the Dumbarton Oaks Conference in May 1944, at which delegates of the United States, the Soviet Union, Britain and France studied draft proposals for the UN Charter. Finally, after an additional year of diplomatic exchanges, including great-power agreement at the Yalta Conference (February 1945) on the veto provision, the United States hosted the San Francisco Conference (June 1945) for the formal signing of the Charter.[31]

American interest evolved from two directions. First, there were those believers in the grand design of continued Soviet-Anglo-American cooperation who anticipated great-power enforcement of the peace and who looked upon the veto in the Security Council as insurance against unwilling involvement in war. Second there were others who more realistically assessed the postwar situation. Why, they asked, ought we to expect that the Soviet Union will not return to its prewar attacks upon capitalism and on the West? The other side of this question, which plagues revisionist scholars of the Cold War, was this: since the postwar bipolarity was likely to necessitate a *pax Americana,* why not create international machinery through which American foreign policy toward the Soviet world could be pursued with collective legitimacy? Depending upon one's historical outlook, therefore, the American interest in the UN originated either from naïve expectations of Soviet-American cooperation in power politics or from the American intent to establish global institutions for facilitating American foreign relations.

It stands to reason that in an American-dominated world, Washington would consistently seek to enlarge the UN's authority insofar

30. Senate Resolution no. 192, as amended, 78th Congress, first Session, vol. 89, p. 9222, November 5, 1943. This resolution was offered by Senator Tom Connally of Texas, and is generally referred to as the Connally Resolution.
31. For a comprehensive study of the American role in the founding of the UN, and of the various political and diplomatic forces that shaped that role, see Robert A. Divine, *Second Chance: The Triumph of Internationalism in the United States During World War II* (New York: Atheneum, 1967). See also Ruth B. Russell (with the assistance of Jeannette E. Muther), *A History of the United Nations Charter* (Washington: The Brookings Institution, 1958). Ms. Russell was a staff member of the Leo Pasvolsky Committee, which prepared the American draft proposal.

as such increases helped American policy. This explains the American approval of the ICJ's interpretation of UN legal status in the *Reparations* case, in which the UN was held to be a subject of international law with certain characteristics resembling those of states, and having implied powers to fulfill specified functions and responsibilities. It also illuminates American sponsorship of the Uniting for Peace Resolution, which created a recourse in security matters in the General Assembly, free from Soviet veto. The American reaction was similar to the ICJ's advisory opinion in the *Certain Expenses* case, which rejected the Soviet argument that security measures that circumvent the special prerogatives of the Security Council are illegal.

In organizing the economic sector, the United States also played a leading role. It hosted the Bretton Woods Conference in 1944 which created the International Monetary Fund (IMF) and the International Bank for Reconstruction and Development (IBRD). Washington rejected the founding of the International Trade Organization in 1948, which would have limited the exercise of unilateral restraints to trade. The General Agreement on Tariffs and Trade (GATT), now with permanent institutional structure, has adopted much of this function.

This Western economic structure was created in an era when the United States was undisputed king among the trading partners. It was the most productive and largest exporter; it enjoyed the most favorable balance of trade (income from exports greatly exceeding cost of imports); and the American dollar was not only in great demand overseas, but was virtually the standard medium of international exchange.

Recently the American position has deteriorated. Inflation has reduced export potential; Western Europe and Japan have regained productivity and favorable trade and payments balances; the European Community has enough combined strength to spurn the American dollar and to compete with American manufactures. All of these contributed to a reversal of the American balance of trade in 1971, when imports exceeded exports for the first time in sixty years. Furthermore, the export of capital has brought on disastrously high balance-of-payments deficits.

Looked at from abroad, American reactions to these problems have been retaliatory. Western Europeans in particular feel that after years of attempts to persuade Germany, Japan, France and other countries to alter their currency values in relation to the dollar, the United States in 1971 undertook vigorous changes which either frankly or marginally violated international economic rules. The imposition of a 10 percent surcharge on all imports—a unilateral act designed to reduce the imports that were throwing the trade balance into deficit—was clearly a violation of the GATT. Furthermore, only months later Washington forced wholesale changes in the world's currency valuations by informing other governments of the changes that the United States would expect in return for an American devaluation. All of this was done without formal adherence to the rules of the IMF.

Washington's interpretation of these events differs. The official view is that because of its postwar economic superiority and Europe's need for special trade conditions, the United States has voluntarily endured trade discrimination. Now, however, having restored Europe's economic vitality through its foreign assistance programs and having encouraged the European Community to establish still further trade restraints disadvantageous to the US, the American competitive position has been eroded to the point that Washington must demand international trade equality. The official view holds that the United States started from a weak position and is bargaining back to equality.

On other economic fronts, the record of the United States is unsurpassed. No government contributes more to the economic programs of the UN than does the United States (although relative to its total wealth American contributions are not great). Overall, the United States bears about 40 percent of the total burden of financing UN programs. Thus, it has resisted proliferation of UN programs, having worked assiduously to prevent the founding of the Special United Nations Fund for Economic Development (SUNFED) and having shown little if any early enthusiasm for the UN Conference on Trade and Development (UNCTAD). The motive for this resistance is that such changes in institutional structure do not contribute to American interests, but turn the collective voting strength of the less developed nations into a bloc intent upon availing itself of American wealth.

The General Assembly's decision of 1972 to reduce the American share of the *apportioned* budget (as contrasted with total budget, which includes voluntary contributions) from 31.5 percent to 25 percent, at American request, ought not to be interpreted as acquiescence in a reprisal based on declining American confidence. The request was made as part of the Nixon administration's general distaste for UN activities and as a domestic budget-cutting measure. While the organization needs American money, the proposal was acceptable to the General Assembly mainly because payment of one-third of the apportioned budget symbolizes American domination. Immediately after the Assembly's decision, the Soviet delegation announced that it would reserve the right to request reduction in its apportioned share as well.

But just as the members of the United Nations do not want their organization dominated by the United States, so too does Washington look with disfavor upon the current trend in which the Third World uses the UN as a forum for global anti-Americanism. Throughout

1975 in particular, the string of American embarrassments over economic questions and over policy with respect to Israel and the Palestine Liberation Organization resulted in outspoken counterattacks by Ambassador Daniel Patrick Moynihan. Washington made clear its dissatisfaction with the United Nations as an instrument of global diplomacy. Whereas Washington once used the UN in the battle against the Eastern (communist) world, it is now being used against the United States by the Southern (underindustrialized) world. American governmental and popular reactions to this reversal add up to public hostility to the UN and declining willingness to fund its programs.

The greatest American frustrations with the United Nations General Assembly have occurred over North-South issues and over efforts by the underindustrialized world to adjust the world economy such that the industrialized West pays not only the economic price of development, but the social price as well. The degree to which the United Nations and its agencies are the forum for this policy explains the deterioration of American public opinion regarding the United Nations. Ultimate frustrations occurred in 1979 and 1980 when the United Nations was unsuccessful in securing the release of fifty-three Americans held hostage by Iranian militants, even after the formation of a presumably responsible government.

Among the presidential administrations in post-Korean War years, that of Jimmy Carter attempted most, and in the most difficult times, to improve relations between Washington and the United Nations. Perhaps because of his concern for human rights as a cornerstone of foreign policy and perhaps out of a broader faith that the United Nations might once again become consistently useful to American foreign policy, Carter was quicker than his predecessors to refer to the UN or to utilize its capabilities. Needless to add, much of this occurred over issues on which the US had little alternative: use of the General Assembly and of the International Court of Justice in attempts to secure the release of Americans held hostage in Iran, protest over Soviet occupation of Afghanistan, attempts to limit the impact of the New International Economic Order of the American domestic economy, etc. But in other areas, such as in the general effort to improve relations with the Third World, Carter took unprecedented steps, such as the selection of two black Americans, Andrew Young and Donald McHenry, as Washington's ambassadors to the United Nations. In other areas, however, Carter was notably resistant to UN participation, particularly in respect to the Middle East, a matter on which he rested politically and diplomatically on the Camp David accords. These were a series of agreements forged by Carter with the leaders of Egypt and

Israel on which he pinned long-range hopes for a peaceful Middle East.

The Reagan administration's view of the United Nations reveals a very different attitude. Apart from having named the first American woman ambassador to the UN, the administration has treated the organization with disdain. It has lost patience with Third World and Eastern bloc resolutions on the Middle East, particularly on Israel and the Palestinians; it has been frustrated by failure of the UN to reverse Soviet policies; it has withstood Third World efforts to use the UN to resolve civil wars in Nicaragua and El Salvador; and it has resisted further American obligations to the New International Economic Order. The conservative frustrations of the administration were summed up by Charles Lichenstein, a member of the US delegation at the UN, when he said in the fall of 1983:

> If in the judicious determination of the members of the United Nations, they feel that they are not welcome and that they are not being treated with the hostly consideration that is their due, then the United States strongly encourages such member states seriously to consider removing themselves and this organization from the soil of the United States. We will put no impediment in your way. The members of the US mission to the United Nations will be down at dockside waving you a fond farewell as you sail into the sunset.[32]

Two other issues created political friction between the US and the UN in 1983. The first was an administration request that Congress authorize additional contributions to The World Bank Group in order to provide added borrowing power for the Third World nations unable to pay their international debts. Liberal factions took the position that this was a request that taxpayers' money be used to drive foreign governments deeper in debt to American banks, the solvency of which was threatened by the mounting inability of the Third World to service its huge debts. Conservatives, on the other hand, wanted to supply the additional money as a form of assistance to American banks, but only on the condition that the new funds not be loaned to communist

32. Mr. Lichenstein's remark is reported in *The New York Times,* September 20, 1983, p. 1. It was made in reference to charges made by the Soviet Union that the United States had violated its responsibilities as the host state of the UN by refusing permission to Soviet Foreign Minister Gromyko to land at a civilian airport in the US on his way to the fall session of the General Assembly. Both New York and New Jersey had announced that in retaliation for the Soviet downing of a Korean civilian aircraft, the Soviet jetliner would not be permitted to land at any of its accustomed destinations. The federal government had offered use of a US Air Force base as a substitute, but the Soviets declined the offer and announced that Mr. Gromyko would not attend the session.

or other anti-American governments. When an amendment to this effect was defeated in Congress, conservative Republicans released public letters to the constituents of the Democrats who had voted against it claiming that they had communist tendencies.

The second issue was President Reagan's announcement late in 1983 that the US would withdraw from the United Nations Educational, Social and Cultural Organization (UNESCO) on December 31, 1984, the mandatory one year after announcement. This declaration capped a long-standing frustration with UNESCO and its Secretary-General over ideological, financial, policy and management issues. Specifically, the US charged the organization with having politicized every issue and allowed itself repeatedly to be used as a Third World, anti-West forum. The US objected to UNESCO's debates on Arab-Israeli issues not related to the organization's charge; to the Secretary-General's attempt to impose a New International Information Order which would have restricted the rights of the Western press operating in Third World countries; and to the position taken by the organization on restricting the activities of transnational corporations. Withdrawal of the United States from UNESCO would mean a loss of 25 percent of the organization's financial support. As a result, global movements began almost immediately upon release of the withdrawal announcement to attempt to dissuade the Reagan Administration.

The deterioration of the American attitude toward the United Nations reflects the general decline in America's satisfaction with the international system. One study of UN effectiveness correlates it with the general decline of American economic and political hegemony and with the rapid decrease in the frequency with which the United States has voted with the majority of the General Assembly on all subjects.[33]

But whatever course any American presidential administration may take with the United Nations, a dangerous paradox emerges in US-UN relations. If the UN system reflects an American-dominated world order, and if the United States is its largest financial supporter, and if the UN is an important element in international progress, American dissatisfaction with the UN may either destroy the organization's role, or drive the United States farther from support of the UN and from willing participation in collective decision making. If the United Nations lacks the authority to compel the United States, and if the United States is unable to manipulate the membership to its policy needs, the disaffection between Washington and the UN may destroy the organization's role in a changing world.

33. Ernst B. Haas, "Regime Decay: Conflict Management and International Organizations, 1945–1981," pp. 189–256.

The Views of America's Major Allies

Because they have generally shared the Cold War preoccupations of the United States, the major American allies have held views of international organization similar to those of the United States. There have been, however, some outstanding exceptions.

The Japanese position has been anomalous. Having been one of the wartime enemies against which the UN was founded, Japan was excluded by the terms of the UN Charter. It was nearly a decade before East-West agreement permitted the seating of a Japanese delegation. Since then, Tokyo has served as a loyal American ally in the UN, though its role has been a quiet one. It has not wanted to serve American interests to the detriment of normal relations with the USSR, and it has not wanted its American ties to make more difficult the problem of working out effective relations with both China and Taiwan. Probably for these reasons, Japan has disavowed any intention of requesting a permanent place on the Security Council, even though its accession to great power status in all but the military sense might otherwise justify such a claim.

The Western European attitude, too, is similar to that of the United States, though there are marked differences. During the peak of the Cold War, trans-Atlantic objectives were identical, so Western Europe clung to the anti-Soviet successes of the United States at the UN. European dissatisfaction with the extent of Washington's commitment to Asia during the Korean War, and American criticism of Britain and France over the Suez venture of 1956, were the only substantial exceptions.

But in the dynamics of world politics, the Western European partners have begun to move away from the United Nations, and away from some of the positions that the United States holds there. Most important, the progress of European regionalism has both altered the focus of Europe's organizational attention from the global to the regional and created the strength with which to pursue policies independent of Washington. On global issues such as petroleum, the Europeans prefer a policy of industrial states' consortia; and on the political issues of the Middle East that threaten the steady flow of oil they have abandoned such major American concessions to Israel as excluding from UN debate representatives of the Palestine Liberation Organization.

The Canadian attitude is genuinely unique among Washington's principal allies. Having for the first ten postwar years been caught in the flow of Soviet-American events at the UN, including participation in the Korean War, Ottawa's independence began to show in 1956.

It was Ambassador (later Prime Minister) Lester Pearson who conceived the idea that Dag Hammarskjöld later developed into peacekeeping, and Canada has since been one of the prime contributors to interventionary peacekeeping. It also served a brief and unhappy term as part of an international (non-UN) truce observer team in Vietnam.

On economic matters the Canadian position is also a unique one. Resource rich but industrially dominated, it is subject to all the fluctuations of American demand and American business. In a peculiar sense, then, Canada is an industrialized state that confronts many of the problems that are typically those of the Third World. On issues of the New International Economic Order, therefore, Canada is defensive when the United States is assertive, and often assertive when the United States is defensive. The role the United Nations plays in Canadian foreign policy, accordingly, is increasingly different from the one it plays in American policy. Consequently, the attitude that Canadians hold toward international organization is gradually diverging from that of its southern neighbor.

The Soviet View of the UN System

The Soviet view differs spectacularly from those of the United States and its principal allies. All of the latter have traditionally taken a Western view of matters of organization, as of law, pertaining to the world confrontation between communist and socialist states, on the one hand, and noncommunist and capitalist states on the other. Because of its sharply divergent perspective on these matters, the Soviet political attitude differs vastly.

The Kremlin sees international organization as an instrument of Western, and particularly American, policy designed to weaken the Soviet Union and to enhance capitalistic imperialism. Traditionally, then, its approach to the UN system has been defensive. Because of the composition of the organs, the Soviets have been able to pursue few if any major policies through the UN; they hope at best to prevent American intrusions in their interests. If they have outdone the American delegations in maximizing the propaganda potential of the UN, it is only because the makeup of the organization makes a negative approach to collective diplomacy necessary.

Several focal points have emerged in Soviet outlooks. The first was opposition to the Uniting for Peace Resolution on the ground that it subverts the prerogatives of the great powers in the very founding spirit. Second, the ICJ's advisory opinion in the *Certain Expenses* case further infuriated the Soviet Union on the ground that it illegally expanded the authority of the General Assembly as the expense of major power domination in security matters. A third major issue has been the principles of peacekeeping, toward which the Soviets have taken the view that the Security Council must control the issue to preserve great power authority. Connected to the issue of peacekeeping finance is the Soviet complaint that the Secretary-General managed the Congo operation in a pro-Western manner.

It would be a grave error to suppose that as the membership has become less sympathetic to American foreign policy, it has become more oriented to the Soviet Union. Although voting patterns in the 1960s gave greater strength to Soviet positions, it was not because increasing numbers of states were adhering to the Soviet line. Yet the Kremlin took a more patient view of the UN during the latter half of the 1960s. Attacks upon the organization were both less frequent and less vehement; and aside from refusal to pay for peacekeeping operations, Soviet willingness to fund the UN improved. Although it is a passive policy, the increasing failure of the organization to support American policy must have raised Moscow's spirits and its view of the UN's viability.

Because of the long-standing conflict between Moscow and Peking, the seating of the Chinese delegation at the UN was not a victory for the Soviet Union—as it would have been in 1950 or 1955. Indeed, the presence of the Peking delegation has changed the Soviet outlook on the UN. It is the avowed intent of the Peking delegation to champion the cause of the Third World; and in the long run this means new losses in the Soviet voting column. The deliberate Chinese strategy of labeling the Soviet Union a "social-imperialist," a concept alien to Marxism-Leninism because all imperialism is regarded as fascist and capitalist, is an ideological and rhetorical device by which China deliberately drives a wedge between the Soviet Union and the Third World countries at the United Nations.

Aside from the political organs and the economic programs, the Soviet Union is not an active participant in the UN system. It has never agreed to submit a dispute to the ICJ. Because of its different economic system, it has refused to participate in the institutions of Western imperialism. Neither it nor its allies takes part in the GATT. It was not until November 1972 that Romania became the first Soviet ally to enter the IMF and the IBRD.

Overall, although the Soviet view has been one of disaffection from the United Nations, there have been only a few issues that have threatened the existence of the organization because of that disaffection. The future is not likely to change. The Soviet Union will gain little new support in the UN, and with the presence of China and its special objectives, some recent apparent support may actually be lost. But being alone at New York is not new for the Soviet Union, and the depth of Soviet dissatisfaction is not likely to bring much change to the UN's role in the international system.

The Chinese View of the UN System

China is the youngest of the major powers. Its development toward full status has been retarded by the United States and the Soviet Union. American resistance was facilitated by the United Nations, through which Washington conducted a consistent anti-Peking policy from 1949 until the General Assembly session in the fall of 1971. It follows that Peking shares the Soviet view of the United Nations as the handmaiden of American foreign policy and of Western imperialism. More specifically, the UN is the forum through which the fraud was perpetuated until 1971 that the nationalist government on Taiwan was the real representative of the Chinese people, while over 800 million Chinese people on the Asian mainland were ignored.

The Korean War is also at the center of Peking's memory. In the hands of pro-American majorities, the General Assembly labeled China an aggressor despite obvious threats to its borders, and despite the urgings of General Douglas MacArthur that the Western allies in Korea attack Chinese targets. The UN, moreover, submitted to American pressures to vote an economic boycott against China. The continued refusal to seat the Peking delegation was the largest single source of China's sense of isolation from world politics, and was interpreted in China as an extension of the Century of Humiliation. Its embarrassment was further heightened by the comparative diplomatic positions of the two Chinas prior to the seating of Peking. By that time, sixty-six states had recognized the People's Republic, of which sixty still had active diplomatic relations. Of these, fifty-five were UN members. Meanwhile, sixty-one states had formally recognized the Taiwan government and fifty-nine had active diplomatic relations, of which fifty-six were UN members.[34]

When finally seated at the UN, the Peking delegation was notably restrained. It insisted before arriving that it would take no part until remnants of Nationalist representation had been expunged from *all* UN agencies (except the IMF and the IBRD, in which Peking has no interest). Its other uncompromising position was refusal to pay for

34. Summarized from Byron S. J. Weng, *Peking's UN Policy* (New York: Praeger, 1972), appendices B1–3, pp. 232–35.

maintenance of military cemeteries in South Korea. Otherwise it announced, quietly but resolutely, that it recognized its duty to pay a larger share of UN expenses than the weaker Nationalist government had, and volunteered to increase its contribution from 4 percent of the budget to 7 percent over a five-year period.

In other respects China's introduction to the United Nations was not quiescent. The first major event that followed the seating of the Peking delegation was the Pakistan Civil War and fighting between India and Pakistan, out of which Bangladesh was born. Because China sided with Pakistan and the Soviet Union with India, Bangladesh's subsequent request for admission to the United Nations was vetoed by China. Second, at the global United Nations Conference on the Human Environment at Stockholm in 1972, China used the opportunity to obstruct the meeting by condemning American use of defoliants in Vietnam.

In many respects, China's early days at the United Nations were characterized by outspoken criticism of the United States and the Soviet Union. It was apparent from the beginning that China intended to use its new status as a permanent member of the Security Council—a proud and prestigious position—as a new and unique opportunity to campaign against the perceived intentions of the two superpowers of dividing the world into two giant armed camps, commanding the allegiance of all others. In those early years, then, China's diplomacy at the United Nations was of two kinds: a bitter invective against the political intentions of Washington and Moscow, and a passionate involvement with the demands and expectations of the developing world. The developing world had already come to command General Assembly majorities on virtually all economic and development issues, and sympathized with China on matters of development and on its dislike of Soviet-American manipulation of the international system.[35] China's intention of taking a world lead among the developing countries was first enunciated at Bandung (Indonesia) in 1955, so the advancement of this policy at the United Nations is consistent with well-established Chinese foreign policy objectives. It is not sheer opportunism, as is often argued by anti-Chinese and anti-United Nations political elements in the West and in the Soviet world. China, after all, is the largest of the underindustrialized countries. It feels that it has been driven into a position of inferiority and that its achievement of national self-fulfillment is tied to nonwhite nations, regardless of

35. For a thorough contemporary analysis of China's role at the United Nations, based on documentary UN information, see Samuel S. Kim, *China, the United Nations, and World Order* (Princeton, NJ: Princeton University Press, 1979), particularly chapters 3–7.

politics or ideologies, more than to the industrialized world or to other Marxist societies.

Quantitative studies now reveal that on matters dealing with security, social policy, human rights and economics, the Chinese delegation at the United Nations has voted more frequently with the Third World than with the Soviet Union and Eastern Europe. The inclination to vote with the Third World is most pronounced on economic, human-rights and social issues, and somewhat less on political and security issues. It has voted more frequently with the Eastern European bloç on colonial and race issues than it has with any particular region of the underdeveloped world.[36]

Within a year or two of the arrival of the Chinese delegation at the United Nations, interest grew for a review of the UN Charter to determine whether or not it would be possible to strengthen both the Security Council and the General Assembly. These efforts were opposed by all other permanent members of the Security Council, but China took an ambivalent position. On the one hand, China wanted to signal its support for the interests of the Third World, which wanted foremost to reduce the abuses of the veto in the Security Council and to increase the authority of General Assembly decisions. In short, China and the Third World favored steps that would "democratize" international decision making at the United Nations.

On the other hand, as a permanent member of the Security Council after twenty years of exclusion from the United Nations, China was not eager to sacrifice the privileges of membership, including its new veto capability in the Council. Prior to admission and in the early years thereafter, China took the position that the veto is one of the building blocks in the Security Council's authority in international peace and security, and that the unanimity of the permanent members is critical to progress. As this position became unpopular with the Third World, which wanted to eliminate the veto, China took the position that the problem is not with the existence of the veto privilege, but with its abuse by the other four permanent members.[37]

China's view of peacekeeping has changed substantially. Since the original peacekeeping initiatives were carried out by the General Assembly in part under authorization of the Uniting for Peace Resolution, a resolution under which China and the United Nations had conducted war against one another in Korea, it should not be surprising that

36. Trong R. Chai, "Chinese Policy Toward the Third World and the Superpowers in the United Nations General Assembly 1971–77: A Voting Analysis," *International Organization,* Summer 1979, pp. 391–404.

37. Suzanne Ogden, "China's Position on UN Charter Review," *Pacific Affairs,* Summer 1979, pp. 210–239.

China's early attitude toward peacekeeping was that it is a form of organized aggression. Not until the end of 1981 did China finally vote affirmatively on extending the mandate of a UN peacekeeping force, after nearly a decade of having abstained on all related questions. Nonetheless, China joins the Soviet Union in insisting that since peacekeeping is an instrument of maintaining international peace and security, it belongs exclusively to the Security Council were it is subject to the unanimity of the permanent members

The Third World View of the UN System

Although the Cold War has left the impression that all international conflict is arranged along East-West lines, it is the feeling of the less developed states that the focus of world politics is really North-South. The bulk of the world's industrial power is in the northern hemisphere, while most of the southern half of the globe languishes in poverty. As a result, the less developed states have a mixed view of the UN system. On the one hand, they see it as the special preserve of the major powers, through which the latter have promoted economic domination and resisted adequate development programs. But on the other hand, much of the Third World enjoys national independence principally because of the UN's activities in promoting self-government; and they see in the UN agencies hope for relatively depoliticized programs of aid, trade and technical assistance. Thus, while the ideologically uncommitted states play an active and often vocal role in higher politics, their principal energies in the UN are reserved for the organs and agencies that serve their development needs.

The Third World's relations with these agencies are not entirely smooth. Since the funds for these programs come from the industrialized states, attempts to control the politics of assistance are never far off. The developed states, insisting upon maximum efficiency in the expenditure of funds, impose difficult criteria. They insist upon preinvestment development, designed to mature the nonvisible aspects of an economy so that larger and more productive projects can follow with maximum probable success. Less developed countries view this sequence with impatience. Likewise the LDCs, in their long-range planning, seek commitment of funds from plan to completion, while the lending agencies generally prefer to fund in stages and to require successful completion of each stage before releasing money for the next. More recently, the lending institutions have required consideration of ecological hazards in development projects. The LDCs view this requirement with disdain, since in their quest for rapid development they view environmental protection as a luxury appropriate only to developed economies. All impediments to accelerated development are viewed by the Third World as attempts to retard the pace of economic sovereignty in the southern hemisphere, and as methods of collective neo-imperialism. Nevertheless, acquisition of funds through the UN system is less costly, both economically and politically, than attaining them directly from other governments.

The need second to capital is trade concessions. The Third World has a difficult time trading in a world dominated by enormous economies in which trade regulations serve industrial states. To counter this situation, the Third World pressed for the establishment of the United Nations Conference on Trade and Development (UNCTAD), which provides a collective voice in confronting the GATT for more advantageous terms of trade with industrial countries. Specifically, UNCTAD seeks to press upon the GATT a unified program of preferential trading conditions. As we have seen, in 1974 and 1975 the underindustrialized states succeeded in focusing the attention of two special sessions of the General Assembly on economic problems, and achieved passage of the Charter of Economic Rights and Duties of States and the Declaration on the Establishment of a New International Economic Order, together with a Programme of Action.

Technical assistance is the third principal area of need. The UN's contribution began in 1949 with the founding of the Expanded Program of Technical Assistance (EPTA). Technical assistance continues to be provided through the Technical Assistance Board (TAB), the United Nations Industrial Development Organization (UNIDO), and appropriate offices of such functional agencies as the Food and Agricultural Organization (FAO) and the World Health Organization (WHO). Administrative personnel are offered to governments through the OPEX program (Operational and Executive Services), which locates administrative talent and places it on loan to Third World governments.

To meet the combined needs of the LDCs with respect to aid, trade and technical assistance, the United Nations General Assembly designated the 1960s the "development decade," and combined the Special Fund, the TAB and the EPTA into the United Nations Development Program (UNDP). The aim was to achieve 5 percent per year economic growth among the LDCs and to raise foreign assistance to a level of 1 percent of the annual gross national products of the industrialized states. During this period, however, unilateral nonmilitary aid did not increase substantially, and the UN's own programs were only a little more successful than they had been. The modest successes of the UNDP did, however, restore hope for collective advancement, and the 1970s were designated the "second development decade." UNDP II was launched. UNDP III is now in progress for the 1980s.

In all of these undertakings, the Third World nations are engaged in the difficult process of turning the United Nations to a goal that in practice has taken a decidedly secondary role to the great-power struggle. Now as the world recedes farther from bipolarity, the hope is kindled that the UN may turn to saving "succeeding generations from the scourge of war" by employing "international machinery for the promotion of the economic and social advancement of all peoples," as envisaged in the preamble to the Charter. Patient and long- suffering, the LDCs look to the UN system to lift them above exploitation by the great powers and to carry them over the seemingly impassable barriers of neo-imperialism.

16

International Integration and Transnational Participation

Centuries of study of the nation-state system have raised doubt regarding governments' ability to preserve international peace and stability. International law and organization have assisted, but neither has ensured lasting international harmony. What, then, are the alternatives to the nation-state system? What new political contexts might be framed through which familiar international transactions might continue, but in which peace might be a closer prospect?

At present, attention is focused upon two possible alternatives: international integration and transnational participation, the subjects of this chapter. Will political history reach beyond the nation-state?

International Integration

International integration is the process by which a *supranational* condition is achieved, in which larger political units conduct the business now carried out by national governments. Defined succinctly, it is

> the process whereby political actors in several distinct national settings are persuaded to shift their loyalties, expectations, and political activities toward a new and larger center, whose institutions possess or demand jurisdiction over the pre-existing national states.[1]

1. Ernst B. Haas, *The Uniting of Europe: Political, Social and Economic Forces 1950–57* (Stanford, Calif.: Stanford University Press, 1958), p.16.

Unlike international organization, which establishes institutional machinery among states, international integration provides decision-making machinery above them. It constructs procedures and institutions capable of making obligatory decisions on behalf of national governments. It consists of the merger of separate authorities and jurisdictions, usually in a well-defined geographic region, into a larger unit, a higher unity and a single polity. This slow and gradual process, which may occur unevenly in different sectors of interaction, leaves different states intact, but progressively blurs the distinctions of international policy among them.

Before commencing an analysis of the theory and progress of international integration, a note is appropriate regarding the frequency of integrating efforts. Most have begun with economic integration. Among the market (nonsocialist) economies of the world, progress toward economic integration is most easily observed in Western Europe, where two collaborations of different memberships, the European Community (EC)[2] and the European Free Trade Association (EFTA), are well on their respective paths to integrated economies. Because the progress of the EC has so far exceeded others, and because of the rich theoretical and analytical literatures that it has inspired, the sections that follow rely heavily upon theory and data pertaining to the EC. In fact, however, outside of Western Europe there have been no fewer than fourteen efforts of regionally related market economies at some level of integration, involving virtually every part of the nonsocialist world except North America. Among these the Andean Group, formed in 1969 and composed of Bolivia, Colombia, Ecuador, Peru and Venezuela (Chile having withdrawn in 1976), is generally considered the most advanced and the one that has most effectively limited direct foreign investment in order to maintain regional control over the economic future.[3] In the analysis that follows, occasional

2. The integrating states of Western Europe are conmmonly referred to in the aggregate as "the European Community." However, the larger community consists of a number of functionally organized activities, each of which is also labeled a "community." As a result, the European Community consists, in part, of the European Economic Community (EEC), which Americans call the Common Market, and the European Coal and Steel Community (ECSC), through which coal and steel resources are regulated. Hence if one wishes to speak of the community as conceived totally, one refers to the European Community; but if one wishes to connote the specific functional activities, the reference is instead to the European Communities. In this book, the singular form is used except where technical accuracy calls for the plural.
3. Lynn Mytelka, *Regional Development in a Global Economy: The Multinational Corporation, Technology and Andean Integration* (New Haven: Yale University Press, 1979). Also see Elizabeth G. Ferris, "Foreign Investment as an Influence on Foreign Policy Behavior: The Andean Pact," *Inter-American Economic Affairs,* Autumn 1979, pp. 45–69.

references are made to economic integration efforts outside of the European Community, but only when they are more instructive than are similar observations about the EC.

Integration and the Functional Model

Integration by any means is a long and arduous process. Although some observers have predicted integration through federation, most hold that integration is a testing process tied to compiled successes. This functional model of integration rejects rapid constitutional consolidation and looks instead to progress in specific sectors. The functionalist view holds that even compatible societies cannot integrate all public functions simultaneously. Collectivization may be based on economics, on politics or on security. Gradual and parallel progress in several sectors may converge into general, cross-sectoral integration. Without this convergence, integration is encapsulated or isolated, having no carry-over effects in other sectors.[4]

1. The Sectors of Integration

What functions have been given over to the integrative process? What purposes, normally served by national governments, have been entrusted to higher political levels? The answers to these questions lie in the different sectors of integration.

Economics

Historically, the sector most frequently integrated has been the economic sector. The most familiar integrative organizations are "common markets," in which the member states consolidate all or part of their economic activities. The European Economic Community (EEC), the Central American Common Market (CACM), the Latin American Free Trade Association (LAFTA) and the European Free Trade Association (EFTA) are among the most familiar.

4. For a study of the distinction between the federationist and the functionalist approaches, see particularly David Mitrany, "The Prospect of Integration: Federal or Functional?" *Journal of Common Market Studies* 4, December 1965. A useful study of the multivariate nature of integration is found in Leon N. Lindberg, "Political Integration as a Multidimensional Phenomenon Requiring Multivariate Measurement," *International Organization* 24, 1970, pp. 649–731. The neofunctionalists hold that federation can ultimately occur upon a well-established and solid functionalist base. See for example Joseph S. Nye, "Comparing Common Markets: A Revised Neo-Functionalist Model," *International Organization* 24, 1970, pp. 796–835.

The function of a common market is to raise economic potential through policy consolidation. Two particular instruments are used. First, the members eliminate barriers to trade among themselves, so that goods flow freely in trade. Second, they agree to treat outside states with a single economic policy; their economic policies concerning nonmembers are not only coordinated, but are identical and mutually enforced.

Because economic interaction is highly complex, it is instructive to consider economic subsectors. In the European experience, for example, progress toward a full free trade area has developed at different rates and with vastly different amounts of enthusiasm in the industrial and agricultural subsectors. Although it has not been easy, principles for industrial free trade areas were more readily achieved than those for agriculture. In addition, Britain's entry into the Common Market was delayed not only by French politics (on Britain's first serious attempt to gain entry in 1963, President de Gaulle vetoed its membership), but by British fears of the impact upon its agricultural subsector. Upon entry in 1973, Britain suffered inflation in food prices, but anticipated that gains in industrial trade would favorably affect its balance of payments (increase exports over imports), and would stabilize the British economy.

Another distinction involves production and producer. Though an economy consists of production of goods and services, goods and services are produced by people. Therefore there are important labor aspects to a free trade area—standardization of wages in industries, community agreement on fair labor practices, free flow of labor across national boundaries and agreement on pension and unemployment benefits.

In addition to labor and produce, another aspect of economic integration is the availability of capital, without which efficient, coordinated growth cannot occur. If this means borrowing from abroad, then one state (even perhaps an outside state) may dominate growth by controlling both capital and decisions about capital utilization. Creation of a common medium of exchange among participating central banks facilitates payments. Western European integration achieved this milestone in 1971 with the establishment of the E-note (Ɇ), which is exchangeable only among the member treasuries.

Social Considerations

The second major sector is the social sector. Although it may be technically feasible to integrate economies, ultimate integration requires mutual toleration and common social and political values. Social integration means transforming national preferences into loyalty to the larger political community. Supranational attitudes must evolve.

There is considerable evidence that such a process is now occurring in Europe. Studies reveal that the degree of "Europeanness" among nationals of various European states—the degree to which people sense themselves part of a larger political community—is growing steadily. They also demonstrate variations among age groups, with younger people generally more favorably disposed toward supranational attitudes.[5] Furthermore, available data suggest that the growth of supranational consciousness is accompanied by outward-looking attitudes: A united Europe is seen not only as a political community for self-service, but as a stabilizing force in the international system.[6]

Politics

A third sector of concern to integration theory is the political sector, though it is not neatly distinguished from other sectors. Societies are replete with bonds of patriotism, loyalty, historical mythology and a sense of national difference. Political integration refers, therefore, to the relatively narrow concept of integration of basic political institutions—with transfer of sovereignty over external policy to common international institutions. It aims not to eliminate national governments, but to alter their control over specific functions. These changes may affect internal matters of the state, such as fiscal policy or production policy. In integration short of full federation, there is no pretense to transfer of full sovereignty over internal matters.

Despite this limited expectation, political integration is more difficult to achieve than is economic integration, chiefly because the latter is expected to strengthen the national economy, thus encouraging dual loyalty to nation and larger community. Political integration, in contrast, directly affects the state's sovereignty over decision making with respect to its nationals. Its institutional effects are more visible, and the assault upon nationalism is more nearly frontal. The state is reduced in stature. Only where this is regarded as a desirable objective has the concept of political integration caught on.

A variety of interpretations exists about the relationships among political integration, social integration and general governmental cooperation.[7] Some hold that social predisposition is the critical measure

5. See, for example, Ronald Inglehart, "Public Opinion and Regional Integration," *International Organization* 24, 1970, pp. 764–95, and "The Silent Revolution in Europe: Intergenerational Change in Post-Industrial Societies," *American Political Review* 65, 1971, pp. 991–1017.
6. Ronald Inglehart, "The New Europeans: Inward or Outward Looking?" *International Organization* 24, 1970, pp. 129–39.
7. See, for example, the discussion of Karl W. Deutsch's "sociocausal paradigm" in the section of this chapter entitled "Background for Integration."

of integration potential. Others insist that the creation of institutions among generally sympathetic states will create the social conditions necessary for political integration.[8] Empirical studies now indicate, however, that improvements in intergovernmental relations must precede both institution building and changes in societal attitudes.[9] Western Europe integration illustrates this point.

It was apparent by the mid-1960s that political unification of Europe required a revival of internationalism in France. Always conscious of French historical and cultural uniqueness, President de Gaulle's view of European organization was pragmatic: How much can France profit from integration without sacrificing national identity? Toward the end of his long public career, de Gaulle confided to Christopher Soames, British ambassador to France, that he anticipated as an ideal "a looser form of free trade area with arrangements by each country to exchange agricultural produce, and a small inner council of a European political association consisting of France, Britain, Germany, and Italy." Broad political integration was not part of Gaullist politics, and both the entry of Britain into the EEC and French governmental receptivity to political unity awaited the passing of the Gaullist era.[10]

The forthcoming entry of Britain along with Denmark and Ireland in 1973 set the stage for a forward-looking summit conference in October of 1972, at which ministers from the three incoming states participated. There a general agreement was signed calling for a phased schedule of political unity by 1980. Details of the unity were to be culminated in the first phase, scheduled to end in 1975. The departure of de Gaulle, the enlightened attitude of his successor, the willingness of the British Conservative government to withstand the attacks of the Labour opposition in entering the EEC—these and other events converged to give new life to the spirit of political supranationalism among the Nine.[11] By January 1976, major achievements had been scored: the Tindemans Report on progressive integration was pub-

8. This is the original functionalist model, propounded especially by David Mitrany in *A Working Peace System* (Chicago: Quadrangle Books, 1966).
9. See Barry B. Hughes and John E. Schwarz, "Dimensions of Political Integration and the Experience of the European Community," *International Studies Quarterly* 16, 1972, pp. 263–94.
10. The words are those of British Foreign and Commonwealth Secretary Michael Stewart, as he reported the de Gaulle-Soames conversation to Parliament in February 1969, as described by Hugh Corbet, "Role of the Free Trade Area," in Hugh Corbet and David Robertson, editors, *Europe's Free Trade Area Experiment* (Oxford: Pergamon Press, 1970), pp. 1–42.
11. Studies of de Gaulle's attitudes toward the European future, and of the European Community in particular, are many. For a succinct and lively discussion of the topic, see Walter Laqueur, *The Rebirth of Europe* (New York: Holt, Rinehart and Winston, 1970), especially pp. 328–36. For a general study of the political union question from the Fouchet Plan through 1967, see Susanne J. Bodenheimer, "The 'Political Union' Debate in Europe: A Case Study in Intergovernmental Diplomacy," *International Organization* 21, 1967, pp. 24–54.

lished; a formal agreement had been made for direct election of the European Parliament in 1978 (as contrasted to assignment of members from the respective national parliaments); and the members had intentionally presented a common front at the United Nations on the economic matters considered at the special session on the new international economic order.[12] In addition, within the community new political alliances had formed, and on matters of deliberation there had developed a tendency for cross-national parties and interest groups to discuss policy on the basis of shared interests rather than to resort to the more primitive device of national caucuses.[13]

As is not uncommon, however, progress toward political integration has failed to keep up with the plan. The direct election of the European Parliament was postponed to 1979, but even in advance of the event some observers expressed the view that the very preparation for such elections had had a profound effect upon the national politics of the member states. One such observer noted that in the preparations, European subjects had become more important in public debate, that European voters were aware that Europe itself would soon become a fourth level of politics for their consideration—local, state, national and now continental. In addition, it was apparent that the forthcoming elections were promoting latent transnational links among European political parties.[14] All of these trends seemed to revive earlier attitudes about the probable political spillovers of economic integration, and seemed to give new life to the notion of at least partial transfer of loyalty from the nation as the source of services and economic vitality to the union of nations.

Another little-noticed trend gives added evidence of progress toward political union. By the end of 1978, based on a nine-year-old agreement on European political cooperation, a substantial EEC diplomatic presence was discernible around the world, which might in time result in the development of a structure for a common foreign policy. Working principally through a presidential commission, the directors-general responsible for various aspects of the Community's affairs (such as external relations, agricultural trade, international development and the like) had begun consulting regularly on behalf of the Community in several capitals including Washington, Tokyo, Peking and Ottawa. They had placed fifty representatives in the developing world and elsewhere, and had stationed conferences with several international

12. *Christian Science Monitor,* December 31, 1975, p. 13. See also Robert R. Bowie, "Program for a Federal Europe," *Christian Science Monitor,* February 4, 1976, p. 27.
13. *New York Times,* February 9, 1976, pp. 1 and 18.
14. See, for example, Karl Kaiser, "Europe's Parliament," *New York Times,* February 18, 1979, p. E10.

organizations. In the words of two commentators on the subject, "Without any clear or agreed plan for developing the Commission's role in bilateral diplomacy, incremental growth has nevertheless produced an extensive pattern of Community missions in [nonmember] countries."[15] In 1981, the EC's diplomatic activity resulted in an elaborate proposal, presented to the Kremlin, for the withdrawal of Soviet forces from Afghanistan.

Security

The fourth major area in integration is the security sector. Integration may follow from existing alliances, but it implies considerably more than mere alliance. Generally, an alliance is a political instrument through which the dominant member gains political access to the decision-making processes of the lesser members, in return for which the weaker states are guaranteed strategic assistance. Integration calls upon all members, whatever their relative power potentials, to contribute to decision making at all levels of planning, deployment and command.

Integrated alliances are rare. Despite the frequency of alliances since the Concert of Europe (1815), governments have generally resisted giving total strategic control to common institutions. The Warsaw Pact—the military alliance of the Soviet Union and its Eastern European allies—is about as integrated as an alliance can be. The Soviet Union, through its political control and economic supremacy, regulates the power and the respective roles of the other allies, thus virtually dictating policy. The North Atlantic Treaty Organization has more collective decision making, though in nuclear affairs Washington has consistently clung to unilateral control. Much of the recent history of NATO diplomacy has revolved around attempts by the Western European members to break down this American position. While troops and conventional war materials have been integrated to a considerable extent, fully integrated decision making does not yet exist.[16]

These observations lead to preliminary conclusions. First, considering the importance of strategic policy to national survival and to powerful national elites, security integration must follow political integration. The mere creation of alliances does not ensure integrated policy making, integrated commands or integrated allocation of re-

15. Christopher Hill and William Wallace, "Diplomatic Trends in the European Community," *International Affairs* (London), January 1979.
16. For an extensive treatment of the NATO experience, see Francis A. Beer, *Integration and Disintegration in NATO: Processes of Alliance Cohesion and Prospects for Atlantic Community* (Columbus, Ohio: Ohio State University Press, 1969).

sources. Second, given the same political realities, moves toward security integration occur mainly in times of crisis. They are the result not of political and social preferences, but of immediate vital need.

2. The Momentum of Integration

What causes integrating energy to continue to gain? If the impetus exists for sector integration at all, what forces permit it to surpass mere organization and to enter into supranationalism? And what are the prospects that success in one sector will "catch on" in others?

Each of these questions is answered by a single word, though neither connotes a simple process. Sector integration, once begun, gains steam by *feedback*. This is analogous to gravity: a falling object gains velocity. In like manner, if a snowball rolls down a sharp decline, it gains mass. Put simply, integration theory posits that if a formal process of sectoral interaction is allowed free forward propulsion, it will gain in intensity by strengthening itself.

The analogy is oversimplified, of course. Social phenomena are obstructed from free forward propulsion, in the same way that wind alters the free downward fall of an object or as friction reduces the energy of a rolling snowball. Social scientists have as their laboratory only political systems, and the data invariably show the feedback process to be halting and sporadic. The ideal condition is continuous, growing and mutually perceived success, and equal sharing by all the participants in the continuing benefits. Generally, these inside conditions must by accompanied by external inducements. The impetus to advancement must, on the whole, exceed occasional setbacks.

What of the second question: What forces carry the energy of integration from one sector to another? The answer is found in the *spillover* phenomenon, in which integrative successes in one sector awaken integrating objectives in another. The integrative energy from one sector spills over to another. But once spillover has occurred, there is no assurance that feedbacks within the new sector will keep pace with the first, or that one spillover will energize the next.

Thus far we have considered four basic issues of the integrative process: (1) the distinction between organization and integration (or internationalism and supranationalism), (2) the notion of sector differentiation, (3) the concepts of feedback and (4) spillover. Behind these concepts is an array of social and political conditions that determine the start of the process, as well as its pace, progress and end products.

3. Goals of Integration

Since integration is a conscious process, nations and governments must have explicit motives for seeking it. This is especially true since self-preservation is one of the major aims of statehood and of governmental activity. What expectations are sufficiently intense to motivate governments toward integration?

Economic Potential

Historically, the largest single motive has been the desire to maximize economic potential. In the presence of a few giant economies, smaller states have been unable to keep pace with competition. Whether they are underdeveloped states or old industrial states, the hope of fully competing may be a call to integration.

After the Second World War the Western European states rebuilt their industries only to discover that once-great national economies were lost in the American shadow. The economy of the Western world had become asymmetrical, with the United States commanding the greatest produce for export, the largest and most technically developed labor force and the most innovative entrepreneurial skill. For reconstructed Western Europe to compete, it was necessary to merge national economies. Though this meant hardships for agriculture, six governments agreed in 1957 to establish the European Economic Community (the Common Market), with an elaborate plan for integrating trade among themselves and for a common trade policy with respect to nonmembers. In the first sixteen years of their integrating experience, during which the Economic Community consisted only of the original six members, they were able to develop combined economic potential second only to that of the United States.

Political Potential

A second major motive for integration is the desire to maximize political potential. With rare exception, small and politically powerless states have had little impact upon the international system, especially during the bipolar era that followed the Second World War. Small states have felt either left out of, or victimized by, a world of two massive power centers. Some view integration as the route to reestablishing a multipolar world in which their diplomacy may achieve more favorable results.

Conflict Resolution

A third impetus to integration is the desire to resolve potential conflict among territorial neighbors. If there be nascent conflict among states forced by geography to be interdependent, integration of vital sectors of their interaction may outweigh the existing sources of strife.

The most notable instance of such motivation was the founding in 1951 of the European Coal and Steel Community by the same six states that founded the EEC a few years later. Though the ECSC was the first implementation of a long-range plan for European economic integration, it was addressed more immediately to a specific problem: the age-old Franco-German rivalry over coal and steel resources. At a press conference in 1950, French Foreign Minister Robert Schuman declared:

> The gathering of the nations of Europe requires the elimination of the age-old opposition of France and Germany. The first concern in any action undertaken must be these two countries.
>
> With this aim in view, the French Government proposes to take action immediately on one limited but decisive point. The French Government proposes to place Franco-German production of coal and steel under a common "high authority," within the framework of an organization open to the participation of the other countries of Europe.

The Schuman Declaration, previously approved by the French Council of Ministers, resulted in the ECSC. Most important, however, is the specific intent that Schuman emphasized—the interdependence of European economic integration with elimination of this historic cause of war.

How effectively does progress toward supranationalism actually diminish conflict among the participants? While integration does not eliminate strife, it does reduce its frequency. Denying that this proves a casual link, one scholar, examinining a non-European context, contends that "when combined with awareness and concern on the part of Central American elites about the relationship between economic integration and violent conflict, it does provide some useful evidence for the existence of the probable relationship."[17]

But not all students of integration are persuaded that organizations reduce the likelihood of war among members. Using five measurements of integration (common institutional membership, proximity, eco-

17. Joseph S. Nye, *Peace in Parts: Integration and Conflict in Regional Organization* (Boston: Little, Brown, 1971), p. 120.

An example of economic integration: the oil pipeline from Alaska to Washington State runs over Canadian territory, and had to be planned in conjunction with Canada's interests.

"The pipeline debate? . . . Oh . . . going fine, Mr. President . . . Having a little problem with the routing?"

Source: Donato © *Toronto Sun*/Rothco

nomic interdependence, sociocultural similarity and UN voting behavior), for example, another scholar reviewed the history of conflict among forty-one pairs of states. He found that "all five of these conditions may be necessary to prevent war between states . . . , but not even all five together are sufficient to do so." The greater the interdependence among nations, the more sensitive their interests become, and the greater their prospects of conflict.[18] Unfortunately, the closest

18. Bruce M. Russett, *International Regions and the International System* (Chicago: Rand McNally, 1967), Chapter 12, "Conflicts and Integration," especially pages 198–201.

neighbors may have the largest number of chances to fight—and may do so despite their interdependence. Thus, the desire to resolve conflict is not invariably an adequate cause for integration. Even in such circumstances the duties, expectations and so on placed upon integrative processes may exceed the stabilizing capabilities of organization.

Even though Western Europe now exemplifies a high degree of integration, conflict has not disappeared. Raymond Aron, French political scientist, has warned that Europe is a place and an idea, but it is not a unity. Another European has written a Ten Commandments for the Nine, the first of which is, "*Do not confuse Europe with Uniformity*. Europe is not uniform and attempts to make it so will be rightly resented and resisted."[19]

Scholars have adopted the same tone. Noting that community is built upon a growing sense of cooperation, we are reminded:

> The members of the Community do not confront each other only or chiefly as diplomatic gladiators; they encounter each other at almost every level of organized society through constant interaction in the joint policymaking contexts of officials, parlimentarians, interest group leaders, businessmen, farmers, and trade unionists. Conflicts of interest and purpose are inevitable. *There is no paradox between the progress of economic integration in the Community and sharpening political disagreement;* indeed, the success of economic integration can be a cause of political disagreement. The member states are engaged in the enterprise for widely different reasons, and their actions have been supported or instigated by elites seeking their own particular goals. Therefore, conflicts would seem endemic as the results of joint activity come to be felt and as the pro-integration consensus shifts.[20]

Progress aside, integration is a dynamic process. Goals change, roles shift, new leaders and elites emerge, old influences wane and new ones burst onto the scene. Integration may thus proceed in a regional system of constant conflict. Indeed, since progress toward supranationalism creates stresses of its own, the process may have negative effects upon the overall relations of members. Reason dictates that while the resolution of regional conflicts may be one of the expectations of integrating members, the very process itself may be the cause of strife.[21]

19. John Pinder, "Ten Commandments for 'The Nine,'" *European Community* 161, December 1972, pp. 18–19.
20. Leon N. Lindberg, "Decision Making and Integration in the European Community," *International Organization* 19, 1965, p. 80. The emphasis has been added.
21. Leon N. Lindberg, "Integration as a Source of Stress on the European Community System," *International Organization* 20, 1966, pp. 233–65.

4. Background Conditions for Integration

Alone, common expectations about regional future are not sufficient to promote integration. Certain preconditions must be satisfied, though subconsciously for the most part.

Social Assimilation

To some observers, the foremost precondition of regional integration is social causation, resulting in so-called sociocausal paradigm of integration.[22] Focusing upon transnational attitudes, this posits that social assimilation is a precondition of integration. Critics of this concept reject the assumed necessity of social assimilation. Nevertheless, most observers agree that minimal social prerequisites do exist, and that among them are mutual tolerance of cultures, common identity of foreign policy goals and generally cordial contacts of governments and respective nationals.

Value Sharing

A second precondition is value sharing, especially among elites. In the economic sector, for example, unless the elites of participating states share common values, such as capitalism or socialism, or free market as contrasted with central controls and subsidies, they will expend little energy toward integration, and little pressure will be exerted upon governments. Again, this is a sociopolitical condition.

Mutual Benefit

Expectation of mutual benefit is the third precondition. Since states will enter into a process that fundamentally alters national prerogatives only with sufficient incentives, states must be able to predict that benefits will accrue from the process. Some states may expect to profit in one sector, while others seek advancement in another. Remember,

22. See particularly the classic study by Karl Deutsch, et al., *Political Community and the North Atlantic Area* (Princeton, NJ: Princeton University Press, 1957). See also Deutsch's several contributions to Philip E. Jacob and James V. Tascano, editors, *The Integration of Political Communities* (Philadelphia: Lippincott, 1964), including "Communication Theory and Political Integration," "Transaction Flows as Indicators of Political Cohesion," and "Integration and the Social System: Implications of Functional Analysis." For an evaluation and critique of the sociocausal paradigm, see William E. Fisher, "An Analysis of the Deutsch Sociocausal Paradigm of Political Integration," *International Organization* 23, 1969, pp. 254–90.

however, that the integrative process involves not only international politics, but intense domestic bargaining as well.[23] While a government may be willing to sacrifice major industrial gains to achieve agricultural integration, the industrial elites may resist. Thus, their expectation of benefit is just as important as aggregate national expectations.[24]

Congenial Past Relations

A fourth precondition is experiential: a history of frequent pacific transactions. This acknowledges the functionalist precept that nothing succeeds like success itself; and it posits that elites, nations and governments are unlikely to integrate without already operating cordiality.

Importance of Integration Itself

Closely related to congenial past relations is the fifth criterion—the salience of transactions. If interests are remotely related, integration is unlikely; but if participants recognize the importance of activities in other countries, impetus for integration may awaken. The prospects for integration in these cases are governed by "the law of inverse salience," which holds that the growth of integration is inversely related to the political importance of the subject matter. Another functionalist proposition, this argues that since integration proceeds only with prior progress, it is seen first in matters that are politically expendable. Only through feedbacks and spillovers does the process begin to invade politically sensitive areas.[25]

Low Relative Costs

Since there are bound to be costs as well as benefits, another precondition must be the anticipation of low costs relative to benefits, mea-

23. Stuart R. Scheingold, "Domestic and International Consequences of Regional Integration," *International Organization* 24, 1970, pp. 978–1002; and Robert J. Lieber, "Interest Groups and Political Integration: British Entry into Europe," *American Political Science Review* 66, 1972, pp. 53–67.
24. Karl W. Deutsch has been in the forefront of scholarship investigating the impact of elites. For major studies see particularly these of his works: "Integration and Arms Control in the European Political Environment: A Summary Report," *American Political Science Review* 60, 1966, pp. 354–65; *Arms Control and the Atlantic Alliance* (New York: Wiley, 1967); and with coauthors, *France, Germany and the Western Alliance: A Study of Elite Attitudes on European Integration and World Politics* (New York: Scribners, 1967). Also see Robert Weissberg, "Nationalism, Integration, and French and German Elites," *International Organization* 23, 1969, pp. 337–47.
25. Nye, *Peace in Parts*, pp. 23–24.

sured economically, socially or nationalistically.[26] Likewise, while such costs will probably be assessed principally in domestic policy, a prospective participant may wish to predict the effects upon other foreign policies, or upon other regions. Britain's delayed entry into Europe resulted partly from the potential affect on the British agricultural sector, on its relations with members of the British Commonwealth and on its special relationship with the United States.

External Influences

The last issue raises what generally has been an underestimated precondition of integration: external influences. Virtually every integration movement can be attributed in part to external stimuli. In Western Europe, for example, painstaking progress toward strategic (military) integration would not have occurred without a threat of war from the East; and with the waning of the Cold War that movement might have stopped by now, had it not been for the interest in Europe's own nuclear deterrent that American dominance of NATO has generated. The European members of NATO have undergone two generations of thought about their security problems since the Second World War, one conditioned by external threats posed by the Soviet Union, and a second by US policy.[27]

Economic integration, too, may have external stimuli. The threat of American domination of European economies after the Marshall Plan was completed unquestionably increased the demand for economic consolidation. Also, the desire to coordinate trade policy with respect to the US contributed to the establishment of the Central American Common Market and the Latin American Free Trade Association. External conditions may even have spillover effects.[28] For example, while French military policies during the 1950s in Algeria

26. For a systematic study of costs and benefits in supranationalism, whether or not in regional settings, see Todd Sandler and Jon Cauley, "The Design of Supranational Structures: An Economic Perspective," in *International Studies Quarterly,* June 1977, pp. 251–76.
27. David Owen, *The Politics of Defense* (New York: Taplinger, 1972) and François Duchene, "A New European Defense Community," *Foreign Affairs* 50, October 1971, pp. 69–82. Both writers are European. See also Chapter 3 of this book.
28. Literature on external preconditions to integration is not abundant. For a seminal inquiry, see Karl Kaiser, "The Interaction of Regional Subsystems: Some Preliminary Notes on Recurrent Patterns and the Role of the Superpowers," *World Politics* 21, 1968/69, pp. 84–107. For a comprehensive study of the interactions between Washington and the European capitals that resulted in integration movements, see Ernst H. van der Beugel, *From Marshall Plan to Atlantic Partnership* (New York: Elsevier, 1966).

and Indochina may have contributed to the French defeat of the European Defense Community (EDC), they also helped to change the older notion of forceful maintenance of an overseas empire and inspired new demands that the de Gaulle government turn French national resources and energies inward to Europe.[29]

5. Maintaining the Momentum of Integration

Starting along the integrative path and maintaining continued progress toward the goal of supranationalism are quite separate issues. In addition to certain preconditions that permit the process to begin, certain combinations of "process factors" must be present to govern steady progress.

Functional Satisfaction

First among these process factors is *functional satisfaction,* that is, recognition by pertinent elites and officials of the degree to which integrated policy is serving their interests. This recognition promotes feedback, thus fueling greater sectoral integration and encouraging spillover.

Public opinion polls taken at irregular intervals during the Western European integrating experience reveal a steady faith in the process. Even during the years following the first OPEC petroleum boycott, when the Western industrial states suffered declining productivity and inclining inflation and unemployment, functional satisfaction continued to be high in the participating countries. Though there were some irregularities in the late 1970s, satisfaction with functional performance was directly correlated with national economic condition and

29. This outline of preconditions of integration is intended not as construction of a new model, but as an eclectic review drawing upon prior studies. Among those works which have been drawn upon, the most important are Haas, *The Uniting of Europe: Political, Social and Economic Forces, 1950–57,* a classic study on the subject of regional integration; Amitai Etzioni, *Political Unification* (New York: Holt, Rinehart and Winston, 1965); Ernst B. Haas and Philippe C. Schmitter, "Economics and Differential Patterns of Political Integration: Projections about Unity in Latin America," *International Organization* 18, 1964, pp. 705–37; Bruce Russett, *International Regions and the International System;* Philippe C. Schmitter, "A Revised Theory of Regional Integration," *International Organization* 24, 1970, pp. 836–68; Joseph S. Nye, "Patterns and Catalysts in Regional Integration," *International Organization* 19, 1965, pp. 870–84.

with the duration of membership in the EC. Satisfaction was lower in the newest three members—Britain, Ireland and Denmark, which joined in 1973—but these were also the member states that suffered the worst inflation during this troubled period.[30]

Increased Pacific Transactions

A second process factor is an increased frequency of pacific transactions. The rate and number of transactions are measures of mutual reliance, revealing governmental willingness to compromise sovereignty in specific sectors. Since increasing interdependence is indispensable, the rate of transactions is a critical measure of progress. One study, however, has cautioned against overvaluing transactions as a causal factor in the growth of integration; increased transactions are more a reflection of integration than a cause.[31] Yet it is probable that satisfaction in these contacts, originally an effect of integration, now encourages additional contacts, and is thus a major determinant of sectoral feedback.

Regulation

Gradually, the transactions of integrating sectors must become institutionalized. Informal regulation cannot continuously serve the objective of formal integration. A third major process condition is the proliferation of institutions with sufficient authority to regulate. Ultimately, these institutions must assume the national governments' normal legislative and executive prerogatives. Complete transfer of such authority from national governments to common institutions is the final stage of the integrating process; and with its completion a supranational community may be said to exist. At present, the maximum progress toward complete integration of a subsector is represented in the High Authority of the European Coal and Steel Community (ECSC), which has been authorized by its members to exercise sovereign authority over the allocation of the pertinent resources.

The achievement of full multisectoral supranationalism requires establishment of sufficient institutional machinery to govern the com-

30. Ronald Inglehart and Jacques-René Rabier, "Economic Uncertainty and European Solidarity: Public Opinion Trends," *The Annals* of the Academy of Political and Social Science, November 1979, pp. 66–79.
31. Donald J. Puchala, "International Transactions and Regional Integration," *International Organization* 24, 1970, pp. 732–63.

munity. This means development of legislative, executive and judicial institutions, each vested with full authority in its realm. At present, one of the most interesting developments in Western Europe is the drive, inspired principally by Great Britain, to wrest legislative control from the Council of Ministers of the European Communities and to invest full legislative authority in the European Parliament. Advocates of the ultimate federation of Europe hope that eventually this body will be a true multinational legislature.

Bureaucracy

The institutionalization of a political process requires the creation of a bureaucracy, specially trained to manage sectoral activities. Since a high degree of technical competence is needed in addition to administrative skills, these bureaucracies are customarily referred to as technocracies. Technocrats, not only manage the day-to-day affairs, they must also coordinate the expectations of elites, soothe the sensitivities of governments and make the unremitting case for further development. They are at once technical experts, intergovernmental managers and the guardians of the integrative process.

Bureaucratic development in a community that is both multinational and multilingual is far from automatic. From the start, the integrating European states have established national formulas and quotas for employment in several of the important organs of community. While these were designed for equity and balance, they have had some divisive consequences. The tensions of multinational staffing have accentuated the contrast of national loyalties to community loyalty. In addition, it has been shown that nation-based informal organizations of staff members develop spontaneously, and the tensions among these groups have significant impacts upon community work.[32] Moreover, such organizations may serve as vehicles for special interest groups in the decision making of the community.[33]

Community Jurisprudence

Another, though less visible, process condition is the development of a community jurisprudence, a commonly recognized body of law that

32. Hans J. Michelmann, "Multinational Staffing and Organizational Functioning in the Commission of the European Communities," *International Organization,* Spring 1978, pp. 477–96.
33. Juliet Lodge and Valentine Herman, "The Economic and Social Committee in EEC Decision Making," *International Organization,* Spring 1980, pp. 265–84, deals generally with the role of interest groups in functional integration.

governs legal relations of the respective states. If governments or corporations of different states become involved in legal problems, it is not productive in an integrating community to rely upon the judicial practices of one state or another. Furthermore, if a community institution and a state have a legal disagreement, the development of a body of law and of community courts is eventually necessary in the development of supranational politics. The Court of Justice of the European Communities serves this need, and has already developed a large body of case law governing the relations of the communities, the member states and individual technocrats.

The evolution of a community legal system that supersedes the legal systems of the member countries is fraught with collisions of nationalism and the political primacy of the state. After all, the goal of integration is to subordinate many of the state's traditional functions and prerogatives to a higher political community, but the complex conditions of this evolution ensure that there will be setbacks, periods of little progress and occasional conflicts between state interests and community goals.

In the area of jurisprudence the potential for strife between state and community is particularly acute, especially when basic constitutional premises are at stake. Though the primacy of community jurisprudence was firmly established as early as 1963, a decision of the Court of Justice of the European Communities in 1978 provoked a sharp constitutional debate in Britain, which at the time had belonged to the European Community for only five years. In the *Simmentha* case, the Court declared that "every national court must, in a case within its jurisdiction, apply Community law in its entirety and protect rights which the latter confers on individuals and must accordingly set aside any provision of national law which may conflict with it, whether prior or subsequent to the Community rule." Such a prescription boldly subordinates all acts of Parliament, those that occurred before entry into the Community as well as those that secceeded entry, to the law of the European Community. Membership had, indeed, had a deep impact upon Britain, whose tradition of common law is centuries old.[34] However, all member states are affected by ascendency of Community law. One study uses the case law of the Court of Justice of the European Communities to demonstrate the extent to which the Commission of the Communities and the Advocates General for the

34. J. D. B. Mitchell, "The Sovereignty of Parliament and Community Law: The Stumbling Block That Isn't There," *International Affairs* (London), January 1979.

Communities have expanded the Court's power on matters of direct application of Community law, on supremacy of Community law over national members' law, and even on treaty making.[35]

Increased Decisions

Increased transactions, formation of institutions and technocracies, and the establishment of a common core of jurisprudence all point to the next process condition: increased decisional output. It cannot be said that integration is under way merely because of institutional appearances; rather, measurable and reliable decisions, upon which governments and pertinent elites willingly depend and with which they comply consistently, are indispensable. Institutions can have no productive effect upon national elites unless they are able to command the external transactions of those elites. Only through actual decisions does the institution become the authoritative vehicle of an international process.

Mass Attitudes

All of the foregoing process factors imply increased relations and communications among elites. But the process of integration requires that mass political and social attitudes also be nurtured. Thus, a seventh important process factor is the development of mutual mass attitudes. Though progress toward integration may build upon elite pressures, governments are not likely to sacrifice national prerogatives or to respond to narrow demands for supranationality until appropriate attitudes have been established among their electorates. This development must take place in most or all of the participating nations. In this way, mutual expectations are regularly communicated across national boundaries, the benefits of continued progress become more familiar to individuals and nationalistic attitudes begin to recede.[36] British entry into the Community was paradoxical in this regard, since polls showed in 1973 that the population did *not* favor membership. It was thus expected that while Britain's membership might eventually accelerate integration, there would be a time lag during which British

35. Eric Stein, "Lawyers, Judges and the Making of a Transnational Constitution," *American Journal of International Law,* January 1983, pp. 1–27.
36. A pioneering effort to measure the impact on the individual reward structure of internationalization of business enterprise in Europe (specifically Germany) is found in Bernard Menns and Karl P. Sauvant, "Describing and Explaining Support for Regional Integrations: An Investigation of German Business Elite Attitudes toward the European Community," *International Organization* 29, 1975, pp. 972–95.

elite and popular attitudes would need to catch up with those on the continent.[37] In fact, it was not until 1975 that a British referendum demonstrated decisively the public desire for full membership in the European Community.

External Factors

External factors of either of two types may influence the integrative process. First, they may be external events that absorb the energies of one of the participants in community. These events may prevent full and earnest participation or in some cases accentuate regional preferences. French foreign policy provides examples of both phenomena. Before the Gaullist era, French participation in European integration was impeded by preoccupation with problems in North Africa and Indochina. But for a decade commencing in the mid-1950s, President de Gaulle turned these problems around and directed energies inward. Those years witnessed the most vigorous steps toward European supranationalism. Thus, integration may depend on external events in which one of the community members is vitally engaged. These are member-centered external events.

Other external events are not member centered, but may nevertheless have major impacts upon the integrative process. The foreign policies (potentially even domestic policies) of other nations may touch upon one or more of the members of a growing community with either integrative or disintegrative effects. The unpopularity among Europeans of American policy in Southeast Asia during the 1960s heightened the sense of Europeanness and correspondingly diminished the psychological bonds with Washington. Except in the security sector (NATO), then, the Vietnam War (as a non–member-centered external factor) had integrative effects upon Europe. Warsaw Pact occupation of Czechoslovakia in 1968, a resort to long invisible Soviet politics, was an event of similar meaning to Western Europe. Conversely, the Soviet-inspired imposition of martial law on Poland in response to the liberal demands of the Solidarity Labor Union (which resulted in a 1983 Nobel Prize for Peace for the movement's leader, Lech Walesa), had little integrating impact upon Western Europe. Indeed, these events unfolded even while a new peace movement resisted the deployment in Western Europe of new American nuclear-tipped missiles.

37. For a study of mass opinion as well as elite opinion with respect to European integrative progress, see Donald J. Puchala, "The Common Market and Political Federation in Western European Public Opinion," *International Studies Quarterly* 14, 1970, pp. 32–59.

A most instructive non–member-centered external event occurred in 1962, with telling effect upon European economic integration. Already concerned about future competition from Europe, American merchants sought long-term relief from tariff barriers. As a result, the Kennedy Administration sought and secured from Congress discretionary authority to negotiate substantial reciprocal tariff reductions. The Trade Expansion Act of 1962 authorized executive discretion for a period of five years, during which major changes in American trade policy might be negotiated.

The EEC members entered into the subsequent negotiations, called the Kennedy Round, with full awareness of the American intent to safeguard industrial exports against future competition. This awareness sparked renewed activity in the EEC toward eliminating internal restraints to trade, and resulted particularly in resolution of many of the thorny agricultural problems that had previously retarded progress toward a full free trade arrangement.

These negotiations, together with American direct investment in Europe designed to "get behind" the tariff barriers, comprised a clear signal to EEC members that major industrial competitors feared the successful culmination of the free trade area, and provided added incentives for conscious development. Resentment over this form of exploitation also sparked European attacks upon the American balance-of-payments deficit, accentuated European criticism of American policy in Vietnam, gave credence to President de Gaulle's efforts to "de-Americanize Europe," and generally raised the level of Europe-consciousness. These were significant social and political spillovers.

Transfer of Loyalty

The final process condition is really the measure of all of the others: the transfer of loyalty gradually from national to community values, objectives and institutions. It means the adoption by national majorities of far-reaching supranationalist attitudes. As this itself is a functional requisite, such a development does not occur except through individual recognition of the profitability of integration. Nor will it occur in several nations unless there is sufficient communication by which societies can measure attitudinal progress in neighboring lands. Social communication is thus vital to the transfer of loyalties.[38]

38. For a study of the impact of international events upon the loyalty problem, see John Herz, *International Politics in the Atomic Age* (New York: Columbia University Press, 1959). The foremost study of communications in nationalist and supranationalist attitudes is Karl W. Deutsch, *Nationalism and Social Communication* (Cambridge, Mass.: MIT Press, 1953).

The loyalty-transfer process is one of continuing socialization in which positive value communication substantiates the need for community-oriented attitudes. Several studies have concluded that Europeans look less and less to national governments for critical decisions and increasingly to community institutions. Socialization data point almost incontrovertibly to further integration in economic, social and political sectors in Western Europe.[39] Public opinion polls in 1962, for example, showed overwhelming preference for unification and widespread expectation that it would occur within ten or fifteen years. Furthermore, responses to questions pertaining to internal matters of the European Communities showed huge favorability of integrated policy.[40] More recently, a survey of French attitudes has been conducted (within three weeks of British entry in 1973). On questions of direct election of the European Parliament, the evolution of a formal community government and community supremacy in such critical areas as defense, diplomacy, economics, and nuclear and space development, the number of respondents who preferred community-oriented solutions consistently exceeded those who favored state-oriented policy though approximately one-third of respondents gave no opinion.[41] Repeatedly, therefore, socialization data have underscored public preference for, and acceptance of, regional integration to the extent of spillover from the economic to the political sector.[42]

Although it has become a common accusation that the European Community has become stagnant (by economic recession, high unemployment, slowed progress toward political union), the more recent public opinion surveys show optimism about the future of union. Generally, however, the support and optimism reflect uneven national attitudes. Rather consistently, Italy, Luxembourg, Germany and France record a strong preference for integration, for mutual assistance

39. Leon N. Lindberg and Stuart A. Scheingold, *Europe's Would-Be Polity: Patterns of Change in the European Community* (Englewood Cliffs, NJ: Prentice-Hall, 1970), especially chapters 8 and 9; Carl J. Friedrich, *Europe: An Emergent Nation?* (New York: Harper and Row, 1969); Deutsch et al., "Integration and Arms Control in the European Political Environment," *American Political Science Review* 60, 1966, p. 355.
40. *Communauté Européenne,* December 1962. For well-organized reproduced data, see W. Hartley Clark, *The Politics of the Common Market* (Englewood Cliffs, NJ: Prentice-Hall, 1967), pp. 111–13.
41. *Le Figaro,* February 27, 1973, as reproduced in Ernest H. Preeg, *Economic Blocs and U. S. Foreign Policy* (Washington: National Planning Association, 1974), p. 109.
42. For summary socialization data pertaining to transfer of loyalties, see particularly Ronald Inglehart, "An End to European Integration?" *American Political Science Review* 61, 1967, pp. 91–105. The paper is framed as a response to the article by Deutsch et al., also Donald Puchala, "The Common Market and Political Federation in Western European Public Opinion"; and Inglehart and Rabier, "Economic Uncertainty and European Solidarity."

and for transfer of loyalty, while Denmark, Britain and Ireland show less than majority preference. Dutch voters show marginal optimism.[43] Despite these differences, however, it is apparent from public opinion inquiries that Western Europeans have not abandoned the goal of integration, and that even the economic dislocations from 1978 to 1985 had not dampened their enthusiasm for substituting supranational loyalties for the traditional national ties.[44] The admittance of Greece in 1981, while evidencing expanded interest in common economic progress, should not be confused with enlarged expectation of political union.

With the conclusion of this discussion of sectors, objectives, preconditions and process conditions of integration, we are now ready to summarize the critical issues of the supranational quest. (See Table 16-1.)

TABLE 16–1
Summary of integration factors.

Integration Sectors	*Momentum*	*Objectives*	*Preconditions*	*Process Conditions*
Economic Social Political Security	Feedback (intrasector) Spillover (intersector)	Maximize economic potential Maximize political potential Regional conflict resolution	Social assimilation Elite value sharing Expectation of mutual benefits History of pacific transactions Favorable ratio of costs to benefits External influences a. member-centered b. not member-centered	Functional satisfaction Increased frequency of transactions Institution-building Technocracy-building Community jurisprudence Growing decisional output Mass attitude assimilation External factors a. member-centered b. not member-centered Transfer of loyalty

43. Ronald Inglehart, *The Silent Revolution: Changing Values and Political Styles Among Western Publics* (Princeton, NJ: Princeton University Press, 1977), especially Chapter 12, "Parochialism, Nationalism, and Supranationalism," in which the author explores the history of public opinion surveys on the subject.
44. For a comprehensive summary of European progress toward integration, see Phillip Taylor, *When Europe Speaks with One Voice* (London: Greenwood, 1979).

Before turning to an evaluation of integration, a few theoretical notes are necessary. Earlier in this chapter it was noted that the integration of Western Europe has generated the greatest interest and the richest literature among the fifteen supranational movements in the nonsocialist world, with the result that virtually all of the foregoing presentation concentrated on the European Community. The apparent implication is that the Western European model is reproducible elsewhere, and that to understand the integrative trends of Western Europe is to understand similar phenomena in other parts of the world.

Studies of integration in the Third World suggest, on the contrary, that the Western European model does not have universal application due to the fundamentally different political economies of Western Europe and of the developing world. While Europe has its own technological and industrial bases, integrating economies in the Third World are dependent economies, dependent for growth and development upon the spread of technology from elsewhere, as well as upon foreign capital and aid. As has been demonstrated earlier in this book, these circumstances produce political strains between integrating developing economies, on the one hand, and the industrialized economies which control the flow of capital and technology, on the other, and limit the capacity for political and economic independence of the former. Thus, integration without dependence calls for extraordinary political cooperation among the participating states. The process must begin with political cooperation among transnational coalitions which, together, are able both to promote the integrative objectives and to overcome the sources of dependence. The patterns of underlying political cooperation in the Third World thus differ from those in Western Europe, where spillover from the economic sector to the political sector has been the norm. Hence it may be that the nature of integration in the developing world undermines the assumption of political spillover in the neofunctional model, as demonstrated in the experience of Western Europe.[45]

Furthermore, the theory of functional integration as applied to Western Europe may no longer be viable. Ironically, the scholar who first postulated the theory for the European Communities has called into question the adequacy of the theory given the profound global political changes of the past decade. It may now be that integration theory must be thought of as subsidiary to interdependence theory.[46]

45. W. Andrew Axline, "Underdevelopment, Dependence, and Integration: The Politics of Regionalism in the Third World," *International Organization*, Winter 1977, pp. 83–105.

46. Ernst B. Haas, *The Obsolescence of Regional Integration Theory*, Research Series No. 25 (Berkeley: University of California, 1975). See also the detailed review of the Haas study by Henry R. Nau, "From Integration to Interdependence: Gains, Losses and Continuing Gaps," in *International Organization*, Winter 1979, pp. 119–47.

Several reasons are advanced for this hypothesis. According to this new view, the current objectives of the European Community are not consistent with the original goals. The emphasis has passed from the concept of a customs union designed to improve the combined industrial capacities of the members to one that focuses upon the distribution system in the nonindustrial areas, particularly agriculture. Furthermore, the theory addresses only growth questions, and is not competent to deal with questions concerning quality of life, environmental impacts in a multinational setting and other important societal issues that are not directly economic in character. Finally, the growth of supranational institutions has slowed drastically, principally because of changed national motives and improved administrative skills at the national level.

External factors may also call into question the adequacy of the theory. Among them is the power of OPEC to influence the industrial productivity of the Community members. This and factors of comparable importance raise the necessity of a regional foreign policy that calls for interdependence beyond the geographical boundaries of the Community. Moreover, the Community members are beginning to appreciate more than at any other time during the period of their integrative activity the benefits of economic relations with economies that are not part of their geographic region and which, therefore, cannot contribute to the efficiency of solving problems within the territory. The Yaoundé and Lomé Conventions extended the tentacles of the European Community virtually worldwide, yet without regional integrative benefits. And while the admittance of Britain, Ireland and Denmark in 1973 extended the contiguous boundaries of the Community, the "Mediterranean Phase" of membership enlargement—consisting of admittance of Greece in 1981 and the still pending admittance of Spain and Portugal—will not do the same. Hence the enlargement of membership by these means will not necessarily increase the Community's integrative capacity, and may actually diminish it.[47]

An Evaluation of Integration

This examination of integration assumes that supranationalism is healthy and that it is to be encouraged and lauded. But if integration occurs, its impact upon people and upon international order is worth exploring.

47. William Wallace and I. Herreman, editors, *A Community of Twelve?: The Impact of Further Enlargement of the European Communities* (Bruges: De Tempel, 1978).

First consider the effects of integration upon the population of an integrated community. Although it is conventionally assumed that these persons will, for the most part, profit from integration, some observers raise negative aspects. Integration may very well raise standards of living, indices of production and so on, but what will life be like? Does supranationalism necessarily make the individual's life more pleasant?

Although these questions remain unanswerable, perhaps skepticism is appropriate. The consolidation of economies and politics does, to be sure, have the effect of eliminating competition and some differences among participants, but it creates a new form of political community. Is this new form merely an enlarged nation-state? Is there anything fundamentally different between an integrated community and a large nation-state that is multilingual and culturally and socially heterogeneous?

These are not merely abstract questions. In their concerns with mass anxiety, crises of identity, breakup of the nuclear family, lack of pride in work and the generation gap, social observers today have begun to explore the social and psychological consequences of mass industrialization. They have turned their attention to whether there are ill effects from the philosophy of the modern industrial state: "There's more of it where that came from!" Does integration for purposes of successful international economic competition rush a society blindly toward these effects? Does it hasten the alienation of men and women from the politics, institutions and lip-service ideals of mass society?

Another concern is with the antidemocratic effects of centralization and bureaucratization. As policy becomes less the result of public participation and more a consequence of administrative pragmatism, does a society relinquish to functional technocracies its grip on its own destiny? What is the likelihood that increased reliance on technocracy will degenerate into new forms of oligarchy? Are there major divergences between the values, needs and expectations of technocrats, on the one hand, and those of society on the other? What is the future of the political role of nonelite social sectors?

These and other quality-of-life questions have led to a call for a normative critique of integration theory and for research into the social consequences of regional supranationalism. To be socially tolerable in the long run, life in supranational communities must be preferable and superior to life in contemporary nation-states. Otherwise, the achievement of higher political community may be merely a new organizational stage in the destruction of societies.[48]

48. These questions have been broached in a most incisive manner in John W. Sloan and Harry R. Targ, "Beyond the European Nation-State: A Normative Critique," *Polity* 3, Summer 1971, pp. 501–20.

The view from outside raises equally troubling questions. Even if one accepts the intragroup benefits of integration, what are the effects upon intergroup relations? Do the consolidated policies of like-minded states necessarily contribute to international order, or do they merely accentuate the effects of the nation-state? What are the prospects that European economic integration will lead to trade warfare even with the United States if European production and trade volumes should have long-term detrimental effects upon the American economy, its exports and its balance of payments? Perhaps we have already been introduced to this possibility in Washington's unilateral policies of 1971 and 1972, when unilateral increases in tariff were attached to imports from all industrial countries, and the United States forced reconsideration of the international monetary system. If regional integration tends to have associating characteristics among its members, its external policy may have a disassociating effect on overall international stability.

The potential for global disassociation is especially apparent in security communities, which exist as the result of previously identified enemies. Because the enmities exist before the security arrangements, disassociation is a product of earlier political relations. Yet like all other institutions in society, security institutions tend to become self-sustaining. The elites that manage them continue to have interests, and their operations may depend upon perpetuating the initial causes. In security communities, the original cause is threat; and the perpetuation of security institutions may thus depend upon the ability to convince publics and appropriating agencies of the persistence of potential crisis. Should this occur—if persons propagandize and even romanticize crisis potential for institutional or personal aggrandizement—then institutions may prolong crises, contributing to the disassociating effects of the original antipathy. Institutionalized alliances always carry this danger; and since integrated institutions magnify the political potential of elites, supranational security communities may impede global stability.

There may also be a dangerous aspect to the connection between supranational institutions and domestic institutions. Since successful integrative trends require close cooperation between regional technocrats and domestic leaders, they may learn to use one another for personal purposes. Thus the command officers of an integrated military community may gain inordinate access to legislative politics, to the great detriment of domestic policy. Strong and semisecretive national-regional competition among interacting elites may hasten the erosion of beneficial aspects of national life.

Despite the dangers implicit in integration from both domestic and international perspectives, at present the prevailing attitude is that regional integrative trends are healthy, productive and promising of a brighter future for national peoples and for global stability. Indeed, one French student of EC affairs has gone so far as to write that "Europe as a whole could well become the first example in history of a major centre of the balance of power becoming in the era of its decline not a colonised victim but the exemplar of a new stage in political civilisation."[49] But two others have entered an incisive condition: "the Community's capacity to act constructively in the world depends in the last resort on its success in establishing within its boundaries a more united and more just society."[50] It is safe to conclude that integration over any geographical region will encounter a similar variety of pressures.

The American Perception of Integration

Having maximized its own political, social and economic potentialities through federative integration and having undergone a bloody civil war to preserve union, it is natural for the United States to favor integration. Indeed, at the close of the Second World War the United States not only encouraged but also paid about $15 billion to reconstruct Europe through the Marshall Plan (European Recovery Program). From the start the United States assumed that the Western European participants would plan together a forerunner to the economic integration that the United States intended to encourage. Taking cues from Winston Churchill, Jean Monnet and others, Americans such as Secretary of State George C. Marshall, William L. Clayton and Christian Herter joined from this side of the Atlantic in constructing the foundations for a United States of Europe.

The dramatic recovery of Western Europe depended in large measure on America's assistance and willingness to undergo a decade or more of disadvantageous trade principles so that Europe might speed its reconstruction. Although the principles of the international monetary system and of free world trade were dictated principally by the United States, they benefited Western Europe even more. They opened wide American markets to European produce; and they protected the infant European industries from American competition. Now that the EEC has matured, time has come to restructure the system, for the United

49. François Duchêne, "The European Community and the Uncertainties of Interdependence," in Max Kohnstamm and Wolfgang Hager, editors, *A Nation Writ Large? Foreign Policy Problems Before the European Community* (New York: Wiley, 1973), pp. 1–21.
50. Kohnstamm and Hager, "Conclusion" to *A Nation Writ Large?* pp. 256–64.

States ought no longer be asked to bear the burdens of trade and monetary disadvantages. For economic purposes, a USE (United States of Europe) now exists, and its competitive ability has surpassed the American concessions to its maturation. So that the EEC might not produce disassociating effects in the Western hemisphere, the rules of the road must be changed. Negotiations for the new codes of economic behavior between Europe and the Americas commenced at the close of 1971, precipitated largely by justified American insistence and partly by European responses to Washington's unilateral policies in the two preceding years.

Other than in Europe, the United States continues to encourage economic integration, though successful industrial competition that might alter American attitudes has not arisen from any other integrated region.

On the matter of political integration, the United States takes a somewhat dimmer view. Washington is ambivalent about political supranationalism, even in Europe, that would deprive Washington of the ability to negotiate with European capitals individually on certain matters, and would remove the traditional rite of playing one power against another. Preservation of the American role in the larger trans-Atlantic community thus dictates a cautious approach to European political integration.

The Perceptions of America's Major Allies

As the world's prime promoters of integration, the attitude of America's Western European allies is in the record of their experience. But what of Japan and Canada?

The Japanese view is not entirely clear, though logic would seem to predict a negative attitude. In the first place, just as the United States had retaliated against Japanese economic success, so too has it retaliated against the resurgence of Europe. Since the target of such actions is rarely specified, any Western-oriented industrial producer is likely to feel the brunt of American protection. Second, Japan's exports are industrial and Europe is a large industrial market. The efficiency of European industry, together with the common barriers to trade raised against external competitors, reduces the probable sales of Japanese goods in Western Europe. And third, because of Japan's huge balance-of-payments deficit to the oil-producing states, it desperately needs to compile surpluses by its industrial trade to places like Europe. Though it cannot be said the Japan is hostile to European integration, it appears that integrative success is detrimental to the distribution of Japan's industrial exports.

In its own region of the world, Japan is actively promoting development through both public assistance (largely through the Asian Development Bank) and private capital flows, but its interest is not now in integration. Instead, Japan is attempting to construct industrial markets, particularly in places rich in natural resources.

Canada's view of integration is typically restrained. Itself a federal state, integrative experience is understood by custom. Yet the British entry into the European Community placed economic strains on Canada which, as a member of the British Commonwealth, had previously enjoyed a free-trade relationship with Britain and had particularly profited as an agricultural supplier. British entry not only removed those advantages, but presented the added strain of making industrial trade more difficult at precisely the point when Canada was undergoing a major phase of industrial development. Even in 1973 (the year of British entry), Canada's balance-of-trade surplus with respect to Britain continued to rise. Since Canada suffers a substantial deficit with respect to the world at large, it is probable that the European Community will eventually present costly barriers to Canada's industrial trade.

The Soviet Perception of Integration

The forced integration of the Soviet regions in the civil war that followed the Bolshevik Revolution, succeeded by years of intense "Russification" of the non-Russian peoples of the Soviet Union, speaks vividly for the Soviet tendency to favor integration, at least among its friends and allies. Post-Second World War incorporation of Eastern Europe in a related economic supranationalism directed from Moscow, as capital of the Socialist commonwealth, accentuates this view. But as for integration in the West, the Kremlin's view is mixed, and has changed with progression from the Cold War to the era of peaceful coexistence and back to Cold War.

Initially, the Soviet Union saw American interest in the integration of Europe not as a move toward economic stabilization, but as part of the effort to subject the Soviet Union and Eastern Europe to capitalist encirclement. In the wake of the Second World War and the division of Europe, the United States sought to isolate the East politically and economically by strengthening Western Europe as a huge economic colony and political puppet of American interests. In a view increasingly shared by Western Europeans, the Soviets see American economic restoration of Europe as a way not to create international trade or capitalist competition, but to extend the American economy overseas. And in a view increasingly shared by American revisionist historians, the Kremlin sees economic restoration principally as a step toward preventing the kinds of economic and social conditions that might have made Marxism an attractive doctrine to Western Europeans. American motives were, therefore, either imperialistic or ideological, or perhaps both.

Comparisons between the integration of Western Europe and that of Eastern Europe are fraught with hazard and risk. While in the European Community the ultimate objective is supranationalism, which benefits all of the participating national peoples equally, the central principal of Eastern European integration is that it advances the socialist commonwealth, of which the Soviet Union is the unquestioned political and economic leader. As a result, the distribution system is not fully interdependent and is not operated by equal participation of all the Eastern European governments. Instead, the system is justifiably tilted to the Soviet Union, the industrialization of which carries the burden of defending the socialist commonwealth against capitalist encirclement, imperialism and aggression. The embarrassment of 1980, during which the Polish government was compelled to recognize the legitimacy of independent (non-state-controlled) labor unions, in Marxist terms a victory of the proletariat, but in Leninist terms an unjustifiable repudiation of the Communist party as the vanguard of the proletariat, was but a temporary interbloc disturbance. Yet the Western support of the workers' strikes, especially through the International Mineworkers, resulted in a brief deterioration of East-West trade relations, particularly in Europe.

Apart from these periods of internal crisis, however, the Kremlin and its allies have derived benefits from Western European integration. The combined strength of the European Community countries weakens the world economic stature of the United States and, at the same time, diminishes the dependence of Western Europe upon the United States. These in turn facilitate trade between East and West Europe without involvement of American capital.

But to the Soviets, Western European integration has one characteristic that is especially important. The Kremlin is aware of the partial incompatibility of European integration, on the one hand, and security dependence upon the United States through NATO, on the other.[51] If integration is to proceed, Washington's domination of NATO must be minimized. The spinoff effects of integration upon the American security role in Europe are negative as viewed from Washington, but positive from the vantage point of the Kremlin.

51. Otto Pick, "Atlantic Defense and the Integration of Europe," *Atlantic Community Quarterly* 10, Summer 1972, pp. 174–84.

At present, therefore, the Soviet Union favors Western European integration because it tends to reduce the American role in Europe, principally in the security sector, but in the economic as well. If the aim of Soviet foreign policy is to divide the Western allies, then European progress that causes any division from the United States—particularly that reduces American dominance—is to be encouraged. Hence the fundamental paradox of the Soviet perception: while the Soviets use coerced integration to keep Soviet allies in line on political, economic and security matters, they expect voluntary integration in Western Europe to divide the Western alliance, reducing the United States as a European actor.

The Chinese Perception of Integration

As with most aspects of China's foreign policy, Peking's view of international integration is evolving rapidly. In the past, China has looked upon Western European successes principally as a means of reducing American economic hegemony, and thus as one means of ensuring against Soviet-American domination of the world. More recently, however, as China and the United States have normalized their relations and established numerous economic and even military ties, a strong American presence in Western Europe has meant both as-

International scientific cooperation: Chinese public health officials visit the Harvard School of Public Health, 1980.

Source: Wide World

surances against ambitious Soviet military policies in the east and guarantees of brisk economic competition among Atlantic allies.

Apart from containment of Soviet power and adventurism, pragmatic considerations govern the Chinese perception. Faced with the huge problem of industrializing rapidly, China's trading needs are large. And although Japan is a natural target for trade, a long history of Sino-Japanese antipathy, coupled with the humiliation of Japan's close relations with the United States during the years when the US isolated China, mitigate against full reliance on Japan. Industrial trade with Western Europe, as productive as Japan and as much in need of China's raw materials, is an available alternative. And, paradoxically, with the vacuum left by American withdrawal from Southeast Asia, China expects to benefit from any strong Western coalition that will divert the attention of the Soviet Union from the Asian theatre, even if pan-European stability enables the Soviets to station more divisions along the Chinese border.[52]

As to China's view of integration elsewhere, its policy is not yet clear. While integrated economies in Asia and the Pacific would both accelerate development and reduce foreign interference, such trends would rely heavily upon Japanese capital, goods and political superiority. This is unacceptable to China. Hence, while somewhat reticent on the subject, China for specific political reasons does not look favorably upon integration in its own geographic region.

The Third World Perception of Integration

Although there is considerable regional organizational activity in the Third World, progress toward integration is beset by a peculiar dilemma. The governments are confronted simultaneously by a need for rapid development and by the careful nurturing of nationalist spirits required by modernization. While integration of the economic sectors might increase the pace of modernization, the need for nationalism prevents such progress. In the older regions of Central and South America the dilemma has been bridged, with the resulting Central American Common Market, the Latin American Free Trade Association and the Andean Pact. But in the new independent areas, only the East African Common Market (EACM) has achieved much integrative progress. The merger of Tanganyika and Zanzibar into Tanzania has had little external effect, and the Arab states have not successfully integrated either politicaly or economically. While the Asian

52. See also Alain Bouc, "Peking Now Wants a United Europe," *Atlantic Community Quarterly* 10, Summer 1972, pp. 167–73. Briefly considered in Robert S. Elegant, "China, the U.S., and Soviet Expansionism," *Commentary* 61, 1976, pp. 39–46.

and Pacific Council (ASPAC) and the Association of Southeast Asia (ASA) may eventually embark upon supranational paths, they have made no measurable progress to date.

Yet Western Europe continues to be a focus of forward-looking Third World statesmen, both as a model of economic promise and as a symbol of the passing of bipolarity and of superpower imperialism. Virtually since the establishment of the European Community some Third World states, particularly the former colonial possessions of France, have enjoyed the status of associate members. This has always been a controversial status, for it required the less developed participants to offer tariff preferences to the European Community members in return for selling their exports at low tariff prices within the Community. More recently, through the Yaoundé and Lomé Conventions the European Community has tied itself economically to more than one hundred developing countries with trade preferences and concessions that advantage European trade with these nations in contrast to the trade of these nations with other industrialized economies.

There is one aspect of the European Community that is of undeniable benefit to the Third World. In recent years the members of the Community, acting in a coordinated but nonintegrated way, have become major providers of development funds. By 1970, the total foreign assistance offered by the Six exceeded the annual foreign aid budget of the United States for the first time. Generally, however, such lending is limited to associate members and to former colonial possessions of the members. Thus, it is enjoyed only selectively by the Third World.

Transnational Participation

Every structure of world order that we have thus far considered presumes as its central feature the nation-state, intergovernmental organization or the integration of states into higher political units. Sovereignty, power and official diplomacy lie at the heart of each of these systems. All of them are considered to be state-centric models of world order. Yet every traveler, every student of other cultures, every devotee of the creative arts and every businessman or businesswoman is aware that many transactions of the international system do not involve governments alone, and that much that happens across international boundaries is removed from sovereignty and intergovernmental negotiations. Despite the omnipresence of governments and official regulations, many international transactions occur on a people-to-people basis, or between one government and the corporations of another state. This process, referred to as transnational participation, has recently become the focus of new forms of research and observation in international relations.

Transnational interaction is defined as "the movement of tangible or intangible items across state boundaries when at least one actor is not an agent of a government or an intergovernmental organization."[53] It may involve contact between two or more nongovernmental actors, or between one official actor and one or more private actors. The nongovernmental participants may be corporations, social organizations, interest groups, political parties, elite structures or formally instituted organizations designed to facilitate private relations. An agreement between an oil company and a foreign government falls in this category, as does contact between the International Red Cross and the government of Cuba. An International Youth Conference, involving no governments, is also transnational.[54]

Goals of Transnational Participation

While these forms of international contact have always taken place, their impact has traditionally been minimized because of state domination of the global system. Now it is acknowledged, however, that such contacts contribute to the quality of coexistence, either directly (by improving perceptions and tolerances) or indirectly (by affecting intergovernmental relations). With increasing private contact, ubiquitous international trade and social communication, transnational participation can no longer be overlooked as a major aspect of international stability or of integration.

These interactions have six kinds of prospective impact. First, transnational contact is assumed to promote changes in attitude among the actors. Contact may break down perceptions, erase social and cultural barriers, enlighten outlooks and dissipate animosities. In general, such attitudinal changes may help to transform the international system by raising levels of tolerance among peoples, especially elites.

The second identifiable impact is the promotion of international pluralism. More and more linkages will be developed between do-

53. Joseph S Nye, Jr. and Robert O. Keohane, "Transnational Relations and World Politics: An Introduction," *International Organization* 25, 1971, pp. 329–49. This section borrows extensively from this article.

54. The Summer of 1971 edition of *International Organization* is devoted to the subject "Transnational Relations and World Politics," under the editorship of Robert O. Keohane and Joseph S. Nye, Jr. Among its many papers it considers the Ford Foundation, the Roman Catholic Church, airlines flying international routes, labor unions and scientific societies as transnational actors. Though these papers are not specifically cited here, the reader is alerted to this edition of the journal as the best single source of papers on the theory and illustrative studies of the transnational phenomenon.

mestic political processes and the international system. More interests will come to be involved in decision making; more national elites will gain contact with their counterparts abroad; and more services will be provided for more people.

The creation of new avenues of dependence and interdependence is the third expectation. Transnational contact illuminates mutual needs, and in the long run it may obviate some causes of intersocietal conflict. In addition, reliance will be built upon other societies, upon their productivity and upon their unique forms of creativity. In this manner, transnational contact may assist in "denationalizing" the energies of national peoples, thus taking governments out of the center of international transactions.[55]

Fourth, increases in transnationalism may create beneficial side-effects for those aspects of the international system that remain state centered. Specifically, stabilization of relations among peoples, with increasing intersocietal dependence, may enlarge the peaceful contacts of governments, and actually create for them new avenues of influence. A dramatic and unusual example of this impact was President Nixon's trip to the People's Republic of China in 1972, a trip that, in American public opinion, was made possible by the prior amicable visit of a table-tennis team. Following the president's sojourn, informal contact was utilized further to break down long-standing barriers by exchanges of scientists, physicians and surgeons. This feature of transnationalism has led one observer to describe the process as "transactions which bypass the institutions of government but strongly affect their margin of maneuver."[56]

Fifth, transnational participation, when institutionalized, may create new influential autonomous or quasi-autonomous actors in the international system. Among these are scores of nongovernmental organizations (NGOs) and informal institutional arrangements through which transnational interactions are regulated. The International Red Cross is the best-known of these, one which not only conducts its own relief operations, but to which governments frequently turn to arrange official contacts. Another important NGO is the International Chamber of Commerce, which has already contributed to international stability and amicable exchange by formulating norms of international business relations.[57]

55. These first three features of transnationalism are especially well illustrated in the study of Robert C. Angell, *Peace on the March: Transnational Participation* (New York: Van Nostrand Reinhold, 1969).
56. Karl Kaiser, "Transnational Politics: Toward a Theory of Multinational Politics," *International Organization* 24, 1971, pp. 790–817.
57. Percy E. Corbett, *From International to World Law* (Bethlehem, Pa.: Lehigh University Department of International Relations, research monograph no. 1, 1969).

The sixth possible effect of transnationalism is the gradual institutionalization of intersocietal transactions which may become the private counterpart of functional international organizations. While public single-purpose organizations go about formulating international norms in their respective fields, transnational groups may proceed to develop the norms of their own relations. Furthermore, the national elites that direct functional organizations will be identical in some instances to those that regulate transnational contact. Such a process would maximize the linkages between national and international decision-making processes.[58]

Types of Transnational Participation

Having noted the functional characteristics of transnational research, we may now classify and exemplify types of transnational participation. Most informal among them are the sociocultural activities, of which there are thousands annually. Most common is individual travel, which has some cumulative effect upon international attitudes. Other sociocultural activities of significance are international visits of symphony orchestras, touring exhibits, lecture series, touring dance companies and so on. International athletic events, particularly the Olympics, the Pan-American Games and the Soviet-American games, also are in this category.

Political transnational activity is another. The earliest events were the International Peace Congresses of the nineteenth century, which met to formulate treaties for world peace. These were returned to national societies and national governments, with the Congress members serving as interest groups. At present, the World Peace Through Law movement does much the same thing. Other political transnationalism involves the international communications and meeting of some political parties, such as the Socialist parties of Western Europe, National Communist parties and the several National Liberation Fronts. International Youth Conferences sponsored periodically by the United Nations and other organizations are also examples of political transnationalism, since they present and discuss the political attitudes of young people from different lands.

By far the most important transnational activities are in the economic realm. Though many aspects of the international political economy are conducted by governments, and while most are regulated by official norms, much of the modern international economy is privately regulated. At present, the transnational actor with the greatest power to affect national economies and the flow of international transactions

58. The functional character of transnationalism is also stressed by Karl Kaiser, "Toward a Theory of Multinational Politics," p. 803.

is the transnational (or multinational) corporation (TNC). Its center of operations is in one country, but it has subsidiaries in several others that have major effects upon international economics and upon the host economies. At present there are more than four thousand corporations whose tentacles reach out in this manner, many of them American. In 1979, of the twenty largest corporations in the world (this excludes, of course, the state-owned enterprises of socialist states), twelve were American. In addition, of the largest 300 such corporations in the world in 1978, excluding those which are American based, twenty-six were wholly owned subsidiaries of American firms. Table 16-2 lists the top twenty companies, their countries of origin and their

TABLE 16–2
Twenty-five leading transnational corporations, 1982, measured by total world sales and net earnings in billions of US dollars.

Corporation	*National Base*	*World Sales (US$, bil.)*	*Net Income (US$, bil.)*
Exxon	US	97.2	4.2
Royal Dutch/Shell Group	Brit./Neth.	83.8	3.5
General Motors	US	60.0	1.0
Mobil	US	60.0	1.4
British Petroleum	Britain	51.3	1.2
Texaco	US	47.0	1.3
Ford Motors	US	37.1	(0.6)
IBM	US	34.4	4.4
Standard Oil, California	US	34.4	1.4
E. I. duPont	US	33.3	0.9
Gulf Oil	US	28.4	0.9
Standard Oil, Indiana	US	28.1	1.8
ENI	Italy	27.5	(1.2)
General Electric	US	26.5	1.8
Atlantic Richfield	US	26.5	1.7
IRI	Italy	24.8	NA
Unilever	Brit./Neth.	23.1	0.7
Shell Oil	US	20.1	1.6
Française des Pétroles	France	20.0	(0.8)
Petrobras	Brazil	19.0	0.6
U.S. Steel	US	18.4	(0.4)
Occidental Petroleum	US	18.2	0.2
Elf-Aquitaine	France	17.8	0.5
Siemens	Germany	17.0	0.3
Nissan Motors	Japan	16.5	0.5

Source: Fortune, August 22, 1983, pp. 170–171.

Figures in parentheses represent annual financial losses. NA indicates amount not available at time of publication. Note that 1982 was a year of deep worldwide recession. As a result, General Motors fell to third place from second in 1979, in which year its world sales were $66.3 B. and its net income $2.9B. Ford Motors fell from fifth place in 1979, when its total sales were $43.5B and net income $1.2B. In 1983, General Motors rose to $74.0B., with a net of $3.4B.

annual sales volumes. There are few countries in the world that have gross national products as large as the annual sales of General Motors or Exxon. And in 1972, when the domestic and overseas operations of ITT came under fire, the solicitor-general of the USA remarked that the company was so big that it was beyond the laws even of the United States!

Looked at from the viewpoint of a host government, the power of these corporations is equally great. An anecdote may suffice to illustrate. The British Ford subsidiary manufactures approximately 650,000 automobiles per year, slightly fewer than the Belgian and German subsidiaries. In 1971, when corporation president Henry Ford II arrived in Britain during a strike, he warned that unless the British economy presented less threat to productivity, Ford would consider closing the British operations and expanding productivity on the continent. Though labor reacted with a "we're-not-afraid" attitude, Mr. Ford was generally "treated more like a visiting head of state than an ordinary industrialist."[59] The story illustrates the immense power held by these corporations.

What about the relations of the transnational company to the parent government—that is, the government of the state where the corporation is based? American-owned TNCs produce abroad goods amounting to three times total annual American exports, and these companies are growing at an average rate twice that of the world's most vigorous national economies. By the year 2000, it is estimated that the transnationals will produce upwards of one-half of the gross world product.[60]

These companies have had another effect upon the world economy. Many of them, if not most, do not produce a commodity from start to finish at a single site. Instead, they build some parts in some areas and export them to second subsidiaries, where they are joined to other parts of the whole, and then exported to yet a third place. It is not at all unusual for an automobile made by an American-owned corporation to consist of a transmission made in one country, a motor made in a second, a body made in a third, and tires and fixtures made in a

59. As related in Christopher Tugendhat, "Transnational Enterprise: Tying Down Gulliver," *Atlantic Community Quarterly* 9, 1971/72, pp. 499–508.

60. Similar data are explored by Raymond Vernon, *Sovereignty at Bay: The Multinational Spread of U.S. Enterprises* (New York: Basic Books, 1971). The estimates used here are summarized in Elliot R. Goodman, "The Impact of the Multinational Enterprise Upon the Atlantic Community," *Atlantic Community Quarterly* 10, Fall 1972, pp. 357–67. For a comparative review of the book-length literature on the multinational corporation, see Robert O. Keohane and Van Doorn Ooms, "The Multinational Enterprise and World Political Economy," *International Organization* 26, 1972, pp. 84–120. The literature has grown substantially since this was published.

fourth. Twenty-five percent of all American exports are to the overseas subsidiaries of American-based TNCs. Meanwhile, as much as one-fourth of all exports from Britain consist of international transactions within companies.[61]

More than merely uncloaking the enormity of these corporations, these characteristics reveal the extent to which they—largely unregulated by governments or by international agreement—are able to control the world economy and the economies of host states. Often their operations lead to political controversy, as in de Gaulle's insistence upon "de-Americanizing" Europe, ITT's CIA-assisted coup d'état in Chile and rampant scandals resulting from corrupt business practices abroad. In both developed and underdeveloped economies TNCs are able to penetrate fiscal policy and labor relations; they are able to profit by dispersing earnings and losses among subsidiaries without regard for the host economy; and they are able to remove their economic activity to the detriment of the host. While they are able to contribute to economic development, they are also able to globalize such injurious phenomena as inflation and to use their economic might for political intervention. As a result, many governments have experimented with restrictions on foreign ownership of production, and the governments of the Third World have heightened their demand for international regulation of multinational corporate activity. Both the United Nations and the Organization for Economic Co-operation and Development have labored long over this issue, and in 1976 the OECD adopted a series of declarations comprising guidelines for behavior of multinational enterprises.[62] Despite this progress, and in spite of annual review of performance under the guidelines by the OECD, the Group of Seventy-Seven continues to consider this a major area of need, and treated it with high priority on the agenda of the 1979 UNCTAD meeting.

The capital-lending institutions also affect the world economy and the domestic economies of the host states. Though no one disputes the need for operating capital in industrial modernization, some would argue that the rapid growth of branch banks overseas is an instrument

61. Reported in Tugendhat, "Transnational Enterprise," p. 503. See also Tugendhat, *The Multinationals* (London: Eyre and Spottiswoode, 1971).

62. The OECD guidelines and the review documents for 1979 can be found in "Review of the 1976 Declaration and Decisions on Guidelines for Multinational Enterprises, National Treatment, International Investment Incentives and Disincentives, and Consultation Procedures," OECD, 1979. For background information, see particularly Robert O. Keohane and Van Doorn Ooms, "The Multinational Firm and International Regulation" *International Organization* 29,1975, pp. 169–212, and Paul A. Tharp, Jr., "Transnational Enterprises and International Regulation: A Survey of Various Approaches in International Organization, " *International Organization* 30, 1976, pp. 47–74.

of neo-imperialism. If American capital is the only available source of funds, then American banks and American fiscal policy actually regulate interest rates and growth rates overseas. Furthermore, both in the banking business and in commodity industries, profits are siphoned off and returned with minimal reinvestment, with the result that the principal gains from the multinational enterprise accrue solely to the country of origin.[63]

Considered from political and economic perspectives, the multinational corporation is a mixed blessing.[64] But what is it when viewed from the perspective of transnationalism? What is its value as a nongovernmental actor capable of creating new intersocietal communications?

At present, the transnational corporation may contribute to integration through its ability to forge shared values among participating elites. There is a growing consensus that the managers of overseas subsidiaries must subordinate nationalistic attitudes to corporate profit, regardless of the country of central operations. Since the principal decisions are economic rather than political, and since the function of capitalist business is to achieve profit in competitive markets, the tendency in these corporations is to minimize national feelings.

Yet it is also probable that this attitude does not filter down very far within the company. Below uppermost management, few employees are aware of the full meaning of their participation in a multinational enterprise. Their objective in most cases is to progress in the plant rather than in the corporation, or in the industry rather than in the conglomerate. Furthermore, at the consumer level, few in Britain, for example, who eat cornflakes realize that the company that made the product is a wholly-owned American subsidiary.

The multinational business enterprise has not had a deep overall impact upon national economic attitudes. There are many who feel that such organization is vital to efficiency in a technological world,

63. The most incisive critique of the political-economic effects is found in Harry Magdoff, *The Age of Imperialism: The Economics of U.S. Foreign Policy* (New York: Monthly Review Press, 1969). For a critical but less bleak European view, see J. J. Servan-Schreiber, *The American Challenge* (New York, Atheneum, 1969). For a study of U.S. banking abroad, particularly the growth of branch banks in other economies, see Table1–1 of this book.

64. Theodore H. Moran, "Multinational Corporations and Dependency: A Dialogue for Dependentistas and non-Dependentistas," *International Organization,* Winter 1978, pp. 79–100. Moran attempts to clarify the debate between the advocates of the dependency theory of development and the role of the TNCs and the more liberal or traditional view. He categorizes the charges against the TNC in the Third World as made by the dependency theorists and develops each into a testable hypothesis for nondependency-theory inquiry. Though the paper is inconclusive, it offers a logical procedure by which to explore the controversy between the two bodies of interpretation.

and there are those who insist that regional supranationalism is dependent upon multinational business.[65] But there is little evidence to suggest its positive effect upon international stability through attitudinal change at the mass level. The opposite may be quite the case, in fact, because these huge operations tend to be exploitative and ready to use their considerable political weight. Often they make themselves unwelcome guests by aggravating existing tensions. While there is considerable evidence that the TNCs are effective agents for the transfer of technology from the developed economies to the developing, the overall effects of national and international political economies remain controversial, as does the broader role of the TNCs in social change and in the emerging world order.[66]

To whatever extent transnational participation contributes to world stability, then, its virtue must be found in less visible places. Most such progress at present is found in the sociocultural sector. At its roots, the transnational process is one of awareness; and the indications are that at the individual level, maximum attitudinal change through awareness occurs through sociocultural contact only.

Governments cautiously safeguard their prerogatives and prevent escape of political functions to external agencies. But the intersocietal linkages created by the movement of persons, information, goods and capital across national boundaries challenge the purely state-centered model of international stability. They may ultimately alter the supremacy of the state as an actor in the international system, though to date such transformation is minimal. All in all, however, the several alternatives to absolute sovereignty that we have studied in the last three chapters (international law, international organization, supranationalism and transnational participation) all press in upon the nation-state and challenge its ability to remain the paramount actor in international relations.

65. On the relation between the multinational corporation and the progress of European economic integration, see particularly Werner J. Feld, *Transnational Business Collaboration Among Common Market Countries* (New York: Praeger, 1970), and "Political Aspects of Transnational Business Collaboration in the Common Market," *International Organization* 24, 1970, pp. 209–38. See also a discussion of "The Multinational Corporation and World Economic Development," *Proceedings of the 66th Annual Meeting of the American Society of International Law,* September 1972, pp. 14–22, especially the remarks by Jack N. Behrman.

66. David E. Apter and Louis W. Goodman, editors, *The Multinational Corporation and Social Change* (New York: Praeger, 1976), consisting of eight coordinated papers; Lewis D. Solomon, *Multinational Corporations and the Emerging World Order* (Port Washington, N.Y.: National University Publications by the Kennikat Press, 1978); and Raymond Vernon, *Storm Over the Multinationals* (Cambridge, Mass.: Harvard University Press, 1977).

17

The Future World Order

During the era of the Apollo moon probes, an American astronaut told mission control that the most remarkable thing about space travel is looking back upon earth as a planet without boundaries. From his vantage point deep in space, temporarily removed from armed conflict and the rhetoric of enmity, he voiced the long-standing view of many people—if enduring peace is to dawn, the international system must first be substantially altered. If war is a product of the nation-state system, then the role of the state must be diminished and that of other governing and social processes increased. Disillusioned with the balance of power, the balance of terror and all known power distributions, observers ranging from nineteenth-century utopians to contemporary futurist scholars have sought alternative worlds, all focusing on one problem: how to supplant the nation-state's capacity for disruption.

But war/peace issues no longer monopolize scholarly examination of the future. On an overcrowded planet nearing depletion of resources and extinction of species, the dynamics of the international system have come upon new emergencies. Stability relies not only upon the willingness of governments to put aside their arms, but upon their ability to correct anarchical ways. Consider briefly a few areas in which the records of nation-states are dismal, and which now cry out for international regulation.

1. Ecology

First among them is ecological anarchy. States have exploited the earth's natural riches without regard for the problem of exhaustibility and with little consideration of future generations or of the needs of others. Growing energy demands deplete fossil fuels; deposits of hard metals have been used up; supplies of fresh water are dangerously low. Meanwhile, we have poisoned air, despoiled most of the major rivers of the world, toxified vast areas of the seas, made urban living a painful clatter and outgrown designated dumping areas. These problems have become so nearly universal as to make clear that national regulation is too little and too late. Without new levels of cooperation, and without international regulation, we are bent upon ecological suicide.

Sadly, international cooperation on this issue has scarcely commenced, despite the best efforts of the United Nations. Under its auspices, after fully four years of preparation, the Global Conference on the Human Environment was convened at Stockholm in 1972. Fraught with politics over the seating of East Germany (not then a member of the UN) and over Chinese charges against the use of defoliants in Vietnam, and beset by the insistence of the less developed states that environmental preservation is a luxury for the industrialized, the conference achieved but modest ends. It established the seeds of a global environmental monitoring system, promulgated an Action Program and a Declaration, and established UN oversight machinery. But beyond dramatic recognition of the need for international cooperation and the establishment of functional machinery, the Stockholm meeting itself was a less compelling impetus to cooperation than were subsequent events.

The years that followed Stockholm saw a number of dramatic environmental calamities. French ports and wildlife were menaced by the cargo of a disintegrating supertanker. Nuclear fallout from a Chinese nuclear explosion was measured more than halfway around the world. Lakes in the northern United States became lifeless as the result of "acid rain" contamination. And the United States government was obliged to commit funds to move hundreds of families away from the chemical-contaminated Love Canal in New York and from Times Beach, Missouri. Then there were the near disasters. The Three Mile Island nuclear power station in Pennsylvania released radiation through its cooling station in amounts so high that the long-range consequences are still not known. Terrorists penetrated the security of a West German nuclear station, accentuating concern for the possibility of nuclear blackmail or terrorism. An American Titan ICBM

Source: Wide World

A container of radioactive material is lifted onto a barge after being brought up from a sunken French freighter off the Belgium coast.

exploded in its Arkansas silo, reportedly throwing its nuclear warhead several hundred yards, but without exploding.

Less dramatic but equally alarming are the quieter cumulative effects of environmental spoilation. In the industrialized state, the last fifteen years have seen considerable progress in industrial smoke discharge; in control of health hazards in mines; in diminished stripmining or, alternatively, stripmining followed by reconstitution of the landscape; and in reduction of waste release into rivers and bays. But these familiar evils have been overtaken by new revelations, such as the extreme long-term effects of toxification and irradiation of soil, air and waterways. The genetic, carcinogenic and other pathogenic consequences of these problems are only now becoming issues of public policy.

Rapid industrialization and increased dependence upon synthetic fertilizers for agricultural advancement have inspired a new concern for ecology in the Third World since Stockholm.[1] The environmental consequences of unplanned urban growth, involving such things as industrial discharge, waste disposal and treatment, etc., have stimulated this concern. Yet because environmental spoilation knows nothing of national boundaries, rising concern in both industrialized and developing countries can do little more than underscore the fact that national solutions to environmental problems are inadequate.

2. Science and Technology

The dramatic improvements in standards of living that have characterized the current century are attributable in large measure to advances in science and technology. Particularly since World War II scientific discovery and application have reached into every facet of life in new ways. Biomedical science and engineering have produced chemical compounds that prolong life and machinery that sustains the ill. Recombinant DNA techniques that produce new forms of microbial life will soon produce enzymes, hormones and other chemical compounds that afflicted organs fail to produce. Supersonic aircraft have reduced the duration of intercontinental travel to a few hours. Communications have been revolutionized to a point where home computer

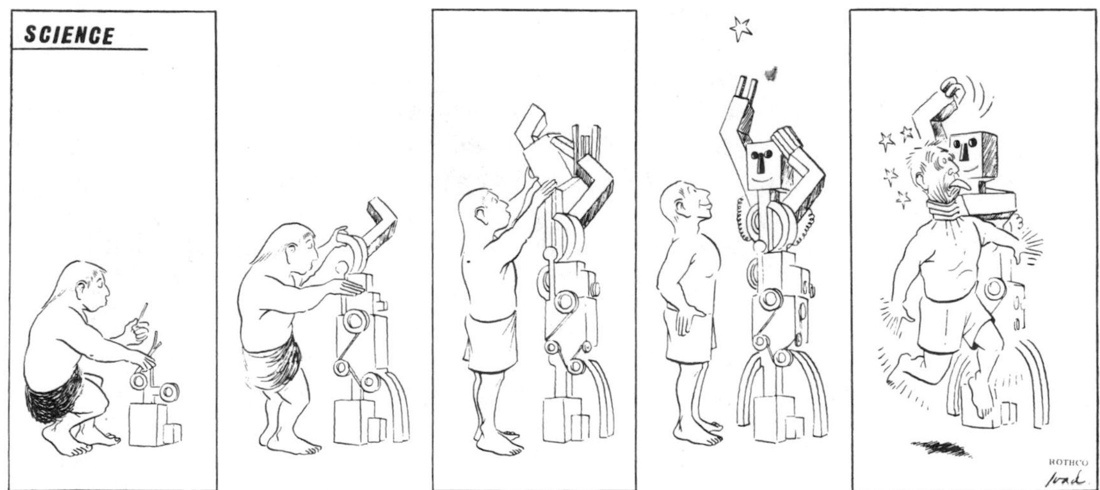

Source: © Vadillo *Siempre,* Mexico/Rothco

1. Whitman, Bassow, "The Third World: Changing Attitudes Toward Environmental Protection," in *The Annals* of the American Academy of Political and Social Science, July 1979, pp. 112–20.

terminals will replace daily newspapers. New synthetic fertilizers have enabled farmers to increase their yields substantially.

But these miracles of the modern age are not without their liabilities. In the industrialized countries in particular, disposal of chemical waste poses dangers to plant and animal life. Because dumped chemicals eventually find their way back into the human food chain through soil and water and through ingestion by lower species, the long-range consequences of carelessly planned dumping may be catastrophic. In 1980 the Surgeon General of the United States declared for the first time that the uncontrolled consequences of scientific and technological development are multiplying the disease burden of the American people and the annual national cost of health care. But it is the long-term results of toxification that are most alarming. With the United States alone producing over 300 billion pounds of synthetic chemicals annually, and other nations producing amounts in proportion to their economies, it is certain that national solutions to these problems will be inadequate.

The long-range genetic consequences of chemical and radiological contamination are particularly threatening and inconclusively understood. Mutations brought on by these hazards have the capability of altering species, including humans, fundamentally. The increased use of nuclear fuels to replace diminishing supplies of conventional fuels is fraught with distant implications. While we continue to be concerned more with the immediate consequences of irradiation, the more serious risks may not be visible for generations. One recent prediction centers on freshly demonstrated leaks of radiation from barrels of nuclear substances dumped in the Pacific Ocean over a period of twenty-five years. By 1980 the leaked radiation had gotten into the human food chain; edible fish tissues were shown to have radiation levels hundreds of times more than normal. Scientists expect that the genetic consequences for humans as well as for lower animals will evolve in unpredictable fashions for thousands of years.

Not all of the consequences of scientific and technological modernization are physical or physiological. In recent years social scientists have begun to focus upon their social and political consequences. For some time "futurists" have attempted to postulate the characteristics of the postindustrial or technological societies. More recently, as some of the liabilities of the age have become so alarmingly apparent, they have begun to focus on mechanisms of social control and forms of decision making that will preserve philosophies of government rather than simply respond to technological change. Increasingly they argue that socially responsible decision making is falling danger to decisional reactions necessitated by the lure of scientific discovery.[2] The use of nuclear fuels, for example, was scarcely a topic of public debate until *after* its dangers became apparent. But by that time so many billions of dollars had been invested in it that rational decision making had no practical application. By the same token, international exchanges of nuclear fuel were licensed by governments largely as a form of commercial competition until controls were demanded after India used fuel provided by the United States for peaceful purposes to construct and explode a nuclear weapon. The prospect of nuclear fuel falling into the hands of terrorists has further prompted demands for controls, yet these have been demanded only after nuclear fuel exchanges have become common and only after reprocessing plants and breeder reactors (which permit certain types of nuclear fuel to be rejuvenated for second use) have been completed and put into use.[3]

The dilemma becomes apparent. Science and technology are largely responsible for the rapid improvement in national standards of living in the current century, and are major hopes for the improved economic competitiveness of the Third World; yet the cost of such progress is measured not just in economic terms, but in human and social terms as well. We have grown deeply dependent on these advances; yet unless we control their long-term physical and political consequences, their forces may be as destructive as they are progressive.

3. Population

It took until the year 1800 for the world population to reach one billion. A level of two billion was reached in 1925, three billion by 1960, and four billion in 1976. It is predicted that by the year 2000, at current rates of reproduction, the global population will have reached nearly seven billion. Even more alarmingly, population densities are most stable in industrialized areas and least stable in the poorest sectors of the world. Current projections, for example, are that by 2000, the population density of North America will have increased by only four persons per square kilometer, while in South Asia there will be an increase of one hundred and forty persons in a

2. See particularly Langdon Winner, *Autonomous Technology: Technics-Out-of-Control as a Theme in Political Thought* (Cambridge, Mass. MIT Press, 1977); and Roger Benjamin, *The Limits of Politics* (Chicago: University of Chicago Press, 1980).
3. Louis R. Beres, *Terrorism and Global Security: The Nuclear Threat* (Boulder, Col. Westview, 1979) and *Apocalypse: Nuclear Catastrophe in World Politics* (Chicago: University of Chicago Press, 1980).

Population control in the Third World: a family planning clinic in Tunisia.

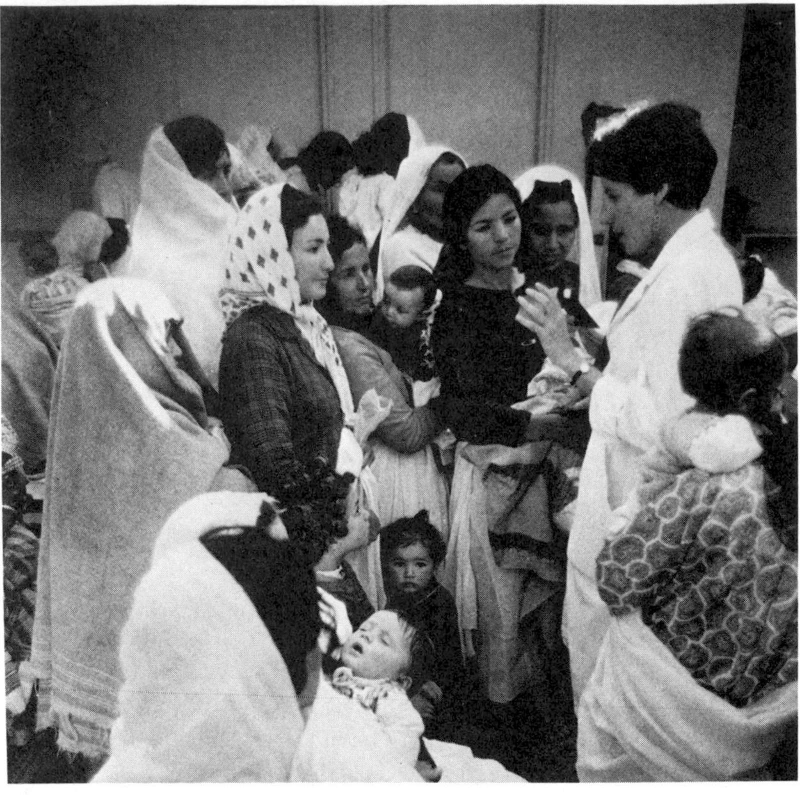

Source: Paul Conklin

similar space.[4] One elaborate UN study undertaken to predict the conditions of life a century hence concludes that in the industrialized world the population will start to decline before the year 2000, and will become constant by 2025. In the underindustrialized world, however, the population decline will commence only in the first quarter of the next century, and stability will not be achieved until 2075.[5]

The world order consequences of these astounding projections are manifold, though not entirely clear. With respect to food, mineral resources and other consumable commodities, there exists a spirited debate as to the world's capacity to sustain a growing population.[6] It

4. Mihajlo Mesarovic and Eduard Pestel, *Mankind at the Turning Point: The Second Report to The Club of Rome* (New York: New American Library, 1974), Chapter 6.
5. Wassily Leontief, et al., *The Future of the World Economy: A United Nations Study* (New York: Oxford University Press, 1977), summary conclusions on p. 4.
6. See, for example, the debate as presented by *The Christian Science Monitor,* November 3, 1975, between Herman Kahn (optimistic view) and Dennis Meadows (pessimistic view).

is a demonstrable fact, nevertheless, that in the most overpopulated regions, even accelerating economic growth rates are being offset by population increases, with the result that per capita wealth continues to diminish. It is apparent, therefore, that apart from the global ability to sustain larger numbers of people, overpopulation retards economic growth, perpetuates squalor and generally restricts the improvement of living conditions. In addition, poverty facilitates the spread of disease, limits educational opportunity, reduces life expectancies and invites imperialism and autocracy. The seriousness of the problem is underscored by a decision in one of the states of India in 1976 to apply coercive sanctions, in which families will be penalized for the failure of at least one spouse to secure permanent sterilization after the birth of a third child. Despite efforts of contemporary international organizations to control population growth, effective progress on the issue remains a matter for the future. Religious objections, superstition, inadequate understanding of the sexual origins of pregnancy, cultural approval of large families and other factors converge as impediments to effective global population control.

4. Food

Preoccupation with the world's mineral distribution only serves to obscure the global nutrition crisis. In November 1974, just one year after the first major petroleum crisis, the United Nations convened the World Food Conference at Rome to deal with the long-term threat of dwindling food production relative to need. The UN had projected that by 1985, an increase of production per year of 2.5 percent globally would barely offset the increased demand of the industrialized states, thus leaving none to contribute to the 3.6 percent increase in need from the industrializing states.[7] More recent UN estimates take into account the results of the Green Revolution and of increased land yields resulting from modern agricultural techniques. The experts now seem confident that available agricultural land can be increased by 30 percent during the remainder of the century, and that yields can be improved by as much as 60 percent. With massive investment, the study concludes, major crop staples might be produced in amounts as much as twice to three times the current annual global yields.[8] Already major strides have occurred. By 1977, for example, Bangladesh, once considered beyond hope with respect to staple-crop sufficiency, pre-

7. *Assessment of the World Food Situation: Present and Future,* Item Eight of the Provisional Agenda for the World Food Conference, p. 225.
8. Wassily Leontief, et al., *The Future of the World Economy,* pp. 4 and 5.

dicted that it would be self-sufficient in rice production within five years. In 1979 American agricultural scientists announced soybean hybrids capable of 15 percent increases in yield. And China announced in 1980 what it considered to be a realistic plan to double its rice production.

What the Green Revolution was to world food supplies in the 1960s and 1970s, new agricultural applications of genetic science may be in the 1980s and 1990s. The same research techniques used to produce new therapeutic agents, when applied to agriculture, may result in major advances in productivity. In one massive effort, for example, so large as to be compared with the war on cancer, scientists are trying to move from soybean into corn a particular nitrogen fixation gene. Since nitrogen fixation is an essential step in the energy and photosynthetic cycles of the plant, successful transplantation of the gene, and the subsequent successful expression of its normal function in a new host, would have profound consequences for corn production worldwide.

Although closely tied to the problem of population growth, global food shortages also present problems of their own. Aside from the obvious consequences—such as starvation, squalor, retarded economic growth—maldistribution of food resources introduces other potential difficulties. At present a major fear is that those states enjoying plentiful food supplies will use them coercively to ensure steady flows of mineral resources from the mineral-rich Third World countries. The introduction of food into the global formula of competitive embargoes would represent a major change in the power resources of international politics, but with individually measurable human costs. In 1979 the prospect of using food as a weapon became starkly realistic. As part of the American reaction to the Soviet invasion of Afghanistan, the Carter Administration terminated unilaterally a trade agreement with the Kremlin, and in so doing discontinued bulk grain sales to the Soviet Union. At almost the same time, as Americans became impatient with the Iranian government for holding American diplomatic personnel hostage in retaliation for permitting the deposed Shah to enter the United States for surgical treatment, there was a growing demand to discontinue food shipments to Iran. As this became a more popular thought, some political forces in the United States advanced food embargoes as a general policy in dealing with the OPEC countries in response to petroleum embargoes or uncontrolled price increases of raw petroleum. Except in the case with the Soviet Union over Afghanistan, however, no such policy has been applied.[9]

9. On the general subject of food export policy as an instrument of international diplomacy, see Raymond F. Hopkins and Donald J. Puchala, *Global Food Inter-*

Despite the efforts of the World Food Conference to establish an international food production program, the large producers have made it clear that food production will remain a matter of national policy. Indeed, because food comprises a large portion of international trade volume, national agricultural policies are linked directly to the international problem. As recently as 1979, for example, the United States publicly recognized the extent to which its international trade balance was deteriorating due to the very successful agricultural policies of the European Economic Community, and Washington requested that Western Europe *reduce* its agricultural production of such staples as grains and butter. Such nationalistic policies ensure that effective international planning of food production and distribution is a matter for the future. Until such planning is feasible, the industrializing world will have to depend on declining terms of trade, scientific development of synthetic protein and other sources of nutrition and foreign assistance in developing crop yields through soil programs and irrigation.

5. Mineral Resources

Although food may be in short supply at present, the world nutrition problem at least enjoys the advantage that scientific advances will be able to increase the annual world yield. In the case of mineral resources this is not true. Mineral resources are at present being expended at record rates, even at a time of reduced economic activity throughout the West and declines in national productivity. That this is most popularly evidenced by the diminishing world supply of petroleum is due to the fact that individuals are so directly dependent upon petroleum to fuel their cars, heat their homes and drive the industries that employ them. But the shortages are becoming critical in other areas as well, such as among the nonferrous metals. Although it is probable that in the long run the exhaustion of fossil fuel supplies will be compensated for by a combination of energy from nuclear fuel, solar power, synthetic fuels and ocean thermal energy, many of the basic elements may not be replaceable in manufacturing and other socially important processes.

dependence: Challenge to American Foreign Policy (New York: Columbia University Press, 1979).

It is difficult, perhaps futile, to assess the impact of the American grain embargo upon Soviet behavior. The American secretary of agriculture has gone only so far as to label it "a significant inconvenience." For a critical assessment, see Robert L. Pearlberg, "Lessons of the Grain Embargo," *Foreign Affairs,* Fall 1980, pp. 144–62.

It is important to stress that the deterioration of world mineral supplies may have potential consequences beyond national and international economics. These minerals are not found equally distributed about the globe any more than petroleum is. While the United States, China and the Soviet Union have been rich in both coal and petroleum (though only China among them now appears to have significant untapped supplies of oil), Britain and the continental powers of Western Europe have been rich only in coal (until discovery of oil in the North Sea). Japan, in contrast, has until the advent of nuclear power been wholly dependent upon foreign sources of fuel. Metals are also distributed unevenly about the planet, many of the unutilized supplies are now limited to the territories of the Third World countries. And while rapid increases in export of these materials has contributed to economic development, dependence upon them has led to imbalanced exports and has raised the prospect of export paralysis upon depletion.

Beyond these potential consequences, it is important to note that the external quest for raw materials has been one of the major causes of war in the industrial age and is generally understood to have been one of the principal causes of imperialism. We have seen that the modern efforts to integrate the economies of Western Europe were inspired in the first instance by the desire to eliminate the repeated Franco-German competition for coal and steel. Similarly, it has long been understood that Japan's imperialistic behavior from 1931 to Pearl Harbor in 1941 was provoked in large measure by the paucity of mineral resources in the Japanese territory.[10] More recently, it has been argued that the Americanization of the Vietnam War in 1964, and the general interventionist trend of American foreign policy in that era, were driven mainly by the need to control political events in those areas which may still be abundant in natural resources.[11]

To the extent that these observations be accurate, then, deterioration of the globe's mineral supply may portend more than fundamental changes in world economic productivity. Surely, the uneven distribution of oil has already brought a major transition to the world measured both politically and economically, particularly with the rise of the oil-exporting countries as political-economic powers despite their social and industrial underdevelopment. But such changes may be little more than the first phases of major new alignments in world politics heralded, among other things, by the Soviet occupation of Afghanistan and the remarkably rapid reversal in Sino-American po-

10. Herbert Feis, *The Road to Pearl Harbor* (Princeton, NJ: Princeton University Press, 1950).
11. Gabriel Kolko, *The Roots of American Foreign Policy* (Boston: Beacon Press, 1969).

litical and economic relations. Without rational control of the politics of declining resources, new forms of imperialism and conquest could emerge.

6. Autocratic Government

From a humanistic viewpoint, another problem looms just as large. Traditionally, each political system has determined its governing philosophy, and has established the quality of relations between the government and the governed. Many political systems—if not most—have justified stern restrictions on human freedoms and rights. Autocratic politics has been history's rule rather than its exception. In an era of growing literacy, improved mass communications, national liberation and domestic protest, can the peace of national peoples be preserved against the brutality of governments? At present the Philippines and South Korea are enjoying economic growth rates of 10 percent, twice that of Japan and almost two and one-half times that of the United States, yet these are two of the world's most repressive regimes. At what price progress? Furthermore, can the world's peace be preserved in the face of government brutality, the ever-present danger of insurgency or revolution followed by foreign intervention? What role is there for international politics in building a global regime of human rights and dignity in face of absolute state control over national subjects?

In the last decade, much of the world's political consciousness has been riveted upon the question of human rights. This has resulted in part from the communications revolution, which has made public spectacles of brutality and political repression. *Apartheid* (the policy of racial separation practiced by South Africa), the murder of popular black leader Steve Biko in a South African prison, the Nobel Prize-winning revelations of Amnesty International regarding the practices of some governments in imprisoning political enemies, and worldwide sympathy for Soviet Jews who have been prevented by their government from emigrating to Israel—these have all been issues of popular attention, fanned by the news media.

There have been official stimulants to the world conscience, also. The Vladivostok accords called upon the United States and the Soviet Union to treat their nationals according to agreed international standards. A quarter-century after the passage by the United Nations General Assembly of the Universal Declaration of Human Rights, two international covenants (the International Covenant on Political and Economic Rights and the International Covenant on Social and Cultural Rights) finally secured enough signatories to come into effect. The 1978 Belgrade Conference on Human Rights, resulting from the Vladivostok Conference in 1978, was conducted amid much popular acclaim, but produced little of significance. And finally, President Carter's emphasis upon human rights in American Foreign policy (even to the extent of chilling Soviet-American relations) kept the general issue in the forefront of international news, even if more as a political matter than a humanistic one.

But with what practical result? Despite the expansion of international standards for the protection of human rights, political imprisonment, denial of due process, unethical (and perhaps illegal) economic exploitation of minorities and other violations of basic human rights abound. This is due in part to the variety of ideological interpretations given to international standards, and in part to the impulse of powerful factions to defend their position against rising expectations of political freedom. Without international sanctioning authority competent to monitor the proliferation of declaratory international standards, the protection of human rights will continue to suffer from inconsistencies of national policy and the maldistribution of political power in national political systems.

7. World Economics

Yet another form of contemporary anarchy is the international economic system. Despite foreign aid and international development programs, a powerful few dominate the world economy. Self-serving autocracy of the economically powerful states and of their political elites, together with central planning and allocation, is the guidepost of world economics. Imperialism, neo-imperialism, exploitation, discrimination and manipulation—these are the instruments used by the powerful to subordinate the weak.[12] Stability in economic relations cries out for international supervision and new modes of decision making.

Already new patterns are emerging. The dependence of the Western industrialized nations upon the wealthy but socially and economically underdeveloped petroleum exporters of the Third World has changed the face of global economic relations. But this reverse dependency is

12. Particularly with respect to Western capitalism, theories of imperialism and structural imperialism abound, which focus on the collusion between the elites of the industrial states with the oligarchs of the developing world to exploit the producing peripheries of the latter. See especially Johan Galtung, "A Structural Theory of Imperialism," *Journal of Peace Research* 13, no. 2, 1971, pp. 81–118.

marked by forms of anarchy of its own: manipulation, retaliation for a century of subordination and decisions of global impact made as much out of competition within OPEC as out of cooperation. Only in 1979 and 1980 did there begin to emerge a rational pattern of decision making with respect to quantity of oil production and price, based at first on the general principle of trying to force the industrial states to control inflation, and subjected later to efforts to establish complex formulas giving attention to inflation, declining values of currencies, anticipation of resource depeletion and correlation of export trade with rate of internal economic development. But this progress declined in 1982 and 1983 when internal disagreement among the OPEC members flared up, sparked by the radicals who wished to maximize and the moderates who wanted to stabilize the world petroleum market. As a result, prices dropped and incentives for exploration of new sources of oil were removed.

A second new pattern centers on the activities of the transnational corporations. Though they are chartered by states of origin and licensed to operate in host economies, the magnitude and complexity of their operations place them virtually outside the legal control of any government(s), and subjects them only to regional controls to the extent of their operations within those regions which have attempted to apply controls.

A third pattern, though perhaps less new, pertains to the imperatives of the welfare state. As the welfare-state concept has spread throughout the industrial world, individual nation-states have strengthened the arsenal of public policies by which they control and maintain the loyalty of their nationals.[13] The political imperatives that follow from this observation ensure that the state's commitment to more rational international economic order may be secondary.

A closely related phenomenon is the "new protectionism." While the interdependence of economies and the activities of transnational corporations have generally stimulated technology transfer and industrial productivity, they have had detrimental consequences for some developed economies. At a time when American industrial sales at home and abroad have been challenged by imports from Japan and the European Economic Community, rising imports and troubling balance-of-payments deficits with respect to the Third World (particularly the OPEC Third World) have led to new demands for protection

13. Melvyn B. Krauss, *The New Protectionism: The Welfare State and International Trade* (New York: New York University Press, 1978); and George R. Neumann, "Adjustment Assistance for Trade-Displaced Workers," in David B. H. Denoon, editor, *The New International Economic Order: A U.S. Response* (New York: New York University Press, 1979), pp. 109–40.

of the American economy. And the pattern has been repeated elsewhere.[14]

The demand for trade restrictions on the developing economies by the developed economies reveals the abiding problem: the forms of social and political organization that make up the state-centric international system are resilient obstacles to effective interdependence. Only reform of basic attitudes, structures and patterns of interaction can transform the processes of global economic interaction. Contemporary system dynamics are self-destructive.[15]

Despite the remedial efforts of statesmen to overcome these vexing problems through organization, law and integration, the magnitude of the problems and the antiquity of national solutions further highlight the dilemma of traditional international remedies. So long as the unique sovereign attributes of the nation-state are preserved, the pace of deterioration will continue to outrun proposed solutions, rendering them always ideas after their times. Accordingly, research has centered upon wholly new approaches, though they vary considerably in scope. Some, labeled *maximalist* proposals, seek a fully structured world government; the *minimalist* proposals advocate upgrading existing international machinery; and the *reformist* proposals would generally retain the current systemic features, but would subject the nation-state to global law.

The Idea of World Order

Though two world wars and the nuclear arms race have prompted new interest in the world order movement, the idea is an ancient one. It has arisen repeatedly in history from peace groups, governments, philosophers, religious thinkers, imperialists and nationalistic zealots. Until recently, the world order movement has been synonymous with the quest for world government. One of the earliest known forms was that of ancient Rome, whose imperial quest sought to bring all of the known world under Roman political control. Other imperial impulses

14. Vincent Cable, "Britain, the 'New Protectionism' and Trade with the Newly Industrialized Countries," in *International Affairs* (London), January 1979, pp. 1–17; and Melvyn B. Krauss, *The New Protectionism: The Welfare State and International Trade.*
15. Students of international organization generally emphasize, in contrast, the progress that has been made through a complex web of official and unofficial organizations. See, for example, Harold K. Jacobson, *Networks of Interdependence: International Organizations and the Global Political System* (New York: Knopf, 1979), particularly Part 4, "International Organizations and the Growth and Distribution of the World Product." Chapter 11 in that section is entitled "Steps Toward the Creation of a World Economy," pp. 244–92.

to world domination have been grossly maniacal, such as that of Adolf Hitler, whose aim was to rule Europe and then the world on behalf of the Aryan race.

Several other sources of universalist sentiment have also emerged. Theologians have posited concepts of control, though not through governmental superiority. St. Thomas Aquinas propounded the concept of a universal Christian spirit forging a human community, and supplying the ideals and benevolence of Christian rulers throughout the world. He distinguished the power of the state *(imperium)* from that of the church *(sacerdotium),* leaving room for separate governments in different lands, even though as a papist he viewed papal power as superior to secular power. Even in a Christian Europe, however, and writing a half-century later than Thomas (about A.D. 1310), Dante saw the only hope for world peace (meaning essentially European peace) in the consolidation of all power in the Roman emperor. In the words of one eminent student of political philosophy, "Neither by birth nor breeding was Dante a partisan of the imperial cause. His imperialism was purely an idealization of universal peace."[16]

Thinkers in more modern times have frequently revived these ideas. The Spanish theologian Francisco Suarez, writing in the absolutist era bridging the sixteenth and seventeenth centuries and imbued with Bodin's notions of sovereignty, moved from the concept of moral law to the hope of world government. Later in the seventeenth century, the English philosopher Hobbes wrote in *Leviathan* that the political nature of society is that of war of every man against every man, and that through social contract men form governments to which they entrust the security of all. Applied to international relations, Hobbes' social contract extrapolates to a theory of world government.

The German thinker Hegel, whose dialectical method formed the basis of Marx's arguments about class conflict, included in his theory of history the concept of a world spirit of the governing class. Though Hegal was a nationalist, he nevertheless found a universal morality in political leadership, freedom and even the arts. Despite his nationalistic fervor he saw every state falling to the universal logic of the world spirit. Marx not only adopted Hegel's system of argument, he also made similar historical predictions. Rather than concentrate on a governing class and a mystical world spirit, Marx looked to the working class and the eventual elimination of class conflict. When power resides in the hands of the proletariat, states will wither away and all people will be ruled in classless harmony. In this utopian prediction, government becomes not state centered, but spirit centered.

16. George H. Sabine, *A History of Political Theory,* 3rd ed. (New York: Holt, Rinehart and Winston, 1961), pp. 257–58.

But visions of universal political morality and utopian harmony have not arisen exclusively in philosophical abstraction. Indeed, the popularity of world government schemes has paralleled certain events: the frequency of war, the destructiveness of modern industrialized warfare, imperial competition and the irrationality of ideological fears, to name only a few. There is at least impressionistic evidence of a correlation between world government enthusiasm and warfare. The activity and popularity of such proposals seem highest toward the ends of, and upon conclusion of, major wars; the longer and more tranquil postwar periods are, the more rapid the decline in popularity of world government ideals. This correlation seems guided by a simple rule of world politics: when states serve their functions satisfactorily and with minimal external disruption, only a handful of activists advocate world government; but when the nation-state system breaks down, more people share the world government sentiment.

It follows from this "rule" that the present century has been one of consistently high interest in world government. The destruction caused by the First World War was unprecedented, and the vision of further industrialization of war potential forged a solid core of sentiment for some form of central government. In America, a group known as the League to Enforce Peace considered several alternative forms of international organization, with some of its adherents arguing for virtual international government. Intent upon retaining their sovereign prerogatives, however, national governments were willing to do no more than subscribe to President Woodrow Wilson's League of Nations. Predecessor to the United Nations, the League of Nations (1) prescribed mechanisms for the peaceful settlement of international disputes, (2) called upon its members to guarantee the territorial integrity and political independence of all other members, (3) looked forward to general arms limitation, (4) authorized its Council to undertake enforcement action against aggressors, and (5) mandated member states to impose sanctions against violators of the peace.

As an instrument of world order, the League of Nations was generally a disappointment to the advocates of world government. They viewed it as little more than a smokescreen for power politics. Its voting provisions, especially on matters of greatest interest to members of the Council, restricted progress toward effective international decision making, and encouraged great-power domination of policy. Though many saw in the assembly, where all member states were represented, an opportunity to sow and to germinate the seeds of international society, there was general discouragement over the decentralization of sanction procedures and over the great-power control of peace/war issues. But of major long-range interest was the network of functional organizations (single-purpose agencies with specific technical tasks), which seemed to promise greater person-to-person contact around the world, and to offer an opportunity for the development of loyalty to a political entity outside of nation-states. Ultimately, the problem of the nation-state system is not simply the existence of multiple sovereignties, but the ability of governments to monopolize the secular loyalties of individuals and to mobilize them for nationalistic rather than universalistic purposes. *Any* institutional structure that might erode this pattern is acceptable to the advocates of world government and to the proponents of most other doctrines of world order as well.

Some universalists viewed the League of Nations with even deeper suspicion, principally because of its collective security provisions. Collective security could not govern, they argued; it could only maintain peace by the threat of force. Thus it was a negative approach to international stability, still built upon nationalistic preferences. It did not address the causes of conflict; it was powerless to legislate preentative social, political and economic changes; and it was impotent when international norms were violated, except by the unanimous consent of the Council members. Hence some saw the League not as a steppingstone between the nation-state system and world government, but as a threat to world government.

Although the League of Nations failed to prevent war, its history was partly successful from a world order perspective. It made modest but positive contributions to self-determinism, previously little more than a platitude. Its social, scientific and economic projects made inroads in problems of squalor and disease. Postwar relief programs, assistance to refugees and the League's management of intellectual exchanges all earned for the organization a reputation as a helpful intermediary among governments in matters not directly related to national security. One of the celebrated events of the League was its acceptance in 1939 of the Bruce Committee Report, which advocated a broad reorganization of authority for social and economic development. Though the Second World War prevented its immediate application, the report formed the rationale for establishing the Economic and Social Council as a permanent organ of the United Nations.

Despite these League successes, the concept of intergovernmental organization was not generally popular with advocates of world government during the interwar period. Like other critics of the League, they found its failings more notable than its successes. But more than that, the Second World War was testimony to the intrinsic weaknesses of collective security in particular, and of intergovernmental organization in general.

The war and its aftermath further heightened the vigor of the world order movement. While the State Department was planning, at first secretly, for revitalizing collective security in an organization to be known as the United Nations, the United World Federalists were organizing in support of world government. That the war had been global rather than continental demonstrated the need for universal regulation. The unprecedented devastation, including the use of atomic weapons, accentuated the need for world government before technical advances led to world domination and centralized imperialism. The polarization of world politics and the Soviet-American stand-off, along with the growing reality of a balance of terror, convinced many people that this might be humanity's last half-century to achieve effective world order.

Vigorous advocacy was untimely. At the end of the Second World War hopes were high for the United Nations, dedicated in part to the principle—the Grand Design—that the major powers, despite their differences, could cooperate in peacetime to preserve stability as they had cooperated during wartime to establish it. Remembering the problems of 1918, advocates of world government had to contest this sentiment. Their first major effort occurred in October of 1945 at a conference in Dublin, New Hampshire. Attended by both "world federalists" and proponents of a "world law" movement, the Dublin Conference derogated the adequacy of the United Nations, called for a world federal government of limited powers, and urged that either the United Nations Charter be amended into federalist form or that a world constitutional convention be called. Only five months later, in March 1946, a second conference was held at Rollins College in Winter Park, Florida. There, delegates reaffirmed the necessity for world federal government, but found the United Nations Charter the most practicable route.[17]

For the moment, the world government movement remained almost exclusively the province of a few committed activists. In the United States, especially, sentiment seemed to lean toward intergovernmental organization, with the specific hope that this time, with the backing of American power, the UN experiment might prevent cataclysmic war. But the promise collapsed with the onset of the Cold War and the desire of like-minded nations to cluster into defensive alliances outside the United Nations. A new threat to the concept of world order emerged: the willingness of states to entrust the preservation of their sovereignty to their most powerful allies.

17. For a review of early events, see Edward McN. Burns, "The Movement for World Government," *Science 25,* 1948, pp. 5–13.

One result was the movement for a union of the Western democracies, which frightened the proponents of world government by the threat of a regional central government which, because of ideological inspiration, would harden the polarity of the world and further delay the universalist dream. There was fear that the North Atlantic Treaty Organization might form the base of such a movement.

Faced with two competing movements—intergovernmental organization (UN) and the possibility of counterproductive regional supranationalism (NATO)—the universalists took to the offensive. In pursuit of the findings of the Rollins College meeting, Cord Meyer, Jr., president of the United World Federalists, offered testimony before the House Foreign Relations Committee (May 1948) in which he called upon Congress to champion greater strength for the UN through Charter amendment, not to strengthen its intergovernmental quality, but to advance it toward world government. A year later (October 1949) Grenville Clark, distinguished lawyer and later director of the World Peace Through Law Movement, sat before the same committee to testify on two bills: *for* the World Federation Resolution and *against* the Atlantic Union Resolution. The former called for an American initiative for the evolution of world government, and the latter for a union of Western democracies. In an eloquent plea, Mr. Clark argued that "the distinction is of basic importance. It marks, I believe, the difference between peaceful evolution and a probable or possible third world war." He concluded:

> We ought always to remember that there are only two ways for the West and the East to be brought into cooperation. One way is an enforced cooperation, following the conquest of one by the other. But we know that the West cannot be conquered in the foreseeable future. And we know that while the West might well completely subjugate the East, after unprecedented slaughter, the West has no wish to do so. We realize that, as Henry L. Stimson [former secretary of state in the Hoover Administration and secretary of war to President Franklin Roosevelt] has said: "Americans as conquerors would be tragically miscast."
>
> The only other way is that of cooperation by the free consent of both sides, to be achieved, slowly perhaps but steadily, by mutual toleration and without requiring either the sacrifice of honor or principle. That can be done and when it is achieved, the basis will exist to create the universal world federation by fundamental amendment of the United Nations Charter.
>
> One other thing we should never forget—that however necessary our present policy under the Atlantic Treaty (NATO) may be, that policy can be no more than a stopgap. It embodies no element of world order under law. On the contrary, it is the essence of power politics. It may well be helpful in gaining time to seek the solution. It is in itself no stable solution at all.

> The world federalism resolution fully recognizes this in calling for a more fundamental objective of our foreign policy, namely, the development of the United Nations into a world federation open to all nations.[18]

As the United States Congress entertained world government resolutions in its sessions of 1948 and 1949, private groups were busily drafting universal constitutions. Some of these, such as that of Grenville Clark, aimed at reordering the United Nations. Others started from scratch, constructing world constitutional models as though the experience of intergovernmental organization were not at hand.

It is one thing to propound the establishment of government, but quite another to equip it to achieve the desired ends in a heterogeneous world. How much power should there be? How should it be divided among governmental organs? To what extent should authority be left to "local" government of the former nation-states? What limitations on power ought to be prescribed? How can these limitations be preserved? What sorts of incentives to compliance should be arranged, and what kinds of punishment for violations? Even more fundamental, what aims and values is world government to pursue? One contemporary observer, a well-known international law scholar deeply concerned with problems of world order, has expressed his troubled feelings:

> I believe *that it is no longer a question as to whether or not there will be world government by the year 2000. The questions are rather, how will world government come into being and what form will it take?*[19]

Still, however, not all world order concepts embrace the idea of world government, though such a tendency is typical of maximalist proposals.

World Order: A Maximalist Proposal

Committed to the need to restructure international order, some students of the future have considered maximal alternatives. Inasmuch as many of the serious proposals have come from Americans, the federal model of government pervades most investigations. Harking back to US constitutional heritage, the federal model has gained wider

18. Mr. Meyer's testimony is reprinted in Julia E. Johnson, editor, *Federal World Government* (New York: H. W. Wilson Company, 1948), pp. 86–94. Mr. Clark's can be found in Appendix B of his *Plan for Peace* (New York: Harper and Brothers, 1950), pp. 78–83.
19. Saul H. Mendlovitz, "Models of World Order," in Richard B. Gray, editor, *International Security Systems* (Itasca, Ill.: Peacock, 1969), pp. 178–92. Emphasis in the original.

popularity through the United World Federalists and through implementation elsewhere. This is a system of government in which the total sovereignty of the state is divided in such a way as to make the central government sovereign over some transactions, other smaller units sovereign over some other transactions, and the two cooperatively sovereign over still other matters. This system is designed primarily to prevent absolutism or a drift toward full centralization. Moving from this model, Vernon Nash, then vice-president of United World Federalists, wrote this disclaimer of absolute central world government:

> Conscious, sharp aversion to the idea of world government arises mainly from two false assumptions. The first is that national governments would be abolished, or entirely subordinated, in the creation of a world state. The second is that nationality would thereby be wiped out. Both fears are baseless. We do not need nationalism; *we need only modify the present absolute nature of national sovereignty.*[20]

Hence the movement for world federalism draws a distinct line between world government and the formation of a world state.

But in addition to its frontal assault upon absolute sovereignty, world federalism seeks to supervene strident nationalism. Effective peace through government requires more than changes on the political map. It means changing national perceptions, enlightening national views of the ideals and expectations of other peoples and so on. In a symposium on the world community in 1947, one observer expressed a vivid notion that typifies the attack on nationalism:

> The person I cannot get out of my mind these days is the young man who dropped the first atomic bomb. I suppose he is a nice young man . . . yet the odd thing is that, if he had been ordered to go and drop it on Milwaukee, he almost certainly would have refused. . . . Because he was asked to drop it on Hiroshima, he not only consented but he became something of a hero for it. . . . Of course, I don't quite see the distinction between dropping it on Milwaukee and dropping it on Hiroshima. The difference is a "we" difference. The people of Milwaukee, though we don't know any of them, are "we," and the people of Hiroshima are "they," and the great psychological problem is how to make everybody "we," at least in some small degree. The degree need be only extremely small. I don't think we have to love our neighbor with any degree of affection. All that is necessary to create the psychological foundations of a world society is that people in Maine should feel the same degree of responsibility toward the people of Japan or Chile or Indo-China as they feel toward California. That is pretty small, really, but it is apparently enough to create the United States.[21]

20. Vernon Nash, *The World Must be Governed,* 2nd ed. (New York: Harper and Brothers, 1949), pp. 44. Emphasis added.
21. Kenneth E. Boulding, "Discussion of World Economic Contacts," in Quincy Wright, editor, *The World Community* (Chicago: University of Chicago Press, 1948), pp. 101–12.

Though world federalists customarily place the formation of world government chronologically ahead of the formulation of a world society, their intention is to eradicate the nationalistic consequences of sovereignty as well as national sovereignty itself.

Separation of Powers

A second fundamental concept is also borrowed by the world federalists from the American constitutional model: the separation of powers. A concept traditionally ascribed to the French philosopher Montesquieu, separation of powers divides the power of the federal government into three branches—legislative, executive and judicial—in order to avert tyranny by a single political authority. As James Madison argued in *Federalist Paper No. 47,* a pamphlet written to argue for ratification of the American Constitution, "The accumulation of all powers, legislative, executive, and judiciary, in the same hands, whether of one, a few, or many, and whether hereditary, self-appointed, or elective, may justly be pronounced the very definition of tyranny." Imbued with this spirit, major proposals for world federation usually include separation of powers.

The first attempt at world constitution making emerged from the Committee to Frame a World Constitution, formed at the University of Chicago in 1945. Its chief author was in Italian émigré, G. A. Borgese. Equipped to reveal its work publicly through its publication *Common Cause* (in no way related to the contemporary American populist movement), this committee announced in 1947 and 1948, in serial fashion, a preliminary draft of a world constitution for the Federal Republic of the World.

In addition to prescription of the organs of government, the preliminary draft specified the areas of substantive power. In normal federal fashion the draft stipulated, after enumeration of specific powers, that "the powers not delegated to the World Government in this Constitution, and not prohibited by it to the several members of the Federal World Republic, shall be reserved to the several states or nations or unions thereof." This provision was intended to guarantee within the federal scheme the integrity of traditional governmental units and political communities. A few years, later addressing the same point, another advocate of world federalism wrote:

> The crucial need is for an effective division of the internal and external sovereignty of all nations. This would leave to each nation its internal sovereignty while helping all nations to pool their separately held fragments of international sovereignty for transfer to world federal govern-

> ment. Generally speaking, any problem national governments are unable to solve acting separately, requires international solution and ought to become a responsibility of world government.[22]

Inis L. Claude, Jr. expressed this sentiment somewhat more succinctly when he wrote: "Federalism symbolizes functionally-limited centralization, but centralization nonetheless."[23]

Highly institutionalized maximalist schemes such as the Borgese proposal have been rather common in the history of the world order movement. Yet in their ambition to restructure the international system, they have run afoul of the same criticisms time and again. Principally, there have been three attacks. One concerns the social practicability of these schemes. A second relates to the slender probability of successful implementation. The third deals with the issue of the philosophical desirability of world government.

The Social Practicability of World Government

The theologian and social observer Reinhold Niebuhr once wrote: "Virtually all arguments for world government rest upon the simple presupposition that the desirability of world order proves the attainability of world government."[24] Even if one accepts the desirability of world government, which we will examine subsequently, what is the link between desirability and attainability?

The critical issue in addressing this question is the relation between society and government. World federalists tend to argue that if people will look beyond their governments, they will be able to shape a supranational government capable of maximizing social integration, effective compliance with law and perpetual peace. Critics hold, on the contrary, that governments have little ability to integrate communities; rather, the merger of diverse value patterns and heritages is a sociopsychological process to which governments may give direction, but which cannot be legislated into effectiveness regardless of the type of government. Integration is a matter of will rather than of power.

Studies have been conducted in a number of countries on the images that national peoples have of one another. Two of these, undertaken fifteen years apart, used essentially the same technique. Respondents

22. Edith Wynner, *World Federal Government in Maximum Terms* (Afton, N.Y.: Fedonat Press, 1954), p. 38.
23. Inis L. Claude, Jr., *Power and International Relations* (New York: Random House, 1962), p. 207.
24. Reinhold Niebuhr, *Christiam Realism and Political Problems* (New York: Scribner's, 1949), as reprinted in Arend Lijphart, editor, *World Politics,* 2nd ed. (Boston: Allyn and Bacon, 1971), pp. 71–80, "The Illusion of World Government."

to questions were asked to describe their feelings about their own nations and about people in other countries by placing in order several adjectives. In the earlier study, the frequency of selection of particular descriptive words was reported in percentages. For example, when Americans were asked to rate themselves, only 2 percent chose the word "cruel" and only 2 percent the word "backward." But when the same people were asked to rate the Russian people, no fewer than 50 percent selected "cruel" and 40 percent "backward." By the same token, 39 percent of British questioned thought the Russians cruel, and 36 percent thought them backward. Only 12 percent of both British and Americans thought the Russian people intelligent. In the polling among people of eight different Western countries (Australia, Britain, Germany, France, Italy, the Netherlands, Norway and the United States), positive adjectives were applied most frequently to the subject's own people. Consistently, the Soviet people and the Chinese people were assigned positive adjectives least frequently and negative adjectives most frequently.

But even among Western neighbors and allies there appeared to be social barriers to complete trust and mutual respect. Not surprisingly, given historical relations, the German people held the French in low regard. German respect for the French was only a fraction above that for the Russians and the Chinese, though Germans thought the French more intelligent, less cruel and less backward than the Russians. However, Germans thought the French less brave, less self-controlled and less peace-loving than the Russians, even though the polling was done during the Korean War.[25]

A similar questioning technique presents subjects with pairs of adjectives that have opposite meanings, such as cowardly and brave, stupid and intelligent, lazy and industrious. In a study in which people were asked to select preferable adjectives first to describe foreign peoples and then to depict their governments, both ethnic images (people) and national images (governments) were determined. Among Americans polled, the results were tabulated in decreasing order of preference (see Table 17–1).

Note that in the ethnic ratings all noncommunist peoples are higher than all communist peoples with the exception of Nationalist Chinese, who rank behind the European communists but ahead of the mainland Chinese. By contrast, in the national ratings there is no exception. *All noncommunist governments rate higher than all communist governments.* The Soviet people and the Soviet government both rate con-

25. For a full tabular report of results, see William Buchanan and Hadley Cantril, *How Nations See Each Other* (Urbana: University of Illinois Press, 1953), pp. 46–47.

TABLE 17–1
Ranking of ethnic and national images by Americans in decreasing order of preference.

Ethnic (peoples)	*National (governments)*
Finnish	United States
West German	Finland
American	West Germany
Russian	Nationalist China
East German	Soviet Union
Nationalist Chinese (Taiwan)	East Germany
Chinese	China

Source: Adapted by permission from Richard H. Willis, "Ethnic and National Images: People *vs.* Nations," *Public Opinion Quarterly,* 32, 1968, p. 190.

sistently above the peoples and governments of the other communist states about which questions were asked.[26]

Results concerning images and trust among allies have been substantiated even more recently. In a study reported by NATO in 1973, Europeans have the highest trust for the Swiss, with the United States ranking second. Although the polling was conducted prior to British entry into the European Economic Community, trust for Britain ranked third among people questioned in Belgium, France, Germany, Italy and the Netherlands. Though engaged in the process of economic integration, none of the Common Market members on the list received a majority expression of trust in all four other countries.[27]

These data underscore the fact that governments are not alone in their resistance to world government. Among allies as well as among enemies, there are still barriers to mass perceptions that are sufficient to rebut the assumption that if national governments were subordinated to a world government, antipathies among the peoples would fade, and that an integrated world society would result. We must be cautious in presuming the social practicability of world government.

Probable Success Upon Implementation

What if the social and political barriers to the implementation of a world government were superable? Would the maturation of a world society be sure to deter further warfare? Most critics of the world government ideal argue that on the national level, central government

26. For a full report of findings, see Richard H. Willis, "Ethnic and National Images: Peoples *vs.* Nations," *Public Opinion Quarterly 32,* 1968, pp. 186–201.
27. For a full summary of findings, see "Swiss, Then Americans Most Trusted by Europeans," *Atlantic Community News,* March/April 1973, p. 2.

has not invariably deterred civil war. Even in a world state, to say nothing of a global federation, occasional warfare will erupt.

Advocates respond to this objection in a utopian way. On the assumption that an effective federation would achieve universal justice (though by what value standards?) and adequate distribution of authority and goods, they insist that the contemporary causes of war would be eradicated. They assume that the absolute centralization of military force will provide adequate deterrence to the use of force by members. But this blanket assumption overlooks that hostilities often involve the use of power at other levels—that the ability of force to deter force is not absolute, but relative to conditions, situations and perceptions. Furthermore, these assumptions trip upon the same snares as does collective security: those who threaten the peace are not always identifiable; self-defense may justify use of force, just as it may be used as camouflage for aggressive intentions; states sympathize with one another's interests and perceptions, thus minimizing the efficiency of global decision making. The expectation that world government might invariably avert war in untenable in light of these observations. On this subject Claude concludes, "The hard fact is that the record does not support the generalization that the establishment of government, within a social unit of whatever dimensions, infallibly brings about a highly dependable state of peace and order."[28] The skeptics agree that world government and monopoly of force would not ensure perpetual peace.

Philosophical Desirability

Not all observers concur that world government is desirable. Some begin with the expectation that central government will gradually erode even the beneficial effects of different nation-states and of systems of government, leading to a dreary, uncompetitive and dull political community. More acutely, however, they differ with the universalist assumption that world government is necessarily good government, either in efficiency or in quality. In the American federal system the delicate balance between executive and legislative prerogatives has undergone fundamental change; why might not the same occur in a world federal system? If political conflict is capable of turning even ideal democracy into tyranny or constitutional authoritarianism, is there any prospect that global problems might produce a world government of universal tyranny? How would coalitions of like-minded states utilize their share of political power in a world

28. Claude, *Power and International Relations,* p. 220.

system? Does world government necessarily eradicate the threat of worldwide absolutism?

These and scores of other related questions plague the theoretical integrity of the world government philosophy, just as does the claim that there is virtue in peaceful diversity. The critics of world government concepts agree that the idea carries an interpretation of Hobbes' social contract to logical absurdity. Inis Claude has observed, for example:

> Hobbes was right; when a community is so poorly developed that its pregovernmental condition is one of intolerable warfare, and its urge to establish government rests on no other foundation than a desperate desire to escape the perils of anarchy, the only theoretically adequate government is Leviathan, an omnipotent dictatorship. Locke, too, was right; when a community is held together by strong bonds of agreement concerning what is right and just, and common life is reasonably satisfactory, a limited and mild kind of government, based mainly upon consent, may suffice to supply its needs. World governmentalists describe the world's situation in Hobbesian terms, with a view of emphasizing the urgent need for a global social contract, but they decpict the resultant government in Lockean terms, with a view of making the social contract palatable. It would be better to recognize that in so far as this is a Hobbesian world, it is likely to require a Hobbesian government.[29]

Yet there are many who hold that supranational world order *short of total world government* is both desirable and feasible. One such movement is that of World Peace Through World Law, and the other is the growing sentiment of globalism in the United States. We turn now to those alternatives of the future world order.

World Order: A Minimalist Proposal

The objective of the world order movement is the centralization of political authority for avoidance of war. However, because of the practical barriers to federation, other movements have proposed partial centralization of authority addressed to the specific problems of arms in international politics. The best known among these is the World Peace Through World Law movement, founded by Grenville Clark and assisted by Professor Louis B. Sohn of the Harvard Law School. The student is cautioned, however, that *world law* is not synonymous with *international law*. International law purports to interpose norms of behavior between states; the world law movement,

29. Inis L. Claude, Jr., *Swords Into Plowshares,* 4th ed. (New York: Random House, 1971), p. 429.

in contrast, is concerned explicitly with the removal of arms from international politics, and the establishment of collective security. In the words of Saul Mendlovitz:

> World law thus ties together two very important notions: disarmament and a collective security system. It argues that the present system of international relations . . . [is] based on unilateral decision-making sanctioned by armaments, and maintains that this situation results in a spiralling arms race that may very well set off a cataclysmic war. The world law model therefore posits the need for complete and general disarmament of all the states in the world down to the level of police forces, and proposes the establishment of a transnational police force that can maintain the territorial integrity and political independence of each state.[30]

The emphasis us upon elimination of arms, rather than their mere limitation.

The structural plans for the world law movement are found in the well-known volume *World Peace Through World Law,* prepared by Clark and Sohn.[31] The plan involves two steps. First, it calls for revision of the United Nations Charter to grant the General Assembly full authority of overseeing total disarmament, and with full power of enforcement through weighted voting. Thereafter, the General Assembly would establish an inspection commission that would begin by taking a world census on quality, quantity and deployment patterns of national arms. The inspection would be accompanied by a truce on further arms production. Upon completion of this preliminary stage, actual disarmament would consist of a decade in which each state would reduce its national arms stockpile by 10 percent annually, all reductions being distributed evenly among the several military services so that all are reduced at the same rate. Verification of compliance both during and after the actual disarmament stage would be conducted by the United Nations Inspection Service, operating in national territories without governmental barriers. An alternative plan calls for the establishment of a special World Disarmament and World Development Agency with powers similar to those of the other plan.

Though the Clark-Sohn proposals would impinge only upon states' freedom to prepare for war, the plans run into several insuperable barriers. Can there be security without arms? Is international inspection trustworthy in a technological age? What are the possible political consequences of secret unilateral violations that result in clear military

30. Saul H. Mendlovitz, "Models of World Order," in Richard B. Gray, editor, *International Security Systems* (Itasca, Ill.: Peacock, 1969), p. 191.
31. Grenville Clark and Louis B. Sohn, *World Peace Through World Law,* 3rd ed. enlarged (Cambridge, Mass.: Harvard University Press, 1966).

superiority, even monopoly? And there are still other problems. National armaments are the special possessions of arms manufacturers and certain elites in society, such as rival armed services. What are the prospects of weakening these groups to levels sufficient to make world disarmament proposals attractive to national governments? Do domestic political relationships bode well for the future of total disarmament? The skeptics—and they are legion—see little hope in current national perceptions. Thus the Clark-Sohn proposals, though humane, remain futuristic, persuading diplomats to concentrate their efforts on international law rather than world law, and upon arms limitation rather than arms abolition. The piecemeal attack on sovereignty remains the method of practical choice, despite the increasingly urgent need for major transformation of the international system.

World Order: A Reformist Proposal

In addition to the maximalist and minimalist proposals for world order, there have arisen other reformist ideas, each of which concentrates upon adaptation of existing national and international machinery. The prevailing idea at the moment is *globalism,* a movement which is tied to the United Nations by virtue of the UN's growing role as a center of international planning. While the UN has not achieved the level of authority proposed by Clark and Sohn, and while it has had little effect upon the world's armaments, its record as an innovator and as a clearinghouse for planning and activity on other issues has been modestly good. The UN has been most successful in economic development, through its Development Program (UNDP). Other areas to which globalism might spread are the allocation and preservation of national resources and distribution of the world's produce.

But there is another dimension to globalism. As societies develop, they overcome problems; but at the same time they create new ones. Industry, the prime aim of underdeveloped states, is a case in point. While industrialization may eradicate poverty, disease, starvation and lack of the conveniences of life, it also causes environmental degradation, marked economic disparities of domestic social groups, problems of urbanization, depletion of natural resources and scores of other potentially critical problems. The philosophy of globalism attempts to transform concern for these issues from the national level to the global level. The UN began to tackle these problems in the Stockholm Conference on the Human Environment (1972), which was to coordinate a global attack on ecological problems. Outside of the UN, the only coordinated attempts are regional, most important among them being the NATO Committee on the Challenges of Modern Society. The CCMS already has done significant work toward improving urban transportation, and is working on methods to contain and clean maritime oil spills.[32]

One globalist philosopher, Lester R. Brown, holds that the need for global planning is evident in a five-item "inventory of mankind's problems": environmental crisis, the widening gap between rich and poor, unemployment, urbanization and malnutrition.

> Given the scale and complexity of these problems, the remainder of the twentieth century will at best be a traumatic period for mankind, even with a frontal attack on the principal threats of human well-being. At worst it will be catastrophic. At issue is whether we can grasp the nature and dimensions of the emerging threats to our well-being, whether we can create an integrated global economy and a workable world order, and whether we can reorder global priorities so that the quality of life will improve rather than deteriorate.[33]

Although Brown sees the solution to this problem in part as one for supranational institutions (agencies that exercise the sovereignty of governments), he is principally concerned with the development of global planning that is acceptable to governments, and that does not alter their status as the principal actors in world politics. He looks ultimately to the creation of a globally planned economy and of a global infrastructure consisting of transport and communications systems. These, he suggests, will improve the quality of life through central planning, and will usher in a new world order—not through fear of threat, but through universal satisfaction.

Others who accept the philosophy of globalism have given more attention to its institutional needs. One well-known British author, for example, enumerates some of the social requisites to this globalist world order.[34] In fields of human rights, labor standards and monetary controls, in particular, United Nations coordination is crucial to the implementation of the philosophy. It seems, therefore, that the development of globalism is tied to the future of some universal organization, most likely the United Nations. It is agreed that if the philosophy is to rise above futuristic platitudes about the human instinct for survival, then institutionalization is essential.

32. For an eloquent plea for development of a globalist philosophy, see Philippe de Seynes, "Prospects for a Future Whole World," *International Organization* 26, 1972, pp. 1–17.
33. Lester R. Brown, *World Without Borders* (New York: Random House, 1972), pp. 11–12.
34. C. Wilfred Jenks, *The World Beyond the Charter* (London: George Allen and Unwin Ltd., 1969), especially Chapter 4.

All of the proposals thus far studied have one thing in common: they are all *political-structural* concepts of world order; that is, each deals with international anarchy by adjusting the system's structural characteristics, and by prescribing mechanisms for addressing existing evils. More recent research, however, focuses upon the *universal cultural* aspects of international relations, recognizing that international events are often nongovernmentally motivated. It assumes that there are universal cultural similarities and, further, that cultural imperatives underlie many international events. Richard Falk characterizes the cultural perspective in this manner:

> The creation of a new system of world order must draw its animating vision from the long and widespread affirmation that all men are part of a single human family, that a oneness lies buried beneath the manifold diversities and dissensions of the present fractionated world, and that this latent oneness alone can give life and fire to a new political program of transformation.[35]

Contemporary research into the future of the international system rests upon the concept of universal culture as a basis for effective political cooperation.

The World Order Models Project typifies this new concern. To restore a humanistic view of the international system, WOMP focuses not only on peace and disarmament, but also on social justice and welfare. One participant argues that, "In a sense, social justice is prior to economic welfare and minimization of violence. Welfare will not be equitably distributed nor violence averted unless justice is done or is in prospect."[36]

Even if one accepts the need for conscious international transformation to achieve peace, justice, welfare and ecological restoration, many troubling questions remain about transactions in a world without sovereign states. Historically, values have been allocated by power, conflict and war. How will these values be achieved in a warless world? Will merely eliminating absolute sovereignty necessarily be more effective for allocating global values? How will crucial value decisions be made? Will such a world be better than the one we have now?

35. Richard A. Falk, *This Endangered Planet* (New York: Random House, 1971), p. 296.
36. Ali A. Mazrui, "World Order Through World Culture," *Proceedings,* American Society of International Law (1972), pp. 252–53. A comprehensive study of the traditions and contemporary ideas of futuristic research, especially with the universal cultural orientation, appears in Louis René Beres and Harry R. Targ, *Reordering the Planet: Constructing Alternative World Futures* (Boston: Allyn and Bacon, 1974).

The Problem of Sovereign Transfer

Whether by structural change or universal culture, the creation of world order requires fundamental alteration of individual states, especially the more powerful. The state, after all, serves many functions, both internally and externally. And while the international law of a nation-state system strives to *regulate* at least the external functions of statehood, effective world order may have to *deprive the state of control* over those functions. If contemporary international law is only modestly successful in its quest, the drive for comprehensive world order faces the same problems in far greater magnitude. While international law seeks to intrude in the exercise of functions with the consent of states, comprehensive world order attempts to abridge the absoluteness of states' sovereignty. And because this requires new institutional arrangements, world order schemes share with the world federalist notion the problem of transfer of loyalties away from the state to a culturally and politically heterogeneous entity.

But the picture need not be altogether bleak. Since world order ideas imply a rejection of world government, the transfer of loyalties, along with the readjustment of states' sovereignty, need only be both gradual and united. In this sense, the world order idea is consistent with the philosophy of functionalism, except that the reassignment of public tasks and the redirecting of individual loyalties are determined not by the political innocuousness of issues but by (1) the importance of the subject matter as a potential cause of war or as a preventative of war and (2) public and governmental support attainable for transfer away from the nation-state.[37] Even so, unanimity on such issues is unlikely. If issues of transfer are decided by international conventions, it makes little difference whether delegates are appointed by governments or elected by publics. Sentiment to alter fundamental attributes of statehood is not rampant. In addition, delegates are likely to differ on whether or not certain issues cause war.

Mechanisms of Sanction

Under institutionalized world order, by what means will the cooperation among nations be ensured? It is assumed that punishment of violators is the responsibility of all members of the community through both centralized and decentralized means. Besides the use of force by

37. Norman L. Hill, "The National State and Federation," in Howard O. Eaton, editor, *Federation: The Coming Structure of World Government* (Norman, Okla.: University of Oklahoma Press, 1944), p. 131. This World order standard is part of the world federalist intellectual tradition.

legitimized military control, however, the world order advocates prescribe various lesser sanctions. Foremost among these is the old-age technique of ostracism—economic boycott, censure, cultural isolation and so on.

Power and Justice

There is probably universal agreement that power and war, the mechanisms by which international decisions have traditionally been made, have resulted in many unjust decisions. But what guarantee have we that some other mechanism will not occasionally be unjust? Presumably, core values of different national peoples will continue to collide. In the absence of war and traditional power struggles, what standards of justice are to be used? Whose concept of justice ought to prevail in a political process without coercion? International decision making may require a functional equivalent to war, since we know that war has settled fundamental questions at critical historical moments. This

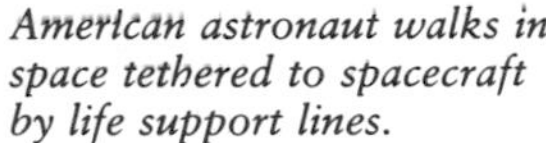

American astronaut walks in space tethered to spacecraft by life support lines.

Source: NASA

is not to suggest that victory is the equivalent of justice; it suggests, rather, that war has been a prime instrument of decision making and the allocation of values. Without it states will require a functional equivalent or they may be prompted to desert cooperative world order in favor of their individual abilities to coerce.

Furthermore, if states sacrifice their warmaking ability by vesting central coercing authority in some supranational agency, we are confronted with the problem of that agency's capacity for justice. Might not such an authority be dictatorial, and thus prone to injustice? Alternatively, could it fall under the command of an influential minority of states? Or the converse, could it succumb to the avarice of a tyrannical majority of states that disdain the values and interests of others? These problems especially plague maximalist proposals for world order, but they are only relatively less critical for minimalist and reformist views.

Value Standards and Value Objectives

Underlying all other problems and questions is the matter of what standards are to be used and what objectives pursued in comprehensive world order. Order requires more than simple institutional mechanics; it reflects the value patterns that create it, and it is expected to perform in accordance with some values. The feasibility of world order depends largely upon the pertinence of the larger values to their particular political and social cultures, their economic systems and expectations, and their philosophies regarding rights, freedoms and other elements of public life. Proposals of world order cannot ignore the sociological imperatives of the international community.

Despite lingering sentiment for a world republic, most formal proposals have been products of the early Cold War—an age of extreme ideological sensitivity. As a result, most of them lean heavily upon the philosophy of government that is broadly characterized as the Western liberal tradition, with emphasis upon civil liberties and economic individualism. At the same time, however, they attempt to attract socialist attention by including collective responsibility for economic development, allocation of natural resources and distribution of wealth. Nevertheless, there is a distinct Western tone to them, with patent leanings toward an idyllic Western model. Proposals that call for upgrading the United Nations as an instrument of world order, on the other hand, are more realistic in accepting diverse domestic ideologies and political heritages. This realism has been imposed upon the Western world largely by the growing solidarity of the left-leaning Third World on economic issues at the UN.

The Problem of Internal War

Traditionally, students of international relations have distinguished sharply between international war and internal war, and a body of international law has arisen regulating each. In more recent years, especially in the revolutionary international system of the past quarter-century, the sharpness of the distinction has faded because of the tendency for internal wars to become international wars through intervention and third-party belligerency. It is by now evident that internal wars are a major threat to international peace and security. Can effective world order instruments avert this threat by resolving internal problems? How much authority should be vested in the international community to intervene for such a purpose? Would the authority of centralized enforcement be tantamount to a dictatorial world state, or a menace of the majority?

A related problem—and from the viewpoints of justice and welfare perhaps a larger one—is the relation of world order to insurgent groups in strife-torn countries. If insurgency threatens world or regional peace,

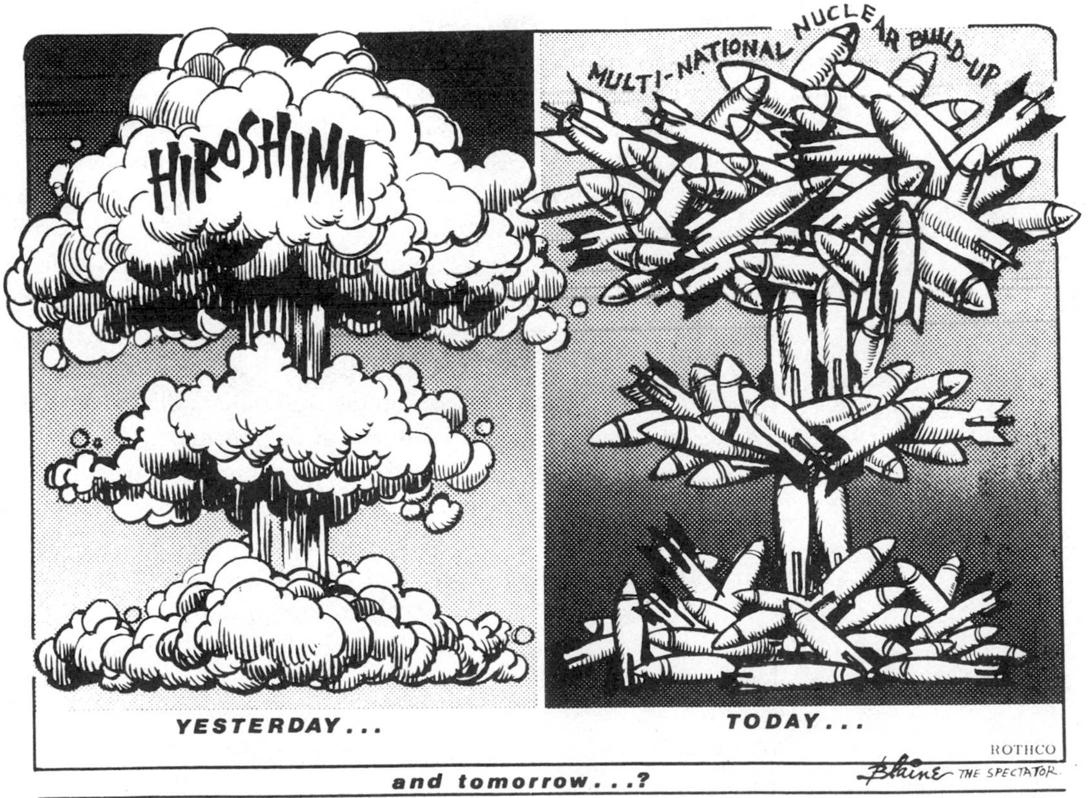

Source: © Blaine: *Hamilton Spectator*/Rothco

and if international agents have authority to intervene, are they *bound* to intervene on behalf of incumbents? Or ought they to act upon their judgment as to the relative merits of conflicting claims for social justice? What ideological and philosophical standards ought to be invoked? Who ought to create them? Furthermore, in internal situations, what will be the mechanisms for determining and executing value standards in the absence of unchallenged national authority?

Conclusion

In this section of the book, we have considered several approaches to world order, and we have concluded by exploring some existing proposals for alternative world futures. Despite the contributions made to international peace and stability by intergovernmental organization, international law, transnational participation and regional integration, it is apparent that the international system presently points toward self-destruction. This is not due entirely to the potential for war in a balance-of-terror system. It is also attributable partly to the widening gap between the wealthy countries and the poor, with resulting social and political antipathies. Moreover, the presence of egalitarian ideals in the minds of virtually all peoples has heightened the demand for international protection of human rights in light of the failure of national governments in this matter. While all this political demand burgeons, the delicate balance of the human environment is deteriorating at an alarming rate. It is abundantly clear that the international system is in jeopardy unless statesmen and those whom they represent accept the critical need to rise above the narrow psychology of nation-states and nationalism.

In deciding among alternative world futures, we are faced with several choices. We may proceed in the traditional political-structural manner, through maximalist, minimalist or reformist means. But the social imperatives, the problems of loyalty transfer and fears about life in the future retard progress on these choices even while the need becomes clearer. Our choice, it now appears, is not between perpetuation of the present structure and vague alternatives, but between (1) world order based on piecemeal erosions of states' sovereignty and (2) highly institutionalized and expansionist world government. The longer the choice is delayed, the more the alternatives narrow to two: expansionist world government or systemic destruction. Since neither is desirable, the wise use of precious time is essential.

INDEX